Strange Genius

Hayden at the height of his power and prestige in 1875. Courtesy National Portrait Gallery.

Strange Genius

THE LIFE OF FERDINAND VANDEVEER
HAYDEN

Mike Foster

ROBERTS RINEHART PUBLISHERS

International Standard Book Number 1-57098-004-7
Library of Congress Catalog Card Number 94-66097

This book is for
Michele Foster Oakes

Contents

Acknowledgments

THIS BOOK WOULD not have been possible without the courteous and professional assistance of numerous librarians, archivists, and curators across the country. They made available the various manuscript collections on which my research depended. Many of the published books and articles I consulted came to me through the good offices of the Interlibrary Loan Department at the Denver Public Library.

I want to thank Ellen Morris, Patricia Anne Dean, Jay Marks, and Lisa Beth Ferstenberg for reading parts of the manuscript and making valuable suggestions. Marlene Merrill critiqued the three chapters on Yellowstone and saved me from several errors. Howard Lamar offered good advice at a crucial time. I also want to acknowledge Norman Cantor, my best teacher, who had nothing specific to do with this book but whose influence on my thinking as a historian has been fundamental. Alice Levine has been a model editor, not only for her attention to the smallest details but often for helping me to find a better way of expressing what I have wanted to say. Terry Vogel and James Cassidy helped with the proofreading. I cannot thank Rick Rinehart enough for believing in this book.

Significant Events Concerning F. V. Hayden

1828	*7 September*	Born in Westfield, Massachusetts.
1838		Parents separate.
By early 1841		Sent to live with relatives in Ohio.
1841	*May*	Mother remarries.
1845	*September*	Enrolls in Preparatory Department of Oberlin College.
1850	*August*	Graduates from Oberlin.
1850	*September*	Enrolls in Theological Department at Oberlin. Teaches in district schools of Ohio for next year and a half.
1851	*December*	Begins studying in Cleveland with Kirtland.
1852	*March*	Settles in Cleveland.
1853	*April*	Visits James Hall in Albany.
1853	*May–August*	First journey up the Missouri River and first visit to the White River Bad Lands (modern South Dakota).

1854	*January*	Earns M.D. from Albany Medical College.
1854	*June*	Begins 20-month venture to Upper Missouri Basin, going as far as the confluence of Bighorn and Yellowstone rivers the first summer. Winters at Fort Pierre (South Dakota); explores the Bad Lands, the Black Hills, and the Fox Hills. During second summer ascends Missouri as far as Fort Benton (Western Montana). Finds first fossils of American dinosaurs in several locations.
1856	*March*	Elected a corresponding member of the Academy of Natural Sciences of Philadelphia.
1856	*March*	First joint publication with F. B. Meek.
1856	*April–November*	Explores Upper Yellowstone River with Lieutenant Warren as far as mouth of the Powder River in Wyoming.
1857	*May*	Publishes his first geological map.
1857	*May–December*	Collects in eastern Nebraska, then ascends Loup Fork of Platte River with Warren. Explores around Fort Laramie, the Black Hills, and the Bad Lands. Returns along the Niobrara River.
1858	*March*	Beginning of the Permian controversy.
1858	*September–October*	In Kansas with Meek.
1858		Founding member, Potomac Side Naturalists' Club in Washington.
1859	*May*	Begins 15-month expedition with Captain Raynolds. Explores drainages of the Yellowstone in southeastern Montana and northeastern Wyoming. During winter layover at Deer Creek on the Platte takes first trip into Colorado. In spring ascends Wind River, crosses Jackson Hole, Pierre's Hole (Idaho),

		and Raynolds Pass, descends along Madison River to Three Forks (Montana). Explores several branches of the Upper Missouri.
1861–1862		Lives in Washington.
1861	*July*	Finishes *Geology and Natural History of the Upper Missouri* (1862).
1862	*October*	Finishes *Contributions to the Ethnography and Philology of the Indian Tribes of the Missouri Valley* (1862).
1862	*October*	Enlists in the Union army.
1863	*February*	Commissioned a surgeon of volunteers.
1863	*April*	Takes charge of hospitals at Beaufort, South Carolina. Later post surgeon.
1864	*February*	Appointed assistant medical inspector, Department of Washington.
1864	*October*	Appointed chief medical officer, Army of the Shenandoah.
1865	*May*	Resigns his commission a month after Lee surrenders to Grant.
1865	*June*	Honorably discharged with the rank of lieutenant colonel by brevet.
1865	*November*	Appointed auxiliary professor of Geology and Mineralogy, Department of Medicine, University of Pennsylvania.
1866	*August–October*	Collects in the Bad Lands and other regions of South Dakota.
1867	*March*	Appointed to direct the Geological Survey of Nebraska.
1867	*June–November*	Travels across Nebraska; also explores in Colorado and Wyoming.
1868	*August–November*	His survey officially expands to southern Wyoming. Unofficially, he surveys part of William Blackmore's Sangre de Cristo grant in Colorado.
1869	*July–November*	Work continues in Wyoming and Colorado. The survey has now become the Geological Survey of the Territories.
1870		*Sun Pictures of Rocky Mountain Scenery.*

1871	*May–October*	Leads survey to country surrounding the headwaters of the Yellowstone.
1871	*9 November*	Marries Emma Woodruff of Philadelphia.
1872	*July*	Resigns his professorship at the University of Pennsylvania.
1872	*June–October*	Returns to the Upper Yellowstone region.
1873		The survey's name is changed to the U.S. Geological and Geographical Survey of the Territories.
1873	*June–September*	With the survey in Colorado.
1873	*November*	Elected to membership in the National Academy of Sciences.
1874	*July–October*	With the survey in Colorado.
1875	*August–September*	With the survey in Colorado.
1876	*August–September*	With the survey in Colorado.
1877		Spearheads creation of the Entomological Commission, which is attached to his survey.
1877	*Summer*	Leads botanists Asa Gray and Joseph Hooker on a naturalists' tour of the West. The survey works in Idaho, Montana, and Wyoming.
1877		*Atlas of Colorado.*
1878		Awarded honorary Doctor of Laws from Rochester University.
1878	*July–October*	In Wyoming with survey.
1879	*April*	Senate confirms Clarence King as first director of the U.S. Geological Survey.
1879	*July*	Retires to Philadelphia.
1879–1880		Contributes to *The Great West* (1880).
1882–1883		Contributes to *Stanford's Compendium of Geography and Travel* (1883).
1883	*July–August*	Fieldwork in Montana with A. C. Peale.
1883		Completes his final geological map, summarizing the survey's work over twelve years.

1883	*December*	Founding member, American Society of Naturalists.
1884	*August–September*	Fieldwork with Peale in Montana.
1885	*July–September*	Railroad tour of Colorado, Utah, and Montana with Emma and the Peales; then fieldwork in Montana with Peale.
1886	*August–September*	Fieldwork in Montana with Peale and George P. Merrill.
1887	*June*	Awarded honorary Doctor of Laws by the University of Pennsylvania.
1887	*22 December*	Dies in Philadelphia, age 59.
1888	*May*	Emma donates $2,500 to the Academy of Natural Sciences of Philadelphia, establishing the Hayden Memorial Geological Fund and the Hayden Medal.
1890		James Hall awarded first Hayden Medal.

1
INTRODUCTION

IT IS ODD that the seat of our democratic government should repose atop Capitol Hill, from which the only view is downward. But the irony of that situation probably never occurred to Abram Stevens Hewitt. In most respects Hewitt was an observant man, who would have noticed, for example, the classical ornaments in the House of Representatives and the austere beauty of the Speaker's dais, which was made of white Tennessee marble. He felt at home in that impressive chamber, where space flexed and flowed so easily across the room that the galleries, which could accommodate twenty-five hundred visitors, were scarcely noticeable. He also appreciated the furnishings, such as the bird's-eye maple in the main doors to the chamber and the individual oak desks assigned to each member of the House.* Hewitt sat in a cane chair that was at once comfortable and elegant: its armrests swirled into delicate vortices, the seat could swivel through a complete circle, and

*Notes are at the back of the book. Those that give sources of quotations, comments on sources, and elaborations of discussions are not announced by a digit in the text but are keyed to the text by page number. Note numbers, which appear infrequently, draw attention to ancillary material that may be of interest to the general reader.

four bold but graceful legs coasted on rollers. Even the rump of a congressman was worth pampering.

On 11 February 1879 Hewitt raised the hinged top of his desk, pulled
out some notes from its inner recesses, and rose to deliver one of his more
memorable speeches. Hewitt was a Democrat who espoused an unusual
amount of sympathy for labor and the common man, yet he was also a captain of industry who had made a fortune in the manufacture of iron. He was
a philanthropist and a well-connected merchant prince; his personal friends
included Andrew Carnegie, President Rutherford Hayes, and Henry
Adams—a notable scholar and himself the grandson of a president. In politics Hewitt was ever the friend of sound money, efficient and honest administration, and reform, whether in the civil service or municipal government.
Typical among men of his station, Hewitt embodied a paternalistic philosophy, which held that the country's progress depended upon righteous leaders
capable of developing America's material wealth—men like himself. His
speech was an eloquent reflection of that philosophy, no doubt a sincere one,
and at the same time a forceful argument for reorganizing the government's
several surveys that were concerned with geological resources and map making. Here is the epitome of that speech.

> When we consider how measureless are the values which spring into
> being at the touch of modern industry, and how these values when
> once created are solid and real and become incorporated into the en-
> during structure of human society, we may begin to estimate properly
> the measure of responsibility which rests upon this nation and its cho-
> sen rulers, not merely to preserve unharmed the priceless boon of civil
> liberty which leaves the individual free to do his share in work of de-
> velopment, but to adopt such measures as will prevent the waste of
> natural resources, clear the way of progress, and promote the triumphs
> of civilization. It is to these immeasurable elements of national wealth
> that we wish to direct the new surveys. It is to a rigid, profound study
> of these great fundamental problems of national progress that we mean
> to turn the new organizations.

Reorganizing the surveys was a controversial business, and though many
members did not see the issue the way Hewitt did, nearly all of them endorsed his wider assumptions. He sat down to thunderous applause.

When, on 3 March, a bill establishing the United States Geological
Survey as a permanent federal bureau came to a vote, a majority of Hewitt's
colleagues approved. The USGS was not everything reformers like Hewitt
had wanted—not by a long shot; it represented the most a recalcitrant

group of western congressmen would allow for the moment. A direct result of creating the USGS was to put out of business four separate agencies, each of which had been doing similar kinds of work.

The next issue was, who should direct the new USGS? Though any number of prominent geologists might have stepped forward for the job, surprisingly few did. It soon became apparent that the heads of the now superseded agencies were likely candidates. Four dynamic and capable men had made their reputations directing these rival surveys, but now only one of them would continue the endeavor.

Lieutenant George Montague Wheeler bore all the prestige and a good deal of the arrogance of the army's Corps of Engineers. Between the War of 1812 and the Civil War, the army had dominated exploration of the West, and Wheeler, who took the field in 1869, was only the most recent in a proud column of officers who resented the intrusion of civilians into what the military viewed as its monopoly. Wheeler mapped vast areas of the West, adding to the impressive number of maps previously compiled by the army. Naturally, he plotted features primarily for their military significance; geologists complained that his charts provided insufficient scale to show their newly discovered formations.

From 1867 the army also sponsored the 40th Parallel Survey, under the direction of a civilian, Clarence Rivers King. Shortly after the outbreak of the Civil War, King graduated from the Sheffield Scientific School at Yale, where he became one of the new breed of scientist who learned geology through training at a university. King's survey focused on economic geology and mining, and King himself yearned to amass a fortune through private consulting in mining ventures. Unlike Wheeler's, King's maps proved quite acceptable to geologists; they were all prepared by civilian topographers.

John Wesley Powell was older than King, and he lacked King's specialized training in the sciences, having found his way to geology through the broader path of natural history. With funding first from the Smithsonian Institution and later from the Department of the Interior, Powell managed a geological and topographical survey of the high plateau country surrounding the Colorado River; his descent of the river's treacherous rapids had brought him fame. Though he became an accomplished geologist, Powell's deepest absorption was always with American Indians, and most of his survey's publications concerned ethnology rather than geology. When Congress abolished the four rival surveys by creating the USGS, it rewarded Powell alone with another job: the first directorship of the newly created Bureau of American Ethnology.

The fourth candidate was Ferdinand Vandeveer Hayden. Taking the traditional path for naturalists trained before the Civil War, Hayden earned a bachelor's degree from Oberlin College and then pursued the only graduate work in science available in America—medicine, which he completed at the Albany Medical College in 1854. Independent of mind and fiercely ambitious, Hayden lost no time hitching his star to the field of western exploration. The oldest of the four candidates, Hayden espoused the most catholic outlook: he embraced the entire province of natural history as his own, and he began collecting artifacts of Indian culture even before Powell. By the beginning of the Civil War he had established himself as the most formidable collector of rocks, fossils, and natural history specimens in America. After the war, by carefully cultivating members of Congress, Hayden built up the largest, best funded, and most resplendent of the four rival surveys operating with a probationary federal patronage.

Wheeler had never been a viable candidate to direct the USGS, mostly because everyone but the army wanted to get the Corps of Engineers out of the business of western surveying. Powell also faded quickly, partly because of his preference for ethnology but also because he had become the leading spokesman for reforming the western lands, thereby alienating most of the western lawmakers. Both men will reappear in this narrative, but the contest for director was always between King and Hayden.

For the first three months of 1879 sponsors of Clarence King waged an intense campaign directed at President Hayes, trying to offset Hayden's advantage as the more experienced naturalist and the clear favorite of most members of Congress, especially the westerners. At the time, King enjoyed the solid repute of a scientist, the prestige of an intellectual, and the giddy acclaim of a brilliant drawing-room raconteur. In 1872 he had exposed the infamous "diamond hoax," thus saving investors huge sums of money they would otherwise have poured into the hands of swindlers. The incident earned King public recognition, which he enhanced through some glamorous writing about the American West. King had a number of elitist friends, who were always ready to lionize him. One of his greatest admirers was Henry Adams; another was Congressman Hewitt.

Hayden lacked King's ties to the literati and to the most socially prominent, but he was recognized as *the* man, more than any other man, who had revealed the structure of western geology. After the Civil War his explorations in the Yellowstone region brought him international renown. Always keen to expand the public's appreciation of science, Hayden saw to it that his reports were written in popular language, and he circulated them widely, not only to scholars and learned societies but also to journals, newspapers, colleges, and even secondary schools. A diverse readership eagerly awaited these annual updates of his explorations, and the broad range of his survey's publications earned him kudos as one of America's best known and most versatile naturalists.

During the contest that followed, sponsors of Hayden and King mouthed a lot of platitudes about their respective candidates, their professional reputations and general experience, and their specific interests and skills. But the noisy and sometimes heated talk amounted to a ritual, the kind sponsors always go through for their candidates when they realize the real issues cannot be discussed, at least not publicly. Those more fundamental questions had been buzzing in the air for months, long before Congress created the USGS. To King's backers the real issues were these: could a zealous but unscrupulous naturalist be replaced as the head of the nation's largest geologic and natural history survey? Or, because of that naturalist's great power and popularity, would it be necessary to abolish his survey entirely in order to get rid of him? From the other side, to Hayden and his friends, the real issue was equally simple: should yet another upstart rival be allowed to distract the nation from the progress of its most celebrated scientific enterprise? Though men of different experience and achievement, both Hayden and King displayed adequate qualifications for the job of directing the USGS. Had the unspoken agenda not preempted questions of general ability, Hayden would probably have prevailed. But that is not what happened.

What happened was that King unseated Hayden as the reigning champion of western scientific exploration. He managed this surprising upset with the assistance of some powerful friends. The USGS had been quietly conceived by men whose interests favored economic geology; that is, they wanted a survey that would develop the "immeasurable elements of national wealth," as Hewitt put it. From his previous experience on the 40th Parallel Survey and because of his well-known expertise in appraising mines, King was the obvious man to head such a survey, and the men who established the USGS wrote out the guidelines for that survey with King in mind. They even consulted King on the wording.

King and his conspirators only succeeded, however, because they made Hayden's personality an issue in the campaign. Despite his great popularity with the public and most of Congress, Hayden was disliked by a hidebound portion of the intellectual community who disdained popularizing science, at which Hayden was an acknowledged master. Professional jealousies were also involved; for instance, three of the men who chartered the USGS were bitter enemies of Hayden. It is undeniable that the slanderous lies they circulated about him contributed to King's victory. However, Hayden was anything but an innocent victim. Without revealing too much prematurely, I will say now that Hayden was a self-absorbed man, often an insensitive friend, and always an aggressive adversary, who could employ devious tactics of his own.

But there is another point. After all, had Hayden become the first director of the USGS instead of King, there would probably be no need for this book. In a reversal of fortune, King—not Hayden—might have turned out to be the neglected man. King and Powell collaborated to unseat Hayden, and both men enjoyed the fruits of their joint victory, including the power of high office and a goodly share of attention from historians and biographers. But in the process of demeaning Hayden in order to snatch a prize from him, his enemies ignored his achievements and exaggerated his faults sufficiently to leave him with an unenviable reputation. Accepting that reputation at face value, biographers have snubbed him.

Other writers have relied on a little knowledge of Hayden to round out their studies of other men or other topics. Hayden was actively involved in a number of matters concerning the American West and the maturing of American science. Accordingly, authors who write on such subjects have been obliged to mention Hayden. Because none of these writers have come to know him, however, their sketches have borrowed from the available grab bag that mixes hackneyed images with biased distortions.

Numerous authors have mentioned Hayden, but no one has ever fully portrayed him. Many have noticed his energy and enthusiasm. A few have guessed at the almost magical spell he could cast over congressmen, fellow scientists, and especially women. None have imagined the demons within that drove him so relentlessly; none have revealed the destructive conflicts between his ambition and his idealism. Hayden remains an enigma. Vying with Clarence King for leadership of the USGS brought his career to a climax, but it also posed a dangerous crisis—one of two Hayden endured at the time. The other crisis was personal: though profoundly private, it influenced every aspect of his public struggle with King. Each crisis resolved itself in a very different way and with quite different implications for understanding this strange genius.

It is time we did understand Hayden, for he was the man who put Yellowstone National Park on the map, and the man who provided the model for our national geological survey. His reports on exploring the West directly affected the blossoming of that region, how it was viewed aesthetically, even how it came to be understood in the popular mind. Hayden influenced the lives of many politicians, scientists, explorers, scholars, businessmen, and artists, as well as thousands of ordinary people—from farmers and miners in the West to school teachers and book readers back East. His impact on American science has been enormous, not just because he dug up the raw materials that explained so much of Earth's history and the evolution of its life but also because he molded government policy. He was one of those archetypal figures whose force of character shapes events into larger issues. He was also a fascinating and complex personality. Hayden deserves the kind of sustained attention that can penetrate his surviving image, as well as his own public masks, to reveal the whole man.

It is easy enough to make such points now, after spending eight years researching the man and three more digesting the results and gradually articulating my understanding of him. Have I made him into a somebody just to justify my possibly extravagant expenditure of time? I don't think so, though I suppose any biographer becomes more satisfied with what he discovers than what he encountered in the first place. At the beginning, I must confess, I had no reason for thinking Hayden was all that important, and I certainly had no idea of the time I would spend on him.

The best way of explaining why I wrote this book would be to relate how I got involved with Hayden. One of my passions is climbing mountains. Another is research. I realized the first as a boy, growing up in Colorado. I discovered the second during graduate school, studying history. Decades later, after teaching for a number of years and then working at a second career in business, I returned to history through the back door as an "independent scholar." I began working outside of the academy at freelance writing on various subjects, including mountaineering and western history. I kept encountering Hayden's name sprinkled freely across maps of the West—maps I used in charting routes to the tops of mountains, many of which Hayden had climbed before me. In his wide travels around the West, lasting over thirty years, Hayden compiled a long list of first ascents, and his fieldwork established a number of surveyed locations (called benchmarks and triangulation stations) on which our modern maps depend.

Initially then, I admired Hayden as an outdoorsman, an explorer, a vigorous physical creature, some of whose feats I was having fun emulating. What puzzled and fascinated me, though, was finding that Hayden was so unknown. At best, he seemed to be a bit player, not a major actor in any particular drama of life. My experience in pursuing him across mountain ranges suggested there might be more to the man than meets the eye. I resolved to give my curiosity its sway.

A biographer doesn't spend years pursuing some person just to satisfy a curiosity, though, or just to sell some books. A biographer is drawn to another person by a complicated set of internal needs and desires, some of them only vaguely understood, others not at all. The research and writing are necessary expressions of an author's personality. As writers we relate to our subjects in different ways, sometimes like a patient to a therapist or a protégé to a guru, but more honestly than either of those because we are not obliged to talk overmuch about our relationship. At other times we develop the kind of bonding that exists between close friends or spouses, but ours is different because we think more deliberately, also more speculatively, about those bonds.

Confronting the demons that inhabit another's soul inevitably disconcerts the investigator, because no inquiry regarding somebody else succeeds without some degree of self-discovery. That process can be embarrassing or even perilous. For these reasons, biographers often wrap themselves in a protective literary tradition that allows them to avoid difficult subjective problems by concentrating on more objective bits of milieu. Though this passive approach is justified in some circles as impartial, I believe it only confuses the reader and leaves the subject hanging in limbo. Therefore I am going to write only selectively about surroundings because they tell altogether too much—and ambiguously at that—but scarcely anything about Mr. Hayden. Besides, isn't it folly to place your subject in a series of contexts without ever saying what you think about him? Is it honest to ask readers to make up their own minds when you have selected all the contexts for them? Better to gather materials as thoroughly as possible; to organize, analyze, and synthesize in a judicious manner; and to admit that insight depends more on intuition than erudition. It is a process of being "an artist upon oath," as someone once put it, in that intuition is always guided by strict fact, never invention.

I view biography as the history of a life, and in constructing my history I have used contemporary materials pertaining to Hayden: his published works, to be sure, but even more his numerous unpublished letters, as well as whatever comments about him I could find in the private letters of his acquaintances. From these, and a number of official records, I have established his deeds, his accomplishments, even his mundane acts; but I have always been curious about more than what he did. In all the sources I have tried to catch Hayden revealing himself: when he was writing, thinking, acting, or failing to act, while chasing down some exotica in the field or plodding through his daily routines. I have attempted to discern his mood and manner at such times. In short, I have been mostly interested in Hayden's inner life. In the late twentieth century I would guess no one's point of view is untouched by modern psychology in the general sense, but mine owes no allegiance to any particular school of thought. My interpretations are based on my own experiences in life, my own insights about people and circumstances, and my own intuitions about Hayden.

That intuition—which has grown more confident after prolonged exposure—has taught me most of what I know of Ferdinand Hayden, "the Doctor," as his colleagues called him. I have also learned something about him by following in his footsteps across parts of the land he explored, at times as a comfortable tourist, at times encountering it raw, pretty much as

he did. I won't boast of any mystical insights that resulted from this reenact-
ment, nor will I deny that I had a few. The value in following him around
was to authenticate parts of his experience and make that experience part of
my own.

Even after eleven years of my best efforts, what I know of Doctor Hayden
is imperfect. Writing a biography of anyone seems a most presumptuous
act, given the fact that sources are never complete and considering that all
biographers—no matter how much they respect objectivity—are bound to
filter reality through their own perceptions. Someone else, with a different
set of talents and limitations, will see qualities in Hayden I have missed,
and historians in the future will find things that have not even occurred
to me.

This cumulative but imperfect process of historical understanding may
strike some readers as an exercise in futility, but I believe it is an accurate reflection of reality. The truth is that uncertainty is always with us, though
the despots and the salesmen of this world willfully urge us to believe otherwise. At the same time, perpetual uncertainty is no excuse for a feckless slide
into relativism—no excuse, in other words, for abandoning the timeless effort to know ourselves and others. We are never more human than when we
look critically but sympathetically, ponder what we find, and wonder without restraint about what it all means.

Ultimately, long after I had been on the trail of Hayden, I realized what
was important about him, in addition to the particulars of his unique life. It
was the insight he offered me into the human condition. What sustained my
enthusiasm was the quest to know and understand another human being and
the desire to experience the intense aliveness that accompanies such work.
Writing a biography became a vivid expression of being human, as well as a
commitment to this fragile treasure we call humanity.

I want to say also that Hayden and the experience of writing his life have
enhanced my appreciation of biography as an absolutely vital tool for understanding the past. Of course, a long-term grasp of economic developments, political structures, social, spiritual, and intellectual changes is the foundation
for historical understanding. Yet such institutional forces work invisibly until
attention is drawn to their impact upon particular human beings or groups of
them. At the same time individual human beings influence the direction and
intensity of these larger forces. But no such force, however powerful or hoary
with the weight of tradition, is truly impersonal, for each of them has been set
in motion and sustained by particular groups or individuals.

Recently, by borrowing the skills of social scientists, historians have devoted a larger attention to groups of people. This has been, on the whole, a
valuable endeavor, but it would be a disaster for the world of learning if histo-

rians were to forget (or renounce) their unique heritage as discoverers and interpreters of the particular. This is nowhere more true than in appraising particular human beings. By reasserting their natural vocation as biographers,
historians will reinvigorate their profession and reveal new meaning in all
fields of knowledge.

2
A FOULED NEST

He was coarsely dressed, not overly clean, [and wore] a kind of downcast, furtive expression as if ashamed of his circumstances in life. He had a kind of stooping, awkward gait when he walked.

—Manly Root (Hayden's classmate at Oberlin) to
Professor Albert Allen Wright of Oberlin, 31 March 1888

DESCENDING FROM THE Berkshire Hills in western Massachusetts, the Westfield River flows south and then east to join the Connecticut River, just below Springfield. Eight miles west of Springfield is the town of Westfield, set in a rich agricultural region, which, except for hills on the east and west sides of town, partakes of the broad, flat flavor of the Connecticut Valley.

Though Westfield today is larger than it was in the 1820s by a factor of six or more, it has changed less than its larger eastern neighbors. The natural surroundings of the town and the denizens of the region have probably not changed much from the nineteenth century. At that time blue and white violets grew along the banks of the Westfield in springtime, cowslip and skunk cabbage not far away, and higher up, azalea, dogwood, rhododendron, mountain laurel, and viburnum. Deer, foxes, porcupines, racoons, skunks, rabbits, and muskrats roamed in the ample forests, while fishermen exploring the waters around town found sport with trout, large- and smallmouth bass, pickerel, perch, and bullhead. Hayden never said whether he climbed Mount Tekoa, three or four miles to the northwest, but in view of the many summits he later reached its very existence raises the question.

Over the past century and a half the human dimension has changed most around Westfield. During the 1820s Joseph Joker found a way of making whips by machine, thereby transforming his hometown into "The Whip City," manufacturer of nearly all the whips sold in America before the demise of horse-drawn transportation. The industry's first steps coincided with Hayden's boyhood in Westfield.

At that time only one other institution contributed to the town's uniqueness. The Westfield Academy provided, in the spiritual universe, the same kind of discipline and signaling that whips conveyed to horses. The Academy was founded by the Massachusetts legislature in 1793 "for the purpose of promoting piety, religion, and morality."

There was one bank in town and one newspaper. No Episcopal church yet existed, nor a Lutheran, and no synagogue either. Father Blenkinsop's Catholic mission would not come for another generation. Although the Baptists and the Methodists had established churches there during the late eighteenth century, the spiritual life of Westfield, plus the six other hamlets and villages that made up the township (accounting in all for fewer than 5,000 souls), centered upon the Congregationalists. They settled the town in the 1660s.

It was in the First Congregational Church of Westfield that a Hayden child born in the community would have been baptized, but Ferdinand Hayden missed that initiation. Tradition holds that he was born in Westfield on 7 September 1829. But no contemporary record confirms the event. Of course, his parents may have misremembered the date, or, because of moving around, have confused his place of birth with a place of residence. Innocent mistakes, all too familiar to a biographer. But Hayden's birth is not recorded at any time, anywhere in New England.

Supposedly, his parents, Asa Hayden and Melinda Hawley, married on 26 November 1826 in Enfield, Connecticut. I say supposedly because no record of this marriage exists. Census records fail to show Asa Hayden heading a household anywhere in Massachusetts during 1830, a year after the birth of his son. "Asa Hayden" is a very common name in the deeds of more than one Massachusetts county, but none of the individuals who bore it can be identified decisively as Ferdinand's father, who was born in 1798 at Blandford.

Men of substance and probity take pride in leaving their mark on history's scroll. They establish themselves, engage in business and buy property, pay taxes, marry in the church, and have their children baptized. Even if they move, they reestablish themselves and do more of the same. But Asa Hayden apparently did none of these things. In the petition she eventually filed to divorce him, Melinda Hayden accused Asa of neglect, and she claimed he was then in prison, not for the first time. Though blurred in outline, the image that emerges of Asa Hayden is not flattering, and this impression gains tedious confirmation in later years.

Ferdinand's grandfather, Joel Hayden, left a more solid record. Brought up in eastern Massachusetts (Sudbury and Sutton), he fought in the Revolutionary War, earning a wounded leg and the rank of sergeant. After the war he married Jemima Nugent (possibly an orphan of Scots-Irish descent), moved to Blandford, in Hampden County, where he lived and farmed for forty-five years and raised five children, before heading west to Lee, in Berkshire, where he spent the last fifteen of his eighty-five years. Beyond Joel, a search for the patrimonial line dissolves amid a plethora of inconspicuous Haydens spread over five counties of Massachusetts, including at least three Joels of the same generation, one of whom shared the same year of birth with Hayden's true grandfather.

From the standpoint of young Ferdinand, by far the most important act of Grandfather Joel was granting him a $50 legacy in his will. Fifty dollars was not a great deal of money even in 1834, but it was the lion's share of the $153 that Joel allocated among twelve descendants, mostly grandchildren. Ferdinand's younger brother and sister would each receive $25, suggesting Joel felt a particular responsibility for the children of wayward Asa. That Ferdinand was promised twice as much as any other recipient, when he was only five years old, speaks of more than a grandfather's sense of duty. The boy was obviously striking, surely not in appearance (to judge by later photographs) but in personal traits and marks of ability.

The sources of such talent must always excite curiosity, but in Ferdinand's case no answers are forthcoming, and few clues. If family tradition can be trusted, Hayden's great-grandfather, Elias, was a doctor; his uncle, Gardner, was a graduate of Williams College and a minister of both the Congregational and Presbyterian churches. Supposedly, the family came to America in the early seventeenth century from Devonshire, prospered by farming, and married into families that had done the same. Even assuming all the stories about their lineage are true, the Haydens seem to have been a God-fearing, sober, moderately prosperous, but unremarkable lot.

Even less reliable information survives about Melinda Hawley and the matrilineal line. Melinda was one of six children, and she married well before her twentieth year. From the evidence of her later letters, she never completed much schooling. All else about the mother's side derives from family lore. The Hawleys came from Berkshire County, and one of them married Elinor Van de Veer, whose ancestors had emigrated from the Netherlands during the eighteenth century and eventually settled around Springfield, in Hampden County. In due course, this Elinor became the mother of Melinda Hawley. Elinor's father, or perhaps her brother, was the last male of the line, and in keeping with tradition, his name was bestowed upon the next male child to appear in the family. That happened to be Elinor's grandson, Ferdinand Vandeveer Hayden (the middle name now one word). Incidentally, most writers, not appreciating his Dutch ancestry, have spelled the name "Vandiveer," and even Hayden once wrote his name with that spelling, which may derive from the way some people pronounced it. By the end of his life, however, Hayden was writing "Vandeveer."

If this genealogy leaves something to be desired, it is nonetheless an accurate composite of the earliest and most powerful shaping force of any man's life. Even from the incomplete records at hand, one conclusion emerges forcefully. Hayden's innate abilities made up a far richer endowment than anything the family was able to give him in the way of connections or material advantages. So great was the discrepancy between these halves of his heritage that in realizing his potential, Hayden could only distance himself from his origins. From early on he was a loner. For the duration of his life he grew by looking inward for inspiration. And despite his eventual success in the practical world, the sequel suggests that his lack of a strong family bond, and the absence of a clear sense of belonging, may have denied him those deep satisfactions that derive only from sincerely cooperative endeavors.

How long Asa and Melinda Hayden continued living together is unknown; it is not even clear where they lived. There are no documents to prove they lived in Westfield, only Hayden's later assertion that he was born there. The family was in Lee, Massachusetts, on 16 April 1836, when their second child, William Henry, died—at the age of six years, nine or ten months, meaning he was born during June or July 1829. This fact is of some importance, as it proves Ferdinand could not have been born on 7 September 1829, as he claimed. The family was also in Lee on 29 August 1837, when Melinda gave birth to her fourth child, Henry Franklin. Ferdinand also had a younger sister, Frances, who had been born about 1832, place unknown.

The sketchy details about the family's residence and the lack of reliable evidence about Asa's occupation make it appear they moved from place to place. Asa had relatives sprinkled across Massachusetts and one brother in New York. Melinda had family in Springfield and New York. Possibly, the couple stayed with one or more of these relatives from time to time. Eventually, Melinda took the children and moved to Rochester, New York, where she lived briefly with one of her aunts, who had married a man named Joseph Putnam. During May 1840 she returned to Massachusetts long enough to file a petition of divorce.

Divorce was a difficult and harrowing experience for a woman, and ordinarily Melinda would not have endured the ordeal. Recently she had been living without Asa anyway, and under such circumstances she could have raised her children alone and gone on quietly with her life. Except for the appearance of a new suitor.

John Marchant was born in New York, later spent some time in Philadelphia, and moved to Rochester in 1828. A widower and a man of property, he was an agreeable contrast to Asa. It is not known when or how they met, only that they married in Rochester on 23 May 1841 and settled on his farm in Greece, just north of town. She was thirty-three or thirty-four, he fifty-four. His eldest daughter had already married, and his second came to the altar only five days before her father's remarriage. Melinda's petition for divorce in Berkshire County had been dismissed earlier in May. Perhaps she obtained a divorce somewhere else. Perhaps, after giving a nod to respectability, she did not feel the need of a formal dissolution anyway, if her previous union had never been legalized.

Around the time of Melinda's remarriage, Hayden was sent west to live with an aunt in Ohio. The timing, though important for what it would reveal, is impossible to pinpoint. It is tempting to think it occurred after 11 February 1842, when Grandfather Joel Hayden died and the legacies in his will would have made it possible for Melinda to board out her eldest son. But I think Hayden went to Ohio earlier, even before his mother remarried. Probably she sent him away in early 1841 to reduce her financial burdens and to increase her chances for a favorable remarriage.

Melinda, like many women who start birthing at a tender age, found more anguish than joy in her children. This is not speculation. The few letters she later wrote to Hayden show little affection, and she took little personal interest in him. Hayden's sister, Frances, once wrote to him that the only trouble their mother complained of was her children.

And though they never recorded it, Melinda's children may well have been troubled by her. From all we know, Ferdinand was a sensitive and spirited child. Imagine the impact on him of being uprooted from familiar surroundings (not for the first time), of moving to a new home in Rochester, and of seeing his mother deliver what little love she could muster to a man old enough to be his grandfather.

No doubt Melinda felt better about remarriage after she was able to board out both of the two elder children. Frances, the only girl, stayed nearby; the obliging Joseph Putnam offered her a place in his home in Hansford's Landing. Ferdinand, whose behavior may have matched his troubled emotions, was sent farther away. Only Henry Franklin, being younger than four, needed to stay with his mother.

Rochester, Ohio, is in Lorain County, in the northcentral part of the state, situated on good farm land between the Vermilion River and the East Branch of the Black River. About forty miles to the northeast is the great city of Cleveland, a day's journey by horseback or buggy, though few around Rochester had any reason to go there. Young Ferdinand lived on a farm with an aunt, Lucretia Stevens; another aunt, Philena (or Phileny) Perry, lived on an adjacent farm. Both were sisters of his father, Asa.

During the nearly five years he lived there, Hayden hunted, studied in the local secondary school, and found a secure home, probably for the first time in his life. Aunt Lucretia made his clothes and loved him as one of her own. She was also free with spiritual counsel. Even after he went off to college, her homilies followed him: "Don't look for great things, be humble, trust in the Lord . . . bear always in mind that this is not your home (the Christian lives for Heaven)."

But Hayden did aspire to great things. Whether because of some inner drive or because his curiosity soon soaked up whatever was nearby, Hayden later reported that "at sixteen years of age I started for Oberlin College on foot, without a change of clothing or a dollar in my pocket, with an Adams arithmetic under my arm." Thus, twenty-eight years later did Hayden romanticize his entry onto a larger stage. But in that same recollection he deliberately distorted his past: he said he "moved to Ohio when about twelve years of age, and assisted my parents in opening a new farm during the four following years." His parents never opened a farm in Ohio, never lived there together. Hayden's only residence in Ohio, before Oberlin, was with Lucretia Stevens and her husband.

Hayden chose to weave illusions around certain embarrassing facts of his early life. He then reported a more suitable mythology to various colleagues, but he neglected to contrive a consistent story. For instance, he told another associate, Albert Charles Peale, that "his father died when he was about ten years of age, and about two years later he went to live with an uncle at Rochester, in Lorain County, Ohio." He gave a modified account of that second version to Charles Abiathar White, who noted: "Ferdinand's father died when the former was about ten years old, and his mother, marrying again, went to live in New York State. Two years after his father's death the boy, finding his home uncongenial, went to live with his uncle on a farm near Rochester, Lorain county, Ohio."

The chief difficulty here is that Asa Hayden did not die when Ferdinand was ten years old. He lived to plague Hayden and his siblings for a long time before he died in 1857, when Ferdinand would have been almost thirty. In each of the altered stories of his past Hayden was trying to hide his parents' divorce and the far uglier reality of his father's drunken, shiftless way of life. The report of Asa's "death" when Ferdinand was ten probably indicates the time of his parents' separation (in about 1838) and Melinda's resettlement in Rochester, New York.

Because the records are inadequate, and Hayden's own summaries of his past are unreliable, his biographer is left in a quandary about the true events and chronology of his early years. Yet Hayden did not recreate his whole past, only selected parts of it; if the myths can be identified and discounted, what remains should be a useful guide. The key to the puzzle is his true birthday, for 7 September 1829 is too late by at least a year. In the only account of his life that supplies a different date, his birth is given as 27 September 1828. This year seems correct, but was he born on the 7th or 27th of September?

Both Peale and White have Hayden entering Oberlin in 1846 at the age of eighteen, which would appear to contradict Hayden's own statement that "at sixteen years of age I started for Oberlin College on foot." But what Hayden did not acknowledge is that he spent his first year at Oberlin in the Preparatory Department and only began as a freshman in the fall term of 1846. If, as seems likely, he "started for Oberlin" shortly before his birthday on 7 September 1845, he would have been sixteen, as he said; a little over a year later, at the beginning of his actual entrance into college, he would have been eighteen, as he told Peale and White.

Then how to explain the one reference to his birth on 27 September? The 27th was only cited once, and the author of that article admits to basing his remarks on an interview around a campfire in Colorado, which he reproduced "from the unwritten book of memory." If we can allow that author a slip of the pen or a lapse of attention, we can settle on 7 September 1828 as Hayden's birthdate.

The confusion over the year of his birth arose because Hayden desired to appear younger than he was. Later in his life he courted and married a much younger woman; apparently he wanted to narrow the gap between them. Their marriage certificate, of 9 November 1871, shows him as forty, but he was, of course, forty-three. His bride hid the truth, too, for she recorded her age as twenty-one, though she was actually twenty-seven.

To summarize my reconstruction of Hayden's early life: he was born in 1828, out of wedlock, in the town of Westfield. His father and mother had a residence in Lee for several years, but Asa moved around, pursuing a number of bootless schemes. Was Asa Hayden a doctor? It seems unlikely, but one of Hayden's classmates opined as much in a reminiscent letter written years later. His only source for such information would have been Hayden himself, and Hayden may have invented a profession for his father to clothe him in respectability. At any rate his parents seem to have resided in Lee longer than anywhere else. They finally split up in 1838. Melinda moved to Rochester, where within two years she met John Marchant, and she married him in May 1841. Hayden was sent to Ohio when he was twelve, probably in late 1840 or early 1841 at the very time his mother was making serious preparations to remarry.

Meanwhile, after Melinda left him, Asa continued to drift. In February 1842 he was said to be living in Syracuse. In October 1849 he turned up with a new wife and "two pretty boys" in Rochester, Ohio, living near his sister Lucretia, who remarked that he would not be exposed to "bad society" there. Lucretia hoped Ferdinand would not stay away from Rochester on his father's account, but none of Asa's children had any desire to see him. About this time Ferdinand's younger brother wrote, "Better write father, too, tell him not to come near me." Ferdinand felt the same way. He would spend the next eight years trying to avoid his father.

3
COLLEGE OF DREAMS, 1845–1850

He always had an intense, self-absorbed air, indicating a devotion to his own lines of thought and to subjects of special interest to him, which interfered with the hearty comradeship that students are fond of.
—Jacob Dolson Cox (Hayden's friend at Oberlin, later his boss as secretary of the interior, 1869–1870) to Professor A. A. Wright, 24 February 1888

ONE OF THE talents of a good lobbyist—and Hayden became one of the best—is the ability to tell a good story. While cultivating that skill, Hayden applied it to his own past and fashioned a history more attractive for public consumption. His arrival in Oberlin, as narrated twenty-eight years later in the same report that glossed his family origins, sounds like an episode from a fictional boyhood created by Horatio Alger, who started writing his popular rags-to-riches tales in the 1860s.

Arrived at Oberlin late at night, a perfect stranger, hungry, tired and footsore. In this condition I accosted a gentleman whom I chanced to meet upon the sidewalk, and who seemed to have a kind, benevolent face, and asked for shelter during the night. To my request he quickly gave assent, and I lodged in an unfinished back-chamber upon that, to me, eventful night. In the morning I agreed to haul sawdust from the mill to the backyard of my host, two days, for twelve York shillings. At

the expiration of the two days I received my money promptly, which
was the largest sum I had ever had in my pocket at one time. With this
money, thus earned, I bought a second-hand Latin grammar and reader,
and commenced fitting for college. . . . Through my entire course I
boarded with the man that sheltered me so kindly during the first
night I spent in Oberlin, and occupied the same back-chamber.

There are some difficulties with this account. College records show Hayden
residing in Tappen Hall for three of his four undergraduate years, and fellow
students mention visiting him in Tappen. But lodging in a "back-chamber"
makes a much better story, especially for a poor boy on the make. Nevertheless, Hayden may have told a partial truth, because he would not have been
allowed to room in Tappen during his preparatory year. Though Hayden does
not identify the kind gentleman who sheltered him that first night or during
his entire first year, Professor George Nelson Allen was head of the Preparatory
Department in 1845, and Allen and his wife filled their home with boarders
to collect additional income.

Hayden's account implies that he came to Oberlin as a result of the happy
coincidence of having settled previously in Rochester, only fifteen miles
southwest of the college. That may be. There is no way of knowing how
young Hayden heard about Oberlin. However, like Hayden, most of the student body at the time came from New England or upstate New York. It may
be that he was sent to Ohio in the first place by well-intentioned family
members who foresaw that Grandfather Joel's legacy of $50 would make a
down payment on an education for the boy who seemed gifted enough to
make something of himself.

Whatever the circumstances of his entrance to Oberlin, an anecdote
Hayden did not relate is far more revealing about the young undergraduate.
He was enraptured with the study of flowers and became so exuberant about
all growing things that, according to one professor, "the other members of
the class were rather inclined to amuse themselves a little in a superior way
over his demonstrative interest in 'common weeds.'"

Many of his fellow students seemed to look down on him in one way or
another. In a recollection penned twenty years after their graduation, one
classmate said flatly, "Hayden was the boy of the class. He was the youngest
and was peculiarly boyish in feelings and manner." One perceptive friend
pointed out, "His mind seemed to be occupied with something else besides
what was in the regular course." Another mentioned that "his eye calls to
mind the 'Ancient Mariner.' On entering a scene it wanted to take in everything in it." A valuable talent, this, for a future naturalist, though scarcely
anyone who lived around him for five years noticed it.

Which tells as much about his classmates as it does about Hayden. People notice what their experience trains them to expect, and some of the more prominent among his peers had a profoundly different background than Hayden. They had come to Oberlin because of its reputation as a nursery for religious and social reform. Oberlin was founded in 1835, at the tail end of the Second Great Awakening, less than a generation before Hayden's arrival. Among the original faculty members was Charles Grandison Finney, one of America's leading revivalists and a man intent upon freeing the human spirit from the harsh determinism of traditional Calvinism. Another was Asa Mahan, selected as the college's first president, who became a leader of the movement for spiritual perfection, which many sober Calvinists equated with heresy.

Not by coincidence the leading financial patrons of the institution, the Tappen brothers of New York City, who amassed a fortune in the silk trade, were dyed-in-the-wool abolitionists. So were Finney, Mahan, and most of Oberlin's first faculty. Cofounder John Jay Shipherd was a revivalist preacher with a passion for temperance, and from the start the college welcomed experimental ideas. In particular, the founders wished to admit women on an equal basis with men and to recruit black students. Manual labor should supplement mental studies. Health must be buttressed through physical exercise, ventilated sleeping quarters, and a moderate diet, which called for decreasing the intake of fats, meats, and gravies. All students would attend chapel services twice daily. The atmosphere surrounding the early community has been captured by Oberlin's premier historian: "The serious-mindedness of early Oberlin is appalling. The consciousness of a wicked world and an approaching day of atonement clouded the spirits of students and teachers. . . . Anything which diverted the attention from religion was sinful."

The physical setting bore no resemblance to a garden of earthly delights, so diversions were minimal. The town rested on a flat glacial plain, consisting of poorly drained clay soil that was splattered with swamps; roads crossing the plain became quagmires. The geography of the place reinforced the earnestness that is the trademark of all reformers, even as it reminded residents that their first priority must be to rise above such mundane matters. Oberlin was a perfect spot to settle a religious colony.

By 1850, the year Hayden graduated, the town sheltered some 1,700 souls. The college, intended from the start to be the spiritual spearhead of an experimental community, gathered an additional 500 or more, most of whom enrolled in the Preparatory and Female departments. Only sixty-nine engaged in undergraduate studies, and perhaps twenty pursued graduate training in the Theology Department. Few of the students arrived with any experience of social reform or any sophisticated understanding of religion. Most were poor but ambitious and came to Oberlin because of its reputation. In those respects at least Hayden was utterly typical of most of his fellow students.

But he was also different, in ways even his closest friends did not discern. What his classmates did notice was a boy all steamed up about the wrong things. None of them foresaw much of a future for this "enthusiastic dreamer who could never conquer in practical life." Ferd, as they called him, was careless about his dress and appearance; he sputtered his words; he spent a good deal of time alone—all signs of immaturity to his peers, who puffed themselves up for cultivating the social graces. Just as apparent to his conventional friends was Hayden's utter disinterest in religion or leading issues of the day. As one classmate put it, "Oberlin was thoroughly Abolition; Hayden cared nothing for it. It was thoroughly religious; he was almost unmoved, not a sceptic nor a sinner, but other things filled his thoughts. He was upright and moral. He was sentimental, but there was no reverent, deeply religious element in him, so long as I knew him."

Most who knew him misjudged him, and one friend admitted, "Ferdinand was little understood. To most of his teachers and classmates he was an enigma." The solid men of his generation—trained by their Oberlin experience to accept women's equality and to work for the abolition of slavery—embraced public service and social awareness as a duty. Many later extended their beliefs into careers, especially the ministry. But not Hayden.

Other classmates reported he worked hard, became a good student, and read widely beyond what was required. With some fondness, a tutor remembered that Hayden suggested new books for *him* to read. Others recalled an inner intensity and ambition to improve himself. But most saw him as an outsider whose most notable effort at social life was a habit of regularly falling in love. "Fond of the beautiful in nature and art, open to affection, eager for the society of women, it became sport to play on his susceptibilities," reports one. That same classmate recalled that an attractive girl in the school who had not yet met Hayden wagered with some friends that within a week she could extract a proposal of marriage from him. Supposedly, she won the bet.

Surviving letters to Hayden from this period attest to his adolescent infatuation with women, but these epistles were written in a playful spirit by fellows similarly smitten. The letters he received from women strike an entirely different chord: besides expressing concern and affection for him, they show genuine regard for a friend. Like other men who are uncomfortable with the bravado and backslapping comradery of their own sex, Hayden reserved his most intimate revelations for women. And they reciprocated. Such men are often discounted by more traditional men, and Hayden's more conforming classmates overlooked some of his accomplishments. For example, at only the beginning of his sophomore year Hayden joined the Union Society, one of two literary groups at Oberlin, formed for the "cultivation of the moral and intellectual powers." No one remembered that Hayden went on to serve regular monthly terms as secretary and vice president, that he was elected corresponding secretary for a year, or that he was one of three chosen to speak for the senior class at the Society's annual anniversary. So he was not quite the effete loner his classmates liked to remember, though his choice of a curriculum showed that he had a mind of his own.

Because of Hayden's inadequate schooling, President Asa Mahan had accepted him into the Preparatory Department of what was then styled the Oberlin Collegiate Institute; it did not become Oberlin College until Hayden's senior year in 1850. In the Preparatory Department Hayden found an accelerated exposure to geography, math, English, elementary Latin and Greek, history, and the four gospels. No dishonor darkened this probationary experience. On the contrary, most Oberlin students started in this way, since another desire of the founders was to extend education to the poorer classes. As the institution grew, an increasing number came endowed with poverty and cultural bleakness. After two terms, however, Hayden was one of forty senior preps who passed exams admitting them to freshman status in time for the fall term of 1846. Four years later (another fact his classmates overlooked), only thirteen of those forty graduated, including Hayden.

A part of Hayden's seeming dreaminess was genuine: he could scarcely believe his good fortune in being encouraged to spend hours learning and reading. What a delightful contrast to the grim and dreary life he had known. No wonder he was enamored with poetry and whiled away hours reading novels. Of course he indulged in pure escapism, but a curious mind needs to snap its shackles and soar before it can embrace discipline and focus itself. His undergraduate studies included a more plentiful diet of what he had already tasted as a prep. He probably took President Mahan's course on Intellectual Philosophy (because almost everyone did), possibly Mahan's course on The Will, and Studies in the English Bible. It seems likely that he studied Hebrew grammar during his senior year (again, most did), heard lectures on Hebrew poetry, and delved into Moral Philosophy and Political Economy. To judge by his graduation thesis ("The Benefits of a Refined Taste"), he spent a lot of time on literary criticism and poetry, so he probably took Professor James Monroe's courses on rhetoric and literature, thus establishing a link with the future congressman who became a strong proponent of Hayden's later surveys in the West. One classmate thought he began French. The full range of his studies will never be known, because from the 1840s, students could pursue independent courses beyond the curriculum. To his friends he appeared a dilettante, affecting aesthetic inclinations; but in embracing both the traditional liberal arts and some of the newer sciences, Hayden gave notice of the versatile capacities that would become his hallmark.

The only hint he himself gives about his actual course of study is the statement, "I graduated in 1850, with a decided taste for the natural sciences." The College Catalogue lists several courses in science, though no personal transcript survives to show in which of these he may have enrolled: astronomy, chemistry, anatomy, physiology, mineralogy, and geology. In addition, there was his extracurricular interest in botany, and whatever he absorbed of biology or zoology must have come in the same manner. Even at such eastern colleges as Yale, from which Oberlin borrowed much of its curriculum, no separate texts in biology, botany, or zoology existed until the 1840s, and not plentifully even then. Natural history was slow in finding an established place in the curriculum at all American colleges, because few accepted its practicality—a fact of some interest, since Hayden himself was thought to be impractical. Given his early lack of self-confidence, he felt uneasy in studies that implied a heavy dose of social action, such as the ministry, where most of his classmates inclined. In pursuing natural history Hayden could gradually build up knowledge in a field where he felt at ease without running into professional anxieties about a specific career. At the same time he could study the practical sciences of chemistry and mineralogy—even geology, a collateral discipline. At Oberlin, beginning in 1847, geology was taught by George Allen, professor of music, geology, and natural history.

Allen was a kindly man, remembered for his devotion to children and young people, especially their musical education. More than anyone else, Allen laid the groundwork in both instrumental and choral music for the celebrated center Oberlin has become. But he was a sickly man who suffered terribly every winter, and he lacked confidence in his abilities as a teacher and administrator. Regarding Christian doctrine, however, he suffered no doubts at all, and his understanding of geology rested on bedrock religious faith. For Allen, geology merely illustrated the Creator's work, and his method of instruction was to review the first twenty-eight verses of the Book of Genesis to show how each was upheld by the known facts of geology. He summarized: "The various secular changes and modifications to which the matter of the globe has been subjected, in the animal, vegetable and mineral kingdoms, as we have just seen in our study of historical geology, can only be referred, as a final cause, to an all-superintending, infinitely-wise and almighty creator."

This approach was typical of traditional teaching in geology before the Darwinian revolution. Though some geologists had begun, by the time

Allen taught, to question the extent and significance of the biblical flood, and simultaneously some theologians were beginning to doubt the usefulness of geology in understanding Genesis, still no new worldview had yet emerged to challenge natural theology. Natural theology provided the only guiding principle for understanding physical matter—namely that the deliberate and purposeful design of the Creator was responsible for the entire universe in all its detail and complexity. The role of natural history was to discover and illustrate that design in nature. Since the early nineteenth century these views had been widely respected in learned circles, thanks mostly to two books by the English theologian and archdeacon William Paley, called *Natural Theology* and *Evidences of Christianity.* Paley's teachings circulated at Oberlin, too, in a course with the same title as his second book.

Allen taught that species existed in all climates and all regions of the Earth, which demonstrated the Creator's perfection and completion. God had left nothing unfinished; all was fixed and stable, even if wonderfully intricate. There was an order behind all creation, an order that was sensible to rational understanding, and it was man's opportunity to master that knowledge because, as Allen said, "What God has so carefully planned and executed is worthy of study. Especially important to religious teachers and ministers."

In view of such ideas, the student of natural history should not question why anything was created or devote much attention to how species behaved. Instead, he should marvel at the very breadth and complexity of what existed, especially its structure. In practical terms this meant emphasizing classification, and Allen's courses on natural history contained abundant physical descriptions of species in their respective kingdoms: animal, vegetable, and mineral. He divided the animal kingdom into four subkingdoms (the term phylum was not used until the 1870s): Vertebrata, Articulata, Mollusca, and Radiata. Vertebrates in turn separated into four classes: mammals, reptiles, birds, and fishes; mammals into eleven orders, from the first of which, Bimana, derived one genus, Homo. Man could be classified with the mammals because of physical similarities, but his existence owed nothing to such creatures and he did not evolve from them; rather his being was due to a separate and special creation through which man gained his unique spiritual and intellectual qualities.

What an impact all this must have made on the bright, impressionable youngster who had shown no inclination for the calling of a minister, a lawyer, a doctor, or a teacher. Later, he would become both a doctor and a teacher, but he did so in each case to commit himself more completely to the only career he ever considered and whose devotee he became at Oberlin—the as yet impractical business of natural history.

Why impractical? In part because few could make a living by collecting

beetles or birds or bones. Studying the anatomy or behavior of living creatures might prove an enjoyable outlet for curiosity, but it yielded nothing
substantial. The meaty stuff—causation and meaning—already were known,
thanks to natural theology. Further study could only provide confirmation,
in endless detail, of the Creator's design, and while a little personal exposure
to some fragment of this arcana suited the Christian gentleman and lady, the
details could be left to professors, whose job it was to teach. No right thinking man of the world in 1850, no one with any sense, certainly no college
graduate, would step out into the world as a bug collector.

Perhaps not in 1850, but after Charles Darwin published his *Origin of
Species* in 1859 things began to change. Once the answers to all basic questions were no longer assumed, research had a top priority; collecting samples
became practical, even profitable. Natural history became the key to understanding the secrets of life. Hayden would play an important part in that
brave new world, but the time was not yet, and to read back into his undergraduate years a purpose he showed during his mature years would be a mistake. Even if he was utterly absorbed with natural history at Oberlin, his
motive at the time was a personal urgency to fill the void within himself. It
was the first step in a lifelong process of trying to rise above his origins and
be somebody.

How suitable it was, this natural history. His supple mind was challenged
to learn the schemes of classification, to sharpen his eye for telltale distinc-
tions, to learn for himself by collecting in the field, to solidify his perceptions by mastering the Latin names, and to memorize it all: descriptions,
characteristics, habits, species, genera, families, suborders, and so on. Even
as the myriad wonders of nature quickly enthralled him, this solid empirical
work gradually trained his mind and set the course of his future. And how
perfect for his first mentor was Professor Allen: a gentle man interested in
the welfare of boys, a teacher of natural history, an ardent collector, yet a bit
of a mystic, unsuccessful enough in the normal material concerns of life to
appeal to a rudderless youth.

Certainly it was Allen who unlocked the door to nature's charms for
Hayden, and he may have been the first to suggest the possibilities of making
a living at natural history. It was still risky and would have seemed fool-
hardy to more conventional men, but discoveries are made by those who follow a star not a herd. Already President Jefferson had sent Lewis and Clark
across the continent, and an important part of their work had been to gather
as diverse a collection of fauna and flora as possible. John Charles Frémont
captured the imagination and sympathy of his more sedate countrymen for
his brave and sometimes rash exploits, and he also returned burdened with
samples of natural history. As did many other bold members of the U.S.

Army's Corps of Topographical Engineers, who were carving out new careers for themselves as naturalist-explorers in that scenic, expansive, dangerous, mysterious, unexplored place called the West.

News of these explorers was trickling back east—even making headlines in some places—while Hayden was in college. Probably Hayden did not read the accounts, for in Oberlin newsreaders and newsmakers more likely were pondering the latest arguments about perfectionism, as detailed in the *Oberlin Evangelist.* Talk of abolition, prohibition, and other social reforms buzzed around the town and campus, and Hayden could not have avoided having opinions and discussions on these subjects or on the more personal questions facing undergraduates: What of your own salvation? Will you make a spiritual commitment, take up the ministry, and lead in the battle for souls? If not, what path will you take, worthy of your education, and suited to the terrible urgency of the times?

Such questions would have intruded rather rudely into the life of young Hayden, who had found intellectual feasting such a joy, flirtations with women so consoling and college life in general such a pleasing change from his previous existence. But there was another inescapable side to the life of a student. He had to eat, to live somewhere, and to pay his tuition and expenses. Yet Hayden was desperately poor. And he had to think of some feasible direction for his future, no matter how much he loved natural history.

The College Catalogue showed the tuition at $15, board in the Public Hall at $1 per week (slightly more in the village), and room rents from $4 to $6 a year. Incidental expenses were estimated at a modest $2. This meant an annual investment in excess of $50, perhaps closer to $75. How did Hayden manage?

His poverty was not exceptional for the time, and many boys worked to earn their way at Oberlin. Hayden said later that he survived by "doing chores for my board, and laboring five hours per day upon the college farm at six cents per hour . . . I sawed two hundred cords of wood twice in two and split the same during my college life." He also reported that he "taught district school during each winter of my course," which was during the long November through February vacation. Perhaps he exaggerated about the woodcutting, and it is doubtful if he would have been prepared to teach during his first few winter vacations. There is no evidence he taught before his junior year, when he did teach in a district school while visiting his family in New York over winter 1848–1849. His younger half-brother, John Marchant, was among the pupils. During the equivalent period of his senior year he taught in the schools of Sullivan and Huntington, south of Oberlin, not twenty miles from campus.

But even working during term and teaching during vacations did not bring in enough money. Thus Hayden sought sponsorship from two relatives on his mother's side. John Martin of Holidaysburg, Pennsylvania, had a painting and paint supply business and was doing well enough to send his daughter to a boarding school. Later he bought a piano for her. Martin sent $5 on three occasions, but he spurned the larger support Hayden sought. Instead, Martin chastised Hayden for writing on the Sabbath, and he offered platitudes: "Be not discouraged. With but few exceptions the young men who meet with most obstacles in youth become the most persevering and useful citizens in after life." He also recommended that Hayden find a trade, not a profession. But John Martin was generous compared to Joseph Putnam of Rochester, who would give nothing and treated Hayden coldly while affecting what Martin called "aristocrat feelings."

Aunt Lucretia gave him $20 on one occasion and probably as much more as her meagre means allowed. Hayden also borrowed from several of his friends, but the sum of all these expedients fell short of his needs. He was able to continue his education only by throwing himself on the good graces of the college, which allowed him to accumulate a debt. In a note to the treasurer written six months after his graduation, Hayden acknowledged owing the sum of $100. There is no record of his ever repaying this debt, by the way, though years later he donated books, photographs, and fossil samples generated by his Survey of the Territories.

Though natural history obviously suited him, he did nothing while at Oberlin that suggests he saw a way of making a living from such interests. For all the inspiration George Allen provided Hayden, he had no specific suggestions about a job, and apparently neither of them knew much about explorations going on in the West. In the year following his graduation, Hayden concentrated on keeping himself employed as a teacher.

While earning his living in the district schools at Johnston and Hartford, Hayden also enrolled in the Theology Department of Oberlin. This move may have surprised some of his classmates, who found him rather indifferent to religion, but given the powerful evangelical setting at Oberlin and Hayden's introduction to science as the handmaiden of religion, it is not surprising at all. Also, at mid-century, an easy alliance still existed between clergymen and naturalists. Both could boast more education than most members of society, and some of the best naturalists were clergymen. Natural history offered work enough for a lifetime, and once committed to its causes, many clergymen and naturalists found rewards of a deeper kind. Here was consolation and glory far beyond what might be gained in the perpetual but petty squabbles over issues of the moment. Given his eager but uncritical mind, it seems impossible that Hayden should not have been moved by religion. In finding him wanting in that regard, his classmates simply misread him. Hayden brandished no general hostility for religion itself; he reacted bitterly toward the preachy and stingy behavior of his uncles, which made him appear irreverent and even impious. His upbringing provided him no common ground with fellow students who had grown up taking Christian dogma for granted. Hayden resented their condescending attitudes, and it showed.

Besides, the Theology Department held out a practical allure as well. No spiritual commitment was required to gain entry into the department, and the curriculum included a variety of general studies. His teaching jobs, which kept him away from Oberlin, dictated a leisurely pace for his studies, thereby postponing any serious considerations of a religious career. During the year and a half following his graduation, Hayden seems to have had only two months during summer 1851 for uninterrupted study at Oberlin, though he may have returned for shorter periods when he found time. Even if piecemeal, this arrangement was attractive on several counts. It gave Hayden a chance to continue his education while supporting himself. Theology students often tutored the preps, and they lived inexpensively because the college waived their tuition. The Theological Society, which Hayden joined, had its own library, and it contained books on a great many subjects beyond religion, including various memoirs, volumes on history, even geology. Hayden's postgraduate experience prolonged a congenial academic life while he pondered his future. During autumn 1851 he made some new acquaintances in Cleveland; they would change his life.

4

CONNECTIONS,
1850–1853

Careless fellow
You waste your precious hours in bed
In pouring over some foolish book
When you should strike to get some bread
Your dress is as good as you need
Your face from sorrow is freed
And some attentions you neglect
To steal the time a novel to read
Learn industry and be wise
For little good in romance lies

Your Valentine
—Hattie Brooks to Hayden, 1850

AFTER GRADUATING FROM Oberlin on 28 August 1850, Hayden appears to have taken his time breaking with the agreeable lifestyle he had developed there. For the rest of his life he would look back fondly on his undergraduate years, and he never hesitated to say so to various friends. "You will no doubt look back upon the time spent in O. as the happiest period in your life, at least I did," he wrote a friend two years after his own graduation. He expressed an attitude that would endure for his lifetime: "It is a valuable thing to have a good education. I can think of nothing in this world that can be compared with [it] at all. Wealth is nothing although it furnishes the means. Still wealth without an intelligent and well cultivated mind would be but a poor consolation to me."

In retrospect it seems almost inevitable that Hayden should have seized upon natural history, as taught by George Allen, and later reinforced by Jared Potter Kirtland, John Strong Newberry and James Hall, in order to consolidate a career for himself as one of the foremost naturalists of the day,

30

in the process organizing the largest scientific survey of the West, which itself later served as the model for the U.S. Geological Survey. But few things (perhaps none) in human experience are truly inevitable, and if we are to understand the man behind the deeds, we must try to put ourselves in his boots and follow his steps one at a time.

Despite his restless nervous energy, Hayden did not spring straight from Oberlin to Cleveland and a career in natural history. What he did for those intervening months has not interested those who have written about him, yet his behavior at the time reveals much about his inner life, especially the private elemental forces that raced in tandem with his public ambitions and in part determined their course.

It would help a great deal in understanding Hayden's mind at the time to know precisely when he met Jared Kirtland and John Newberry in Cleveland and began studying medicine and natural history with them. Kirtland was a professor at the Cleveland Medical School, Newberry a recent medical school graduate and a budding geologist. Undoubtedly, George Allen was the intermediary who brought them together; certainly this happened by autumn 1851, though it may have been somewhat earlier. If it were earlier, one might ask why Hayden delayed so long in establishing himself in Cleveland. Granted he needed money to stay independent, which his teaching jobs in the district schools of Ohio provided. But he could have found employment in Cleveland, as he later did. Perhaps the spell of Oberlin was too strong to break at a stroke. Not only did Oberlin offer an inexpensive way of continuing his general education, but life there provided a stimulating intellectual environment and a comfortable setting of friends. These are reasonable suppositions, but they overlook something.

Hayden was at the time, and would remain for most of his life, an impetuous, impatient man whose way of dealing with anxiety was to swallow more activity, and who, in the face of uncertainty, scorned staid reflection and kept on moving until his unfailing intuition sent him the right signal. This period of about a year and a half after graduation was a time of anxiety and uncertainty, the heart of his difficulties being what we now call "relationships." There is no more revealing difference between our time and Hayden's than the approach to this always vital subject. Of course, we are talking about sex, marriage, children, and love, though in Hayden's day the order would have been love, marriage, sex, children.

On its surface Hayden's love life seems to epitomize that of an adolescent. Recall the testimony of Oberlin friends about his inability to resist—and his habit of seeking—female attention, lots of it. Later on, a colleague at the Smithsonian, would make a similar observation. "He is as eccentric (outrageously so) as ever. . . . A jolly good fellow is Hayden who always falls desperately in love several times a month and is always just about to marry, but will never do so I'll bet a hat, for he would have a new loveliest ere the wedding preparations could be made." Even after allowing for the teasing exaggerations of a close friend, Hayden's yearning for women is evident—and not always playfully innocent. Among the letters Hayden saved from this period is one exchanged between two of his friends and of apparent interest to Hayden himself: "Tell Bob . . . old Sarah sends her love to him & wants to know how his penis is." The letter ends by suggesting that two of the pals are going to Twinsburgh, Ohio, "to see little Wetmore"—no doubt the euphemism for a prostitute or an endearing name for a regular lover.

It is not necessary to rehearse all the particulars, for these examples are mere spurts from a well-charged battery of evidence. But it would be a great mistake to write off Ferdinand's passionate obsession with the opposite sex as adolescent growing pains or to look the other way as one unsuccessful affair followed another. And equally wrong to treat him with derision or the kind of locker room jocularity that often hides our embarassment at such formidable thrusts of passion. Problems of love and sex consumed much of Hayden's life. He never successfully resolved them even after a conventional marriage; eventually they contributed directly to his premature and tragic death. No matter how our modern sensibilities may judge his romantic behavior, we must regard Hayden's escapades as clues to the inner man. The boy who enjoys little attention from his mother may, as a man, turn frantically to other women to make good the loss. Yet he may also thrust them aside in succession, for if the primal woman in his life proved unworthy, how could others do any better? Hayden was looking for a career, but at the same time he was discovering Eros, and the two were pulling him in opposite directions. Science might promise worldly success, even renown, but at the cost of lonely work in far-off places, while the rewards of love might ease and console. No wonder Ferdinand needed a little time to decide where to channel his energies.

Following graduation he turned up in Hartford, Ohio, teaching in the district school, where he labored during the fall and early winter of 1850. While at Oberlin, in addition to however many flirtations he engendered, he also had a serious encounter with Hattie Brooks. Sophronia H. Brooks started at Oberlin with Ferdinand's class, then dropped out for some reason but returned two years later to resume her studies. At some point—probably while still undergraduates—they resolved to marry, and though they shared their decision with friends they never set a date for the wedding. Instead, in fall 1850, Hattie remained in Oberlin while Ferdinand went off to Hartford, a town due east of Oberlin but near the Pennsylvania border, close to a hundred miles away by even the best of slow roads.

Effectively separated from his fiancée, Ferdinand was soon attracted to another young lady. Esther—one of his students at Hartford—sent a most affectionate letter to Ferdinand who was in Johnston (a few miles north of Hartford), where he held another brief teaching position during the winter of 1850–1851. She complained of her current instructor: "He teaches a very good school, but we don't get around that table and talk with him at intermission as we did with you." Calling him "a particular friend," Esther hoped Ferdinand would return to teach in Hartford, and she urged him to come back for a visit during the week after Christmas. Two months later Ferdinand added another valentine to his collection, this one unsigned but probably from Esther.

Not surprisingly, the engagement to Hattie Brooks was broken off. Expressing shock amid lots of pompous talk, one friend warned Hayden that because of the break with Hattie "you will lose the good will of more than one of your dearest and most valuable friends." Another said that Hattie now "considered herself entirely free from her pledge to you on account of your cruel neglect." All this fuss worried Ferdinand, and he wondered aloud whether he should return at once to Oberlin to see Hattie, implying that he still loved her. The friend in whom he confided thought not, saying in effect: if you want to patch things up, start writing her every week. Ferdinand was back in Hartford for spring 1851, but by June his correspondence evaporates, suggesting he returned to Oberlin for the summer and early fall.

It is not known what happened between Ferdinand and Hattie when he reappeared in Oberlin, except that their reconciliation failed—for the time being. In January 1852 the friend who had formerly scolded him over his treatment of Hattie wrote, "You grieve too much over the folly of an act in your past life. You have repented of it, we have all forgiven you, and now think no more of it. Give your attention to your studies." That's just what Hayden did. The break with Hattie impelled him in the direction of science. Certainly the tension between love and science did not dissipate. Nor did Hattie disappear entirely from his thoughts either, and a few years later she returned to his life. Meanwhile, the man had a hole in his heart, and it wanted filling, if not with love, at least with activity.

Prior to his return to Oberlin in summer 1851 there is no hint of Hayden having met any of his future mentors in Cleveland. It was probably during that summer, and likely the result of Hayden imploring him for help in finding employment, that George Allen arranged an introduction to Kirtland in Cleveland. Prior to that summer Ferdinand showed little serious interest in science. At this time he still perused literature in preference to science. Just what Hayden was reading at the time is suggested by an interesting list of thirty books he bought at auction for $17. It includes a heavy dose of literature, poetry most of all, including Shelley, Keats, Coleridge, Longfellow, and Poe. The Romantic poets: how appropriate. And how perfect that he should have encountered Poe's "The Raven," with its brooding over the loss of love, and other poems idealizing women. But science was not entirely excluded, for Ferdinand also bought a geology text and one of Asa Gray's books on botany.

Hayden appeared in Cleveland by at least December 1851, if not somewhat before. Kirtland advised him that any serious student of nature would betake himself to medical school, for nowhere else (at least in America) could someone keen on science find advanced courses in botany and biology. Kirtland introduced Hayden to Newberry, who would have reinforced that opinion. Hayden made arrangements to begin studying with both of them before the end of the year.[1]

During winter 1851–1852, Hayden attended Kirtland's lectures at Cleveland Medical School. These lectures summarized much lore and learning, and repeated recipes for herbal treatments of specific illnesses. Some of the suggested remedies harken back to textbooks of the Middle Ages, which in turn relied on ancient folk medicine. In another respect, however, Kirtland's lectures were right up to date. They upheld the Victorian mixture of medicine and morality, for diabetes was called "a nervous disease," brought on by "intemperate eating & drinking and injuries, etc." And constipation resulted from that clandestine exercise in selfishness—masturbation.

The lectures made no recognizable impact on Hayden, but Kirtland's concept of natural history did. Kirtland saw all living creatures as part of an indivisible though invisible whole. He studied as many different species as possible in order to arrive at a better understanding of the divine force that put breath in all of them. Like George Allen, he believed that every species enjoyed a unique creation and that each lived within fixed behaviors and environments as set down by the Creator. In connection with his work on the first geological survey of Ohio during the 1830s, Kirtland compiled lists of the fauna inhabiting the state, which included 585 vertebrates, 222 birds, and a number of fishes. Kirtland wrote over seventy papers on zoology and a number of others on agriculture and horticulture.

Another side of Kirtland probably influenced young Hayden too. Beginning in 1850 Kirtland and two partners published a weekly magazine called *Family Visitor,* which, besides a carefully selected notice of national news, featured articles supportive of family values. Even after Kirtland retired, Hayden was sending his former teacher samples from his western collections and remembering him warmly. This kindly but forceful man became a model of the manly rectitude Hayden missed in his own father. Certainly Hayden would have heard a number of informal homilies from Kirtland, including this one: "Science keeps the mind active, . . . allowing no time for idleness or vice. Her pursuits soon establish a taste for knowledge which increases with every new attainment." Whether pursuing women or pursuing science, Hayden was making up for a painful sense of inadequacy, and the wider his reach—and the greater his grasp—the better he felt about himself.

This encyclopedic, or what I will call the broadbrush, approach to natural history, which Hayden absorbed so readily from his mentors, rested on two related assumptions. First, despite the complexity of their circumstances, all creatures lived according to fixed laws; second, God had promulgated those laws. It was a tenet of these assumptions that all creatures exhibited a sort of unity, if only the mysterious essence of life itself, and it was not forbidden for man to try understanding that linkage. Indeed, many asserted it a duty to do so. Furthermore, since a benevolent deity would have promulgated just laws, those laws would seem to be discernible through rational inquiry, more specifically through the empirical method. Thus all fields of knowledge lay open to the naturalist, and each offered some insight into the Creator's plan, which is why naturalists had been sweeping with as broad a brush as possible, to collect the large and the small, the old and new, the familiar and the exotic.

Hayden gleaned this spirit of the times from his mentors, and he began his career by thinking along traditional lines of a unified world designed by God. In 1852, like virtually all other naturalists of the time, Hayden busied himself trying to learn the most basic aspects of the natural world, without asking or even considering any deeper questions. Surrendering to the ample bosom of Mother Nature meant entering a stimulating and rewarding career. It also brought a warm companionship, the sort he had missed in his own family; his colleagues became a substitute family. Thus, with all her dazzling wonders did fair Nature bid to fill his heart as well as his mind.

From spring 1852 until spring of the following year, Hayden began to find himself. He went on listening to Kirtland's lectures. Simultaneously, he studied medicine with Newberry and a little geology too. He collected fossils among the limestone rocks at Sandusky, found what turned out to be a new species of the Chara plant, and sent it to Asa Gray for identification; it was eventually named for Hayden. Hayden began an ambitious correspondence with other naturalists around the country, picking their brains, asking for scientific books, and boasting of his collections; he even proposed a collecting trip in the South to a more experienced botanist and offered himself as assistant. Even before his colleagues met him, Hayden was gaining a reputation as a serious and eager naturalist. Wrote one, "You have been very successful this season in that study, having detected and determined a larger number of plants (species) than I have ever known a person to do before, in the same length of time." He added prophetically, "At this rate, you will sigh (with Alexander) for other worlds to conquer."

Hayden's medical studies with Newberry for two terms amounted to an apprenticeship. Apprenticeship was the traditional entrée to the profession, and until well into the second half of the nineteenth century most practitioners took this route to the M.D. in preference to medical school. Hayden probably assisted Newberry on his rounds, ran errands, prepared pharmaceutical remedies, and followed him on his hospital rounds—even into the operating theatre to assist with dissections and operations. But the personal relationship between Hayden and Newberry is more interesting than the medical one, especially in view of Newberry's torrid hostility later. The man who shared Newberry's medical practice remembered Hayden did an indifferent job of cleaning up the office and looking after their affairs. "In fact," he continued, "so brassy was he that he always considered us his debtors." The anecdote could just as well have come from Newberry himself. Not quite six years older than Hayden, Newberry had finished his medical degree in 1848; no doubt he expected Hayden to be the deferential protégé.

In order to understand his relationship with Hayden, one yearns to know Newberry better. For an objective appraisal of his character or a frank discussion of his idiosyncrasies, one cannot rely on the adulatory cliches written by his Victorian colleagues, who disguised all warts, all skeletons, and anything else that would have made Newberry an interesting, believable human being.[2] But reading between the lines of even these fulsome eulogies, one surmises that Newberry was, to put it in modern language, a condescending authoritarian. Yes, he was said to be cheerful to students and always ready to give of his time for their concerns, but it was also admitted that he liked to hear himself talk and that he was not skilled in stimulating discussions. Significantly, he never attracted—or would likely have tolerated—a close professional relationship with a student or younger associate the way even the cantankerous James Hall did with several of his protégés. Jealous and secretive, Newberry worked alone and without assistance from anyone on the research projects that interested him.

All Hayden's mentors outranked him in age and scientific experience, but he came to work with all of them as a true colleague, a peer—all but Newberry, that is. That becomes the first clue in explaining their later estrangement. Another is that Newberry came from a wealthy family. His grandfather was an original purchaser of lands on the Western Reserve in northern Ohio. His father successfully managed mills, mined coal, and founded the town of Cuyahoga Falls. Newberry was typical of scientific men Hayden would encounter again and again as he rose to prominence. Most came from comfortable families. Most had studied in prestigious universities on the eastern seaboard, and a number, including Newberry, added postgraduate experience in foreign universities, at a cost that would have been beyond Hayden's fondest dreams.

While he delved into natural history, Ferdinand kept in touch with several chums from Oberlin as well as some former students in the district schools. Cleveland was the largest city Hayden had ever lived in, and as one friend said, "You with your fine exquisite sense of the beautiful will no doubt appreciate its beauty." Indeed he did, in more ways than one. He would often go walking in the Cleveland cemetery, and one day he encountered Louise, a former student from Cuyahoga Falls, and that meeting encouraged him to begin a fond correspondence with their mutual friend Myra Holloway. Hayden told another friend, Mary Scranton, of his tie to a Prospect Street Church Society—probably the same group Hayden met with on Thursday evenings to discuss Nature and God. He also became very close to one Maria, who must have been a stimulating intellectual and spiritual companion, for she wrote of music and her teaching. She also wondered (on the Sabbath) whether Hayden was in church that day and wished she were there to share in his devotions. Maria and Ferdinand seem to have stimulated more than each other's minds. She confides, "Yes, I do visit you, not in dreams alone, but daily, in imagination," then adds, suggestively, that she has nearly finished her affair with Benton Hunt. Ferdinand lost no time pursuing that hint, for within two weeks Hunt was writing indignantly to deplore Hayden's recent behavior.

On the darker side of his personal life, Hayden's father reappeared several times during this year. In Rochester, after surviving a bout with tremors for six to seven weeks, he moved into the late stages of alcoholism, pawned his clothes to get money, and spent all he got immediately. He was hallucinating about being Melchizedek (a strong father figure in the Old Testament—an ironic choice), communing directly with God, meanwhile running around the streets ranting and swearing. "You can have no idea," Hayden's Aunt Lucretia wrote, "what a trial we have had with him." Pathetically, Asa himself wrote a short time later, acknowledging his deteriorating condition and imploring, "If you wish to see me any more, you will have to come here, for I am failing pretty fast." Actually, he lived another five years.

Easily the most fateful of all Hayden's early connections was with James Hall, which took place in late autumn 1851, at the home of Dr. and Mrs. Newberry. Hall had visited at the home of Newberry's father years earlier and encouraged young John in his observations of natural history. Now it was Hayden's turn to meet one of the strangest men in the history of American science. In 1836, at only twenty-five years of age, Hall was chosen to head one of the four districts of New York's geological survey. By the time he met Hayden he had become the leading spirit of that survey as well as New York's paleontologist, and he had published a classic study on New York's Fourth District, which demonstrated the great utility of invertebrates for correlating layers of rock and established an early stratigraphic column that would become widely used in other parts of America.

Archival work is rarely dull, but to sit in Albany and read through Hall's papers is nothing short of electrifying. The man was at times raving mad, vengeful, deceitful, and always suspicious, pugnacious, petulant; yet all the while he marched vigorously under the banner of self-righteousness. He excelled at sarcasm and character assassination. There was not an assistant with whom he did not quarrel—usually furiously—no scientific institution that escaped his criticism, and no patron who could boast of his unremitting gratitude. On the contrary, it seems that Hall saved his crudest damnations for the New York legislators, regents, and other officials who sponsored him. John James Stevenson, a younger geologist who became adept at writing obituaries of his senior colleagues, once wrote of Hall (in a confidential letter):

> If JH had lived in Philadelphia among men, and not in Albany among politicians, he would have been a very different man. But he never met anybody: he was isolated. Whenever any busybody in science found no devil's work to do elsewhere, he would put a suspicion into H's mind respecting some friend and make the poor man miserable. If H. had had half a chance he would have been a loveable man. You think I was wrong in calling him childlike. A man possessing his confidence could do anything with him. He was the most tractable man I ever met.

This insight is valuable from a man who never had to cross swords with Hall and may explain the happy circumstances of Hayden's early friendship with Hall.

Nearly forty years later Hall still remembered his first meeting with Hayden in 1851. He was especially impressed with Hayden's zeal, and they talked of sending him to the Bad Lands of Dakota to collect fossils. Hall said to Hayden, in effect, I think I can find some work for you in Albany as soon as you have finished your studies here with Kirtland and Newberry; contact me then. Rightly seeing this informal offer as an unparalleled opportunity, Hayden wrote Hall in early January 1853, almost two months before he would finish his studies in Cleveland, to remind Hall of their conversation and nudge him toward some practical offer. Hall replied promptly that a collecting trip to the Bad Lands now seemed less expensive than he had thought, meanwhile "I will promise you that I will either give you the means of going on this expedition, or upon some other nearer home." Enticingly he added that Hayden might want to finish up his medical studies in Albany, for which Hall could make the arrangements, and that Hayden could then assist him with his New York fossils.

Rather than being swept off his feet by such promises, Hayden evinced the same native shrewdness Hall had shown at the same age, when Hall had insinuated himself into a leading position on the New York Survey. About the time he wrote Hall, Hayden also wrote Charles Christopher Parry, the botanical collector, to inquire whether Spencer Fullerton Baird, assistant secretary of the Smithsonian and in charge of organizing all the specimens brought back by the western explorers, could attach him to any scientific expeditions. At the same time he had Kirtland write Baird on his behalf, asking the same question. "He is truly enterprising," Kirtland assured Baird, in an understatement neither he nor anyone else could have appreciated at the time. Then Hayden calmly sat down to answer Hall, saying he was eager for anything Hall could arrange for him, but he wondered (thinking about his other options) whether it might be better to go to the Bad Lands *next* year and study geology in some field closer to home this season. In short, he was holding out for the best offer, and he closed by urging Hall to write soon, saying he was eager for fieldwork.

Two weeks later, having heard nothing from Hall or Baird, he wrote Baird himself, making up for his lack of experience and knowledge by a disarming boldness. "I am extremely anxious to spend a few years in the study of natural history. I feel as though I could endure cheerfully any amount of toil, hardship and self denial provided I could gratify my strong desire to labor in the field of a naturalist . . . Were it necessary to accomplish my purpose, I could live as the wild Indian lives and endure any amount of exposure and trial without a murmur." Thus in February 1853 began a long and mostly harmonious friendship that would profoundly impact the study of natural history in America. But he still had no job. Replying in late February, Baird said there were no openings on expeditions at the moment and no way to employ Hayden at the Smithsonian itself; but Baird was encouraging without committing himself to anything. In his next letter to Hall, in early March, Hayden rehearsed his financial dilemma and wondered, should the Bad Lands trip be delayed, if he might work for Hall in Albany for the next several months. He offered to do so for $150, plus expenses.

The availability of an enthusiastic young naturalist prompted Hall to ponder the feasibility of a collecting trip to the White River Bad Lands (then in the Territory of Nebraska; today they are in South Dakota). The first fossils from this region, retrieved in 1843, stirred up enormous excitement among scientific men. Geologist John Evans, who collected there, made clear the extraordinary nature of this boneyard. "At every step," he said in his report to David Dale Owen, "objects of the highest interest present themselves. Embedded in the debris, lie strewn in the greatest profusion, organic relics of extinct animals. All speak of a vast fresh-water deposit of the early Tertiary Period." Joseph Leidy of Philadelphia, who described the first mammal remains from the White River area, wrote feverishly to Baird on 5 December 1851, "I think it must be the greatest cemetery in the world for Eocene mammalia. . . . You can have no idea how much my mind has become inflamed upon this subject. Night after night, I dream of strange forms: Eocene crania with recent eyes in them." He asked Baird if they might cooperate on a future venture to the Bad Lands, splitting costs and the resulting proceeds.

Baird had already been thinking of the Bad Lands, but not of sharing any collections. He granted Smithsonian sponsorship to a small private party to go there in 1850, and he pestered George Engelmann to do what he could for the Smithsonian. Engelmann was a German-born naturalist and physician who had been collecting for German museums from his base in St. Louis. Baird's plan was to promote private ventures until a government-funded trip could be organized, which would cost the Smithsonian nothing, yet return all the collections to Washington. By law the Smithsonian was the official repository for all collections brought back by government expeditions. Consequently, Baird ignored Leidy's suggestion about a joint venture. Baird also chose not to reply to Hall's queries about the Bad Lands, even though he knew Hall was considering sending Hayden there.

Rumors from St. Louis galvanized Baird into action; he had heard that two Germans were planning a private collecting trip to the Bad Lands in spring 1853. To circumvent the men he called "outside barbarians," Baird arranged in early April for John Evans to be attached to the northern survey, which was to search for the most practical railroad route between the Great Lakes and Puget Sound; Governor Isaac Stevens of Washington Territory was the leader of the survey. Learning of this, Leidy renewed his offer to provide some of the funding for Evans, and Baird was pleased to accept. As a result, Baird would eventually take two-thirds of the Evans collection for the Smithsonian, and Leidy one-third for the Academy of Natural Sciences of Philadelphia.

In their eagerness to divide up the spoils, neither Baird nor Leidy bothered to inform James Hall about the Evans venture until the second week of May. Meanwhile, Hall had also learned about the Germans during March, and their potential competition stimulated him to go forward. As he wrote to Leidy on 10 April, "I feel a little patriotic just now and am anxious to prevent all these things from going to Europe." The nod to patriotism conveniently disguised Hall's ambition to be the first to gather and describe a really significant load from the Bad Lands.

In this competition between self-interested giants Hayden played the part of a catalyst. With little professional experience to recommend him, he pushed himself forward and offered to undertake a risky and expensive expedition. Did Hayden genuinely charm Hall with his contagious enthusiasm, as he would afterward charm (and later antagonize) so many others? Or did Hall amuse himself in encouraging Hayden, without revealing much of his own plans for him? Hall wrote in flattering terms of the young naturalist: "He is ardent, enthusiastic and untiring in his industry," he wrote to one colleague, and to another he described him, even before they had worked together, as "a young man, a friend of mine."

But while doing all he could to stoke Hayden's vanity and ambition, Hall was checking up on his young friend. Newberry responded to a query from Hall with the warning that "in a subordinate capacity Mr. H would be excellent. He has enthusiasm, industry, and untiring perseverance, but has had little experience in the ways of the world & little practise in the field." Newberry went on to make a useful suggestion. "After a little training I think he would serve you as a collector in New York, Ohio, or the western states very efficiently, and would probably do as well for you in the far west as any one who would take the place of an employee." Three days later Hall got another letter, a very bold one from Hayden himself, announcing his intention of coming to Albany. He would study with Hall before entering the field, he said, and he would start right away for Albany unless Hall told him not to come.

So confident was Hayden of working with Hall that he began announcing his good fortune to his friends even as early as February. His friends congratulated him on his new career in science. From his mother, however, came a different reaction. "I could not find out what you was going for. When you write again you writ it plain so that I read what it is," she replied after learning he might be going west. She thought it would be dangerous and concluded, "I hope you will live to come back. If you goe I think great deal about you. I shal be glad when you finish your profession . . . I don't work as hard as I use to. I am a going old. I hope I shal spend my last days with you." So in addition to an embarrassing father, Hayden had to think of an aging mother, a woman who had virtually abandoned him, had never shown him much affection, and now was expecting him to take care of her.

Hayden spent about two weeks with Hall during April, at which time he met and became favorably inclined toward Hall's chief assistant, another older man named Fielding Bradford Meek. By coincidence, Joseph Leidy came up to Albany from Philadelphia that spring to see some of Hall's fossils. He and

Hayden may have met at that time. Even if they did not, by now they were known to each other. Within a year and a half of coming to Cleveland, therefore, Hayden had made several valuable connections in the scientific world—with Kirtland, Newberry, Baird, Gray, Parry, Hall, Meek, and Leidy. To these he would add George Engelmann when he arrived in St. Louis.

In this way Hayden recruited a substitute family, to which he would now look for guidance and patronage. He became dependent on these men not only for professional advancement but also for approval and friendship. Largely to please his sponsors and also because he needed something to throw himself into, he embraced the prevailing broadbrush ideas about natural history. As yet he showed none of the self-confidence or curiosity that breeds an independent approach to science. The seeds of a more creative side of Hayden were planted during his earliest exposures to the West, though they grew slowly and even Hayden scarcely noticed them during a long and at times painful apprenticeship. In the beginning he had only his boundless energy, his enthusiasm, his boldness, and his ambition.

Just after Hayden returned to Cleveland near the end of April 1853 to complete his preparations for the Bad Lands, he wrote to assure Hall he felt capable of undertaking the expedition alone. By that time Hall had made other plans, and he replied that he would be sending Meek along as chief of the Bad Lands trip. If Hayden was miffed at this, he hid it well. He wrote warmly to Meek just before leaving for St. Louis on 29 April and showed he was already thinking of how Meek's presence could be turned to his own advantage: "If you bring along your paint brushes, etc. we may make drawings of shells rainy days and give me a chance to learn something of the art."

5
IN THE
BAD LANDS, 1853

These words [Bad Lands] signify a very difficult country to travel through, not only from the ruggedness of the surface, but also from the absence of any good water and the small supply of wood and game.

—Hayden, *The Great West* (1880), 43

THE WHITE RIVER Bad Lands were to occupy a special place in Hayden's heart. Their awesome piles enchanted him. Their desolate appearance disguised the fertile formations running beneath the surface. Their mysteries challenged his resourcefulness, but also yielded fruitfully to his persistence. Hayden visited the Bad Lands many times, more than any other single location in the West, and the sum of his work there contributed mightily to his knowledge. But this first journey was chiefly important to Hayden in proving that he could succeed as a collector of natural history specimens. His experiences were exciting, but in several respects did not live up to his expectations. And a number of unpleasant surprises occurred.

The first, which came before the expedition even got under way, concerned its leadership. Despite giving Hayden the impression that he would be sending him alone to the Bad Lands, Hall had been looking around for an experienced naturalist to head the expedition, to whom Hayden would be an assistant. In replying to one of Hall's letters, Newberry wrote on 23 March he was sorry to hear Hall's "friend" had decided not to go on the trip: "If of the right stamp his cooperation with Hayden would be of the utmost importance." The identity of this friend is not mentioned, but it was probably Dr. H. A. Prout of St. Louis, who had described some of the early fossils retrieved from the Bad Lands. Prout sent Hall some cost estimates for a Bad Lands trip, but added he was very sorry he could not go; his language suggested that Hall had offered the trip to him. On 24 April, Hall wrote Hayden that Meek would be in charge.

So it seems Hall never intended to let Hayden go alone in the first place, and that the mantle of leadership only came to Meek as a second choice. Hall may have turned to Meek because he had heard rumors of what soon became a fact, namely that Evans wanted Meek as one of his assistants. Indeed, Evans mailed a formal offer to Albany on 2 May. Meek got it well before leaving for St. Louis on 9 May, and he told Hall about it. That offer confirmed for Hall that Evans would be going to the Bad Lands.

Since Hall knew about the offer before Meek left Albany, Hall was less than truthful when he later claimed that he would not have sent his own expedition had he known about Evans's plans. In an undated letter to George Engelmann, probably written during late May, Hall further claimed to have telegraphed Meek in St. Louis to cancel the expedition. This would have been in reaction to hearing from Hayden that Governor Stevens opposed his plans and to learning the costs of the expedition, which Hayden thought might run as high as $1,200. But it is most unlikely that Hall sent Meek any such instructions; certainly Meek never received them. Hall could not look on rivals with equanimity, and his intemperate language stemmed from anger. As he fumed to Engelmann in the same letter, "I am so utterly disgusted with this whole affair that I shall make an effort to dispose of all the collection, should one be made, without ever seeing it." It was a rash promise, which he must have known the moment he uttered it he would not keep.

Meanwhile, things were not going well in St. Louis for Hall's two protégés. Hayden arrived on 4 May and promptly reported that it had been a mistake to buy so many supplies in advance in Cleveland and other places (all with Hall's money), for everything was cheaper in St. Louis. Then Meek arrived 14 May and went directly to Governor Stevens with the impossible task of mollifying him concerning the trip that James Hall was sending out in competition with his own. No one had the courage to tell Hall how near his venture came to being eclipsed, but Hayden came the closest when he reported that the Stevens party was "violently opposed to our going to Bad Lands." More of the explosive details trickled out in Engelmann's letter to Baird of 28 June, in which he said that Stevens had behaved "in an overbearing and by no means conciliatory way" and had threatened to throw more money and men into the Bad Lands to destroy Hall's chances there.

What dissipated the tension was both surprising and ironic. Louis Agassiz, the Swiss-born naturalist then at Harvard, who had made a reputation studying fishes and glaciers, was in St. Louis at the time on a lecture tour. Blessed with a congenial disposition and beloved by many of his fellow naturalists in Europe and America, Agassiz offered a pleasant contrast to the coarse ambition that motivated many of his colleagues. He and George Engelmann stepped into the fray and made two suggestions in order to defuse the rivalry and maximize the collections. They suggested that the Evans party absorb Hayden and Meek into its ranks and that Stevens compensate Hall for his expenses so far. It was a sensible and honorable solution for all concerned and could have succeeded. Evans especially liked the idea; after all, it would have brought Meek into his camp, which is precisely what he had wanted from the beginning. But Stevens was unwilling to share the glory that would accrue to a successful party of collectors. Too conventional to acknowledge such naked greed, he voiced some unspecified quibble about Hayden. Overnight, Evans seems to have persuaded Stevens that some accommodation with Meek and Hayden was desirable. The next day the two parties considered a second proposal from Evans on a cooperative venture, but this time it was Meek who rejected it. He did so because he realized that Hall was every bit as reluctant as Stevens to share glory and, therefore, that he had to insist (on behalf of Hall) on an independent expedition.

No one on either side backed down. Engelmann captured the heart of the matter in writing to Hall on 23 May, "I was deeply pained to witness the spirit of rapacity, envy and sickly emulation evinced by most of the persons interested. And of this Mr. Hayden is not free himself. . . . There is a want of the true spirit of science, the pure love for science in all this; there is on the contrary a selfishness and rapacity manifested in this, which grieved me much. And I am afraid that this is not the end of it yet." At this point Agassiz and Engelmann, tactfully endorsing what was going to happen anyway, suggested that each party take its own separate path.

Next Hall himself nearly scuttled the expedition, for somehow he neglected to send his letter of credit to the American Fur Company, to compensate the company for its cost in carrying Hayden and Meek up and down the river, with all their freight and collections. The letters Hall exchanged with Engelmann made no specific arrangements for transferring funds, and Hall probably assumed he could settle up with Engelmann and the fur company later. To meet this emergency, Engelmann stepped into the breach and guaranteed the expenses of Meek and Hayden; as soon as Hall learned of it in mid-June, he replied, "I shall attend to any drafts by the Fur Company."

He explained his oversight by adding, "I had supposed that this was all fully arranged by Mr. Chouteau." Charles Chouteau was head of the American Fur Company.

On 21 May, after several delays, the steamer *Robert Campbell* departed St. Louis for Fort Pierre, carrying over one hundred passengers, two hundred crew, and three hundred to four hundred tons of freight. The rival parties embarked on the same ship as did the mysterious Germans, who turned out to be the twenty-year-old Prince of Nassau, a traveling companion, and two servants—no threat to professional naturalists. The Germans disembarked just west of the Vermilion River; in the end they collected fishes for Agassiz in Missouri, Arkansas, and Texas. Thus the group that had stimulated so much chauvinism and rivalry among American naturalists never went near the Bad Lands. A further irony is that Louis Agassiz should have been instrumental in intervening on behalf of his friend James Hall to assure the journey of Meek and Hayden. Agassiz, the gentle proponent of a creationistic view of natural history, thereby unleashed a formidable team whose collections over the next several years went a long way toward undermining the traditional notion that science only revealed the workings of God in the world.

At last Hayden's first voyage could begin. Alas, for days he was bottled up on board most of the time. The river was full of snags and sandbars that could have destroyed the steamboat, so the captain had to proceed slowly and tie up each night. During the day they advanced at only three to four miles per hour through monotonous scenery. "Nothing is to be seen but low alluvial bottoms, and islands clothed with a dense growth of gigantic sycamores, cottonwoods, oaks, maples, etc.," Meek wrote to Hall. Occasionally they viewed cliffs at a distance, which only whetted their appetites for a closer look at rock formations. Nevertheless, the boat stopped several times a day to cut and take on wood for fuel, and at these times Hayden and Meek eagerly scampered overboard to grab anything in sight. Some of the passengers helped, especially with plants and flowers.

Carrying as much human cargo as it did, the *Robert Campbell* offered opportunities for those ambitious to form new connections. In St. Louis Hayden had already met several of the leading officials of the American Fur Company, including Alexander Culbertson and Captain John Sarpy, and an Indian agent, Major Alfred J. Vaughan, all of whom were on board. Hayden must have made a favorable impression on them, for each would become valuable to him in future trips on the Upper Missouri. Though only of moderate height and possessing no striking physical features, Hayden commanded a lively intelligence. With his contagious enthusiasm and his desire to please those who could help him, it is easy to imagine Hayden making lots of new friends during this time on the river. Meek's letters (our best source on the upstream voyage) say little about Hayden, but they reveal Meek as somewhat aloof. He was an upright gentleman who expressed shock at seeing how many of the fur traders had married Indians or half-breeds, and who disdained a feast of dog meat with the natives when two hundred of them came on board at the invitation of Captain Sarpy. "I do not envy them their supper," he wrote dourly.

Regular encounters with Indians provided relief from the slow churning upriver. Major Vaughan dispensed presents to the Sioux at several points along the way, and the passengers often amused themselves by throwing crackers to them, which were always gathered up and handed over to an elder for later distribution. Once in a while Meek permitted himself a certain admiration: "Some of these Indians are mounted on good horses and cut quite a figure as they sweep across the prairies with their long hair and trappings flying in the wind." But Indians did not provide all the excitement. On the fourth day a fire burst out in the bow; apparently started by careless smokers, it threatened to reach ten thousand pounds of powder stored just below in the hold. Passengers crowded to the stern and would have abandoned ship had Sarpy not extinguished the fire promptly. On another night a strong wind nearly capsized them. The neophytes were learning the dangers of a strange new world.

Gradually, they were also relaxing, sitting back, and learning to appreciate the outdoors on its own terms. Although initially bored with the scenery, toward the end of the second week Meek expressed a different mood.

> Frequently the eye wanders over a vast expanse of level prairie with here and there long, narrow belts of scattering trees and island-like groves beyond which the view is bounded by dimly seen ranges of hills, or less elevated rolling prairie. Although the prairie grass is not less than two feet high, when we look at the prairies and distant hills the whole surface appears as smooth and soft as velvet. All these objects when viewed in a proper light, present a scene which is beautiful beyond description.

At the same time the two naturalists took every opportunity to amass specimens. Before arriving at Fort Pierre, they accumulated over 350 plants and several bottles filled with insects. Just north of the present site of Sioux City the Missouri takes a decisive swing toward the west, and before turning north again into the present state of North Dakota, it welcomes three large streams—the Big Sioux, the Vermilion and the James rivers—near each of which Hayden and Meek found interesting fossils. Farther upriver, shortly before the Big Bend, they ascended Bijoux Hills, where they discovered in

Tertiary rocks some teeth of a large reptile or mammal of uncertain age. Leidy later determined they belonged to a true ruminant, and were therefore relatively recent. At the Big Bend of the Missouri they left the boat and walked across the land encircled by the river, finding one of their richest stores of fossils, different from those located elsewhere. Near Red Cedar Island, thirty-five miles south of Fort Pierre, they found still others.

The animals these fossils represented had once lived in specific niches, in unique relationships with other animals. To a trained eye the fossils revealed much about early environments, including the general setting of climate, temperature, topography, and so on. They also disclosed the comparative ages of the animals they represented and of the formations in which they were found. Specific time dating, possible today by measuring radiocarbon deterioration, was unknown in Hayden's day.[1] Instead, geologists had only a comparative idea of which rocks were older than certain others, based on the principle that older rocks usually lie deeper down. Geologists in England first learned to "date" formations by the characteristic fossils within them during the early nineteenth century, and in America the technique was most successfully amplified by none other than James Hall.

Hayden got his first lessons about fossils from Newberry and Hall, from whom he learned such rudiments as the names and characteristics of key species and the kinds of rock in which to find them. But the Missouri River gave Hayden his first experience with formations that spread over hundreds of miles and whose composition had to be gleaned from occasional outcrops in cliffs or exposures at riverbanks. From the hurricane deck of the *Robert Campbell* Hayden examined the breadth and structure of the country, and he began to practice the art of quickly identifying isolated features, synthesizing them in his brain with scores of others, then unifying them all into a coherent, dynamic picture. This was the grand sweep of geology, which carried a man from horizon to horizon, from week to week, and from the small representative fossil to the grand vision of a geological map.

Meek instructed him further about fossils, but no one could teach vision, for vision is an inner response to the external environment. It enables the geologist to engorge and transform the disorganized facts of nature. It is a process both intellectual and intuitive, ritualistic, and imaginative, frustrating but enormously stimulating, and ultimately romantic—at which Hayden became the highest of high priests. He did not so much learn the methods as he discovered within himself the ability to invent them. It is a gift, and one that has been insufficiently appreciated by historians of science, who have paid more respect to theorists, such as James Dwight Dana, John Lawrence LeConte, Henry Rogers, or Hall himself, or to the classifiers, like Amos Eaton, J. Peter Lesley, Josiah Dwight Whitney, or again Hall, or even to the administrators, like Baird. Yet none of these deservedly eminent men could look at virgin country and read it the way Hayden learned to do. A few of the great collectors, like Othniel Charles Marsh or Edward Drinker Cope, Charles Sternberg or John Hatcher, also combined intuition with intellect to reap mighty results, but these men became specialists; none of them approached Hayden's versatility as a collector or his breadth of vision.

On 19 June the *Robert Campbell* arrived at Fort Pierre, having covered the 1,600 miles in two days less than a month. Fort Pierre sat at the mouth of the Teton River, later known as the Bad River. Culbertson provided the pair of naturalists with six horses, three carts and appropriate tack, as well as three men who would serve as guides and hunters—one a quadroon, "who is as dark colored as an Indian" and who took along his own wigwam and squaw. At the suggestion of Evans—now more friendly since he had separated from the proud Governor Stevens—the rival parties traveled in tandem, camping nearby and sharing the kills of the hunters. The first day out an axle on one of the carts broke while they were crossing a stream. They returned to the fort for another, then recommenced. They traveled along the main road to Fort Laramie, heading for the White River Bad Lands, some 50 miles east of the Black Hills.

Meek's diary—covering a period of twenty-nine days—provides the only record of their experiences in the field. He filled it with notes on formations (which became the basis for the first vertical section depicting the stratigraphy of the Bad Lands, later published by Hall and Meek), but he conveyed only a general outline of their daily work. Along Sage Creek, in the heart of the Bad Lands, they found entombed in beds of clay "fine specimens of Ammonite, Baculite, Scaphite, Inoceramus, Nautilus, Dentatum, etc., . . . Some of the Ammonites are very large, in nodules, not less than 3 ft in diam." They found other fossils near the head of Bear Creek, but Sage Creek proved the richest lode.

Two educated but urban naturalists could not resist commenting on the sometimes bizarre circumstances in which they found themselves. For instance, at a spontaneous dinner with two Sioux they were offered "a tin pan full of jerked buffalo meat and pome de prairie boiled together. The dish did not look very clean nor was it very savoury, but as it would have been a great breach of etiquette to have appeared displeased with it, we ate of it and pronounced it very fine." Meek found prairie dog "only tolerably good," but of antelope he said, "I am very fond of it, think it more savory and delicate food than deer meat." The guides preferred buffalo meat, arguing that it gave them greater strength, though one of them found tripe "a delicate morsel," and he ate it "raw and without washing." They saw the tracks of grizzly bears and more wildlife than either of them had ever imagined, including lots of wolves. The wolves "prowl around within a 100 yds of our camp soon after sun set, and at night come up and help themselves to pieces of fresh meat left hanging on the carts within two or three steps of the tents."

The Bad Lands exuded mystery, and Meek deliberately recorded his first impressions of them. "The appearance was very much like that of the ruins of Ancient Castles and fortifications of gigantic dimensions. . . . These hills and peaks appear to be entirely destitute of vegetation, and are light grayish yellow, almost white in col[or]." Hayden's first observations of the Bad Lands do not survive, but a later description (*The Great West,* 1880) harks back to Meek's. "But it is only to the geologist that this place can have any permanent attractions. He can wind his way through the wonderful cañons among some of the grandest ruins in the world. Indeed, it resembles a gigantic city fallen to decay. Domes, towers, minarets, and spires may be seen on every side, which assume a great variety of shapes when viewed in the distance." Possibly suggestive of the conditions he and Meek encountered in 1853, Hayden added, "In the summer the sun pours its rays on the bare white walls, which are reflected on the weary traveller with double intensity, not only oppressing him with the heat, but so dazzling his eyes that he is not infrequently affected with temporary blindness. I have spent many days exploring this region when the thermometer was 112° in the shade and there was no water suitable for drinking purposes within fifteen miles. Lack of water plagued Hayden during each of the subsequent expeditions he made to the Bad Lands.

He collected in virtually all horizons, but he made some of his best finds along Bear Creek and on lower Sage Creek, where the abrupt pinnacles of the true Bad Lands yield to gentler prairie to the west and south. Here it was cooler, and he could let his horse graze, though the water was not much better until one reached the Cheyenne River.

The lack of potable water and other natural resources was especially discouraging during his first visit to the Bad Lands. On their last evening in the wilds, finding little water and no wood, Meek grimly recorded, "Isadore burned up his lodge poles to make a cup of tea for supper." An equally serious problem, and one that finally drove them back to Fort Pierre just short of a month, was the danger from Indians. Meek's diary makes ominous references to various groups of Sioux, known or thought to be in the region. His fears were justified, for some tribes regarded the Bad Lands as sacred territory, and they viewed wanderings there by the white man as intolerable. Knowing this, and remembering vague threats voiced by several natives at Fort Pierre, the two naturalists were nervous from the start. The end was in sight when anxiety crept into the minds of even their guides. Fearing trouble at the end of their first week, one of the guides advised the party to go back. Meek's terse summary showed the expedition was living on borrowed time: "Some dissatisfaction amongst our men almost amounting to mutiny. Have succeeded in getting them to go on."

And on they went, feeling they must gather some specimens to justify all their troubles in getting to the Bad Lands, not to mention Hall's expenses. But another week brought greater tensions. "Our camping place and the locality where we are at work is between two large bands of unfriendly Indians. . . . We are constantly in dread of them. If they find us they will probably not kill us but will rob us of everything." And loss of those precious specimens, they may have joked aloud, would have been far more serious to Hall than any threat to their own lives. At any rate, by 18 July they were back at the fort, noting uneasily that the campsite they used that very morning had since been occupied by "unfriendly bands consisting of about 1000 to 1100 warriors."

It was time to come home. Culbertson had already arranged a mackinaw-type boat for their descent, and they got away on 27 July, reaching Council Bluffs on 7 August. A mackinaw was normally around 40 feet by 10 feet and drew 15 to 20 inches, large enough to carry the 10 to 15 tons of cargo the fur company commonly shuttled up and down the river. The large craft would have provided plenty of room for all the specimens Meek and Hayden had gathered, but it also required a steersman and four oarsmen. The boat that actually brought them downriver was somewhat smaller, for it carried a total of only five men: Meek and Hayden, "one good pilot and two stout men to row." Meek called it a "mackinac."

Away from bands of hostile Indians and able to select from among numerous campsites, the naturalists found the descent more pleasant and also more fruitful for their collections. They stopped for longer looks at several cliffs and exposures of rock they had only glanced at on the upstream voyage, and they garnered more fossils at several promising sites. They also witnessed one of the strangest migrations ever recorded in the West, millions of frogs moving across the Missouri during the month of July. Others remarked on the phenomenon several hundred miles west of the river, where the frogs congested springs and wells and, according to one observer, crowded the ground in damp places to a density of fifty to a square foot.

Near Council Bluffs they left their mackinac and unloaded all their specimens at Peter Sarpy's trading post, above the mouth of the Platte. They intended to transfer immediately to a fur company boat, which was expected at any moment. It did not arrive for another nine days. On 16 August they loaded their precious cargo onto a steamboat, which brought them safely to St. Louis on 21 August.

One of their immediate problems was how to tell Hall about their unexpectedly large expenses. Before the voyage began, Hayden had written from St. Louis that $1,000 to $1,200 would probably cover everything, but Meek later revised the estimate downward by several hundred dollars after conversations with Culbertson. Then something went wrong. As they anxiously confided to Newberry after reaching Cleveland, total expenses now stood at $1,500. Years later, Meek revealed what had happened. The fur company had simply taken advantage of them, regarding them "rather in the light of intruders on ground belonging to others and consequently charged us unheard of prices." The charges at Fort Pierre were double what had been quoted in St. Louis. At first sight the trip seemed a disaster, costing much more than expected and lasting too short a time to enable the collectors to compensate for the large expense. No matter how Meek and Hayden smoothed it over with him, initially Hall could not have been pleased. In the end, Hall recouped some of his expense by selling part of the collection.

Hall noted in his formal report, "One of the principal objects of this expedition was the discovery of the fossil flora of this period, so prolific in remains of Mammalia, as well as to determine more clearly the relations between Cretaceous formations of the Missouri Valley and those of the region especially known as the Mauvaises Terres." As he had written to Meek on 12 August, he especially wanted samples of Carboniferous fossils, in order to connect the geology of the Missouri with that of New York State. The fossils brought back were mostly Cretaceous, but insufficient to compare the Bad Lands with the nearby Missouri Valley, and certainly not enough to justify any generalizations about similarities with the eastern states. The flora were interesting, but, like the whole collection, not nearly as substantial as had been hoped. Hall summarized, "Circumstances . . . over which the writer or the exploring party had no control, frustrated in a great measure the original objects of the expedition."

But there were some positive results of the trip, especially for Hayden. Hall acknowledged Hayden's ability to find specimens, by naming one of the new mollusks for his talented young collector—*Avicula haydeni,* a pearl oyster. Hayden and Meek brought back thirteen boxes of fossils and more than one hundred vertebrate heads, including those of titanotheres (extinct mammals related to the rhinoceros), plus numerous reptiles, insects, and a few fossil plants. Most important for geology were the thirty-four new species of invertebrate shells they found embedded in Cretaceous rock. This precisely doubled the number of Cretaceous shells then known to science and was more than five times the number of new species Evans retrieved.

The applause of those who had sponsored the rival Evans party was especially gratifying. Leidy (who had put $100 of his own money at Evans's disposal, and who procured an additional $500 from a colleague at the Philadelphia Academy) wasted no time in writing Hall to ask for permission to describe the vertebrates, which Hall granted. Leidy found the collection contained better specimens than any he had been able to examine before. Baird, who had so brazenly tried to brush aside Hall's efforts on behalf of Meek and Hayden and had done all in his power to equip the stronger hand of Evans, also paid his respects by traveling to Albany to see the trove, which he pronounced "magnificent." This recognition was more important than anything else, and for Hayden the sweetest fruit of his short journey was the favorable attention of Spencer Baird, the greatest Midas in the history of American natural history—if not of the world. Baird would provide critical assistance for Hayden's future ventures.

6

SOLO ON THE UPPER MISSOURI, 1854–1855

I have not the slightest doubt but that I could bring as large and valuable [a] collection as has ever [been] brought from the West. It is a glorious country for a naturalist.
—Hayden to Baird, 27 January 1854

UNEXPECTED FALLOUT CAN be far more important than the formal results of any enterprise. Hall continued to complain about the costs of the Bad Lands journey, but more than a year after its completion he admitted to Engelmann a more serious consequence: "My Mauvaises Terres expedition . . . has been the means also of taking Mr. Meek from me."

No sooner were they back in Albany than both junior naturalists began looking for other employment. Meek sent word to Baird in mid-September, saying he needed more outdoor work for his health and adding that Hall would have released him the previous spring to go with Evans, had he known of Evans's plans in time. Perhaps so, but Meek was bending over backwards to avoid sounding like he wanted to run out on Hall, which, as events proved, was precisely what he intended to do. He began laying the groundwork with Baird by grousing that Hall paid poorly, only $600 a year.

Hayden also drew up a list of grievances. Hall was a skinflint, yes, but worse "neither Mr. Meek nor myself, after all our diligence and success, have yet received so much as a single plant, nor do we expect to." Any putative naturalist required his own collection of specimens as a handy cabinet of study materials and as a source of duplicates to sell or trade for new specimens. Further, if a naturalist wanted to make a living he required a reputation, but a reputation depended on recognition by colleagues. That, thought Hayden, would never be forthcoming from Hall. "He [Hall] will rob us of all the credit he possibly can."

It turned out to be an accurate assessment. After learning of their initial success in the field, Hall promised Meek and Hayden he would help them prepare a paper for publication. However, after examining the surprising number of new Cretaceous fossils now at his disposal, Hall wanted his own name on the report. He arranged some recognition for Meek by listing him as coauthor, but gave Hayden only a perfunctory nod for his role as a collector. In fairness to Hall, that was about all Hayden deserved at the time. But how quickly grow the weeds of ambition. Waiting on the docks at St. Louis not eight months before, yearning to head upriver but embarrassed at the costs he had incurred, and fearing the conflict with Evans and Stevens might kill his chances, Hayden sheepishly wrote to Hall, "I shall refuse to receive any credit for what may be done this season, however successful the expedition may be." Now he wanted more; but seeing no way to get it while serving Hall, he determined to get away from Albany.

Unfortunately for the impatient tyro, he had no other opportunities. Under the circumstances he needed credentials even more than credits, so he resolved to complete his medical degree, which he did at Albany Medical College during January 1854. Incidentally, a term of medical school in Albany cost Hayden over $100, which he earned by working for Hall. Hall obligingly wrote letters on his behalf, trying to find him another expedition to the West. This effort seemed to aid Hayden's desire to get out of town, but it also served Hall's purpose in separating Hayden from Meek. Hall was no fool. As he watched the two naturalists in his own house, he would have noticed their growing compatibility. They had survived an exasperating and dangerous adventure and now showed signs of wanting to work more together.

Their experience led to the second unintended result of the Bad Lands trip: Meek and Hayden agreed to forge a professional relationship and to become independent of Hall as soon as possible. As early as January Meek confided to Baird that he would be describing Hayden's future collections. Over the next year Meek often reiterated how much he wanted to work up Hayden's new fossils, just as Hayden constantly encouraged Meek's efforts to free himself from Hall, so that they might collaborate in earnest. Hall learned only gradually of what was happening, his first inkling coming in May 1854 when Meek demanded a revision of their contract that would permit him to work part of each year for the Missouri survey.

The different way each man handled Hall reveals their temperaments. Though occasionally cowed by Hall's intimidating ways, Meek was cool, determined, able to focus himself on one thing at a time, and extraordinarily patient: he did not finally break with Hall until spring 1858. By contrast Hayden burned with a fervid ambition, and even though he had no other employment, he found Hall's presence so intolerable that he left Albany in late February 1854. Having nowhere else to go, he traveled to Rochester for an extended visit with his family.

Given Hayden's need to please older men who could serve as patrons and father figures, the break with James Hall might have induced a personal crisis had Hayden not already identified his next mentor: Spencer Fullerton Baird. Baird had ambitions of his own and could be single-minded for a purpose, but he was utterly absorbed in the same broadbrush approach to natural history that captivated Hayden. As assistant secretary of the Smithsonian, he resolved to agglomerate a pile of natural wonders second to no other institution's, and his personal gifts seemed to assure him of success. Fortified by a strong constitution (even though it required regular alcoholic stimulation), a persistent hunger to know every possible collector, and a strong, steady hand capable of manufacturing a stupendous correspondence on every conceivable aspect of natural history, Baird was clearly a driven man. At the same time he was generous, self-confident, amiable, and genuinely fond of human beings, especially if they were potential collectors, whom he seems to have ranked with his own family, if not somewhat higher. In view of the large number of collectors associated with the U.S. Army, Baird was fortunate, too, in his marriage, for his father-in-law, Sylvester Churchill, was inspector-general of the army. As such, Churchill could use his influence to arrange a man's orders pretty much the way Baird desired.

Given Hayden's inclinations and talents, he would have been drawn into Baird's orbit sooner or later, although he could never be content for long as anyone's satellite. His approach to Baird and the development of their relationship are instructive on several counts, especially as they typify his behavior with several other mentors. During the first five months of 1854, first from Albany and then from Rochester, Hayden pleaded, fawned, flattered, pestered, and badgered until he got what he wanted. While asking Baird's advice on his future career, he stated baldly, "Our past correspondence leads me to look to you as my best and safest advisor in matters of science." Or later: "I have the most perfect confidence in your friendship and interest in my welfare, and that thought has encouraged me much. I trust you will always feel an interest in me and aid me by your counsel." When Baird suggested Hayden should sharpen up his medical skills in order to pursue natural history as an army surgeon, Hayden was quick to answer, "I look upon the Army as the principle [sic] object of my efforts." But in the next breath he added, "Though I passed a very creditable examination this winter at my graduation, still I do not feel prepared to attempt it for the army." I want something else, he meant, but what he said was, "I think best to follow your advice and wait some other opportunity," which was sheer chicanery because Baird's only advice up to that point had concerned the army. Hayden began building his case carefully, asking how else he might be employed, where "I could be more useful to science than in the Army." "Some position in an expedition however humble would I think be much better for me," he offered; then later, to be sure Baird got the message, he wrote, "I shall have it understood that I can learn and should have an appointment under government."

Bold talk, but no doubt Hayden would have taken almost anything, even a position that paid only his expenses, just to be engaged with an expedition. Once at home in Rochester he was "out of business and consequently somewhat dependent, which is unpleasant," and his family opposed his interest in natural history. His relatives "appreciate nothing which does not bring in an immediate return of cash," he explained. While biding his time, Hayden worked gratis for Professor Chester Dewey at the University of Rochester, arranging and labeling materials. He conjured up a number of job possibilities and bombarded Baird with the details. He might collect for Sarpy; he might go with Culbertson to Blackfoot country; he might be a surgeon on one of the fur company's boats or even become a fur trader himself; perhaps he would accept an offer from George Swallow to work for the summer on the Missouri survey. Or should he hold out in hopes that Captain Randolph Marcy would get funding for a Green River expedition or that Congress would authorize explorations in the recently purchased lands of southern New Mexico and Arizona? He sent similar missives to Leidy in Philadelphia and Engelmann in St. Louis.

Naturally, he hoped for a government-endorsed expedition, which would pay better than a private one and do more for his reputation. However, a private collecting venture up the Missouri River with Indian agent Alfred Vaughan emerged as his best possibility. He and Vaughan had discussed it while on the *Robert Campbell,* though they had not codified terms at the time. Before Hayden left Albany, Vaughan made an informal offer along the lines of their earlier discussions, but Hayden delayed accepting it in order to see what better situations might exist in Washington or Philadelphia. After finding nothing else, Hayden decided to settle on something with Vaughan, but he was frustrated at not being able to locate him. Knowing Vaughan would turn up in Washington sooner or later, Hayden alerted Baird in early February to keep an eye out for him, adding, "A few words from you on the importance of such a plan as he proposes would set him right." Hayden also had a few words for Baird on the subject: "Under your patronage and that of Maj. V. it seems to me large results might be obtained," which was a rather cheeky way of suggesting the Smithsonian throw additional resources into Vaughan's private venture. Baird himself had said previously he might lend "essential assistance," without defining what that meant, but after such encouragement Hayden did not slacken his pressure until Baird contributed an entire collector's outfit and arranged cash advances from several other naturalists.

Meanwhile Vaughan was having difficulties organizing the expedition; for a time it was doubtful he would go anywhere in 1854. Consequently, in April Hayden accepted an offer to work for Swallow in Missouri, only to learn a few days later that Vaughan would be going after all, assisted by the Smithsonian, and that he wanted Hayden to accompany him. Hayden knew he would evade the agreement with Swallow, though he allowed a month to pass before doing so in writing, meanwhile rationalizing his behavior with a curious mixture of idealism and self-interest. "I am confident that if he [Swallow] feels any interest in science, he will not hesitate one moment to release me from my obligation to him," he wrote to Baird and then added to Meek, "Prof. Swallow may object, but Baird says it is my duty to go," which, let the record show, Baird never said, at least not in any of his extant letters.

After visiting Vaughan in New York City in early May, Hayden described their agreement as only "satisfactory." Hayden was not sure he trusted Vaughan, so he asked Baird to get something in writing from him, explaining, "If he states our bargain to you I shall have proof and he will fear to do anything less than he agreed." Baird honored Hayden's request to secure a written statement from Vaughan. There was no reason for thinking Vaughan dishonest, but Hayden's uneasiness with him was genuine, though probably based on nothing more than an idealistic youngster's antipathy for the bluff and blunder style of a politician.

Putting the agreement with Vaughan together with certain other facts gleaned from private correspondence gives us a good idea of what Hayden expected as he left Rochester on 13 May, bound for St. Louis. He would spend the first year getting to and collecting in the vicinities of Fort Benton and Fort Union, then descend the following spring or early summer to Fort Pierre in order to collect again at the White River Bad Lands, until a boat would take him back to St. Louis in July 1855. Hayden would receive $300 for the expenses of collecting, which he would be doing essentially on his own and under no direct supervision. Vaughan would pay the cost of shipping all collections back to St. Louis, even if the shipping bill exceeded Hayden's allowance of $300. Hayden would keep half of all collections made, and he would classify the entire lot once it arrived in St. Louis, which meant Hayden would determine which half would be his and which Vaughan's. The Smithsonian would receive plants, peltries, and various specimens stored in alcohol. Engelmann would get a suite of plants. Leidy would write up the vertebrates, and Hayden had his own agreement with Meek about the invertebrates.

Once in St. Louis Hayden found an inexpensive way of ascending the river on the *Genoa,* a boat that did not belong to the American Fur Company. He arranged with Captain Sarpy to carry his freight up and down the river at no cost. Financially things fell into place nicely: Vaughan spent $40 on Hayden's collecting outfit; in addition to what Baird had provided, Engelmann gave him $50; and Baird arranged another $60 in donations from six naturalists who hoped to share some of the returns.

Hayden's second voyage up the Missouri began 1 June, and he arrived at Fort Union in good time, a little over a month later. The biggest adventure along the river was the killing of a grizzly bear, part of which Hayden ate—without commenting on its taste. Despite the rapid ascent, which meant few stops for collecting, Hayden managed to capture some fish, reptiles, mice, "a fair lot of bugs and some birds, a prairie dog's skin," and most extraordinarily "500 spec's of plants," by which he meant specimens, not species. He had little chance to gather fossils below Fort Pierre but accumulated "three good sized boxes" of them before arriving at Fort Clark, south of the junction with the Knife River, where he found a number of new shells and made a vertical section of the rocks; then for comparison he made another section at Fort Berthold, upstream between the Knife and the Little Missouri. These sections held no particular significance geologically; rather they represented places Vaughan called for a stop in order to deal with the Indians. Fort Clark was near a village of Arikaras, and Fort Berthold near a group of Gros Ventres.

Though operating on his own, Hayden was not flying blind. He carried with him Meek's notes on the order, thickness, and composition of the beds they had observed during the previous summer as well as a number of detailed questions and suggestions to keep in mind as he collected. For example, he and Meek were not yet sure if the Tertiary material collected a year earlier was deposited by rivers, in lakes, or beneath an ocean. Baird also submitted suggestions, much more generous ones. He wanted just about everything that moved, though he especially craved fishes, beetles, reptiles, large mammals, birds, and birds' eggs. "I need not remind you," he added, "to keep copious notes of the habits and peculiarities of each species, referring to the specimen by number." Which raises a troublesome question: what became of Hayden's notes from the field? Of course Hayden kept notes. He could not have coped without them, and he referred to them from time to time in his correspondence. He even quoted from them in some of his later publications, but the original journals he compiled over nearly thirty years have never surfaced.[1]

Baird also suggested making notes on Indian vocabularies, which Hayden began during winter 1854–1855. His long-standing interest in the manners and customs of Indians dates from this trip. Passing by the Chalk Bluffs near Omaha, Hayden observed strange carvings in the rock, 50 feet above the water level and as far from the top of the cliff. He called them "Indian hiero-glyphics" and thought they depicted "pipes, canoes, various kinds of ani-mals, rude representations of the Indians themselves, etc." (From these same Cretaceous rocks he would later extract fossil plants that showed the Mid-west once enjoyed a nearly tropical climate.) Somewhat south of Sioux City he recorded the legend of Blackbird, the Omaha chief who predicted the deaths of his enemies, then fulfilled the prophesy by inviting them to a feast at which he poisoned them. Chief Blackbird reposed atop a nearby hill that still bears his name.

It was probably during this trip that Hayden got his nickname from the Sioux. The incident has often been mentioned but usually misquoted. It is worth getting the facts right because an innocent bit of storytelling has grown into some mischief. Let me start by quoting in full the first report on the nickname (1888).

> Dr. Hayden had many adventures with the red men, but none resulted in bodily harm to himself. His occupation as a geologist excited their curiosity, which was generally satisfied by the conclusion that he was not entirely sane. The Sioux gave him the name of "The-man-who-picks-up-stones-running." On one occasion, while he was engaged in an exploration of the beds of the Laramie formation of the upper Missouri, he was chased by Indians for many miles. When at last they overtook him, they were surprised to find him armed only with the ge-ologist's pick and hammer, and proceeded to search him. They exam-ined the bags which he carried, and turned the fossil bones and shells which they contained out upon the ground. Finding nothing of value to them, they concluded that he was crazy, and left him without harm.

Much of this is apocryphal, of course. Hayden did not usually go unarmed, for instance. Also, although it is appealing, the image of him swirling across the prairie like a whirlwind, picking up whatever lay in his path, is exagger-ated. As to his insanity, the Indians may have found him a bit odd, but it is interesting to trace the origin of this report. After interviewing Hayden in early 1856, a reporter for the *Daily Missouri Republican* wrote that Hayden "was frequently among hostile tribes of Indians, who watched his movements with great curiosity, and formed very absurd notions of his sanity."

So it was Hayden himself, doubtless amused at his reputation among the Sioux, who laid the foundation for what became part of his exaggerated lore. Thereafter the matter of his insanity was mentioned as a lighthearted joke, raised in the spirit of puzzled admiration that often surrounds a figure who has become legendary, if not somewhat troubling. Often friends and sympathizers liked to remember the anecdote as if it helped them understand a man they wanted to know but could not quite get hold of.

But what started as an amusing throwaway line took on credence and accumulated power with the retelling and has given unwitting support to a false picture of Hayden. Half a century after Hayden's death William Berryman Scott cited the incident, with elaborations: "Hayden had the great advantage of being regarded by the Indians as a madman and therefore sacred, and this enabled him to visit many places which were inaccessible to other white men." As recently as 1986 John McPhee reiterated the tale with his own flourishes, thereby adding an additional layer of myth to the formidable series now overlying and obscuring the original truth of the matter. Relating the Sioux's discovery that Hayden ran around filling his bags with rocks, McPhee said, "In that instant, Professor Hayden was accorded the special status that all benevolent people reserve for the mentally disadvantaged . . . and to all hostilities thereafter Hayden remained immune."

Certainly Hayden scorned such nonsense in private, and oddly it was another perceptive geologist who never knew Hayden personally, Charles Doolittle Walcott, who best captured Hayden's own mind on this subject: "Often laughed at by his fellows and treated as of unbalanced mind by the red man, he ignored the one and smiled at the childishness of the other, and went forward as though neither were in existence." But note the cruel irony here: with Hayden's own blessing an insignificant anecdote is inflated beyond its competence; at first, humor and a touch of humanity add to a legend-in-the-making. But with retelling and loss of context, the anecdote becomes distorting and belittling.

Arriving at Fort Union near the mouth of the Yellowstone, Hayden was somewhat embarrassed by the modest size of his collections thus far and even more so by the presence of large boils on his knees and rump, which he attributed to dirt and a change of climate. But Vaughan had no cause to complain about his young collaborator, and he wrote to Baird of "the indomitable perseverance of Hayden," which boded well for the future. Hayden himself, already looking ahead to the next trip scarcely had this one commenced, queried Baird again about appropriations for government expeditions and boasted that with $10,000 he could explore "the whole country this side of the Rocky Mountains."

But his ability to explore depended upon whatever logistics Vaughan devised for dealing with the Indians. He was an Indian agent after all, and his job was to distribute government supplies, maintain a dialogue with the tribes, and keep an eye on their moods and movements. Fortunately, the Crow were not at Fort Union when Vaughan and Hayden arrived there on 3 July, so Vaughan resolved to go up the Yellowstone to find them. Hayden was overjoyed. Originally he had intended to go back down the Missouri on one side as far as Fort Clark, then back up on the other side, to look more carefully at whatever outcrops he could find. Apparently Vaughan made his plans more rapidly than expected, for Hayden reported spending only seventeen days exploring the region around Fort Union, which included the day or two before the *Genoa* actually reached the fort. Then on 18 July they headed up the Yellowstone, bound for Fort Sarpy some 300 miles away, near the mouth of the Bighorn.

Progress was slow. A keelboat carried all their supplies, but the wide, flat-bottomed craft had to be hauled by men pulling on a cable, or cordelle. Only 6 to 12 miles could be gained in a day, which allowed Hayden to explore on both sides of the river as the party advanced. Hayden found the Yellowstone very different from the Missouri. He described volcanic formations for the first time, saw lots of petrified wood, marveled at the amount of gravel thrown up by the river, and identified the lignite coal beds that would later claim so much of his interest. But generally the country around the lower Yellowstone did not excite him. "Of the country bordering on the [Lower] Yellowstone, I would say that there can be none more barren in the world; none of it could be made subservient to agriculture, or even grazing purposes. The land is even more sterile than on the upper Missouri; the timber is very scarce, and of diminutive growth . . ."

He acknowledged the wealth of shells found along the Yellowstone, and by the time the party reached Fort Sarpy on 15 August Hayden had found significant fossils at the mouths of the Powder, the Tongue, and the Bighorn. Because of space limitations on the keelboat, he had to discard much of what he collected, yet he gathered an estimated two and a half to three tons of fossils. Included were remains of deciduous trees dating from the late Paleozoic, now known to be well over 250 million years old. He found a few mammal and reptile bones for Leidy and amassed a menagerie of animals including beavers, bears, prairie dogs, numerous birds, foxes, wolves, antelopes, bighorn sheep, and an astonishing "12 or 15 hundred spec's of plants," all of which later filled "a good sized room at Fort Pierre." Unfortunately, many of the fish, reptiles, insects, and other specimens confined to bottles or barrels were lost in an accident. Remarkably, he gathered most of this treasure alone, and his own self-portrait leaves a lively image. "I was obliged to take my pick in one hand, my bag in the other, my note book in my side pocket, my bottle of alcohol in my vest pocket, my plant case around my neck, and with all these carry a gun to defend myself from bears and Indians."

About only one aspect of the collection was he troubled. "I must have at least 50 different species of plants," he reported to Meek, by which he meant fossil plants. "Can we describe them? Or must I send them to Dr. Newberry? If we can, I think we had better do it." He gave no explanation for his uneasiness with Newberry, though a letter received from Newberry on the eve of his departure provides a clue. Newberry had cautioned him: "Remember your bible and your prayers daily. As I should regard the gain of any share of fame or wealth as infinite loss, if thereby your Christian hope was forfeited and lost—a loss [of] faith which the loss of life or health or failure in your specific objects would be infinitely incomparable."

Despite considerable danger from hostile Blackfoot warriors (they killed two of his Crow guides four days after arrival at Fort Sarpy), Vaughan kept his party at the fort for more than a month, not beginning the homeward passage until 19 September. By 8 October Hayden was at Council Bluffs, having come down from Fort Pierre in a small skiff carrying important mail from Vaughan. Hayden volunteered for the task because "the excited state of the Indians rendered it unsafe for me to operate around Fort Pierre" and because the river was running low, which enabled him to study a few new outcrops. By the time he returned to Fort Pierre for the winter he claimed to have sketched a continuous series of rock outcrops (vertical sections) from Council Bluffs to the mountains around the Bighorn.

Once settled, however, Hayden began to show signs of agitation, especially regarding his future. He issued a steady flow of queries, suggestions, and reminders to Engelmann, Leidy, Meek, and especially Baird concerning his need for steady employment. Meek was now working with Swallow in Missouri, and Hayden was keen to join his friend there if something could be arranged. He talked with Colonel Cummings, superintendent of Indian agents in St. Louis, about a salaried position of some kind; several openings existed. Baird suggested to Lieutenant Gouverneur Kemble Warren of the army's Corps of Topographical Engineers that he include Hayden in his expedition to Nebraska Territory, which was to begin in spring 1855. Warren agreed, but the two explorers missed each other at Fort Pierre, and after an exchange of letters all Hayden could show for it was Warren's informal hope that they might connect the following year.

By far the most exciting possibility Hayden uncovered was organizing a geological and natural history survey of the entire Nebraska Territory, along the lines of the several state surveys already in existence. Politicians in Nebraska were pondering such a scheme. Before going into winter quarters at Fort Pierre (from early December 1854 into the latter part of May), Hayden did some snooping at Bellevue, the territorial seat. He talked to a number of people about his suitability to direct such a survey. The territory was then in a frenzy, for the Kansas-Nebraska Act, which created the two territories on 30 May 1854, stated that a popular vote should determine whether slavery would be allowed in each. Nebraska Territory included parts of the Dakotas, Montana, and Wyoming, and some doubted the practicality of asking voters in those distant and isolated regions to exercise their franchise. Being familiar with the land and knowing he was headed back there in any case, Hayden volunteered to act as an election official if needed. He also promoted the idea of a survey with the local newspapers and even spent a week in Sargents Bluff and Karnesville discussing the plan with key politicos. To keep his name favorably before the public, he donated a few of his specimens to the new territorial museum; he saw them displayed in the very house where the first governor had recently died.

During the winter, after storing his collections, Hayden put his notes in order and looked ahead. Thinking well beyond his reach, he planned a map of the Missouri Basin that would show every important locality and stream from the mouth of the Platte to the sources of the Yellowstone. And he began work on an ethnological survey of the tribes he had encountered, which would include comments on their languages along with grammars and vocabularies.

During the long nights he became acquainted with several fur traders at Fort Pierre, especially Charles Galpin and his wife, Matilda, a full-blooded Sioux known as Eagle Woman. Hayden taught the children who lived there, most of them the offspring of mixed Indian and white parents. Collecting specimens around the fort itself provided no novelties, so in January Hayden and Galpin headed for the Moreau Trading Post, "14 days travel from Fort Pierre," and about 90 miles northeast. He visited Thunder Butte, the nearby streams, and for the first time examined the Fox Hills (between the Cheyenne and Moreau rivers), whose geology he would make famous. He found a parcel of new shells and added some large bones to the stack for Leidy. As soon as he returned he began planning another junket to the Bad Lands. He made three attempts before pronouncing his efforts successful; his energy amazes.

On 11 February he set out with two men, four horses, and a cart. Despite storms that dumped two feet of snow and dropped the thermometer to twenty below zero, they reached Sage Creek where Hayden spent nearly a week. Next he made "a splendid collection" around Pineas Spring, on the north fork of what is now called the Bad River. Because of terrible weather, he sent the men back at this point and pushed on alone with one horse; he became lost and ate nothing for three days but reached settlements along the Cheyenne where he met Galpin and an interpreter. The three of them headed west for a look at the Black Hills. There another storm greeted them, but Hayden gathered specimens at Bear Butte anyway and made his first assessment of the geology around the Black Hills. Then they began a retreat of 150 miles to Fort Pierre via the Belle Fourche and the Cheyenne. For ten days they had little to eat. For four days they ate nothing but scraps of one prairie dog.

They reached Fort Pierre on 22 March, and by 9 April Hayden had saddled up for the Bad Lands again, taking only a guide. At Grindstone Hill they encountered a trader who told them the Brule tribe intended to rob everyone on the road between Forts Pierre and Laramie; Hayden reluctantly turned back. From Fort Pierre he complained bitterly to Baird of these "rascally Indians" and bemoaned, "Perhaps I shall have to give it up until the government sends troops up here and wipes out two or three hundred of them." He also seized the opportunity to remind Baird, "I labor under great disadvantages. I have to lose at least half of my time and much of that is without profit. I cannot do as I wish and could do if I had means." To Meek he was more candid about his plans as well as his fears that someone else might beat him to the punch in collecting something new and writing it up: "As I said before, do not show my letters to anyone, not even Hall, for I do not even write Baird much of my operations."

Unwilling to give up, he departed again for the Bad Lands on 7 May. Accompanied by an Indian guide, one other man and a boy, and horses to drag two carts, this time he took the southerly route across the Teton (Bad) River, thence to the White, and on south to the overlooking ridge, which he then followed mostly west and finally north to the same areas around Bear and Sage creeks he had visited twice before. Having filled both carts after five days of collecting, the party returned to Fort Pierre on 6 June via the road from Fort Laramie. Although they traveled through the heart of Brule country, Hayden could congratulate himself on having taken a slower but less conspicuous route, for he saw only three Indian lodges during the entire journey. The fossils he brought back enabled him to sort out distinct layers in the Tertiary rocks of what he named the White River Group. The oldest belonged to the titanotheres, the succeeding layers to turtles and what Leidy called "ruminating hogs" (later classified as oreodons).

But frustrations piled up. It was more than the threat of Indians and more than not working under the banner of government. It was a question of self-esteem, all the more insidious because outwardly all seemed well. As Hayden said in an unguarded moment, "I am treated here with respect, yet I am well aware that here a man without money is a bore, and with money [one becomes] a great gentleman let him do what he will. And my industry only makes me a greater bore . . . because they [the traders] can make no money out of me." It was this bitter feeling of humiliation that caused him to exaggerate the novelty of his collections, that provoked impatience with Vaughan, and even led him to scold his mentors for not sending him enough letters, not finding him a better position, and not appreciating him sufficiently. "It seems as if I was excluded from the world, an exile as it were. And I sometimes feel lonely."

Yet his ingratiating manner and enthusiasm won him the practical support he needed to keep collecting. Baird, Engelmann, and several other naturalists made outright gifts of cash, Vaughan and Chouteau covered his daily expenses for the better part of two years, and several of the traders did other substantial favors. Galpin covered the costs of the two outings they undertook together, and he contributed far more to Hayden's general upkeep. Other traders occasionally donated cash, apparently with no return expected, so that by the time Hayden returned to St. Louis in January 1856 he could boast of having $165 in his pocket. Also his energy and determination were making a favorable impression on the men whose benevolence could open the country to him. Alexander Culbertson had been a fur trader since 1830, and from 1848 he was the agent in charge of all forts on the Upper Missouri and Yellowstone rivers, specifically the superintendent of Fort Union. After Hayden's return from the successful trip to the Bad Lands in June, Culbertson invited him to spend summer 1855 around Fort Benton, nearly 800 miles on the Missouri above Fort Union. It was a wonderful opportunity to explore entirely new country, and Hayden made the most of it.

Until that point, his collections had been valuable, sometimes new, but, rather like his concentration—uneven. Baird, Leidy, and Engelmann had each written to chide him gently about taking more care in preserving, wrapping, and labeling his material, and Hayden freely admitted that he wasted many samples because of his lack of experience. He yearned, quite sincerely, for some leisurely time with Baird to master the proper techniques. Nonetheless when he returned to St. Louis he brought an extraordinary harvest: six tons of specimens accumulated over two years, including more than a thousand pounds of fossils he wanted to work up with Meek, which he expected would occupy them for five years. Naturally, he wanted Meek, Leidy, even Baird to drop everything and come at once to see his treasures in St. Louis.

Having seen part of the plunder, Baird wrote Leidy of the fascinating bunch of teeth Hayden had found, "some of which will make your eyes water." Baird also mentioned that Hayden had found the first soft-shelled turtle known in

America. But that was only the beginning. On closer examination, Leidy found that some of the teeth came from saurian creatures, the first dinosaurs found in America. These seemed to be of Cretaceous age and came from the Judith River Badlands, near the Judith's confluence with the Missouri. Hayden found other saurian remains along the Milk, Musselshell, and Little Missouri rivers and more at several points within 40 miles of the mouth of the Yellowstone, others within 10 miles of Fort Union, and some around Fort Benton too. In addition to dinosaurs he found pachyderms, fishlike reptiles, various marine mammals, true fishes, hippopotami, a crocodile, peccaries, camel-like animals, and rodents, among them several extinct species, many of which were new to science. Included was only the second Hipparion found in America—the small, three-toed equine then thought to be an ancestor of the horse.

A prodigious haul to be sure, but also a significant one. Leidy thought the reptiles from the Judith Basin suggested the Wealden formation, or the lower Cretaceous, not yet known in America. Meek wrote excitedly, "You will probably have more species than all now published from the Cretaceous formations in this country." Many of the mollusks Hayden found were regarded in Europe as belonging to the Tertiary, but as Meek said, they lay "in the same beds with Ammonites, Scaphites and other genera regarded as Cretaceous, or earlier." Americans were now teaching Europeans some new things about science, instead of the other way around.

Meek's reaction to seeing the new invertebrates is revealing. In January 1855, before seeing any of Hayden's collection, Meek had been uncertain whether he could find the time to work on this new material, given his obligations in New York and Missouri. After seeing the first batch of Hayden's shells in early February 1856, Meek changed his tune. He exclaimed, "They are grand—magnificent. All of them as perfect as recent shells. There are not less than 50 species most of which are new." To make time for writing descriptions of this trove, Meek was now willing to give up his work in Missouri provided Hayden could arrange publication in a government report, which would mean pay for Meek's time. Three weeks later he stuck his neck out a lot further: "The contribution we will be able to make to geology and palaeontology is, I think, of such importance that if I possessed the means, I would be willing and much prefer to publish it [our report] at our own expense." During February Hayden arranged with Lieutenant Warren to return to Nebraska Territory again that summer, and Warren agreed to pay Meek for his research and drawings. Hayden insisted that Meek keep quiet about all this, fearing that a rival might attempt to get to the field before him. Hayden, rushing to Albany where he had already shipped the invertebrates, urged Meek to open the boxes and begin studying the shells immediately, even before he arrived.

With solid accomplishments behind him, and having shown his resourcefulness and tenacity, Hayden seemed assured of a career as a naturalist. Congratulations poured in from all quarters. Governor Isaac Stevens, who had been so unfriendly to the young naturalist previously, wrote to Baird in fall 1855: "I have met your friend, the naturalist Mr. Haden [sic], who has won golden opinion from all intelligent men, for his persevering labors on the Missouri and its tributaries. He is a man of the right stamp: enthusiastic, forceful, and modest. Should the Northern Boundary line be run another year, he is the man for its geologist. Look to it, as I know you will." How satisfying it was to hear those words. The recognition of his colleagues meant even more. During March 1856 Leidy sent him the happy news that he had been elected a corresponding member of the Academy of Natural Sciences of Philadelphia; Leidy and Baird stood as his sponsors. Thus, through immersion in the depths of western wilderness did the emotional needs of a neglected and unfulfilled man begin to be satisfied.

Simultaneously, he nearly made some serious missteps with the same colleagues who sought to push him forward. In fact, his behavior threatened to rupture virtually all his close friendships at the very moment when his careful cultivation of them was about to begin paying dividends. On 25 January 1855 John Newberry wrote to James Hall complaining that Hayden had never given him any specimens, even though Newberry had contributed to Hayden's collecting outfit with the understanding that he would receive some samples. On 13 March Hall in turn wrote to Joseph Leidy, saying he had learned of Hayden's large haul of fossil plants, which, Hall claimed, Hayden had promised to him, but he had heard nothing from his former protégé.

We have seen the beginnings of awkward feelings between Newberry and Hayden as well as a proto-rivalry between Hall and Hayden, each stemming from the paternalistic circumstances of Hayden's early relations with both men. The dilemma Hayden experienced about the disposition of his fossil plants shows his continuing discomfort with the two men. On 25 March 1855 Hayden expressed the wish that Meek would work up the fossil plants (even though plants were not Meek's specialty), so that Hayden could avoid sending them to Newberry. By the following January, however, Hayden seemed inclined to send the plants to Hall on the assumption that Hall would coauthor an article with him on the plants. Unfortunately, Hall and Hayden had misunderstood each other. Hall had no intention of coauthoring an article with Hayden. Instead, he offered Meek and Hayden the use of his home and office for their own research in hopes that in return Hayden would hand over the plants for Hall's own collection. This arrangement was unacceptable to Hayden, who wrote to Baird on 20 March: "I send you all my fossil plants that I have here for Dr. Newberry to describe. He [Hall] can't have them . . . I thank God that I still feel confident that there are some men of soul as well as intellect in this world of ours, or I should be a misanthrope."

Hall was absent from Albany during the time Meek and Hayden worked there together that spring, but when he returned he was furious, especially at what he considered Hayden's insufficient gratitude and his quest for independence. He composed a rambling and angry letter to Hayden, dated 22 April, which also raked up his unresolved bitterness toward Baird over events leading up to the Bad Lands trip of 1853. Hall enjoyed holding a grudge, and the letter served as a memorandum of grievances, but he never mailed it. Though not normally shy about spitting his hostility in the face of opponents, Hall preferred to stoke his resentments in this case.

The incident further estranged Hayden and Hall, and both men turned their backs on each other. The circumstances were different with Leidy and Baird, whom Hayden treated very badly over their mutual interest in the rodents brought back from Nebraska. Although no one had asked specifically for the rodents, Hayden realized both men would have an interest in them: Leidy in the fossilized specimens, including any extinct species, Baird in the more recent ones still living. So when Baird asked for permission to describe the rodents, Hayden rashly replied that nothing would give him greater pleasure, then added, remembering an obligation, "Still I would feel extremely sorry should Dr. Leidy have any hard feeling about it," and concluded cleverly but not so wisely, "Perhaps you can arrange that matter better." Baird finally asked Leidy directly about the rodents, and when Leidy rebuffed him and asserted his own right to them, Baird yielded gracefully and sent on the specimens from Washington. Clearly, by being careless or forgetful or both, it was Hayden who had created the problem between Leidy and Baird. Hayden was often impulsive, self-centered, and remarkably blind to the effect he had on others, and the result was he all too frequently created similar dilemmas.

About this time he made the same mistake with Meek. Returning to St. Louis loaded with fossil treasures, flush with satisfaction, acclaimed by important men who had previously scorned to know him, and with cash in his pocket, Hayden let his good fortune impair his judgment. He told Meek on 20 January that naturalist Benjamin Franklin Shumard wanted to describe his freshwater fossils from Pineas Spring; "but I cannot do it without your consent," he added, almost as an afterthought. Any arrangement with Shumard would have violated the entire understanding Meek and Hayden had been developing for two years and would have contradicted Hayden's specific pledge of 1 July 1854 to give Meek the exclusive right to describe all his invertebrate fossils. Only a forgetful man, or a very foolish one, would have considered a proposal from Shumard under these circumstances—unless he were trying to

show a little annoyance with Meek for not hurrying to St. Louis as he had requested earlier or not being quick enough to rearrange his time for Hayden's
convenience. For his part, Meek acquiesced in the plan, knowing he could not
stop Hayden if he were serious about it. Even before he received Meek's reply,
however, Hayden had second thoughts, saying Shumard "is an able man but
has not the true scientific spirit. Do not say a word. He is very sorry when a
western fossil does not first pass into his hands." A few days later, having just
received Meek's permission to go ahead with Shumard if he chose to (which
had the effect of calling Hayden's bluff), Hayden changed his mind and wrote
reassuringly to Meek, "You always have the preference in all things that I collect, and I feel it a benefit to me rather than conferring a favor on you."

Subsequently, during February or early March 1856, Shumard published
a catalog of new fossils from the Upper Missouri, anticipating Meek and
Hayden in several descriptions. The incident reveals how readily Hayden
could bounce from a naive idealism about science to cynical observations
about particular men. While in St. Louis, he arranged a large part of his entire 1854–1855 collection in a room specially made for the purpose in the
home of Charles Chouteau. He allowed Shumard to see as many of his things
as he wanted, and he left town without giving a thought to the confidential-
ity of his material. It was not until he reached Washington and after he read
an anxious note from Meek about protecting the collection from public
scrutiny that he wrote to Engelmann to have the room secured. Privately,
Hayden admitted to Meek his own indiscretion may have given Shumard
the information he needed for several descriptions, but to others, especially
Baird and Leidy, Hayden proclaimed that Shumard had "stolen" several
species from him.

Hayden and Meek's first two publications came to print in March 1856.
More extensive and better received than Shumard's, these initial articles were
an auspicious debut for their coauthors, but the team of Hayden and Meek
was still groping toward partnership. So many projects vied for Hayden's attention that he could devote little time to sustained work with Meek in
Albany. In Washington he was looking after the bulk of his recently arrived
collections, arranging his summer plans with Lieutenant Warren, and working on a report he had promised Warren, to be delivered before he took the
field again that spring. That report would summarize his work as a naturalist
over the previous two years, but he only finished a first draft of it before leaving for the West; he asked Baird to handle corrections and proofreading.
After hurrying through his business in Washington, Hayden wanted to spend
a few days in Philadelphia with Leidy, discussing the large vertebrates he had
found. Meek had been working on Hayden's gastropods and cephalopods
since early February, and by the time Hayden finally arrived in Albany a

month later, Meek had virtually finished their first two papers. Hayden confirmed the locations of the described species, and they mailed the completed
articles to Leidy.

Originally Hayden had thought of spending two months in Albany, but
he managed a little less than three weeks. Still, after they worked together
for that short period, Meek was able to assemble a total of five substantial
articles based on Hayden's collections, all of which appeared in the *Proceedings* of the Philadelphia Academy before the end of the year. Because Hayden
had to hurry back to the field, it became Meek's responsibility to correct,
proofread, and see each article through the press. Hayden left Albany to
spend some time with his family in Rochester, then hustled back to
Washington for a few days, leaving there in time to arrive again in St. Louis
on 9 April. There he met Lieutenant Warren, with whom he would visit
some new parts of Nebraska Territory.

7

IN THE COMPANY
OF SOLDIERS,
1856–1860

I will make a somewhat nicer collection this year but I can never explain to you the vexatious things which a naturalist must endure on one of these government expeditions. . . . I have been pressed too hard for the last 4 or 5 years & I cannot stand it.
—Hayden to George Engelmann, 9 November 1859

STRANGE—AND UNPREDICTABLE—are the events that determine men's lives. In summer of 1856 Hayden began a promising association with Lieutenant Gouverneur Kemble Warren; but what originally brought Warren to the field was not science but a stolen cow. The Sioux stole the cow, said to belong to a Mormon settler, near Fort Laramie in 1854, and when Lieutenant J. L. Grattan went to retrieve it he overplayed his weak hand by firing weapons into the Indian encampment. A superior force returned his fire, leaving him and twenty-nine men from his detachment dead, which commenced the so-called Sioux Wars. To avenge these deaths General William S. Harney came west in summer 1855, with Lieutenant Warren assigned to his party. Brought together by Baird during winter 1855–1856, Warren and Hayden consummated a working agreement for the following summer.

Before the Civil War the army's elite Corps of Topographical Engineers dominated exploration in the West; the men in the corps excelled at surveying and mapping. After graduating second in his class from West Point, Warren joined the corps and began to learn his craft by working on the Mississippi Delta. In assigning him to assist General Harney, the army wanted Warren to traverse unfamiliar territory. A number of surveyors had already worked along the Platte River, and Joseph Nicollet, a Frenchman, had produced a valuable map of regions north of the Missouri, but little was known about the country between the two rivers, especially those areas drained by some of the Missouri's prominent forks—the Yellowstone, the Loup, and the Niobrara (called Running Water, or L'eau qui court, in Hayden's day). The Sand Hill country of Nebraska awaited exploration, as did the Black Hills to the north. Both offered Hayden pioneering opportunities.

They were a dynamic pair, Warren and Hayden, who shared more than appears at first glance. Both had eager, intelligent minds and slim bodies capable of enduring hardship. Both were bold in the face of adventure. Neither could tolerate fools, each could be tactless, and both yearned to make a name. Both loved art and literature, enjoyed the company of women, and ardently studied natural history. Of course they differed too. Though they had similar physical builds, Warren had a thin face, with sharply lined features, and a rigid posture, which made him appear deliberate and meticulous, which he was. He wore his hair long over the ears but carefully brushed down, and he sported a thin moustache. Hayden was fuller in the face, had a distant or dreamy gaze in his eyes, wore his hair longer and looser than Warren, and sported a beard. Warren started life with the advantages of a close, supporting family and a prosperous father. He grew into a pompous martinet, who, at the ripe age of twenty-two, was lecturing his own mother on dressing and caring for his younger siblings. He adored the regimented life of the army, which completely exasperated the more freewheeling Hayden. Warren and Hayden could not avoid a clash: their similarities seem to have exacerbated their natural differences into a warm hostility.

Warren hired Hayden as geologist and naturalist for his party at a salary of $1,000 per annum, starting 1 April 1856. Warren paid Hayden's costs of transportation to and from the field, plus his subsistence while on duty; Hayden had to provide his own horse. On 22 April Warren hired Jim Stevenson as Hayden's assistant, thus beginning a partnership that would last more than two decades. Warren specified that he himself, in addition to Hayden and Stevenson, would be making natural history collections. Things started out well enough, with Warren writing Baird, "We intend to do great things this summer," and Hayden saying in his letter to Baird, "Warren takes hold with the true spirit."

But the slow pace of a military troop, coupled with unexpected delays, irritated Hayden. The party left St. Louis in mid-April on the steamer *Genoa*, but because of low water the boat tied up about 160 miles below Fort Pierre, to wait for safer conditions. Warren led a small advance party overland to reach the fort without delay, but they underestimated the distance and the provisions they would need. They arrived after a grueling march of seven days, during which they dined mostly on birds they killed along the way. It is not known whether Hayden accompanied Warren or remained with most of the party aboard the *Genoa*. All assembled at Fort Pierre by mid-May; then Warren descended to Fort Lookout, ordering Hayden to stay at Fort Pierre. Hayden found little to do there and complained about the "sad deficiency in management of affairs" that kept him idle for nearly six weeks. He gathered a number of birds and refined his notes on geologic sections along the river.

Finally, on 28 June the party departed on the fur company's steamer *St. Mary,* which reached Fort Union on 10 July. Years later Captain Joseph La Barge remembered Hayden as "a man of rather small stature, talkative and companionable, well informed, and very energetic and eager in his work." La Barge also reported a close call for the naturalist. At Fort Clark as Hayden was fossil hunting beneath a bank overhanging the river, some Arikaras threw pebbles at him. Hayden aimed his rifle at them and might have shot had not La Barge yelled to him. "If he had fired," La Barge recalled, "he would certainly have been killed, and as it was, the Indians were greatly incensed that he should have leveled his gun at them."

Arriving at Fort Union, Hayden was in an agitated state. He was pleased to hear from Baird that his skills in taxidermy were improving, but aside from 400 bird skins he had gathered little. His pleasure in learning of his recent election to the St. Louis Academy of Science was overshadowed by despair at working with an organization that never seemed to know what to expect from one hour to the next. Although all his old friends in the fur company welcomed him warmly, Warren vexed him, making him feel "that I hold my position only by courtesy." Hayden began campaigning with Baird for an opening on the Northern Boundary Survey.

Getting back to work cooled him off. On 25 July they started walking up the left bank of the Yellowstone, accompanied by wagons carrying their supplies. After a hundred miles the terrain dictated leaving the wagons, and a small party including Hayden and Warren pressed on another 30 miles to the mouth of the Powder River. At Fort Union Warren had enlisted Jim Bridger to act as guide along the Lower Yellowstone, and at night Bridger recounted "wonderful tales, that . . . sharpened the curiosity of the whole party." Bridger told of the boiling springs and exploding mudholes of the Upper Yellowstone, wonders few had seen by 1856, and fewer believed. But Hayden listened and resolved to see them for himself one day. After returning to Fort Union, the group left on 1 September for Fort Pierre and arrived on 2 October. Some traveled in a mackinac, others walked along the shoreline with the animals; all reassembled in the evenings for camp. After Warren disbanded his men at Fort Pierre, he, Hayden, and a few others took another mackinac to Sioux City, which they reached on 15 November, and from there a steamboat carried them to St. Louis. Hayden had in tow three live pets: a prairie dog, a sage rabbit, and a large-tailed fox, which he managed to bring back to Washington.

He also had a little political dynamite up his sleeve, which he proceeded to explode as soon as he reached civilization. Hayden granted several press interviews in St. Louis, which, by the time they were in print, made it sound as though Hayden, not Warren, had been in charge of the expedition. Outraged, Warren wrote a very peevish note to Hayden, threatened to fire him, and ordered him to keep his mouth shut regarding the expedition until he gained specific clearance to publish something. Probably Hayden had not deliberately misled the journalists, but if as he warmed to the subject with his usual enthusiasm, the reporters saw an interesting slant in playing up the flashy naturalist, Hayden certainly did nothing to deter them.

The summer's work was commendable. The expedition brought back 600 birds skins (135 species), skins and skeletons of all the large quadrupeds of the plains, a number of important skulls, more than twice as many fossil plants as he had found previously, and 80 new shells—despite the fact that the Flat Head Indians had thrown a number of Hayden's specimens into the river. Leidy was exuberant with Hayden's finds: 2 new mammal genera from Bijoux Hills and 3 other new species. Writing to Hayden on 1 December, he said he had now examined 55 vertebrates from Nebraska Territory, 26 of which Hayden had found. Indeed, as he was recounting six weeks later, Leidy realized that of the large vertebrates, "You have discovered more than half the species brought from the Upper Missouri country, including all explorers back to the time of Major Long." By the end of March 1857 Leidy had arranged for the Philadelphia Academy to pay Hayden $1,200 for part of his collections made in 1854–1855, including vertebrate fossils from the White River Bad Lands and the Judith River Basin, plus a set of fossil plants from the Lower Yellowstone. Hayden and Warren donated a miscellaneous assortment of zoological specimens to the Academy.

Hayden reached Washington by 26 November and at once began planning several projects. He needed to sort his materials and write up results for Warren; he had to deliver to Meek and discuss with him his latest fossils; he wanted to visit Leidy in Philadelphia to show him the vertebrates; and he felt obliged to visit his family in Rochester. Upon returning to Washington, Hayden lived in a boardinghouse owned by William Stimpson, at 280 F

Street. Since 1852 Stimpson had been the naturalist to the North Pacific Exploring Expedition, headquartered at the Smithsonian, and he was Hayden's closest personal friend in Washington. Stimpson selected as boarders only those young naturalists who would make a congenial group, and by spring 1857 they had affectionately nicknamed their home The Stimpsonian. Hayden lived there during winter 1856–1857 whenever he was in town, and he missed the pleasant company whenever he was away. As he said to Baird, while visiting family in Rochester, "I feel sorry to spend any time [here], still I owe them a visit and must grant it to them." He then concluded he was "quite anxious to return to W[ashington] again. I feel more at home there."

Relations with Meek were a little strained. Hayden wanted Meek to come to Washington to help select the best samples to carry to Albany, where Meek would work up published descriptions. Meek could not afford to come unless someone paid his expenses. Hayden arranged for that, but then Hall balked at letting Meek go. Meanwhile Hayden was making it difficult for Meek to know what to expect. First he said it would take a week for them to sort his material; then he hinted he himself might not stay the whole week; then he asked Meek to bring to Washington a labeled set of everything they had previously examined for comparison with the new things. This was too much for Meek. Meek stayed in Albany and wrote with annoyance on 17 January that he would not be able to study Hayden's new things until May or June, by which time he knew perfectly well Hayden would be on his way back to the field. It was an effective way of telling the impetuous Hayden: if you want my help on your new materials, bring them to Albany—which Hayden finally did. He arrived around 24 February and stayed seven weeks, until 15 April, though Hall allowed Meek only two of those weeks for Hayden's fossils. During that time Meek wrote their joint paper on the parallelism of the Cretaceous across the United States (published in May 1857). While Meek worked on Hall's materials, Hayden used the time to prepare his report for Warren and to complete his first geological map (published in May) as well as an article on the geology of the White River Bad Lands (published in June).

They laid the groundwork for future publications as well. Warren had provided sufficient funding for Meek to hire an assistant and begin stockpiling important fossil illustrations; by early summer 1857 Meek had five hundred drawings as the basis for what he termed "a grand memoir." When eventually published in 1865, it offered a comprehensive review of virtually all Paleozoic and Mesozoic invertebrates known at the time.[1] During that winter Leidy proposed to Hayden that the two of them publish a summary of the vertebrates of Nebraska. Hayden agreed, though his sense of what still lay hidden in the field persuaded him to reply, "I am making my preparations to go into the upper mo. region for [a] two years trip, and if I succeed I think we had better let that Memoir rest until I return, for I am sure I can double the number of new species of vertebrates in that time." That joint effort appeared in 1869 and was one of Leidy's most important contributions, for which Hayden wrote a geologic introduction.

The two-year trip Hayden alluded to would have been for the Indian Bureau. He had been thinking of it since April 1856, when Colonel Cummings, the Indian agent, had offered him a position inoculating the Indians along the Upper Missouri. After enduring a season with the army, Hayden yearned to revitalize his own individualistic style of fieldwork. His many friends among the trappers offered hospitality and conveniences, and the salary from Cummings would give him the means he needed. Even after Warren wrote on 9 March 1857 to assure Hayden of a place for the forthcoming season, Hayden continued looking for something else. He did not want to accompany Warren again, despite mumbling polite phrases to Baird about Warren having his heart in the right place. Rather than go out again with Warren, Hayden preferred transferring to the Northern Boundary Survey, and he urged Baird to secure that post for him, should he not get his first choice—the vaccination position with Cummings. He pestered Baird to lobby the Indian commissioners on his behalf, which Baird did, no doubt sincerely. The vaccination job would have been ideal in all respects. Certainly his high expectations for that position explain the anger he expressed when he did not get it. Writing to Baird from St. Louis, on the brink of embarking for a second season with Warren, he moped, "Col. Cummings felt quite badly that I did not secure that vaccine appointment." Then he closed by saying, "He [Cummings] thinks there was not a sufficient effort made," which was a bitter slap at Baird himself.

Warren arranged for his team to assemble at the mouth of the Loup Fork of the Platte, near present-day Columbus, Nebraska. It would be a large party, including thirty soldiers for a military escort. Hayden wanted to arrive early enough to do a little investigating on his own. Passing upriver, he made some notes that are interesting to modern students of natural history.

> Annually thousands of buffalos, in attempting to cross the Missouri River and some of its large tributaries on the ice as it is breaking up in the spring, are drowned. For many days their bodies are seen floating down the river by Fort Union or Fort Clark and lodging on some of the islands or sandbars, fill the air with the stench of their decay. In the spring of 1857 thousands of their bodies floated down the Kansas River past Fort Riley and were carried into the Missouri River.

He disembarked at Bellevue, spent a week ascending the Platte about 40 miles to the Elkhorn River, which in turn he ascended to about the latitude of Bellevue, then turned east to complete a circle trip. From there, still on his own, he traveled up the Missouri as far as Sioux City, stopping frequently to examine cliffs and outcrops and gather more fossils near Dakota City, Decatur, and Tekamah, and particularly in the Blackbird Hills, where he wanted another look at some puzzling red sandstone formations.

Meanwhile Warren was having a terrible time. The wagons he had purchased to haul his party up the Platte proved to be of poor quality, the mules became sick, twelve of the military escort deserted, and thieves stole two of the horses. The entire party did not gather at the mouth of Loup Fork until 17 July. While waiting for the military escort in this swampy region, many of the men became ill.

More hardships awaited them on the trail. Quicksands delayed their ascent of the river, and narrow gorges made it impossible to travel beside the river. Around the headwaters of the Loup hundreds of small lakes perforated the landscape but offered a disagreeable saline taste. Timber, potable water, and game were scarce. Mosquitoes so aggravated the animals that to save their lives the men had to smear them with tar and grease. Several men came down with fever, and one nearly died. Moving painfully northwest, they finally arrived at the Niobrara River in the vicinity of modern Rushville, and from there they enjoyed a good trail to Fort Laramie. The journey had taken a month. Hayden came through in good health, and along the way he found the White River Formation about 20 miles above the mouth of the Loup, which he traced all the way to Fort Laramie.

Fur traders had built Fort Laramie in the 1830s, but by the time Hayden saw it the army had purchased it and altered it dramatically. The old traders' fort, built in the traditional stockade fashion, deteriorated ungracefully at one end of an open parade ground. Around the parade ground but unprotected by a surrounding barricade were the barracks, officers' quarters, arsenal, stables, and so on. At least the place offered some welcome amenities, including laundresses, whom the army hired at the rate of one for each twenty-five soldiers. It is doubtful Hayden halted long enough to have his clothes washed. He had his eye on Laramie Peak, whose massive bulwark thrust so forcefully into the skyline that it was visible even though it was more than 50 miles from the fort. It only stood a bit over 10,200 feet, but it rose ominously 4,000 feet above the prairie.

While the party rested and resupplied at the fort, Hayden—ignoring the obvious dangers from Indians—took a small group to explore the region around Laramie Peak. First he went north to collect along Cottonwood and Horseshoe creeks, then moved south and returned via the Laramie River.

During the six-day trip he found a number of birds he had never seen before, but the geology especially excited him. "You know that the geology about Fort Laramie," he wrote to Baird, "has never been known. It is now before me as clear as day. I have also got the key to the Mts [Laramie Mountains] and I am making good use of it." Typically confident of his judgments after the slightest encounter, Hayden nonetheless had a sharp eye for the distinguishing fossil and a remarkable ability to synthesize a whole region, as he proved once again a few weeks later in the Black Hills. There he found the Potsdam sandstone, so familiar from upstate New York. He also found the first Jurassic fossils in America. He correctly assessed the Black Hills as an eastern extension of the Rocky Mountains rather than a separate range, an "outlier" as he called them.

The effectiveness of Hayden's reconnaissance methods, rapid though they were, can be appreciated if we follow his route around the Black Hills. From Fort Laramie he traveled with Warren north up Rawhide Creek, then along Hat and Old Woman creeks, then up Beaver Creek to its source near Inyan Kara Mountain, which he climbed. While the main party moved deliberately and as a unit, Hayden had authority to search on his own wherever he wanted. He examined whatever buttes or hills could be reached by horseback, and he wandered up nearby drainages to observe deposition. For instance, he branched west to examine the country where the Cheyenne River formed, southwest of the Black Hills. Indians refused Warren's request to proceed north and east from Inyan Kara, so the party turned south for about 40 miles to explore along the western side of the Black Hills. Turning east, they came around the southern flank, then headed north along the eastern slope as far as Bear's Peak (or Bear Butte). From here they explored east beside the Belle Fourche River a number of miles before turning south to rejoin the Cheyenne at Sage Creek. From that point they ascended the Cheyenne about 30 miles to French Creek.

The importance of the Belle Fourche (known at the time as the North Fork of the Cheyenne) was that it drained the country immediately north and west of the Black Hills. Hayden would have had a view of its headwaters when he stood on the summit of Inyan Kara. So he nearly circumvented the Black Hills and examined two key outcrops at Inyan Kara and Bear Butte and tramped along the two rivers that hold the Black Hills in a geographic vice. It may have been a rapid survey, but it included significant features and a diversified group of clues. In later years his opponents would criticize his reconnaissance surveys, but none of those critics mastered the same intelligently selective approach to fieldwork that brought Hayden such rapid and comprehensive results.

The last portion of the journey allowed Hayden to distinguish and categorize much that he had recently seen. From the mouth of French Creek on the Cheyenne Warren's party turned southeast across the Bad Lands, then continued along the sources of White Clay Creek and Porcupine Creek to rejoin the Niobrara. Hayden made another profitable haul of vertebrates in what he described as Pliocene rocks in the vicinity of the Niobrara, distinct from those previously found in the White River Formation (which he called Miocene). Descending to the mouth of the Keya Paha, he found the same formations there that he had earlier found at the mouth of the Niobrara, about 55 miles east. Wanting to see something new, he left the river and marched overland with Warren directly to Fort Randall on the Missouri. Doubting they would encounter a steamer so late in the season, Hayden and Warren began walking downriver on 7 November, reaching Sioux City on 16 November and Leavenworth by 4 December, where they boarded the steamer *Florilda* on its way to St. Louis.

At some point during the summer, relations between Hayden and Warren soured. In August, while they worked around Fort Laramie, Hayden had reported favorably on Warren, but by the time they reached Fort Randall in early October Hayden was vowing never again to go out with Warren, whom he said the whole party now hated. Their difficulties probably began during the trying conditions of their final march downstream. After telling Baird that Warren had called him a fool, accused him of lying and gross neglect of duty, Hayden seethed, "I intend now either to whip him or shoot him, or else consider myself no more as a gentleman." Three weeks later from Council Bluffs, Hayden reported Warren had drunk too much and scuffled with one of the men. "His egotism and tyrannical disposition is his ruin," Hayden crowed. In St. Louis, after another three weeks, Hayden still fumed. "I shall cease my connection with Lt. Warren. There will be no open difficulty between us, I think but it is utterly impossible for me or anyone else to live [with] or endure him. He has much the character of H [Hall] only more meaner qualities, will descend to meaner tricks and has a <u>diseased</u> idea of his own abilities and importance."

Despite his difficulties with Warren, Hayden returned with another fine collection. Among the vertebrates Leidy identified many creatures that differed from those previously found in the White River deposits, and he counted at least 16 extinct species, including rhinoceros, mastodon, elephant, and a camel approximately one-third the size of the modern animal. There were more ruminating hogs, one larger than any living species, 2 felines, and 4 canines, including a huge extinct wolf, which he named for Hayden, describing it as "of more robust proportions than any now in existence." Perhaps most interesting were the equines, of which Hayden had found 8 species belonging to 6 genera. "One of them was a horse undistinguishable by its remains from corresponding parts of the ordinary domestic animal; and a second was a horse not larger than a Newfoundland dog." After looking over some of the smaller mammals, Baird said, "Your collections and results are prodigious, but not more than past experience would lead us to expect." Hayden completed this extraordinary season by presenting to the Philadelphia Academy a valuable group of insects.

Returning to Washington by 18 December, Hayden moved into another house belonging to Stimpson. While Hayden had been roaming across the West, Stimpson had written periodically to relate the latest news of their lady friends and to report on their scientific friends who worked in Washington. The compatible group of naturalists who lived with Stimpson made a habit of dining together. Thus was born the Megatherium Club, named for an extinct sloth.[2] Hayden and Newberry were among the first members of the group (they joined at least as early as winter 1856–1857), which later included William Phipps Blake, James Graham Cooper, and Robert Kennicott. Meek joined in spring 1858, when he finally broke with James Hall. The group consisted mostly of bachelors, though it included Baird, who had been married for a decade and who brought in some of his close friends, such as William Turner, the philologist, and Anton Schönborn, the artist. Naturalists from out of town joined in the club's festivities while working in Washington.

In fact, Meek stayed with the Megatherium for a three-week working visit with Hayden during January 1858. Hayden did not go to Albany that winter, for by this time an irreparable breach had developed between Hayden and Hall. The Permian controversy commanded most of Hayden's writing efforts over the winter, though he published a second edition of his geologic map in June and at the same time brought out an improved geologic section of the Tertiary beds of Nebraska, based on his exciting new vertebrate finds of the previous summer.

As in past winters, his most worrisome problem concerned employment for the forthcoming summer. No agency of the federal government carried on continuously funded explorations of the nation's geography or its resources. More than any other group, the Corps of Topographical Engineers existed for this purpose, but it depended on annual appropriations from the War Department, whose priorities changed from year to year. The railroad and boundary surveys operated with only short-term objectives. Various geologic and natural history surveys functioned at the state level, but none enjoyed long-term funding.

The business side of natural history before the Civil War was precarious at best, and the life of a naturalist insecure and uncertain. For that very reason the profession tended to attract risk-takers and entrepreneurs, at least until after the founding of the U.S. Geological Survey (still a generation in the future). Even when flush after selling a collection, Hayden complained to a colleague, "Science is not lucrative, furnishing but a bare support." And to another he confided, "There is a terrible stir here about so much natural history being published in the government reports."

As soon as he returned to Washington, Hayden began scrambling again, trying to find a benefactor who might support his explorations. He revived the vaccination project, and he lined up an important new sponsor in Joseph Henry, the secretary of the Smithsonian. He also talked about venturing out alone under the patronage of the American Fur Company, which stood ready to offer the same kind of indirect assistance that had sustained him in 1854–1855. He might have swallowed his pride and gone again with Warren, who had plans for entering the unknown country of the Upper Yellowstone. Alas, the army failed to dispatch Warren to the field in summer 1858.

Because he could find no government-funded expedition to offer him a place, Hayden spent two months in Kansas. Meek had resettled in Washington during May, in the aftermath of a bruising battle he and Hayden had been carrying on with James Hall. When Hayden found no paying position for the summer, Meek probably persuaded him that it would be wise to solidify their claims to the Permian by gathering more evidence. Thus in June Hayden started soliciting private support for their journey, which he got from Leidy, Baird, and James Dana in New Haven. Once Hayden got an idea into his head, he could be quite relentless about it, and his pestering of the gentle Leidy elicited this uncharacteristic response in July: "I must beg you to be occasionally indulgent when I do not immediately answer your letters."

Though Hayden and Meek intended to be in Kansas only about a month, they left Washington at the end of August and did not return until early November. They wanted to examine and take samples of the entire series of rocks from the Carboniferous up through the Cretaceous, a period of 300 million years, which included the Permian.[3] Compared to Hayden's experiences of the past summers, they had few adventures. They saw some antelope and wolves, but mostly buffalo, which were always in sight. Grasshoppers abounded, and Hayden commented in their joint journal, "The hogs and fowls devour them in immense numbers and, strange to say, their flesh was very poor to eat. The chickens had a bad taste, and the pork was stringy and poor." Prophetically, he feared grasshoppers would be "the curse of this western country." With good humor Stimpson had directed Hayden to "be virtuous among the Shyennes and see that Meek don't get — ," an obvious reference to venereal disease. Other than fossil collecting, Meek's biggest adventure was shooting a buffalo, which he did at Hayden's insistence. They also observed a comet and kept track of it for several nights.

Over the winter the usual uncertainties about the next summer lingered until March 1859, when Hayden heard the army would be sending a group to explore the Upper Yellowstone. Captain William Franklin Raynolds replaced Warren at the head of the party, and by late April Raynolds had hired Hayden as the party's naturalist at $120 per month, plus all travel and field expenses. Hayden was issued a revolver with belt and holster, two blankets, an overcoat, a pair of boots, a knapsack, two pair of trousers, a knife with sheath, a canteen, and mosquito equipment. His old friend Culbertson gave him a double-barreled shotgun.

The party left St. Louis on 28 May on the steamer *Spread Eagle*. Typically in a hurry at the last minute, Hayden left behind two shirts at the Virginia Hotel, and he forgot to endorse a money order for his mother. He imposed on friends to set things right. Once underway though, he resumed his dedicated collecting habits, as one of his fellow passengers recorded in his diary. "This morning we were detained by a fog till after 6 o'c and Dr. Hayden while the rest of us were asleep went on shore & shot four small birds which he gave Piersol to stuff. Dr. H. is very energetic & active & at the moment the boat reaches land he is on shore with his gun."

After reaching Fort Pierre on 18 June, Raynolds distributed presents to the Dakota tribe (Sioux) and gave assurances on his intentions and his route. The Indians approved; they even gave him a guide to take the party to the Crow country.[4] As the party left Fort Pierre, Raynolds kept it together by moving in the traditional military column. This enhanced security, but it did not suit the needs of a collecting naturalist. As a result Hayden diverged from the column to explore creeks, rock outcrops, and other sites likely to yield fossils. Normally, he returned within a few hours, but on 12 August he and three others departed for the Little Wolf Mountains (in southeastern Montana) and did not return until the next day. Raynolds noted the facts in his diary with disapproval; then in his official report he had the satisfaction of recording, "I improved this incident to issue an order forbidding any one to be absent from the train over night without explicit permission." This was especially galling because Hayden normally roamed wherever and whenever he wanted; even Warren had permitted that.

Raynolds was a bit of the fish out of water, for in none of his previous assignments had he shown the initiative or love of adventure so necessary for a successful commander in the West. Though he had worked outdoors for the Northeast Boundary Survey, had made maps in the field for five months during the Mexican War, and later plodded along the Great Lakes to complete several specific tasks, Raynolds performed best when sitting behind a desk. Probably his most notable contribution had been supervising the construction and repair of lighthouse facilities along the East Coast. He carried out a number of other minor assignments, none of very long duration, and it is difficult to believe that this moderately endowed bureaucrat was the officer most qualified to replace Warren as commander of the Yellowstone expedition. As his diary shows, from the moment the party left Fort Pierre he was uncomfortable, constantly worrying about something: the route, the Indians, sufficient pasturage for the animals, or getting to winter camp in good time. His portrait shows a man with a full shock of hair worn long in the back, a broad forehead, thick moustache, and a prominent nose. He displays none of Warren's keen intelligence; instead he projects the flat countenance and overly confident demeanor of a man who has never suffered curiosity. He resembles a biblical prophet more than a frontiersman.

Indeed, he subordinated exploration to his grander religious goals. "I feel that my attempts to do good are feeble and few, and that my precepts are not properly seconded by my example," he confided to his diary on 17 July and then concluded, "May I have grace to live more in accordance with my professions and may I be the means of doing something in my Master's cause." Consistent with that purpose, Raynolds hoped to inculcate a respect for the Sabbath among his men, which meant abstaining from work of any kind on Sunday: not marching to another camp, not writing up notes or studying maps, not working on specimens—in short, doing nothing. To the practical, worldly men under his command, this approach seemed utter nonsense. Yet Raynolds was sure enough of his mission that he wrote in his official report for Sunday 31 July: "I find that the entire party eagerly anticipate throughout the week the welcome rest of the Sabbath, and upon Monday morning our labors are resumed with renewed vigor, an illustration of the physical advantages of this heaven-appointed day of rest." Maintaining his zeal even in private, he wrote in his diary for the same day, "Quiet in camp. Read the Service as usual at 9 o'clock. Attendance not as good as I would like, yet hope it may be made the means of doing good."

After Hayden's dash to the Little Wolf Mountains, the party marched north to find the Yellowstone but had to kill time at Fort Sarpy, where they awaited fresh supplies. Leaving the fort on 31 August, they turned away from the Yellowstone, south then west, to explore two minor tributaries, Sarpy and Tullock creeks, before encountering the Bighorn River and beginning its ascent on 6 September.

Sunday the eleventh found them near the place where the Bighorn emerges from the mountains, an ideal place to geologize. Here distorted and contorted rock threw up new challenges, for "almost all the country is more or less disturbed and it requires much patient study to work out the formations," as Hayden told Leidy. Hayden and one of the army topographers, J. H. Snowden, proposed to approach the mountains. As it was Sunday,

Raynolds balked, and he prevailed upon Jim Bridger to pronounce the idea dangerous. Hayden said he would go unless specifically forbidden. Snowden backed out, however, making it more awkward than dangerous for Hayden to proceed. It was the second time Raynolds had quashed Hayden's desire to work on Sunday, and the commander took pains to summarize the incident, concluding, "I do not imagine that the gratification of curiosity or even the determination of the dip of the rocks or bearing of a hill is of sufficient importance to risk going out when we know the Indians are watching us." Raynolds failed to realize that each day was precious to an exploring naturalist. Forbidden to work on Sundays and prevented from making extended side trips, Hayden was disappointed with his collections. But time was running out on their first summer. Arriving at Deer Creek on the Platte River in mid-October, Raynolds decided to establish winter quarters there.[5]

As soon as the party found time to catch its breath at Platte Bridge, Hayden began to vent his frustrations. He could not resist telling Baird, "Capt. R. is an old <u>fogie</u> and can't quite appreciate my large views about the importance of various branches of science." Hayden still bristled at whatever or whomever seemed to block his own self-appointed mission. Comparing Raynolds with Warren elicited a newfound respect for Warren: "Capt. R. is by no means the man we all supposed him to be. It is quite difficult sometimes to know when one is well off. Warren, I now think, was a perfect trooper." Or again, "I am not happy on this trip," he confided more honestly to Meek. "My Christian Captain is in trouble with someone all the time. About all he cares for is to get back with his wife. I do not think I shall ever go out again unless Warren were to go." Of course, had Warren been in charge of the Yellowstone expedition, Hayden would have found cause to complain, too; it was his nature. Warren stirred up intense feelings precisely because he was a kindred spirit, one Hayden could respect even while he argued with him, but for Raynolds Hayden could summon only contempt: "Warren you know got right at last, but this man has not a tithe of the good sense or intellect of Warren."

At Deer Creek Raynolds established winter quarters opposite the Indian agency, along the Platte Road, so that regular mail came through. Raynolds's party took over cabins some Mormons had constructed and fortified them against an oppressive winter. "We are totally shut up with cold and snow," Hayden told Meek. "Thermometer 30° below zero. We are going to have a hard winter. All well, though doing nothing. I would give much to be with you." Making the best of it Hayden spent the nights reading *Harper's Weekly, Century,* and a variety of other magazines and newspapers Baird and others sent him. He also made four exploring trips over the winter: one for about three weeks shortly after they reached the Platte, presumably along that river; another in February to the Sweetwater River country, not far to the west; then during March into Colorado Territory, down the eastern slope of the Rockies, probably as far south as the Arkansas River; and finally, during April, south across the Laramie Plains to inspect the Medicine Bow Mountains.

Raynolds found less productive ways of occupying his time. He worried about having enough money to finish the expedition, and he brooded about discipline among the soldiers, especially their proclivity to drink and their lack of spiritual concern. He paid off and released several of the unruly ones and court-martialed the insubordinate leader of the military escort. Raynolds suffered through a painful urinary disorder at this time. For consolation, he looked forward to Sunday services, played the flute, and talked religion with the four Lutherans sent out by the German Evangelical Synod of Iowa as a mission to the Crows. And Raynolds recorded this vignette about Hayden: "He seems to live only for the world and worldly fame, and I tried my best to argue in favor of living for a higher and better end. He admits readily but does not feel. I fear his whole aim is this world's rewards. God grant he may see his error." Hayden saw no error, of course, only that he must become more politic; he had a great deal to lose by alienating Raynolds, not least his valuable collections, which for a while Raynolds thought of keeping for the army instead of delivering to the Smithsonian as was required by federal law. So Hayden temporized, did small favors for Raynolds, talked with him infrequently, and confided his opinions only to trusted friends back East. He even attended services on Sundays, not regularly but as often as anyone else over the course of nearly sixteen months in the field.

Resuming its march on 10 May, the party was destined for disappointment but also some striking encounters with western geography. They wanted to ascend the Wind River[6] to its source, then cross over the divide to the north to enter the Upper Yellowstone, approximately in the manner of U.S. Highway 287 today, though traveling on that road hides from the tourist the unforgiving enormity of the country. A few miles west of Dubois (still in modern Wyoming) they crossed the Continental Divide at Union Pass, which Raynolds named. It was 31 May. Jim Bridger was guiding but could find no route across the steep amphitheaters that barred the way north. For the next week they worked their way painfully west and a little north, trying to find an alternate route, but everywhere deep snow or swollen streams harassed and slowed them. On 7 June, climbing along the North Fork of the Gros Ventre River, they regained the divide somewhere in the vicinity of Togwotee Pass, only to come face to face with defeat. "A single glance was sufficient to satisfy me that if I proceeded the loss of my party would be the result," Raynolds later told his superior, Andrew Atkinson Humphreys. "As far as the eye could reach nothing but snow and pines was visible, and as my guide (Mr. Jim Bridger) told me that even if the snow was gone we could not get out of the pines for weeks, I was reluctantly compelled to change my route."

Retreating down the Gros Ventre, they came into Jackson Hole with the intention of swinging north, up the west side of the Teton Range to a point that would permit them to turn east again, thus finding a back door to the Yellowstone. But a couple of barriers intervened. In its spring runoff the Snake River raged downhill in three separate channels, all deep and treacherous. In trying to find a ford, one man drowned. Clearly, some kind of boat would be necessary. Rafts were tried, but proved unsuccessful. Finally, the men constructed a craft about 12 feet long by 3 feet wide, covered its bottom with blankets and hide, and smeared it with resin to improve its ability to resist water. Three men working in shifts manipulated the craft across the channels, but its capacity was so small that three exhausting days passed before they completed the crossing on Saturday, 16 June.

Once across the Snake the country to the west and north proved even more difficult. Finding a notch through the lower part of the Teton Range, they came down into the Teton Basin, known as Pierre's Hole, then moved north to Henry's Fork and beyond it to Henry's Lake, crossing the Continental Divide again at what Raynolds called the Low Pass (now known as Raynolds Pass). This gave them access to streams that eventually debouched into the Madison River, which they followed to Three Forks, arriving on 29 June. At what point in their trek from Pierre's Hole they abandoned the idea of crossing back to the east to find the Yellowstone is not known. The northern portion of the Teton Range is formidable as are the mountains running north from Raynolds Pass, parallel to the Madison Valley. But the Madison itself, which they encountered a few miles north of Raynolds Pass, gave direct and easy access to the Yellowstone had they but realized it. Though Jim Bridger knew this part of the country as well as any man, even he had not seen enough of it to imagine how the Madison might lead to the Upper Yellowstone. The region presented a staggering geographic conundrum, involving a mental integration of the headwaters of the Jefferson, Madison, Gallatin, and Yellowstone rivers—a feat of sufficient difficulty that it was not unraveled until the early 1870s, when, after repeated efforts, Hayden himself turned the trick.

Rations now ran dangerously low, discouraging further explorations around Three Forks. Raynolds sent one group east to find the Yellowstone, with orders to descend it to Fort Union, while he pioneered a new route up the Little Green River (now Sixteenmile Creek) and Smith River to rejoin the Missouri near Great Falls. From Fort Benton his group came down the river in a mackinac to Fort Union. At that point Raynolds assigned the river survey to one of his lieutenants, and he took a land route all the way down to Omaha, where the party dispersed on 4 October.

After a quick visit with his family in Rochester, Hayden returned to Washington by mid-November 1860, and he lived there for most of the next two years until he enlisted in the army and was transferred to Philadelphia in mid-October 1862. Once back in Washington Hayden had intended to live again with Stimpson, until Meek suggested he stay with him at his boardinghouse, to which Hayden readily agreed. With the approach of the Civil War various members of the Megatherium Club drifted out of town and the club dissolved. After the formal outbreak of war in spring 1861, Hayden, Meek, and the other megatheres remaining in Washington gave up their separate residences and flocked to the Smithsonian's castle, where they roomed and boarded for the duration of the war.

Hayden's job prospects, always uncertain, virtually evaporated as war became more certain, though the possibilities he pursued give an insight into his thinking. While still in Nebraska Territory with Raynolds, he spoke of returning to collect again under the partial auspices of the American Fur Company, but he also thought he had amassed enough savings to launch the kind of independent survey of which he had always dreamed. As much as he enjoyed collecting on his own, however, he realized that too much independence could hinder him, that government sponsorship provided more amply for his physical requirements in the field—not to mention a number of intangible benefits, such as connections with colleagues, ready access to publication, and recognition from the scientific world. Uncertain what to do, he rehearsed aloud on the same day (5 May 1860) two different options for his future: the first to Baird, regarding a collecting trip on his own; the second to Meek, wondering about working for Newberry on the forthcoming survey of Ohio or for Whitney on his new survey of California. In fact, Hayden pursued neither of these possibilities, which remained but ideas in a fertile and sometimes frantic brain. Another possibility was to visit Hudson's Bay. Hayden only thought of it because Baird mentioned that another of his field men might be going there. It was a fantasy, plain and simple, but in boldness it foreshadows some of Hayden's more deliberate plans during the 1870s.

Only a few other options remained. Hayden still wanted the appointment as Indian agent to the Blackfeet. That came to nothing despite strong endorsements from the scientists he enlisted to back him. Actually, Hayden was too independent and too highbrow to be an Indian agent; most men gained those positions as a reward for allegiance to a prominent politician. Still ruminating, he wrote to Leidy, suggesting he might again go up the

Missouri should the Philadelphia Academy support him. But as the war got under way in earnest, Hayden, like so many other young men, was genuinely confused about his future.

Against this background of frustration and uncertainty, Hayden and Meek decided upon a collecting trip during May and June 1862. Leidy even managed a modest underwriting from the Philadelphia Academy. Of course, a firsthand comparison of the Cretaceous beds of New Jersey with those they knew from the West would be valuable, and certainly the acquaintance of the brilliant young man Leidy sent along from Philadelphia, Edward Drinker Cope, would be stimulating; yet this junket was more a brave assertion of a threatened way of life than a serious scientific endeavor.

Under the circumstances it was especially gratifying that during 1862 Hayden became a corresponding member of the Lyceum of Natural History in the City of New York (after 1876 known as the New York Academy of Sciences). He had now been recognized by each of the most prestigious institutions of science in America, for he had recently become a corresponding member of the American Philosophical Society in 1860 and earlier of the Boston Society of Natural History, the Essex Institute, the American Association for the Advancement of Science, the Academy of Science of St. Louis, and the Academy of Natural Sciences of Philadelphia.

Besides being highly honorary, corresponding membership in these learned bodies publicly acknowledged important contributions to science, which in Hayden's case meant a combination of his collections and his publications. By the outbreak of the Civil War Hayden's versatile interests and abundant talents had moved him to the forefront among American naturalists. Strictly as a collector, Hayden was already in a class by himself. As a coauthor with Meek he had stamped his name on history in connection with the rocks of the Upper Missouri. Hayden also published several works on his own, and these are worth assessing, especially because they epitomize his interests as a broad-gauge naturalist and foreshadow his role as a scientific publicist after the Civil War. But first it is necessary to draw together several other strands of his life during the middle and late 1850s, which set the context for his emergence as an author.

8
FRIENDS
AND ENEMIES

His old game is going on still. Well, I think he [James Hall] will certainly die one of these days and then the coast will be clear of one <u>monster</u>. However I do not fear him. If he can attack me in any way directly or indirectly I will publish a card with the names of every man who will dare to be my friend attached.

—Hayden to Meek, 12 April 1858

As for Hall I do not care a fig for him now. Every blow he may hit at us falls upon his own head. The mere fact that he is our enemy is making us friends, and helping us all over the U.S. and Canada, as well as in England and in Europe.

—Meek to Hayden, 2 December 1859

HAYDEN NEVER DOUBTED who his friends were. They were the men who sponsored him, supported him, above all agreed with him. Perhaps because he staked so much of his personal happiness on professional success, Hayden confronted life as if it were a battle, a risky battle in which colleagues were either for or against him and from which he could emerge victorious only by adhering to his own severe standards of right and wrong. This pattern of thinking bedeviled his work with Vaughan, then Warren, then Raynolds, with each of whom Hayden fussed and fought. But he could not afford to dismiss Leidy, to turn his back on Baird, or to quarrel very long with Meek, for these men were more crucial to his success, and in his relations with them Hayden reveals other sides of himself.

Although Baird set similar goals for all his collectors—broadly, to increase the holdings of the Smithsonian—he worked with each in different ways, appropriate to the men, their specialties, and the regions they scoured. Until someone volunteers several years of his or her life just to read Baird's mammoth correspondence, it will not be possible to say whether his relationship with Hayden was typical or exceptional; I suspect it was exceptional. After all, Baird treated Hayden rather coolly at first and never developed the personal closeness with him that he did with other collectors. It was not until after Hayden had separated from James Hall in 1854 that Baird regarded him as potentially useful, and even then he only smoothed out some of the details of a scheme Vaughan and Hayden had already conceived. This offered Baird a chance to reap a harvest without having to invest much in the planting, and his commitment of time and resources to Hayden's first venture amounted to very little.

Perhaps Baird's common sense told him to give a wide berth to a man like Hayden. Perhaps he was put off by Hayden's persistent and petulant manner. He could hardly fail to see a pattern in Hayden's behavior, a pattern of deliberate stroking. Hayden began by asking for advice regarding his career as a naturalist, then he offered to collect various specimens in which Baird had an interest, and he promised to deliver far more, especially if he could be properly funded. He pestered relentlessly, but flattered consistently. He demanded attention to himself but did not forget to express gratitude. Most of all he created an image of himself as the dedicated naturalist, interested in science at all costs, even including risks to his life. The stroking was not exclusively for Baird, for that behavior runs through Hayden's relationships with other patrons and men of eminence.

Other young protégés of Baird adopted deferential postures toward the great man, but I have not found this steady stroking in any of them. The more Hayden is compared to them, the more he differs from other naturalists. Some collectors—Robert Kennicott especially comes to mind—were ill at ease in the presence of urban civilities and frivolities, and they could hardly wait to get back to nature. By contrast, Hayden seems to have regarded his fieldwork as a necessary preliminary to the real rewards, which derived from being in Washington or Philadelphia. Perhaps other collectors felt this way sometimes, but their letters exude an absorption with the tasks at hand, and they write in detail of their outdoor life and habits, people they met, adventures and dangers they encountered. They were intelligent men in lonely circumstances, and their letters often read like diaries, full of observations on their work, thoughts about life, and so on. I base these impressions on the letters of a variety of naturalists, men like Kennicott, John Xantus, William Stimpson, Henry Wood Elliott, and William Healey Dall. But Hayden's letters are not like theirs, despite his obvious intelligence and the wide variety of his interests.

Instead Hayden reveals himself as incapable of enjoying the moment. He looks ahead constantly—to the next week, the next season, the next place to mail and receive letters—and always he yearns for better employment in the future. Even the physical appearance of his letters betrays a self-imposed urgency. He writes atrociously, he wanders from topic to topic in a stream of consciousness, then doubles back to repeat himself in unexpected places, showing little respect for organized discourse and disdaining the clarity of good grammar. Alone on a wild and unknown frontier, he appears oblivious to the uniqueness of his position, except to complain of its hardships. Of course he understood his singular opportunities as a collector, but he was stingy in sharing his thoughts about the frontier with his friends, which contrasts with his generous comments for the general public in his later publications. Despite his abundant skills at coping, he was restless in the wilderness, acting as if he could hardly wait to enjoy the comforts of home and the pleasures of fame. He constantly asks for newspapers and begs for news of friends. He fears he will be forgotten. He frets that others may pre-empt him, and he wants immediate word on the latest articles relating to his interests. He tells his sponsors little about his collections—how taken, where, the circumstances—except to say they bulk large in importance for science, I hope they interest you, and, by the way, do look after the expense of shipping them. In addition to the calculated stroking he applied to all his patrons, especially Baird, his tone could also be demanding, peremptory, and downright rude, with the result that others found him impulsive, exasperating, suspicious, quarrelsome, and self-centered.

No wonder Baird was rather cool toward him. Why, for instance, did he not place Hayden on any of the numerous Pacific Railroad Surveys during the 1850s? Without question, and more than anyone else, Baird had the influence to do so. There was always room for a good collector in the right field, and Hayden had plenty of talent. But Baird had to work closely with men recruited for the railroad surveys because he himself organized and published their materials. It could be that Baird balked at working so closely with Hayden, though he did not mind placing him in harness for others, whose collections would eventually wind up at the Smithsonian.

All this tells only half of Hayden's story, the half that is revealed through the eyes of others. What about Hayden's view of himself? Being the restless wanderer he was, he did not indulge in self-evaluation, or if he did, he never committed such thoughts to paper. Yet his very activity, or better, the style in which he expressed it, vividly portrays his inner self. At his core burned an aggressive ambition, a desire to be recognized and acclaimed. His was the sort of appetite that mere achievement cannot satisfy. He had won praise from his colleagues, had seen his name in print, had been welcomed into the company of learned and important men, but so far he had secured no island of inner peace, no beachhead of self-satisfaction that could be expanded through exploration. Some of this would come, but by 1860, at the end of his apprenticeship, his worldly circumstances did not yet permit any psychic comfort. Despite successful employments, he had located no secure base for future operations, no particular sponsor. Despite a growing circle of acquaintances, where he found praise and even financial endorsement, he lacked a sense of belonging, for he was frustrated by the very men who promoted him. Several of the fur traders and Indian agents generously paid his expenses and opened the doors for his travels, but they were frontiersmen, often friendly and helpful but imbued with an earthy, sometimes coarse outlook, who scoffed at the high-minded pretensions of a young idealist pursuing scientific truth. Those who sympathized with his loftier aspirations lived back East and thus were distant from his immediate field of activity; while they rejoiced in his collections, they could not be trusted to advance him without constant reminders of his needs.

So another pattern emerges. The strength of Hayden's character, the very qualities that assured him worldly success, made him unpopular with the men on whom he depended to get ahead. Thus he advanced in a kind of fox trot: two steps forward and one step back. Gradually an uneasy accommodation evolved, because no matter how annoying he could be, he also delivered on his promises. Year after year and from regions widely separated and distinctly endowed, Hayden brought back large and important collections. Remembering his urgent personal anxieties to succeed, to rise above his sordid origins, it does not seem farfetched to say he used these priceless natural history specimens to buy the respect and attention he so desperately needed. In the process mentors were made over into patrons, and sponsorship gradually raised Hayden to the level of a colleague, at least for those, like Baird and Leidy, who cooperated in his acquisitive enterprises.

A more complex relationship existed between Hayden and Meek because of their similar needs and ambitions, mutual respect, a bit of jealousy, and certainly the exasperation that explodes when mixing such different temperaments. Meek was unique among Hayden's circle of colleagues and deserves the most attention. He could not muster the boisterous good humor of Stimpson or teasingly rejoice in Hayden's libidinous nature the way Stimpson and James Graham Cooper did, yet he became Hayden's closest associate, his staunchest ally, and his only true partner.

Ever since their return from the Bad Lands in fall 1853, Hayden and Meek had been planning to work together. To achieve that goal, they each needed regular employment. Working for Hall served Meek well at first, but Hall looked jealously on anything that took Meek away from his assigned work, and he did not pay well. Meek's part-time position with the Missouri survey under Swallow gave him additional income and the time to study

Hayden's fossils. For his part Hayden realized that to use Meek most effectively he had to find funds for him, and beginning in spring 1856, when he signed on with Warren, he also arranged for regular payments to Meek. Over the next five years the War Department became an important source of support for Meek.

Despite their increasing independence, neither Meek nor Hayden were able to break away from Hall for a while. Meek labored in Missouri only during summers; in the off-season he continued to work for Hall in Albany and had less time to write descriptions of Hayden's fossils. Meek's double employment annoyed Hall, who complained frequently about it, but it also permitted Hall to look over Meek's shoulder, as it were, to examine Hayden's fossils and expand his own knowledge of western geology at little cost to himself. Hall cordially invited Hayden to stay at his house again and released Meek for two weeks so that he and Hayden could work together in spring 1857. Hayden looked forward to his time in Albany as Hall's guest, and he treated Hall graciously, almost obsequiously, clearly anxious to patch up their quarrel of the previous spring over the fossil plants. Hayden acknowledged his obligations to Hall, said he would like to work under him again, and then overdoing it a bit, said, "There is no one whose good opinion I more earnestly desire." Hayden offered to communicate facts at his command for Hall's forthcoming geologic map of the West, which Hall was preparing for William Hemsley Emory's Mexican Boundary Survey.

But all these good intentions disappeared during spring 1857. The details elude us; only the fallout remains. From Philadelphia Hayden wrote Meek of the relief he felt to be out of Albany. "I tell you there is an entire difference between being in Albany and in an atmosphere like Pa or Washington." He urged Meek not to submit to Hall's bullying and went on at some length about his favorable prospects for the next three years, implying there would be money enough to fund their joint work and plenty of publishing opportunities. The trip to Albany in the spring had been significant for Hayden. He saw he could not work with Hall, could not abide him personally, and subsequently he urged Meek to keep quiet around Hall about their own discoveries. No more talk of sharing information with Hall; instead only the deepest suspicion of him. Hayden now began an earnest campaign to get Meek away from Hall as soon as possible. "It is the request of all my friends that hereafter I carry out all investigations either in this place or Philadelphia," he wrote from Washington, "so you will have to meet me in one of these places." He emphasized that his friends were Meek's friends, that others wished to see Meek free of Hall too, that there would soon be room for Meek in Washington. He also started mentioning job opportunities for Meek, which he picked up from his contacts in Washington.

However, Meek was not yet ready to leave Hall, and during May 1857 Hayden and Meek suffered one of their periodic crises. Hayden's first geologic map was about to be printed, and Hayden wanted Meek to put his name on it. After all, Meek had done all the paleontological research for it, and Hayden viewed it as a joint effort, like their previously published articles. But Meek hesitated. Wanting to see more fossils from certain problematic areas, such as the Platte Valley, he asked Hayden to refrain from coloring those areas on the proposed map. Hayden balked, saying Warren and other friends in Washington urged him to publish everything, and, besides, he wrote, "If it is not published as full as possible I shall be blamed." Meek also feared Hall might possess fossils from some of the same regions and that Hall might claim they had used his own materials to preempt him. Hayden pointed out that the only specimens of Hall's they had used were ones Hall had already published in his reports for Frémont and Howard Stansbury; furthermore, he noted that the War Department was prepared to defend the claims Hayden wanted to make on the map.

Meek swayed back and forth and almost accepted Hayden's arguments. At the height of the crisis Hayden learned from the public printer that Hall was trying to use his connections to sneak a look at Hayden's map, with the obvious intent of copying anything Hayden might have discovered that he had not yet confirmed for himself. This news, coupled with Hayden's other pleas, persuaded Meek to place his name on the map. Alas, four days later in a fit of anxiety, Meek lost his nerve and asked Hayden to remove his name. Hayden put a good face on the matter, saying Meek probably had done well not to collide with Hall; "but at the same time you can see for yourself how important it is for you to be firm and stand to your rights." Such pep talks became a regular tonic from Hayden over the next year.

During the summer, while Hayden was in Nebraska Territory with Warren, events took a fateful turn. Meek received some curious fossils from Frederick Hawn, who had been collecting for Swallow and knew Meek through their joint association with Swallow's survey in Missouri. The fossils came from the Smoky Hill Fork of the Kansas River, and Meek thought they might represent the first Permian formations in America. His hunch was reinforced by some fossils Hayden brought back from the base of the Black Hills and others from the banks of the Missouri River, which also seemed to be Permian. Better still, Hayden had brought back evidence of the first Jurassic in America, and he and Meek both realized at once that these facts gave them a decided advantage in explaining the geology of the West. Specifically, they now held the key to an improved geologic map, which they intended to publish before Hall could publish his own for the boundary survey. The race was on.

Hawn had promised to send additional samples of the doubtful fossils from Kansas, and Meek would have preferred waiting for these in order to make the best case for the American Permian. But the longer he delayed, the greater the risk that Hall might learn of the Permian on his own and anticipate them. To forestall that possibility Hayden and Meek decided to establish a paper trail. They obtained a note from Baird at the Smithsonian, stating that on 19 January 1858 they had shown him "forms indicating Permian," and on 8 February they wrote Warren with the same news. While they were preparing a formal paper, Meek also wrote Leidy on 16 February, asking him to announce the Permian on their behalf to the Philadelphia Academy. These communications were private because they did not want to inform Hall of their discovery. Leidy subsequently read their paper publicly on 2 March, and the Academy published it at the end of the month in the *Proceedings*. All this was arranged without ever alerting Hall. They had clearly taken a huge step along the path to the kind of recognition they both wanted, and, best of all, they had stolen a march on James Hall.

But they had reckoned without "Major" Hawn. Hawn cared nothing for the niceties of a priority dispute, and power struggles among rapacious rivals did not concern him. Hawn was a civil engineer with experience building railroads, who after learning some geology on his own, began locating coal for railroads and collecting fossils for Swallow. The fact that the shells he sent Meek might represent the first American Permian only enhanced their potential market value as far as Hawn was concerned, for he added to his income by selling such collections. Therefore he wanted the shells determined and described as soon as possible. During fall 1857 he pressed Meek several times to publish descriptions right away. To Hawn, Meek seemed to be taking an inordinately long time to make up his mind about the fossils. Hawn was mistaken, for Meek had recognized the possibility of the Permian immediately and promptly confided that fact to Hayden. Being a methodical and cautious investigator, however, Meek wanted to consider all the possibilities; meanwhile he decided to play down the Permian a bit, lest news of it turn up in Hall's hands before Meek and Hayden were ready to make an announcement. Accordingly, in fall 1857, he told Hawn at least twice that the fossils *might* be Permian, but then again they *might* be Carboniferous. The news was significant to Hawn, for in the agreements he had struck with Meek and Swallow, Hawn had promised to send anything resembling Cretaceous material to Meek and anything Carboniferous to Swallow.

The fact that the Permian lay somewhere between the Carboniferous and the Cretaceous may have suggested Hawn's next move. Clearly misunderstanding Meek's deliberate temperament, and having no idea of the game that was going on with Hall, Hawn assumed Meek had "abandoned the investigation, either for want of time, or of confidence in the final result," as he later explained to Meek. Previously, he had shown Swallow only his materials that seemed to be Carboniferous, but around the end of January 1858 he also produced samples of the curious shells he had sent to Meek and beseeched Swallow to publish descriptions. Little more than two weeks later Swallow wrote a St. Louis newspaper to make the first public announcement of Permian fossils in America. Swallow also wrote a notice for the *American Journal of Science and Arts,* which appeared there by the first of March. Shortly afterward, he published his more elaborate scientific descriptions in the *Transactions of the Academy of Science of St. Louis.* Having assured himself of priority in the announcement, Swallow then informed Meek of the facts on 23 February. As he explained later, "I then felt you could not have the evidence I had or you would have announced the fact long ago."

Meek was furious, for he felt Hawn had betrayed the agreement between them. "Is it not as clear as daylight that they were availing themselves of our study?" he wrote to Hayden on 2 March. Though caught off-guard by Swallow's initiative, Meek and Hayden resolved to produce their publication on the Permian as soon as possible, which they hoped would be before Swallow's could appear in a scholarly journal. Swallow's earlier newspaper announcement would not carry the same weight in a claim for priority as a learned discussion of the evidence, complete with descriptions of the relevant fossils. Meek read his and Hayden's joint paper to the Albany Institute on 3 March, and it was published the next day in the institute's *Transactions.* It is quite important to notice that on the very day this paper was read, the secretary of the institute dutifully recorded that "in the last number of Silliman's Journal [the *American Journal of Science*] Professor Swallow makes a similar announcement," which of course means Swallow's paper preceded Meek's, and both Meek and Hayden knew it.

But few other people knew positively which article appeared first; therefore, the issue of priority remained up in the air. Swallow certainly knew he had won as his correspondence proves, but he wanted to put the quarrel behind him in order to rebuild a shattered relationship with Meek, whose expertise in paleontology he still needed on the Missouri survey. Meek also knew it, and he could ill afford to offend a potential employer; so they each made gestures of conciliation to the other. A formal truce emerged from the May 1858 meeting of the American Association for the Advancement of Science, when Swallow publicly acknowledged Meek's pioneering role in identifying the American Permian. Soon after Swallow passed the word through Hayden that he wanted Meek to come to Missouri to do drawings, and on 1 July he sent a formal offer. Meek accepted. But the controversy was not put to rest; it raged in print for another decade and smoldered in the hearts of the antagonists even longer. The highlights, summarized here, underline Hayden's role in the story.

Not a month after Meek and Swallow patched up their quarrel, Hayden published the second edition of his geologic map. In a supplementary essay he recited a brief history of the Permian matter, which inexcusably failed to mention Swallow. Then, nine years later, hoping to take advantage of the residual uncertainty about whose article had been published first (Swallow's in Silliman's *Journal* or his and Meek's in the *Transactions of the Albany Institute*), Hayden introduced the false notion that Swallow's article had appeared between 4 and 10 March, which would have been after his and Meek's of 4 March. In truth, Swallow's was published by 1 March. The net result of this deception, however, coupled with the impact of a first-rate monograph on the Permian that Meek published in 1872, was to persuade geologists at the time that Meek had spoken the final word on the American Permian, as well as the first.

Despite all the heat it generated, the conflict with Swallow (which temporarily distracted Meek and Hayden) had always been a sideshow to the more crucial battle with James Hall. The longer the dispute with Hall continued, the more intolerable Meek's subordinate position at Albany became and the more Hayden stepped up the pressure on Meek to leave Hall once and for all. Knowing Meek was cautious and likely to be intimidated by the prospect of a showdown with Hall, Hayden fired off morale boosters to Albany, adding that other men of science agreed. He reminded Meek that as long as he remained under Hall's thumb, their future work was in jeopardy. Meek had his own perspective on Hall and did not need Hayden to tell him what kind of man they were dueling with. In mid-March Hall interrogated Meek thoroughly on the results of Hayden's discoveries around the Black Hills, which included Permian and Jurassic shells. Hall was trying to avail himself of anything new that he might incorporate into his map for the Mexican boundary report. Failing to learn much from Meek, he again tried to prevail upon the public printer to give him an unauthorized look at Hayden's forthcoming geologic map (second edition, published in June 1858), just as he had done in May 1857 with the first edition. This was probably the final straw that persuaded Meek he had to escape from Hall. At the AAAS meeting in May Meek saw for himself how informed opinion favored his break with Hall, and by mid-May he had boxed up all Hayden's fossils and moved from Albany to Washington—to take a position at the Smithsonian.

Bringing Meek to Washington—a cherished goal of Hayden's—had important consequences for both men. By any standard Hayden and Meek had won a substantial victory. Their knowledge of the Permian, though not announced or published first, was widely accepted as the earliest. The second edition of Hayden's geologic map, bolstered by Meek's research, was superior to anything else in print or to anything that would appear soon after. Best of all, they had weathered a potentially ruinous competition with the formidable James Hall, had relocated on a more comfortable basis in Washington, and were now poised to enlarge their professional territory through further joint efforts.

Though they could not have realized it then, the Civil War proved to be a watershed in Hayden's career. Hayden and Meek developed in different directions after the war, but they maintained close professional ties. Hayden continued to ask Meek to work up the invertebrates his survey brought back from the field each season. Through affiliation with ten other geological surveys, Meek became the most respected invertebrate paleontologist in America, but his most important research was published under the auspices of Hayden's survey. Hayden remained excitable, impulsive, and self-centered, but the Permian controversy had matured him sufficiently that, though younger than Meek by twelve years, he now emerged as the senior partner in guiding their future collaboration. Meek was almost constantly negotiating with a variety of employers for work, and Hayden gave lots of advice and coaching, partly out of genuine concern for Meek but also in order to preserve enough of Meek's time for his own purposes. He even took the liberty of asking one of Meek's employers to delay appointing him until Meek could finish some work for Hayden. Such actions caused flashes of resentment in Meek, especially as Hayden was becoming better known, but cooperation and mutual respect had brought them a long way and would carry them even further.

It was different with some of Hayden's other associates. His relationship with George Engelmann illustrates what happened when a colleague chose not to keep in step with Hayden's parade. Their mutual interest in plants drew them together, and Engelmann admired the energetic young collector, just as Hayden looked up to the experienced naturalist. Engelmann intervened in a timely fashion to save the 1853 journey to the Bad Lands and offered encouragement during Hayden's first solo venture during the following two years. Engelmann showed his friendship in other ways. He looked after various shipments of Hayden's collections as they arrived back in St. Louis before being sent back East, and he did not hold a grudge when Hayden sold his first haul of specimens to the Philadelphia Academy instead of to the St. Louis Academy where Engelmann was the guiding light. Hayden proposed that they collaborate on a catalog of all the plants of the Upper Missouri, for which Hayden would provide notes on geographical distribution; Engelmann would write the actual descriptions based on several different collections, most prominently Hayden's. During January 1856, with Engelmann's help,

Hayden compiled an extensive list of plants in his own handwriting, which amounted to a first draft of the catalog.

Engelmann subsequently agreed to write up the plants Hayden gathered during the Warren expedition, which would include but enlarge upon the list he had already helped Hayden compile. Like all the men with whom Hayden collaborated, Engelmann worked on several reports simultaneously; he could not afford to devote himself exclusively to Hayden's business, no matter how interesting. Yet Engelmann's multiple projects led to delays in publishing any one of them, which exasperated Hayden—justifiably. The circumstances under which Hayden worked, both before and after the Civil War, demanded a rapid accounting of past work in order to secure future funding. Thus Hayden pestered Engelmann to finish the catalog, and when it remained unfinished Hayden appealed to the dean of American botany, Asa Gray, to prod Engelmann.

Eventually, Engelmann completed the catalog and sent it to Hayden in December 1860, but this act led to more commotion. Hayden was now working on his natural history reports for Warren, and he wanted to incorporate the plant catalog into them. Hayden made a few changes in the catalog as submitted by Engelmann and published the revised version in his *On the Geology and Natural History of the Upper Missouri.* But his revisions gave Engelmann cause for complaint. Though Engelmann was listed as the author of the catalog, it was obvious to him that Hayden had rearranged some of the species. As author of the catalog, Engelmann would be blamed for errors in the notes on geographic distribution, yet Hayden alone had written these notes. Hayden acknowledged, "The catalogue was not just as you prepared it." He had not shown Engelmann the revised version before it was printed, Hayden explained, because "I had very little opportunity to read my own proof." Inasmuch as he received Engelmann's catalog in December 1860, and the book was not published until 1862, this was a terribly lame excuse. Embarrassed, Hayden offered to make things right: "If you will make out a critical notice, I will make the proper statements and send it to Silliman's Journal." Engelmann ignored him.

Similar problems developed between Hayden and Newberry, beginning with the fossil plants Hayden had gathered in 1854–1855. Having finally resolved to have Newberry describe them, though reluctantly and after flirting with the idea of giving them to Hall, he then worried that Newberry would never get the job done. Newberry delayed work on Hayden's fossils because he had accumulated plenty of work from three expeditions of his own between 1855 and 1859. Along the way, he did manage to look at enough of Hayden's angiosperms to pronounce them Cretaceous, which confirmed Meek and Hayden's stratigraphic column of the Upper Missouri. At least on the surface, therefore, relations with Newberry appeared smooth. Whenever in Washington, Hayden socialized with him, even boarded with him, and he usually spoke kindly of him to others.

But signs of a deeper incompatibility kept emerging. Writing as though Hayden would be amused to hear it, Stimpson reported in June 1857 on a hike taken by members of the Megatherium. "Poor Newberry got the blues & went home. He worked too hard on his report, & his mistaken religious ideas would not permit [him] to go out on Sunday mornings to recupe & walk with us." After Hayden returned to the field, isolated conditions encouraged his already suspicious mind to run rampant. In March 1859 he commented to Meek about Newberry's reputation for using specimens without giving proper credit to others and decided not to send Newberry any of his Tertiary plants. Hayden had already entrusted his Cretaceous plants to Newberry, and he often wondered aloud if he should ever see the reports. Hayden seemed to forget that Newberry had paying work from the government, and Hayden never offered to pay Newberry to speed things along. He didn't pay Engelmann or any other assisting experts before the 1860s— except for Meek—which testifies as well as any fact to Hayden's method of dealing with colleagues.

Did Hayden show the same exploitive tendencies toward women at this time? Only vague and mostly unconnected hints survive regarding his love life. A biographer yearns for a full and candid correspondence to reveal the nature and extent of the subject's emotional life, but in Hayden's case somebody deliberately attempted to destroy evidence of personal intimacies. Over the entire period of his otherwise ample correspondence, no bundle of letters survives from any woman in Hayden's life, not even his wife of sixteen years. What survives is a letter here and a letter there, from different women, written at different times—but no serial collection from any of them. Such a void becomes the emotional equivalent of a black hole in space, swallowing up all evidence of the past, yet further stimulating our curiosity with each gulp.

For now let me record the few relevant facts and postpone interpreting them until we have explored a few more years of Hayden's life. The one certainty is that Hattie Brooks reappeared, though the entire evidence for their renewed relationship derives from two sentences in a letter from Newberry to Hayden, dated 8 August 1858. After discussing other business, Newberry says, "I found a letter from you to Meek here on my arrival in which you speak of receiving no letters from me and attributing my silence to disapprobation of your treatment of Miss Brooks." Newberry said he knew little of Hayden's involvement with Hattie, but noted, "I must say that little was not quite creditable to you." He concluded the matter "was no affair of mine, and whatever my private opinion might be of that matter it could have no effect in interrupting pleasant intercourse between us."

This passing reference tells us nothing about how Hattie and Hayden got back together, only that it did not work out, and it implies Hayden initiated the break. We know nothing of timing, duration, or intensity, though circumstantial evidence can fill in some of the gaps. Between the time Hayden left Cleveland in spring 1853 and the time he enlisted in the Union army in October 1862, he may have visited in Ohio on two occasions, both times on the way to or from the field; but neither visit was very long, not long enough to carry on a romance. If Hattie was living in Ohio during this period, there would have been letters to sustain whatever a visit may have rekindled—letters that have since disappeared. Perhaps Hattie no longer lived in Ohio. Where then? New York State is the most likely possibility because Hayden could have called on her during his annual visits to family near Rochester or while he worked with Meek in Albany. Again there would have been letters had anything serious developed. Certainly Hattie did not move to Washington; the megatheres would have mentioned her. Instead, they speak of Hayden among a bevy of mostly nameless ladies, and they joke about his penchant for intense but short-term liaisons. And, in the end, that is all even Hattie amounted to. She may have endured a bit longer than the rest because she lived beyond Washington, thus sustaining through letters what would have evaporated sooner in the heat of physical presence. Their final breakup seems to have been in early 1857, for Hayden wrote Baird on 4 March from Albany, "I have concluded to remain a <u>single man</u> and devote my energies to western explorations."

Even by his thirty-fourth birthday, in 1862, Hayden had not yet discovered the bliss and consolation of a loving relationship. True, some people live their entire lives without this experience, and probably Hayden had no idea what he was missing. He was addicted to intense but brief affairs and always hoped the next would bring him lasting happiness, just as he assumed a permanent government job would result in security. Too restless to savor his moments, too ambitious to know what he really wanted, Hayden drove on like a powerful freight train racing into the night without a headlight.

His single-minded thrust for recognition was succeeding, but at the cost of crippling his emotions. He made room in his life only for his work and the activities and associates tied to it. For the most part his work was a lonely and self-absorbed obsession. From it he did gain a sense of something larger than himself, the great cause of natural history, but even causes can be made to serve the hidden demands of self. Hayden's life lacked the simple, direct commitment to another human being. He seems to have been fond of his younger sister, and he made use of some connections to promote his brother's career, but generally his relations with family remained perfunctory and distant. His serial romances may have stoked the fire of his ego, but they brought no lasting satisfaction, no belonging, no caring.

But what about his colleagues? Could not someone cut from the same raw cloth, colored with the same interests, and dressed with similar accomplishments have drawn out the inner man? Hayden used colleagues artfully and relentlessly, but cast aside those who would not cooperate in his self-aggrandizement. If anyone could have jerked him out of this rut, could have broken through to the inner man, it should have been Stimpson—the brilliant, fun-loving, warm-hearted spirit behind the Megatherium. Stimpson enjoyed a comfortable upbringing and was secure in his family's affection (pleasures that eluded Hayden), but he was generous with his associates and offered a friendship, if not a model for living, that might have appealed to a neglected but talented young man. Moreover his fascination with conchology enabled him to assist Hayden in his professional concerns. Yet, except for arranging playful encounters with the opposite sex, Hayden did not relax with Stimpson and never completely trusted him. In May 1862 Stimpson offered to take Hayden to Europe to see the sights and to meet some of the world's leading naturalists. Hayden declined but not because he had anything better to do. Perhaps Stimpson was too perfect a foil for Hayden, too secure in himself, and therefore not to be manipulated.

The colleague that was closest to Hayden as a young man, and the only one that even approached becoming an intimate friend at this time, was Meek—a man of similar disadvantages, a man whose professional gifts so perfectly balanced his own, and a man who implicitly recognized Hayden's hold over him. So Hayden remained emotionally isolated, imprisoned by his ambitions, as the inner man devoted himself to gathering bricks for his proud tower.

9
REACHING
FOR FAME

I wish to propose Dr. Hayden as a correspondent of the Academy. Will you permit me to use your name in recommendation, together with my own? No one knows him at our Academy except myself.

—Leidy to Baird, 13 February 1856

HAYDEN'S COLLEAGUES AND friends also included Joseph Leidy, who, following Allen, Kirtland, Newberry, Hall, and Baird, would be the last of Hayden's mentors. Leidy was a gentleman as well as a gentle man, full of consideration for others, and apparently immune to the poisonous effects of strong ambition. At the same time he had a healthy appetite for achievement: one does not become professor of anatomy (later of zoology also) at the University of Pennsylvania, publish over 600 scientific works, and lay the foundations for vertebrate paleontology in the United States without an ego and an unusual amount of drive.

Hayden admired Leidy more than any of his mentors, and certainly his broad approach to natural history was reinforced by this man who developed expertise in minerals, mollusks, plants, and insects—not to mention anatomy and paleontology, his chief specialties. With his microscope Leidy pioneered the study of protozoans. It was Leidy who first identified the cause of trichinosis in the tiny parasitic worms that infest pork. Later he was one of the first Americans to call attention to the public health implications of newly discovered bacteria. In 1853, six years before Darwin's *Origin of Species,* Leidy published a short essay illustrating evolution in animals; it effectively demolished the notion of spontaneous generation of species. Not surprisingly, he was among the first to hail Darwin for his revolutionary achievement. And this line of thinking would leave its traces on Hayden.

So Leidy would seem to be, like Stimpson, a colleague ideally suited to become more than a close professional associate, more than a scholarly collaborator. But he did not, at least not for many years. Hayden's manner of using people discouraged personal relations of any depth, but there was another barrier. Leidy had a deeply rooted fear of close human contact. Soon after getting his M.D. degree in 1844, the appearance of his first patient caused him to flee into a back room. Within three years he gave up medical practice entirely to concentrate on research. While living in the home of the man he assisted in anatomy, he realized a passion for the man's daughter; but he avoided the crisis by moving out of the house. Years later he turned down an opportunity to deliver the prestigious Lowell Lectures in Boston (which would have earned him $1,500), because he despaired of having to socialize and take meals at strange places while away from home. Obviously, Leidy never developed a taste for extended fieldwork. He also despised professional meetings. Though elected one of the original members of the National Academy of Sciences, he dropped out after its first meeting. He never joined the American Association for the Advancement of Science. For Leidy the study of nature was attractive and safe compared to the dangers and conflicts he saw lurking behind human encounters. No, this was not the man to lure Hayden out of his shell, though he set an example that profoundly influenced young Hayden, at least in his broad approach to nature.

Like all Hayden's previous mentors, Leidy saw the world whole and interconnected. Leidy especially saw separate disciplines as complementary tools, each different but all necessary to produce a rich and balanced harvest of knowledge. For Leidy, and for Hayden too, gaining expertise meant accepting an unending apprenticeship, which never culminated in mastery, never permitted the naturalist to comprehend more of nature's mansion than a carpenter who worked on every room, every closet, every fixture, but saw only one thing at a time. After years of experience, perhaps the gifted builder might gain an imaginative vision of the entire structure. But what a structure! It moved and changed, even as the craftsman caught a glimpse of it.

Those who have seen Leidy only as an accomplished empiricist, a man who supposedly scorned theories, have missed something in the man. Leidy was a resourceful investigator who respected all avenues of knowledge, empirically derived facts as well as theories of operation. All were useful in gaining understanding, but no single idea explained everything. This is why Leidy could welcome and applaud Darwin's theory of evolution, even the mechanism of natural selection, without becoming a rigorous Darwinian. Darwin had fashioned a valuable tool. Let us use it, Leidy thought, even as we search for others.

There is no doubt Hayden learned this way of thinking from Leidy. In the dutiful way he had of telling patrons what he thought they wanted to hear, Hayden reported in a letter of 13 March 1856, "Our collection of Cephalopoda is very large and will doubtless clear up many obscure points in reference to species and their progress of development." I do not mean to say that Hayden was simply a parrot, only that when he met Leidy he was a young and impressionable man, eager to soak up whatever learning was available. Evolutionary thinking provided Hayden with a way of making sense of what he was finding in the field: the chaotic diversity of life and its confusing abundance, in which many creatures scarcely differed from others; nature's feverish fecundity, yet also the relentless evidence of countless species gone extinct.

It is tempting to see Leidy as a personal model for Hayden, too. Leidy married late in life, a month short of his forty-first birthday; Hayden followed suit, at forty-three. Leidy never became a regular churchgoer, neither did Hayden. Leidy avoided professional meetings; so did Hayden. But we can also see differences between the two. Leidy was warm-hearted, remarkably tolerant in an age of moral rectitude, but sincerely shy and comfortable only in the quiet cocoon of research he had built around himself. He hated controversy of any kind, unlike Hayden, who thrived on it. Hayden was suspicious, unyielding once he had made up his mind, but outgoing and high spirited, the sort who draws energy from being around others, even in controversy. As for professional meetings, Hayden did not avoid them because he feared controversy, but because he did not have much to say, at least not to a clatter of scholars. The convoluted formalism of academic debate—its unremitting polemics, all couched in clever remarks and rhetorical flourishes—annoyed and frustrated Hayden. He was the kind of man who kept his thoughts to himself, and his larger ideas developed slowly, unprovoked by discourse. He was primarily an active creature (he reminds me of the shark whose survival depends on constant motion) whose understanding of any subject depended more on his direct experience of it than any subsequent reflection on that experience.

Besides borrowing from Leidy's example and style, Hayden made great use of Leidy, just as he did with all his mentors and friends. What Leidy offered in particular was fame through publication. Hayden collected most of the specimens, many new to science, that Leidy described in the *Proceedings* of Philadelphia's Academy of Natural Sciences. And Leidy's pioneering descriptions served to enhance the reputation of Hayden the collector. Leidy was already one of the brightest stars at the Philadelphia Academy, and he exercised considerable influence over what appeared in the *Proceedings*. Naturally, he encouraged Hayden to publish his fascinating and novel results in the same place. Leidy's friendship with Hayden had begun in early 1854 and that personal tie led Hayden, two years later, to choose the *Proceedings* for his first joint publication with Meek. As a journal devoted to the empirical method, and one that announced miscellaneous scientific intelligence, it suited their needs perfectly.

Between March 1856 and February 1862 Hayden and Meek published sixteen major articles together, thirteen in the *Proceedings*. In 1865 the Smithsonian brought out their last joint effort, *Palaeontology of the Upper Missouri*, a sort of summa of early life as revealed by the invertebrate record. Meek alone did virtually all the work for this volume, though he retained Hayden's name as joint author, partly out of respect for their continuing partnership but also because this learned essay built on their earlier collaborative efforts.

Written to provide accuracy and detail regarding the new species they were discovering, Meek and Hayden's work embodied a rigorously empirical approach to science. In the days before photographic reproduction, and in advance of the time when a huge number of specimens were available for study in museums across the country, the illustrations they produced were of particular importance to scholars in promoting their own fossil studies.

In order to assess Hayden as a maturing geologist and a writer, it is important to know his particular role in the partnership with Meek. He collected all the fossil samples, labeled them, and described their physical settings in his field notes. He noticed such facts as the kind of rock in which each fossil appeared, the thickness of the beds surrounding them, the width of adjacent beds, as well as the composition and structure of each layer of rock. In other words, based on his knowledge of conditions in the field Hayden analyzed lithology and stratigraphy. Even if Hayden's notes on such things had been perfect, before writing up the fossils Meek would have needed to know much more than any notes could tell. How did one layer of sandy, gray clay at one location compare, for example, to an apparently similar one tens or even hundreds of miles away? Were they the same formation? What was the wider environmental setting of each? How did the kind and quality of other fossils found in similar sites compare? To answer such questions required both experience and judgment, and the perspective of the collector was invaluable. As Hayden became more adept in reading various terrains and understanding the possible configurations, his input became indispensable. So even if we assume Meek wrote most of the fossil descriptions, which he undoubtedly did, he would not have been able to start without Hayden's information from the field.

Next, which of them wrote the specific parts of each joint article? I have summarized the particulars in the notes, but the gist can be reviewed here.[1] Although Meek wrote most of the fossil descriptions, the letters the two men exchanged suggest Hayden helped write descriptions for the second article of March 1858. He probably assisted with several others, namely those of May 1857, December 1858, the second article of January 1859, and December 1861. The evidence for the collaboration on these articles is that Hayden and Meek spent a good deal of time together prior to their publication. Meek alone wrote descriptions or prepared a catalog for eight of the articles, but only once did he add more than a brief geological commentary. On the nine occasions when a significant amount of text appeared, Hayden shared in its composition five times, and he wrote all of it three other times.

Whose work was more significant? The answer will depend on one's predilections. The paleontologist will likely appreciate Meek's exacting descriptions and careful drawings, while the geologist will admire Hayden's alertness, imagination, his sheer endurance in gathering the raw data, and his ability to generalize about what he found. Ultimately, I don't believe a convincing case can be made for either Hayden or Meek being the more important partner in these articles. The work of one would have generated slight interest without the supplementary input of the other, and their publications depended on a truly joint effort.

Such carefully crafted and deliberately focused pieces eventually enabled the authors to draw conclusions of broad interest and great significance. In the vast country between the Mississippi Basin and the Rocky Mountains, earlier explorers, going back to the time of Lewis and Clark, had correctly identified Carboniferous, Cretaceous, and Tertiary formations known in Europe or the eastern United States. To these Hayden added discoveries of the oldest Paleozoic rocks in the region, as well as Permian and Jurassic formations, and he found that Carboniferous and Triassic beds existed on both sides of the Rockies. In reporting on Hayden and Meek's trip to the Bad Lands in 1853, James Hall and Meek had produced the first geologic section for the Cretaceous rocks of the Upper Missouri Basin. In their November 1856 article Hayden and Meek refined Hall's strata and added two identifiable formations of the overlying Tertiary rocks. Over the next several years they further refined their stratigraphic column, so that by 1861 (Hayden's article of March, and Hayden and Meek's of December) they had identified four separate formations of the Tertiary and added much detail on the extent, structure, composition, and setting of each layer in the Cretaceous-Tertiary sequence. Their stratigraphic column for the Upper Missouri Basin became the standard for the whole trans-Mississippi West, and the names Hayden and Meek announced for these formations in the December 1861 article endure to the present.

The implications of their work went far beyond the Missouri Basin. As early as their article of March 1856 they began to wonder whether, and to what extent, similar formations in different places were laid down at the same time. In their November 1856 article, and more comprehensively in those of May 1857 and December 1861, they showed that the Cretaceous of the Upper Missouri was equivalent to the Cretaceous of New Jersey and Alabama, and that some parts of the Cretaceous extended into Kansas, Arkansas, Texas, and New Mexico.

A result of their comparative studies was to raise fundamental questions about the understanding of geology itself. Because many of the established formations had first been found in England, and because British geologists were the first to synthesize a knowledge of their own and Europe's formations into a sequence, British geologists assumed, rather imperially, that their findings provided an all-inclusive history of the Earth's development. Not so, showed Hayden and Meek. Notable differences existed in the strata of western America, enough to indicate that American formations might be the standard against which to judge local variations in Europe and elsewhere. For example, of the 191 species of mollusks[2] discovered from the Upper Missouri by November 1856, only 9 occurred in the eastern states and another 4 in Europe. In their article of October 1860 Hayden and Meek reemphasized the same point, using additional evidence. Study of Hayden's fossil leaves disclosed that some flora emerged in America before they appeared in Europe. When added to a growing body of evidence gathered by others, these facts challenged the Old World's understanding of geology.

One of the more dramatic implications concerned the progress of living forms. The traditional wisdom, based largely on fossils of European dinosaurs, held that an abrupt and massive extinction of life took place at the end of the Cretaceous, dramatized by the death of the dinosaurs. But the invertebrates Hayden found showed no extinction of life, rather a shift—sometimes a rather abrupt one—from marine to estuary to freshwater types, as a receding Cretaceous ocean gave way, under pressure of a rising continent, to freshwater lakes and streams typical of the Tertiary. Hayden toyed with his findings for years before expanding them into a revolutionary explanation for the geological evolution of the High Plains and Rocky Mountains.

His work with Meek was already producing large and daring conclusions. It may seem surprising that he and Meek chose not to speculate in other directions. The many subtle variations they noticed between different samples of the same species, and the seemingly senseless abundance of similar life forms, certainly raised questions about the nature and origin of species, their development and demise. Especially after 1859, when Darwin provided a theory explaining much of the apparent disorder, Hayden and Meek realized how powerfully their diverse findings buttressed Darwinian thought. Yet they remained silent on this subject in their printed works and even in their correspondence. In light of the controversies they had already stirred up over discovering the Permian and reinterpreting the end of the Mesozoic era, they may have felt they had their hands full.

Meanwhile, Hayden began writing some articles on his own. The ones with Meek accentuated structures and extent, which sketched the static side of geology. This approach involved Hayden in a series of careful observations, which he later translated into laboriously constructed sections, tables, and lists. But he was not satisfied just to lay the foundations. He wanted practical results. What could be more useful than a map? All Hayden's early maps were geologic maps. They depicted accurately for the first time the physical realities of vast stretches of country, as well as an attractive visual picture of the major formations in the Upper Missouri Basin. From the moment of their publication these maps became the basis for all future studies of western geology. For the duration of his career Hayden would seek ways of delivering practical results from his lonely work as a naturalist, and maps became a favorite means.

At the same time he wanted to paint a sweeping, vivid picture of the land in motion over time—upheaving, sinking beneath the waves, rising again, only to be worn away by rivers, and so on. It was not by accident that most of his ideas on the dynamic side of geology appeared in different places than his joint work with Meek. The *Proceedings* continued to publish most of their collaborative efforts, but only three of his own articles appeared there out of some twelve important essays that he wrote before the Civil War. (For the time being I ignore "A Brief Sketch" of 1856 and "A Catalogue of the Collections" of 1858, both completed for Warren and both published by the government.) The timing is interesting too. Hayden brought out the first edition of his geologic map in the *Proceedings* (May 1857). A month later his very first independent article (on the White River Basin) appeared there, as did the second edition of his geologic map a year later (June 1858). That was all he cared to give to the *Proceedings*. Afterward, he wrote six articles for the *American Journal of Science and Arts* and three monographs for the *Transactions of the American Philosophical Society,* two of them book length. By spring 1858 the Permian controversy had brought Hayden's name to the attention of all American geologists. Although that struggle strengthened his partnership with Meek, Hayden took advantage of his growing reputation to begin publishing articles on his own.

Branching out on his own enabled him to broaden his circle of connections, but he relied on his old friends to arrange the necessary introductions. Through Meek, for instance, Hayden met James Dwight Dana, the chief editor of the *American Journal of Science,* which was published in New Haven. The editors, members of the Yale faculty, prided themselves on prompt announcements and critical appraisals of new developments in science. Probably the most widely read scientific magazine in America, the *Journal* boasted a diverse readership of professionals and amateurs who would delight in learning of Hayden's discoveries in the West. The American Philosophical Society offered an entrée of a different kind, for its *Transactions* was probably the most prestigious read in America. It was the oldest scientific journal in the country and was justly celebrated for printing the works of such luminaries as Thomas Jefferson, Benjamin Latrobe, and Robert Hare. The editors wanted monographs, or as they put it, studies on "the importance or singularity of subjects." This suited Hayden's increasing fascination with natural history and Indians, and, yes, it was Joseph Leidy who opened the door for Hayden to this other Philadelphia patron.

Being a curious as well as an observant man, Hayden could not wander over the land and think only about its structure. How did it get the way he found it? What forces alternately massaged then crumpled the surface? How did these titanic forces operate? The land did not yield answers to such questions all at once, and his writings reflected his changing thoughts as he encountered different territory. Some people criticized him for publishing before seeing more of the country and before organizing his thoughts about it into an orderly treatise. But Hayden was compiling pioneering reports on a vast region, and he justified his rapid-fire, piecemeal technique on the grounds that no geologist would ever see the entire picture. As he put it, "Some erroneous statements, growing out of our limited knowledge of the structure of these mountain chains, may be made, but these when known, will be corrected. Geology is a progressive science and even our best efforts are but approximations to truth rather than the truth itself." At the same time Hayden hoped a regular appearance of his articles would enhance his name and stimulate the sponsorship he needed to continue his collecting ventures.

Some of his perceptions were quite sharp, even though he failed to elaborate on their implications. For instance, in March 1859, writing on the Judith River beds, he dropped the news that the whole chain of the Rocky Mountains resulted from a huge uplift. He gave no details, no evidence, and his remarks were rather out of context, but they provided a correct and brilliant insight. Earlier, in June 1858 (in remarks accompanying the second edition of his map), he showed the similarity between the core rocks of the

Black Hills and the Laramie Mountains, and he opined that both were up-lifted by the same forces at the same time. He went on to suppose a series of uplifts, culminating in one at the end of the Cretaceous, which he later equated (in May 1862) with the beginnings of a general upsurge that even-tually produced the Rockies. While pondering these upheavals he also real-ized that some of the West had remained dry land, above the dominant oceans. He showed that the seas were shallow during most of the period they held sway over the land, only deepening briefly (in relative terms) during the Cretaceous. He demonstrated that formerly, and for a long time, the Upper Missouri basked in a near tropical climate, close to that now enjoyed by the Gulf states.

In another series of loosely connected revelations he first defined the White River Basin as a lacustrine deposit, that is, formed at the bottom of a lake (May 1857 commentary on his map). He repeated this assertion in June 1857, this time with some evidence; then in March 1859 he announced that the entire Upper Missouri consisted of three major basins: the White River, the Judith, and the most extensive of all, the Great Lignite—all three of Tertiary age. It required only a step from here to argue that all the great basins of the West were lacustrine, a position he did not formally take until 1862, with implications we shall examine later.

Though he has never gained the credit he deserves for them, Hayden made other valuable contributions in his early publications. The numerous vertical sections he compiled were the first of their kind to penetrate the depths of the land from Kansas to the Dakotas and from the Missouri River to Montana. He pioneered an understanding of the Black Hills as well as many ranges in modern Montana and Wyoming. He was the first to distin-guish two basic types of mountains in the Rockies: the dominant backbone of granitic and metamorphic rocks, whose uplifted fractures carved a regular outline across the terrain, and the eruptive igneous ranges with their jagged peaks that punched dramatic but irregular patterns into the landscape. The former he identified in the Black Hills, the Big Horn, Laramie, Wind River, Medicine Bow, and Sweetwater mountains. The latter he located in the Wasatch Range, the Green River Mountains, the Tetons, in a number of val-leys like Pierre's Hole and Jackson Hole, in several groups between the headwaters of the Yellowstone and Missouri rivers, and in "the mountains all along the sources of the different branches of the Columbia."

Sometimes Hayden's choice of words disguised his novel insights. Take laccoliths, for example. These are formed when molten igneous rock pushes up layers of older sedimentary rock, forcing them into a bulging domal shape. No one recognized the distinctive nature of these forms for a long time because often the igneous mass stays concealed beneath the outer layers it has swollen up. Usually erosion peels back the covering layers near the top of the dome first, so that the underlying tilted rocks look "trappean" (that is, the sheetlike masses of igneous rock one on top of another look like traps or steps, and their overall appearance suggests a stairway). Here's how Hayden said it in 1857: "The Black Hills furnish the only examples on our route of the outburst of trappean rocks. Stone Peak, on the north eastern side of the Black Hills, is an isolated protrusion . . . The highest portion of the peak is composed of trap rock . . . Near Bear Peak, on the north-eastern side of the Black Hills, is another example of the protrusion of these basaltic columns." Modern geologists now use the word "intrusive" in connection with laccoliths; Hayden called them "protrusions," but he obviously realized the intrusive nature of the formation, for he said, "All the Cretaceous beds and all the Jurassic . . . are upheaved around Bear Peak." He didn't use the modern jargon, but he grasped the concept.[3]

Similarly with antecedent streams. An antecedent stream is one that established its path before the emergence of modern features around it, and it stayed in that path despite the changing topography. Thus if a mountain range starts to rise across the path of such a stream, the stream immediately begins cutting through it in order to maintain its riverbed. In the following passage Hayden gave a powerful rendering of the idea and, incidentally, the first mention of the Rockies as an anticline.

Another illustration of the gradual and long continued rise of the country may be found in the immense chasms or canons which have been formed by the streams along the mountain sides. We can only account for them on the supposition that as the anticlinal crest was slowly emerging from the sea, the myriad sources of our great rivers were seeking their natural channels, and that these branches or tributaries began this erosive action long before the great thoroughfares, the valleys of the Mississippi and the Missouri, were marked out. The erosion would go on as the mountains continued slowly rising at an almost imperceptible rate, and in process of time the stupendous channels which everywhere meet us along the immediate sides of the mountains would be formed.

To Hayden, scientific insight and literary impact went hand in hand. The passage just quoted exemplifies his maturing style, his greater success at describing discoveries in words that would attract wide attention. But he was trying to move in this direction from the start. In his description of the White River Bad Lands (June 1857), he deliberately combined technical analysis of rocks with portraits of the scenery and geography over which he walked while gathering his facts. Not long afterward (January 1859), he showed the specific relationships between surface topography and the underlying geology, in the varying quality of soil, for example. Always alert to the practical, he spoke of coal deposits where they seemed to exist in quantity (as in Kansas, but not in Nebraska), as well as the location of other economically useful rocks, such as gypsum and limestone. In the introduction to his second geologic map he gave excerpts from his field journal of 1857 in an attempt to recreate the immediacy of that living laboratory in which the naturalist delved.

It was as a naturalist that Hayden found his voice and developed the style that felt right to him. His style, or his larger vision of things, did not emerge all at once, indeed he never expressed it clearly and thoroughly in any single work that might epitomize his philosophy as a naturalist. Restless by nature and easily distracted, he lacked the mental discipline to compose anything that systematic. So his insights tumbled out piecemeal, and his style must be pieced together from disparate works. One of the most useful in this respect is *On the Geology and Natural History of the Upper Missouri,* for it successfully summarized all his early work before the Civil War. It deserves sustained attention.

10
TWO EARLY
TRIUMPHS

I have got my memoir nearly ready and hope to bring it on with me early in July. You
know it is the summing up of all my labors in the West and the consequence is that it
embodies the small papers already published. The consequence is that there is a good
deal of extracted matter from other papers. The question arose in my mind, will some
old fogy in looking over the memoir say, "Well this paper has been published before"?
—Hayden to Leidy, 27 June 1861

ON THE *GEOLOGY and Natural History of the Upper Missouri,* which came into
being because of some unusual circumstances, took its inspiration from two
earlier works. The first of these—"A Brief Sketch of the Geological and Physical Features of the Region of the upper Missouri, With Some Notes on its
Soil, Vegetation, Animal Life, etc."—was published as an appendix to Warren's annual report to the War Department in March 1856. Hayden began
working for Warren in summer 1856, but during their talks of the previous
spring Hayden promised to prepare for Warren a description of the country
he had visited on his own over the past two years. The result was "A Brief
Sketch," for whose contents Warren set down only very broad guidelines,
leaving Hayden free to do pretty much what he wanted. Hayden had already
been thinking about a book summarizing his early work on the Upper Missouri. He had written to Baird on 26 December 1855 proposing "a large octavo volume, say 300 or 400 pages, entitled 'Wanderings in the Far West,
or Three Years on the Mo. R[iver] & its Tributaries.'" *Geology and Natural*

History was the realization of that ambition, and "A Brief Sketch," though only fourteen pages long, can be considered an experimental first draft.

"A Brief Sketch" permitted Hayden to try out a new form. Though he mentions the principal geological formations and major areas of their appearance, he includes no sections, no detailed account of formations, and he provides no explanations for changes in the land over time. Geology is subservient to geography but also blended with it in such a way that the reader understands, for example, that the rich bottom lands along parts of the Missouri are due to "a mixture of the calcareous and silicious marls of the Tertiary, and the clays of Cretaceous beds brought down by the river from the Upper Missouri." Or that, farther upstream, a black Cretaceous clay holds the soil in such a death grip for about 350 miles that "the soil, if there be any, is exceedingly sterile, producing very scanty vegetation, and sometimes considerable areas present a bare, blackened appearance, without trace of tree or shrub." Such remarks anticipated the practical needs of the settler, as did other comments on the climate and the extent of forests. But pragmatism is no excuse for dullness, and Hayden adds immediacy and adventure by quoting from his journal of 1855, telling of capturing a strange lizard, eating antelope and bighorn sheep, and struggling to free horses from the mud. He mentions a few of the typical fossils he found and identifies numerous flowers, trees, shrubs, the most common mammals, and tells of their geographic distribution. It was scientific exposition through travelog.

His next effort along these lines departed dramatically from the form of "A Brief Sketch." Nonetheless, "A Catalogue of the Collections in Geology and Natural History" (published in late fall 1858) planted another seed that came to fruition in *Geology and Natural History*. After Warren finished his explorations in the West during summer 1857, he still faced the task of codifying a final report of all his results. Wanting to show the War Department something more than another annual report, he asked Hayden to prepare a summary of what he had accomplished over the past two years, which he could attach to his own Preliminary Report on work done during 1855–1857. By the time he received Warren's request, Hayden was busy writing three pieces with Meek summarizing their trip to Kansas during 1858; one appeared in December 1858, two in January 1859. He devoted less than a month to "A Catalogue" and limited himself to what he could put his hands on quickly. Thus "A Catalogue" rehashed conclusions about the Cretaceous and Tertiary he had already published on his own or with Meek, and he lifted the key vertical sections entirely from his earlier articles. To these he added some new tables from his notes, which placed each fossil in the appropriate vertical formation. Also from old notes he compiled some tables on the Judith River beds, and he mentioned new facts he and Meek had just encountered in

Kansas on the questionable formation at the bottom of the Cretaceous, bordering the Jurassic.

Most of "A Catalogue," however, is a series of lists, which Hayden outlined in a table:

77 fossil vertebrates, 50 thought to be new
251 fossil mollusks [186 new]
70 fossil plants [all new but none named in text]
423 mineral and geological specimens
47 recent mammals
186 birds
65 recent mollusks
24 fishes
28 reptiles
1,500 recent plants [49 new, but only 593 listed]

The number of fossil vertebrates and mollusks actually mentioned in the text differs slightly from what Hayden claimed in this table, and his "1,500 recent plants" was an estimate of how many species would eventually be identified from the many yet unstudied. Only 781 were later enumerated in *Geology and Natural History.* Still, when we remember that Hayden gathered nearly all the various specimens himself, often working alone, "A Catalogue" is a staggering testament to his ability as a collector.

It probably would not have occurred to Hayden to combine "A Brief Sketch" with "A Catalogue" had he not needed to assemble a new publication in a hurry. Upon returning to Washington in November 1860, after two years in the field with Raynolds, Hayden immediately began working up his results, which appeared as articles in March and December 1861, January and May 1862. Meanwhile, he was thinking about two other reports. (Actually, three: the third was his book on Indians, the subject of the next chapter.) First was the final report for Warren; second was a separate memoir he would publish with Leidy, to be based on the extensive vertebrate collections from the White River Bad Lands. Hayden had done most of the collecting there, but John Evans had done some, too; for that reason Leidy planned to report on both collections at once, if Evans would have the combined report printed at government expense as part of the final report of Evans's explorations. When Evans suddenly died in April 1861, the government shelved plans to publish the memoir. The Academy of Natural Sciences came to the rescue, promising to publish it in its *Journal.* Meanwhile, a series of delays and frustrations intervened: worst of all, the War Department lost Leidy's original manuscript. Bravely, Leidy rewrote the entire monograph, to which Hayden attached an introduction on geology; finally the project came to a happy conclusion, but not until 1869.

One bit of bad luck followed another. By a stroke of coincidence that must have seemed cruel to Hayden, at virtually the same time Evans died, Warren realized that his final report might never see the light because the Civil War had altered the priorities of the War Department. Ever since his own explorations were finished in 1857, Warren had been rendering essential support for Meek's study of Hayden's fossils, which included the production of hundreds of drawings. Now, rather than see all this go up in smoke, Warren authorized Hayden to bring out his own portion of the final report, covering geology and natural history, provided Hayden could make arrangements for publication. Hayden talked to friends and persuaded the American Philosophical Society to publish the work, but he had to act fast. He knew that even private sponsors of scientific work would soon go into hiding because of the oncoming war. These frantic circumstances gave birth to Hayden's *Geology and Natural History.*

The book is a pastiche, and its contents pure collage. Being as busy as he was on several projects, Hayden abandoned the idea of writing an extensive volume about his "Wanderings in the Far West" (though fragments of that idea appear in several later works), and he decided on something else. He liked what he had done in "A Brief Sketch" to bring the layman into contact with geology, to point out practical matters, and to emphasize the adventure of fieldwork by adopting a travelog style. He resolved that *Geology and Natural History* would build on that initial step to further popularize science. This important decision deserves a brief digression to clarify Hayden's role.

By the middle of the nineteenth century a long-standing tension still existed in America between those who pursued a scholarly interest in science and those who aimed at useful results. On the one side were theoretical, even speculative investigations, often with no particular result in mind; on the other side, existing knowledge was applied to produce new techniques, practical devices, measuring instruments, work-hungry machines, and other results of interest to a shrewd people, who, of necessity, had been do-it-yourselfers for more than two hundred years.

As a science, geology had a foot in both camps; so did Hayden. He was absorbed in collecting and cataloguing, even though few people would ever appreciate his laborious work. Similarly, the careful correlation of fossils to rock strata might enhance awareness of stratigraphy, but only specialists noticed such esoterica. At the same time a knowledge of rocks and their layers had implications for mining, agriculture, and various applications of engineering. Hayden understod the practical curiosity of a people moving west, and he tried to anticipate the kinds of information they would need. That is the first sense in which he popularized science, in quite a traditional way; but in going a step farther he helped to pioneer something new. What he aimed at was nothing less than enlarging the audience that could understand and appreciate what had previously been the preserve of experts. He wanted to teach science in such a way that it would excite a mass audience.

Part One of *Geology and Natural History* expands on Hayden's own fruitful precedent in "A Brief Sketch." In six chapters, taken from his journal of summer 1857, he takes the reader on an excursion up the Missouri River, then heads west along the Platte River, branching off to follow the Loup Fork to the Sand Hills, then to the Niobrara River and eventually to Fort Laramie. On the return he traverses the Black Hills, before returning to the Missouri by way of the Bad Lands and the Niobrara. Though he reproduced a number of valuable sections and descriptions that must have come verbatim from his field journal, Hayden did more than simply abstract that journal. He knew he had interesting material, and he obviously took pains to select and polish the parts that would be most useful, most instructive, most appealing.

The flavor of these chapters is strikingly modern. They remind me of the *Roadside Geology* series, which began in the 1980s. Like *Roadside Geology*, Hayden's *Geology and Natural History* has the amateur reader in mind. At times it reads like a field guide, though it does not describe features with the detail of a modern guide. Still the analogy with *Roadside Geology* is apt in emphasizing how much Hayden was concerned not just with popularizing science but with acting as a teacher. He loves his subject, and he wants to share it with as wide an audience as possible. His examples are clear, his text is smoothly written, he draws the reader in with anecdotes and recollections of his personal experiences.

This approach was quite novel. Other writers of his time described geography and the physical details of the country, sketched the length of formations, and discussed lithology, stratigraphy, and paleontology. One thinks especially of John W. Foster and Josiah D. Whitney's *Report on Lake Superior* (1850) and of David Dale Owen's *Report of . . . Wisconsin, Iowa, and Minnesota* (1852); but these works were not so closely organized around routes of exploration, and they usually overlooked the dimension of scenery. John Evans sketched the scenery of the Bad Lands in his portion of Owen's report, but the text of both these impressive works lacks the personal flavor so distinctive of Hayden's *Geology and Natural History*.

The deliberately pedagogic tone of Part One even taught Hayden something. In assembling it, he realized he had discovered a popular model for reporting the results of a reconnaissance survey whose purpose was to take a rapid glance at geography, geology, and natural history over an extended territory. When he took to the field again after the Civil War, this time with his own government-supported survey, he became the acknowledged master of the reconnaissance technique. Therefore while summarizing much of his knowledge so far, *Geology and Natural History* also provided a model for his future work.

Part Two of the book concerns historical geology. In other words, it follows the traditional method of describing the strata, layer-cake fashion, from oldest to most recent. Here Hayden summarizes conclusions on structural geology he had previously published, either with Meek or in his own earlier articles on dynamic aspects of the region's geology. Part Two flows less smoothly than Part One because it patches together excerpts from other published works, but it weaves an impressive garment of knowledge. In one convenient text Hayden presents many of his ideas, gradually crystallized since his first visit to the Bad Lands of Dakota during summer 1853. The language struts a bit to the tune of professionalism rather than skipping along as in Part One. Part One whets the appetite by introducing the adventure of geology, while Part Two sets out a curriculum for the advanced student. Taken together, the two parts offer the earliest example of Hayden's passion to combine fresh research, which scholars would esteem, with informative travelogs, which everyone would enjoy.

The last chapter of Part Two and all of Part Three consist of zoological and botanical lists, which derive directly from "A Catalogue," with additions. He adds substantially to the number of plants. He gives a fuller account of the geographic range of his specimens, and he affixes notes on the habits of many species. He cites the scientific literature on birds and mammals. It took time to note these small changes, which witnesses his concern for accurate detail. The map accompanying the volume amounts to a third edition of Hayden's geologic map. On it he extends the area of the Great Lignite farther south, to approach the west side of the Black Hills. He also shows for the first time the metamorphic and granitic base to the Rocky Mountains between Pikes Peak and Laramie Peak, with an exposure of sedimentary rocks ranging from the early Paleozoic to the Cretaceous running parallel to the Front Range.

As Hayden said in the book, he had finished most of it before setting out with Raynolds in spring 1859. Of course, at that point he intended to publish these results in his final report for Warren. After two years with Raynolds, he had some new facts to put in place.[1] Blending in these additions would have cost him little time, but Part One polishes a raw field journal and Part Three colors more of the background. Considering all the other pots he was stirring, Hayden may have spent up to seven months revising *Geology and Natural History,* going back and forth from it to other projects.

His private correspondence suggests he became serious about finishing it around April 1861. He delivered it to the American Philosophical Society for a formal reading on 19 July. Thereafter he made no other changes in the text before its publication early in 1862.

Though each is distinctive, all three parts of *Geology and Natural History* adhere to a common purpose: to teach aspects of natural history. Previously, Hayden had experimented with different ways of doing this; in this book he integrated all of them. That is why *Geology and Natural History* says little that is new, but its form is completely new and unique. Though mostly a rewrite of material Hayden had published earlier, the book adds up to more than the sum of its parts. For one thing, combining the results of separate articles made a greater impact and offered a more comprehensive treatment of the subject matter. And even though Hayden had hinted before of his interest in the practical and the popular, *Geology and Natural History* gave the first indication that he wanted his publications to instruct. Also the sheer enormity of his observations—the numerous geological sections, the descriptions of rock (thickness, color, lithologic character, and stratigraphic position), the prodigious enumeration of mineral and geological specimens, birds, mammals, fishes, reptiles, and above all plants, the notes on geographic range of his specimens, and the elaborate tables relating hundreds of fossils to specific strata—forces us to see this man as a determined empiricist.

But not a theorist. He was a depicter, not an analyst. Even in his discussions of dynamic geology, what interested him was what had happened, not how or why. In this respect Hayden was typical of his era. Geology at the time favored the empirical observation over the grand theory, and even the few men who produced theories spent most of their time dutifully building up their layer-cake diagrams. Hayden joyfully endorsed this emphasis on accumulating facts. Where he differed from most of his colleagues was in conveying scientific insights through popular language, which implied that an intelligent reader could draw conclusions from the data.

Although *Geology and Natural History* focused on subjects of great contemporary concern and did so in a novel way, it is curious that surveys of nineteenth-century literature never cite the book. No doubt it was written in too popular a style to have been appreciated as strictly "scientific." At the same time it lacked the romantic approach—and the literary pretension—of works by men like William Cullen Bryant, Washington Irving, Thoreau, John Burroughs or John Muir, who cultivated the "natural history essay."[2] History has overlooked *Geology and Natural History* because it does not fit into any of the traditional genres of the nineteenth century. Like its author, it is unconventional and idiosyncratic.

Hayden did not find it necessary (perhaps he thought it would be imprudent) to spell out all the implications of his findings. The concept of evolution existed, and questions about speciation floated in the air, especially the essential question: how do new species form? Not every naturalist wondered about such issues in Hayden's day, and most who did refrained from risking any answers, at least in print. An exception to this reticence was Charles Darwin, who confronted these questions and answered them dramatically, in a way that gave birth to an intellectual revolution. Darwin published his *Origin of Species* in 1859, about the same time Hayden finished the bulk of *Geology and Natural History.* In view of the timing, one cannot help wondering if any Darwinian influence crept into Hayden's book.

It is an enticing question, but the answer is a solid no. Yet to judge by his book, Hayden had been wondering about many of the same questions that puzzled other naturalists in the days before Darwin's bombshell. *Geology and Natural History* is pregnant with observations that would provoke questions in a thoughtful mind, though Hayden does not allude to those questions, at least not explicitly, preferring to present his facts without comment. But Hayden had already moved away from the creationist's traditional viewpoint regarding the natural world, and the evidence is in his book. For this reason *Geology and Natural History* becomes a "secret" book, the sort that communicates on two levels. There is one message on the surface for all to read, which concerns the facts of nature. Another (cryptic) message lies beneath the surface, concerning the meaning of those facts; only a few will see the second. We can disclose the deeper structure of his intentions if we do what Hayden himself was not bold enough to do: namely, juxtapose some of his conclusions with the questions they would seem to be addressing—questions, I repeat, that were already floating in the air.

Over unimaginably long periods of time, regular deposition under the sea or in lakes alternates irregularly with catastrophic periods of volcanism, melting, uplifting, crushing, and overturning. Is an orderly creation possible in the face of such irrational violence? Some rock formations in America and the Old World seem to show that similar fauna might have existed at different times in different places. How is this possible if life has enjoyed a uniform, purposeful development? Almost all fossil shells are found in numerous locations, but the environments of these locations often differ in age and character. Could all members of the same species have originated in the same place, at the same time? Fossil drawings show subtle differences between members of the same group. Do they all belong to the same species?

How deeply Hayden pondered such questions is uncertain, for he never recorded his thoughts about them, but there are reasons for saying such questions intrigued him. One friend remarked on Hayden's extensive grasp of theological literature around this time, and that literature spoke freely of the potential conflicts between religion and science. Since his undergraduate days Hayden had been an omnivorous reader, and the footnotes to many of his learned articles show he read widely beyond the requirements of scholarship. Perhaps the best indicator of his thinking on the deeper meaning of science is his reaction to Darwin after *Origin of Species* appeared. Hayden said nothing specific about Darwin or about the debate his book engendered, in either his published works or his large correspondence. On the one hand, he refrained from taking a public stand in favor of what many regarded as anathema; initially, few naturalists in America were brave enough to endorse Darwin. On the other hand, Hayden shunned the reaction of more fainthearted geologists, which was to condemn Darwin and emphasize that their own understanding of the natural world upheld biblical teachings. Hayden's avoidance of this second approach, I believe, signifies a tacit acceptance of Darwinian thought, without any fuss or agonizing, as though it were all too obvious to bear discussing. Because Hayden never had any theoretical pretensions, it is probably closer to the truth to say he found Darwin interesting, even useful, but not paramount to his work. Hayden was one of those naturalists who lived to accumulate information. With one major exception, and several minor ones, he was content that others should interpret the information.

That major exception was his view of the Great Lignite. The Great Lignite beguiled him for years and with good reason: its complicated structure suggested to Hayden a reinterpretation of the geological timetable for that curious interval between the Cretaceous and the Tertiary. His contribution to the Great Lignite was Hayden's second early triumph, which, unlike *Geology and Natural History,* did not announce itself with the publication of a book; rather it emerged as a synthesizing idea that slowly made sense of some very intricate beds at the mouth of the Judith River in Montana. The story is a fascinating one, and I will tell it in pieces, beginning here with his solution to the Judith conundrum and later in another chapter relating how he generalized from that solution to a theory about the Great Lignite itself.

Hayden's ideas on the Judith River beds probably meant more to him than any of his other fruitful gifts to geology. The fact that he misjudged these perplexing beds should not distract us, for most geologists who confronted them were equally bewildered until well into the twentieth century, when their secrets were finally deciphered. Hayden's mistake is one of those fortunate incidents that reveals much about the way he thought, the way he behaved, and how he was perceived by others at the time.

Hayden first found the dark red sandstone beds he later called the Judith River Group[3] during summer 1855. Sorting through the fossils from these beds, Leidy identified some teeth belonging to dinosaurs, and Meek and Hayden thought the shells suggested a freshwater deposit. From that fragmentary evidence Hayden supposed he might have found the equivalent to Europe's Wealden, a formation of early Cretaceous age. This news was important on several counts, especially in showing the continent had remained above the encroaching ocean for a substantial period, long enough to give rise to large life forms. But he was not yet ready to discuss such implications openly, because, as he reported in the June 1856 article coauthored with Meek, "It was found impossible to devote to the examination of these formations time enough to determine their relations to the Cretaceous and Tertiary strata of this region, without running the risk of being cut off from the party and murdered by the Indians."

Another season in the field persuaded Hayden to abandon such cautious language. In his own publication of May 1857 he had no difficulty turning around and declaring the entire Judith Basin to be Tertiary. He came to this conclusion after noticing that widespread erosion in the Cretaceous rocks across the West had produced basin-shaped depressions and that Tertiary deposits filled in those depressions. The Judith Basin presented difficulties to the geologist because there was no clear demarcation between marine Cretaceous and freshwater Tertiary deposits. As Hayden admitted, "The most remarkable feature of this basin is the wonderful disturbance of the strata. So much are the beds disturbed and blended together by forces acting from beneath, that it seems almost hopeless to obtain a section showing with perfect accuracy the order of superposition of the different strata." Hayden particularly acknowledged the difficulty of understanding the strata at the mouth of the Judith itself, where the upheavals had mixed older and younger layers in a most confusing way. The predominant sandstone there appeared, on lithologic evidence, to be similar to the oldest Cretaceous rocks found farther down the Missouri, and the dinosaur remains from these beds also suggested early Cretaceous. The presence of one shell even suggested rocks as old as lower Jurassic! But then some of the shells seemed to be similar or identical to much later types found in the Great Lignite Basin, then thought to be middle Tertiary.

Hayden solved this dilemma with the notion of an estuary bed (that is, a place where a freshwater stream entered a saltwater ocean). Such beds would contain a mix of creatures that had lived and died in the ocean along with others that had lived on land and whose remains had been washed downstream to the sea, like the dinosaurs and freshwater mollusks, to become entombed along with marine shells. The complicated uplifting at the site helped to account for the coexistence of otherwise incompatible fauna, whose enclosing beds had been "disturbed and blended together."

After this brilliant explanation, it only remained to determine the age of the freshwater and estuary beds. Over the next few years Hayden several times rehearsed the conflicting evidence, compiled more vertical sections for comparison, and wavered between the early Cretaceous and the early to middle Tertiary. He devoted one entire article in March 1859 to the difficult problems of the Judith beds.

Soon thereafter he returned to the field with Raynolds and resolved the uncertainties to his satisfaction. As he wrote to Meek on 5 November 1859 the Judith beds were definitely Tertiary. He based his conclusion, interestingly enough, on a similar estuary formation he had recently found at the mouth of the Bighorn River. He made this correlation on the basis of similar environments, not on any similarity of the fossils, and the boldness of his announcement is an indication of how much he was coming to rely on his observations in the field, even when they conflicted with paleontological teaching. Hayden had not been back to the Judith itself, but that did not prevent him from writing to the *American Journal of Science* on 3 March 1860 that the Judith beds were Tertiary (as were, by implication, beds at the mouth of the Bighorn and some others he had not yet seen), and they seemed to be ̇equivalent to the lower portions of the Great Lignite Basin, which he now thought to be early Tertiary, or Eocene. So, at a stroke, the problem of the Judith beds was solved (or seemed to be), and new issues were opened by connecting them to the Great Lignite. By the way, Hayden called it the "Great" Lignite Basin to distinguish it from numerous earlier but less significant deposits of lignite and to emphasize its widespread expanse. Hayden thought the Great Lignite included other Tertiary lignites found as far west as Fort Bridger, as far south as the Arkansas River, and to the north nearly to Hudson's Bay, and, of course, plentifully along the Upper Missouri, where he had first encountered it, and where, even before announcing his latest discoveries of it in the Wind River valley and the Sweetwater Mountains, he estimated it encompassed some 60,000 square miles.

Hayden did not instruct his readers about the implications of his dramatic new conclusion. No doubt he realized those with a sympathetic turn of mind would see where he was going; there was no need to antagonize anyone else by being too specific. Since the Great Lignite contained a combination of estuary and freshwater beds and, therefore, amounted to a transitional layer between true Cretaceous (marine) and true Tertiary (freshwater), its widespread existence argued for the gradual passage from one era to another, at least in America, where the evidence seemed to offer different conclusions than in Europe. And a gradual change, especially when accompanied by a fauna showing transitional forms, which Hayden had more than once noticed in the highest Cretaceous rocks, argued strongly against the catastrophic view of geology that was compatible with a creationist's view of life.

Hayden's connection of the Judith beds with the lower part of the Great

Lignite eventually proved faulty. He conceived the linkage on the basis of apparent similarities between formations he had previously seen along the Grand and Cannonball rivers (in the Dakotas) and on some new discoveries at the mouth of the Bighorn, not at the Judith itself, which he had seen only once, under harried circumstances back in 1855. Nonetheless, he remained confident of his conclusions. In his publications of the 1850s Hayden several times pointed out that he alone was responsible for determining the age and reach of the Great Lignite. Though he acknowledged its discovery by others, he sounded downright proprietary about it.

A subsequent chapter will give the sequel to this first episode of the Judith beds, but some conclusions are already apparent. His inclusion of the Judith beds in the Great Lignite relied on an almost intuitive sense of parallelism between formations and demonstrated two things that had become characteristic of Hayden by the outbreak of the Civil War. He was increasingly confident regarding his insights in the field, and he was anxious to establish an exclusive physical domain (the Upper Missouri) in which to exercise his manifest talents. He was thirty-four years old.

Over the course of the 1850s Hayden's methods in the field changed in specific ways. In compiling his first geologic map of the Upper Missouri in May 1857, for example, he was willing to color in the extent of formations based on fossils gathered by others from sites he had not visited. But as he said in the preface to the second edition of the map (in June 1858), "A much larger surface might have been colored on the map with a good degree of confidence, but I have preferred to confine myself, for the most part, to the results of my own observations in the field, leaving the blank portions to be filled up by future explorations." Other similar changes in his attitude occurred as he was exploring new territory with Raynolds, and he confided these in letters to Meek. He said he wanted to digest more thoroughly what he had already gathered before going out again on future expeditions, and he admitted that some of what he had already published for Warren now needed revision. Most revealing was something he wrote to Meek on 12 May 1860. Speaking of Meek's collaboration with Captain Simpson, who explored the wagon road routes of Nebraska and Utah territories in 1858–1859, he said:

> Of course you can publish what you choose and as far as you choose, but I will tell you one thing sincerely that it is utterly impossible to give much defin[it]e information from a set of fossils collected here and there. It is true that what they teach is correct, but the information is of little use for the purposes of a map. Nearly all we have done in that map has been wrong. I shall hereafter place my confidence mostly in actual observation in the field.

The map he speaks of is the 1858 edition, and the errors he mentions are in the measure of the Great Lignite.

These examples show Hayden relying on his own examinations of a formation in the field rather than trusting the strict evidence of paleontology. Such behavior approached arrogance because it implied that he understood geology better than mere scholars, who knew the Earth only through their books. We are witnessing here a new level of Hayden's maturity and boldness, but his attitude is not quite as preposterous as it may seem. Dating rocks by fossils was relatively new, going back to William Smith's publication in England of *Strata Identified by Organized Fossils* (1816–1819), an innovation recognized by American geologists only in 1828, but not with universal approval at first. The science was still new enough in the 1850s that careful practitioners acknowledged they did not yet know enough about the upper or lower extensions of a species throughout the column of geologic time. (Meek was still voicing this caveat in the 1870s.) It was only sensible, therefore, to use the evidence of paleontology cautiously, in combination with the techniques of a good field man, whose firsthand observations of stratigraphy and lithology could distinguish what was normal from what was exceptional.[4] And by the time Hayden went off with Raynolds, he was not just a good field man, he was a superb one and getting better with experience. And he knew it.

With rising confidence came a willingness to take stands, even controversial ones, and stick with them. The geologist for Captain James H. Simpson's explorations in Utah, Henry Engelmann, opined that the Great Lignite was Cretaceous, not Tertiary. In drafting a review of Engelmann's preliminary findings for the *American Journal of Science,* Hayden blasted this view and argued that *all* the lignite of the Green River country was Tertiary. A daring statement indeed, in view of how little of that country Hayden had seen for himself. The remark was not published, however, because Meek edited Hayden's draft severely ("punched the pith out of it," according to Hayden), then wrote Hayden to say that Engelmann's collection *did* contain some coal from the Green River country that might prove to be Cretaceous.

Hayden was not convinced, and the dispute only made him eager to gather more evidence. Not long after his return to Washington, he was angling for an appointment as an Indian agent. In addition to a few specific duties, the job would permit him plenty of time to continue collecting. But the Civil War intervened, and he did not return to the field again until summer 1866.

By the outbreak of the Civil War Hayden had sketched the territory he regarded as his and demonstrated skills as a naturalist, but other topics still attracted him. One of those interests never bore fruit, but it testifies to the breadth of his roving mind. It was another publication project. Who initiated the idea is uncertain, but in summer 1860, having recently met with Hayden in the field, James Graham Cooper wrote Baird to say that he and Hayden were considering a new edition of Lewis and Clark's journals, complete with modern notes on the natural history.[5] Nothing happened. By February 1862 Hayden had nearly finished all his back work from Nebraska and was casting about for something else to do. He asked Leidy to inquire if the Lippincott Company would publish a new edition of Colonel Stephen H. Long's report, which, Hayden said, Long had asked him to edit and reissue. When Lippincott turned the idea down, Hayden countered with another query: Would they publish Long's report along with a new edition of Lewis and Clark's journals? No mention of Cooper as coeditor this time. Lippincott agreed to do so, if Hayden could guarantee 500 subscribers. By this time it was April, and though Hayden received some encouragement from the likes of Joseph Henry, he was too distracted to concentrate on finding 500 subscribers for the book. The civil conflict had now moved to the forefront of his thinking. Before seeing him off to war, however, we should examine the other book he published in 1862.

11
GOING TOO FAR

My Indian memoir started yesterday. Please look after it, I do desire to see it out soon. Talk with Mr. Bridges about it and interest him. It is a memoir that will give me a position among ethnologists at once.

—Hayden to Leidy, 8 May 1862

ALTHOUGH HAYDEN THE man has baffled and eluded biographers, his published works have been sufficiently read, at least among specialists, to have generated no little reputation for him. Particularly in geology, where he emerges as an important pioneer, and in natural history, where he epitomizes a dying breed of generalists, Hayden has commanded an attentive, if limited, audience. But no similar devotion has followed his work on Indians. Little of Hayden's fascination with Indians translated into published results, and the one large work he did write—the Indian memoir, as he called it— has not been widely read. This is unfortunate in a way, for Hayden's *Contributions to the Ethnography and Philology of the Indian Tribes of the Missouri Valley* is the most perverse thing he ever wrought. For Hayden's biographer *Contributions* offers a rare insight into its author and as a confession it is more eloquent than he might have imagined.

Hayden first mentioned a book on Indians in a letter to Baird of 6 April 1855. He wanted to do "a comparative view of all the languages on Mo. [the Missouri River], with small grammars, and vocabularies of each for the American Ethnological Society, which I have already about half completed." Knowing Hayden, he probably exaggerated the extent of his progress in so short a time. He wrote Baird again on 26 December, giving more details.

> I have paid attention to the Indian languages. I do not know what has been done in that way, and perhaps others may have anticipated me, but I will tell you I have obtained large vocabularies of the Grose Ventes of the Prairie [Atsina], Grose Ventes of Mo. [Hidatsa or Minitari], Assinniboin, the Arrickara & the . . . [word uncertain] . . . dialects of the Dakota. Pretty good grammars & dictionaries of the Blackfoot, Crow & Mandan languages. The whole would make quite a volume.

How large his vocabularies were at this early stage is questionable, but there is no reason to doubt he had made a preliminary collection in each of the languages he mentioned. His travels took him to the right places, and he could improve on his own gatherings by learning from the fur traders and missionaries who had been collecting similar materials for a longer time. The key point is that in all the early descriptions of the Indian memoir, it is obvious Hayden intended a volume on languages, or "philology" as he rather grandly called it in the title for *Contributions.*

Nearly seven years passed before he finished the book. As long as he could geologize outdoors or spend the winters in Washington, he seems to have neglected the Indian memoir, for it did not excite his attention again until the next winter he had to endure in the field (1859–1860), when he was marooned with the Raynolds party at Deer Creek. Then he showed a new flurry of activity: interviewing Cheyennes and at least one Arapaho at the nearby Indian agency, assembling vocabularies and notes on grammar, and obtaining a 1,200-word vocabulary of the Crows from missionaries and another of the Osage from an unnamed source. Once back in Washington he began searching the published literature on vocabularies and grammars to discover how much of what he had gathered was original. He worked in fits and starts, for he was juggling the Indian memoir along with four articles on the geology he had observed while with Raynolds and was finishing up *Geology and Natural History* at the same time. In October 1861 he reported he had nearly finished a study on Indian languages, but toward the end of November he was still saying the same thing. He thought he would finish it in December, but by March 1862 it was "nearly done;" he finally delivered it to the American Philosophical Society, the publisher, in early May. He was correcting proof by late summer but could not start sending out complimentary copies until October, just before he enlisted in the army. Like everything he wrote during that frantic period (autumn 1860 to autumn 1862), *Contributions* suffered from the pressure he felt to get several things in print before the opportunity for publication should disappear, perhaps forever.

In producing *Contributions* Hayden portrays himself as a modest and dutiful worker in a large vineyard. In the introduction he salutes the recent grammar and dictionary of the Dakota language by Stephen Return Riggs and Professor William W. Turner and justifies publishing his own collections on the grounds that "only brief vocabularies of the languages spoken by these nations [of the Upper Missouri] have been published." Disarmingly, he adds: "I am well aware how incomplete these Contributions are, and would not at this time suffer their publication, did I not believe that there is contained in them much useful information which ought to be given to the world in advance of a more elaborate work." He then proceeds to survey fourteen tribes and list whatever published vocabularies and grammars exist for them. In the text he names a number of individuals whose grammars or vocabularies he has used, and in the index he carefully cites each of the authors who have published similar work. Separating his own efforts from what was obviously a broad compilation, Hayden tells us that he himself produced the following: the grammar of the Blackfeet, everything on the Cheyenne and Arapaho including vocabularies and grammars, vocabularies of the Atsina and Arikara, and a part of the Minitari vocabulary. In a book of 230 pages, including the introduction and index, this amounts to only 84 pages, or a little over a third. Nonetheless, this much of the book is a useful reference on Indian languages.

But most of *Contributions* concerns "ethnography," or a broad history of customs and habits, tied in with notes on the geographic range of each tribe, the physical character of the land, even the weather. The concentration on ethnography is interesting because in all his private communications about the Indian memoir Hayden always emphasized its linguistic content. Writing to Leidy on 8 December 1861, he said the various papers "will consist of philology for the most part, with a historical & ethnographical introduction to each language." Because "philology" takes up only a third of *Contributions,* Hayden's claim that it was "the most part" of the book can only be accepted as a subjective judgment, by which he meant that philology was the heart of the book. Philology was the part he liked most, so perhaps it was natural that he should highlight it. But he had another reason for diverting attention from the ethnographic sections. He stole most of them from another writer.

This flabbergasting fact did not come to light for sixty-eight years. In the 46th Annual Report of the Bureau of American Ethnology (1930), J.N.B. Hewitt published a manuscript entitled *Indian Tribes of the Upper Missouri,* which was completed around 1854 and was written by a fur trader named Edwin Thompson Denig. Hewitt said Hayden plagiarized "numbers of pages" from Denig, without being specific about how many or from which parts of the manuscript. A generation later John C. Ewers edited and published another manuscript of Denig's, entitled *Five Indian Tribes of the Upper Missouri* (1961), originally written in 1855–1856. Ewers's grim conclusion was that "page after page of Hayden's descriptions of the Sioux, Arikaras, Assiniboines, and Plains Crees are nearly verbatim renderings of selected portions of the Denig manuscript in the Missouri Historical Society. Hayden's entire brief description of the Crow Indians, comprising pages 391–94 of his 1862 work, is but a slightly edited version of the early pages of Denig's 'Of the Crow Nation.'" With a growing sense of amazement and curiosity, I confirmed what Ewers had discovered by checking Hayden's book against Denig's manuscript (as published by Ewers). A simple bit of arithmetic gives Hayden a pretty dismal batting average for the originality of the ethnographic backgrounds he printed: he assembled five (Blackfeet, Atsina, Pawnee, Omaha, and Iowa) from other workers whom he acknowledged; he stole five from Denig without any attribution (Cree, Arikara, Sioux [Hayden called them Dakota], Assiniboine, and Crow); probably stole two others from Denig (Minitari, or Hidatsa, and Mandan); he did the research on the Cheyenne and Arapaho himself. Two out of fourteen. But that is not the worst of the matter.

Hayden's greatest crime was the wanton butchery he performed on Denig's essays. No one who reads Denig's full accounts could prefer Hayden's excerpts, either for content or on stylistic grounds. Hayden changes paragraph order indiscriminately, he leaves out sentences willy-nilly, and he cuts whole sections without rhyme or reason. In return he gives back little more than connectives and summaries of what other writers have published. The sad truth is that Hayden mutilates and mangles a body of writing that is superior to his own in every way.

Why? After compiling his vocabularies and grammars, even including those he had borrowed from others, Hayden lacked sufficient material for a book. He still needed something that would make appealing reading, something "that will give me a position among ethnologists at once." He lacked the time to do the research himself; besides, an excellent source was at hand. It was not necessary to reproduce all of Denig's essays, because what he wanted was a context for his own "philology." In fact, to judge from the manner of Hayden's cuts, it seems he was in a terrible hurry to extract just enough from Denig to make his own pastiche palatable.

Hayden chose to disguise his theft behind a cloud of generous acknowledgments. Besides thanking a number of specific fur traders and missionaries (including Denig for the Assiniboine vocabulary), he pens the following blanket statement.

In all my researches in the Northwest, most important aid has been rendered to me by the different members of the American Fur Company. All their stores of knowledge of Indian life, language, and character, which they had acquired by years of intercourse with the different tribes, were freely imparted to me, only a small portion of which is given in the following pages. I am especially indebted to Mr. Alexander Culbertson, the well-known agent of the American Fur Company, who has spent thirty years of his life among the wild tribes of the Northwest, and speaks several of their languages with great ease. To Mr. Andrew Dawson, Superintendent of Fort Benton, Mr. Charles E. Galpin, of Fort Pierre, and E. T. Denig, of Fort Union, I am under great obligations for assistance freely granted at all times.

Are we dealing here with an ingenuous fool or an impetuous knave? Perhaps a fully matured Iago.

Other questions arise. How did Hayden get the opportunity to steal so freely from Denig? Didn't he realize he was jeopardizing the reputation he had been cultivating so assiduously? Assuming he knew what he was doing and understood the risks, how did he justify it? And apart from *Contributions,* what assessment can we make of Hayden's work on Indians?

As to opportunity, events played right into his hands. Hayden told Baird on 9 January 1856 that "Mr. Denig is now collecting and preparing material for a great work on the Indians of the Upper Missouri for Mr. Culbertson. Mr. C. has with him manuscript for one volume which I have requested him to show you at W[ashington]." Hayden went on to praise Denig's tome, then added, "Mr. C. has agreed with me to write a physical description of the country, essays on Indian languages etc. and revise the whole and see it through the press as joint author." Culbertson never followed through as joint author, but it is valuable to learn he once intended to publish a book on Indians and that he deemed Hayden a suitable coadjutor. Perhaps that accounts for the praise Hayden poured over Culbertson in his introduction to *Contributions,* quoted above. Perhaps Hayden's ample but unspecific praise also hints that Culbertson provided more assistance than he wanted Hayden to acknowledge.

But the biggest clue in Hayden's letter is that he says Denig is preparing his Indian volume *for* Culbertson. Culbertson was the bourgeois of Fort Union, who had encouraged Hayden's collecting activities and invited him to Fort Benton during summer 1855 to further those efforts. Culbertson was also a longtime friend and older colleague of Denig. He probably brought Denig into the fur trade; both men came from nearby towns in Pennsylvania. Culbertson, indeed his whole family, also knew Baird well, and they had cooperated in gathering specimens for the Smithsonian. So we have a co-operative, and, from all appearances, a friendly group in Hayden-Culbert-son-Denig.

Then Denig falls out of the picture. Apparently for family reasons, Denig decided to leave the Upper Missouri after twenty-three years and move to Canada, which he did during summer 1856. That September Denig prepared a will in which he mentioned such personal items as his tools, clothing, utensils, and a watch, but not a word about manuscripts. Hayden's letter to Baird of January 1856 suggests Culbertson already had possession of Denig's manuscript on Indians. Denig had been thinking about migrating to Canada since at least 1854, and probably Culbertson knew of his intentions that early too. He and Hayden doubtless discussed the implications of Denig's move for their joint publication on Indians. They had plenty of opportunity to do so, particularly at the end of the 1856 season, when Culbertson accompanied Hayden on his downstream voyage and then traveled with him for several days after their arrival in St. Louis.

It is not certain when Culbertson handed over the Denig manuscript to Hayden and encouraged him to finish it up. Perhaps it was in January 1856, but possibly it was not until June 1859, when Hayden spent some time with Culbertson at Fort Randall. We can be sure of four things, though not about the timing: Culbertson delivered the manuscript to Hayden; Hayden copied large parts of it for his *Contributions;* Hayden then returned it to Culbertson; thereafter it came with Culbertson's papers to the Missouri Historical Society, where Ewers discovered it years later. Regardless of when he got it, Hayden lacked the time to begin selecting from it until he got back to Washington after the 1860 season. On 8 April 1861 he wrote to Leidy that he had "just begun to prepare some papers on the Indians and Indian languages of the north west. My first paper will contain the Crow language with a long account of their history all of which is new to science."

How did Denig feel about Hayden taking over and publishing part of his work? Did Culbertson say anything to Denig about the arrangement with Hayden? And how was Hayden going to disguise his plagiarism from Denig? As it happened, none of these questions ever arose, for Denig conveniently died in 1858, thereby removing the one person most likely to reveal Hayden's theft. And one of only two people who even knew of it. What about Culbertson? There is no record of his agreement with Hayden regarding Denig's manuscript. It was doubtless informal—probably never written down. Being interested in Indians himself, Culbertson wanted the seeds of his friend's research to bear fruit in some form. Because he had no literary experience or pretensions, he probably turned over the ways and means to Hayden, who did. And unless Culbertson had previously read Denig's manuscript carefully, he would not have seen Hayden's book for the artless expropriation it was. Even if he did, he may have kept quiet about it because he was the one who had provided Hayden with Denig's manuscript in the first place.

But the biggest question concerns Hayden and how he understood what he was doing. To begin with the most obvious point: Denig's work came to Hayden in manuscript form and quite incomplete. The introduction Denig wrote for it served as an outline of all he intended to cover, but much that he promised is not delivered. In adding the vocabularies and grammars Hayden would be compensating for the topics Denig never completed. By incorporating Denig's work into his own book, even if he ignored large sections of it, Hayden would be saving from oblivion the valuable research Denig had already done. Publishing Denig's research would not only benefit Hayden personally, it would advance science, a justification Hayden was fond of reiterating for all his work.

Furthermore, Denig's manuscript was itself a compilation, based mostly on Denig's own work, we assume, but also relying on other anonymous fur traders. More specifically, Ewers suggests that Denig learned much from Robert Meldrum, James Kipp, and Culbertson himself. Hayden may not have realized the extent of Denig's indebtedness to others, but Denig himself made no secret of having relied on colleagues for much of his material. Hayden might have thought he was merely extending the process, completing a history of Indians in the same cumulative fashion as Denig had begun it.

Recall how much Hayden used the compilation method in producing his *Geology and Natural History*. At least he borrowed only from himself there. But his general style of research often depended on borrowing from others. In 1858, while still trying to decide if he had good evidence of the Wealden formation, he wrote Leidy on 24 June asking for a letter "on the Wealden affinities of those vertebrate remains." He promised to use Leidy's exact words: "I will insert it bodily just as you write as proof"; then he concluded, "I suppose you would be as willing to put your remarks in that form as any other, and it will aid my remarks very much." Hayden seems to have had a communal understanding of information: if it came from a colleague it could be incorporated as one's own and published as one's own, with only the most general of attributions—all for the greater glory of science. More than that, publishing information obtained from a colleague seemed to reinforce bonds of common interest. That reasoning may sound strange, but this is a man whose earliest experiences in scientific activity grew from his need for collegial relationships.

Does this mean Hayden got so caught up in the spirit of joint enterprise that he made a habit of plagiarism? I think not. In several of his writings he borrows material from others, just as writers often do in summarizing research on a particular point, but usually Hayden gives citations or the context identifies the authority. I know of no similar instance of outright plagiarism in his other writings. Does this suggest that Hayden did not know what he was doing to Denig, did not realize in his enthusiasm to "save" Denig's work from oblivion that he was really stealing it? No again. Hayden was well educated and well read, and he grasped the concept of plagiarism. In practical terms, he certainly realized the dangers inherent in losing one's proprietary rights to information, as he vehemently demonstrated at the time of the Permian controversy.

Temptation will test the mettle of any virtue. And so will pressure. Denig's manuscript was an enormous temptation to Hayden, especially because it would complete his own meager linguistic gatherings. Hayden was greedy for reputation and drastically pressed for time. He was writing up four articles on the geology of the Upper Missouri, which would have been demanding enough. At the same time his vocabularies and grammars lay idle on the desk, near the manuscript that might transform them to something quite attractive. Suddenly, Warren gave him an opportunity to bring out another book, so he scrambled to put together *Geology and Natural History.* All the while the country was slipping into civil war: lives were changing, careers disintegrating, and no one knew what the future would bring. By May 1862 *Geology and Natural History* was published, and his other geological work was nearly done: three articles were already published and the fourth would come out that month. Several reviews he had promised to write were finished and in print. Now he lacked only some tangible sign of his interest in Indians. He had already abstracted material from Denig's chapter on the Mandans for his *Contributions,* but the whole book was not yet ready. So he abbreviated part of his chapter on the Mandans (amounting to an excerpt of an excerpt) and sent it off to the *American Journal of Science,* where it appeared in July. After completing a very rough draft of *Contributions* in May, he wrote urgently to Leidy, "It is of vital importance that it should come out at this time to go with 'American Linguistics' of Shell of New York, which is now attracting much attention." But his anxiety had not yet abated. *Contributions* would not appear for another five months, and it seems his own haste was partly to blame. For the better part of two months he had to sit in Philadelphia correcting proof of his draft before it could be published in October.

Let us return to May for another perspective. Hayden has finished up virtually all his outstanding work. He has a draft of his Indian memoir. He has shown no burning patriotism that would induce him to volunteer for the fighting. There is nothing to do in Rochester or Albany. His friend Stimpson invites him to come along on a trip to Europe. It is the chance of a lifetime, an almost obligatory journey for young gentlemen who aspire to careers in science. Many notable naturalists have preceded him on the European tour. Yet Hayden declines. His decision not to go to Europe would seem short-sighted; his refusal of Stimpson ungracious. Yet Hayden had many times been painfully reminded that he was not born a gentleman; if anything, Stimpson's well-intentioned offer stirred Hayden's bile. He was not a gentle-man-naturalist. He was different, and he knew it. But he would triumph in his own way. He would show them.

How did Hayden feel when it was all over, when *Contributions* was finally published? Relieved, certainly, and possibly proud that he had achieved something he had very much wanted. Did he feel any remorse about what he had done to Denig? Did the manner of the accomplishment detract from his enjoyment of it? Apparently not. On the contrary he was quite pleased with the book and certainly not afraid he would be exposed. On 15 October 1862 he wrote to Henry Rowe Schoolcraft, the prominent geologist and ethnolo-gist, "I return to you the books you so kindly lent me [on Indians]. Sorry am I that I have kept them so long, but I wished to have my book published be-fore the reference books left my hands . . . I enclose a copy of my work. I would call and see you in person but leave the city immediately to join the army." And six years later, in presenting a copy of the book to Henry Wadsworth Longfellow, he boasted, "The materials of the volume are en-tirely original and cost me much labor." Hoping for an opportunity to trade compliments, he added, "Your beautiful poem of 'Hiawatha' induces me to believe that you will look into this work with interest and I very much de-sire your opinion in regard to it." He had read *Hiawatha* many times, Hayden said, and regarded it "as the only poem expressing the real spirit of the Indian character in our language." Which was flattering rubbish, for Hayden's letters several times bemoaned the impediments the "savages" put in his way, and his writings on Indians reveal him to be a hard-boiled collec-tor of artifacts with no trace of sentimentality.

Hayden looked forward to publishing more on Indians. Even after the war he was trying to think of ways to use the parts of Denig's manuscripts he had not yet touched. In his *Contributions* he alluded to other materials at his disposal, which contained more information than he could use at the mo-ment, and he implied several times that he was working on another book, specifically at page 380, where he says, "Inasmuch as an extended history of the Indian tribes of the Missouri Valley is in process of preparation, . . . " His correspondence shows him trying to enlarge his holdings, and he wrote to Martin Brewer Anderson on 3 July 1866: "I hope to gather some material for the second part of the Indian memoir." He probably would have brought out another volume, had he been able to find something fresh to add to

Denig's material, in the same way his vocabularies and grammars balanced Denig's ethnography the first time. He never found enough for another book, for he wrote only two more short articles on Indians. In October 1867 he described for the *Proceedings of the American Philosophical Society* the remains of an old Pawnee village, where, over time too long to remember, the ancestors of living Indians had chipped arrowheads with stone tools. In April 1868 he published in the same place "Brief Notes on the Pawnee, Winnebago, and Omaha Languages." Though he did not acknowledge the fact in the article, a Dr. T. T. Miner did the work on the Winnebago for him.

That article was the last of Hayden's publications on Indians, but not the end of his interest in them. His emphasis on linguistics seems to have grown out of a desire to classify the various tribes. Because language was an obvious measure of difference between them, and one of the easier aspects to collect, that is where he focused. In this frankly taxonomic approach, the vocabularies became analogous to his lists of species. To carry the comparison a little farther: in studying the natural world Hayden was a good empiricist, looking more to collect facts than interpret them; similarly as an ethnologist, he looked more for the tangible, physical artifacts of language (words, phrases, definitions, grammars) than the broader ideas or meanings of Indian culture. In reading Hayden I have the distinct impression that he sees Indian languages, and their components, like so many geological formations, to be sorted according to their physical relationships. He said at one point in *Contributions* that he intended "to work out the history of their migrations from all the materials within my reach," as if it were their physical location and spread across the land that made the tribes fascinating to him—again rather like geological formations. In this analogy the natives themselves become like fossils—to be collected, classified, written up, and displayed.

Ah, yes, and displayed—the most dramatic and popular way of materializing the Indians. No wonder Hayden grew so eager to build up a photographic record of the tribes. Shortly after the Civil War Hayden urged the American Philosophical Society and the Academy of Natural Sciences to start collecting photographs that would illustrate the rapidly vanishing ways of the Indians. Both institutions complied by putting him in charge of committees to raise the money and start the work. At the same time Hayden started accumulating his own collection, with financial help from his friend William Blackmore, an English entrepreneur who also collected Indian artifacts. In Washington Hayden acquired glass negatives of Indians from photographer Zeno Shindler, and he employed C. M. Bell to make prints. After 1870 he began adding pictures from the field, which were largely the work of his survey's photographer, William Henry Jackson. By 1877, when Hayden stopped collecting in this genre, he claimed to have amassed 1,400 photographs of seventy-eight tribes.

On the literary side Hayden sponsored several writers by publishing their works through his survey. For instance, he published George Ainslie's grammar of the Nez Percés, Garrick Mallery's "Calendar of the Dakota Nation," and Cyrus Thomas's article on "Ancient Mounds of Dakota." Edwin A. Barber wrote several pieces on Indians of the Four Corners region for Hayden's *Bulletin,* while William Henry Holmes and W. H. Jackson wrote up archeological remains of the Anasazi civilization for Hayden's annual reports. All three men worked for Hayden's survey. Going further afield, Hayden encouraged four other contributions on Indians of the desert Southwest and West Coast. The most ambitious undertaking was Washington Matthews's *Ethnography and Philology of the Hidatsa Indians* (1877), which appeared in Hayden's *Miscellaneous Publications* series.

Hayden went on boasting of his interest in Indians for quite a long time. As late as 10 June 1877, when he wrote the preface for Matthews's volume on the Hidatsa, he would say: "It was originally intended to publish this treatise as a portion of a general work on Indian ethnography now in course of preparation by the undersigned." Thus, nine years after his last publication on Indians, he was still broadcasting the fiction that a second volume of *Contributions* was in the works. He said this to inflate his reputation as an all-around naturalist, of which he was always proud, but about which he may not have been entirely secure—at least regarding Indians.

After 1868 Hayden wrote nothing more on Indians, nor did he do any more research on them. Even as that last article appeared, Hayden had already redeployed his energies into natural history and geology.

12

AN INCONVENIENT
WAR, 1862–1865

If you see Gen. Hammond [Surgeon General William Alexander Hammond] at any time, <u>do</u> express my thanks to him for sending me here, for I am very pleasantly situated and am now learning very rapidly. I think Gen. H. will locate me where I can continue my scientific operations—at least for a few hours per day.

—Hayden to Baird, 31 October 1862,
writing from the West Philadelphia Hospital

THE MOST REMARKABLE THING about the Civil War, from Hayden's point of view, was his willingness to have anything to do with it. He had devoted a decade to establishing himself as a naturalist of the first rank. Why should he now throw himself into a brutal war? Despite the conscription, substitutes could be hired if the net did catch an unwilling recruit. Hayden did not have a lot of money, but his influence and connections could surely have assisted him, had he chosen to use them. But the draft did not catch him; he volunteered immediately after finishing the Indian memoir, under circumstances suggesting he may have been a bit off balance. Stepping back and listening to what he said about the war over a period of nearly two years, however, puts his enlistment into a different perspective.

From near the end of 1860, four months before the firing on Fort Sumter, Hayden began bemoaning the likelihood of coming violence. He was mostly concerned with the personal impact of war: "At any rate our country is broken up for the present and science must suffer." Or, touching the same theme a week later, "I see no decrease in scientific effort as yet, though war is the only profession that pays at the present time." Even as President Lincoln issued the first call for volunteers in mid-April 1861, Hayden noted the excitement in Washington but told Meek, "We are all well here and hard at work"; then showing where his priorities lay, he added with mild annoyance, "I have not got my appointment [as an Indian agent] as the President has not acted on the agencies yet." By 5 May he was piping a more belligerent tune, though probably with the intention of making an impression. Alluding to the rumor that southerners thought any one of them could whip any twenty Yankees, he wrote another correspondent, "Let them try it on. I shall enlist if needed, and my services are already offered, but I do not wish to leave my work until war is actually begun."

As others got caught up in war fever, Hayden received conflicting reactions from his colleagues. Newberry wrote, "We are tremendously excited by the war news . . . If there is to be any fighting at Washington, I want a hand in it and shall mount guard in the Old Smithsonian as soon as I can get there." And in just over a month Newberry was in Washington, but probably to lobby for the surgeon generalship of Ohio, which he did not get. Typically, Newberry's mind was untroubled by any ambiguities: "The most perfect unanimity as regards action now prevails in the North. Since we must fight we shall go at it in earnest and as one man." But most naturalists had little taste for war. As Meek said, "So it seems war is at last upon us, as I so long have anticipated. Well, let them fight it out. I have no blood to spare in fighting my own countrymen, on either side."

All the excitement and the conflicting views took their toll on Hayden's concentration, as he admitted to Meek in late May. "There is no voice for science here now, the cry is all war! war! . . . I am at work all I can but there is so much going on that my mind is very much diverted. I did not get my agency. I am glad now. I feel too much of an interest in this movement to be away." Hayden did not need to impress Meek, so we can assume this statement was from the heart, though it is difficult to see what he meant by asserting "an interest in this movement." Despite his years at Oberlin—a hotbed of abolitionist sentiment since the 1840s—he never showed any emotion regarding slavery, one way or the other. Unlike a number of gentlemen on both sides of the conflict, he never appealed to honor or duty or righteousness to legitimize belligerence. (Hayden's near contemporary, Oliver Wendell Holmes, Jr., justified the war in such ways, as did a number of other New England Brahmins.) When it came to scientific combat, Hayden might succumb to the pretensions of honor, but regarding actual war he took a more sensible view. Its greatest evil was that it interfered with his work. So what was his "interest in this movement"? Like many young idealists at the time, he seems to have been caught up in the enthusiasm to preserve the union. Years later, on the eve of the election of 1880, he admitted that he had only voted twice in a presidential election—both times for Lincoln, in 1860 and 1864.

As the country settled down for a long siege, individuals adjusted careers according to their true interests. Hayden returned to work, finishing up articles on his exploits with Raynolds, tackling *Geology and Natural History,* and then putting together the Indian memoir. By November he was telling a friend that he was too busy to notice the war, and by March 1862 he was writing the wife of Rochester University's president: "I do not now intend to take a commission even if I could get one, though if the offer was made me, perhaps so. I have many projects on hand which can only be accomplished by patient labor."

No doubt he did, but by late summer his business was winding down. He and Meek and Cope had taken their brief excursion down the Potomac and into New Jersey during the spring. He had paid a long visit to his family in Rochester over the summer. He had finished up everything but the Indian memoir, with no prospects of doing anything else as long as the war lasted. He could have stayed on at the Smithsonian at little cost but for no pay, as others of the Megatherium did, though with not much work either. What to do? Where to go to escape this menacing war?

The answer occurred to him by late summer. Hayden first mentioned it while writing to ethnologist Lewis Henry Morgan, with whom he had been swapping favors ever since he started his Indian memoir. "I may go to New Mexico this fall. If so something may be done for you in that region. The Surgeon Gen. wishes to send me there, and I am much inclined to go. Let me know what you wish at any rate and I will do all I can." Of course! How better to keep active and avoid the more hazardous theaters of war than by enlisting for duty in some out-of-the-way place, where the danger of snakebite probably exceeded that of bullet wounds. He did not go to New Mexico after all, but had he gone there the likelihood is Hayden would have spent the entire war collecting natural history samples. Therefore his decision to volunteer was not so rash after all. On the contrary, to a man who seemed to fear inactivity more than death itself, enlistment was the only solution. Besides he did not anticipate going eyeball to eyeball with Johnny Reb. The last letter he wrote before leaving Washington was to the Topographic Bureau, asking for whatever maps the bureau could send him on explorations west of the Mississippi.

Doctors entering the army offered certain skills and an invaluable source of manpower, but most physicians brought little expertise to the practice of medicine on the eve of the Civil War. Considering the realities of the time, one can only breathe a sigh of relief for the care received today. Anesthetics were new in the mid-nineteenth century and not yet widely used; antiseptic procedures (like doctors washing their hands before surgery) virtually non-existent, because the germ theory of disease was still unknown. Medical schools had no entrance requirements; besides, many physicians never attended medical school, preferring to enter their profession by completing an apprenticeship. Effective licensing of the M.D. was still two generations away. Students attending medical school had few opportunities to work in a laboratory or to develop any clinical experience under supervision. Mostly they memorized lectures. They learned pat formulas and prejudices that had passed into the medical mythology centuries ago. Scientific knowledge was growing dramatically at the time, but it made no impact on the curriculum of medical schools until the fourth quarter of the century.

Hayden's training at the Albany Medical College seems to have been superior to that of most of his contemporaries. Anatomy was a required course, and Albany boasted an anatomical theater. Chemistry got more attention than at most schools, and connection of the college to the Albany Hospital guaranteed some exposure to clinical practice. Hayden had to pass an oral examination on his subjects, which showed more rigor than most schools, and to submit a successful thesis, though his essay on the digestive system was only a rehash of various textbooks. Typical of theses written at the time, it required no research beyond the school's library.

As a result, like virtually all "private physicians" hired by the army, Hayden needed a crash course in the military applications of his craft. For that the army sent him to the general hospital at West Philadelphia, where he received $80 a month during training. The work did not tax him greatly, or his time. Meanwhile he enjoyed his time in Philadelphia, and he managed to visit the Academy of Natural Sciences occasionally, though he did no specific work of his own. He wrote encouraging notes to Meek regarding Meek's forthcoming masterwork on the fossil invertebrates of the Upper Missouri, and he talked with Leidy about the joint work they would eventually complete on the Nebraska vertebrates. He wrote a few pieces for a periodical called *Hospital Record,* and he may have helped edit this journal for two or three months. After successfully completing his three-day examinations at the end of November, he became a surgeon of volunteers. (In formally accepting this commission the following March he gave his age as thirty-two; he was actually thirty-four.)

Having won his commission, he knew he could not remain in Philadelphia. "I wish I could be stationed at Washington, or put in charge of a small hospital there," he wrote Baird. "Do not tell Dr. Hammond that I write you anything, but if he consults you I wish you would suggest what you think is best. If I had charge of some hospital I would have even more time than now." He got his hospital, all right—in Beaufort, South Carolina—along with a bellyfull of bureaucratic rivalry he had not counted on.

Beaufort served as the beehive for all of Port Royal Island; the rebels abandoned both early in the war, including some 15,000 acres of cultivated land. Before the end of 1861 General William Tecumseh Sherman swooped in and put the slaves to work harvesting the corn and cotton that otherwise would have gone to waste. The island remained in Yankee hands throughout the war, and the hospitals erected there became important during the long siege of Charleston. From mid-April through mid-August 1863 Hayden was in charge of first one, then two hospitals, each of only fifty beds; but at first he had no medical assistants.

Despite a nearby war, for a while it seemed that natural history would reassert its hold, albeit with the strange creatures and exotic perfumes of a southern coastal climate. Hayden started gathering everything in sight, having requested all the necessary collecting apparatus from Baird, who was only too glad to oblige, as the Smithsonian had no samples from that region. Dr. J. J. Crane, medical director at Beaufort, was Hayden's immediate superior. Interested in natural history and already possessed of a good collection of specimens, he fell easy prey to the congenial attentions of Hayden. Before long Hayden was writing Leidy arranging a corresponding membership in the Philadelphia Academy for Crane, who in return would surrender his collection. Hayden also went after bigger game, by asking Baird and Joseph Henry to smooth his approach to the top military commanders in the department. Hayden asked Baird to use part of the cash he was holding for him to purchase and send him some good claret. By the end of summer he was getting things under control. "I am very well contented down here, doing well and gradually gaining favor I hope." As fast as new commanders were shuffled in, Hayden played his trumps and had another suit of flattering introductions dealt around. Hayden also got some pleasing news from home: in 1863 he was awarded an honorary M.A. degree from the University of Rochester, doubtless due to the initiation of Chester Dewey.

On the whole, things began quite well for Hayden at Beaufort. True, natural history collecting tapered off with the heat of summer, which coincided with the arrival of more injured soldiers. Then there was a puzzling confrontation with the nurse, Mrs. Lander. Apparently the lady differed with medical authority regarding the proper treatment of the wounded. She was clever enough to gain support from some officers, but countermanding orders squelched her. Hayden seems to have sympathized with her cause initially, until she crossed swords with him too. Nurses were new to American battlefields, and apparently Mrs. Lander's presence disrupted the clubby routine of the officers. As a woman confronting a rigid male hierarchy, she had her work cut out for her. It should have been the perfect scenario for a rescuing knight, armed with more than the normal ammunition required to win over the fair sex. Alas, this one got away and left a few scars. "The only trouble we have arises from women, the curse of our existence. Chaplains come next. Most of them are gossiping old women." Still the tempest was a tiny one and quickly forgotten. On 6 September Hayden could write to Leidy, "I have now one of the prettiest positions a man could possibly have; neat, respectable and only half my time occupied, and senior member of Gen. Saxton's staff [medical staff]. Sincerely hope I will not be relieved until sent north." In the same letter Hayden inquired about the background of Dr. Meredith Clymer, the new medical director at Beaufort, who had just come down from Philadelphia. He hoped Leidy knew him and would be able to "influence him in my favor, as it might save me from being disturbed." Leidy knew the gentleman all right, but even his considerable influence, if indeed he chose to use it, could not prevent the clash that was coming.

Despite the personal bitterness that arose between them, Hayden's quarrel with Lieutenant Meredith Clymer, M.D., was essentially a professional one. Especially in critical posts like those of medical practitioners, the army depended on volunteers; it could not have functioned without them, given the inadequate number of army doctors and the frenzy in which the military found itself in gearing up suddenly for an all-out war. But the full-time soldier has always scorned the amateur, no matter how necessary. And consider Hayden. Freshly trained, more than competent, probably better organized than most of his new comrades, he was not intimidated by the brass hierarchies that kept more conforming men in awe. He had powerful friends in Washington, both civilian and military, and he didn't mind dropping names. He was articulate, charming, could converse on a number of subjects, and had the knack of making himself at home among the powerful men he was trying to please. He had his own mind and interests. Besides the natural history collecting, which must have seemed bizarre to his more warlike colleagues, he was reading Henry Buckle's paean to progress, *History of Civilization;* it was also at this time that he managed to find a copy of Darwin's *Origin of Species.* In short, among regular army men, Hayden stuck out like a cornstalk in the cabbage patch. Watching this dandy prance around, so full of himself, so comfortably out of place, provoked as much amusement as annoyance, at least among the general officers. To the lower ranking commanders, whose authority overlapped this stranger's, he was more disturbing, clearly a threat.

Furthermore, Hayden had erected a nicely fortified position. He had moved up from manager of a hospital or two to post surgeon at Beaufort, which made him head of General Rufus Saxton, Jr's, medical staff and gave him wider responsibilities. He attended sick and wounded officers at the post; he also decided who should be moved to other hospitals. Being ambitious, and taking advantage of undefined jurisdictional boundaries, Hayden briefly extended his authority all over Port Royal Island, until 15 August—when the bureaucracy cranked out official orders limiting his activity to the hospitals at Beaufort.

That was the situation when Lieutenant Clymer arrived in early autumn 1863. Clymer brought with him more than the line officer's normal contempt for a flashy volunteer. He had a large chip on his shoulder, an angry growth formed by general hatred for the whole new system that made Hayden possible and in particular for the man who commanded it—the surgeon general himself, William Alexander Hammond. It is worth saying a little about Hammond because Hayden admired him and openly sympathized with his efforts to reform the truly desperate condition of the army's medical department at the outbreak of the war. Because we lack Hayden's records as a volunteer, Hammond's initiatives suggest some of the ways Hayden might have worked with actual patients.

Hammond displayed a scholar's interest in physiology and botany, he had experience in university teaching, and he was an accomplished author. He wrote medical articles, of course, but much more: he was a novelist and a playwright. No wonder Hayden idolized him. When promoted, Hammond vaulted from first lieutenant to brigadier general over a host of more traditionally qualified officers. He was thirty-three when confirmed as surgeon general in April 1862. No wonder the medical establishment despised him.

Not shy of controversy, Hammond waded into troubled waters with bold reforms. He wanted to separate the delivery of medical supplies from the quartermaster's department; he introduced women as nurses; he wanted more educational requirements for army doctors; he emphasized medical research and wanted hospitals set up according to specialties, instead of dumping all the sick and wounded into general hospitals. His most controversial reform came in May 1863, when he banned the use of calomel by army surgeons. Traditionally prescribed in cases of fever to act as an emetic, calomel contained mercury, whose poisonous properties were understood at the time. Hammond argued that inexperienced physicians would certainly administer improper doses. Behind the use of calomel was the desire of the reforming physicians to rely on nature's own healing mechanisms and on preventive approaches, both of which implied prescribing fewer drugs. Generally, younger physicians embraced Hammond's reforms, as did many of the volunteer surgeons who, like Hayden, were recruited for the war effort. Conservatives like Lieutenant Clymer angrily opposed Hammond, and they controlled most medical associations as well as the army's medical department.

Another of Hammond's reforms initiated the war between Hayden and Clymer. Traditionally, line officers made ultimate decisions regarding the sick and wounded, even though most of these officers were not doctors. Hammond wanted complete responsibility for all patients' treatment transferred to the surgeons, regardless of whether they were volunteers or regular army doctors. Like many of Hammond's reforms, this one made excellent sense, but it tweaked the wart-infested nose of tradition.

No sooner had he arrived in Beaufort than Clymer began contesting Hayden's authority within the regiment. No dramatist could have staged a more antagonistic setting, and during the next three months the leading characters played out their roles with increasing rancor. Obviously the catalyst in the affair (because things had been smooth before his arrival), Clymer appears as the devil incarnate, naturally: our main source on him is Hayden. Clymer is a petty schemer, a vengeful man obsessed with his own anger, finally a "vicious, bad man." Meanwhile Hayden played to the hilt the part of wounded innocence and whined to his friends up north to back him or rescue him by having him transferred. His friends did eventually rescue him, because they continued to like him, though they must have wished Hayden were less troublesome.

Hayden's military superiors also liked him, but they could not tolerate a disruptive personal quarrel. The short-term result was that Hayden retained responsibility for treating the officers at the post, but Clymer took over control of the hospitals. Clymer was eventually court-martialed for his troublemaking and relieved, while General Saxton "fully approved of my course and my labors," Hayden reported. At the same time Saxton said he "would be sorry to have me leave the department but would advise me to do so if I could." Hayden got the hint; he stepped up the pressure on his friends to get him back to Washington. Even with Clymer out of the way, things were different. The bubble had burst. Though he found time to resume his collecting over the winter, Hayden now felt he was wasting his time, and he yearned to get back to the West. He considered quitting, but realized his resignation would probably be refused. Besides, such an act would alienate the friends on whom he had leaned to get him involved in the first place.

Fortunately, those friends did not abandon him, and by February 1864 he was posted back to Washington. For the better part of nine months Hayden served as assistant medical inspector for the Department of Washington, under Augustus Choate Hamlin, another naturalist-doctor, who happened to be the son of the current vice president, Hannibal Hamlin. Hamlin was about Hayden's age and shared a sympathy for Hammond's reforms. Apparently the two men were compatible and worked effectively together, looking after the sanitary conditions of hospitals, barracks, and other places of temporary resort for soldiers and arranging their transport within the district. The job kept Hayden busy enough that he could neither grouse about his circumstances nor do any natural history work.

However, back in the congenial surroundings of Washington, he was able to enjoy the company of the Megatherium from time to time, as well as another overlapping group of naturalists. The members of the Potomac Side Naturalists' Club (formed in 1858) hoped to perpetuate the spirit and activities of an earlier organization, by then defunct, called the Botanical Society of the District of Columbia. Hayden was a founding member of the Potomac Club, along with his friends Stimpson, Kennicott, and J. G. Cooper. Titian Peale seems to have been the guiding light of this group, which met at members' residences on Monday nights to hear a paper or examine collections. Simplicity dictated no permanent offices, no regular meeting place, and no monetary expenses. Perhaps the club's most essential function was to give a mostly idle group of naturalists something to do during the war and to remind them of their professional priorities during these discouraging times. The club lapsed after 1865, when members resumed their regular occupations. Hayden's relaxed state of mind during these months of 1864 certainly derived from his activities with the Potomac Club and the Megatherium.

Doubtless Hayden would have enjoyed serving out the war in his position as medical inspector. It was not to be. How and why he was assigned to the Army of the Shenandoah is a mystery, but in mid-October he moved to Winchester, Virginia, to become chief medical officer of the region, reporting directly to General "Little Phil" Sheridan. By the time Hayden arrived, Sheridan had just won several celebrated victories over the Confederacy and had driven them from the Shenandoah Valley. Apparently, Hayden was called in to organize a field hospital in Winchester, necessary in the aftermath of recent battles.

But the war was winding down, and Hayden could begin turning his attention to other matters. Life was quiet enough at Winchester that his chief preoccupation became the compilation of casualty statistics and medical histories of all surgery cases in the district. He geologized in the region, and for a while he had notions of investing in "a company for mining and other purposes." Nothing came of it. Shortly after Lee surrendered to Grant in early April 1865, Hayden prepared to resign. He left Winchester by the end of the month, and according to General Orders of 19 May the army officially accepted his resignation, saying his service was no longer needed. In the fall he received a formal and honorable discharge with the rank of lieutenant colonel by brevet. He returned to Washington and lived at the Smithsonian for most of the summer, but his thoughts were now shifting toward Philadelphia. In the immediate aftermath of war Hayden realized that government would not be funding any expeditions, and he was anxious to get back into harness. Private sponsors held out better hopes for the near future, and the Academy of Natural Sciences seemed the best bet. Hayden had been suggesting to Leidy since January that he would like to move to Philadelphia, and by November a new career had been arranged for him in the City of Brotherly Love.

13
THE ENTERPRISING
PROFESSOR, 1865–1872

My explorations in early years were made under unfavorable circumstances, when there was but little interest in such matters among our people, and it is only within a few years that I have begun to reap the rewards of those labors. The survey now under my direction began in a very small way in 1867, and has gradually attained its present size and position through my most strenuous personal efforts. It was, however, founded largely on my labors during the first eight years, or from 1853 to 1860.
—Hayden to Carl Schurz, 29 October 1878

THE END OF the Civil War found Hayden in the same dilemma he had been in at its start. He was still trying to further his career as a naturalist and geologist, but in 1865 he had no idea what to do next. The natural history and geological surveys of the states had gone to bed during the war, and the revival of the army surveys in the West seemed uncertain. Even the irrepressible assistant secretary of the Smithsonian had no projects afoot in which to enlist Hayden. In a letter to a friend in Boston Hayden summarized his mood and prospects: "I am floating on the tide and where it will land me I know not, perhaps in perdition." During the next seven years Hayden engaged in a number of enterprises and tried out the career of a college professor. It was an experimental period—with mixed results. He finally found regular government employment, and he adjusted several professional relationships to his advantage. But his personal relationships seemed to suffer.

He began by poking around the Great Lakes during July, where he "visited all the iron mines, made good collections of ores & rocks." Later he gathered books on the geology of the region with the apparent intention of forming some kind of mining venture. It never materialized. He also considered a scheme involving oil tracts in West Virginia, but it came to nothing. He talked vaguely about a real estate development. Though he mustered some interest for all these projects, making money for its own sake failed to excite Hayden. Besides, thanks to selling various collections, living frugally, and saving most of his salary as a volunteer surgeon, Hayden had more than $3,000 in savings. But his restless temperament dictated staying busy. He followed through on only one consulting venture at this time: a journey through Tennessee, Alabama, and Georgia, which lasted from early November through mid-December. He undertook it because he had nothing else to do and because he persuaded his wartime colleague Augustus Hamlin to accompany him, thereby transforming a business trip into a naturalist's tour of new territory. On the eve of departure Hayden collected $300 for his expenses, and he may have earned some fees for reporting on mineral lands and an oil tract along the Cumberland River. The only lasting result of the journey was that the Smithsonian added some specimens to its collections.

Before he began this trip another possibility had captivated Hayden. From mid-August the thought uppermost in his mind had been to gain a professorship at the University of Pennsylvania. It came about through the initiative of Joseph Leidy. In addition to holding the chair of anatomy, Leidy had been delivering general lectures on natural history. No one else taught natural history courses regularly, though Leidy believed more should be done in this line through an expanded medical curriculum. Leidy approached his friends on the board of trustees and lobbied for an auxiliary to the Department of Medicine. The board granted his request and created five auxiliary professorships to begin in spring 1866: zoology; botany; geology and mineralogy; comparative anatomy; hygiene, medical jurisprudence, and toxicology.

The leading candidate in geology was the incisive and irascible Peter Lesley, an impressive polymath who combined expertise in coal and iron deposits with an appreciation for philology and poetry. He had worked on the first geological survey of Pennsylvania. He had also served as a Congregational pastor in Massachusetts, where most parishioners found his ideas too liberal. Lesley shirked at nothing and gave freely of his opinions, in which he had a fond confidence. He wanted to teach geology, he wanted to do it at Penn, but at the time he feared for his health; therefore he recommended Hayden. "It is needless for me to urge his value, for it is well known. His health is perfect, his energy untiring, his experience & knowledge large. He is loyal & has served his country in the field. He has done a great deal for science & I think he must be a good teacher."

In a frenzy of anticipation Hayden began lining up support. In addition to Lesley, Leidy, and John Lawrence LeConte, all of Philadelphia, he also secured endorsements from Baird and Joseph Henry in Washington, and Dana and Benjamin Silliman, Jr., at Yale. Yet he could not relax and trust the network he had called into being. "I look upon the success or failure in this scheme as the turning point in my life . . . I shall be entirely unsettled until after the appointment is made." He proceeded to imagine rivals, despite the assurance of his patrons that he was the only candidate. He imagined that his old enemy at Beaufort, Dr. Clymer (a Philadelphia resident), might stir up trouble. He gave numerous suggestions to Leidy on tactics, all of them tactless, then apologized in a fit of embarrassment. "Please pardon my anxiety, but feel like leaving no stone unturned which will aid toward a favorable result." To the relief of all, the appointment sailed through, and Hayden got the good news at Atlanta in the middle of his consulting trip. Once back in Philadelphia, he forgot about business schemes and plunged into preparations for his lectures.

Hayden recorded little about his course of lectures. At the end of his first week he reported having finished three lectures "with moderate success, hope to improve as I go on." The fullest statement he made about his initial efforts as a teacher was: "I had a good class to the close and feel delighted with the idea of teaching. I have been requested to open a school of instruction in those branches (natural sciences) and possibly I may do so." How were these lectures received by the students? "To the satisfaction of all apparently."

From every indication both Hayden and his lectures received a warm reception. While preparing his first lectures, he told Leidy he would not write out more than six or eight of them. This respect for spontaneity doubtless made him a popular teacher. Not content to lecture, which would have been the norm, Hayden displayed minerals, maps, fossil drawings, and other materials he had accumulated in the course of his work. Naturally, he brought specimens from his own collections and from the Philadelphia Academy; he even prevailed upon Baird to contribute some from the Smithsonian. Hayden obtained additional sketches and drawings from Warren and Dana. Beginning in 1868 Hayden added to this rich trove of pedagogic tools the drawings of Henry Elliott, whom Hayden called "one of the most remarkable and rapid diagram drawers I have ever known." Elliott's illustrations of topography and geology enliven many pages of the Hayden Survey reports; no doubt they did the same for his lectures.[1]

Between early April and the end of June Hayden delivered thirty-eight lectures for which he earned $500. That pattern continued for each of six succeeding years, through 1872, except that in a couple of years he managed to finish during May, in order to get a head start on his western surveying.

Despite his initial eagerness and apparent success at teaching, before the end of his first course of lectures Hayden yearned to return to the field.

For summer 1866 he arranged for the Philadelphia Academy to sponsor a collecting trip to the Bad Lands. After reaching Fort Randall by steamer in early August, he obtained the services of a couple of men to help with cooking, route-finding, and logistics, but he took along only one colleague, his old friend Jim Stevenson. Despite being drenched by heavy rains for much of their journey, they returned after thirty-five days with about 1,800 pounds of specimens and a number of new insights into the Bad Lands.[2]

But summer 1866 was not yet over. Having recuperated briefly at Fort Randall, he and Stevenson embarked at the end of September on another junket for just over two weeks. From Yankton on the Missouri they went up the James River to Fort James (near modern Mitchell, South Dakota), then headed east to explore the drainages between that point and Fort Dakota (Sioux Falls). From there they headed up Pipestone Creek to find the distinctive pipestone quarries. Hayden returned to Philadelphia in late October. His summer's work had cost $1,000, more than half of which came out of his own pocket; the Academy contributed $500.

To recover his expenses he intended to sell part of the collection after giving the Academy first choice of his accumulated treasures. This involved some sleight of hand, whereby he tried to do two rather incompatible things. He told Dana and Marsh at Yale that they would have first option on purchasing specimens after Leidy made his selections for the Academy. This offer implied he had some valuable, even original, samples to sell. At the same time he told Baird he had found little that was new, which provoked Baird's understandable reply, "If neither Leidy nor you can give me anything for the collection [of the Smithsonian], it will not be much encouragement to me to interfere to promote the success of another expedition." Hayden answered that the Smithsonian already possessed better samples of everything in his current collection and, besides, he had to raise some money to cover his own large investment in the trip. Baird accepted Hayden's statement without asking to see the evidence. In 1867 Hayden sold some large vertebrate fossils to Yale for $1,000, and some unspecified collections to the Boston Society of Natural History for $400.

The Academy's backing in 1866 had been a useful stopgap, but from the moment he returned to Philadelphia in October 1866, Hayden began scrambling again. He sounded Baird on the chances of succeeding Robert Kennicott as the Smithsonian's collector in the Arctic; Kennicott had died there in 1866 during his second journey. Hayden must have been desperate to find steady work in the field, for taking the Arctic position would have meant abandoning his professorship. Fortunately, he found something far more suitable early the following year. On 1 March 1867 Congress admitted the state of Nebraska to the United States. It was a momentous event on the national stage, for the two new Republican senators could be expected to vote with their colleagues on several vital issues in opposition to President Andrew Johnson. Some radicals already spoke of impeaching Johnson. Not surprisingly, Johnson vetoed the Nebraska Statehood Bill. Congress struck back by overriding the veto with the necessary two-thirds majority.

The admission of Nebraska was equally momentous for Hayden, for it led directly to the creation of his own survey in 1867. Many private individuals and public officials in Nebraska desired an inventory of the state's natural resources, and a reconnaissance of this kind had been talked of for more than a decade. Using the connections he had been cultivating since the middle 1850s, Hayden kept his own name prominently before the political leadership, and he did all he could to promote the idea of a geologic survey under his direction. A particular admirer of Hayden was Julius Sterling Morton, secretary of Nebraska Territory from 1858 to 1861. Morton gave Hayden a jump on the competition by informing him of a proposal to use the unexpended funds of Nebraska Territory for a geologic survey of the state. Hayden lost no time in mounting a lobbying effort, and he shrewdly instructed his friends to point out to Congress "how much it would aid emigration [i.e., increase population in the new state] to have a good scientific report of that region." The names of the men he recruited to support his bid for the survey attest to Hayden's widespread influence and his ability to promote himself and his ideas: Baird, Dana, Marsh, and Leidy from the scientific community; Warren and Raynolds, his former field colleagues; more importantly General J. H. Simpson, chief engineer of the Department of the Interior, and General A. A. Humphreys, chief of the Corps of Army Engineers; and perhaps best of all, Governor Alvin Saunders of Nebraska.

Hayden stepped into the Nebraska survey virtually uncontested because everyone recognized his unique pioneering abilities, but questions of jurisdiction and money persisted even after his appointment. Eventually it was decided that Hayden would report to Commissioner Joseph Wilson of the General Land Office (in the Department of the Interior) instead of to the state of Nebraska. The possibility of additional funds from the state of Nebraska or Congress never entirely disappeared, which accounts for the utopian ambitions Hayden voiced periodically for this brief survey, whose total expenditures over two years amounted to only $11,500. Hayden earned $2,000 in salary for each of the two years.

Thus began in 1867 a series of surveys under Hayden's authority. First was the Geological Survey of Nebraska, which reorganized and continued in 1869 as the Geological Survey of the Territories of the United States. Hayden cleverly altered the style of his survey to the informal United States Geological Survey of the Territories. No one objected; besides, the new name sounded better. In 1873 the survey evolved into the U.S. Geological and Geographical Survey of the Territories. The name kept changing to reflect expanding operations, but from its inception everyone recognized it as "the Hayden Survey."

Shortly after the Civil War, as the nation turned its attention to the vast interior resources of the country, Congress resolved to sponsor scientific surveys of the West. Though not yet prepared to create a single permanent bureau for these broad purposes, Congress wanted the benefits of continuity, even though for more than a decade it insisted on funding its surveys on an annual basis only. This cumbersome procedure set up roadblocks to smooth operations, but the nation's lawmakers had no idea how to administer this kind of work; they depended on individual entrepreneurs to show them the way—men like Hayden. Building on the reputation he had established before the war, Hayden did his job so well and made such effective use of publicity that more than anyone else he drew attention to the importance of western surveying. By making his exploring activities interesting to a popular audience, he eventually drew rivals into the field: men like John Wesley Powell and George Montague Wheeler. Clarence King's survey began on the same day as Hayden's (2 March 1867, authorized by separate legislation), but King's survey never approached Hayden's in attracting public attention.

Hayden's formal instructions from Commissioner Wilson underlined how much his new survey would be a continuation of his earlier work. In calling for a survey of geologic formations, a collection of minerals, fossils, and barometrical observations, an appraisal of coal deposits, and a geologic map, the government endorsed Hayden's established track record. In directing him to study the potential for farming and to recommend how best to grow timber, the government asked him to elaborate on observations he had already published. True, he would now have to emphasize the economic value of the coal more than its geographic expanse, and in performing analyses of soil he would be breaking new ground for the future of agriculture.

Hayden deployed some interesting innovations in 1867 that went beyond his instructions. He began purchasing photographs of Indians for the Smithsonian, the American Philosophical Society, and the Philadelphia Academy. He also hired an unnamed photographer from Chicago to accompany him for part of the season, though the man seems to have worked on geologic and geographic subjects, not Indians. In the larger context of Hayden's evolving work to this point, these innovations are merely expansions on his old desire to create an all-purpose natural history (and now ethnological) survey. Incidentally, though not justified in doing so by his instructions, Hayden continued to collect a variety of zoological and botanical specimens, which he tactfully promised to Baird. Finally, with solid funding from government, Hayden could begin to implement the scientific extravaganza he had envisioned years before.

Actually, the government played right into Hayden's plans for a popular survey. In an addendum written two weeks after he penned Hayden's original orders, Wilson urged Hayden to get as many illustrations as possible of landscapes, outcrops, strata, specimens, and so on, which, Wilson thought, "would be of great service in showing to Congress and to the country the beautiful results of a judicious expenditure of money in prosecuting such inquiries as those which have been confided to you." Of course, the idea originated with Hayden, who had been gathering such materials since at least 1866 for use in his lectures at Penn. It only reinforces the point to note that on his own initiative Hayden would soon hire landscape artist Henry Elliott and photographer William Henry Jackson.

The following year—1868, Hayden's second as U.S. geologist in charge of the Geological Survey of Nebraska—he created his own instructions. Commissioner Wilson based his official orders on Hayden's detailed suggestions, drafted three weeks before his appropriation was approved. All of which shows something more than Hayden's initiative, something that looks remarkably like the tail wagging the dog. The situation deserves emphasis because it is unfamiliar and seems to defy conventional wisdom about institutional behavior. The government was trying to accommodate the urgent public desire that the West be populated and settled, yet its powers were limited. Having provided such incentives as homestead acts and railroad charters, the best the government could do was contain the Indians and stand clear of the unstoppable forces pushing west. Men like Hayden were indispensable. Essentially he was an intermediary between the raw and unbridled materialism underlying western migration and the devices that legitimize and stabilize such relentless forces. He offered inventories of the land and descriptions of the resources, which encouraged the profitable development of private property. He showed the railroader, the land developer, and the town planner where to do their work, and through his enthusiastic advice to the miner, the farmer, and the rancher he provided the railroads and the developers with plenty of customers. Commissioner Wilson summarized it succinctly: "Your labors cannot fail to promote the public interest and will be appreciated by the Department."

Despite their common interests, Wilson and Hayden developed a mutual antagonism. Hayden chafed under bureaucratic regulations. He wanted money advanced to him in the field, but he was told to accumulate receipts for expenses and wait for reimbursement; he wanted samples shipped directly to the specialists who would write up those materials, but the department collected everything in Washington; he wanted assurances about using plates to illustrate his reports, but the department authorized only what had been specifically provided by appropriation. At the same time it cannot have been easy for Wilson to ride herd on a man constitutionally incapable of accepting any authority he could not manipulate. Wilson wanted Hayden to restrict his activities to the letter of his instructions. Hayden could not resist playing to the crowd, whether in addressing the Nebraska legislature on the importance of his survey, giving promotional talks at a county agricultural fair, or speechifying in various towns along his route. Most of these activities were harmless and probably reinforced the purposes of the commissioner, but at this time Hayden also chose to vent in the Kansas newspapers his private quarrels with George Swallow over the Permian rocks. Wilson was annoyed, but there wasn't much he could do. Besides, in some respects Hayden was a model employee: he prepared practical plans, accomplished what he set out to do, kept up with his correspondence, and filed timely reports.

He did these things not just to satisfy the demands of his employer but to promote his own plans. Because his reports were prompt and popular, he saw to it that they were widely circulated and summarized in magazine articles. Such publicity stimulated the appetite for practical knowledge of the West, which in turn increased the pressure on his employer to keep him occupied. Hayden applied this fine instinct for publicity to his other publications. He reissued some of his work with Meek on the invertebrates of the Upper Missouri. He arranged for Leidy to send their joint publication to England in time to be reviewed by Thomas Huxley during his year as president of the British Association for the Advancement of Science. He prepared specially bound copies of several of his works (and later virtually all his survey's annual reports) for presentation to congressmen and influential friends. After 1869 he made sure that his survey's publications reached learned societies, libraries, universities and schools, museums, journal editors, popular magazines, newspapers, publishers, and mapmakers. A constant theme of his correspondence with Baird in the 1870s is the widest possible dissemination of his works. Baird wanted this too, because by broadcasting Hayden's many volumes the Smithsonian qualified for exchanges from the recipients. All this redounded to Hayden's personal benefit. In fall 1866 he was elected a member of the Dakota Historical Society and the next January of the Buffalo Society of Natural History. It was only the harbinger of much wider recognition.

Publicity worked both ways. Once the demand existed, Hayden could scarcely keep up with requests for his works from countless individuals: congressmen, western governors, state officers, federal officials, land offices, county assessors, state geological surveys, teachers and professors, amateur naturalists and ethnologists, doctors, railroad agents, land agents, miners, travelers, farmers, ranchers, army officers, Indian agents and commissioners, authors, a variety of businessmen and lawyers, and a host of foreign governments, societies, and individuals. Before 1870 only a trickle of Hayden's publications reached eager readers compared to the deluge that began early in that decade, but the pattern was established as soon as Hayden got his hands on the public floodgates. Once a hungry public began to seek his works, Hayden knew how to take advantage of the situation. In return for sending his publications he asked the recipients to write reviews of them or to send them to other influential people or to mention to their congressman how much they appreciated them. He understood perfectly the connection between making an impression with his publications and generating annual appropriations.

After two seasons in the field—1867 and 1868—Hayden completed the work of the Nebraska survey. Once its appropriations were spent and its legal authority had expired at the end of January 1869, Hayden was temporarily out of a job. In order not to miss fieldwork in 1869, Hayden lined up several private sponsors willing to fund him should the wheels of bureaucracy fail to provide a prompt appropriation.

He need not have worried. Though official instructions did not reach him until April, Hayden knew by early March that he would return to the field that summer. He would have $10,000 and would now be free of the General Land Office, reporting directly to the new secretary of the interior, Jacob Cox, who, by a happy coincidence, had been a friend of Hayden's while both were students at Oberlin. Hayden also had strong support from a group of western congressmen who could see the advantages of continuing the work of this enterprising professor. One of Hayden's chief boosters shortly after his arrival in Washington in 1867 was Representative (later Senator) John A. Logan of Illinois. Another early friend was Congressman (later Senator) Henry L. Dawes of Massachusetts. Despite the vicissitudes of political leadership and the turmoil surrounding civil service reform that raged through the 1870s, Hayden became a fixture in the Interior Department, doing some of its proudest work, bringing it recognition from home and abroad, and outlasting several secretaries in the process. Hayden was now firmly in the saddle.

His relations with English capitalist William Blackmore illustrate not only other entrepreneurial schemes but also Hayden's method of combining public responsibility with private interest. Blackmore already had a reputation as a bold and acquisitive developer. During the Civil War he had proposed to Congress to raise a series of loans for the Union cause from foreign sources, taking land from the public domain as security. Later he helped to market the stock of the Union Pacific Railroad in Europe. He met Hayden in Laramie during September 1868, while consulting with officials of the Union Pacific regarding a merger with the Central Pacific. It was through his railroad connections that Blackmore heard of the vast Sangre de Cristo Land Grant in New Mexico and Colorado owned by William Gilpin. He conceived a plan to purchase part of the grant and develop it for resale to European immigrants. Before proceeding, he enlisted Hayden to do a resource survey of his proposed property.

Wasting no time, Hayden dashed through a part of the grant (the San Luis Valley in Colorado) during late October and November, finishing up in the field on 19 November. By 5 December he had completed a five-page report, which was published the next year in London as part of Blackmore's promotional book *Colorado: Its Resources, Parks, and Prospects*. Despite the enthusiastic endorsement by a United States geologist and university professor (which exaggerated the economic prospects for the region), Blackmore had trouble recruiting investors.

Blackmore paid Hayden $500 in cash for his report and gave him shares of stock in one of the companies organized out of the grant. The stock seems to have been worth no more than several hundred dollars, and Hayden sold his shares after a year. Although he cheerfully took the money, his motive for cooperating with Blackmore was not financial gain. In 1871 Blackmore offered him far more dazzling prospects: the leadership of a thorough survey of his entire holdings, doubtless more stock, and the directorship of a proposed geological institute in Colorado that Blackmore would establish to advance science. But Hayden turned him down and kept saying no when Blackmore persisted.

Blackmore's appeal was more in his manner than his money. He was a cosmopolitan man of the world who took pleasure in the rugged outdoor life of the West. Blackmore also boasted an interest in science. His collection of Indian artifacts and his quick appreciation of photography made an immediate impression on Hayden. Running off to examine the San Luis Valley for Blackmore had been a spontaneous gesture, a personal favor for an admired friend. If he was paid for it, fine; if science benefited in the long run, as Blackmore certainly hinted, so much the better. But Hayden never showed much inclination for the risks of high finance; therefore he hesitated to ally himself too closely with a man whose business success depended on cultivating foreign investors. It also occurred to Hayden that if Blackmore persisted with his grandiose ideas, he might become a rival for that precious favor of Congress on which Hayden had staked his career. He decided to stay independent in a line of work he understood and for which he had gained wide reputation.

As soon as he returned to Denver after surveying Blackmore's land, he gained something far more valuable than any money he earned through the Sangre de Cristo estates. During the course of an interview with the *Rocky Mountain News* (published 20 November), Hayden praised the quality of coal around Marshall and Boulder, both in Colorado. Those deposits had nothing to do with Blackmore's holdings, but Hayden shrewdly used the interview to call attention to an important resource. That kind of publicity paid large dividends in Washington.

Meanwhile, though he would not enter into a partnership with him, Hayden maintained ties with Blackmore. He invited Blackmore to accompany him as a personal guest during his 1872 sojourn on the Upper Yellowstone. In 1873 Hayden brought his survey to Colorado Territory in large part to examine the San Juan mining districts, and it happened that some of those mining districts lay within Blackmore's Sangre de Cristo Land Grant. In 1875 Hayden authorized his second-in-command, James Terry Gardner, to prepare a *Report Upon the Southern Coal and Iron Fields of Colorado Territory.* Gardner did the field inspections during June and promptly sent Hayden a copy of his report, which endorsed the economic potential of coal mining between the Cucharas River and the Raton Mountains. It so happened that the Denver and Rio Grande Railway was looking into the feasibility of building an extension of its line to Trinidad to take advantage of these mines and that Blackmore was heavily involved in developing the Denver and Rio Grande. The railroad quoted Gardner's report in its promotional literature justifying the Trinidad extension.

These private dealings caused a commotion within Hayden's survey when Fred Endlich, the geologist in charge of the region where the Trinidad mines lay, got wind of the whole affair. He wrote an indignant letter to Hayden, asking whether he had authorized Gardner's irregular and (to Endlich) unsavory behavior. Hayden responded (untruthfully) that he had not; the answer satisfied Endlich. Hayden was not concerned about a wider scandal, only with keeping things smooth within his survey. By the standards of the time, he had done nothing improper and no conflict of interest existed.

Did Hayden take a fee from the railroad? There is no evidence of any payment, but that is hardly decisive. I suspect Hayden did not ask for a fee and probably did not get one. Hayden was a strange bird from several points of view, especially his ability to blend private interests with public duties and justify both as furthering science or bolstering development in the West. Of course, promoting science or development also helped Hayden because both translated into publicity that he could use to justify the continued sponsorship of Congress.

Meanwhile, Hayden's growing professional success was effecting changes in his relationships with colleagues, friends, and family. His relations with both Meek and Newberry showed signs of strain. In 1867 some of Meek's colleagues, especially Stimpson, encouraged him to apply for the Nebraska survey: "Why don't you go in <u>as chief</u> on the Nebraska survey? Don't let Hayden get ahead of you this time, you furnishing the brains and he getting the pay." But Meek was not a political animal, and he knew it; he "did not wish to enter upon a scramble with an old friend," as he put it to Dana. Besides, Hayden offered him the position of paleontologist for the Nebraska work, in which Meek would be more comfortable. Meek accepted that offer at a salary of $1,000, but on condition that his results would be published in his own name. It was a significant departure: never again would Meek and Hayden write an article together. Hayden could still show flashes of his old self with Meek: his enthusiasm, his temper, his ambition, and certainly great respect (and need) for Meek's professional assistance. But more and more his tie to Meek was all business.

Hayden asked Meek to prepare a careful analysis of the coal deposits in Nebraska. Hayden doubted that Nebraska possessed useful quantities of coal, but he realized the citizens of the new state thought otherwise.[3] "This coal business is most important," he wrote Meek, with a sharp appreciation for the political implications. "In examining the pit sunk at Nebraska City, if you find no signs of coal, let them down gently, for it will almost kill the Survey to come out boldly with the statement, 'no coal.'" After Meek confirmed his own suspicions about Nebraska's coal deposits, Hayden announced the discouraging news in three different articles for the *American Journal of Science*. Apparently satisfied with their recent cooperation, but perhaps missing some of the warmth of their earlier years, Hayden wrote toward the end of 1867, "Whatever success I have I will always <u>share</u> with you and I am anxious you should do the same by me. Our names will be ever identified with the geology of this country. When I have power I will always do by you whatever you <u>yourself</u> will say is right."

Meek must have found this remark somewhat disingenuous for he groused about Hayden to Charles Abiathar White, state geologist of Iowa. His exact complaint is uncertain because we know of it only through White's reply. Meek probably feared Hayden would reap the public credit for work he had done. Such resentment flared in Meek from time to time and with good reason. He had every bit as much professional pride and ambition as Hayden, yet none of the pizzazz needed to translate ability into public acclaim. Few scholars did. As Hayden became more and more successful, he became more and more cordially despised by many of his colleagues for this very reason.

And by none more than Newberry. Right after the Civil War Hayden and Newberry managed briefly to meet on a beach of friendship before resuming their downstream drift toward estrangement. Forgotten for the moment was the antebellum rivalry of two pioneering geologists as they both rejoiced in being back in harness at the work they loved. Not long afterward, however, the rivalry recommenced. In his first postwar publication on his favorite subject, Hayden stated that the lignites in Colorado and Wyoming were part of the same basin he had called the Great Lignite on the Upper Missouri and that the Great Lignite was Tertiary in age. On the basis of some work in New Mexico, Newberry countered that the lignites were Cretaceous. He later drew the same conclusion regarding fossil plants from the Green River Basin. Hayden would not budge.

Newberry had often treated him condescendingly, which only irritated the proud Hayden. Then there was Newberry's annoying habit of keeping specimens for a long time without reporting on them. This behavior had embarrassed Hayden more than once, especially when it seemed Newberry's tardiness would delay one of Hayden's publications. To avoid such difficulties Hayden arranged for Leo Lesquereux to study his first fossil plants from Nebraska, and he made sure Newberry knew it. Thus began another partnership similar to that with Meek, whereby Hayden provided materials and Lesquereux wrote them up; Hayden then published the results in his reports. Lesquereux was a most congenial collaborator: not only did he complete his studies promptly, but his view on the lignites came close to Hayden's.

With Hayden's survey gathering momentum and acclaim from the late 1860s, Lesquereux and Newberry were competing for the prize in paleobotany: the exclusive right to publish Hayden's fossil plants. When it looked like Lesquereux would get the advantage of the fresh materials from Nebraska, Newberry volunteered to contribute $1,000 to Hayden in case he needed private sponsorship to return to the field in 1869. This offer came in the interval between the end of Hayden's Nebraska survey and the official continuation of his work under different supervision. This generous favor caused Hayden to soften his attitude toward Newberry, and he let Newberry look at his plants from 1868 with the promise of seeing more from 1869.

The subsequent rivalry between Lesquereux and Newberry caused the final rupture between Newberry and Hayden. For six years beginning in June 1870 Hayden gave all his new fossil plants to Lesquereux for study; simultaneously he offered Newberry the chance to publish other results through various outlets of the respected Hayden Survey. Though Newberry did write two insignificant pieces for Hayden, he failed to provide the detailed reports Hayden wanted on the fossils still in his possession. Instead he began to dislike Hayden and disparage his survey. He circulated a very nasty series of calumnies based on his own hurt feelings and his desire for revenge. Hayden wanted "the monopoly of the palaeontology of the West and nothing is to be given to the public on that subject except through his reports, and thus no views except his are to have a hearing," Newberry wrote to James Hall on 10 June 1874. "Meek has been chastened by Hayden and will do nothing for anybody else," he continued; therefore, in "the best interests of science" Hall should undertake to write up Clarence King's Paleozoic fossils. That he was deliberately stirring up old hostilities between Meek and Hall and new ones between Hayden and King, Newberry understood full well.

Meanwhile Newberry played a delaying game with Hayden, asking to see some of Lesquereux's materials in order to make comparisons with his own. The request was sensible in view of scientific questions of duplication and synonymy, but it disguised another purpose. By late 1875, if not well before, Newberry had abandoned any idea of publishing his results with Hayden, for he had been negotiating with Powell to bring out a catalog of fossil plants through Powell's survey. As he candidly admitted to Powell on 11 January 1876, the catalog had to wait "till I have Lesquereux's plates which (between ourselves) I shall then know precisely what he has described and what is new." He then unabashedly wrote Hayden asking for Lesquereux's material.

Lesquereux saw at once what Newberry was trying to do. "That demand of the Tertiary plates by Newberry troubles me much," he wrote Hayden on 17 February 1876. "You know well enough that he is unworthy of any kind of confidence and I do not believe that he will be more disposed to work his report with my plates in hand than without." He went on to say Newberry "has fooled you with promises" for the past ten years. Still trying to play peacemaker, Hayden asked if Lesquereux would either loan materials to Newberry for his inspection or allow him to see them in Lesquereux's home. Lesquereux's response of 29 April 1876 seems to have exhausted Hayden's efforts to gain concessions for Newberry: "I will not have him here ransacking my specimens for his own pleasure . . . Newberry has not any right to know about my work or to look over its materials before it is ready."

More than a year earlier Lesquereux had warned Hayden: "I will have nothing whatever to do with Newberry. You have many times wondered at my antipathy against this man. It comes from old acquaintance with his character. But you will still have more to do with him. If he can do anything to harm you be sure that he will not miss any opportunity offered to him for that." And he repeated the message frequently. By 1876 Hayden seems to have given up on Newberry. Lesquereux went on to write up a number of results for Hayden's *Annual Reports* and his *Bulletin*. Most importantly, he wrote the three substantial volumes for Hayden's *Final Reports* on the Cretaceous and Tertiary flora of the West. All of which only added to Newberry's resentment and encouraged him to dip his pen deeper into gall.

With the exception of the disgruntled Newberry, Hayden's colleagues joined in the general chorus of acclaim for his survey. Reflecting on the early years of the survey's success, Dana wrote Hayden, "I should like to see you employed there for ten years to come." Shortly afterward Dana was writing Hayden's boss, the secretary of the interior, to credit Hayden as the principal source of his own information about the Rocky Mountains. In January 1870 Charles Henry Hitchcock asked Hayden to collaborate on a geologic map of the United States. Hayden agreed, and he eventually provided information for the maps of Kansas, Nebraska, Dakota, Colorado, Wyoming, Montana, and Idaho. Josiah Whitney, head of the California Geological Survey, suggested a cooperative venture with Hayden, to produce a "geological map and section of the region west of the Mississippi River." Whitney wrote again in February 1870 praising the "brilliant results" of Hayden's recent reconnaissance work, and he hoped Hayden would be adequately funded to continue. He also wrote Secretary Cox saying as much. Whitney found Hayden's work on mining engineering (a particular interest of Whitney) inadequate, and he hoped Hayden would provide more detail on the correlation of topography to geology. A direct result was that beginning with the next field season, in 1871, Hayden hired Anton Schönborn as his chief topographer. Hayden's closer interest in producing good topographic maps dates from that season.

Although Hayden was gaining the general approval of his colleagues, he was losing opportunities for closer personal ties. Certainly his relationship with Baird cooled after Hayden moved to Philadelphia, even though he still spent parts of each winter in Washington arranging his collections. But gone was the fawning respect Hayden had formerly shown for Baird, gone the vulnerable confessions of the enthusiastic naturalist. In their place Hayden communicated mostly a series of impatient demands. Unlike some men who enlarge their circle of acquaintance as they become successful, Hayden turned the other way. He rarely wrote to George Engelmann any more. His letters to James Hall spoke pure formality, even though Hall had spent a few days in the field with him during 1868. He did not take advantage of their mutual interests in western geology to move closer to Dana, or Lesley, or William Barton Rogers, or John Lawrence LeConte. Mutual suspicions ruined a budding friendship with Marsh. With the exception of the young Edward Cope, no new colleagues became friends. Interestingly, the few new friends to emerge later in the 1870s fell into two distinct groups. Some seemed to appeal because of their physical or professional distance: a Scot, an Englishman, and a Yale philologist; others because of their personal commitment to the Hayden Survey. We will meet these men in subsequent chapters.

A declining interest in family and old friends reveals the shift in

Hayden's personal orientation. He no longer made the dutiful trips to Rochester as he had done so often in the 1850s and early 1860s. Except for helping his brother get a job in Washington, he showed no interest in his family at all, and he only heard about them through Chester Dewey. When that old friend died in 1867, Hayden could not find time to go north for the funeral; and he did not visit his mother later that same year when she became a widow. An Oberlin friend wrote to scold Hayden for not visiting in St. Louis on his way back from the field. Reminiscing, he gave Hayden the chance to revive a close friendship.

> Now Ferdinand write me a long old fashioned letter of friendship. Let me know how you are getting along, all about yourself as you used to write. It will do me a world of good. You need not tell me of material prosperity for that I know, nor of professional success, for that all the country knows, but open the long shut chambers of the heart and tell me how you enjoy life. Whether you are married or still single. Whether as life becomes shorter you feel the satisfaction of having realized the fond dreams of college days.

Alas, a year and a half later his old friend in St. Louis was still asking for the open-hearted response that never came. Hayden did not even bother to tell him of his recent engagement or subsequent marriage.

Hayden had certainly realized "the fond dreams of college days"—no doubt much more than he could have dared to dream—but it is questionable how much satisfaction he took in his accomplishments. Satisfaction goes hand in hand with confidence; it brings with it a certain amount of contentment and expansiveness as the ego proudly proclaims the newfound dimensions of self. But Hayden was closing down, narrowing more than he was opening up. Even as his survey successfully encompassed more territory, he became obsessed with fears of being replaced by rivals.

14
TO CAPTURE THE
WEST, 1867–1870

Never has my faith in the grand future that awaits the entire West been so strong as it is at the present time, and it is my earnest desire to devote the remainder of the working days of my life to the development of its scientific and material interests, until I shall see every Territory, which is now organized, a State in the Union. Out of the portions of the continent which lie to the northward and southward of the great central mass, other Territories will, in the meantime, be carved, until we shall embrace within our limits the entire country from the Arctic Circle to the Isthmus of Darien.
—Hayden, in the preface to his *Fourth Annual Report,* pp. 6–7

HAYDEN HAD BEEN a long time finding the means to do what he wanted. Starting out with only his dreams and gradually recruiting assistance from influential patrons, he found employment as a collector of natural history specimens. His curiosity and boundless energy made him a superlative collector, the more so because he ignored specialization and embraced the whole natural world for his province in ever-expanding regions of the American West. He was much more than a collector, however, and his studies of geology and paleontology led him to ponder and write about the dynamic natural forces that wrought structure and wreaked havoc on the Earth and among its creatures. By persistently badgering his colleagues, by exploiting his talent for making friends from all walks of life, by exerting raw courage and presumption, he managed to find sponsors who would keep him employed in the field. During that time he probably gave little thought to any ultimate goals, beyond writing up the materials he constantly collected. What would he do if given a relatively secure and growing sponsorship?

While working on his Survey of Nebraska and then unfurling his Survey of the Territories he was groping for an answer to that question.

The first thing he had to do was adjust his thinking to longer term projects. He had become known as an individual entrepreneur for science, adept at launching his own ventures or attaching himself to any expedition that would suit his purposes. Now he needed to become more of an organization man, capable of building something and making it last. He learned to do that, but even as his survey became a respected institution it retained very much the imprint of Hayden's individuality. That was its beauty, its strength, and ultimately its downfall.

At first glance Hayden does not resemble the successful departmental administrator. Impatient and impetuous, he strained against the restrictions of bureaucracy. And he did not manage his own time well. While rushing to prepare himself for the field each spring, he frequently had to impose on Meek or Leidy to revise some of his writings at the last minute or correct proof on an article and see it through the printer. He misplaced important documents, he forgot to arrange forwarding addresses for his mail, he underestimated his expenses in the field, and even after a decade's experience he was still damaging some of his specimens by packing them hastily. Such telltale examples of carelessness did not disappear when he took charge of his own survey. But focusing too closely on his warts neglects the overall ability of the man. What he might lose through carelessness, he regained by resourcefulness. Beyond his innate shrewdness was a relentless intelligence, which enabled him to confront new circumstances and adapt to them. And when convinced of its necessity, he could plow his way through acres of the most tedious work. For instance, in tackling his correspondence.

Over the twelve years of the survey's existence, Hayden amassed a pile of nearly 19,000 pages of manuscript materials, mostly letters. These papers are preserved at the National Archives and constitute the in-basket of his correspondence, which came from more than 1,500 different writers. He might have dictated to scribes some of the formal responses required by the secretary of the interior, the prefaces to his annual reports, and miscellaneous memos designed to influence congressional opinion; but he himself seems to have directed the entire paperflow of the survey. Hayden's out-basket letters are widely dispersed and have not survived in the same quantity as the letters to him, but the survivals suggest that Hayden personally handled a high percentage of this correspondence. If we assume that every incoming letter generated a reply, the survey responded to an average of 125 correspondents every year for twelve years, and many wrote more than once. A great many letters requested the survey's publications; congressmen often wrote on behalf of their constituents. Because the publications offered the chief means of promoting his survey, Hayden answered many of these letters himself, especially when his correspondent was in a position to give the publications wider exposure. He also liked to reply personally when a university or a society or a library requested one of his publications. Hayden let his staff respond to most of the job inquiries, which came from young adventure seekers as well as established geologists and naturalists from all over the country. For the most part Hayden reserved to himself the task of answering important individuals and the bigwigs who sponsored them.[1]

He adopted standard language for a number of responses, but he also crafted individual messages for many correspondents. Even the standard language changed from time to time or from one colleague to another, and no scribe could balance all the subtle nuances as well as Hayden. Besides, he seems to have done his letter writing during the evenings, long after his staff had gone home. (I say "staff," but there was only one other person or perhaps two, and they only became available in 1873.)

So the sobering routine of the survey's work cured Hayden of some of his sloppiness and impatience. But efficient clerking is not the same as successful administration. For that he needed to build ideas, sell them to his sponsors, then bring them to fruition in the field. These tasks admirably suited his strengths, which were in promotion, lobbying, and what we now call public relations, a new art form in Hayden's day; he understood PR far better than most of his contemporaries. Hayden was an interesting mix of the old and the new. On the one hand his natural ambition led him in the direction of the old-fashioned entrepreneur who builds his own exclusive empire; on the other hand he carved out that empire by effective use of publicity. A final assessment of Hayden as administrator must wait for another chapter, but it is clear he possessed all the requisite skills. To the extent that he failed in his larger designs, we can blame his judgment, not lack of ability.

A good measure of administrators is the quality of people they recruit and the ability to keep them. By inclination self-centered and ambitious, and not always easy to work with, Hayden might have driven away the best people. Quite the reverse happened. He began with very little help, depending at first on his old comrade Meek, whom he hired to estimate whether the coal beds in Iowa continued into Nebraska. By now Meek was perhaps the best invertebrate paleontologist in the country, and Hayden managed to keep him in harness for the remainder of his life. He contributed many articles and monographs to Hayden's reports. Cyrus Thomas was a naturalist with a particular talent for entomology. Before making Hayden's acquaintance, he had founded the Illinois Natural History Society in 1858 and had shown admirable versatility as a county clerk, school administrator, and minister of the Evangelical Lutheran Church. Baird had recommended him to Hayden. He wrote reports on agriculture and entomology for four of Hayden's annual reports and managed Hayden's Washington office during the summers of 1873 and 1874. He remained a loyal supporter of Hayden throughout the life of the survey and became a member of the Entomological Commission—created in 1877 as an adjunct to Hayden's survey. During the mid-1870s he was also a professor at Southern Illinois Normal School and held the post of Illinois state entomologist. Later on, he became best known for his skill in anthropology, especially for his work on the mound builders of Illinois.

Artist Henry Elliott signed on in 1868 and worked with Hayden for three seasons. Photographer William Henry Jackson worked with Hayden all through the 1870s, while making his reputation as one of the premier landscape photographers of America. They met in Cheyenne during summer 1869 in a brothel, where Jackson had been negotiating with the madam regarding some pictures of the place and its girls. Jackson recorded their meeting. "In the evening had to go around to Madame Cleveland's & was much surprised to see Dr. Hayden come in with some military friends. He acted like a cat in a strange joint." And, of course, Hayden's longtime field assistant, Jim Stevenson, continued with him for the duration of the survey, graduating to general field manager in 1869.

Hayden invested quite a lot of time in his experts, who prepared various natural history reports for his publications. These men had to be recruited, oriented, dispatched, paid, and heard from. They required frequent reminders about details and deadlines. For instance, after Hayden and a writer agreed on the idea for a report, they had to discuss its length, extent of coverage, and use of illustrations. Would illustrations be produced from woodcuts or stone engravings? Would a steel engraving be preferable? Who would do the actual artwork? Would it be necessary to borrow illustrations from a third source? What costs could be expected? Once he received a text from each author, Hayden had to work with the public printer on scheduling its production. Proofs went back to the author for correction, and it was not uncommon for pages or illustrations to be misplaced in the process. As deadlines approached, a nervous Hayden pestered his colleagues, warning them of the delays that would ensue if they interrupted the schedule of the public printer. No one seems to have trusted the postal system; thus typically a flurry of worried letters flew back and forth between Hayden and his authors. (In Hayden's day letters arrived more promptly than ours do today, at least for short distances between major cities on the eastern seaboard.)

Meanwhile Hayden's personal prestige attracted a number of prominent men to collaborate with the survey. Charles White, then state geologist of Iowa, assisted Meek on questions of Nebraska coal in 1867. White later became a permanent member of Hayden's survey. For that first year the leading botanist of the day, John Torrey, agreed to work up Hayden's lignites. Samuel H. Scudder did the same for insects, and Samuel W. Johnson of Yale agreed to analyze the soil samples. James Hall and the great Louis Agassiz both visited Hayden in the field and traveled with him for several days during 1868. For a while in 1870 three of America's leading artists sketched with the survey: John Frederick Kensett, Thomas Worthington Whittredge, and Sanford Robinson Gifford, who remained a friend of Hayden's long afterward. From 1870 Hayden's annual reports announced the latest finds in paleontology, zoology, and botany of the West and provided a collection of miscellaneous articles on natural history. To mention only the contributors to the 1870 report, Hayden assembled a tribe of prominent naturalists consisting of Meek, Newberry, Lesquereux, Leidy, Cope, Thomas C. Porter, Charles Christopher Parry, and James Thatcher Hodge, as well as others just coming into their own, like Cyrus Thomas, S. R. Roberts, George Henry Horn, and Philip Reese Uhler, men who enhanced their reputations through work for Hayden.

Hayden's ideas about what to do with his survey congealed between 1867 and 1870, and his experience in the field influenced those ideas. We need to watch him at work a while in order to understand the evolution of his plans. More precisely, we need to listen to what he said about his work and note the change in his manner of reporting on it. In the various articles and reports he published before 1867 Hayden gave only a cursory account of his travels; he squirreled away many of the more important details in his private correspondence, which wound up in scattered manuscript collections. After 1867 he continued in the same manner, but as he realized the value of publicity he learned to record most of the facts in his annual reports. By the end of the 1870 season, which he summarized in his *Fourth Annual Report,* he had worked out the routine he wanted for his fieldwork and found an attractive format for communicating his deeds to the public.[2]

In 1867 he compiled a sweeping commentary on the geology and natural resources of the whole state of Nebraska. By then settlers had formed pockets of population in the southeastern part of the state. Hayden began by walking through all but one of the settled counties, commenting on whatever resources he could find. Then his report took flight, as he extended his remarks to the entire state. He summarized the geology north of the Platte River, along the Missouri, which he had observed many times during the 1850s. In places that had agricultural potential, he discussed soil quality and carefully identified the surface layers and their age. He opined that the western half of the state was too high and dry for agriculture, though it would be suitable for pasturage—except for the 20,000 square miles in the extreme northwestern corner where numerous alkaline lakes rendered the land barren. Still, most of this huge new state beckoned the settler: "Surely the great West, with its broad fertile acres, to be had almost for the asking, through the generosity of our Government, is the poor man's paradise." However, he candidly admitted Nebraska lacked rich mineral resources, including coal; the seams in Nebraska were either too thin or too deeply buried to be of commercial value. For not telling them what they wanted to hear, newspaper editors in Nebraska blasted Hayden as a "charlatan and humbug." Many citizens had convinced themselves (on no evidence but faith) that large stores of coal existed, but Hayden courageously refused to knuckle under to their pressure. Time proved his views to be correct.

He thought most hardwood trees familiar in the East could flourish in Nebraska and take the place of coal as a fuel. Several times he recommended extensive tree planting in his report, and Commissioner Wilson picked up the thought and passed it on in his annual report. Meanwhile, there was enough peat to use as a fuel. The chief economic resources Hayden identified in quantity were limestone, potters' clay, and sand. Although the Tertiary layers discouraged agriculture, they yielded treasures that fascinated the thoughtful citizen: camels, rhinos, the largest elephant ever known, wolves larger than present species, and numerous horses large and small. All of that he published in his annual report.

His letters reveal how far afield he traveled while working on the survey of Nebraska. After tramping through the settled counties of the state, he obtained railroad passes to the end of the line, near Julesburg, Colorado, where he looked for fossils. Regarding Julesburg, he wrote to a friend, "This place has been called the hardest place on earth. There is somebody killed here almost every night." But it was just Hayden's kind of place: "This wild instinctive life suits me splendidly and I shall follow it up, I think, for many years to come." Indians frustrated his plan to hunt for more bones near the headwaters of the Loup Fork. From Julesburg he made a dash to Fort Sanders (near modern Laramie), then took the railroad west to the Green River area, again looking for fossils and making geological sections. He even had time for a sprint south into Colorado, where he looked quickly at coal along the Front Range, probably as far south as the Pikes Peak area. From there he took the stage and railroad back to Omaha, where he and Jim Stevenson obtained a skiff and descended the Missouri to the mouth of the Kansas River, making more geological sections along the way.

He financed his wanderings in creative fashion. Because Wilson would not advance him funds, Hayden paid his assistants from his own pocket and took out loans to keep operations afloat until he could receive cash for approved expenses. He economized by hunting wild game. But he wasn't suffering. In Pawnee City he was able to buy bacon, coffee, tea, sugar, soda crackers, gingersnaps, dried beef, ham, and cans of oysters, jellies, and peaches. Later he purchased fresh milk, butter, eggs, beef, bread, flour, and vegetables from farmers, and in Omaha he found such delectables as tartar sauce and syrup.

Hayden's Nebraska work was such a success that Commissioner Wilson recommended, on Hayden's suggestion, that he continue his survey into Wyoming and Colorado in 1868. The Sundry Civil Bill authorized $5,000 for the purpose. The Smithsonian laid on an additional $1,500 for natural history samples—which stirred up a bit of controversy. Ever since Congress accepted the half-million-dollar bequest of James Smithson, the French-born British scientist, to found an institution for the "increase and diffusion of knowledge among men," there had been questions about the proper use of such a fund and such an institution. The first secretary, Joseph Henry, successfully resisted for a while the idea of building up a large library. He also opposed the notion of collecting whatever animals, vegetables, and minerals struck the fancy of naturalists. On the occasion of receiving Hayden's collections for 1868, Henry recorded in his private diary: "Stated to Dr. Hayden that my policy in regard to collections is that the Smithsonian fund must be guarded from absorption in a museum. We cannot accept specimens on the condition that the Smithsonian fund is pledged to forever preserve them." Of course, since its inception in 1846 the Smithsonian had been doing just that: becoming the nation's official repository for specimens that flowed east in the wake of exploring expeditions. Joseph Henry thought a better use of the institution would be to sponsor original research, not dissipate limited resources on such limitless objects as books and fossils. On the other side, Assistant Secretary Baird had always wanted to create a museum, and every year the not-very-subtle pressure of his collecting friends, like Hayden, made Henry's position more and more untenable. By the time Baird succeeded as secretary in 1878 the National Museum was an established part of the Smithsonian.

Hayden did not reach the field in 1868 until early August. Starting from Cheyenne, he worked his way to the Green River area in southwestern Wyoming, using the stage routes. He made three major diversions along the way: to explore the Chugwater Valley near Cheyenne, then the recent gold strikes near Laramie, and lastly the North Park area of Colorado. After reaching the Green River, he turned around and came back to Cheyenne, boarded the railroad and repeated his western thrust beyond the Green River as far as the tracks would take him. He knew the general trend of the Rockies was northwest to southeast, but he observed ridges running off at every angle from the main spur, reflecting a variety of local forces throughout the mountains. "It becomes, therefore, quite important to describe the geology of every locality with minuteness, even at the risk of repetition and tediousness. . . . So little is known even of the outline of the great formations along this route, that any information, however brief, will be of interest." Whatever formations he found, he related to familiar outcrops surrounding the Upper Missouri. Though he continued his habit of describing features in the order encountered, he paused now and again over something exceptional, like glaciers. In the 1840s Louis Agassiz had drawn attention to the erosive power of glaciers in the Alps, and Hayden was among the first to translate Agassiz's perceptions to an understanding of the American landscape. In noting the evidence for glacially eroded valleys, Hayden was more alert than most of his contemporaries, including some members of his own survey who later overlooked numerous examples of glacial action in Colorado.

In the open country of southern Wyoming the geology presented fewer complications. Here the staggering coal and iron deposits and the potential for precious minerals captured his attention. Rich pasture land existed in the high valleys of the mountains, but the plains west of Laramie would never support agriculture. Hayden discussed the details in his 1868 report, but he prefaced that report with a succinct appraisal of the geography and geology of the entire country between the Missouri and the Rocky Mountains, emphasizing the major drainages in the Missouri Basin and the nature of the mountain ranges of Wyoming. That broad summary was not new: he assembled the facts from his previously published work, but the summary enabled him to place his discoveries of 1868 in a wider setting.

Hayden completed his assigned duties by late September, but he did not return immediately from the field. Because geologic and topographic features do not end at state borders, and because winter had not yet moved in, it was an efficient use of his time and money to extend his research into adjacent regions. The money was not actually his, of course, because it derived from a public appropriation, but he used it now for a couple of private ventures. He took a quick trip to Salt Lake City, apparently at the invitation of railroad officials who wanted advice on how and where to expand their track. He took a longer foray through Blackmore's land grant in the San Luis Valley. The two trips kept him in the field another month and a half. Technically, he was now fulfilling his agreement to gather specimens for the Smithsonian, but everyone realized he was also conducting private business. But no one objected, not even Commissioner Wilson. Everyone accepted the quasi-public nature of Hayden's work and realized that for the public survey to go forward it would have to accommodate various private arrangements. What has become intolerable to the ethics of our day (though still practiced) was permitted in Hayden's.

By the opening of his third season Hayden found his work widely appreciated, and other rewards followed recognition. His appropriation of $10,000 doubled that of the previous year, and he now reported directly to the new secretary of the interior, Jacob Dolson Cox. Commissioner Wilson had been reluctant to advance Hayden cash at the start of his fieldwork, but Cox found that by bonding Hayden he could advance him half his appropriation at the beginning of the season. Wilson and Cox were alike in one respect, however: both insisted on prompt summaries from Hayden, which they would then incorporate into their own annual reports. As a result, Hayden wrote most of his first three annual reports while still in the field. This urgent deadline permitted only tentative conclusions in the annual reports, and Hayden soon realized he needed another outlet to publish more systematic information at a later time. These would be subject reports, summarizing the work of several years on significant topics. (Three separate series eventually answered his needs in this respect: his *Final Reports,* the *Miscellaneous Publications,* and the *Unclassified Publications.*) Because the specialized studies would appeal largely to scholars, Hayden resolved that his annual reports should have a broad popular appeal. In the annual reports he would publish new discoveries and provide timely practical information on a regular basis.[3]

In his *Third Annual Report* for 1869 Hayden concentrated on the geology between Cheyenne and Santa Fe—including the San Luis Valley, the Arkansas Valley, South Park, and Middle Park. He described local outcrops of the major formations he identified in the region and gave provisional names to each of them. He depicted the relations between the major formations. His overall picture of the geology along the Front Range was sketchy, but in describing its basic structure and outline he provided the first scientific evaluation of this country. He obviously had an exciting summer: "To the geologist Colorado is almost encyclopedic in its character, containing within its borders nearly every variety of geological formation." Though incomplete, Hayden's report painted a clear and vivid picture, sufficient to enlighten any geologist. For the prospector the report of Persifor Frazer, "Mines and Minerals of Colorado," gave additional information. Frazer's report was the first example of an addendum on some specialized topic, and with each succeeding annual report Hayden made greater and greater use of this device to crowd in popular information or timely scientific announcements.

After finishing up the 1869 season in Denver by mid-October, Hayden made another excursion on his own. He never mentioned it in any publication, but the experience had a profound effect on his evolving ideas about the purpose and scope of his survey. He boarded the Union Pacific in Wyoming and went all the way to San Francisco. Keen to examine rock exposures in canyons and other places where the soil had been torn back, he persuaded the railroad to let him use the handcart, so he could follow the train but stop at interesting outcrops. Seeing new regions, especially the very different basin and range country on the far side of the Continental Divide, obviously had an expansive effect on Hayden. In the preface to his very next annual report, the *Fourth,* he shows symptoms of having contracted a kind of scientific manifest destiny. It was there he penned the extraordinary statement that appears at the head of this chapter.

Back in the field for summer 1870, Hayden wanted to complement his thrust of 1868 across Wyoming by two other parallel lines of exploration, one to the north, the other to the south of his previous route. He started from Cheyenne, headed north along the eastern slope of the Rockies to the North Platte River, then swung west along the Platte and Sweetwater rivers to South Pass, then along Big and Little Sandy creeks to the Green River, then west to Fort Bridger. For over a month he explored in the Green River region of southwestern Wyoming and in northeastern Utah, where he climbed several summits of the Uinta Mountains. He found former shorelines of the Great Salt Lake and demonstrated the lake's greater extent in Pliocene times. He argued that the lake had once been freshwater and only accumulated its saltiness in recent times when the outlets of the lake disappeared. He gave names to all the major formations between the lake and the Green River Basin in Wyoming. He showed a sharp understanding of the powerful forces of erosion that shaped the region, including what geologists now call aerial and subaerial forces—those that work in the atmosphere and on the surface. He was particularly perceptive about glacial erosion in the Uintas and in the Laramie Range. To return east he marched parallel to the southern border of Wyoming through the Medicine Bow Mountains, which he crossed at Bridger Pass, then traveled across the Laramie Plains back to Cheyenne. After dismissing his party at Cheyenne in early November, he remounted the Union Pacific with his artist, Henry Elliott, and rode to Salt Lake and back, studying and sketching important geological features and returning with "an excellent pictorial section of the entire road."

A number of Elliott's sketches appeared in the *Fourth Annual Report,* the first of Hayden's annual reports to carry illustrations. Apparently Elliott did not accompany the field parties during the 1868 season, but he did go west during the summers of 1869, 1870, and 1871. Most of the many illustrations he contributed to Hayden's reports were based on his own sketches, but the inspiration for several of his earlier illustrations is uncertain. One is based on a sketch by Meek. At least one other is based on a photograph by a Mr. Carbutt of Chicago, which Hayden purchased during summer 1868. Some others may have been inspired by Hayden's drawings. Also some of what Elliott later did in Yellowstone can be traced to Jackson's photographs.

After the 1870 season Hayden announced that his survey would do nothing less than chart the entire West, creating an extensive series of maps. His survey would "prepare a map of the districts explored, on a scale of two miles to the inch, not only to express the details of the geology with suitable colors, but also to show, for the benefit of our legislators, the amount of land that can be redeemed by irrigation, timber land, bottom land, etc." Hayden never adopted a uniform scale for his maps, but he used 4 miles to the inch on his sweeping renditions of the territories. More original than the 4-mile scale was his creation of "economic" maps with designations for the best use of the land: arable, pastoral, mineral, and timber. Hayden's idea for topical maps came several years before John Wesley Powell announced his plan to reclassify the lands of the West according to their potential uses. Such maps, Hayden pointed out, "would be of great importance in determining the value of land grants to railroads and other corporations, and would save to our Government many times the cost of the entire survey."

In several other respects the *Fourth Annual Report* (published in early 1871) announced the shape of things to come. In his first three annual reports Hayden identified formations by equating them with those already known in the Upper Missouri Basin; he described resources where encountered, like coal and iron, and he commented on the quality of soil and the likely crops it would support. But the *Fourth Annual Report* contained two very different geological reports. The first continued the style of the previous three annual reports by describing formations and resources. The second returned to the approach of *Geology and Natural History* (1862), which had been Hayden's first attempt at a popular blending of science and scenery. It was this second approach he adopted for all subsequent annual reports. For example, in the *Fourth* he followed the route of the railroad from Omaha to Salt Lake, summarizing the geology and geography in bold strokes, describing some of the extinct animals that once roamed the land, and planting teasers everywhere for tourists.

> The little streams [draining into the North Platte] that flow from the mountains have in many places quite broad valleys, which afford an abundance of hay and pasturage for all kinds of animals, wild and domestic. The wild animals often descend into the beautiful grassy bottoms to feed in large herds, and at the least approach of danger retire to the almost inaccessible ravines and gorges of the mountains. The big-horn or mountain sheep may often be seen in flocks, peering from some mountain peak upon the traveler below. Early in the morning these animals descend into the valleys to crop the moist grass, but during the greater portion of the day they will be found, if discovered at

all, upon the most precipitous crags and ridges of the mountains. The little streams are full of fine trout, which are easily caught, they not having learned as yet the cunning arts of self-protection, like their eastern relatives. . . . The close proximity of this delightful region to the railroad must make it a desirable place of resort for sportsmen during the summer.

Henceforth, Hayden added a large number of special reports by different experts. The *Third Annual Report* had contained only two: Frazer's on mines and minerals, and Cyrus Thomas's on agriculture. The *Fourth Annual Report* contained numerous specialized essays and catalogs on subjects ranging from fossilized plants and animals to living plants and such creatures as mollusks, insects, fishes, reptiles, mammals, and birds. Included were Cyrus Thomas's second analysis of agriculture in the West, James Hodge's essay on coal in Wyoming and Colorado, and J. W. Beaman's discussion of meteorology.

Most of these reports had a direct bearing on fieldwork done by members of Hayden's survey, but Hayden also introduced material of a broader nature. Neither Newberry's appraisal of ancient lakes west of the Mississippi, nor Richard Smith Elliott's survey of industrial resources in parts of Kansas and Colorado had anything to do with Hayden's survey. Indeed, looking closely at the fossil reports of Leidy, Cope, and Lesquereux, we find that they discuss samples gathered from many regions of the West, and by several collectors, not all of them members of Hayden's survey. Naturally, this scope made for better scientific reporting, and it signaled Hayden's wider ambitions.

By 1870 Hayden had set two goals for his survey's publications. First, they should summarize everything his survey chose to tackle: geological reconnaissance, geography, map making, resource inventories, and catalogs of natural history—broadly interpreted to include zoology, botany, paleontology, eventually even ethnology and archeology. He encouraged his specialists to publish through the survey rather than in scholarly journals. In this way he emphasized his own role in sponsoring diverse research, and he touted the versatility of his survey. Secondly, the survey should sponsor a separate shelf of books and articles on natural history that derived from research done outside the survey itself. The very fact that such a heterogeneous library could be amassed and paid for out of the survey's public funds demonstrates again how Hayden's personal proclivities dictated the scope and form of his survey. It was another example of Hayden instigating and the Department of the Interior providing.

In short, Hayden made a deliberate transition in 1870, and the *Fourth Annual Report* became the prototype for his future annual reports. The combination of his own popular reviews of geology with illustrations and numerous specialized reports from diverse experts proved a successful formula, and the survey prospered. The *Fourth Annual Report* boasted eighteen separate reports from various collaborators, the *Fifth* had nineteen, the *Sixth* twenty-two, and the *Seventh* twenty-six. Meanwhile appropriations increased accordingly: $25,000 in 1870; $40,000 in 1871; $75,000 in 1872, plus $10,000 for publication expenses; $75,000 in 1873, plus $20,000 for publications. As the survey expanded, Hayden built up a staff of geologists and topographers who gradually took over more of the fieldwork and the report writing. His last personal contribution came in the *Eighth Annual Report* for 1874 (published in 1876).

As the Hayden menagerie swelled so too did its need for field and fodder. To provide for his growing survey the leader now began honing some new skills. Flattery was among the most useful, and Hayden used it generously. He thanked the military authorities at several western posts for invaluable supplies he could not have obtained otherwise and also for intangible support: "At every military post we visited we were received with great attention, and numerous favors, so indispensable in the performance of our duties, were granted to us everywhere." He praised the railroad barons as enlightened patrons of science, from whom, "with comparatively few exceptions, I have received . . . every mark of appreciation I could desire." He praised individual journalists, businessmen, and citizens by name. He was astute enough to point out that the sum of all these favors reduced the actual costs of his publicly funded survey. Most of all he hailed each of his principal assistants and told the significance of their work. Behind the public eye, he was sharpening his lobbying skills as well. Increasingly, he visited congressmen, he wrote to them, and he persuaded his colleagues to coax them on his behalf. Regularly, he supplied them with his annual reports and the other offspring of his survey. To his inborn genius as a collector of fossils, Hayden now added a talent for gathering votes.

We might pause a moment to reflect that Hayden might easily have gone in another direction or in one of several directions. Professional success was encouraging most of his colleagues to specialize, and Hayden might have chosen to concentrate exclusively on geology. Or he might have opted for the simple life of a field collector, gradually augmenting his innate skills while extending his competence to an ever-widening circle of new species. Or he might have turned instead to writing—interpreting the output of science for a growing lay audience or depicting the wonders of the West for a swelling tide of tourists. He might have grown rich as a consultant, selling his knowledge of resources to developers and settlers. In a sense he did all those things except the last, but he did them within the context of a versatile scientific survey, a kind of empire that he personally created, administered, and ruled. The survey provided the only machinery with enough instruments to occupy Hayden's ambition, for he was a man who would not willingly give up anything once acquired.

He would like to have stayed on at the University of Pennsylvania, enjoying the trappings of a professor. Even though he knew his temperament was unsuited to the life of a scholar,[4] he did not resign from Penn for another two years (July 1872). By then he had accelerated his survey into high gear. There had been some talk of moving Hayden to a chair of geology in the college, which would have suited the illustrious leader of a government survey rather better than the auxiliary professorship he held in the medical department. The talk was mostly on Hayden's part, however; he wanted Leidy to lobby Provost Charles Stillé on the matter, but nothing came of it. He departed with the reputation of a popular teacher, and he took along one of his students who would become an important member of his survey: Albert Charles Peale.

Hayden's seven years in Philadelphia coincided with an experimental period in his life. He tried the life-style of a professor, but found it unsuitable. Even had Penn found a more honorable position for him, Hayden would not have rooted himself in Philadelphia. As his survey enlarged its appetite and added muscle, he realized his destiny was in the West. Only the encyclopedic sweep of his survey offered him an enterprise big enough and showy enough to satisfy his hunger for accomplishment and recognition. Hayden also swam in two of the most famous ponds open to learned gentlemen of scientific disposition: the Academy of Natural Sciences and the American Philosophical Society; but he only splashed around on the surface and never submerged himself seriously in either organization. He found the formality of these societies tiresome and their agendas limiting, and he could not transform himself into a gregarious bon vivant.

Hayden's marriage to Emma Woodruff was the most significant event of the years in Philadelphia. Emma was the daughter of a prominent Philadelphia merchant. She and Hayden met some time during 1867 and became engaged in January 1868. They were married on 9 November 1871.[5] Possessing few details of their early years together, I can only sketch some paths that wander across the wider landscape of their lives. Even before their marriage, Emma and Ferdinand saw a good deal of the Leidys (Joseph had married Anna Harden in 1864). A cordial relationship between the four endured. Emma, the youngest of the group (some fifteen years younger than Ferdinand and twenty-one younger than Leidy), would appear almost the child of her companions. Though attractive in her own way, she did not possess the good looks and easy social graces that would have earned her a squadron of suitors. She was twenty-seven when she and Ferdinand married, old by the standards of the time, but probably not by hers. She looks like someone with a mind of her own. The Leidys were probably quite fascinated by her, and Ferdinand quite proud. Only an accomplished woman could have entertained two of the country's foremost naturalists and been received repeatedly by the Leidys in their home.

Emma Hayden moved easily in the circles of Philadelphia society; it was home ground to her. To a bright girl of independent disposition, Ferdinand offered plenty of stimulation, and she probably wanted to show him off. No doubt she introduced her famous husband into those staid circles with a certain relish. Around the campfire he was a celebrated raconteur, and in the halls of Congress a skilled talker. He possessed an intense curiosity, and he read widely—well beyond the limits imposed by orthodoxy. He brandished ready opinions about politics, religion, and science. No doubt he enlivened many a parlor in Philadelphia with his tales of the frontier. Emma was probably a bit in awe of him, and she remained his loyal admirer. Even after his death (she outlived him by forty-six years), she busied herself erecting monuments to his memory.

If Emma did not already share Ferdinand's love of natural history, she soon caught his infectious enthusiasm for the subject. It is easy to imagine their taking walks in the countryside, collecting together, his teaching her about fossils at the Academy, and their reading aloud from interesting books. Emma went west with Ferdinand the first summer after their marriage, but she never became anything like a collaborator—the way Matilda Stevenson did with Jim Stevenson after he turned to ethnology and archeology. In fact, for all her apparent devotion to Ferdinand, Emma remained her own person and did not lose herself in his life. During the winters, while Ferdinand sorted his specimens and wrote his reports, she lived with him in Washington from time to time; but she preferred Philadelphia, and it was he who periodically rode the rails between the two cities. Unfortunately, I cannot say how often they lived separately or for how long. The question and its implications will recur, however, as we search for some plausible explanation for the fact that the couple never had children. For the time being, it is enough to note the immediate impact of the marriage on Hayden. He no longer filled his spare time casting about for money-making schemes. Gone were the obsessive and frustrating flirtations with various and sundry women. Emma brought a calm and satisfaction to Ferdinand's personal life he had not known before. Even before their marriage, Emma's novel and stimulating companionship began to provide a comfortable backdrop for Ferdinand's center-stage performances with his survey.

Hayden catching bugs by the light of a candle. Sketch by one of his field companions, probably while working with Lieut. G. K. Warren in 1856 or 1857. Courtesy the National Archives.

Watercolor by Anton Schönborn, showing Hayden collecting fossils in the Black Hills while working for Captain W. F. Raynolds, summer 1859. Courtesy the Beinecke Library, Yale University.

C. 1859. Photographer E. R. Morgan. Courtesy National Portrait Gallery.

Probably during winter of 1859–60 at Deer Creek. Courtesy National Portrait Gallery.

About the time he became a professor at the University of Pennsylvania in 1865. Courtesy
National Portrait Gallery.

W. H. Jackson depicted (in 1935) Hayden's first encounter with Yellowstone in 1871. Jackson reconstructed the scene from his own contemporary photographs. Courtesy Department of the Interior.

Jackson's photograph of Hayden on horseback, c. 1872. Courtesy Bancroft Library, University of California.

Summer 1872. Emma traveled to the field for part of the season following her marriage to Hayden. Around the table in this typical camp scene are A. C. Peale, Jim Stevenson, and Hayden. Photograph by W. H. Jackson. Courtesy U.S. Geological Survey.

His formal portrait taken upon initiation into the National Academy of Sciences, 1873. Courtesy National Academy of Sciences.

1885, after his retirement to Philadelphia. Courtesy National Portrait Gallery.

15

CONTROVERSIES AND CONTRIBUTIONS

It is believed that all unkind criticisms of the labors of other scientific men are out of place in an official report, and in no instance will they receive the sanction of the geologist in charge. Each assistant is held responsible for the correctness of his statements in his report, and it is presumed that his love of truth is superior to his personal feelings.
—Hayden, in his *Seventh Annual Report,* p. 13

AFTER SUCCESSFULLY REORGANIZING his survey in 1870 and restructuring his reports with the *Fourth Annual Report,* Hayden could concentrate on the topics he cared about most. Thereafter his survey's publications would provide a forum for discussing ideas and developments in the West. They would also showcase a variety of specialized studies on living plants and animals as well as fossils. We begin with a fascinating but controversial idea Hayden helped to publicize.

In the course of a twenty-two-page report ("Agriculture of Colorado") published with Hayden's *Third Annual Report,* Cyrus Thomas made an interesting observation. He noted that settlers at diverse points along the Front Range testified to a greater volume of water in the streams during recent years. It was not just the immigrants who thought so, for "it is a common expression of the Mexicans and Indians that the Americans bring rain with them." Pondering the causes, Thomas said: "All this, it seems to me, must lead to the conclusion that since the Territory has begun to be settled, towns

181

and cities built up, farms cultivated, mines opened, and roads made and traveled, there has been a gradual increase in moisture." Thus was Hayden's survey affiliated with the now infamous theory that "rain follows the plow."

Hayden himself had given some support to the wider implications of the theory in his *First Annual Report,* when he cited evidence in the West and in literature from around the world that planting trees encouraged the forces of nature that increased rainfall. Both Thomas and Hayden pointed to an increase of moisture—not strictly rainfall—because on lands bordering the Rockies snowfall was the major ingredient. The theory that settlement increased rainfall originated with Josiah Gregg in his book *Commerce of the Prairies* (1844) and by the 1870s it was a popular idea on the plains. The theory was finally discredited (but not until the 1890s), and for that reason it seems foolish to those with no appreciation for historical context. But for half a century the idea that settlement might actually increase rainfall was widely believed. By contrast, a number of early explorers had spoken of the western plains as a Great American Desert, including Lewis and Clark, Zebulon Pike, and most of all Edwin James, who wrote Major Long's report and originated the phrase. Scholars of the stature of Francis Parkman accepted the desert concept, as did publisher Horace Greeley. Obviously, even to careful observers around the middle decades of the nineteenth century, the climate of the Great Plains was a mystery.

What most critics of the "rain follows the plow" theory have overlooked is that for nearly two generations (just at the time settlement increased) rainfall on the plains *did* increase, according to contemporary testimony. Meager climatological records for the 1860s and 1870s confirm what many experienced. The Department of Agriculture began compiling better statistical records in the 1870s, which also indicated a modest increase in rain over the plains during that decade and early in the next. Thomas acknowledged (correctly, as it turned out) that the phenomenon might be due to a climatic cycle. He urged scientists to observe rainfall over time in regions of growing population. He encouraged the Department of Agriculture to study the situation, which probably accelerated its more effective recordkeeping. Neither Hayden nor Thomas made any commitment to the veracity of the theory, and neither used it irresponsibly, as some promoters did, to stimulate western migration. Both men simply called attention to empirical evidence that seemed to support an interesting theory, and both insisted, whenever discussing agriculture on the plains, that irrigation would be necessary for successful crops.

After first mentioning the idea, Thomas referred to it four years later— more critically—in the course of another lengthy report for Hayden on the agriculture of the West. Hayden called attention to the popularity of the theory twice more without giving it any endorsement. But two other writers publishing reports for Hayden's survey spoke of it more sanguinely. R. S. Elliott noted the apparent climactic changes due to settlement but added, "Whether the change has been already spread over a large enough area, and whether our apparently or really wetter seasons may not be part of a cycle, are unsettled questions."

The following year Elliott gave an unqualified endorsement to the theory, which, coupled with the fact that his job was to prepare promotional literature for the Kansas Pacific Railroad, has made it easy for critics to dismiss his views. But critics overlooked the fact that the railroad performed a number of valuable experiments regarding climate and moisture accumulation. The railroad dug and measured wells, studied rainfall, and planted vegetables, cereals, and a variety of trees. Of course the work was done rapidly and over too short a period to judge fairly of the prospects for agriculture on the Great Plains. But potential farmers were not looking for long-term guarantees. Most were seeking a new life and were willing to take chances. Because the prevailing view of the plains as Great American Desert discouraged the pioneering spirit yearning to unleash itself over the land, settlers were as quick as promoters to seize on any evidence of arability in the western lands. Certainly hucksters spoke beyond the limits of veracity, but Americans wanted to believe western settlement would increase rainfall. Elliott was not regarded as a huckster or a quack. Joseph Henry published his opinions in the 1870 *Annual Report* of the Smithsonian Institution. The settlement-rainfall issue was a very hot topic, and even the most cautious men realized it would require years of results to be sure of anything. Meanwhile, publishing Elliott's reports enabled Hayden to march with the standard-bearers of popular science.

Publishing the work of Professor Samuel Aughey had a similar effect and endeared Hayden to westerners, among whom Aughey was highly regarded. Aughey was another pastor-naturalist whose religious zeal seems to have intensified his scientific interests. He moved to Nebraska from the East in 1864 and was a professor of natural sciences at the university in Lincoln for years. His particular loves, like Hayden's, were botany and geology, and for Hayden's *Eighth Annual Report* (1876) he wrote an essay on the recent geological deposits of Nebraska and their relationships to soil quality. Only one page of his twenty-seven-page report mentioned the settlement-rain issue, but he made some useful observations based on his own research. Many streambeds in the territory that had been dry for years were now full of water. Springs were more frequently found bursting out along the base of cliffs. The grasses and sedges typical of dry regions were retreating before flora that required more moisture. Aughey believed that plowed land absorbed more water than virgin prairie and in turn released it back to the atmosphere by evaporation to encourage more rain. "There is little room to doubt that the atmosphere is becoming more moist or the rain-fall is increasing, or both, all over Eastern and probably Western Nebraska," he concluded. With the publication of his *Sketches of the Physical Geography and Geology of Nebraska* in 1880, Aughey became the leading proponent of rain following the plow, at the very time when better government statistics gave objective support to the theory, at least for a short period of time.

Unfortunately and unjustly, after the theory was overthrown in the 1890s, some critics ignored the context of Aughey's original work in order to discredit him along with Thomas, Elliott, and Hayden. Reputation is a fragile garment, and several historians have been all too ready to believe the worst about Hayden. Judged by what was known at the time, however, Hayden behaved quite responsibly. By bringing public attention to the matter he undoubtedly stimulated scientific testing of the theory.

A more embroiling topic, and one much closer to Hayden's heart, was the Great Lignite, on which he lavished enormous energy. For years he had been struck by the apparent connectedness of the great Cretaceous and Tertiary periods through the ubiquitous spreading of the Great Lignite. Since before the Civil War, he and Meek had been arguing for bridging these critical periods, in contradiction to received opinion. Now he focused on the Great Lignite with a fury. In the *Fourth Annual Report* five of the special reports spoke directly to this issue and three others touched it indirectly. Hayden was determined to gather and publish all the relevant information on the topic he could find, and he was not shy about searching for it. Over the next few years he sent Leidy, Meek, Lesquereux, and Cope into the field at the expense of his survey to continue the research, and he himself kept his ever-vigilant eye open, even if his mind was now mostly made up. In order to introduce a major subdivision for paleontology the format of the *Fifth Annual Report* was changed slightly, and this format persisted in the *Sixth, Seventh,* and *Eighth Annual Reports* (published between 1872 and 1876), with most of the emphasis on the Cretaceous-Tertiary issue. In the *Tenth* the reports of Charles White and Lesquereux returned to the same theme, and both the *Eleventh* and *Twelfth* annual reports (1879 and 1883) contained important contributions to the issue. Meanwhile Leidy's first volume in the *Final Reports* series, *Contributions to the Extinct Vertebrate Fauna of the Western Territories* (1873), spoke directly to the issue, as did six more of the final reports between 1874 and 1883, written by Cope, Meek, and Lesquereux. More than a score of articles appeared in the survey's *Bulletin* on the same subject, many of them slightly revised and reprinted in subsequent annual reports. It was with more than professional satisfaction then that Hayden could announce, in the preface to one of the final reports, "The conclusion, therefore, becomes more and more apparent that while the principal groups of the Mesozoic and Cenozoic formations in the West have each peculiar characteristics, and are readily recognized by the geologist, they really form an unbroken series of strata, not separated by sharply defined planes of demarcation, either stratigraphical or palaeontological."

To understand Hayden's contributions to this issue it will be useful to conclude now the story of the Judith River beds, begun at the end of Chapter 10. Recall that prior to the Civil War Hayden had encountered a varied group of rocks at the mouth of the Judith River in present-day Montana. He described the character of the rocks accurately, but their age baffled him for five years. Then in 1860 he decided they were early Tertiary, or Eocene, and belonged to the lowest part of the Great Lignite. It is clear from the start that in describing the top portion of the Judith group as "fresh water and estuary beds," Hayden saw these rocks as transitional between the marine Cretaceous formations below and the freshwater Tertiary above. By the time he resumed his study of the Judith beds, he had extended even farther the range of its close associate, the Great Lignite, which, during the 1850s, he had traced all across the Upper Missouri and assumed its equivalency in all the coal-bearing rocks near the eastern slope of the Rockies from Montana to New Mexico.

Thus even before the Great Lignite was renamed the Laramie Formation in 1877, Hayden had staked out his position in a dispute (the so-called Laramie Question) that would exercise geologists for the next fifty years. Confident in his views because of encountering the formation for years in many places, Hayden modified details of his original position but never changed his basic understanding of the formation and its extent. Assuming this uniform and widespread formation at the bottom of the Tertiary permitted him to propose a gradual, orderly transition between the Mesozoic and Cenozoic eras; it also gave him a handy benchmark by which to date the first upsurge of the Rocky Mountains (soon after its initial deposition). Hayden's early, and by now proprietary, interest in the Great Lignite no doubt stiffened his resolve not to change his essential views about it, but so comprehensive were the implications of his ideas that he held geologists in thrall for nearly half a century. While they quibbled with his dating, they could only correct it after two decades of detailed work.

Dissent from Hayden's opinion that all the lignite-bearing coal beds of the West were part of the Great Lignite began in the late 1860s after a number of investigators started looking in different places. In New Mexico and Colorado John L. LeConte and John James Stevenson both found invertebrate fossils in coal-bearing rocks that seemed to be Cretaceous. Clarence King reached similar conclusions for the Green River Basin of Wyoming Territory. Cope looked at the vertebrate evidence and also favored the Cretaceous. Newberry looked at fossil plants in the lignites of New Mexico and found the rocks to be Cretaceous. Newberry was the first to see that the lignites were not all part of one enormous formation, for he had also testified to the Tertiary age of the Great Lignite on the Upper Missouri, even calling it Miocene. Regarding the Colorado lignites, Newberry thought them all Cretaceous, and he tried his best to get Meek to endorse his views, knowing how delicious it would be to discredit Hayden's views through his closest colleague.

Meanwhile Hayden got ardent and continuous support for his Tertiary views from the Swiss paleobotanist, Leo Lesquereux, who had been living in America since about 1848. During his long residence in Ohio he met Newberry, became an expert on coal plants, and wrote reports for no less than seven different state geological surveys. Stone-deaf and suffering from time to time from poor eyesight, Lesquereux was nonetheless a most meticulous worker and a stubborn one. He learned to read and write English accurately, though he was never comfortable speaking it, and perhaps it was the resulting social isolation that caused him to become a deeply suspicious man. He went to work for Hayden in 1867 and published on Hayden's flora throughout the 1870s, becoming gradually more and more distrustful of Newberry, whose place as Hayden's expert on fossil plants he gradually took over.

I believe Hayden's personal difficulties with Newberry may have influenced his professional judgment on the whole issue of the Great Lignite. Lesquereux's views on the Great Lignite were more compatible with his own, even though they rested on older assumptions of geologic chronology, which used European evidence as the world standard. Ironically, Hayden had been a pioneer in casting doubt on the applicability of the European chronology to the American West; but in continuing to support Lesquereux's opinions on the West's fossil flora Hayden seems to have forgotten his earlier critical insights. His hostility to Newberry may be part of the explanation.

Meanwhile Hayden modified his position slightly without giving up his general ground on the lignites. During 1868 he himself found in northeastern Utah lignites that were undoubtedly Cretaceous, and he duly reported that fact in his review of the season. Replying to other suggestions that the entire Great Lignite might be Cretaceous, not Tertiary, he said: "It is quite probable that the coal-making period began in the later portion of the cretaceous era and extended up into the tertiary. . . . That there is a connection between all the coal beds of the West I firmly believe, yet until much clearer light is thrown upon their origin than any we have yet secured I shall regard them as belonging to my transition series or beds of passage between the true cretaceous and the tertiary." In other words the Great Lignite, or the Fort Union Group as Hayden now called it, was *one* formation, and the fact that it partook of Cretaceous and Tertiary characteristics only reinforced the case for its great geographic extent, not to mention its importance in the geologic column as an intermediate series.

Thereafter Hayden's position on the matter remained essentially unchanged. He managed to interpret all the new evidence as supporting his idea of transitional beds. And many agreed with him. Clarence King disagreed on their age but accepted Hayden's ideas on their structure and position, and even their great extent, at least in the areas of Utah and Colorado with which he was familiar. Wanting to focus greater attention on these important beds, King persuaded Hayden to come up with a new name for his Great Lignite where it occurred in areas they were both mapping. They agreed on the term Laramie, but Hayden clearly understood this name as only a refinement of the Great Lignite. In 1878 he wrote, "The facts as we understand them at the present time would seem to warrant this general division, viz.: a marine series, Cretaceous; gradually passing up into a brackish-water series, Laramie; gradually passing up into a purely fresh-water series, Wahsatch." To some geologists the newly recognized Laramie identified a regional group, albeit an extensive one, that was not necessarily coextensive with Hayden's older Great Lignite. But Hayden still considered them the same: "It is also probable that the brackish-water beds on the upper Missouri must be correlated with the Laramie, and that the Wahsatch Group as now defined and the Fort Union Group are identical as a whole, or in part at least."

Having set in motion a rethinking of one of the most pivotal periods in geologic history, Hayden took enormous satisfaction in all the new research that was going on, much of it sponsored by his own survey. Meek refrained from endorsing the sweeping views of Hayden, but he also resisted Newberry's attempts to discredit Hayden's dating, preferring instead to examine and date particular outcrops. Regarding only the Judith River beds, for example, which had initiated the whole inquiry, Meek decided they were Cretaceous. Peale agreed, but he also viewed them as a transitional series, part of which linked up with what Hayden originally established in his Great Lignite. White accepted the integrity of a single series of transitional beds and even extended their geographic range well beyond what Hayden had proposed. White also emphasized that these beds were unique in the world.

In the process of debating the Laramie Question, geologists greatly increased their knowledge of how structures succeeded each other through time. In addition to these empirical refinements, geologists added sophistication to their methodology and a greater appreciation of complexity in the processes that shaped the Earth. Research on the Laramie produced conflicting evidence on the age of rocks, depending on whether one relied on vertebrate, invertebrate, or floral fossils; therefore the whole question of biological benchmarks came up for review. As new biota emerged that did not readily fit into the traditional chronology, improved standards of classification and periodization had to be found. As research expanded and specimens accumulated, it became more and more obvious from the geographic distribution of particular fossils that the same periods of time gave rise to different creatures in different places (which Hayden and Meek had hinted in the 1850s). Conversely, paleontologists realized that just because the same species appeared in different locations did not necessarily mean they originated at the same time. Naturally, all these discoveries enhanced the singularity of the American evidence, which could no longer be considered a variation on the European standard. Indeed, the evidence raised questions about the feasibility of a universal standard. These fruitful new developments in geological science gained a big push from the evolution of the Laramie Question, which itself grew out of Hayden's sweeping thesis regarding the extent and importance of the Great Lignite.

Eventually, the resolution of these issues meant diminishing the physical boundaries of the Laramie and overthrowing the concept of succession Hayden had used to inflate the Great Lignite in the first place. Hayden's initial error had been to concatenate the many separate outcrops of late Cretaceous and early Tertiary lignite into one grand formation, or series of transitional beds as he called them. Of course it is presumptuous to speak of any worker in a developmental science like geology making "errors," for today's patterns of thought will inevitably crumble before new information, which in turn will usher in new paradigms. According to the standards of his time, Hayden's evidence was good, never completely satisfying, but strongly suggestive. He drew many of his inferences about the extent of the Great Lignite from the similar physical settings of different deposits, especially when the faunal evidence was confusing or lacking; he did not realize that many of these apparently similar deposits accumulated at different times. Not until the 1920s was the once-mighty empire of the Great Lignite (Laramie) reduced by painstaking research to the Denver Basin along the Front Range in Colorado and to Carbon County in Wyoming. However, the Front Union Formation, which Hayden wound up equating with his Great Lignite, is now mapped from northwestern Colorado, across much of Wyoming, into eastern Montana and western parts of the Dakotas; geologists now date it to the Paleocene but admit that it overlaps the Cretaceous boundary. Hayden's larger insight was not far off.

What interests the historian is the pattern of thought that encouraged such a vast agglomeration in the first place. That inquiry must especially provoke Hayden's biographer, because Hayden exemplified that pattern of thought as well as any contemporary. Following the ideology of his day, Hayden believed that once a certain force set to work, it moved forward gradually but inevitably until its work was done.

> If there is a strict uniformity in all the operations of nature when taken in the aggregate, as I believe there is, then this is simply in accordance with the law of progress which in the case of the physical changes wrought out in the geological history of the world has operated so slowly that infinite ages have been required to produce any perceptible change. The position that I have taken in all my studies in the West is that all evidences of sudden or paroxysmal movements, have been local and are to be investigated as such, and have had no influence on the great extended movements which I have regarded as general, uniform, and slow, and the results of which have given the West its present configuration.

The quotation (from 1871) provides a valuable insight into the development of Hayden's thought. In *Geology and Natural History* (1862), his best early work of a general nature, he acknowledged the power of catastrophe in shaping the earth; but now he was showing greater respect for the idea that the present is the key to the past: that an understanding of past geologic events can be gained by discovering the principles that govern present events. This concept, that both past and present are ruled by the same principles, is known as uniformitarian thinking, and it rests on an assumption of gradualism. By the early 1870s Hayden was entirely won over to the gradualist view, and his supporting remarks became stronger.

> I have always expressed my belief in the continuity of all the great formations from the Silurian to the present time, and that the highest privilege of the geologist is to discover the evidence that bridges over all chasms and obliterates all the lines of demarkation. When our knowledge of the geological history of the world is more complete, we may expect to find well-marked beds of passage or transition between all the great groups of the geological scale.

Hayden (and Meek) had early called attention to the blurring of the boundary between Carboniferous and Permian, too, though it was not strictly accurate for Hayden to say that he had "always expressed my belief in the continuity of all the great formations . . ." As his views became stronger on that point, he overlooked his earlier flirtations with catastrophism. His uniformitarian views placed him right in the mainstream of geological thinking. Charles

Lyell had first articulated these views in his *Principles of Geology* (1830), and they steadily gained acceptance and adherents, until, with Darwin's endorsement and enlargement, they reached an unassailable position.

In another respect Hayden also supported traditional thinking, but wound up making his own contribution. I refer to his understanding of lakes. In his *First Annual Report* of 1867 Hayden suggested that from the early Tertiary a series of freshwater lakes, formed from remnants of the retreating Cretaceous seas, covered large portions of the West. Erosion of the Cretaceous rocks shaped the emerging continent into basins, and Tertiary formations took shape in these basins, in the lakes themselves. Why lakes? The answer reflects geological thought at the time. In the eighteenth century Abraham Gottlob Werner of Germany had made a convincing argument that all sedimentary rocks were deposited in the ocean. But in the early nineteenth century French geologists found fossils known to have lived in fresh water or on land, and they found these fossils in stratified sedimentary beds. Gradually the idea emerged that the beds containing these freshwater fossils were deposited in lakes, apparently because no one could yet conceive how else an extensive formation could be laid down, except by a large body of water. Drawing on this European theory, Hayden reinforced and extended it in his explanation of the Tertiary deposits of the West. He inspired other Americans, including Newberry, Cope, and Clarence Dutton, to employ the same theory. It was not until the turn of the nineteenth century that geologists—using the same evidence examined by Hayden, Newberry, and others—began to see that streams and wind could have acted as agents of large-scale horizontal deposition.

As a result of his strong uniformitarian views, Hayden began to take a grand processional view of the forces ruling the Earth. He taught, for example, that the gradual uplift of the continent caused the Cretaceous seas to recede, leaving behind brackish bodies of water, which, with the help of streams and snowmelt draining from the rising continent, eventually became freshwater lakes during the early Tertiary. Hayden identified four great basins that formed successively as the result of this process. Each held a distinct place in time, but each displayed characteristics that bespoke a gradual, inexorable transition from one to another. First came the Judith Basin, a mixed estuary and freshwater deposit, laid down at the end of the Cretaceous or the opening of the Tertiary period—Hayden thought the latter. It was succeeded by the Great Lignite, a mixed brackish and freshwater deposit, whose extent was larger than any of the rest. The lignite had formed from the compressed remains of extensive forests, which had crowded the shores of the early Tertiary lakes. He found the overlying Wind River deposits to be entirely fresh water, as was the White River Group centered around the Dakota Bad Lands. At one time Hayden said, "All the lignite Tertiary beds of the west are but fragments of one great basin, interrupted here and there by the upheaval of mountain chains or concealed by the deposition of newer formations," showing that he felt the rise of the Rockies commenced some time after the initial deposition of the Great Lignite. There were puzzling outcrops that seemed to belie such a ubiquitous deposition, and dating the upthrusts of the continent from the evidence of the Tertiary basins did not always yield convincing results. Still Hayden's was a powerful hypothesis that fit most of the evidence, and no one else had a better one.

In the early twentieth century geologists began to recognize that succession at the end of the Cretaceous was not a strictly progressive process, free from interruptions or reversals. Perhaps a beach thrust above the tide for a time might later be recaptured by a bay, then elevated again only to be covered by a swamp, which itself would later be engulfed by a resurgent sea, and so on. But if Hayden thought in these terms he certainly did not articulate the possibilities clearly, and my reading of him is that he did not think about succession in this back-and-forth fashion at all. Hardly anyone did in Hayden's day, except, oddly enough, Newberry, who was among the first to doubt the extent of the Great Lignite. But Newberry's was a voice in the wilderness, and it is doubtful he realized the implications of his findings. It required years of patient examinations at scores of locations (where for a long time the facts of irregular deposition made no sense) before a new synthesis emerged.

Hayden's ideas about the Great Lignite fit well into the context of his times. Grand themes that mobilized facts into a comprehensive view of Truth appealed to the mentality of late Victorian times, especially when those themes allied with Progress, one of the most cherished of Victorian concepts. But his ideas appealed for an even more obvious reason: his own personal influence. By the end of the 1860s anyone with any interest in the issues knew that Hayden was the kingpin of the Great Lignite, that he was the one who had found most of it, dated it, and made it the gateway to the modern Age of Mammals. Even though his views were challenged from early in the game, still his ideas defined the contest. And Hayden's ideas stimulated his Survey of the Territories, which, under his direction, focused massive and erudite attention on the Great Lignite. It was not until long after his death that his concept of the Great Lignite was superseded. During his later life Hayden was a powerful force in every area he ventured: in influencing geological theory, in promoting studies of natural history, and in widening popular appreciation for science.

Although he did not speak often of it explicitly, he strongly endorsed the theory of evolution. Comparing some fossil leaves of Cretaceous age with modern forms, he concluded, "The inference is, therefore, that this flora illustrates the great law of progress: commencing with great simplicity of form, and advancing, step by step, to greater complexity and beauty." But was this progressive advance directed by a divine plan or did it evolve in harmony with the laws of natural selection? Summing up another paper on "The Geographical Distribution of Plants," he showed his preference for the latter. "It will be seen at a glance from the few observations here made, that most animals and plants are restricted by nature within certain geographical limits. . . . There are also natural reasons why certain aspects of animals and plants are restricted to certain geographical areas."

Once the notion of gradualism gained acceptance in geological thought, an understanding of succession among species by natural selection was accelerated. Hayden gave prominent attention to facts accumulated through his survey that supported the theory of evolution. In particular, these studies made apparent the enormous number and diversity of species. Whether it was Leidy's and Cope's vertebrates, Lesquereux's plants, Meek's invertebrates, or the living creatures of Elliot Coues, Alpheus Spring Packard, Jr., Thomas, and Scudder, the flowers of Porter and John Merle Coulter, or Joel Asaph Allen's seals and walruses (to mention only some of the more prominent studies), a consistent portrayal of life emerged. It teemed in staggering abundance and surged forward in endless, seemingly senseless, variety. Yes, senseless: Hayden could find no rhyme or reason here, which was probably why he avoided bogging himself down in explanations. Significantly, he did not try to impose a design on, or read an order into, the exotic splendor of nature. When he ventured explanations, he found naturalistic causes. As an author he was not comfortable as a theorist, so he contented himself with piling up the facts. As an editor, though, he did not hesitate to promote the evolutionary philosophy, as in his preface to Coues and Allen's monograph on rodents (1877). He pointed out that no elaborate work on rodents had appeared since Baird's twenty years earlier, but that since that time Darwin had established the theory of evolution. He said both Coues and Allen "are well known as leaders among American Mammalogists in this line of research, and their studies have resulted in placing the subject in an entirely new light."

The broad range of specialized studies in natural history Hayden sponsored is impressive. The *Fourth Annual Report* alone published five studies on fossil plants and animals, and seven on living fauna and flora. This scope was typical of his survey's publications over the next few years.

In addition to his Annual Reports in twelve volumes, Hayden edited thirteen volumes of Final Reports (or Monographs), twelve of Miscellaneous Publications, seventeen of Unclassified Publications, and then a journal called the *Bulletin*. Of the 386 separate contributions only 88 (23%) concerned geology or geography. Another 15 covered mineralogy, agriculture, or natural resources (4%), 23 were devoted to ethnology or archaeology (6%), and 17 to miscellaneous subjects (4%). Studies of fossils and different kinds of living fauna and flora—the traditional concerns of naturalists—dominated the Survey's publications: 243 of the total (63%).

In compiling these works Hayden acted as an editor of his colleagues' work. Yet his colleagues were quick to praise his remarkable versatility as a collector of specimens. They mentioned fossil leaves, insects, and fish; the first fossil feather of a bird; a number of turtles, living birds, and insects, even mollusks, and, of course, numerous living and extinct vertebrates. The birds he collected with Warren (1856–1857) formed the backbone for Baird's report in Volume 9 of the Pacific Railroad Reports. Elliott Coues's *Birds of the Northwest* (published in Hayden's *Miscellaneous* series in 1874) was almost entirely based on Hayden's collections. In the preface to that book Coues said of Hayden, "I do not hesitate to say that no one, not an ornithologist, has contributed more to the advance of our knowledge of the birds of the West."

Hayden's own writings after the Civil War show a similar multitude of interests: the pipestone quarries of Dakota, the geographical distribution of plants in the West, a first description of strata in the Bear River Group, his identification of a new rabbit, and his discovery of a modern Indian site associated with Stone Age culture. He wrote three pieces on coal veins in Nebraska. He continued two professional arguments, both begun before the Civil War. One concerned the Permian in America, the other the dating of Cretaceous rocks on the basis of dicotyledonous leaves. Both topics underlined the uniqueness of American geology and highlighted his and Meek's pioneering role in interpreting it. Little of what he said in these articles was original; most of what he wrote relied on research he had done before the Civil War.

He was still flirting with the fantasy of publishing more on Indians. He wrote some "Brief Notes" on three more Indian languages: only two pages of notes, in fact, followed by thirty pages of vocabularies, which he claimed to have collected during summer 1867. He acknowledged help from a Mrs. Platt, a teacher working with the Pawnee, without specifying how much she had done. He alluded to "an extensive work in preparation," which would be a study in comparative linguistics, but it never appeared. The article of April 1868 was his last word on Indians. He seemed to realize it when adding nostalgically, "No pursuit has ever given me greater pleasure than the study of the languages and customs of our native tribes, and it would be my choice to give my undivided attention to those researches, but all my labors in that direction must ever be incidental to other duties." We need not take this remark seriously because by 1868 Hayden realized his future lay in geology and geography, not ethnology. As a versatile naturalist who took pride in his broad capacities, Hayden was unusual in an age of growing specialization. He was also an ardent self-promoter who lost few opportunities to proclaim his multiple talents.

In the first few years after the war Hayden published most of his writings in scholarly journals. Nearly all of them appeared in the *American Journal of Science* and the *Proceedings of the American Philosophical Society.* He seems to have thought the journals offered a wider audience than his government reports. The surprising demand for these reports convinced him otherwise. Each of the first two annual reports sold out promptly; then 8,000 copies of his third sold out only three weeks after its release. As a result, beginning with his next report for 1870, he expanded the format to encompass not just his own original work in geology but also his many miscellaneous interests in natural history. Henceforth he spent more time as an editor than an author, arranging the diverse contributions on all aspects of natural history for which his survey became famous.

While writing articles, Hayden was doing original work through his survey of Nebraska and subsequently of Wyoming and Colorado. His *Final Report of Nebraska* (1872) is a good example. In it he organized his information around the counties he traversed. He described the base rocks as well as the superficial deposits and mentioned quarries, mines, and potentially useful resources he encountered. He noted evidence of glacial scratching on the limestone rocks along the Missouri, south of the Platte River. He mentioned the great range of the yellow marl, or loess, without ever deciding about its origin, age, or relation to other recent formations. Consistent with his broader ideas on the region, however, he thought the loess had been deposited in lakes.

At first glance it might seem Hayden spread himself too widely, but there are patterns to his diversity. For example, the many lists and studies of insects he encouraged seem unconnected until we discover that Hayden was instrumental in establishing the U.S. Entomological Commission in 1877 (and having it attached to his survey); its purpose was to collect and disseminate information on preventing crop damage. Hayden often combined scholarly and practical motives for his natural history work. As he put it in a rather clumsy way,

It is possible to make natural history entertaining and attractive as well as instructive, with no loss in scientific precision, but with great gain in stimulating, strengthening and confirming the wholesome influence which the study of the natural sciences may exert upon the higher grades of mental culture; nor is it a matter of little moment to shape the knowledge which results from the naturalist's labors that its increase may be susceptible of the widest possible diffusion.

At the same time, through an ambitious and attractive series of publications Hayden was educating the public about knowledge and methods of science. It is interesting to see how he slanted these publications. Despite his desire to popularize science, he was not trying to appeal mostly to laymen or amateur scientists, like such new journals as *American Naturalist* (begun in 1867), and *Popular Science Monthly* (1872). He could have edited his *Bulletin* to compete directly with these popular periodicals. Instead, he aimed higher, attempting to gain a share of the growing market for more serious science. As he boasted on the third anniversary of the survey's *Bulletin*: "It has already acquired a character and standing which render it favorably comparable to the regular 'Proceedings' or other similar publications of any of the learned bodies of this country or Europe." In these efforts he was both prolific and original. None of the other postwar surveys funded by the federal government published anywhere near the quantity of Hayden's survey. None of the state geological and natural history surveys published a periodical at this time.

Although he aimed his survey's publications mostly at the professional scientist, Hayden's instincts as an educator were too strong to ignore the growing popular interest in science. Having organized the survey's work to capture the specialist, he published other material designed for a popular audience. His distinction between scholarly and popular was never precise, for as he said in introducing one of his reports: "The present annual report is submitted with the belief that it contains much that is new and interesting to geologists and the intelligent world generally." It was a comment he used frequently. He believed his serious work would command growing attention; sales of his annual reports justified that belief. At the same time Hayden wanted to publish summaries of this serious work where it would be found by those who did not read government publications.

With that thought in mind in 1868 Hayden began planning "a book or album illustrated with photographs of the wonderful scenery along the line of the U.P.R.R." Accompanying the photographs would be "a descriptive text, giving a history of the road, the resources of the country through which it passes, with such incidents as can be interwoven properly, with remarks on each picture in the proper place." Hayden wrote directly to the vice president of the Union Pacific on September first outlining his idea, and boldly asking for the railroad's sponsorship of the book, pointing out: "The sale of the book would, it seems to me, pay all expenses, and probably much more.

At the time of the completion of the road the demand for such a work would undoubtedly be very great."

The railroad agreed to sponsor the book, which consisted of Hayden's text and a number of attractive albumin prints. *Sun Pictures of Rocky Mountain Scenery* appeared in 1870 and was published by Julius Bien. Bien was a talented lithographer and map engraver who had produced the maps for the Pacific Railroad Survey in the 1850s and would later do virtually all the maps for Hayden's survey as well as King's and Powell's. *Sun Pictures* was modeled on Josiah Whitney's *Yosemite* (1868), also published by Julius Bien, and its thirty illustrations came straight out of *The Great West Illustrated* (1869) by photographer Andrew Joseph Russell. In 1868 and 1869 Russell took more than two hundred glassplate negatives of the West while on assignment for the Union Pacific Railroad. Seeing some of those pictures had given Hayden the idea of assembling his own book around Russell's pictures. Hayden stated his purpose for the book on its very first page. "The increasing interest now taken in the science of geology, has led me to believe, that a volume embodying the principal geological facts in regard to a country, which has been and will be visited by so many thousands, would be read with interest." Thus Hayden the teacher. Indeed his comments on the illustrations are apt and instructive, especially in describing the strange forms wrought by erosion.

But Hayden had another purpose, which he was just as open about: to lead the armchair tourist on a journey of discovery through a wondrous new country.

> Now that we have, in as brief terms as possible, constructed our mountain and river system, I shall ask the reader to travel with me along the line of the Union Pacific Railroad, wandering aside here and there, to cull a flower or examine an Indian village or read some wonderful legend which attaches to almost every portion of this country. We shall also delay now and then, to study the rocks and unearth their fossil contents; and in many a locality we shall find the poet's utterance no fiction, that there are 'sermons in stones' etc. Scenes more wonderful than any related in the far-famed Arabian Nights' Entertainments have been performed on these apparently lifeless, monotonous plains.

His first chapter surveys the geology and geography of the whole Upper Missouri region, which Hayden had summarized so many times before and in virtually the same words. He then leads the traveler from Omaha to the Great Salt Lake and delivers on each of his promised asides. Especially skillful is his depiction of former landscapes, replete with fantastic creatures, now known only through their fossil remains. He weaves geological principles and geographic changes into the fabric of the text, including a much bolder statement of evolution than he had printed in any of his scientific papers.

> Ever since the commencement of creation, constant changes of form have been going on in our earth. Oceans and mountains have disappeared and others have taken their place. Entire groups of animal and vegetable life have passed away and new forms have come into existence, through a series of years which no finite mind can number. To enable the mind to realize the physical condition of our planet during all these past ages is the highest end to be obtained by the study of geological facts. It has been well said by an eloquent historian, that he who calls the past back again into being, enjoys a bliss like that of creating.

But Rocky Mountain scenery is the centerpiece of the book, and Hayden enshrines it like a relic, appealing to his readers to discover it, like so many knights seeking the Holy Grail. Time and time again he casts specific lures in front of his readers, mentioning the number of trout to be pulled easily out of a stream and the variety of large mammals to challenge the hunter, and all is placed against a backdrop of soaring peaks, broad vistas, and nearly incredible (were it not for the photographs) landforms.

The timing of *Sun Pictures* is also important. That Hayden utilized photography in this fashion as early as 1868 shows again the innovative quality of his thinking. All the postwar geological surveys eventually blended scientific and aesthetic aspects of landscape photography. Clarence King was the first to institutionalize photography into his survey when he hired Timothy O'Sullivan in 1867. Hayden followed suit by hiring William Henry Jackson in 1870, and Powell later hired Jack Hillers. But with *Sun Pictures* Hayden was the first to publish samples of the dramatic new landscapes all the surveyors were seeking. He did so even before hiring Jackson to work full time for his survey and at least three years before any of O'Sullivan's pictures circulated for public consumption. Hayden was also first to publish a catalog of photographs taken by his survey (in 1874), and he issued two revised editions in the next three years. Of all the surveyors, Hayden was the one who realized first and capitalized most on the popular appeal of photography. Actually, some of his letters from 1859 and 1860, written while in the field with Raynolds, show his early awareness of the camera's potential; but *Sun Pictures* is his first concrete effort to employ photography as a pedagogic tool. Incidentally, his prophesy about the market for the book was quite accurate: before the end of 1870 he was telling Baird that the demand for *Sun Pictures* was exceeding Bien's ability to bind them.

This kind of verbal and pictorial approach to the West has been so often repeated that we ought to have grown tired of it. But we have not; perhaps we never will. Even after the innovations in photographic technology, after the production of thousands of books depicting and trying to define the West, after an onslaught of slide shows, television specials, highway construction, and economy tours, the West still retains its power to dazzle and inspire. Even those of us who live in the West are still mesmerized by its power. That even the blitz techniques of the modern media and eager travel agents have failed to numb our fascination for the West proves that there is something magical here, something beyond our meager abilities to explain or exhaust. If this is still true today, how much more stunning the impact of Rocky Mountain scenery must have been in Hayden's day. The appetite for travel adventure and scenic discovery in the West had just been aroused, and in his many publications Hayden played a large role in stirring up that hunger.

Like *Geology and Natural History, Sun Pictures* hardly contains an original page if we look only at its language or contents. In his first book Hayden blended science and natural history with the beginnings of popular travelog in an attempt to sell science to the intelligent layman. In the second book he married science with tourism in an attempt to sell the West to anyone who could read. In neither book was he the first to make such appeals, though in both he was a pioneer in the creation of what became a new art form.[1]

By 1870, therefore, Hayden had already staked out a unique position. He was the only serious scientist in America trying to promote his professional interests and the wider concerns of science itself by a candid appeal to tourism. Other scientists were popularizing their work at this time by patient and deliberate explanations that did not debase content to attract readers. In his survey publications Hayden took this same cautious approach: he was not willing to water down his geology and natural history the way journalists and other popularizers would soon begin to do with science. With *Sun Pictures* he offered something in between strict science and popular oversimplification. His aim was to recruit a mass audience through an attractive tourism, then educate those readers to the wonders of real science. It was a bold and imaginative step, and as his survey rolled into Yellowstone in 1871 he was determined to make the most of it.

16
YELLOWSTONE
AND THE IMAGE
OF A MAN, 1871–1872

We have examined the yellow stone range of mountains, one of the finest ranges I have ever seen on the Continent. . . . We shall pass on into the head branches of Missouri & Columbia and connect at several points with Col. Raynolds' work, so that we claim that our map will be as good as any ever made by the Engineers' Bureau.

—Hayden to Baird, 20 July 1871

BY THE 1870 season Hayden had developed an effective routine for field-work, and his annual report for that season displayed the fascinations that would become his trademark for the duration of his survey's existence. He had fashioned an institution that reflected his personal interests in natural history, and he had enlisted an army of like-minded specialists to further the work. In short, Hayden and his survey now marched together as a team, ready to advance into any unexplored territory. Yet, except to his professional colleagues and to the Congress that funded him, Hayden was just another naturalist working in the West. This attitude disconcerted him, for he yearned for popular acclaim to complement his enviable reputation as the most versatile naturalist exploring the West. He hoped Yellowstone would bring him the fame he desired.

He got his wish, but he also acquired an image that he came to regret. As a result of his two years' work in Yellowstone, the popular press ballyhooed him into such a celebrity that most people never learned of his more solid accomplishments as a scientist. His popular image was incomplete and misleading, but it was also unforgettable because it cast Hayden in a necessary and believable role, as the interpreter of nature's wonders for the common man. Many people who first heard of Hayden in connection with his explorations in Yellowstone accepted the popular image; so, too, did colleagues who had known him only slightly before. Even Hayden delighted in reinforcing certain aspects of his stylized portrait. The disparity between image and reality, and the tension between them, will concern us until the end of our story.

Let us admit that it has been all too easy to see Hayden as a popularizer of natural wonders. That he stirred up enormous publicity for Yellowstone, and later used it—over and over again—as a sparkling inducement to become acquainted with other wonders in the West, did nothing to discourage the view of him as preeminently a promoter of western scenery and tourism. Similarly, based on the instant fame that Yellowstone brought him, it has been easy to associate Hayden too exclusively with Yellowstone and to assume that he had been lucky to encounter it in the first place simply by being in the right place at the right time. So goes the mythology accompanying the popular image.

On the contrary, Hayden's primary focus for nearly a generation had been on geology and natural history. By taking pains to amass formative collections over many years, he had contributed fundamentally to America's first understanding of the structure and history of the western landmass. Even as he was parading through Yellowstone to much acclaim, he was orchestrating research and planning publications on the Great Lignite, which raised basic questions about the evolution of life. But this was obscure work, scarcely known outside the elitist world of paleontologists and professional naturalists. Hayden differed from most of his more pedantic colleagues in possessing a boyish excitement about nature, an excitement he never outgrew, and which, even in full maturity, was filled with exuberance, boundless curiosity, and a huge sense of awe. Of course he saw Yellowstone as a wonder, especially because of its uniqueness, but wondrous too were the less dramatic marvels he had been describing on the Upper Missouri for many years. His writings on Yellowstone showed a similarity to his *Geology and Natural History* and to his *Sun Pictures of Rocky Mountain Scenery,* both of which pulsed with a vibrant appreciation for nature.

If we were ignorant of those facts and looked only at his Yellowstone writings, we might view Hayden as just a glib popularizer, and instead of sensing his roving curiosity we might catch only the opportunism. Early in his career Hayden had learned that popular science created funding that made possible his more esoteric endeavors. What the popular image does not capture is that his ebullience was genuine, that it originated during his college years and reached fruition in the 1850s, and that it endured, essentially unchanged, even after he was no longer able to benefit from exuding it—which he did, incidentally, for the rest of his life.

Expressing enthusiasm for nature, exploiting the growing taste for popular science and scenery, and undertaking serious research on natural history—these approaches underlay Hayden's work in Yellowstone and, in his mind, always blended together. Let us begin to separate the man from his mythology by discussing why he went to Yellowstone, when he decided to go, and what he accomplished there.

Luck had nothing to do with bringing Hayden to Yellowstone at just the right moment. His previous explorations in the West had aroused his ambition to discover the sources of the rivers that seemed to originate in the same region of northwestern Wyoming Territory. These included the Snake, the Green, the Yellowstone, and the Missouri, along with their major tributaries. As he followed their winding courses ever higher, it seemed to Hayden that the rivers sprang out of nearby watersheds and that all of them might emanate from the vicinity of the Upper Yellowstone. Before the Civil War he had approached this region from three different directions, and in 1860 he almost broke through to his goal. Late spring snows blocked the approach from the south, and perhaps for once in his life Jim Bridger botched the route-finding. At any rate Hayden had been hungering for the Upper Yellowstone country a long time, more to solve the puzzle of its geography than to see its alleged freaks of nature.

After finally managing to launch a vehicle that would spearhead his discoveries, Hayden eventually steered his survey back to Yellowstone country. A resource inventory for the new state of Nebraska led further west into eastern Colorado and southern Wyoming territories, in order to find the coal deposits that were so lacking in Nebraska. By 1870 Hayden had gone up and down the Front Range of the Rockies; he had examined three of Colorado's mountain parks, and he had crisscrossed southern Wyoming several times along different routes and branched off for a preliminary look at the Uinta Range in Utah. Clarence King's Survey of the 40th Parallel was busy working across Utah; thus there were no good reasons at the moment for exploring further south or west, especially in view of Hayden's inclination to look north, back to Yellowstone country. And, as it turned out, 1871 was the right time to return there.

Rumors of boiling mudholes and exploding geysers had been drifting back east ever since John Colter stumbled onto the Upper Yellowstone in

1807–1808 on his way home from the journey with Lewis and Clark. In the 1830s and 1840s fur trappers added descriptions of the country, but eastern publishers dismissed their reports as absurd and refused to publish them. Jim Bridger had several times crossed through the Upper Yellowstone country, and Hayden and Raynolds knew him as a reliable witness. Even though they had been unable to substantiate his tales, the map they published of Raynolds's explorations in 1859–1860 assumed the truth of Bridger's geographic outlines of the region. The Civil War delayed publication of that map; it finally came out in 1869. Its appearance probably stimulated two private tours of exploration of the Upper Yellowstone: the first by David Folsom, Charles Cook, and William Peterson in 1869; and the far more important one of Henry Washburn, Cornelius Hedges, and Nathaniel Pitt Langford in 1870. A military escort, led by Lieutenant Gustavus C. Doane, accompanied Washburn's party. Doane, who was well educated, quite literate, and a good observer, prepared a careful report of the party's explorations. His report documented for the first time the extraordinary geography and geology of the Upper Yellowstone. Through and through the professional soldier, Doane avoided such frivolities as details of scenery and personalities of the party. None of his colleagues had anticipated that their discoveries might excite popular curiosity; for instance, no one in the party had thought to bring along an artist or a photographer.

Once exposed to the enchantments of Yellowstone, however, the members of the Langford-Doane party realized the novelty of what they were seeing, and they hastened to spread the word upon their return. Newspapers in Montana told of their venture during late September 1870, and other papers picked up the story soon after. Hayden probably saw some of these articles or heard of them while still in the field that fall. Langford showed particular skill in publicity. He put together a lecture tour on Yellowstone, and when he spoke in Washington on 19 January 1871 Hayden was in the audience, along with a few political dignitaries. Langford also wrote two articles for *Scribner's Monthly,* which appeared in May and June, both containing illustrations by Thomas Moran, based on sketches made by party members. Of course, Moran had not yet been there himself. Meanwhile Doane finished his report on 15 December, and on 3 March the Senate ordered it to be printed; it became available to the public soon after. Baird read aloud a portion of Doane's unpublished report before the Philosophical Society of Washington, probably during February, and Hayden heard it at that time.

How much did this publicity influence Hayden's decision to go to Yellowstone in 1871? Several circumstances suggest he had made up his mind before all the hoopla began, before he could have heard Doane's report and even before Langford's lecture. On 13 February, for example, he wrote a colleague to say that the appropriations committee had reported in favor of his plans for the forthcoming summer. That committee would not have done so without previously receiving details of his plans; on 3 March the House passed the Sundry Civil Bill approving Hayden's work around "the sources of the Missouri and Yellowstone Rivers." Well before that, on 18 December 1870, Hayden had written Anton Schönborn asking him to accompany his survey the following summer as chief topographer. Hayden's letter has not survived; it is known only through Schönborn's reply of 28 December, which makes no mention of destinations. However, 1871 was the first year Hayden took along a full-time topographer, and he did so because he wanted to map the unknown watersheds that he had good reason to believe contained the headwaters of several great rivers. Schönborn was an old friend, having accompanied Hayden on the Raynolds expedition to the country surrounding Yellowstone in1859–1860. He accepted Hayden's offer gladly, saying in part, "I would much rather go with you to explore some new country than run up and down on these forts here continually." Given the context, it is difficult to imagine his reference to "new country" applying to anything but the Upper Yellowstone. So Hayden had plenty of reason to steer his survey back to Yellowstone in 1871, and certainly he made up his own mind to do so before learning the details of the Langford-Doane exploration.

But a Hayden who thought for himself does not fit the popular image of the man, which historians have swallowed so glibly. Consider four representative opinions. Our first authority states flatly that Hayden went to Yellowstone after being "inspired by Langford's . . . lecture." A second authority says Hayden was "spurred on" by reading Doane's report. The third says Hayden actually changed his survey's program for the season of 1871 in order to go there because of all the publicity generated by the Langford-Doane expedition, without saying what Hayden had previously intended to do. The fourth authority (Wallace Stegner) embroiders upon the third, repeating the notion that Hayden changed his whole plan for 1871 in order to go to Yellowstone, and adds that Hayden invited Moran to join his party.

The point about inviting Moran is misleading, too, so let me clear up that smaller point first before moving to the larger errors in Stegner's statement. A.B. Nettleton, an agent of Jay Cooke (who owned a majority interest in the Northern Pacific Railroad), contacted Hayden in June 1871 and asked him to take Moran along, pointing out that his expenses would be paid by the railroad and *Scribner's Monthly.* Both the railroad and the magazine would benefit from giving Moran a firsthand look at Yellowstone. So, obviously, would Hayden, who cheerfully agreed to take Moran along.

The more disturbing issue is the repeated misunderstanding of Hayden's motives for going to Yellowstone. Ideally, a biographer wants to write his own history, not argue with previous writers about their interpretations. But there has been no real interpretation of Hayden before, only an accumulation of unrelated stories, most of them invented wholesale or based on distortions. Recall how many writers played up the fanciful tale of Hayden traveling unarmed among Indians, from which they drew the conclusion that he was not quite right in the head. The report that Hayden only decided to go to Yellowstone after hearing Langford's lecture or reading Doane's report is equally misleading. As with the earlier mythology surrounding his solitary travels in the West, it becomes important to run to ground the origin of such rumors in order to separate fact from fiction.

Stegner is the only authority of the four who indicates a source for the idea that Hayden decided to head for Yellowstone after hearing Langford's lecture. The source turns out to be William Henry Jackson, specifically an article Jackson wrote in 1936 and his autobiography, published in 1940. In the article Jackson tackled the issue directly: "Although prepared for the continuation of the work of his organization in other localities, he [Hayden] decided, after attending Langford's lecture in Washington January 19, 1871, to make Yellowstone, instead, the field of his operations for the current season." In his book Jackson remembered the facts a little differently, saying that even after Langford's article in *Scribner's* documented Yellowstone's wonders, "the doubting Thomases demanded still further proof! And it was Hayden, spurred partly by the Langford article, who determined to satisfy them." Jackson wrote both accounts so long after the events that we must be skeptical of their accuracy on precise points of chronology. In this case, however, it was more than Jackson's memory that erred; it was his assumptions.

During the 1870 season Jackson had worked for Hayden in southern Wyoming. Not being told anything to the contrary, he assumed he would go back there in 1871. Given the little he knew of Hayden personally at that time, and even less of the survey's history, it was a reasonable assumption. Jackson's first outing with Hayden had been during 1870, and he was concerned solely with making pictures. There is no reason to think he would have read Hayden's four annual reports, which showed how much of southern Wyoming and adjacent regions Hayden had already examined. Nor would Jackson have been aware yet of Hayden's longstanding interest in exploring the headwaters of the Missouri and Yellowstone rivers. Most of all, there is no reason for thinking so secretive a man as Hayden would have opened his mind to a young newcomer regarding a project that was fraught with potential rivals. In his private correspondence Hayden rarely wrote much about his plans for forthcoming summers, and when he did he often warned even his closest friends "not to say a word." I cannot find a scrap

Hayden wrote during fall and winter 1870–1871 about going to Yellowstone, at least not until after his appropriation was approved. He was being even more careful than usual not to tip his hand too soon. But his wheels were turning. He was not back at his desk in Washington until 14 December; thus the letter to Schönborn of 18 December, recruiting him for another try at Yellowstone, was among the first he wrote. A month later, on 11 January, he wrote to Leidy, "All is well with me now and things are moving on gloriously." It is a cryptic statement, not clearly connected to anything else in the letter, but he certainly sounds pleased with whatever plans he has afoot. The letter, by the way, was written more than a week before Langford's lecture in Washington and more than a month before Hayden could have heard Doane's report read aloud.

One anachronism needs to be explained. Jackson's erroneous impressions about Hayden—changing his plans for 1871 in order to tackle Yellowstone—were first published in 1936, then repeated with a somewhat different chronology in his autobiography of 1940. Three of the four authorities I quoted could have borrowed this mistaken idea from Jackson because they published after 1940. But one of these authorities (Hiram M. Chittenden) published his book in 1895. Where did he get his misunderstanding? Come to think of it, where did Jackson get his? Jackson could have been inspired by Chittenden, but the likelihood is that both Chittenden and Jackson unwittingly accepted the popular image of Hayden, an image that stressed only Hayden's knack for publicizing wonders while ignoring his genuine ardor for geology and geography as well as his scholarly passion for natural history. Jackson later came to know Hayden better, but in nothing that he wrote about him did he ever show any appreciation for Hayden as a pioneering geologist or a broad-gauged naturalist. To be generous to Jackson, we could say he was blurring in his mind events that took place much earlier, indeed sixty-five years earlier. But to be fair to Hayden, we must realize that Jackson's primary interest in Hayden and his survey derived from pursuing popular wonders. Hayden had hired him to photograph the wonders, after all, and Jackson made himself a reputation by doing so, a reputation that he enlarged by doing more of the same for decades after his work with Hayden. In other words, we must see Jackson for what he was: one of the perpetuators (if not one of the inventors) of the Hayden mythology.

Because by 1871 Hayden had his own reasons for wanting to try again to reach Yellowstone, the rivalry created by other recent expeditions only added urgency to his planning. He viewed the others as interlopers, poaching on ground he had staked out years earlier; and no doubt the publicity stirred up by Langford gave Hayden an idea about how to take maximum advantage of Yellowstone. In order to bring back vivid images he would take along a photographer and two artists. Congress was swept up in the fervor over Yellowstone: it granted Hayden $40,000 for 1871—a substantial boost over his $25,000 for the previous year.

There now exists a substantial body of print on all the expeditions that have ever visited Yellowstone, and it includes a fairly accurate summary of Hayden's work in the park itself. It documents his march up the Yellowstone from Bottler's Ranch (140 miles north of Yellowstone Lake), his pioneering exploration of Mammoth Hot Springs (which he first called White Mountain Hot Spring), his encounter with Tower Falls, Grand Canyon of the Yellowstone, Lower Falls and Upper Falls, and the first sizable mud geysers near the north end of Yellowstone Lake. His party circumnavigated the lake, plumbing its depth and sketching its shoreline in the process, found the East Fork of the Madison River (which Hayden named for General John Gibbon in 1872), followed it to the Firehole River, which they ascended to the Lower and Upper Geyser basins, discovered several new lakes near the headwaters of the Madison, and explored some of the area between the sources of the Madison and Snake rivers, including the Yellowstone River above the lake. Minor points are still in dispute concerning how much Hayden's party actually discovered and what they named or did not name, but these matters need not concern us.

The interesting fact is that the Yellowstone literature only notices Hayden and his survey working *within* what is today the national park. But when he first arrived on the scene there was no park, and no one had any accurate information about the nature and extent of the Upper Yellowstone. It was Hayden and his men who worked out the geography of the region, and Hayden who suggested the dimensions for the park in the context of his wider explorations of that region—important points that are overlooked in the literature about Yellowstone. So even the substantial body of writing on Yellowstone National Park tends to reinforce the popular mythology about Hayden.

To get a sense of Hayden's true priorities and his broader accomplishments at the time, one has to read his two reports covering the 1871 and 1872 campaigns in Yellowstone. In those reports we find that in addition to surveying the Yellowstone River itself, Hayden's geographers also traced most of its branches for the first time. They also explored the Madison River from Geyser Basin to Three Forks, in Montana Territory, and traveled down the Missouri as far as Helena. From Three Forks they ascended to the source of the Gallatin River; then, recommencing in another direction from Three Forks, they also found the place where smaller streams unite to form the Jefferson River, at whose junction with the Gallatin and Madison at Three Forks the Missouri begins. Hayden went down the Yellowstone to the mouth of the Shields River, which connected with his work for Raynolds in 1860.

One feeder of the Jefferson was traced to the Continental Divide in the Bitterroot Range on the border of modern Idaho and Montana. Another division of the survey examined the nearly forty small streams that come together to form the Upper Snake River, and they clarified the geography around Henry's Fork and the Bear River to the west and south of the park in Idaho Territory. They showed that the headwaters of the Green River also trace to that remarkable part of northwestern Wyoming Territory where the Snake, the Madison, the Gallatin, and the Yellowstone all rise. Hayden personally walked over a lot of the country in order to sketch its geology, in the process taking notes that translated into the first descriptions of the mountain ranges of the Yellowstone region: the Washburn, the Gallatin, and the Absaroka ranges (Hayden called the latter the Yellowstone Range). Other survey members carefully examined the Teton Range south of Yellowstone, finding it to be mostly Precambrian metamorphics and Paleozoic sandstones, thereby modifying Hayden's impression of 1860 that the range was largely eruptive.

All this enabled Hayden's men to work out the first useful maps of the region. In 1872 Hayden published a map of the park and Yellowstone Lake based on his 1871 survey. Several errors appeared on these first maps—most notably the absence of Lewis Lake and the incorrect assumption that Shoshone Lake (Hayden called it Madison Lake) was the source of the Madison River. However, Hayden's second expedition of 1872 corrected these and most of the other errors on the first maps. Over the next few years Hayden issued six other maps of the surrounding country (on scales of 2 to 10 miles to the inch) that included portions of Utah, Idaho, Montana, and Wyoming territories, on four of which he also showed the major geologic formations.

There is another interesting point about Hayden's explorations in the Yellowstone region. A reporter from the *Helena Daily Herald* interviewed Hayden on the eve of his march upriver in 1871. After outlining plans for his exploring parties, Hayden added candidly, "Then, if possible, they are to cross from the head of the Yellowstone to that of the Snake River, and down to Fort Hall, surveying the entire route accurately, at the instigation of J. Cooke & Co., who contemplate running a branch road through this Pass [Two Ocean Pass] to connect with the Central Pacific, if practicable." Never mind that the survey was unable to complete this exploration of the headwaters of the Snake and Yellowstone rivers until the 1872 season. More interesting is Hayden's admission that he set the route of his survey partly for the benefit of a private party. Perhaps Cooke & Co. contributed something to Hayden's expenses in Yellowstone, just as Blackmore had paid Hayden to survey his Spanish estates in Colorado.

From this summary it is obvious how far beyond the immediate area of the Upper Yellowstone Hayden's vision extended. Moreover, in approaching the Yellowstone valley—via Ogden and Salt Lake City, Fort Hall in Idaho Territory, Virginia City and Fort Ellis in Montana Territory—Henry Elliott made drawings along the whole route, while Schönborn summarized the topography and Hayden sketched the geology. At the beginning of his own report Hayden added a short but valuable description of the northern third of Utah, including the Great Salt Lake, the Wasatch and Uinta ranges, some of which lay in the path of Clarence King's survey, to which Hayden made a brief but flattering reference. Previously, Hayden had been the first to describe the terraces of the Great Salt Lake in detail; now in other ancient shorelines he found evidence of the formerly greater extent of the lake. He pointed out the enormous spread of basaltic lava across the Upper Snake Basin and described the mining region around Virginia City, which he connected to the metamorphic basement rocks.

Further describing the geology, Hayden identified the basic volcanic character of the Yellowstone region. He recognized alternating layers of what he called "trachyte, basalt, and volcanic conglomerates," indicating numerous flows, some he thought as recent as Quaternary age, but most he thought were later Miocene at the oldest and more likely Pliocene. After finding numerous extinct geysers, he decided that the major volcanic force had passed from the region and that the existing geysers were gradually declining. Here and there, in places like Tower Falls and at the bottom of the Grand Canyon, Flathead Pass, the Gallatin Range, and opposite the hot springs on Gardner River he found evidence "that the entire series of sedimentary strata, from the lowest Silurian to the highest Tertiary known in the West, has extended in an unbroken mass all over the Northwest." In Cinnabar Mountain in particular he found a continuous series of beds from Precambrian quartzites to Cretaceous coal strata. He found the earliest examples of extensively overthrusted beds, especially at the head of Jackass Creek. In the East Gallatin Range of Montana he noticed inverted sedimentary beds. In the Madison, Gallatin, and Yellowstone valleys he found the best evidence yet of what Powell later called antecedent streams, and he described them most vividly. "The fact that the streams seem to have cut their way directly through mountain-ranges, instead of following synclinal depressions, indicates that they began the process of erosion at the time of the commencement of the elevation of the surface." Between the sources of the Yellowstone and Missouri rivers Hayden encountered repeated evidence of glacial action in smoothed rock faces and in the movement of huge boulders no mountain stream could have budged. Hayden linked the history of the surrounding country, extending north and west all the way to the Pacific Coast, by supposing a series of crustal uplifts that had been rapidly eroded into basins similar to Yellowstone Basin, basins that contained lakes from Pliocene into

Quaternary times. Yellowstone Lake itself was the remnant of a once more extensive lake. All these revelations—after only two seasons in the field, totaling a mere eight months—amounted to an astonishing accomplishment.

Yet the opinion persists that in Yellowstone Hayden worked superficially and that he cared more for popular wonders than careful studies of nature. This lingering popular image has delayed a more balanced appraisal of his work in and around Yellowstone. Having said that, however, it must be admitted that Hayden himself reinforced the popular image by the tone of several of his remarks. Toward the end of his own portion of the 1871 report Hayden says, "Our journey homeward was so rapid that I could not do more than work out the geological features immediately along the route." And two pages later he says, "I shall therefore hasten on, making a few observations from point to point, referring my readers to a more complete and illustrated report hereafter to be prepared for a clearer understanding of my descriptions." Twice more in the next four pages he admits the preliminary nature of his report, seeming to grow more aware of its incompleteness as he brought it to an end. This is a strange attitude to take in view of the fruitful results he has just set down. And why encourage an unflattering view of himself as a man in a hurry? The answer is he was beginning to feel stung by criticisms that his reports appeared too rapidly, that they amounted to reports of progress rather than finished results. Therefore he was anxious to emphasize that his results were tentative. In his introductory letter to the secretary of the interior, written 20 February 1872 and attached to this first Yellowstone report, he elaborated the point.

> The wisdom of the policy of publishing for the people the immediate results of my surveys, in the form of annual reports, even though somewhat crude, has received emphatic sanction by the great demand for them in past years and the general satisfaction they have given. . . . The attempt, also, to give to these annual reports a somewhat popular as well as scientific cast has met with the cordial approval of the students of geology and natural history all over the country. I trust, therefore, that they may be continued from year to year, as long as the survey shall receive the sanction of the Government.

Of course, not everyone agreed with his publication policy; otherwise he would not have defended it in this manner. The unmentioned presence of Clarence King and his survey weighed on his mind. By 1872 King had finished most of his fieldwork and his survey had already issued two final reports (the last of five others appeared in 1880). Disdaining to issue bulletins of progress like Hayden, King preferred to publish nothing short of final reports, and some scientists approved of his restraint. When legislators began to grasp that Hayden's preliminary reports incurred extra costs they too endorsed King's practices. Therefore, the fact that King issued only final reports put pressure on Hayden to bring out his final reports promptly. The first volume in that series would be Leidy's *Fossil Vertebrates*. All through 1872, even while he tramped around Yellowstone, Hayden hammered relentlessly at Leidy, trying to get him to finish up the volume as soon as possible; it appeared in 1873. Another volume of the final reports appeared the same year, and thereafter at least one came out each year for the rest of the decade.

Though he enjoyed it and needed it, Hayden was concerned about all the popular attention to his work in Yellowstone. All the talk about the wonders ignored what he considered his top priorities: the Great Lignite, a comprehensive treatise on western paleontology, and continued study of natural history specimens of the most diverse character. Writing to George Allen, his former Oberlin professor, on the eve of departing for Yellowstone in spring 1871, Hayden characterized the survey's job for the forthcoming season: "All field work must necessarily be of the crudest kind. It is designed to throw some light on matters that are not obvious at once to the eye." At the same time he was reminding Meek of his wider plans, saying that he wanted Meek to "gather together materials for a grand palaeontological report of all that has ever been done west of the Mississippi, make all the necessary comparisons east or in the old world. . . . The great idea in my mind is to have all the geological and palaeontological matter of the far West worked up full and put into such shape that it will be available." What he wanted, in other words, was a volume supplementing the one they had published in 1865, which covered the earliest fossils up through the Jurassic period. The proposed volume would be on the Cretaceous and Tertiary fossils. (Meek completed the work in 1876; it was published as Volume 9 of Hayden's *Final Reports.*) Meanwhile Meek, Cope, Leidy, and Lesquereux wrote up recent collections in their respective departments for the 1871 *Annual Report,* and all four spent summer 1872 in the field, at Hayden's expense, on studies of direct relevance to the Great Lignite issue. The 1872 *Annual Report* summarized their results.

A look at the two annual reports together gives a good indication of Hayden's real priorities. Total pages devoted to all matters relating to Yellowstone amounted to less than 40 percent of the two reports, while natural history and paleontology consumed more than 60 percent. Hayden wanted his readers to give at least as much attention to the latter as to the former because he felt his geology was just as good as King's and his paleontology and natural history probably better. Never mind that King was publishing his final reports more quickly than Hayden. Given time to get his reports through the press, Hayden would come out all right. Meanwhile, the annual reports, even when tentative in their conclusions, provided an enormous amount of current information, and most naturalists valued them highly for that reason.

Although nervous because of his competition, Hayden was confident about his ultimate prospects. Besides, King had authority to survey only a specific block of country, and being nearly finished, he would soon pass from the scene, whereas Hayden admitted only the broadest limitations to his own work. After all, he directed a "Survey of the Territories," and in 1872 no less than ten territories still remained to be explored. As he wrote to Baird near the end of his second season in Yellowstone, "Genl. [James Abram] Garfield told Governor [Benjamin Franklin] Potts and other citizens of the West that my exploration would be continued as long as there was any of the public domain to be explored, so we might as well strike out as free as we can."

17
YELLOWSTONE
AND THE IMAGE
OF THE WEST

I was certain you would speak with enthusiasm of this great West. I feel sorry for the man who must leave this world without having his eyes fed with the grand vision. If I have aided you to the sight, I am glad.

— Hayden to G. N. Allen, 2 September 1871

NOT ONLY HAS Hayden the man been misunderstood, but so too have the reports he wrote about Yellowstone. The stereotype of Hayden as a superficial popularizer has made it very difficult to discover the perceptive originality of his writings. To read his reports on Yellowstone without prejudice is to realize that he had a novel point of view and that his interpretation of nature sprang directly from his manner of seeing it. To appreciate Hayden's understanding of Yellowstone we must first learn how he looked at it. This exercise is of interest because the way Hayden saw Yellowstone had an enormous impact on the way the American public viewed Yellowstone and, subsequently, came to understand the entire West.

Let us begin with the form of Hayden's reports on Yellowstone. He describes features along the immediate route of travel, one at a time in a sequential fashion. From time to time he compares particular features with similar ones elsewhere, but not in the systematic way that would character-ize a topical or thematic approach. As a result, whatever generalizations he offers the reader are provided in the context of an unfolding chronological narrative.

Recording a sequence of encounters along a direct line of travel *appears* to be an uncomplicated process requiring little study or reflection, and it may seem hasty. By contrast, a topical approach *appears* to be more thoughtful, more thorough. But if we are willing to renounce our assumptions about a re-port based solely on its appearance, it is possible to see that Hayden had a se-rious purpose in mind and that he chose his method of reporting quite deliberately.

It is understood today that individuals employ different methods of learn-ing new material. Some people learn more effectively by participating in a give-and-take conversation, for instance, than by listening to a lecture. Oth-ers learn better by watching, others by doing, still others by reading. Even with regard to a preferred learning technique—watching, for example—people use various skills, strategies, and biases. All of which is another way of saying that people "see" differently. The structure of our brains gives us the mechanism for seeing, but it seems that our previous experience influ-ences what we actually see or at least how we interpret what we see. So it is understandable that one man writing up what he saw in Yellowstone might organize his facts around *events* that he had studied (like volcanic eruptions); another might emphasize *ideas* in which he had some expertise (plate tecton-ics, for example); another would prefer *objects* with which he was familiar (like volcanic rocks, but some would emphasize basalt, others rhyolite, still others the tuff). All these are topical approaches, suitable for someone who already knows the material well and now wants to take the explication to a deeper level. By contrast, the taxonomic approach—simply identifying what one sees, pretty much in the order encountered—seems best for someone ap-proaching a subject for the first time, where the ground is not familiar. Hayden was seeing much that was new, often dramatically and overwhelm-ingly new, and in that regard Hayden's meeting with Yellowstone mirrors in a small way America's larger confrontation with the American West in the middle decades of the nineteenth century.

But this only partially explains why Hayden adopted the taxonomic ap-proach. He wanted to keep discovering new territory, and as long as he was constantly on the move progress reports suited his style better than final (top-ical) reports. Also the descriptive approach enabled Hayden to stress practical points of geology, to emphasize the adventure of fieldwork, and to popularize science through a travelog style. But I think all these results may have grown from Hayden's way of *seeing* nature in the first place. Hayden wanted to record spontaneous impressions, and he chose to do so sequentially because that method, and only that method, reflected the way he perceived nature. Even though he had shown himself capable of publishing systematic historical studies, it is revealing that as early as 1856 when he wrote "A Brief Sketch" he had shown an interest in the descriptive, taxonomic approach. His *Geology and Natural History* (1862) solidified this approach and foreshadowed the emphasis of most of his future writings and all his annual reports.

During Hayden's time scholars began to specialize in their studies of the sciences. They divided natural history into botany, biology, zoology, for example, and they subdivided each of these into smaller pieces. Hayden preferred the older unified approach. For him, splitting disciplines into topical specialties actually created separate subjects, separate realities, but destroyed the seamless fabric of nature's flowing gown. To Hayden, the reality of nature was a totality, a wholeness, and the mind could only grasp it by spontaneous impressions. To Hayden, single impressions gradually linked through narrative provided the only picture one could construct of a region.[1]

One of the pleasures in reading Hayden's works, or the works of any of the men whose reports he published, is coming to know their ambitious modesty. Remembering the voracious energy with which Hayden gathered fossils and birds and insects and mammals, and any other creatures he could find, we recognize his ambition. The same tireless endurance breathes across every page of Cope's pursuit of vertebrates, of Lesquereux's comparisons of stony plants, Coues's lists of birds, or Coulter's flowers. These and other sympathetic spirits celebrated their collections as well as their way of seeing nature in the pages of Hayden's voluminous publications. Confident, energetic, rather pedantic, sometimes combative, in every respect ambitious men, but regarding nature itself, always modest. These were keen hunters, gathering facts, noting the setting, sketching in their impressions, sometimes synthesizing the details into a larger picture, but never wishing to paint beyond the immediate facts they could observe.

Here are samples of Hayden's descriptions of hot springs and geysers near the Gardner River, all taken from his *Fifth Annual Report* of 1871.

The sides of the basin are ornamented with coral-like forms, with a great variety of shades, from pure white to a bright cream-yellow, and the blue sky reflected in the transparent water gives an azure tint to the whole which surpasses all art. The little orifices from which the hot water issues are beautifully enameled with the porcelain-like lining, and around the edges a layer of sulphur is precipitated. As the water flows along the valley, it lays down in its course a pavement more beautiful and elaborate in its adornment than art has ever yet conceived.

And then, too, around the borders of these springs, especially those of rather low temperature, and on the sides and bottoms of the numerous little channels of the streams that flow from these springs, there is a striking variety of the most vivid colors. I can only compare them to our most brilliant aniline dyes—various shades of red, from the brightest scarlet to a bright rose tint; also yellow, from deep-bright sulphur, through all the shades, to light cream-color.

Details. Details of light and its shading. Details of color and its variation. Details to look at, indeed to feast upon, along the sides of the basins, in the orifices, in the beds formed by the extruded water. Hayden's eye wanders over surfaces like a video camera, ignoring the larger setting in order to absorb the thousands of sparkling details.

He takes the same approach in describing rock formations. Elsewhere he mentions how basalt poured out massively over the land, but he is not much interested in the wide-angle view. He does not measure the extent of the basalt, for example, or note its thickness, explain its origin, or trace the several flows to their major sources. He does not want to capture the basalt and paint it into its proper place in a wider picture of the landscape. No, he merely wants to touch it, to sketch its many appearances in separate portraits. Here are several impressions of the basalt he met with between Gardner River and the vicinity of Tower Creek, each in different locations.

The summits and sides of the mountain are thickly covered with fragments of dull-brown basalt; but what seemed most strange were the rounded masses of black, very compact basalt, mingled with the less compact angular fragments, broken from the mountain side. . . . The West Fork [of Gardner River] rolls over a bed of basalt, which is divided by jointage into blocks that give the walls the appearance of mason-work on a gigantic scale. . . . On the summit of the ridge the basalt is quite coarse, and decomposes into a kind of sandy clay.

The general mineral character of the igneous material is about the same, but the colors and textures are very variable; some of them are coarse, decomposing easily; others rough, angular, vesicular, or compact; some red, purple, brown, black, etc.

[Tower Falls] are surrounded with pinnacle-like columns, composed of the volcanic breccia, rising fifty feet above the falls and extending down to the foot, standing like gloomy sentinels or like the gigantic pillars at the entrance of some grand temple. One could almost imagine that the idea of the Gothic style of architecture had been caught from such carvings of nature. Immense boulders of basalt and granite here obstruct the flow of the stream above and below the falls. . . . In the walls of the lower end of the Grand Cañon, near the mouth of Tower Creek, we can see the several rows of columns of basalt arrayed in a vertical position, and as regular as if carried and placed in the sides of the gorge by the hand of art. . . . On the west side of the Yellowstone and west of Tower Falls, the basalt is quite massive, sometimes forming columns quite irregular in form and length, differing much from those on the opposite side.

Hayden employed an impressionistic approach, which emphasizes local variations, not just for hot springs and basaltic rocks but for virtually everything. Open his report at random and read a few pages; the pattern reemerges. He provided a bird's-eye view from time to time, but he never lingered over it, never subordinated all the details to a larger composition (the way Thomas Moran painted, for instance), preferring instead to define the space that he would fill with details.

Until his way of seeing is understood, Hayden's prose seems jumbled, disordered, unfocused, hence monotonous and tiring. But Hayden was trying to see nature and then describe it as it was presented to him. And nature is, in the raw state he found it, hugely irrational and confusing, to the point of overwhelming the observer. Order and some sense of comfort, which immediately enables an aesthetic appreciation, is possible only by taking nature one small piece at time: one impression, one image at a time.

Collecting photographs and pictures of the West was similar in Hayden's mind to collecting fossils and natural history specimens. The analogy of the jigsaw puzzle is apt. Just as fitting more and more bones together finally leads to the reconstructed anatomy of a fossil dinosaur, so more pictures lead to a fuller grasp of the bizarre reality that was the American West. For this approach to succeed Hayden had to keep moving, had to keep collecting an ever larger quantity of bones and specimens and images, which meant that he had to keep rolling into new territory. Thus he organized the survey as a whole in the same way he organized his tour through Yellowstone, and for an identical purpose: to gather separate impressions and to link them with others into a grand picture by means of a continuous narrative, eventually designed to encompass the entire West. As a result of this frankly quantifying approach, an image of the West did begin to emerge, an image based on Hayden's impressionistic view of reality.

Hayden's way of seeing nature influenced far more than the style of his report writing. Before I elaborate on that idea, it may be helpful to rehearse the evolution of Hayden's interest in the visual image. He had been quick to appreciate both the popular appeal and the scientific uses of photographs and pictures. Before the Civil War he realized their potential for illustrating principles of geology. On his return to the field after the war, he began accumulating images of landscapes as well as of Native Americans. Although the evidence is not conclusive for 1866, he may have employed a photographer during part of that summer. In 1867 he persuaded a Chicago photographer to accompany him in the field for a time. Simultaneously he took along his former colleague Anton Schönborn, who made sketches of the landscape. For three seasons beginning in 1869 artist Henry Elliott joined Hayden's corps, and he contributed a mass of original drawings of landscape, geology, and scenery. In 1870 three leading American artists, S. R. Gifford, T. W. Whittredge, and J. F. Kensett, accompanied his survey, and that same summer Hayden hired William Henry Jackson, who would work for the survey for the duration of its existence. Also in 1870 Hayden brought out *Sun Pictures*, the first of his publications linking scenic and scientific images of the West. When he arrived in Yellowstone, in 1871, he had Schönborn, Elliott, and Jackson on his payroll, and Thomas Moran would join him for the summer. There was also a plan for Albert Bierstadt to accompany Hayden, but this did not work out.[2] At any rate the artist's perspective would be well represented on Hayden's tour through Yellowstone; that perspective was also becoming fundamental to Hayden's personal outlook on the West.

As a result, Hayden brought back a flood of images to Washington. There is no telling how many exposures Jackson took in Yellowstone, but Hayden had about three hundred promptly made into prints after the 1871 trip. Moran's contribution was more in quality. His large *Grand Cañon of the Yellow-Stone* made a stunning public debut in New York on 2 May 1872, then traveled immediately to Washington, arriving too late to have any impact on the vote to create Yellowstone National Park but in plenty of time to stimulate even further that feeling of awe and wonder that Hayden had been broadcasting across town since his return. The painting hung briefly in the Smithsonian, then was moved to the old hall of the House of Representatives. With help from Hayden on the lobbying, Moran persuaded Congress to purchase it for the nation— for $10,000.

Henry Elliott was being overshadowed by his more illustrious colleagues; nevertheless his workmanlike sketches served Hayden's purposes admirably. Elliott made hundreds of drawings, not only of the round-trip route from Ogden to Yellowstone but of the entire circumference of Yellowstone Lake. No less than sixty-three illustrations graced Hayden's own report in the

1871 *Annual Report* (the only portion of that report to be illustrated), and
Elliott drew most of them, though Moran depicted a dozen of the more dramatic views, such as the Grand Canyon, Yellowstone Lake, and several geysers. Hayden himself may have contributed the illustration on page 73 (a
geologic section); he implies that he did, though the style is strongly reminiscent of Henry Elliott.

The barrage of images continued in the 1872 *Annual Report*. Illustrations
were now sprinkled more generously through several sections, even fossils
and animals commanded pictorial attention. Jackson's photographs appeared
for the first time, now translated to the printed page through lithography.
Elliott no longer worked with the survey in 1872, but William Henry
Holmes took his place, and he saw with the eye of a genius. He captured
broad vistas without investing them with Moran's feeling of epic drama. He
instilled an appreciation for detail and geologic structure that made his pictures even more valuable than photographs. Given the crude contrasts and
the dim depth of field in early photographs, Holmes's drawings offered far
more physical realism. Holmes saw the way Hayden did: his pictures summarized a wealth of detailed impressions regarding rock structure and tex-
ture, faults, uplifts, and erosion.

All this image making enlarged Hayden's renown and reputation and
aided the progress of his survey. Naturally, the cresting of his fame at
Yellowstone spilled over into the halls of Congress, where he gained an even
larger appropriation for his venture into Colorado Territory. By the time he
arrived there, in 1873, the survey had adopted a successful but inflexible routine, one that the Yellowstone experience made irreversible. Beginning with
the report on the 1870 season Hayden combined an annual review of his geologic and geographic work with a series of scholarly reports on paleontology
and natural history. He followed the pattern in the two reports published for
the Yellowstone years. But to continue uncovering new specimens for his collaborators to describe, to fill in more blanks on the map, and to provide more
visual and verbal impressions of the West, he had to keep moving. It was no
longer possible for Hayden to stop or to shift his focus to a particular region
and systematically work up its science—the way King was doing along the
40th Parallel. His previously successful method and his emerging vision of
the West urged him to march along an ever-widening path. And now that he
had a reputation for documenting wonders, that too drove him to find new
curiosities that would excite his growing army of readers. If he had any anxieties about the now-fixed course of his future work, he never committed
them to paper. But why should a man of action have any such doubts, especially when greeted with widespread approval?

Meanwhile another result of his image gathering began to take hold. It was perhaps more significant than anything else he accomplished in Yellowstone, yet no one has ever acknowledged it. All the photographic and artistic renderings of the West that he sponsored necessarily emphasized those qualities that can be captured in a picture: color, space, light, perspective, scale—visual qualities. And because these pictures represented among the earliest self-conscious confrontations between civilized easterners and a fantastic new world, they aroused strong responses, for the scenes were bright, expansive, exotic, powerful, violent, and dangerous. Even when more serene or simply "beautiful," according to traditional canons, the pictures speak with force and clarity. Ambiguity is absent, unimagined. In other words, these pictures offered an interpretation of reality based on visual impressions, and these impressions were sharp, intense, and dramatic.

This imaging of the West continues to be dominated by the kind of focus Hayden and his men gave it.[3] Of course, Hayden did not originate this emphasis. The process of understanding the West as a series of visual images began in Yosemite during the 1850s. As with popularizing science, so with image making, Hayden may not have been the creator of either movement, but he was a most important pioneer and a hugely influential practitioner. His particular interpretation of the West continues to the present day, as witnessed by the endless flood of coffee-table books, prints, and calendars. Sometimes the views are artfully composed and developed with technical sophistication, as in the work of Ansel Adams; more often they contrive to produce a simple commercial impact.

We need to stop for a moment and remember that an object and its image are not the same thing and that all images distort in one way or another the reality of their objects. If there is distortion in the process of making a single image of a single object, how much more is this process magnified when many images are made of many objects. On another level, insofar as an image is meant to convey a meaning, how misleading it is to look for an understanding of the West merely by inspecting its pictures. If the pictures convey anything, it is the imagination of the picture maker, not the reality of the West.

But what is the West anyway? Certainly more than an image or the sum of many images. For Hayden and those who assisted him in gathering images, I believe the West was primarily an experience, an experience most of them never got over and for whom the literary or visual images were pleasing but pale reminders of a series of unforgettable past adventures. Who can blame them for trying to capture in tangible form some hint of the ineffable moments they had enjoyed in the West? But in hauling so many astonishing images back east, Hayden and his colleagues reinforced a particular view of the West, a view that distorted its total reality or at best emphasized only one aspect of it. I say this not to denigrate the grandeur of the West, but to make the point that grandeur is only a small part of its totality, a part that is susceptible to image making. What a camera and a painting really capture—more accurately, contrive to capture—are not parts of reality and certainly not qualities, but images that, if successfully arranged, suggest certain qualities. Yet in the minds of those who never experienced the West for themselves, these pictures and their assumed qualities *became* the reality of the West.

I think it is fair to assume that Hayden and his image makers realized they were rendering only a segment of the West or a slanted view of it. They did not deliberately try to distort reality, at least not very often. There is Jackson's famous first photograph of the Mount of the Holy Cross, several parts of which he altered to make a more interesting picture. In his celebrated oil painting Moran did the same favor for the Grand Canyon of the Yellowstone, and there are other examples though they remain exceptions. In making their selections of reality Hayden and his men were conveying an image, but at the same time creating a mythology for the West.

Let us also look at a verbal portrait to make the point that writers and image makers were producing the same result. In 1872 Hayden took along a young naturalist named Clinton Hart Merriam. His first appraisal of the Lower Geyser Basin is full of the awe that all Hayden's men exuded in the presence of these wonders. Merriam even described his personal experience with geysers and did not flinch from mentioning harsh realities.

> Today for the first time we struck the Hot Springs & geysers. They are wonderful. One can form no idea of their grandeur without seeing them. The geysers are everywhere & the ground is oftentimes hollow between them & it is really dangerous to walk around. I fell through & scalded my right leg, also my hands; when I was in swimming I stepped into the river near a large geyser & the water was so hot that it burnt both feet.

Yet as vivid and realistic as this account is, it omits several gruesome but unromantic details of Merriam's life while at Yellowstone. It is only in his diary that he admitted he had been fighting for weeks a painful infection he acquired when he ran the blade of his knife deeply into his finger; aggressive mosquitoes plagued him and the rest of the party daily; and Merriam had recently managed to smear poison ivy all over his face. That reality of the West seldom found its way into the popular descriptions our heroes brought back home and published so freely in newspapers and magazines. Also ignored were moments of homesickness, fear, and danger; the pain of gnawing hunger when food ran out or the agony of sickness when the food was bad; the terror of becoming lost; the losing battle to stay clean and dry; the monumental effort required to secure even a few moments of comfort; the sheer fatigue, and often boredom, of having to sustain oneself in an inhospitable wilderness. Such experiences are well documented in private letters and diaries, but were rarely offered for public consumption.

In glorifying, prettifying, and thus distorting the West, Hayden and others who assisted him with his imaging work were helping to create a mythology of the West. Those who mythologize can create whatever reality they desire, and for most who experienced the West with Hayden it loomed larger than life ever thereafter, at least larger than the ordinary lives they seemed to live elsewhere. Given all the professional success and personal satisfaction he found there, perhaps it was only human that Hayden should have exaggerated the West's importance, and it is not surprising that the pictures he gathered reinforce a mythology of the West as a heroic, romantic, and exotic place.

For years it has been widely assumed that Jackson's photographs made a decisive impact on the legislators who drafted the Yellowstone Park Act. With one notable exception, recent authors have endorsed this opinion.[4] But no matter how much impact is attributed to a selection of Jackson's photographs, the point is that those pictures only reinforced a mythology of the West that depended on visual images. It was that mythology (to which Jackson and all Hayden's image makers contributed) that so profoundly influenced the origins of the Yellowstone National Park. Ever since the days of Lewis and Clark, stories of the West had been filtering back east through explorers, trappers, prospectors, later settlers, land promoters, and railroad agents. These spokesmen repeatedly told of a new and different country, especially its strikingly larger scale. Gradually, picture makers brought back a growing supply of paintings, sketches, and photographs. As a result, even before the Yellowstone region itself had been brought to the public's attention, the nation had been conditioned to think of the West as something quite wonderful to look at; Congress approved the Yellowstone Park Act because of this thinking—and did so without a dissenting vote, within three months of the bill's introduction into Congress on 18 December 1871. President Grant signed the bill on 1 March 1872. A favorable climate for the idea of a national park already existed, and there can be no doubt the pervasive imaging of the West, so effectively orchestrated by Hayden, played a large part in creating that favorable climate. That is the important point, not which particular individual first conceived the idea of the park.

Nonetheless, several men claimed the park idea was theirs, and Hayden was one of them. Looking carefully at Hayden's claim reveals that the traditional image of the man has stood in the way of appreciating his real importance in creating the Yellowstone National Park. For the background I will summarize the work of Richard Bartlett and Aubrey Haines.

As early as 1833 artist George Catlin (significantly, an early image maker) called for the creation of a national park covering much of the Great Plains and part of the Rockies. A number of other pre–Civil War authors mentioned such an idea in general, and precedents for public preserves immune from private ownership existed from the 1830s, including New York's Central Park (1856) and Yosemite Park (1864), at first a state park. Specifically regarding Yellowstone, Montana Territorial Governor Thomas Meagher said privately to a few friends in 1865 (as recorded in a diary) that if Yellowstone proved to be what explorers reported, it should be protected by the nation. David Folsom, who went there in 1869, made the same suggestion (in another private conversation), as did Cornelius Hedges, who was there in 1870 (in yet another private conversation).

In view of this, what are we to make of Hayden's claim, written to Secretary of the Interior Carl Schurz, on 21 February 1878: "So far as I know, I originated the idea of the park, prepared the maps designating the boundaries, and in connection with the Hon. W. H. Claggett, then Delegate from Montana Territory, wrote the law as it now stands"? William Horace Claggett, by the way, also claimed he initiated the park idea, but he denied working with Hayden on the law. Historians have found no evidence Claggett suggested the idea, and they doubt he had much to do with writing the law. For a drafter of the House bill, historians prefer Henry L. Dawes, representative from Massachusetts, a powerful member of the appropriations committee, and a strong supporter of Hayden. But it was the Senate bill that the House later approved and sent to President Grant, and that bill was introduced into the Senate by another strong Hayden backer, Samuel Pomeroy of Kansas, who also chaired the Senate's Committee on the Public Lands, where the bill was probably drafted in the first place. Everyone—contemporaries and historians alike—acknowledges Hayden's major and probably crucial role in lobbying for the Yellowstone bills. He worked directly with Senate and House committees on the public lands. His formal report on Yellowstone was not printed until after the legislation became law, but a draft of it was available by mid-January, if not somewhat earlier. The House Committee on the Public Lands actually adopted a synopsis of the draft version and submitted it as its own report to the House on 27 February. The House then ordered it to be printed, showing how much importance it gave to Hayden's views. In short, Hayden may not have written either Senate or House bill, but both bills reflected his influence.

But, again, did he suggest the idea for a national park? Bartlett and Haines are both at pains to point out that A.B. Nettleton, the agent of Jay Cooke whom we met before, wrote to Hayden on 27 October 1871 asking him to endorse the park idea in his official report. But this was more private talk behind the scenes. Surely the larger point is that Hayden went beyond the private chatter and began to promote the idea *in public*. How many others among the so-called originators of the park idea did that? Long after the fact, Langford claimed his lectures, in Washington on 19 January and in New York on 21 January 1871, concluded with pleas for a national park, but no evidence supports this claim.[5] That leaves only Hedges, and we will come to his claim in a moment. It is in this sense of the first *public* recommendation for a national park that Hayden's claim must be taken seriously.

Yes, Hayden pushed the idea in public, both in his draft report (and the printed synopsis) and in an article he wrote for the February issue of *Scribner's Monthly*. Importantly, these were the earliest public statements in favor of a specific *national* park, made at the time when the issue lay before the legislature. True, Hedges had published an article in the *Helena Daily Herald* on 9 November 1870 suggesting the region be secured for "public use," but he had in mind to alter the boundary between Montana and Wyoming territories so that the park would lie exclusively in Montana and become a *state* park, along the lines of Yosemite. Under the circumstances, I must part company with Bartlett and Haines in the interpretation of this matter and conclude that private expressions or endorsements of an idea are merely a demonstration that an idea's time had come.

The debate over who first expressed the national park idea privately is interesting but academic.[6] It is important in identifying the several voices that first picked up a tune, voices that soon became a chorus. We know now that Hayden was not the songwriter who first wrote the tune; he may not have been the first soloist to sing it in public either, though I know of no one else who beat him to it. He *was* the leader who took charge of a swelling chorus of voices and directed them, along with his own, at the moment an articulation of the idea made a difference: at the crucial time of advocacy before the Forty-Second Congress.

Until now no one has drawn a distinction between originating the idea for Yellowstone National Park and being the first to promote it in public. I have made that distinction to clarify what Hayden did and did not do. Apparently, he was the first public advocate, but just as clearly he was not the conceiver. Yet Hayden claimed to have "originated the idea of the park." Though he knew this was not the truth, he also knew that among a bevy of similar boasts his own commanded more believability than anyone else's. At the time he asserted this claim he was in the midst of an ominous political struggle, and his reputation needed a fillip.

Before looking at that struggle, we must give Hayden his just desserts. He had been yearning for acclaim, and Yellowstone rewarded him with reputation. At the same time some of his detractors hung around his neck the shingle of a crass popularizer. Both aspects of his fame require further exploration.

18
THE CELEBRITY

Many persons who have seen me grow up from nothing imagine I should do for them the same servile things I did years ago, but I claim some respect now, or I let them alone. There is not a man on earth who has been a true friend to me all the way through who can say that I have ever deserted him. Whenever I have seemed indifferent or arrogant, there has been a <u>persistent</u> reason for it, not one neglect, not one rebuff alone, but a series of them. You know how complicated my relations are getting to be with the world. The consequence is that I get a "<u>sorehead</u>" every little while. I cannot comply with all the demands that are made upon me. Reasonable requests on my part are not respected by some. I must therefore have a fixed line of action and go through with it at all hazards.

—Hayden to Leidy, 26 October 1872

THE ENCOUNTER BETWEEN Hayden and the Yellowstone region made both of them famous. The national and, after 1872, international attention that flowed to Yellowstone National Park resulted directly from Hayden's efforts to focus not just his geographers and geologists on this extraordinary region but especially his team of artists, photographers, and writers, who publicized its scientific and scenic values. Hayden had a great deal to do with forging the nation's first national park. Conversely, his labors on behalf of Yellowstone earned him renown in his own day. Even today, when all his other interests and achievements are mostly forgotten, he is still remembered in connection with Yellowstone.

Hayden knew how to exploit Yellowstone to his advantage. William Tecumseh Sherman was one of those who had heard Doane's report read before the Philosophical Society of Washington during winter 1871, and it fired his imagination. Sherman, commanding general of the army since 1869, was one of many influential men who wanted to see the Yellowstone region explored. Hayden remembered to send him a personal letter from the field summarizing his work. Hayden extended this thoughtful touch to all his important backers. Though brief, these letters carried a message that made a far greater impression than any details of Yellowstone he might have mentioned: "I wish to write you just a few words to show you as unmistakably as I can that I do not forget you even in this far off region." Hayden was becoming a master at these tactics, and they paid handsome returns. For instance, more than nine weeks before his appropriation for 1872 was formally approved, James Garfield wrote to tell Hayden that the appropriations committee had agreed to recommend $75,000 for the survey that summer.

This was all part of the politics of funding the survey, which Hayden orchestrated with keen appreciation for fitting each move into a larger strategy. As he told Leidy, "I am most anxious that your report be full in order that the results may tell on another appropriation." To Meek he said much the same. Meek was considering writing up the fossils of Clarence King at the same time, a prospect that brought this exclamation from Hayden: "Do not touch any other work I beg you, for I must raise more money this winter." As an inducement to stand by him faithfully, Hayden offered, "I may desire you to work up some tough, obscure points in western geology every year, and it will be of great service to your health. If you will stand strong by this work you will not lose anything but make much. Nothing can put my organization down now. It will grow greater and more important every year." No doubt this rhetoric was not nearly so persuasive as the fact that Hayden was paying Meek regularly; in any event, Meek complied and did not take on any further work for King beyond what he had already completed in 1870.

Even congressmen received Hayden's not very subtle directives to prosper by backing a winning horse. He wrote to James Monroe: "I count on your earnest friendship for three (3) terms. Aid me in the good work and the people will sustain you. I have grand plans for the future which ought to succeed." That was the stroking, or gentle side of the tactic, the flip side of which could be more demanding. Here he writes, again to Monroe, on the importance of pressing the government printer to proceed with his report at once: "I will not be near there [Washington] to stir the matter up. Do not let a moment pass without seeking him I pray you." Blunt and distasteful as it may have been to some, the strategy worked, for beginning with the Yellowstone years Hayden prospered mightily.

And everyone wanted to identify with his success, especially the politicians. Garfield traveled west during summer 1872, and though not actually with Hayden during his field maneuvers, he did manage to pass within sight of Garfield Peak, a high point of the Bitterroot Range that Hayden had tactfully named for him. Secretary of the Interior Columbus Delano also wanted to see some to the country whose exploration he was urging Congress to fund;

he met Hayden in Salt Lake City and had a brief opportunity to see the survey in action. So did other congressmen and officials of the Interior Department. Though most could not accompany the survey itself, several managed to place their young friends with Hayden for a summer or two as "general assistants." Thus Garfield found a place for Professor Edmund Wakefield of Hiram College, Representative Monroe did the same for Rush Taggart, and so did a number of other congressmen, including Representative Dawes and Senator John Logan, who placed relatives with the survey. Hayden told one colleague that during summer 1871 he would be taking along six political appointees and he had turned away another fifty.

These general assistants were supernumeraries, of course, though Hayden squeezed whatever useful services he could from them. Young Logan proved an admirable collector of butterflies, and he assisted Stevenson with the paperwork; Taggart was helpful in geology. Hayden took along two cronies of his own: George Allen, his former professor at Oberlin, who helped collect botanical specimens, and William Blackmore, whose presence will call for a more extended comment later on. Blackmore persuaded Hayden to take along his nephew, Sidford Hamp.

But the appearance of the survey as a patronage circus would be misleading. In the wake of success also followed men of outstanding ability. When he joined Hayden in 1872 William Henry Holmes had only his gift as an artist and a number of friends at the Smithsonian, but during the next few years with the survey he blossomed into a talented geologist and discovered a lasting interest in ethnology and archeology. He later became head curator of anthropology at the U.S. National Museum, chief of the Bureau of American Ethnology, curator and then director of the National Gallery of Art. Clinton Hart Merriam was only sixteen in summer 1872, but his report on birds and mammals was so good that Hayden published it the following year. A versatile naturalist, Merriam went on to head the Bureau of the Biological Survey. Henry Gannett came on board the same season as a young topographer, boasting two degrees from Harvard, one from the Lawrence Scientific School, and another from the Hooper Mining School. He stayed in the field with Hayden for seven seasons and later became chief geographer of the U.S. Geological Survey and chief geographer to the Tenth, Eleventh, and Twelfth censuses. Gustavus Bechler came along as a topographer in 1872, as did geologist Frank Howe Bradley at the suggestion of J. D. Dana. Bradley and Bechler took charge of the Snake River Division of the survey that summer; it was the first time Hayden had enough staff that he could delegate some of the field responsibility to others. Albert Charles Peale, a member of the famous family of Philadelphia artists, took Hayden's course in geology at Penn and graduated with an M.D. in time to join Hayden for his first trip to

Yellowstone. Hayden assigned him the task of writing up the first scientific analysis of the hot springs and geysers, and Peale's results spanned all three of Hayden's annual reports on Yellowstone. Peale's report in the *Twelfth Annual Report* was an extended monograph that might just as easily have appeared in the survey's *Final Reports*. John James Stevenson, who later did some geology with Lieutenant Wheeler, considered joining Hayden's survey, as did Grove Karl Gilbert, who decided instead to join Major Powell.

In addition to these regulars recruited for his field corps, Hayden attracted a host of naturalists of the first rank to write for one of the publications of his survey: men like Elliott Coues, Alpheus Spring Packard, Jr., John Merle Coulter, George H. Horn, Philip Reese Uhler, Joel Asaph Allen—to name only a few. Meanwhile the old guard—Meek, Leidy, Cope, Lesquereux, and Cyrus Thomas—continued to produce important work for the survey. Hayden became a powerful patron of science, mentoring younger men and encouraging fresh work from veterans, and between them he managed to bring out a combination of popular and scholarly works that illustrated his broadbrush understanding of natural history.

Naturally, these professional works took time to bring to fruition; meanwhile newspapers and periodicals made Hayden's instant fame as an explorer. Right after his first venture to Yellowstone in 1871 the *Helena Daily Herald* sang his praises. Other articles soon followed in the *Boston Advertiser, New York Times, Cheyenne Daily Leader, Cleveland Herald,* and *Sacramento Bee*—the first wave in a flood of publicity sweeping the county for Hayden and his survey. Several of Hayden's men contributed to the torrent. Henry Elliott wrote four articles in as many months following the 1871 season, two of them for a national illustrated paper. Robert Adams, Jr. (another graduate of Penn, who did not study with Hayden) went to Yellowstone twice with the survey and returned home to deliver a popular illustrated lecture. He also wrote thirteen articles for the *Philadelphia Inquirer* in 1871–1872 on the survey, mostly about Yellowstone. Rush Taggart wrote one article on Yellowstone and may have published another. Hayden's champion publicist in Yellowstone, however, was Peale, who wrote a dozen articles for the *Philadelphia Press* and three more for the *Illustrated Christian Weekly*.

Hayden himself got into the act, beginning with an article in *Scribner's Monthly* (February 1872) and continuing with three more in the *American Journal of Science* (February, March, and April 1872). The former, gorgeously illustrated by the drawings of Thomas Moran, reads much like his first annual report on Yellowstone; indeed he wrote the article at the time he was preparing that report, and he put similar language into both. In emphasizing a tourist's view of the wonders he wrote the article as a sequel to Langford's two articles that had appeared in the same magazine the previous spring (hence the puzzling title, "The Wonders of the West—II: More About the Yellowstone"). A sequel, to be sure, but one that emphasized how much more of the region he had seen than Langford. In a two-part essay for the *American Journal of Science* Hayden again used language that would later appear in his annual report (and he borrowed a bit from the *Scribner's* piece too), but here he concentrated more on the geology of the region and the location and nature of the hot springs. His approach was more scientific, and he attempted to answer some of the questions provoked by the wonders. He did an admirable job of summarizing what he had learned, but cleverly he saved his best examples and most vivid descriptions for the annual report. That was the one he wanted people to read, for in doing so they would be advancing the cause of his survey. In the third essay for the *American Journal of Science* Hayden gave a few particulars leading to the passage of the Yellowstone Act, modestly passing over his own efforts in that endeavor and failing to claim (as he did for the first time four years later) that he had initiated the park idea.

After his return from Yellowstone, many journals and newspapers clamored for articles from his authoritative pen. *Scribner's* wanted at least one more article. The *New York Tribune* wanted an article. So did the editor of *Appleton's Journal.* With none of these requests did Hayden comply. With some publishers, however, he agreed to send copies of his Yellowstone writings and let the editors reprint excerpts. In this way *Picturesque America* published an article based on Hayden. Similarly, a New York newspaper, the *World,* prepared an article called "The Yellowstone: Story of Last Year's Explorations."

The same trick worked in foreign countries, which proved equally hungry for news of Yellowstone. The British journal *Nature* became the first foreign periodical to reprint parts of his series from the *American Journal of Science.* Other Englishmen were quick to show their excitement, enough that the *Weekly Montanian* was amused to print an article called, "English Comments on U.S. Geological Surveys," which summarized Hayden's report and added quotes from the *London Saturday Review.* In Germany *Petermann's Geographische Mittheilungen* carried a summary of Hayden's *Fifth Annual Report.* A short excerpt appeared in Italy, which included early news of Hayden's explorations of Colorado as well, which began in 1873. *Le Tour du Monde* published the most ambitious foreign translation, which excerpted parts of Doane's report, Langford's two articles, and Hayden's two reports, plus part of Hayden's first report on Colorado. In view of all this, there may have been some truth to the remark of William Blackmore that English boys could never remember the names of American presidents, but "all knew intimately the stories of Dr. Hayden's expeditions into the wild Indian country of the far West."

Meanwhile, to keep news before an admiring public, Hayden began preparing advance publicity on the achievements of his field parties. Hayden wrote two articles in fall 1872 that appeared in the *American Journal of Science* and the *Engineering and Mining Journal*. Bland summaries of where the survey had been operating recently, these articles contained little of substance. Their purpose was to whet an appetite for the forthcoming annual report and in that they succeeded. Every year after his explorations in Yellowstone, the leading scientific journals of the country reviewed his reports, and many of the popular ones did too. Regular attention was also drawn to his survey by the *Annual Record of Science and Industry,* edited by Baird and published throughout the 1870s by Harper and Brothers. The Smithsonian's *Annual Reports* also gave the survey regular exposure as did an almost annual review of American explorations published in *Nature,* written by Hayden's good friend Archibald Geikie.

These general reviews also mentioned other American explorers, but the lion's share of attention consistently went to Hayden. A close study of this publicity—comparing newspaper and journal articles about the Hayden, King, Powell, and Wheeler surveys—shows that Hayden's survey received considerably more coverage than the total of the other three surveys combined. The inescapable conclusion from all this growing publicity is that Hayden's survey was stirring up the greatest interest and Hayden's survey was creating a regular and favorable press for all other scientific work in the American West. The implications for increased government interest in science and funding of scientific explorations are obvious. Also obvious at the time, but worth repeating here because it has since been forgotten, is that thanks to Yellowstone Hayden achieved a reputation as the greatest explorer of the American West.

Hayden would not lead his survey back to Yellowstone until 1878, but the region continued to fascinate him. That fascination, coupled with his unfailing instinct for publicity, engendered several other publications, four of which appeared in 1876. The first was an article attributed to Hayden and Peale, written for *The Pacific Tourist: Williams' Illustrated Trans-Continental Guide of Travel.* Though it is apparent the author had at hand Hayden's and Peale's earlier writings on Yellowstone for reference, the text does not read like either of them. The author wrote about unusual sounds, sights, smells, and vistas, but made no attempt, as Hayden had done in his earlier annual reports, to describe the region faithfully through an accumulation of impressions. Instead the author highlighted some of the famous attractions; by tinkering to achieve more popular effects he produced a ragged and clumsy text. Though the substance derived unmistakably from Hayden, I doubt Hayden was responsible for the published form of this book. The illustrations came from Moran, but an inexpensive printing process failed to reproduce their original power. In short, the book was a sloppy piece of work that probably embarrassed Hayden's friends and outraged his scientific colleagues, but because Hayden's name was on it and the text briskly exuded a touristic style, it reinforced Hayden's image as a shameless popularizer.

What few among even his friends grasped was Hayden's sincere interest in tourism. To his colleagues, tourism seemed incompatible with serious science, but Hayden felt differently and continued to speak of the two together long after he or his survey could benefit from the publicity. It was another example of the boyish enthusiasm of the man: he had invented for himself an absorbing career of travel and discovery, and he wanted to share his passion. Unfortunately, his pride in wanting to associate his name with Yellowstone overwhelmed his judgment in allowing so much editorial latitude. But that was typical of Hayden—craving reputation, but being hasty and careless about getting it, which in the long run has undermined much of what he wanted in the first place.

An interesting contrast to *The Pacific Tourist* is the volume Hayden produced in cooperation with Louis Prang, published as *The Yellowstone National Park and the Mountain Regions of Portions of Idaho, Nevada, Colorado and Utah.* Though making a similar appeal to the tourist, even borrowing some of the same material that appeared in *The Pacific Tourist,* the Prang book was expensively produced, enriched with the first color illustrations of Moran's watercolors, and improved by tightly written descriptions and a pleasing style. The text derived from Hayden, but again a distinctive style suggests the hand of a liberal editor, this time at least to the literary advantage of the finished product. A full correspondence with Prang reveals much about the background of the book.

At age twenty-four Prang had taken part in the intoxicating upheavals that shook Europe in 1848; soon afterward, the German-born romantic fled to America to avoid the Prussian repression that followed. Already an experienced printer and engraver, Prang soon established his own business, producing a variety of trade cards and business advertisements. During the Civil War he cultivated a mass market for colored maps of cities in the news and battle plans, a market he harvested at interest after the war by reproducing famous works of art for an increasingly affluent and art-loving middle class. Prang was the first printer in America to employ colored inks in lithography, using a process he called "chromolithography," and the public rewarded his initiative with a fortune, which Prang enlarged by creating the first mass market for greeting cards. Astutely, he also wanted to capitalize on the growing taste for pictures of western scenery.

Thus, the idea for the second Yellowstone book of 1876 was all Prang's.

He wanted to cash in on the soaring interest in Yellowstone, the popularity of Hayden's survey, and the increased popularity of science, all of which he thought would be enhanced by a quality production featuring Moran's superb watercolors. He imagined that Hayden would write a general introduction on the survey, on Yellowstone, and on the geography surrounding the other pictures beyond Yellowstone. From the first he seems to have planned to write extended captions for the fifteen watercolors himself, and these captions made up the bulk of the text. He assumed, naively, that Hayden would open doors and do most of the marketing for the book. Having gained Hayden's enthusiastic approval of the general idea for the book, Prang proceeded with production without making any specific plans for promotion and distribution and without realizing Hayden was unwilling to do much of the work. Finally, Prang extracted from Hayden a promise to write an introduction. After a number of delays, Hayden delivered, but the result proved so unsatisfactory to Prang that he rewrote it and added a preface over Hayden's name, stressing the novel importance of chromolithography. In short, Prang authored virtually the entire book, though he certainly relied on Hayden's writings and even borrowed specific phrases and sentences here and there. Hayden did not object to these liberties, which he had accepted so often before in order to have his name publicly rejoined with Yellowstone without any effort on his part.

As time passed, the lack of a marketing plan left ripe fruit to rot on the vine. Though Prang created beautiful books at a cost of over $15,000, most of them piled up in his warehouse. At last, with stock on hand and preliminary reviews doing nothing to help move them, Prang dragooned Hayden into selling some, which he did at prices ranging from $36 to $60 apiece. Hayden also gave away several copies to friends, like Senator Aaron Sargent of California, General Sylvester Churchill (Baird's father-in-law), Joseph Henry of the Smithsonian, some other officials, and William Henry Holmes. Unfortunately, a fire at the warehouse intervened, destroying all but about fifty copies in September 1877, putting an end to an excellent but ill-planned idea. The few rescued books became collectors' items. It is a pity so few ever reached the public, for they succeed admirably in promoting the link between aesthetics and science, which it had been Prang's insight to notice in the first place.

The third offering on Yellowstone published during 1876 also suffered from natural disaster in New York City. Hayden was planning a picture book based on Jackson's photographs of Yellowstone. A fire at the Alberttype Company destroyed about twenty negatives. Using one illustration, two pages of his own commentary, a map of the park, and a title page, Hayden published *The Grotto Geyser of the Yellowstone National Park.* It could not have carried much impact, though in abbreviated form it outlines Hayden's intention of spreading more images of Yellowstone.

The fourth publication of 1876 aimed straight at the curiosity of the tourist. *Report on the Proposed Yellowstone National Park* carries a publication date of 1872, but internal evidence shows the correct date to be 1876. It discussed routes to the park, gave distance tables, some statistical information about geysers and mountains, and described scenery, geology, and geography in a most cursory fashion. But in this modest book Hayden stated publicly for the first time that he had written the report of the House Committee on the Public Lands, which the House adopted in January 1872 and used as the basis for its own subsequent approval of the Yellowstone Act. Hayden's involvement was no secret to the congressmen who had worked on the act four years before, but the public did not know all the details; neither did some officials in Washington, nor a number of new congressmen. Because of some political struggles he was then engaged in, which we will look at later, Hayden thought it time to reach back for more ammunition.

Though he continued to cooperate with efforts to advertise Yellowstone and simultaneously promote his survey, the initiative for these efforts did not come entirely from Hayden. It did not have to. So great was the swelling interest in the park, its images, and the vision of the West it conveyed that Hayden was swept along by the genie he had summoned. At the urging of another publisher he did write two encyclopedia articles, "National Parks" (1877) and "Yellowstone National Park" (1878), and a few years later, at the request of different publishers, he wrote parts of two books on the West, each of which gave prominent attention to Yellowstone.

All this publicity for Yellowstone and the survey inevitably led to greater recognition for Hayden personally. His survey gained increased funding (he already had much more than any of his rivals), and Congress eagerly printed and reprinted more of his reports. Even before he returned to his desk in Washington after the 1871 season, the Sociedad Auxiliador de Industria of Rio de Janeiro had elected him a corresponding member, as had the Royal and Imperial Geological Institute of Vienna and the French Temperance and Educational Society. These diverse honors reflected his growing reputation, and during the next two years at least eight other societies elected him to corresponding or honorary memberships, including the Anthropological Institute of Great Britain and Ireland, the American Geographical Society, the Royal Society of Sciences at Liège, and our own National Academy of Sciences. These accolades were only the tip of an iceberg. As the result of his early labors on the Upper Missouri and now in Yellowstone, Hayden gathered eighteen such memberships. Between 1874 and 1880 he gained another sixty-seven, including the leading geological and geographical societies of the world. By the end of his life he had accumulated ninety-one memberships.

Another monument to his growing fame was the naming—actually, the attempted renaming—of the highest peak in the Teton Range. Josiah Curtis summarized the interesting circumstances in a letter to Hayden.

> When the party met in Lower Fire Hole Basin in August 1872, and the vote was about to be taken, giving the name of 'Mount Hayden' to the highest peak of the Tetons, you voluntarily and repeatedly promised in your remarks to the assembled members of the survey that each and every one should receive a set of the photographs taken on the expedition.

A "Mount Hayden" would have been a fitting capstone to Hayden's achievements in the region, especially since two members of his survey, Nathaniel Langford and his old friend Jim Stevenson, had climbed the "Grand Teton" only two weeks before.[1] Stevenson probably instigated the renaming; indeed he may have undertaken the climb in part to gain the conqueror's right to name it. Stevenson owed his longtime companion a favor: the previous summer Hayden had placed Stevenson's name on an island in Yellowstone Lake as well as on a high mountain overlooking the lake.[2]

As much as he savored the idea of commemorating himself on a giant peak near Yellowstone, Hayden found himself trapped by his own rhetoric. In his first report on Yellowstone Hayden had written:

> In attaching names to the many mountain-peaks, new streams, and other geographical localities, the discovery of which falls to the pleasant lot of the explorer in the untrodden wilds of the West, I have followed the rigid law of priority, and given the one by which they have been generally known among the people of the country, whether whites or Indians.

He had also written, in that same report, that if "no suitable descriptive name can be secured from the surroundings, a personal one may then be attached," and he candidly said he would give priority to "eminent men who have identified themselves with the great cause, either in the field of science or legislation." No doubt "Mount Hayden" was suitable on any number of counts, especially because the translation of "le Grand Teton," as the French fur trappers dubbed it, may have offended genteel sensibilities. So far, Hayden had not joined his name with any feature of the western landscape, though later a generous bestowal took place, mostly in Colorado. So it is not surprising that he wanted to start in a region where his name had become so prominent.

And try he did. On the map facing page 255 of his *Sixth Annual Report* (1873) "Mount Hayden" stands forth. In the abundant press about Yellowstone and the nearby regions over the next few years, this new name appeared frequently. But it was not to be, and even Hayden realized the futility of overcoming a popular local contender. When he published his *Twelfth Annual Report* (1883), the map of the region restored the "Grand Teton," and so it has remained. All was not lost, however. On a map of Yellowstone National Park in that same report, a broad region between the Yellowstone Lake and the Upper Falls was named "Hayden Valley," and that, too, has endured. William Henry Holmes claimed he named the valley for Hayden in 1872.

Nevertheless, bitterness over losing "Mount Hayden" may have been part of the reason Hayden claimed that he had originated the idea for Yellowstone National Park. As I said in the last chapter, Hayden did not originate the idea for the park, though he was the first to promote that idea in public. Examining the context in which he made his unjustified claim gives insight into his state of mind over several years. He first claimed the idea in 1876 about the same time he realized "Mount Hayden" was slipping away. We know Hayden well enough by now to realize that he yearned for reputation, that he resented rivals, and that he often muddled the chronology of his previous deeds. In his agitated state, it is possible that he sincerely believed he had been the first to imagine the park idea. It is more probable, I think, that he first heard the idea expressed or first heard conversations that hinted at such an idea shortly after men of the Northern Pacific Railroad began to bruit it about, and that could have been as early as 1870, when Jay Cooke took over a majority interest in the line.

By the time Hayden finally claimed to have initiated the park idea (in 1876), circumstances had changed. The idea was an acknowledged success, even though the park itself now languished in a sort of limbo. It was unfunded, in danger from vandals, but largely unvisited by the public because it lacked linkage to a railroad. (The Panic of 1873 forced Cooke to suspend his backing of the Northern Pacific.) Nevertheless, the concept of Yellowstone (as well as its many images) remained in high vogue, and Hayden wanted to remind the world of his role in originating the park. It was a timely maneuver, because at the time he was locked in a deadly professional duel with John Wesley Powell and in 1878 he had an opportunity to impress their mutual boss, Secretary of the Interior Carl Schurz. Thus in the same letter in which he claimed the national park idea, he also said, because it would carry more weight with Schurz, "It is now acknowledged all over the civilized world that the existence of the National Park, by law, is due solely to my exertions during the sessions of 1871 and 1872." He exaggerated to say "solely." "Largely" would have been closer to the mark, but the worldwide association of Hayden's name with the origin of the park was accurate.

Hayden further claimed he had written the Yellowstone Act "in connection with the Hon. W. H. Claggett." Of course, he did no such thing, but his saying so is very revealing. Since the act had become law, Claggett had been enjoying a certain repute for introducing the House bill. In his desperate desire to associate his name exclusively with Yellowstone, Hayden became jealous of even such a small fish as Claggett. He could have said, and more truthfully, that he had worked with *all* those involved in putting the act together. Or, more impressively, he could have said nothing and asked one of his friends to remind Schurz of his ties with bigger fish, like Dawes, Pomeroy, or Mark Dunnell.

How excruciating is this petty jealousy over Claggett! Here is a man (Hayden, that is) who often traveled alone in the field, frequently under threat from hostile Indians, but who courageously went about his business. No trooper was more cool under fire. Yet threatened by a perceived rivalry in a battle for praise, he loses his composure and resorts to hyperbole to carry the day. Having once made the claim, this proud man continued to think of a successful idea he had championed as his own, especially when he feared that his enemies were trying to denigrate his name and his deeds. Thus in 1883, in the introduction to his *Twelfth Annual Report*, Hayden thought it necessary to repeat his claim about originating Yellowstone.

By 1883 Hayden's survey had been legislated out of existence. He had lost the position that once had given him so much political power and through which he had profoundly influenced the government's scientific policy. He was now a mere employee of the federal bureau that might have been his to direct. His personal life had lost the intensity and high resolve that had focused his earlier years. By 1883 there were no more worlds for Hayden to conquer because he had been summarily removed from the battle. Thus, the introduction to his twelfth—and last—annual report was his swan song. And he knew it.

Hayden was also trying to counteract his negative image. By 1883 a whispering campaign had magnified that image and circulated it beyond the confines of a private spite into the arena of a public scandal. That image took form during Hayden's first contact with Yellowstone and was largely created by a frenzied press corps. Subsequently, Hayden's enemies seized on the image and further exaggerated it to suit their own purposes. The letter to Leidy, quoted at the head of this chapter, shows Hayden reacting to a part of that negative image. Leidy's letter, which prompted Hayden's self-justifying response, gives a useful perspective on Hayden and helps explain why a negative image of him could take hold and spread so successfully.

> Permit me as a friend to say a word or two intended for your eye alone. I wish you to be respected and liked as you have always been, but I find some of your friends and acquaintances begin to speak of you coldly. They say in general that you were once amiable and kind, but fear that prosperity is making you indifferent and arrogant. It costs nothing to remain as you always were, but on the contrary pays well!!

Each quote reveals accurately a different side of Hayden. No doubt he did become somewhat haughty as fame surrounded him, but at the same time some of those who criticized him did so out of jealousy or by way of extending older quarrels that had nothing to do with his recent fame. It was among those inclined to dislike Hayden, for whatever reasons, that the negative image took root. Once established, that image fed upon itself, assumed distorted shapes, and cast shadows everywhere. Here is a typical example. "What you tell me about Hayden falls in perfectly with my estimate of his character. He has a demonic nature, and I should never count upon finding him except when jealousy and self-interest push him." Thus wrote Julius Erasmus Hilgard, an official at the Coast Survey, in the midst of a poisonous exchange of letters with Hayden's old enemy, James Hall, in which both men took unguarded pleasure in painting the worst Hayden they could imagine. Hilgard continued, aptly demonstrating how an unfriendly witness will draw the worst conclusions.

> He is deliciously egotistical: he has a very nice, estimable little wife, who recently was thrown from her little carriage and considerably although not permanently hurt. He said naively to my wife, speaking of the accident—"When I heard of it, it came upon me all at once that I should be burdened with a crippled wife all my life"—thus spoke the man who [sic] you know.

We cannot know how accurately Hilgard paraphrased Hayden, but consider the context a little, which Hilgard completely ignored. Emma Hayden fell from a wagon during late June or early July 1872 near Ogden, Utah, while visiting her husband in the field. They had been married only seven months. Shortly thereafter, on 18 July, a more serious incident took place: another guest of the survey, the wife of William Blackmore, died in Bozeman, apparently of fatigue. Hayden had somehow to pick up the pieces, get his

own wife safely home, continue with the survey, and console his friend
Blackmore, whom he described as "the most broken-hearted man I ever saw."
Under the circumstances, might Hayden not have been feeling guilty about
Emma's accident, because she hurt herself while under his charge in the field?
Might he not have been concerned about the long-term effects of her injury,
including the dreadful possibility that she might have miscarried a child or
even destroyed her chances of having other children? The injury, though
never described in any detail, was serious; nine months later she was still re-
covering—at the very time Hilgard made his snide remarks. I suspect
Hayden said something to Mrs. Hilgard about feeling "burdened with guilt"
or feeling responsible for an injury that might have crippling effects on his
wife—or words to that effect. But given Hilgard's frame of mind, even had
Hayden said exactly this, Hilgard would not have heard it that way.

I have encountered a number of similar statements about Hayden that illustrate how his negative image endured and eventually gave shape to a distorted historical picture of the man. Other examples will follow in their
place, for they have much to do with understanding the remainder of his career. One more regarding Yellowstone is especially apt here. In 1950 Joseph
Ewan published his biographical sketches of American naturalists, entitled
Rocky Mountain Naturalists. On page one, as an epigraph for Chapter One,
Ewan framed the following.

> It is grand, gloomy and terrible; a solitude peopled with fantastic ideas; an empire of
> shadow and turmoil.
>> Lt. Gustavus Doane *on* Hayden's Survey (emphasis added)

A classic statement of the Hayden image if ever there was one! And apparently derived from a contemporary source—except that Ewan erred
grievously and made what can only be called a fascinating Freudian slip.
Tracing the quotation to its source, we find it comes from Doane's journal
for 26 August 1870, before he had ever met Hayden and before Hayden ever
arrived in Yellowstone. The clear purpose of Doane's words, when read in the
context of the surrounding paragraph, is to characterize the Black Canyon of
the Yellowstone River, which he was seeing for the first time. The particular
mental steps leading to Ewan's blunder escape us, but they illustrate powerfully the insidious persistence of Hayden's negative image.

To Hayden himself the popular image he acquired through Yellowstone
was less important than a solid professional triumph. Not only had he documented the wonders of the region, he had explained them in a broad geographical and geological setting, which directly connected with his fieldwork
over the previous decade and a half. He had mastered the logistics of scien-

tific exploration sufficiently that he could now turn his survey in any direction, to any task, and he was resolved to extend his reach over the entire West. He had in harness an expert team of scholars to publish on every aspect of his explorations. In short, here was a man hitting full stride in his chosen profession, and he was keen to make the most of it.

19
GLORY, GLORY
COLORADO, 1873–1876

For the last two years the survey has operated about the sources of the Missouri and Yellowstone Rivers, but the expenses of transportation, subsistence and labor are so great that it seems desirable to delay the further prosecution of the work in the Northwest until railroad communication shall be established. The Indians, also, are in a state of hostility over the greater portion of the country which remains to be explored.
—Hayden to Columbus Delano, secretary of the interior, 27 January 1873

WITH THIS LETTER Hayden formally requested $100,000 for the fiscal year 1873–1874 to be expended in moving his survey into Colorado. The letter is more important for what it does not say than what it does and also for what it implies: Hayden is still initiating the ideas for his field operations. He is not told by the secretary where he will explore next season; he does not request permission to move to Colorado. He tells the secretary where he is going and provides ample justification, giving the sort of cost-saving reasons that department chiefs understood. This independence in planning, this autonomy in execution had been the hallmark of the survey since its inception in 1867, and these qualities would endure to its end.

The letter fails to mention the most powerful motivations Hayden felt for moving the survey to Colorado. True, transportation was a costly proposition without a railroad in the Upper Yellowstone, and, yes, Indians had attacked one of his divisions in Wyoming during the previous season, though they inflicted no casualties and took no property. More work remained to be done in the Wyoming-Montana region, but it was not urgent. Yellowstone had served Hayden's purposes admirably; now he was obliged to perform further deeds to justify the public's continuing interest. Boasting soaring peaks and sweeping vistas, Colorado's dramatic landscapes attracted Hayden like a magnet. He had already sampled the geology, and he knew its elaboration would win him another scientific coup and reinforce his notions about the Great Lignite. Now he came prepared to produce maps as well. Nor was it coincidence that Hayden ventured to bring science to Colorado at just the moment prospectors were calling attention to its vast mineral resources. And doing a favor for William Blackmore regarding the Cucharas-Trinidad coalfields in southern Colorado was timely. Even though it was no longer politic to work openly with Blackmore, Hayden realized that his old friend could mention the survey favorably before the British press.

A favorable press continued to be vital to the survey, and not simply to shower glory on its leader. After six fruitful seasons in the field, Hayden could point with pride to a number of achievements, and certainly he was thrilled to hear the likes of James Dwight Dana say, "I look upon your survey as an institution of the country." But Dana's words underlined a major problem: the survey survived only by lobbying Congress each year to renew its funding. Despite the continuity of its operations, despite its progression from one region to another, no institutional basis secured the survey's future. Jim Stevenson, now the survey's executive officer, helped with lobbying, as did the well-connected Fred Endlich, one of Hayden's geologists beginning in 1873. But Hayden shouldered most of this task alone. In interviews, in official reports, in articles, even in private letters, Hayden began emphasizing that to extend the achievements already won, Congress must now provide for a permanent survey. Partly self-serving, of course, this line of argument also made good sense because nothing of value could be done in Colorado without committing several years there.

Meanwhile, showing a confidence that helped his cause, Hayden organized his approach to Colorado as though he would be granted adequate resources to get the job done. For the first season he deployed seven separate divisions in the field. One would construct a geographic overview of the entire territory, three would study geology and geography within specific regions, Jackson's photographic party would roam at will to discover the best images, and Hayden's own division would examine whatever appealed to him. Jim Stevenson took charge of delivering mail to the other divisions, arranging their food caches, and keeping each in touch with Hayden. Each division prepared its own report, and each report appeared as a segment of Hayden's overall annual report. Hayden assigned naturalists to accompany several of the divisions and required them to accumulate more specimens and prepare separate reports. Sometimes naturalists wrote up their own results; sometimes Hayden farmed out that task to specialists who never entered the field.

Hayden established this pattern in 1873, and he followed it, with minor variations, for the four years required to survey Colorado. This plan could accommodate as many divisions as Congress was willing to fund, for as Hayden liked to remind his boss, "Each one of the parties is complete in itself, and may be sent to any portion of the public domain as the needs of the Department may require."

To coordinate all the topographic work Hayden created the position of geographer, and he filled it by hiring James Terry Gardner. Gardner had been an intimate friend of Clarence King's since boyhood, and during the Civil War the two of them departed for the West in search of adventure and employment. They signed on to work for J. D. Whitney's survey of California, where King got his first real taste of geology and Gardner became an accomplished topographer. In particular Gardner mastered the methods recently worked out by a German-born engineer named Charles Frederick Hoffmann for accurately surveying alpine landscapes. When King left California to initiate his own survey of the 40th Parallel, Gardner came along as his chief topographer. When his survey finished its fieldwork after the 1872 season, King retired to New York to begin writing reports, but Gardner wanted more practical experience. In hiring him, Hayden gained more than geographic preeminence, for Gardner had valuable connections at Yale and Harvard, and he used them to bring several new men of talent on board the Hayden survey, most notably Archibald R. Marvine. Gardner also persuaded William D. Whitney to accompany Hayden through Colorado during summer 1873. It was a happy meeting, for Whitney became a staunch Hayden supporter. Joining the leading survey of the West also suited Gardner's ambitions. As he wrote to his mother, "Should my health hold out I will control American geographical work in three years, and make a name that will not be forgotten."

Still the Gardner-Hayden alliance surprised their friends and threatened to fly apart, for they were very different men. A refined easterner who loved music, fine art, and gourmet food, Gardner often wrote with an exaggerated sensibility, which matched his fastidious manners; but he found it difficult to mix with the rougher men he encountered on the surveys. He cherished some beautiful but simplistic religious ideals, which he manifested in a cardboard piety and a determination not to work on the Sabbath. By contrast Hayden was more the chameleon. Back east, he could enthrall congressmen with his adventures and charm women with his vulnerable openness. He had dark moods and could become incensed by the smallest things, but he made friends easily and around the campfire he excelled as a storyteller. Although he had no time for religious ceremonies, he was unafraid to speculate about the metaphysical underpinnings of theology or discuss the vague border between science and religion. Anna Dickinson climbed Longs Peak with Hayden and Gardner and penned a perceptive comparison of the two.

> What a pair of heads had that party! Hayden, tall, slender, with soft brown hair and blue eyes—certainly not traveling on his muscle; all nervous intensity and feeling, a perfect enthusiast in his work, eager of face and voice, full of magnetism. Gardner, shorter, stouter, with amber eyes and hair like gold, less quick and tense, yet made of the stuff that *takes* and holds on.

Clarence King painted a less flattering picture of Hayden. He did so in a long letter to Gardner the previous February, trying to persuade him not to join Hayden's survey. He began by saying Gardner was "in honor bound to complete for them [the Corps of Engineers, who sponsored King's 40th Parallel Survey] the work which is in your head and hands." Then he admitted, "If you combat them you will stab me." He warned of "trouble and vexation to others (I mean you and your family)," though he could not be specific. He went on to opine that surveying was for younger men (King and Gardner were only 31), that moral and spiritual values were not forwarded by such work, and "that science rolls on and progresses at the <u>expense</u> of those absorbed in her pursuit, that men's souls are burned as the fuel for the enginery of scientific progress." He enumerated the joys of a settled life, no doubt sincerely, vowing never again to work on a survey, and said, "The humanity and Christianity which ought to be the fruitage of our careers, needs the influence of home and stability." The rhetoric and the moral rectitude typify King at the time, but beneath the labored arguments one hears a cry of pain, a deep anguish at the thought of losing his oldest friend to a rival, which accounts for his cruel peroration.

> Now of Hayden I know but little except that his geology is hopeless and his private character bad. You cannot fail to be more or less connected with him in the public mind and I feel altogether certain that his future will be <u>bad,</u> for his science is weak and ignorant and men of his character sooner or later have the mask of position torn off. . . . Do not disguise from yourself the fact that H is a selfish and Christless man. Nor underrate the danger of a connection with him.

Though admitting he knew little of Hayden, still King could not refrain from scorning his work and denigrating his character. This is typical of the overblown, emotional reactions Hayden so often stirred up in his rivals, whose resort to outraged generalities betrayed their deep but inchoate uneasiness about him. Criticism of Hayden's geology was a ruse. The final sentence of King's letter articulates his real concern: "Can you bear to be allied with a man far below you in all that makes the Christian gentleman?"

Significantly, Gardner ignored King's protests. Indeed, his private letters reveal genuine respect for Hayden and approval of his science. "Dr. Hayden seems to make friends everywhere," Gardner wrote to his mother, "and I do not wonder, for he is full of good feeling when his belligerent power is not aroused." To Baird he said:

> We are doing a grand piece of work. Hayden is an enthusiastic supporter of accurate topography and geology, instead of liking superficial work. If that was ever his taste, it has certainly changed, for we have worked side by side and I think I am not deceived in my conception of his standards. I think the grade of our work this summer is as high as anything that has been done in the interior. The topography is the best thing that has been. I have made many improvements that the 40th Parallel experience dictated, rendering the results far more complete.

During the next four years, bolstered by the talents of Hayden's old hands as well as the new men Gardner helped to recruit, the survey rolled along with great success. The geologists found evidence of repeated cycles of continental uplift, then submergence beneath an encroaching ocean; they identified and dated strata on both sides of the central Rockies that had never before been studied; they noted the massive carvings of glaciers; and they enlarged current understanding of the forces of erosion. Hayden himself refined his earlier notions about the upheaval of the Rockies' spine of metamorphic and granitic rocks by pointing out that the uplift did not take place as a steady process in one period of time, but with interruptions over several periods of time. On a more practical level, Hayden and his geologists documented hundreds of precious mineral sites, thereby enabling the mining bonanzas that followed during succeeding decades.

Hayden's personal contribution to the field efforts of his survey diminished during the four years in Colorado. He still loved the challenge of collecting, and even a full summer could not satisfy his many curiosities. As Jackson put it, "He made every man feel that each little individual side trip was vital to the whole—as indeed it was, the way Hayden apportioned the work." He still enjoyed the camaraderie, still discoursed with verve on religion, politics, or whatever other subjects came up around the campfire. And he was still capable of sharp insights.

> We may safely assert that at some period comparatively modern, 10,000 or 15,000 feet of sedimentary beds extended uninterruptedly from the South Park across the interval now occupied by the Sawatch range, all of which, but insignificant remnants, have been swept away, while a mass of the granite nucleus, of inconceivable dimensions, has also been removed. The general elevation of the Sawatch range for 60 to 80 miles is 13,000 to 14,000 feet above the sea at this time, and it is highly probable that hundreds and perhaps thousands of feet have been removed from the summits.

His awareness of erosion and, in particular, the enormous power of glacial action has been scarcely noticed by historians of geology, who would appreciate Hayden more if they read his two reports on Colorado. Also insightful is his description of the Elk Range, especially because he foreshadowed the now fashionable theory of "punctuated equilibrium."

> This is a grand illustration of an eruptive range, and appears also to be an example of a sudden violent or catastrophic action. The immense faults, complete overturning of thousands of feet of strata, and the great number of peaks, all composed of eruptive rocks, indicate, perhaps, periodical and violent action in contradistinction to long continued uniform movements of the elevatory forces.

Despite such jewels of insight, Hayden's reports now appear meager compared to those of his three assistant geologists to whom he left the more difficult problems. But the quality of his work is comparable to what he had achieved over the previous three years in Wyoming. Now that he had assistants to amass the basic information, he could write the appealing travelog narratives he preferred. Though walking over mostly familiar ground during the first two years in Colorado, he compiled some original observations, connected newly found strata to familiar formations elsewhere, and described the landscape with his patented impressionistic sketches.

Because his rivals disparaged much of his fieldwork, it is worth noting that later geologists found much in his work to praise. For more than half a century after his death, numerous monographs in the *Professional Papers* of the USGS identified Hayden or members of his survey as the earliest workers worth mentioning in diverse regions of the West, especially in Colorado. Several authors singled out Hayden as the explorer who found the earliest fossil evidence of particular formations. Even when correcting or supplanting his work, later geologists have respected him for making timely observations.

Colorado also provided unparalleled opportunities for popularizing science through scenery. Probably Hayden's most telling contribution in Colorado was to offer up to the public's unquenchable desire for wonders—which he himself had helped to create—such triumphs as the Garden of the Gods near Colorado Springs, the Royal Gorge of the Arkansas River, and the Mount of the Holy Cross.

He described these features for the first time in his annual report, then elaborated on them in a series of acclaimed lectures. He gave the first lecture at Lincoln Hall in Washington in December 1873, just after his first year in Colorado. The following April he spoke before the American Geographical Society in New York and illustrated his talk with slides. A year later he returned to New York to present another series of views at Delmonico's. Unfamiliar with such dramatic western scenery, the public was fascinated, even stunned, with the parade of images. Hayden took full advantage by giving the public what it wanted and at the same time insisting on the scientific value of photography. It is significant that Hayden pressed this point more than any other western explorer. A suspicion still existed in the minds of most scientists that anything appealing to the popular mind could not be good science. Naturally, Hayden and his survey benefited from the wide circulation of images, but he was also a sincere idealist who believed the public could understand science if offered the facts in an attractive context. In pushing that line of thought, Hayden was ahead of his time, but as a result he lost respect among his more conservative colleagues.

He wrote nothing at all regarding the second two years in Colorado. He devoted his time in the field, shorter than usual for him, to reexamining outcrops of the lignite beds along the Front Range and between Cheyenne and the Green River along the line of the Union Pacific Railroad. More and more time was taken up with the survey's administration. "I am driven to death from 8 A.M. to 10 P.M. with executive work," he confided to a friend, "editing the publications & looking after the interests of the Survey." To the secretary of the interior, he elaborated.

> The various changes which have occurred in the personnel of the party during the past year has [sic] thrown an immense amount of executive labor on me, which has exhausted my strength, and consumed my time to such an extent that I have not been able to give the necessary attention and study to my portion of the report. The editing of so many publications is sufficient labor for one person, and yet this is the

smallest duty that has devolved on the geologist-in-charge. The various executive duties, as correspondence, foreign exchange, settlement of accounts, and the supervision of the parties in the field and office, seem to increase from year to year, so that only mere fragments of my time can be devoted to scientific study.

Which raises the question of how large an administrative staff Hayden had to help him. Until 1870 his expenses for secretarial and office staff amounted to less than $1,000 annually, which means that he got by with part-time help for the first three years of his survey. In 1870, however, he paid more than $2,250 for office help, and over the next seven years an average of $7,253 each year for the same. Not surprisingly, the big surge came after 1871 when Yellowstone thrust him upon a world stage. Requests for publications grew sharply after Yellowstone, and along with them came something new: a massive army of job seekers, some of them mere camp followers, but most of them legitimate scholars and engineers. Faced with an embarrassment of riches, Hayden had to refuse almost all these requests, but in a way that would not alienate the political patrons of these applicants.

From the early 1870s Hayden had one and perhaps a few more temporary clerks in his Washington office, but not until June 1873 did he experiment with an office manager. Cyrus Thomas took that job for two summers while Hayden worked in the field; then Theodore Gill wrestled with affairs for about six months. Thereafter Hayden designated no office chief, though he allowed several men to take care of specific tasks. For instance, he put Jackson in charge of organizing the survey's displays at the International Centennial Exposition. Elliott Coues came on board in summer 1876 to help with publications. Generally though, except in handling correspondence, Hayden didn't want a lot of help. For the crucial tasks—motivating professionals to finish their reports on time and cultivating congressmen to keep the survey funded—Hayden was not comfortable relying on anyone else. Being as personally involved as he was in the entire operation of the survey, he felt obliged to look after most things himself.

As Hayden became more interested in geology, he realized that displaying it depended on accurate topographic maps. Since 1871 the survey had been producing maps, but at the start Hayden did nothing to improve upon the reconnaissance method perfected by the army years earlier: that is, surveying along the route of travel, using a compass to set direction, an odometer to determine distance traveled, and a sextant to establish positions of latitude. The system worked adequately in plotting the sequence of features the survey actually encountered. Difficulties arose in trying to plot features that lay beyond the route traveled. For that, surveyors had to construct a network of contiguous triangles, which related features accurately to each other within the limited scale of the triangles. Hayden's survey first used contiguous triangles in 1872 with improved results. The next refinement was to begin the system of connected triangles from a carefully measured baseline whose longitude and latitude were measured, so that all the features within the triangulation system could be related to others anywhere in the world.

That is what Gardner achieved in 1873. He constructed the baseline on a portion of Kansas Pacific Railroad track, just east of Denver, then began extending his network of primary triangles across Colorado. Eventually, Gardner constructed two other baselines in Colorado Springs and Trinidad as a control on the first one. These primary triangles averaged 25 to 40 miles to a side and were based on fifty-nine stations, or high points, which Gardner's team established atop high summits across Colorado. This network of primary triangles spread over 70,000 miles of alpine country, and from it topographers working in each of the separate divisions could create a system of secondary triangles. These smaller triangles averaged 8 miles to a side and permitted measurements of high accuracy.[1]

Four years of diligent measuring and plotting produced Hayden's *Atlas of Colorado,* a triumph of science and art, and arguably the finest published work of his survey. The *Atlas* began by displaying the whole state on four separate sheets: one each for geology, economic features (including mines and agricultural products), the primary triangulation points, and the major drainages—all of which showed roads, railroads, and towns. Then followed the heart of the *Atlas:* twelve sheets covering the western two-thirds of the state, beginning on the east where the plains meet the mountains and moving west to cover all the alpine and plateau regions. First the natural and man-made features were plotted on a series of six topographical maps; then the same six sheets were reprinted with color overlays to show the main geologic formations. The scale of these twelve sheets was 4 miles to the inch, and contour lines showed elevations at intervals of 200 feet. At the back of the *Atlas* a number of geologic sections depicted the geology beneath the surface in regular strips corresponding to the six maps of surface geology. Finally, William Henry Holmes gave dazzling proof of his unique skills as a landscape artist by rendering in six panoramic views several of the more dramatic alpine scenes encountered in Colorado.

Hayden was justifiably proud of this achievement. Holmes recorded Hayden's reaction to the first proofs. "Hayden is in exstacies [sic]. 'Oh! Oh!' says he jumping clear of the floor with a bundle of them in his hands, 'My good God these are gorgeous, extraordinary. This will stir Europe up to the very bottom.'" Hayden went on to prophesy, "When finished, Colorado will have a better map than any other state in the Union, and the work will be of such a character that it will never need to be done again. Colorado will never support so dense a population that a more detailed survey will be required." He was right about the quality of the map; he misjudged the future.

And he was right about the reception the *Atlas* would have both in Europe and America. Virtually every journal of importance in the fields of geology and geography noticed or reviewed it and always with praise. Andrew Ramsay, director of the Geological Survey of Great Britain, said of it, "I know nothing of the kind superior, or even equal to this work, especially when we consider the physical character of the country and the hardships that such a survey must entail." All of the survey's publications stimulated a high demand from scholars and the general public, but the *Atlas* was the most prized of all. After it became known, Hayden was flooded with requests for it.

Another solid achievement of the survey in these years was the photographic record compiled by William Henry Jackson. Not just attractive illustrations to titillate the wanderlust of the tourist or enrapture the esthete, these photographs gave the geologist and topographer their first accurate records of the landscape, which most artists had exaggerated. By 1877 Hayden estimated Jackson had amassed nearly 4,000 negatives for the survey, and most of those would have been of landscape.[2] It was by far the largest collection brought back from the West at the time, and its impact was greater than any other because of the speed with which Jackson brought his images before the public. The pictures showed enough detail to be used in the geology classroom, and when projected as slides (with a steriopticon), they revolutionized lectures and popular education.

Besides alpine scenery, Jackson brought back valuable portraits of Indians and the first views of ancient cliff dwellings in the Four Corners area. Jackson himself discovered the first of these archeological wonders in 1874 in the Mancos Valley, and he also published the first appraisal of them in Hayden's *Eighth Annual Report*. Jackson gave credit to Hayden for the insight to appreciate his findings.

Though more than thirty years were to pass before the significance of Mesa Verde should be suitably acknowledged, there were some individuals who could at once grasp the implications of those canyon houses. One of them was Dr. Hayden. Before he had glanced at half a dozen photographs, my work for the following season (1875) was determined in his mind. I was to go back, take pictures, explore further. Hayden was a dynamic, intense man; yet never had I seen him at such a high pitch of enthusiasm.

Regardless of their subject matter, all of Jackson's huge haul of pictures dramatically enhanced the popular appeal of Hayden's survey.

So, too, did written descriptions of the survey's work. Naturalist Ernest Ingersoll brought back accurate and humorous accounts of daily life in camp, including anecdotes about food, campfire tales, the proper method of getting wrapped in blankets for the night, and the torments of putting up with mules. Geologist A. C. Peale churned out his share of learned articles for scholarly journals, but he also wrote for a wider audience. Here he speaks of hardships in the wilderness.

> With all its pleasures, and they are by no means few, the life of the sur-
> vey has sufficient of hard work. Sharp and rugged ridges are to be as-
> cended; treacherous rock-slides, that give way beneath your feet, to be
> crossed; bluffs to be scaled, and dangerous precipices surmounted, in-
> volving toil and fatigue; weary rides over monotonous wastes of sand
> to be taken; times to be experienced when supplies give out, and salt-
> less beans and fat bacon have to be washed down with black and bitter
> coffee; dreary days to be spent in your shelter-tent, while the gentle
> pattering of the rain falls unceasingly upon your ear; nights when,
> after a hard day's work, camp is not reached, and, supperless and blan-
> ketless, you lie with your feet to the fire with no covering save the cold
> and comfortless vault of heaven.

No less than sixteen of the men accompanying Hayden in Colorado wrote articles for a similar audience. Bonnie Hardwick has ably reviewed this litera-ture, most of which appeared in newspapers or popular magazines. Even some of the survey's formal reports on its fieldwork embodied the combination of scholarly accuracy and vivid description that Hayden himself had long en-couraged. One of the best examples was Franklin Rhoda's absorbing account of the survey's initial encounter with the San Juan Mountains of Colorado. Rhoda's report received wide circulation in Hayden's *Bulletin* for May 1875 and then was reprinted in the survey's *Eighth Annual Report* (1876).[3]

Hayden himself, who could flourish an engaging style when he wanted to, wrote some of the articles that popularized his scientific work. "We were close up to the south foot of the mountain," he reported of Longs Peak, "and the reverberating crash of rolling thunder among its crags and defiles was grandly terrible." On being short of rations, he noted, "With all our enthu-siasm for science, we cannot endure empty stomachs, and the love of natural knowledge, which we have been so long earnestly seeking, oozes out under that influence quickly." And on the need to find a balance between explor-ing and getting a job done, he confessed, "If we should seek the wonderful always, science and economy would go to the dogs."

Professional geologists writing for a more limited audience also hailed

Hayden. In a highly regarded critical summary of "Geographical and Geological Surveys," J. D. Whitney reviewed the history of surveying in America and gave special attention to the four surveys then operating in the West. Hayden emerged with good marks as, to a lesser extent, did King and Powell. The brunt of Whitney's article was an attack on the Wheeler survey and the army's inadequate methodology. Archibald Geikie, head of the Scottish branch of the British geological survey, wrote a similar review in *Nature* that praised Hayden above all other American geologists.

It would be difficult to exaggerate the enormous impact Hayden had on popularizing science in the West. The scholarly reviews and the countless newspaper articles give only a hint of the vast awareness and curiosity he stirred up though the many publications and pictures of his survey. Some additional measure of this impact derives from the 19,000 pages of materials, mostly letters, Hayden received from some 1,500 correspondents. Even without categorizing every letter, it is obvious that well over half of the mail came from people wanting copies of his publications and photographs. The Powell, King, and Wheeler surveys also received many requests for publications, but whether measured as a percentage of incoming letters or as total numbers, the sum of requests for the other surveys does not even approach the volume directed to Hayden.

Let a few samples convey the broad interests of those who wrote requesting Hayden's works. A principal of city schools in Holton, Kansas, wrote for his reports because he wanted "to introduce as much scientific instruction as it is possible in the various departments." A professor of natural sciences at Denison University wanted the reports for the university's Library. The head of the Coast Survey asked that a colleague be allowed to study Hayden's results; he also desired the reports as a gift for his son. The assistant state geologist of Wisconsin wrote for a recent annual report; so did the state geologists of North Carolina and New Hampshire; also someone from the Kentucky survey; someone else from the Peabody Museum at Yale; a zoologist at Harvard; a botanist at Princeton; a professor in the School of Mines at Columbia. Metallurgists, mining engineers, civil engineers, editors, publishers, cartographers, and curators could not get enough of the survey's output. Professors of geology and natural history all across the country begged for his publications and fell over themselves trying to get temporary appointments to work with the survey in the field. All this must be remembered when we hear from Hayden's enemies that he was a charlatan and his survey a sham.

Though it means jumping ahead a bit, this is the best place to add some little known facts about Hayden's impact on two of the nation's major libraries. Hayden was one of those people with an inborn need to collect. We have noticed his voracious appetite for natural history samples, which added significantly to the basic collections at both the Smithsonian Institution and the National Museum of Natural History. Hayden applied the same systematic energy to collecting books, and through exchanges he built up a formidable library on geology and natural history. From the 1850s, even before he had a steady income or regular employment, he was buying books whenever he could afford them. As soon as his survey began issuing reports, he sent them to colleagues everywhere with the request that they send back something of their work. He even placed an advertisement in the *American Naturalist* seeking book exchanges, and he had the Department of the Interior print circulars inviting individuals and institutions, both at home and abroad, to exchange books. So when he confessed in 1874 to his old nemesis, James Hall, "I am most industriously collecting together by begging and purchasing as many works for the Survey Library as I can," he was only acknowledging what had been going on for two decades.

The Centennial Exposition in Philadelphia of 1876 was a great boon to Hayden's book collecting. With the many interested foreign scientists who stopped by to admire the survey's exhibit, he managed to arrange an exchange of publications, often for whole series. The Smithsonian handled these exchanges, both before and after the Centennial Exposition, and one of the major themes of Baird's large correspondence with Hayden during the 1870s and early 1880s was this foreign exchange of books. Did Hayden beg Baird to arrange these exchanges? No, more the reverse. Baird built up the Smithsonian's collections by exchanging Hayden's publications. In the late 1870s it seems that around half the shipments the Smithsonian sent abroad were Hayden survey publications, and most of them presumed a return.

What happened to the superb library Hayden assembled? When his survey was abolished in 1879, the books were boxed up and stored in the Armory. So voluminous was the library, even in boxes, that Baird estimated "it will require the work of two to four men three or four days to straighten out everything at the Armory." Meanwhile, because Clarence King had assumed the directorship of the newly created USGS, Baird told Hayden, "I have, both directly and through others, stated that all the archives of the official books, maps, etc. of the Survey [i.e., Hayden's survey] are at Mr. King's service whenever he wants them." When Powell succeeded King in 1881, he prepared a list of books that would be useful to have on hand in a library, and he started buying them until he discovered "that most of the publications of the list could be found in the library collected by Dr. Hayden and stored in the Armory Building. These facts have raised the general question of establishing here in Washington a geological library." A year of discussion and bargaining went on to determine who would get what. Baird summarized the result.

I have for some time avoided instructions from you in regard to the books coming to your address in our exchanges and will hereafter transfer these to the library of the U.S. Geological Survey. Major Powell is now making large orders for the completion of his library and to this end is securing works which I am quite sure you have previously received. Do you not think it will be better to open the boxes at the Armory, assorting them there and assigning to the Geological Survey everything relating to that branch, and reserving the purely natural history books for the National Museum Library?

Organizing a growing and ever more ambitious survey, extending its focus from natural history and geology to mapmaking, issuing a versatile array of publications, and lobbying Congress for an annual renewal of funding—these tasks preoccupied Hayden during the four years his survey explored Colorado. During those same years Hayden's rivalry with Lieutenant Wheeler raised searching questions about the future of surveying in the West.

Of the four "great surveys" of the post–Civil War era, Wheeler's was the least affected by modern science. Civilians developed novel techniques for mapping alpine terrain, and other civilians working for King, Hayden, and later Powell, refined these techniques. Wheeler's survey continued to devote more attention to strategic questions, such as where to build forts and roads and how to defend certain regions. Geologists found Wheeler's maps of little use in displaying newly discovered formations because the maps took little account of elevations and depressions in the Earth's surface—that is, of topography. The best topographic maps were coming out of the civilian surveys.

From the early 1870s, if not before, both military and civilian surveyors had been anticipating a struggle for the control of future western explorations, and in 1873 tensions came to a head between the two chief contenders, Hayden and Wheeler. King had already left the field, and Powell was too insignificant to worry about. The major antagonists epitomized different interests: Hayden championed the civilian scientists, ambitious to extend their knowledge across the West, unfettered by military rules and considerations; Wheeler represented the Corps of Engineers, making a last ditch effort to preserve its authority in general exploration. "The Engineer Bureau is the only real foe we have had," Hayden said to Gardner in February 1873. Hayden thought pressure from the engineers resulted in cutting his appropriation that year. The secretary of the interior had recommended $100,000 for the first year in Colorado, but Hayden came away with only $75,000. Hayden thought the engineers wanted to strip him of autonomy by consolidating his survey under the War Department. Even before he took the field in summer 1873 he learned that Wheeler intended to overlap his survey in southern Colorado. In order to get there first, Hayden arranged for his field parties to begin work weeks before he himself could be on the scene. The expected confrontation of the surveys finally occurred in South Park, and Hayden dramatized the situation by exchanging heated words with one of Wheeler's men. After that, everyone realized another showdown would take place during the winter before Congress. Hayden began lining up political support while still in the field. "We are going to prepare a piece of work this summer to present to Congress next session, which shall be a <u>test</u> piece, which will show our capacity more fully for the <u>trust</u>. We will look to you for strong aid."

Meanwhile, a few members of Congress had been thinking of exercising greater controls over the rival surveys. "I am troubled to know what to do with the large number of exploring expeditions Congress has on hand," Congressman Garfield confided to his diary after spending several hours discussing the situation with Hayden and others. Garfield thought "there should be a consolidation of all the geological and geographical expedition[s] in their work under one head." But under what head? Representative Clinton Merriam of New York (the father of Hayden's young naturalist) envisioned a scientific board would answer this need; the board would consist of the secretaries of war, the navy, the interior, and twelve members of the National Academy of Sciences. The War Department wanted all explorations subordinated to itself, of course. Thanks to Hayden's prodding, civilian scientists were beginning to speak up, saying they would not work under a military survey.

The collision between Wheeler and Hayden in Colorado prompted the House Committee on the Public Lands to hold hearings on the matter in spring 1874. The chairman, Washington Townsend of Pennsylvania, thought it would be a mistake to restrain the competition between able and ambitious men. He realized Hayden and King had essentially created their own surveys and sent them where they wanted; Powell followed suit shortly afterward. Even Wheeler, who worked under greater bureaucratic constraints, steered his survey pretty much where he wanted it to go. Most of Townsend's colleagues endorsed his hands-off attitude to these entrepreneurs of exploration. I should add that Townsend warmly admired Hayden; he probably thought that in due time Hayden and the civilians would supersede the military in western exploration.

Hayden was shrewd enough to justify his survey to the committee in language that recognized the laissez-faire mood. His survey and Wheeler's could not really overlap, he argued, for both had different concerns: Wheeler's was military reconnaissance, his own was geology and geography. The nation needed both surveys. Insofar as placing all the scientific surveys (i.e., civilian surveys) under one head, Hayden acknowledged that they should be under the Department of the Interior in order to prevent conflict or duplication; but each should be left autonomous, not subordinated to a bureau within the department. A bureaucratic structure, Hayden said, "tends very strongly to crush out and destroy that scientific individuality from which the greatest results have always been derived. It also destroys that healthy emulation which produces extra exertion, gives stimulus to energy, and a proper regard for expenses." He was asked at one point how each party should make use of previous information—that is, information generated by other surveys. Ignoring the intent of the question and turning it to his own advantage, he replied with a tone of supreme confidence, endorsing the ability of his own survey to provide all necessary information. "Our survey is a continuation. We go right along. We know no beginning and no end, and I trust we never shall. It moves along as a unit. All our work of the past is available for the future."

More modestly and with greater effect on the committee, he reminded the lawmakers of the practical benefits of his survey. "I have made it a special object to investigate the value and extent of the coal-fields of this region, its mineral, timber, and agricultural resources, its climate and productions." His testimony was well received, and he emerged not only as a respected scientist but an able executive who knew the details of his survey's finances, logistics, publications, and personnel.

By contrast, Wheeler got off on the wrong foot and never recovered. He evaded a number of questions, and he replied in a surly tone to others. When witnesses compared his maps with Hayden's in a manner unfavorable to Wheeler, he would not deign to explain his purposes; instead he lashed out in personal attacks on Gardner and Hayden. When confronted with the apparently higher costs of producing his less adequate maps, he became defensive and appealed to his superiors. They did not help him. From Secretary of War William Belknap on down, the military witnesses left an impression of consummate arrogance. We don't make mistakes, they seemed to be saying, because we have always done things according to our traditions; anyone else who works in western exploration is presumptuous and incompetent. Hayden could not have asked for better testimony.

An impression of Hayden as a fearless, self-centered entrepreneur, willing to risk his survival on the strength of his results, but unwilling to accept bureaucratic limitations, is largely correct but needs amplification. He acknowledged that departmental affiliation gave him a base of operations, useful connections, a certain respectability, and a sponsor to support his initiatives, though it was frustrating to realize that growing respect for his survey did not win him any greater job security. He still had to go begging every spring to have the survey continued. As to consolidation, Hayden did not oppose it in principle; on the contrary, as the director of the most successful among the several surveys he welcomed it as a means of bringing all civilian science under *his* control, which would have been the likely result of consolidation under Interior. As long as Ulysses Grant remained president, however, Hayden feared being swallowed up by the military and subordinated to "some incompetent man or Engineer officer."

Not much resulted from the hearings. Townsend, speaking for the committee, recommended that the scientific surveys *not* be consolidated under a single department, though he recognized the time for that might be approaching, and he said the Interior Department would be the place. He thought the military should go on with its strategic work but discontinue detailed geographic and geologic studies (in other words, all scientific work). Townsend issued no ringing call for change, however, and Congress ignored the few changes recommended.

Nevertheless, the hearings served a purpose, if only to further polarize the major antagonists. Powell's survey was brought under Interior, and the department issued standardized guidelines for all maps prepared under its authority. The army ignored any suggestion of curtailing its scientific work, and Wheeler defiantly sent a party to explore in Colorado the next season, knowing Hayden would still be there. The larger question of who should map the West went unresolved; indeed it was scarcely asked, though Hayden and Wheeler each had plans to do it.

For Hayden and his survey the results of the Townsend hearings seemed to be all positive. He had certainly made the best impression, and he emerged with a strong endorsement (seconded by the appropriations committee) to continue his work. He had done an effective job of recruiting expert opinion from among the scientific community, both on the deficiencies of military surveys and on the general strengths of his own work. The committee made recommendations that favored his continuing leadership of civilian science, and it doubtless assumed that in time his growing strength, and the increasingly bad odor in which the army found itself among scientists, would relieve Congress of having to intervene again between the hostile parties.

But difficulties were looming for Hayden among the scientific community. Although most civilian scientists backed him in 1874 in order to decrease the military's influence, as individuals they held differing views on Hayden and the virtues of his approach to science. Two of his sponsors during the battle illustrate perfectly the difficult position in which Hayden found himself.

Josiah Dwight Whitney was head of the California Geological Survey, one of the top geologists in the country, and an Ivy League Brahmin to the core. He threw his influence behind Hayden by pointing out publicly the shortcomings of Wheeler's maps, especially their unsuitability for the geologist and general geographer. Yet privately he wrote of Hayden to his brother: "Hayden is an enthusiastic man, ignorant of course, but that is not his fault. He had no advantages of education. This is a question of principle, however, & the sympathies of all non-military men must be on our side." Whitney was one of those traditional scientists who felt that popular work could not be serious work.

Josiah's brother, William Dwight Whitney, saw another side of Hayden. He wrote some of the strongest letters of support for Hayden's survey during the Townsend hearings. More revealingly, a few months earlier he had worked hard in support of Hayden's election to the National Academy of Sciences. A professor of Sanskrit at Yale and a scholar of daunting erudition, William Whitney might seem miscast as an admirer of Hayden. But Whitney also loved the outdoors, collected birds, and wrote competent reports on botany. He accompanied Hayden for one summer in Colorado and summarized his experiences in several lively newspaper articles. He extolled the virtues of science with the same popular voice so often used by Hayden. William Whitney recognized Hayden as a man of talent, even though clothed in unorthodoxy; he realized that Hayden worked with a serious purpose, even if he seemed drunk with enthusiasm; he admired Hayden's enormous productivity, even if he found his results to be of uneven quality. In not scorning Hayden for his lowly origins, William Whitney was more tolerant than his brother Josiah. Perhaps because he was not a rival of Hayden's, as was Josiah, William could be more generous. In any case William did not hesitate to acknowledge Hayden's preeminent position among America's exploring geologists. In 1877 most of Hayden's professional brethren shared that view.

20
TRIUMPHANT BUT
TROUBLED

Powell has developed some most unfortunate qualities this winter. His plans have been given to one of my party by a disappointed member of his. He intended to make an effort to break up my survey entirely but his failure to secure a large appropriation has crippled him.

—Hayden to Meek, 21 July 1876

To THE WORLD at large the Colorado years established the Hayden Survey at the center of American exploratory science and Hayden himself as its undisputed champion. Yellowstone had brought him worldwide acclaim; Colorado kept him in the spotlight. At each end of the Colorado years stood achievements that proclaimed his success and solidified his reputation among colleagues and the wider public. These were his election to the National Academy of Sciences in 1873 and the publication of the *Atlas of Colorado* in 1877.

The fifty founding members of the Academy in 1863 amounted to a self-selected elite, most of whom represented the physical sciences. Naturalists were conspicuous by their absence. Joseph Leidy was tapped, but he was not impressed. "It appears to me to be nothing more than the formation of an illiberal clique, based on Plymouth Rock," he reported to Hayden after the organizational meeting. A few weeks later, Leidy was saying: "I think it will turn out to be a grand humbug, and I intend having nothing to do with it. A society of the kind that leaves out such men as Baird, Draper, Hammond, Lea, Cassin, yourself, and appropriates a number who never turned a pen or did a thing for science certainly can't be of much value."

Beginning with the presidency of Joseph Henry in 1867, things began to change. Membership expanded, and different fields gained recognition. By 1873 the Academy emphasized original research as the key criteria for membership, enabling a variety of men to stand up for Hayden. Upon being asked whether he would support Hayden's membership, James Hall remarked, "He deserves the recognition, and I forgive Hayden much that he has done." After thinking it over, however, Hall rehearsed his past grievances and concluded in more typical fashion: "Simply because Hayden has proved ungrateful, that he has allied himself with my enemies in a sworn effort to crush me, and has never shown any friendship in his actions shall not deter me from supporting him for membership." Nevertheless, the groundswell in Hayden's favor was irresistible. Even Newberry found it expedient to join the four others who nominated him. William Whitney reported the events that took place behind closed doors. "There were four or five very strong speeches made before the Academy in support of your claims: few men have had a heartier backing." Being asked to join the select company of America's scientific elite must have been satisfying, even thrilling. I suspect Hayden also accepted it as a personal triumph.

No less gratifying was the reception that greeted the *Atlas,* which represented the culmination of a very solid effort and established the standard for future work of this kind. Because the need for a complete and uniform mapping of the West was becoming obvious even to Congress, the *Atlas* recommended most powerfully that Hayden be entrusted with that duty. Here, at last, was justification for establishing the bureau that would consolidate all scientific exploration in one place, that would eliminate the rivalry and higher expense of duplicated work, and that would provide Hayden with the security of a permanent survey. With Ulysses Grant out of office, a presidential bias in favor of military surveying had disappeared. No one looked favorably on the Corps of Engineers any longer, except the Corps itself; thus Hayden stood alone as the obvious man to head such a survey. Had the United States Geological Survey been created in 1877 instead of two years later, no doubt Hayden would have become its first director.

Such was Hayden's fame now that he could have increased his income in any number of ways. But he did not. The Haydens were comfortable without being rich (Congress had voted him a personal salary of $4,500 in 1876, the highest he ever achieved), and Hayden was too single-minded about his survey, too idealistic about boosting science, to fritter away his time chasing extra dollars. The Haydens purchased a carriage, which says something of their social life and pretensions, and Mrs. Hayden got her exercise in the fashionable way, by riding horseback. In addition to their home on Grant Street in Washington (which Ferdinand may have owned with his brother), the Haydens also had a residence in Philadelphia to which his wife resorted while he was in the field. Meanwhile, in 1873 the survey moved into its own quarters at 1101 Pennsylvania Avenue. The survey moved again during May 1875 to a larger space in the Second National Bank Building at 509 Seventh Street. By spring 1878 it occupied part of the second floor and all of the third and fourth floors of that building.

During the Colorado years Hayden accumulated more than a score of new memberships in scientific and learned societies. Most of them came from natural history groups and geological and geographical societies, but the American Antiquarian Society wanted to laud him as did the French Alpine Society. The International Geographical Congress at Paris awarded him its gold medal in 1875, and the same year the Geological Society of London elected him a foreign corresponding member. His rivals whined that he gained these honors by virtue of a liberal distribution of his publications. It was the kind of half truth that, repeated often enough, began to gain currency among those who wished him ill. It was true that often the only knowledge these societies had of Hayden was through his publications, but societies received publications from many sources, indeed built their libraries through such fruitful exchanges, without welcoming many of the donors into their memberships. Societies honored Hayden because his publications offered abundant new material of interest to scientists in a number of disciplines. While he was riding high, many of the men who later turned against him were saluting him.

So great was his prestige that he became the subject of jokes. "So you go to Hayden's Park! [Yellowstone]," wrote George Engelmann to a colleague. "Was it you or somebody else who wrote to me about Hayden's grand services to Science, 'still he ought not to consider all he surveys his own.' Pretty good." The joke was prompted by the fact that his survey was naming scores of features around Yellowstone, yet Hayden failed to plant his name atop the Teton Range.[1]

Jokes perhaps, but so great was his repute that no telling criticism would stick. The Corps of Engineers mustered a feeble polemic that attempted to defame Hayden while answering J. D. Whitney's attack on the Corps in *North American Review*. Captain Charles W. Raymond wrote the article; the gist of his diatribe can be seen in this paragraph.

He struggles painfully into national academies; his name and his deeds are continually appearing in the newspapers; his documents crowd the book-shelves of learned societies; he propitiates distinguished professors; he entertains influential scientists; he ingratiates himself with Congressional leaders. He has, in a word, every temptation in the world to be a humbug; and we cannot blame him much if he is one, for it is the system that has made him so. A man may have much ability, much energy and zeal, even a very considerable sense of personal dignity and honor, and not be able to resist such temptations as these.

Raymond's viewpoint is interesting on several counts. To begin, he had a few things backward: Hayden didn't struggle into academies; they sought him. He may have propitiated some professors, but most were vying with each other to win an appointment to his survey or to get his publications. Hayden entertained influential scientists, certainly, but a cordial man could do no less because most were foreigners who demanded to be introduced. Raymond found fault with having one's name in the newspapers or one's books collected in libraries. He made socializing with one's colleagues sound embarrassing and spoke of seeking congressional funds as though it were improper. That Raymond thought he could score points with such charges shows how profoundly Victorian mores differed from our own. In a time when reputations were forged by rectitude rather than public relations, such accusations could matter. After all, most of the "distinguished professors" and "influential scientists" of Hayden's day enjoyed a secure income; they did not have to demean themselves through lobbying. Because he never possessed a secure income, and because he was constantly forcing the government to enlarge its responsibility for science, Hayden had no choice but to assert himself forcefully. He produced, and his achievements impressed his contemporaries, but they worried about his propensity for self-promotion. Such behavior was thought to be unnecessary for a scientist and unbecoming to a gentleman. Hence the "humbug."

Rather than rising above such criticism, Hayden took it personally. "I seem to be so encompassed with enemies now that I hardly know what the result will be," Hayden wrote to Geikie after reading Raymond's article. Perpetually uneasy about enemies and rivals, and insecure by temperament, he brooded over the future instead of enjoying his successes. More than any external struggle, such internal turmoils ate away at the man and reduced his confidence sufficiently that his enemies could finally reach him, could wound him with the scurrilities he had always feared much more than direct competition.

I said that had Congress created the USGS in 1877 Hayden would probably have been chosen its first director. By the time everyone accepted the need for such a bureau, Hayden had lost ground relative to his rivals. A deliberate opposition to him had formed, based on a nucleus of his most devoted enemies, and these men began to imagine replacing him as the nation's leading exploring scientist. In broad outline, that is the story of Hayden's denouement, which will unfold in the following chapters. The particulars are absorbing not only because so little has been known about Hayden's life but especially because they reveal the surprisingly large part Hayden played in his own demise. To take nothing away from his enemies, who orchestrated an effective campaign of vicious slander, it remains true that Hayden lost the prize he sought; no one wrested it from him.

By far the most public sign of trouble was the firing of James Terry Gardner in October 1875. Earlier in the year Gardner had written a report on the Cucharas-Trinidad coalfield for the Denver and Rio Grande Railway. When word of his own indirect link to the report leaked out, Hayden tried to avoid embarrassing questions by shifting the focus onto Gardner. Hayden let the word out that Gardner had "sold the Survey out to a private corporation." Understandably, Gardner reacted bitterly to this announcement because Hayden had arranged for him to prepare the report in the first place. The incident did not help their already strained relationship, but it did not give Hayden grounds for firing Gardner. Another event that same summer triggered the final break. Paiute Indians attacked Gardner's party, killed several mules, and stole some property. The affair was not that serious and would have blown over. Would have, that is, had the popular press not latched onto it. Journalists seized on the details to concoct an adventurous story casting Gardner and his team in the role of heroes. Gardner cooperated with the hullabaloo by granting interviews. It was the latest in a series of incidents in which Gardner seemed to be upstaging his boss. It was bad enough that Gardner enjoyed strutting around the West kicking up publicity. It didn't help that his first publication after joining the survey had been entitled "Hayden and Gardner's Survey of the Territories," as if he and Hayden were co-equals in the enterprise. It was worse that Gardner attributed the success of the survey mostly to himself and didn't hesitate to say so. In departing, Gardner called attention to "those old fires of jealousy and suspicion which ever smoulder in him," meaning in Hayden. Hayden said little, but he resented the smug little aristocrat and was glad to be rid of him. After all, the *Atlas* was nearly done, and he had another superb geographer, Allen Wilson, to finish it up.

A more ominous situation was Hayden's deteriorating relationship with his colleagues. The Colorado years opened with an ambitious plan for a collecting expedition involving several specialists, principally Leidy, Meek,

Lesquereux, and Thomas Porter, the botanist of Lafayette College. Eventually, they did go, but not before a lot of worried talk about travel arrangements, time in the field, and whether wives would accompany them; and not before the original plans were changed, which caused Hayden to quip, "You cannot depend on these old chaps (married) for difficult campaigns." As part of the altered plan, the young and vigorous Edward Drinker Cope also went west, which introduced an awkward competition with Leidy because Cope sought the same vertebrates that interested Leidy.

Because he himself would not be caught up in the rivalry, Hayden showed Olympian disdain for the pettiness of personal emulation. As he wrote in the introduction to his report on Colorado, shortly after outflanking Wheeler so successfully in the Townsend hearings, "It is believed that all unkind criticisms of the labors of other scientific men are out of place in an official report, and in no instance will they receive the sanction of the geologist in charge. Each assistant is held responsible for the correctness of his statements in his report, and it is presumed that his love of truth is superior to his personal feelings." Such high ground struck the right tone for a formal report, appropriate for the leader of a survey whose activity encompassed so many fields and recruited so many men. Hayden was also voicing his personal idealism about scientific methodology, but in doing so was he not exposing his naivete?

Given the conditions of American science at the time, I don't think so. Rivalries sprouted everywhere, often accompanied by animosities, and such fireworks may have stimulated scientific activity. Hayden certainly thought they did, and given that assumption he was not mistaken to push ahead at full speed with the research he sponsored. Besides, the quarrels he found himself in the middle of arose through the ambitions of other men; they were not of his own making. But such an attitude was bound to stir repercussions and resentments.

Hayden's overriding ambition to produce results, and his willingness to let the chips fall where they may, show he was insensitive—perhaps downright indifferent—to the personal implications of professional rivalry. No sooner was Cope unleashed on the field of vertebrate paleontology than Leidy withdrew, embarrassed, annoyed, probably more hurt than he admitted, but willing to yield the field entirely rather than engage in unseemly competition. This crisis led to a distinct cooling between Hayden and Leidy. That it did not precipitate a permanent break resulted more from Leidy's generosity than anything Hayden did to protect their friendship.

Hayden behaved insensitively at best, but saying that only accentuates a familiar theme of his life: he was driven to succeed regardless of the cost. In view of the enemies he created and the bitter professional loss he suffered a few years later—a loss he may have avoided had he cultivated his friends with more consideration—it is tempting to say how recklessly he yielded to that drive. But Hayden could not have foreseen what was coming. From his point of view he was right to push ahead vigorously. As the most successful entrepreneur in a very competitive business, Hayden had risen to the top by consistently employing boldness. And does not fortune smile upon the bold? Anyway, why should he renounce the intensity that had put him ahead of his rivals in the first place?

No, it was not just an insensitive thrusting ahead that defeated Hayden, or even the coalescence of his enemies that made possible his downfall. It was a failure of nerve to continue acting boldly at a particular moment. That moment would not come until 1878, but beginning in 1876 and continuing over the next two years the tide began to turn against Hayden, events seemed to conspire against him, until, at the critical time, his confidence failed. Hayden had always been a self-starter, had always succeeded because he followed through on his initiatives. For such a self-made man, a failure of confidence could be fatal.

Hayden had always used others to get where he wanted to go. From the beginnings of his career, from his earliest serious interest in natural history, he had attached himself to mentors who helped him advance himself. George Allen showed him the advantages of disciplining and focusing his ardor, and he introduced Hayden to a wider circle of compatible naturalists in Cleveland, among them Kirtland and Newberry, with both of whom Hayden studied. Newberry in turn introduced him to James Hall, who arranged the first collecting trip to the Bad Lands and allowed Hayden to finish medical school while working for him. Baird coordinated the second trip to the Bad Lands, which also brought Hayden to the Upper Missouri for the first time with Alfred Vaughan, and Baird brought Warren and Hayden together for the subsequent exploration of that region. Leidy opened the door to a community of scholars and naturalists in Philadelphia, arranged financial support for Hayden at a critical time, and made it possible for him to publish his first writings in the appropriate professional journals. Over time, Hayden either quarreled with these mentors and rejected them, as with Hall and Newberry, or he advanced to a position of greater equality with them, as with Baird and Leidy who became his colleagues.

With both mentors and colleagues a pattern emerged. Hayden was never shy about asking favors, and because he found he had something to give in return he badgered, cajoled, and manipulated his sponsors to get what he needed. This pattern endured as long as Hayden depended on his friends to arrange fresh fields to exploit. But with the aggrandizement of his own well-funded and popular survey, Hayden could stand alone. On the other hand

Hayden had made his survey such an indispensable source of fossils, natural history specimens, photographs, artifacts, books, articles, and information about the developing West, as well as a convenient place for colleagues to publish their research, that they could not so easily do without him—a sure source of resentment.

Added to this difficulty were peculiarities of Hayden's temperament, which eventually turned a number of friends against him. Around the campfire or riding across lonely stretches of the West, Hayden could be a stimulating companion; but when talking about the survey he was always intense, eager, and serious. When stationary, he contemplated action; in the field he brooded about what he might be missing in Washington; at his desk he dreamed impatiently of what could be achieved next season. He was not a man who could easily relax. Despite his quick intelligence, and his ability to converse on any number of topics, Hayden was not comfortable exploring the world of the mind. He never outgrew a feeling of shame about his lowly origins, which is why he shunned clubs and the facile congeniality they offered. He was a man of action, and most of the time he was all business. Because his feverish activity and exciting planning centered on the survey and its needs, he expected his colleagues to share in his enthusiasm, to be swept up in the great cause. If they did not, he assumed they opposed him.

Baird was the first to tire of his cyclonic friend. After years of humoring and encouraging Hayden, and supporting his various projects, most of which benefited himself and the Smithsonian, Baird began to retreat in subtle ways. Their correspondence had always been large but never intimate; it did not taper off after the Yellowstone years, but it dragged on without warmth, focusing on such routine business as the exchange of publications. Baird was no longer responsive to Hayden's constant requests for political aid. Writing to Leidy during the Townsend hearings, Hayden summarized the support he had received from a variety of sources, but he noted "Baird & Henry will do nothing."

Leidy reacted somewhat differently. Because Hayden consistently delivered specimens for him to examine and describe, Leidy could not easily ignore Hayden's wider concerns. Unlike Baird, Leidy did write Townsend a strong letter on Hayden's behalf, but he seems to have done only the minimum demanded of him. Although Hayden continued to encourage Leidy's research and joyfully circulated his writings near and far, the warmth of their relationship diminished. In a friendly but superficial way Hayden went on telling Leidy about his own projects and urging him to get out more publications, but Leidy began retreating from Hayden, obviously stung by the callous way Hayden had arranged the competition with Cope and Marsh and unwilling to smooth it over with conventional talk.

Becoming more apparent with the passing of time was the fact that Hayden had few, if any, close friends. Mentors were used; colleagues were recruited, but for specific purposes that benefited the survey, not for the pleasures or consolations of friendship. After they had performed, Hayden let them go, and as the survey generated different needs, he turned up a new crop of men appropriate to the new goals. He abandoned Engelmann after the latter finally finished up the botanical report for Raynolds's expedition; he ignored his first mentor and early friend, George Allen, after Allen accompanied him to Yellowstone in 1871; he had no time for his fellow alumnus Jacob Cox after Cox completed his service as secretary of the interior; he lost touch with William Whitney after the Townsend hearings, except, as with most colleagues, to send him publications or photographs of the survey. Hayden thought in terms of winning a man's endorsement rather than cultivating his friendship. At the same time, so obsessed was he with potential rivals and the machinations of his enemies that he trusted no one.[2]

With the professionals who worked with him in the field, Hayden enjoyed a happier intercourse, though little more satisfying from a personal standpoint. These men worked for him and were accordingly deferential, even when they expressed exasperation with him (never to his face), and most hailed him as a generous patron and a dedicated naturalist (even beyond his earshot). Lesquereux especially lavished copious praise on Hayden. With all the naturalists who published through his survey Hayden enjoyed the kind of warm cordiality that derives from a successful professional relationship. He stood closer to Holmes and Peale than to others, but he was never steady in his affection for either man and not even forthcoming with Peale concerning the truth of his family background.

With Meek, and only with Meek, did Hayden diverge somewhat from the calculating pattern he followed with his other colleagues. Meek had been his first, perhaps only, close friend. Both men shared modest origins, and both had improved their standing in life at the urging of fierce ambition. They became close in ways beyond their profession: they bought land in Kansas together; Meek loaned Hayden money, and during the war he looked after some of Hayden's personal affairs and kept an eye on his investments. Meanwhile from 1865 Hayden arranged regular funding for Meek's work. At least in their early years together, I believe Meek saw more of the inner Hayden than anyone, possibly more than Emma Hayden ever saw, and for that reason Meek was angered by the grand man Hayden became after Yellowstone. It was not jealousy so much as affront Meek felt as his former comrade became more aloof, more secretive, and yet more demanding of his time and efforts. Hayden wanted Meek to complete his masterpiece on the invertebrate fossils of the West, wanted to publish it through his survey, wanted the satisfaction of completing a lifetime's partnership, and yearned for the glory and respect that would redound to him for doing so. To that end Hayden gave Meek material and emotional comfort, supported him against a careless printer, paid many of his costs, sent him to Colorado for more material, then to Florida for three winters to sustain his fragile health, all the while encouraging him to finish "the great work of your life." Hayden alternately harassed Meek to get on with it, then cautioned him to be "careful of your health, and find some quiet place when you get tired, stop awhile, and then work again." With the book nearly done, Meek's health declined dramatically, jeopardizing its completion. Hayden offered to have Peale prepare the index and introduction.

It would be easy to take the cynical position that Hayden cared for Meek only in order to see his monograph finished and published by the survey. Two incidents that took place after Meek's death seem to recommend this view. Because everyone knew Hayden had been Meek's closest colleague, the editor of the *American Naturalist* asked Hayden to write Meek's obituary for that journal. Hayden agreed, but delayed doing it for so long that the editor eventually had to ask William H. Dall to do it. Dall was a good naturalist and a sympathetic writer, but he had not known Meek as well as Hayden. Similarly, at the April 1877 meeting of the National Academy of Sciences (the meeting following Meek's death), Hayden was named to write the long obituary for the Academy's *Biographical Memoirs* series. The Academy commonly permitted authors several years to complete these articles because they were meant to be extensive reviews of the man's life and work, not just announcements of death. But when, after a generous interlude, it became obvious Hayden would never complete the job, the task was reassigned to Charles A. White, who finally published the memoir nineteen years after Meek's death. So it would seem that once Meek's great work was finished (his death followed only a few months later), Hayden found other pressing concerns to occupy him.

Or was it the complexity of his relationship with Meek that blocked Hayden from writing a tribute to his fallen comrade? During Meek's life, Hayden evinced genuine affection for him. I think Meek was probably the only colleague Hayden ever cared much about and, sensing that, Meek felt bitter about the peremptory manner he perceived Hayden taking toward him in their later years. Meek was a solitary man who lived most of his life without attachments to family or close friends. His work had become his whole life, and the years of joint authorship with Hayden had given satisfaction to his need for emotional richness, much more so than any other period of his life. Those had been extravagant years, filled with fascinating work and exciting discoveries, punctuated by the drama of personal conflicts, and made glorious by almost universal recognition. Together they had enjoyed the kind of intense, dangerous, but thrilling whirlwind few men encounter in a lifetime, and which, if they survive it, bonds men forever. Despite a busy career and many admirers, Meek had fewer opportunities than Hayden to branch out, to find other gratification of his needs and ambitions. Of course Meek resented Hayden's greater worldly success, but that was minor. What hurt the most was realizing that Hayden still yearned for more than what, for him, had been the peak experience of his life.

It is in that context we must understand Meek's snarling remarks about Hayden made at a time when his health was declining, when he could no longer foresee any triumphs on the horizon for himself. Meek and Hayden had always shown pride in their joint work, and though others—then and later—have debated how much each of them contributed to their partnership, it was not a subject of concern to either of them—that is, not until Meek made an issue of it ten years after their last joint effort. We don't have Meek's actual words, only the response of his correspondent, Charles Abiathar White.

> I have not forgotten what you said about credit having been given to Hayden that belongs to you. I have spoken to Maj. Powell about the matter also, he having himself first opened the subject in conversation. He knows well the injustice that has been done you and expresses his intention of vindicating you whenever opportunity offers for him to do so.

The relevant letters make clear White brought up the subject by expressing unflattering opinions of Hayden, apparently designed to draw some confirmation from Meek. (This was one year before White became a member of Hayden's survey.[3]) Meek was terribly sensitive on points of professional credit and capable of great invective when aroused, as he showed at the time of the Permian controversy with Hall and Swallow. No doubt, White piqued his pride sufficiently to elicit the desired response. What is most interesting is that Powell apparently initiated the issue, which White admits, knowing full well that any denigrating bit of gossip he dug up about Hayden, especially from one of Hayden's allies, and no matter how untrue, could be useful ammunition in his campaign to unseat him. Caught temporarily off guard, Meek did not repeat the allegation, and he did not insist on justice formally rendered, which had been characteristic of him in all his previous clashes on points of honor or credit.

The whole incident reeks of Powell's intrigues, and though he gained nothing substantial from this foray, his campaign was building momentum on other fronts. From 1874 he began to cultivate the friendship of Congressman James Garfield, a powerful member of the House Appropriations Committee and heretofore an admirer of Hayden. The culmination of their growing alliance came in December 1878 when Powell transferred one of his own secretaries to Garfield for the express purpose of freeing Garfield to promote Powell's plan for a new geological survey.

Powell and Newberry had been close since the early 1870s. By 1875 Newberry was offering to help Powell enlarge his appropriations and to publish through Powell's survey "a great quantity of interesting material which I have been gathering for Hayden, but would rather publish through some other channel." At the same time, King and Powell were establishing a cordial tie, and Powell was sending fossils to Marsh for identification. At virtually the same time Newberry put Marsh up for membership in the Century Club of New York; of course, he was elected. This coterie of Powell, Newberry, Marsh, and King formed the nucleus of a concerted opposition to Hayden, which came together in 1875 and 1876, the very time when Hayden's renown reached its peak.

Even before Hayden completed his triumphal tour through Colorado, Powell had raised his standard in opposition to him. Hayden knew this. "Major P is very anxious and is raising heaven and earth," he wrote to Meek and added judiciously, "He is more to be feared than any one else." Correctly, Hayden surmised that Newberry had joined the alliance with Powell. He also knew of the longstanding friendship between King and Marsh, which dated back to their undergraduate days at Yale. But in two important respects Hayden misjudged the growing consortium against him. He assumed, wrongly, that Powell and Wheeler would join forces, showing he was still most afraid of a rejuvenated Corps of Engineers, and he failed to see that King and Marsh were also joining ranks with Powell. Oddly, it was an outgrowth of Hayden's final triumph—the publications of his survey—that forged the final links in the alliance against him.

21
PATRON OF
SCIENCE

His fame as a geologist in Europe was extraordinary. It is not too much to say that his name was more familiar to the geological world in Europe than that of any other American geologist. . . . It was due to the exceptional number of his geological contributions, to the freshness of the fields which he explored, and to the untiring energy with which he published his observations as fast as they were made, and communicated them, in large editions, to all the working geologists abroad. The amount of Hayden literature (as it may be justly called) in every library of the world is surprisingly great. More than fifty octavo volumes copiously illustrated with pictures, sections, topographical and colored maps, were published by him, to make known his territorial surveys from 1867 to 1879.

—Obituary of Hayden by J. P. Lesley

FROM ABOUT THE middle of the 1870s Hayden began encountering more trouble from his rivals, particularly Powell, and the survey was having difficulty sustaining the triumphant tone of its work in Colorado. Yet even as the survey returned to Montana and Wyoming in 1877 and 1878 for the important but less spectacular job of completing earlier work, the publications of the survey continued to amaze the country and the world. Several ongoing projects (which I will mention presently) reached fruition in the late 1870s and during the 1880s. Meanwhile, Hayden's own publications are a better barometer of his political struggles at the time, and some of them deserve attention because of inherent merit.

Not counting his contributions to the annual reports or the several pieces on Yellowstone already discussed, Hayden published twenty-five articles between 1874 and 1879, though a number of them amount to duplicate efforts. Like his previous writings, most are either popular accounts of geology and geography, pointing out practical facts and interesting conditions, or specialized studies written for scholars. His promotional writings, which made up a third body of work, increased in frequency during the latter part of the period. Admittedly, these categories are mine, and they reflect the shades of emphasis Hayden chose from time to time, but I am sure Hayden himself would have acknowledged only a single purpose for all he wrote: to encourage a wide appreciation of natural history. Consistent with that aim, Hayden wrote for "the intelligent world generally" and openly appealed to "every attentive reader"; these phrases occur frequently in his writings. He always assumed that what excited the scholar would also interest the intelligent layman.

Notable in many articles was a frank evocation of the picturesque. In "Our Great West, and the Scenery of our Natural Parks" (1874), he verbally recreated the most striking scenes in Yellowstone, then stood on high summits of Colorado to depict the scenery around him. This article grew out of a lecture (illustrated with slides) he had given to the American Geographical Society. In a similar way he wrote other articles to amplify particular illustrations from his survey's publications. Thus, with the aid of pictures did he explain such phenomena as erosion (15 May 1875), the geologic structure of Colorado's Front Range (10 June 1875), and the development of the Miocene-Pliocene lake basins in Montana (5 June 1876).

Even in his works that were devoid of pictures, his style showed the strong impact of large-scale images. Able to see more than impressionistic details, he now wanted to sketch the full extent of major geologic formations and to epitomize the character of countless ranges, river systems, basins, and plateaus. Now geology and geography were to be understood in sweeping vistas of scenery. In this way he explained the "Rocky Mountains" (1875), and he reviewed the fieldwork of the survey in a similar fashion. This broader, more sweeping style answered Hayden's immediate needs. It enabled him to synthesize his understanding of separate chunks of territory, to respond to the many requests for summaries of his work, and to keep Congress and the public informed of his achievements. For these reasons most of what he wrote in the late 1870s conformed to this panoramic style, and these works have become his most familiar efforts.

Some of his other essays, usually overlooked, provide a better guide to the caliber of the man in the long run, beyond the 1870s. He persevered on the momentous issues surrounding the Great Lignite, both in his own writings (especially 9 April 1874 and 8 January 1876) and in the studies published by his survey. He pointed out the potentially vast amount of water lying beneath the arid Great Divide Basin of southwestern Wyoming (5 April 1877), and for the first time he identified true glaciers east of the Pacific coast, which he found in the Wind River Range of Wyoming (15 November 1878). He made a number of astute observations, pioneering insights in the history of geology, though typically he scattered these gems between descriptions of landforms or scenery. He revealed the existence of what are now called the Ancestral Rockies, and he suggested that the many ranges within the Rocky Mountains appeared at different periods of time (10 June 1875, pp. 217, 220). He gave further proof of understanding the concept of antecedent streams, and he saw a connection between the general uplift of mountains and the explosive eruptions of igneous rocks (5 June 1876, pp. 203, 208). Never comfortable as a systematic thinker, however, he failed to mobilize these insights into a fresh theory of mountain building. Instead he paid homage to Dana's theory of crustal shrinkage ("Rocky Mountains," p. 375), and he remained a confirmed uniformitarian (8 January 1876, p. 410).

Hayden displayed the broad interests of a generalist rather than the concentrated focus of a specialist. He showed this inclination in his own publications and demonstrated it even more forcefully in the numerous books and articles he issued through his survey. I will sample the diversity in a moment, but first a few remarks to set the context. Despite general similarities among the four rival surveys, their publications tended to be singular—reflections of the primary interests of their leaders. Thus Wheeler emphasized maps, King focused on economic geology, and Powell, in addition to his interest in weathering and surface geology, managed to bring out nine volumes on American Indians under the aegis of his survey. Hayden's scope was broader than anyone's, and the sum of his publications greater than the total produced by the other three surveys combined.

His devotion to research is Hayden's most distinctive legacy. He looked at the publications of his survey not just as a means of reporting on fieldwork but as an opportunity to sponsor broad research in the natural sciences. He sponsored these investigations in several specific ways: he paid travel expenses to get his colleagues into the field, he sometimes paid monthly stipends to encourage particular projects, and he absorbed all the costs and hassles of publication. Ordinarily, he did not pay fees for specific articles, but he made exceptions to obtain a few essays for the survey's *Bulletin*. Besides giving consistent patronage in these ways to Meek, Leidy, Cope, Lesquereux, and other regulars, he went out of his way to identify and encourage the endeavors of other naturalists, whether or not they were working on materials that derived from his survey. Much of the research he published had nothing to do with his survey.

Hayden aimed to encourage the broadest kind of natural history inquiries. He was interested in locusts and other pests harmful to agriculture, as well as the quality of ore found in Colorado—the sort of popular subjects one expected to find in such journals as the *American Naturalist* and *Popular*

Science Monthly. He also sponsored articles on subjects like the Great Lignite and the geographical distribution of mammals—the sort of thing that appealed to the more scholarly *American Journal of Science.* At the same time he delighted in lists of new species and monographs on fossils and thermal springs—the sort of preoccupation one found in the publications of learned societies. With omnivorous enthusiasm, Hayden wanted to publish the same kinds of studies being done by *all* the leading scientific publications of the day and to reap a cornucopia of recognition.

Such indiscriminate versatility may seem hopelessly anachronistic today, but we must remove the blinkers of our present perspective to appreciate Hayden's vision. Hayden saw himself as the standard-bearer for a group of naturalists who placed an equal emphasis on all the domains of natural history and who wanted to understand each of them simultaneously. It would be wrong to attribute to these broad-gauged thinkers a modern appreciation for interrelated ecosystems, though they did assume, without pretending to grasp the mechanisms, that some force unified harmoniously all the different parts of the natural world. As a result, it made sense to study geology in the context not only of past life (paleontology) but of present life (zoology and botany). Studies of living creatures were essential because "zoology has always been recognized by the Director of the Geological Survey as not only a legitimate and proper, but also very important and practically valuable collateral department of scientific research, the relations of which to geology and geography are natural and intimate." After the formation of the USGS in 1879, a more specialized mentality began to supersede this catholic viewpoint by separating zoology and botany from paleontology. Even before 1879 naturalists argued about the importance of the unified versus the specialized approach. Hayden was the star spokesman for the unified approach, and because of his commanding prestige and the renown of his survey, that approach ruled the thinking of his day—that is, *before* 1879. The specialized approach that later became the hallmark of the USGS was a novelty, a departure from the dominant emphasis before 1879; therefore the creation of the USGS must be seen in a different light than heretofore. It represented not only the institutionalization of a new approach to science but also the overthrow of a rival approach and the deliberate rejection of the man who epitomized that older approach. The one could not have happened without the other.

With his philosophic orientation in mind, we can better appreciate the way Hayden organized his survey's publications. From the start the *Annual Reports* (12 vols., 1867–1883) were meant to give preliminary notice of important scientific discoveries as well as to summarize annual work in geology, paleontology, zoology, botany, and topography. Hayden insisted they be prepared promptly, written in a popular style, and distributed free to the public. The mistakes, inconsistencies, and incongruities of style that cropped up could be weeded out in later reports.

Meanwhile more than 170 articles appeared in the survey's journal, the *Bulletin* (6 vols., 1874–1882), whose contents covered everything from simple lists of species to monographic studies. In the process a number of seemingly disparate facts and observations piled up, many of which would be ordered into topical headings and published in another series.

Some of this material appeared in the *Miscellaneous Publications* (12 vols., 1873–1880), namely studies of birds, flowers, seals and walruses, Hidatsa Indians, a family of fur-bearing carnivores called the Mustelidae, and a *Bibliography of North American Invertebrate Paleontology.* (The other Miscellaneous Publications consisted of catalogs of the survey's photographs and statistics on elevations and meteorology.)

The natural history studies in that series might just as well have appeared in the *Final Reports* (also known as *Monographs;* 13 vols., 1873–1890) because their subjects and methodology were similar. The unspoken distinction between the *Miscellaneous Publications* and the *Final Reports* seems to have been the prestige Hayden associated with the *Final Reports.* Here he published Elliott Coues and Joel Allen's book on rodents (Coues wrote three other volumes for Hayden, which appeared in the *Miscellaneous* series) and individual studies by four of Hayden's favorite collaborators in the survey: Leidy, Cyrus Thomas, Alpheus Spring Packard, Jr., and Samuel Hubbard Scudder. Of course, the seven volumes on paleontology of the West formed the heart and soul of the *Monographs.* Most of the facts and samples for these seven volumes had been gathered by Hayden or members of his survey, and what afforded them so much pride of place in Hayden's mind was their bearing on the Great Lignite, Hayden's consuming interest for more than two decades.[1]

The last series was the *Unclassified Publications* (17 vols., 1872–1879), which Hayden initiated in 1872 as a place to publish his *Final Report of Nebraska.* He finished that report in 1868, though by the time Congress authorized its publication three years later Hayden no longer worked for the General Land Office under whose supervision he had started the survey of Nebraska. Even though it was a final report, it was not a monograph like the studies in the *Final Reports* series. In content and character it closely resembled his first three annual reports; in fact, it supplemented the first of those. Not being an annual report, however, it had to appear in a series bringing together volumes that would not fit readily anywhere else. That pretty well characterizes the other volumes in the *Unclassified* series: catalogs of the survey's publications and photographs, several volumes to do with the Entomological Commission (for reasons to be mentioned shortly), four pamphlets containing illustrations and statistics, and four other essays that amounted to anticipations and revisions of annual reports.

Within this framework Hayden brought out works of remarkable diversity. Snakes of Montana, butterflies of Utah, fishes from the Rio Grande River, and the minerals of Nevada all received attention, as did a flock of birds and countless insects. There were bibliographies of fossils, of birds, even "An Account of the Various Publications Relating to the Travels of Lewis and Clark, with a Commentary on the Zoological Results of Their Expedition," and no less than twenty studies concerning American Indians.

Out of this apparently haphazard abundance, several patterns provide clues to Hayden's organizing ideas. A surprisingly large number of these studies had direct practical implications for the American economy, especially agriculture. This emphasis was most obvious in the many studies of harmful insects; in the attention directed to birds, the natural predators of these pests; and even in the work on rodents, for they had the largest impact on agriculture of any mammal. Nine specific studies expounded on the potential for agriculture in the West, beginning with Cyrus Thomas's essay in the *Third Annual Report*. Even such an arcane work as *Fresh Water Rhizopods of North America* (by Leidy) had a practical bearing to Hayden. In a review of the study he foresaw that a knowledge of these minute animals "may even be of the highest importance to the human race." And all the studies of fossils and geologic sections were hardly random: most threw light on the border between Cretaceous and Tertiary times, which in turn gave geologists insight into the evolution of life on Earth.

Hayden's commitment to the new Entomological Commission followed from this strong practical inclination. As early as 1870 in his *Fourth Annual Report* he issued reports on harmful insects, and every year thereafter the survey published something on the subject, including portions of two of its *Final Reports*. In 1875, when a group of western governors began agitating for federal help in combating pests, all interested parties expected Hayden to be involved significantly. And he was. As early as March 1876 Hayden suggested to Senator John Logan of Illinois that an entomology commission be created and attached to his survey, and everyone accepted that instigating idea.

Everyone assumed that Hayden would name the commissioners too. Of course, he could not do this officially because he held no fixed position in the federal bureaucracy. But his preferences prevailed nonetheless. Initially there was some question about how many commissioners to name, but when it was decided to name three Hayden favored Cyrus Thomas and A. S. Packard, Jr. Both men had written extensively for the survey, and both shared Hayden's broad approach to natural history. For the third slot the choice was between the two men who had done most (besides Hayden) to promote the idea of a federal entomology commission: John Lawrence LeConte and Charles Valentine Riley. LeConte was an authority on beetles and knew Hayden through Philadelphia's Academy of Natural Sciences. Riley had been an official in the Department of Agriculture and by 1875 was the entomologist for the State of Missouri; he did not know Hayden personally, but Cyrus Thomas was a close mutual friend. Thomas and Packard persuaded Hayden to go against his inclination for LeConte on the grounds that the commissioners should be practical men with experience in the field. LeConte, they argued, was more a "closet naturalist." Hayden accepted Riley, and Riley in turn accepted Hayden's survey as the logical home for the commission.

By fall 1876 the congenial team of Hayden, Riley, Packard, and Thomas were working together smoothly, under Hayden's coaching, to formalize the national commission. Their efforts culminated in March 1877, when Congress created the Entomological Commission with a first year's budget of $18,000 and attached it to Hayden's survey, under the umbrella of the secretary of the interior. To no one's surprise the secretary appointed Riley, Packard, and Thomas as the commissioners. They started work immediately, sending bulletins on prevention to farmers in the affected areas and systematically gathering information that illustrated the natural history of the problem.

A year later Hayden managed to get another $10,000 to continue the commission for a second year. It endured for several more years and wound up publishing five annual reports (1878–1890) and seven bulletins (1877–1881). By the time the second annual report was submitted, in fall 1879, Hayden's survey had disappeared; thus the later history of the commission does not concern us except in one respect.

I mentioned that after the creation of the USGS in 1879 it increasingly adopted a specialized attitude to geology, which differed from the more inclusive approach to natural history Hayden had always favored. It might appear from this development that scientists and naturalists would begin moving away from the synoptic view that Hayden embodied. But that was far from the truth. Hayden's broader view lived on in the Entomological Commission, which a few years later evolved into the Bureau of the Biological Survey, appropriately under an old Hayden survey hand, Clinton Hart Merriam. In other words, a number of naturalists continued to think that specialized knowledge should be used to connect, not separate, disciplines, and they wanted to preserve this point of view by creating a government bureau around it: hence the Biological Survey, which perpetuated an important aspect of Hayden's legacy.

Hayden's patronage of his colleagues was intended primarily to produce publications for the survey, but other fruit grew from his nourishing influence. The Entomological Commission was one such product. The maturing of a number of scholars through their association with the survey would be another, and an outstanding example is Edward Drinker Cope. Cope is especially important in Hayden's story because his successful career stimulated the growing alliance between Hayden's enemies.

Born into a prosperous mercantile family and blessed with abundant intellectual gifts as well as boundless energy, Cope early chose the career of a naturalist. In 1860 he attended Leidy's lectures on anatomy at the University of Pennsylvania and soon thereafter began his work on paleontology at Philadelphia's Academy of Natural Sciences. Rich by most people's standards, still he never had enough money to buy all the collections he wanted. For years he managed financially by renting out the farm his father had given him, and he wrote encyclopedia articles when he needed extra cash. Hayden's help with travel expenses during the 1870s, when Cope was an official collaborator of the survey, enabled many collecting ventures, though Cope grumbled constantly of Hayden's stinginess. He also lectured Hayden repeatedly about the necessity of publishing his findings with the utmost speed in order that he might gain priority in announcing new species. Despite the difficulties he caused, he did produce for Hayden: no less than eight separate pieces in the *Annual Reports,* twenty in the *Bulletin,* one for the *Unclassified Publications,* and two hefty volumes for the *Final Reports.* In 1878 he bought a controlling interest in the *American Naturalist,* becoming co-editor with Packard, partly as a convenient outlet for his hastily prepared essays.

A typical golden boy, Cope was fortunate, brilliant, ambitious, and completely unable to comprehend any point of view but his own. He quarreled frequently with the trustees of Haverford College, where he taught for four years. He alienated John L. LeConte and a number of others at the Philadelphia Academy with his outspoken views. He disputed with his church (Society of Friends) and later fought with the directors of mining companies in which he purchased stock. But most of his enmity he reserved for his rival in bone hunting: Othniel Charles Marsh.

Marsh was descended from an old New England family; his immediate predecessors had been reduced to living on modest means, except for Uncle George Peabody,[2] who made a fortune in the dry goods business and then expanded it through various enterprises. Thanks to his benevolence, Marsh attended Andover, a private boarding school in Massachusetts, where he showed a talent for natural history and a proclivity for politics, becoming president of the debating society. Later he attended Yale under the same sponsorship, finishing with a master's degree from the Sheffield Scientific School in 1862. Uncle Peabody financed more education in Europe, which included purchasing books and samples for Yale, and when he established the Peabody Museum at Yale, the university tactfully named Marsh the nation's first professor of paleontology in 1866. Yale had no money to pay Marsh a salary, but with an adequate allowance from Uncle George and later a share in his inheritance, he scarcely needed it. Besides, if Yale wouldn't pay him, he didn't have to teach, which left him free to concentrate on his two grand passions: collecting bones of fossil vertebrates and managing other men.

Marsh and Cope began in a friendly enough fashion, collecting together in the marl beds of western New Jersey in 1868. Showing the hastiness that would become his trademark, Cope worked up his descriptions first and beat Marsh into print concerning their finds. That same year Marsh got a leg up on Cope by undertaking his first trip to the far West. By the time Cope got to Kansas in 1871 and to the Green River area of Wyoming in 1872, Marsh had already begun collecting in both regions, and Marsh always exhibited a strong proprietary feeling about any fossil bed he worked. With the exception of one summer in New Mexico, when he worked for Wheeler, Cope ranged from Texas to Montana during the 1870s under Hayden's patronage, eagerly grabbing everything he could find, though his rivalry with Marsh was concentrated in the dinosaur beds of Colorado and Wyoming. They argued over priority of their discoveries, used different names for the same species, accused each other of stealing samples, collectors, even descriptions. By noisily impugning each other's integrity, they waged the most rancorous war in the history of American paleontology, which had repercussions on Hayden and his survey.

Hayden and Marsh had begun their own little contretemps even before Hayden's sponsorship of Cope gave Marsh additional grounds for enmity. Hayden met Marsh in Philadelphia during December 1866 while Marsh was visiting the Academy in hopes of finding samples he could secure for Yale. Things started well between them, with Hayden offering to collect for the new Peabody Museum and Marsh seeking to work up Hayden's vertebrates—something that he and Cope and Leidy all wanted the exclusive right to do. Hayden handled the rivalry deftly at the beginning by promising to give Leidy first choice of the fossils he discovered and then giving Marsh available duplicates, which would become part of Yale's collection. Cope was encouraged to collect on his own with help from Hayden's survey. When Hayden couldn't supply actual specimens for Yale, he sent lists of the latest collections to Marsh. For his part Marsh encouraged Hayden to write for the *American Journal of Science,* and he provided a strong recommendation for Hayden to direct the new survey of Nebraska in 1867. The cordial relationship lasted not quite three years.

Trouble erupted in fall 1869 when Marsh demanded that Hayden not collect in Kansas where Hayden had intended to gather vertebrates on his way home from Wyoming. Soon after he became irritated that Hayden should collect anywhere near where he intended to work, and he bristled at the fact that Hayden was sending all his vertebrates to Leidy for description. Realizing what a rich haul Hayden was uncovering, Marsh demanded a share—at a time when he had already established a reputation for hoarding collections, working them up in secrecy, and taking credit for the work of assistants. Though willing to provide duplicates to others, Hayden stood by his long-standing arrangement with Leidy to furnish descriptions, and he refused to stop collecting near Marsh, though he made an effort not to be on the same ground simultaneously. For more than two years between 1870 and 1873 they scarcely spoke to each other, and during this time Marsh began his bitter attempts to discredit Hayden behind his back.

Matters reached a climax in December 1873. Marsh wrote Hayden on the third, pointing out that in two of Hayden's recent annual reports Cope claimed discoveries that actually belonged to Marsh. Marsh demanded corrections be printed, which was not so easy for Hayden to do. In his reply of the eighth, Hayden reminded Marsh that Cope was a member of his survey and that he was obliged to print the results Cope provided. If Marsh contested these results, it was up to him to publish corrections. Directly confronting the mischief Marsh was trying to stir up, Hayden added, "You call to me to decide against Cope in a matter which Cope claims to be as much in the right as yourself, and which must be settled by experts." In his letter Marsh had acknowledged the possible need for impartial referees and had said he would accept the judgment of Leidy, Baird, or Gill regarding disputed credit. Hayden accepted these intermediaries, but Marsh failed to follow through. Obviously, Marsh was exasperated by Cope's rapacious rivalry, but just as clearly he was trying to take revenge on Cope through Hayden. Marsh assumed Hayden and Cope must have been conspiring against him; consequently, he resolved to destroy both men.

Marsh allowed his passion to get the better of his judgment in the matter. Though Marsh did not know it, Hayden had been trying to rein in Cope, urging him not to publish with such haste; but whenever Hayden remonstrated with Cope, Cope assumed he was siding with Marsh. Marsh also did not know that Hayden had previously rebuffed similarly impassioned pleas from Cope to side with him against Marsh. It was an impossible situation for Hayden, but he used good judgment in not taking sides between the disputants. Neither combatant could tolerate such neutral behavior.

Trying to stop Marsh from circulating rumors about his survey, Hayden decided to write him in April 1874. It proved to be his last letter to Marsh.

My Dear Marsh,
Your name is being used extensively here at this time by certain parties to sanction a statement that the Survey of which I have charge is a

fraud, etc. It is working to your disadvantage. Is the use of your name in such a connection authorized by you? Please write or telegraph to me on receipt of this at my expense. I wish to make use of your reply for your own good.

Marsh's reply to Hayden was also his final one.

My Dear Hayden,
Your letter of the 20th came duly, and I regretted extremely to receive it. Your language could admit of only one interpretation, and that was an implied threat, that if I did not at once endorse your survey, I should suffer for it at the Academy. As no personal considerations whatever could induce me to yield in such a case, I made no reply, leaving it for you to act as you saw fit. As the Academy will probably adjourn before this reaches you, I now answer your letter, with the same candor, but hardly with the kind feelings that I should have done had you written me a straight-forward letter about the rumors you allude to.

At the very moment Hayden wrote Marsh on the 20th, members of the National Academy of Sciences were meeting in Washington, and on the agenda was a discussion of potential new members, among them Marsh. Because of Marsh's suspicious nature and his recent aggravation with Hayden over Cope, Marsh interpreted Hayden's letter as a threat to blackball his election, and the timing of Hayden's letter only accentuated Marsh's distrustful mood. Yet Hayden wrote what he thought was a "straight-forward" letter. No doubt idle chatter was floating around during the Academy meeting, as inevitably happens when colleagues gather, and no doubt some critical remarks about Hayden's survey were being whispered because Marsh had been circulating his rumors for some time. Hayden was not above making threats, but he also hungered for recognition. After his bruising and personally vindictive battle with James Hall over the Permian discovery in 1858, Hayden could still say to Hall, "I would be glad to regard your appreciation of my labors in the West as expressed in the Iowa report as an evidence of your desire to do me justice." Even when he argued with his patrons or behaved insensitively to them, he simultaneously craved their approval. Therefore I think Hayden crafted his letter to Marsh to be conciliatory. He was saying, in effect, assure me that you are not behind these rumors, so that we can be friends again, and so that I can reassure people here who are uncertain about your intentions. That Hayden thought he could win Marsh over with such a simple appeal—when he knew perfectly well Marsh had been saying unkind things about him—exposes his idealistic side, the side that yearned for approval from colleagues. That he would have written anything at all to Marsh at this time would seem to show how thoroughly he misjudged the depth of Marsh's hostility.

Or did he misjudge it? Perhaps he wrote the letter in order to show it to others later on, to be able to say: no matter how disreputably Prof. Marsh has behaved, I am willing to overlook it, if he will now change his ways. By 20 April the House had passed the Shoemaker resolution, which asked President Grant to consider consolidating the surveys in the West. Hayden had been asked to prepare a response justifying his own survey, and the wheels were already in motion leading to the Townsend hearings that spring, which would deal with the rivalry between the Hayden and Wheeler surveys. In the forthcoming confrontation Hayden would need support from as many colleges and universities as he could muster. In that light, Hayden's letter to Marsh could have served a clever dual purpose: extending the olive branch in hopes that Marsh would grasp it and line up in support of his survey; and providing evidence, if Marsh refused his support, that at least Hayden was taking the honorable high ground.

Hayden was looking beyond the unpleasantness with Marsh to the larger public battle with Wheeler. At the same meeting of the National Academy that April Hayden read a paper entitled "An Outline of the History and Operations of the U.S. Geological Survey of the Territories, with Some Account of the Results." No text survives, but he certainly rehearsed the points he would soon make to the Townsend committee. The results were quite satisfying to Hayden. Not only did he emerge triumphant from the Townsend hearings but he won endorsements for his survey from a number of leading universities, including Yale. That Professor Marsh withheld his signature from Yale's letter only emphasized how isolated he was, for even his Yale colleagues regarded him as peevish.

These events only added to Marsh's bitterness and intensified his loathing of Hayden and Cope. Let us recall at this point the circle of Marsh's friends, among whom he was fomenting his hatred and with whom he would form a clique of conspirators to give practical effect to that hatred. He had been in touch with Newberry since 1866, and Newberry was his chief sponsor before the National Academy of Sciences. He had established cordial relations with Powell by 1871, and in the following year he agreed to write up Powell's fossil fishes. Clarence King had been his classmate at the Sheffield School in the early 1860s, and they kept in touch. Through King's survey Marsh would publish his famous sequence on fossil horses, which Darwin himself regarded as one of the best demonstrations of evolution.

In addition, Marsh was becoming a personage in America and a leader in institutions of American science. His exposé of fraudulent practices among Indian agents resulted in deposing the secretary of the interior (Columbus Delano) and the Indian commissioner (E. P. Smith). By 1877 Marsh was an officer of the American Association for the Advancement of Science. In April of the following year he became vice president of the National Academy of Sciences. A month later, through the untimely death of its president, Joseph Henry, Marsh advanced to acting president. A month after that, fate delivered to him the instrument of revenge he had been seeking for so long.

22
THE BUILDING
STORM, 1877–1878

Ferdinand V. Hayden, M.D., Ph.D., the well-known geologist, died December 22 at his residence in Philadelphia, after an illness which had confined him to his room for over a year and a half. . . . The United States owes to Dr. Hayden the establishment of its Geological Survey. . . . Dr. Hayden's influence was only second to that of Baird in securing for science the aid and recognition which it has received from the government of the United States. . . . And at the period of his greatest success Hayden was always the same unpretentious and enthusiastic seeker for knowledge. He was singularly free from sordid motives, and he left the service of the government a poor man. His retirement was caused by an intrigue discreditable to all who participated in it.
—Anonymous obituary, *American Naturalist* (December 1887)

UP UNTIL THE time of Joseph Henry's fateful death, in May 1878, Hayden seemed to be riding an inexorable tide that carried him from one triumph to another. The successful completion of the survey's work in Colorado during 1876 accentuated his commanding position among scientific explorers of the West. That same summer the International Centennial Exposition at Philadelphia showered further glory on his multifaceted survey. In 1877 Hayden instigated the Entomological Commission and sponsored its work for two years. After sending the survey back to Yellowstone to map the region, Hayden escorted two of the world's foremost naturalists (Joseph Hooker of Kew Gardens and Asa Gray of Harvard) on a well-publicized botanizing tour of the West. The distinguished paleontologist Charles White (who had disparaged Hayden when he worked for Powell) now took the field for Hayden and endorsed his views of the controversial Great Lignite. Demand for the survey's publications continued unabated. An admiring public, on both sides of the Atlantic, raised Hayden's personal prestige to new heights. Tributes continued to pour in, among them more memberships in the leading scientific associations of the world.

Behind the scenes trouble began brewing after 1876. Appropriations for the survey reached a peak during the Colorado years, then fell off somewhat. The decline reflected a growing mood of economy in the Congress and on the part of some members an increasing concern about funding several surveys that might be overlapping each other. Some members of the House Appropriations Committee opposed further grants to the surveys until they were consolidated. At the same time congressmen continued to think highly of Hayden personally, and their admiration showed in their approval of the large printings of his annual and final reports.

But even among Hayden's friends in Congress there was genuine concern over the problems presented by six virtually autonomous surveys. Three of them operated under the Department of the Interior (Hayden's, Powell's, and the surveyors of the General Land Office), two more under the War Department (King's and Wheeler's), and the Coast and Geodetic Survey reported to the Treasury Department. Not only did these surveys operate without much regard to each other, they displayed varying competence, operated in distinct jurisdictions, and relied on distinctive practices in the field. Congress voiced growing dissatisfaction with the situation, but there was no agreement on solutions. Some people wanted to consolidate the surveys, which usually meant combining all of them into one organization; others wanted to leave them separate but under more specific controls. But how to exercise more effective control? Some suggested creating an interdepartmental commission; others wanted a bureau within a specific department.

No one knew what the new secretary of the interior wanted, but everyone realized his influence could be decisive. Carl Schurz burst upon the American political scene in the 1850s, just in time to lend his considerable talents to the new Republican Party. A German immigrant who cut his political teeth during the romantic upheavals of 1848, Schurz found it expedient to flee his native land when the Prussian government began to snuff out the bright lights of reform before they could ignite a conflagration. Schurz was idealistic, honest, hard-working, efficient, forceful, ravenously intelligent, and politically ambitious. With no experience to justify it, he persuaded Lincoln to give him a military command during the Civil War, and he had not been afraid to lecture Lincoln, chastise Johnson, and openly oppose Grant. As a senator from Missouri during Grant's administration, he earned the reputation of an independent, and he threw his weight behind civil service reform. President Hayes, who came into office in 1877, admired and trusted Schurz. It was clear that if his new secretary of the interior developed any strong ideas about how to manage the surveys, the president would listen carefully.

Meanwhile lots of people were trying to plant their own seeds in Schurz's mind. One of them was Hayden's old nemesis, John Strong Newberry. Recently, Newberry had been communicating his hatred for Hayden in circles where he hoped it would do some harm and simultaneously do Powell some good. With that in mind, he wrote to Congressman Abram Hewitt of New York, "Hayden has come to be so much of a fraud that he has lost the sympathy and respect of the scientific men of the country"—at a time when this was manifestly not true. He went on to sketch the survey in an inaccurate and unflattering manner; then, as if to give credence to his slander by broadcasting it, Newberry sent a similar letter to Congressman Garfield of Ohio. (A year later he sent another poison-pen letter to Garfield, hoping to block Hayden's appointment as the geological commissioner to the Paris Exposition. Hayden got the commission anyway, but was unable to attend.)

Powell was most grateful to Newberry for these favors, and before long he found an occasion to reciprocate. As a result of gold discoveries in the Black Hills during 1874, Congress was persuaded to fund an expedition to have a close look at the region. One of the existing geological surveys could do the job, and Hayden's would have been the logical one because it was the largest and most easily expandable. But the gold appeared to be on lands belonging to the Sioux, and for that reason an expedition headed by Walter P. Jenney and his assistant, Henry Newton, was organized by the Indian Bureau of the Department of the Interior. The group did a field survey in 1875 and promptly published a preliminary report. A year later Jenney published a full report on the gold, which addressed the urgent questions and gave Congress what it wanted. Only a description of the general geology of the region remained to be written by Newton.

By coincidence Newton was a student of Newberry's, and by further coincidence the most recent geological reports on the region were Hayden's, the result of his work there in the 1850s and 1860s. Powell (at the urging of Newberry) involved himself in helping Newton complete his report, which was odd because at the time Powell faced critical financial problems in his own survey. Why was he willing to shoulder the additional burden of sponsoring Newton's report? Newton, somewhat embarrassed by Powell's attentions and innocent of Powell's larger motives, unwittingly gives us the explanation in his letter to Powell of 29 March. "I do not like the idea of your paying all the expense for this, especially as if I go back again into the Hills there will undoubtedly [be] much to add that will necessitate an entire new picture." It was precisely his ardent hope for "an entire new picture" that spurred Powell on, for that new picture might embarrass Hayden, the author of the old picture. Meanwhile, Powell and Newberry began circulating the lie that Hayden was delaying Newton's report for fear the old picture would reveal his incompetence. But Hayden had no authority or ability to hold up Newton's report, even if he had wanted to. Publication of Newton's report was delayed simply because it was not yet finished, as Newton himself freely admitted, which is why he wanted to return to the field during 1877 in the first place. For that reason, and at the expense of Powell's survey, he did retake the field in 1877; but he died there of typhoid fever, leaving his work unfinished. Using Newton's notes, G. K. Gilbert finished the report, and Powell's survey published it in 1880. Nothing in it proved embarrassing to Hayden.

All the scheming came to Hayden's attention and worried him. "I do not feel sure of a prolonged existence," he confided to one friend, but he countered the slanders against him by prevailing upon his own allies to write Schurz. Among them were Congressman James Monroe of Ohio and his old college friend and former boss at Interior, Jacob Cox, known to be a close friend of Schurz. At this point, early in his tenure in a big and demanding job, Schurz could only take notice of the rival geologists. He had his hands full keeping track of a most disparate group of institutions, properties, resources, bureaus, offices, and commissions, and simultaneously trying to introduce civil service rules into one of the most graft-infested departments of the federal government. Actually, although the overlapping of the surveys might have annoyed Schurz's sense of efficiency, generally the surveys (especially Hayden's) had brought honor and praise to the department. While in the Senate, Schurz had served briefly on the committee for the territories, so he was acquainted with the major players. Because of his personal love of nature and the outdoors, he was inclined to be sympathetic to the general work of the surveys. At least in the early stages of his regime, therefore, and despite the efforts of Powell and Newberry, there is no reason to think Schurz looked unfavorably on Hayden.

Things began to change as Schurz got down to work with Powell and Hayden on the business of the surveys. Schurz was a much more attentive boss than either man was accustomed to, and he quickly familiarized himself with their work and kept himself informed by asking for regular reports. Hayden and Powell each jockeyed for opportunities to gain an edge over the other. Hayden stole the first march on 26 April by taking advantage of a new appropriation giving the Indian Bureau $2,500 to continue collecting historical artifacts. Hayden boldly asked for half that sum to be used in enlarging his own materials, which he called "the most valuable and important collection of this character in this country," a description calculated to discombobulate Mr. Powell, whose single greatest interest had always been Indian artifacts and culture.

On 22 May Powell made a thoughtful reply to the challenge thrown down by Hayden. He suggested dividing up their work in such a way that both he and Hayden would continue with geology, but in future one of them would monopolize ethnology, the other natural history. This suggestion took Hayden by surprise. He finally replied on 10 July, reiterating his request of April for $1,250 to continue his own collection. He claimed to possess about 1,500 negatives depicting seventy-five to eighty tribes, as well as other photographic and manuscript materials, collected over the previous twenty-five years, which were "impossible to duplicate . . . as the opportunity for securing such material has passed." His collection was "unique in importance as well as in extent; it is regarded as the most valuable extant." In short, if only one of us is to control ethnology, let it be me. Powell had sounded more generous, urging that whoever took over ethnology should have the other's collection, but this seeming openhandedness was a subtle ploy designed to relieve Hayden of his artifacts. The previous year Secretary Joseph Henry of the Smithsonian had agreed to turn over to Powell for study and publication all its ethnological materials. For that reason, Powell certainly had the better case for performing all future work of the same kind for Interior.

Meanwhile Schurz had been asking both men for more information about their surveys, essentially challenging them to justify their present operations and to make a convincing case for taking over all the ethnology. Powell's seemingly diplomatic response found favor, and it had the tactical effect of forcing Hayden to accept his compromise or else appear greedy because he would then be asking to keep ethnology and geology and topography in addition to natural history. So Hayden stalled, calling upon friends to send letters of support and launching a publicity campaign that celebrated the history of his survey and justified its ravenous appetite. Enlarging an article he had written in April for the *Republic,* Hayden now published and circulated the *Sketch of the Origin and Progress of the United States Geological and Geographical Survey of the Territories.*

Schurz was not impressed. On 2 August he reminded Hayden that he had not yet replied to Powell's compromise suggestion in a way that would eliminate duplicate efforts in the future. Clearly outmaneuvered by his rival and threatened with displeasure from his boss, Hayden had no choice but to surrender; but he did not yield graciously. On 28 September he agreed to give Powell any ethnographic material he might gather thereafter, but he reserved "the right to elaborate what matter I have already in hand." And he could not resist enclosing a letter from George Perkins Marsh, the polymath diplomat and philologist, that included an encomium of Hayden's ethnographic work: "[A]nd we shall not do our duty as members of the great commonwealth of knowledge if we suffer a narrow economy to prevent the continuation of work so well begun and so important to the general interests, material and moral, of the old world and the new." It was the kind of rhetorical flourish Schurz himself often made, but his mind was now fixed on deflating some of the puffery surrounding the competing surveys.

Obviously, Hayden was stung by having to give up ethnology and furious that Powell had succeeded in clipping his wings, even if slightly. For nearly two months Hayden brooded and planned his revenge. He dictated at least two draft letters to Schurz in which he tried out various phrases and rationales. The idea he had in mind was clear, and he finally found the right tone for a formal letter on 15 November. In it he made a wholesale conversion to the cause of reform and economy in order to end duplication of effort and eliminate unnecessary costs. Only "one solid organization" was required, he conceded; therefore he suggested that from the beginning of the new year Powell limit himself exclusively to ethnology "and that all geological and geographical work may be assigned exclusively to the survey under my charge." It was a timely suggestion, for it offered Powell what he seemed to want most, appeased those in Congress who cried for consolidation, and paid homage to Schurz's desire for efficiency. As a matter of interest, Hayden's suggestion foreshadowed the reforms of 1879, when the USGS and the Bureau of American Ethnology gained separate existences.

That Powell did not embrace the offer shows he had more in mind than devoting himself to ethnology. Like Hayden, Powell was born and raised with modest means. They both experienced hardship, personal loss, and great frustration; both realized intuitively, long before they found a satisfying career path, that they marched to a different drummer in life. Both found fulfillment in the pursuit of natural history, and both were urged forward by a burning ambition. But by temperament they were poles apart. Where Hayden was enthusiastic, Powell was studious; where Hayden was energetic, Powell was forceful; where Hayden was winning, Powell was persuasive. Hayden was meteoric, charismatic, even explosive at times, whereas Powell was restrained, calculating, systematic. They were perfect foils for each other, and one can only wonder at the powerful partnership they might have forged had fate placed them on the same team.

After the Civil War, Powell also hitched his wagon to the star of western exploration. In enterprise and adventurous experience his career mirrored Hayden's during the postwar years. Like Hayden, he enjoyed sponsorship from the Smithsonian and the Department of the Interior. But Powell found it easier to focus himself, both as to subject matter and territory; thus he became absorbed with the lands of the Colorado Basin and Plateau, and the Indians who lived there. During the Townsend hearings in spring 1874

(Congress's first approach to consolidating the surveys), the differences between Hayden and Powell became more pronounced.

On the surface they appeared as allies because both scorned the scientific value of the military surveys and both foresaw an expanded, exclusively civilian survey to chart the topography and resources of the West. But even in 1874 their enormous difference in style was obvious to anyone who watched them in action. Hayden was a skillful tactician who demonstrated beyond doubt the superiority of his survey over Wheeler's; simultaneously he was an accomplished advocate who knew how to mold the particulars of a situation into a promotional statement that emphasized the practicality of his own survey and saluted Congress for endorsing scientific work. He believed sincerely that his survey could expand to handle any business of the nation, and he yearned for an exclusive jurisdiction in western exploration. At the same time he was perceptive enough to see that not all congressmen were ready, in 1874, to establish a permanent bureau for scientific exploration. Because his own was the largest and most successful of the special surveys, he urged Congress to continue funding these surveys, coordinated by the Interior Department, in the confident expectation that further operations would prove the superiority of his own survey and eventually persuade Congress to give him the direction of a united and comprehensive effort. Hayden took the position of the front runner who has little to gain from drastic change and much to expect from the continuation of present trends.

By contrast Powell had little to gain from the present order of things and potentially everything to lose if it continued. Therefore when he said before the Townsend committee, "There is now left within the territory of the United States no great unexplored region, and exploring expeditions are no longer needed for general purposes," he meant that neither Wheeler's, Hayden's, nor his own survey were "of an importance commensurate with their expense." Instead, he argued, "a more thorough method, or a survey proper, is now demanded." He did not say much about his vision for that "survey proper"; indeed it may not have been fully developed in his own mind yet, but even in 1874 he could outline three tasks for that survey. It must determine "the mineral resources of the country—deposits of coal, salt, ores, precious metals, etc." It must be adequate "for purposes of intelligent legislation on the railroad interests of the country," which meant of adequate geographic detail and precision to enable settlers to buy lands intelligently from the railroads. In 1862 Congress had passed the Pacific Railroad Act, which, among other things, gave the railroads alternate sections of land on both sides of their track, most of which they were expected to sell to compensate themselves for initial capital expenses. The General Land Office had been responsible since the 1780s for parceling and selling public lands, but the railroad lands were private lands and Powell wanted to prevent the rail-roads from simply selling their lands to the highest (probably corporate) bidder; he wanted even private lands sufficiently surveyed that the home-steader would know the nature of the land he was buying.

The third task Powell set for a reformed survey was to take account of the fact, ignored by the General Land Office, that "about two-fifths of the entire area of the United States has a climate so arid that agriculture cannot be pursued without irrigation." Therefore, "it is of the most immediate and pressing importance that a general survey should be made for the purpose of determining the several areas which can thus be redeemed by irrigation."

These were bold ideas, especially for 1874. They implied, first, a survey that would emphasize economic geology; second, legislation that would intrude on the traditional sanctity of private property to insist that such property be used in a manner consistent with the public good; and third, wholesale reforms in the manner of parceling and selling public lands. In 1874 few contemporaries grasped all that Powell's ideas implied, but when he reiterated those ideas in greater detail four years later in his *Report on the Lands of the Arid Region of the United States,* there could be no mistaking his intentions. A few realized what Powell was saying right from the start. Representative Thomas Patterson of Colorado, for example, recalled in a speech of 1879 that Powell had been sowing those seeds since the Townsend hearings and correctly called him a "revolutionist." Other western lawmak-ers had similar misgivings about Powell's ideas. Hayden took no position on the proposed reforms, but he certainly saw that in Powell's scheme of things his own survey must disappear; thus there is some gravity in his remark to Archibald Geikie that Powell was "seeking for the sole command and in the struggle one of us may drop out."

Powell was a clever political animal who could use his considerable rhetorical skills to disguise and mislead as well as to inform. Consider, for example, how he promoted the idea for a consolidated survey. He began with the attractive-sounding idea that science and government could work together better if they did so in a deliberate and coordinated fashion. This implied that most science would be publicly funded science and that any privately funded science would be developed in harmony with (and subordi-nated to) the larger public science. Of course, Powell did not mention that his views on this basic point were not universally accepted, that probably a majority of scientists, and even more of politicians, opposed the kind of pub-lic marriage Powell imagined. Instead he talked as though his views merely summarized the prevailing views of scientists and politicians. The beauty (and forcefulness) of his argument is that its premise about cooperation between science and government leads logically to a number of myths that followed from that premise. Arguing that all science was in the public interest, for example, Powell reasoned that all scientific work could be nonpartisan, even nonpolitical, and further that such work could be divorced from the interests of individual scientists. The actual history of the postwar geological surveys had demonstrated just the opposite.

Attempting to flatter Congress, Powell next implied that most lawmakers were proud of their support of science and that most wanted a reformed geological survey. That was not quite true either. Perhaps those who supported science were proud of it, but many members had doubts about whether government should be in the business of science anyway, and, if so, to what extent.

Then, alluding to the well-known rivalries among the several surveys, Powell managed to convey the impression that these rivalries arose out of personal ambitions and jealousies between the surveys' leaders. It was vital to the credibility of this argument for Powell to deny that he himself had any ambitions and to imply that others (everyone knew he meant Hayden) were preventing a harmonious and progressive unity of science and government by pursuing personal ambitions. This bit of sophistry ignored the fact that the rivalries between the surveys had not originated in personalities or individual ambitions, but in their separate creations at different times, and for different purposes, by a laissez-faire government that looked to individual entrepreneurs to do for the nation what it was not yet willing to do itself. As for Powell's ambitions, we can better judge his sincerity by noting that within a few years he would centralize in his own hands control over the new USGS, the Bureau of American Ethnology, and the Irrigation Survey.

All of Powell's biographers (admittedly, some more than others) have romanticized him into a visionary and a public-spirited reformer, but this approach ignores the needs and ambitions of the man and sees him only as the embodiment of an ideal. It is no disparagement of Powell's genuinely important ideas to point out that they were first articulated in the context of a personal rivalry or to note that of the three rivals he was by far the weakest contender. But these facts give rise to several questions. To what extent did Powell become a reformer because his career as a surveyor-explorer was threatened by more successful rivals? Who supported his ideas, who opposed them, and what was Powell's relationship with both groups of men? What were the interests of his supporters and opponents: in other words, what did they have to gain by supporting or opposing him? Was Powell truly a disinterested reformer or did he stand to gain personally from presenting reforming ideas? Where did he get his ideas: are they original with him? Given his intellectual formation as a versatile naturalist, why did he emphasize only economic geology and separate geology so thoroughly from natural history?

Until some biographer has tackled such questions, we cannot decide whether Powell was an idealistic reformer, capable of standing above personal enmity, or a bitter loser seeking revenge. To be sure, the real man will not fill either of those stereotypes, but it is a pity that this brilliant thinker, this energetic activist, this subtle bureaucrat, this slick salesman, this idealistic and devious man, this richly complicated man, has not yet been discovered. It is almost as though his biographers have found the man himself unworthy of attention and have had to justify their books by clothing him in noble ideals. That approach belittles the real man and denigrates true biography— which begins and ends with the man, the whole man, and recognizes that man for what he was, and was not, rather than making him over to suit the predilections of a biographer.

I would not dwell on the historical picture of Powell if it did not impinge upon an understanding of Hayden. But it does. Powell long outlived Hayden, building up in years after their competition a well-deserved reputation in public service. But Powell's very success, and the fact that Powell bested Hayden in their earlier struggle over the surveys, has made Hayden seem insignificant by comparison, even unworthy of notice. Until now, no one has ever bothered to discover Hayden or relate events from his point of view. I do not intend to raise Hayden by tearing Powell down, for Powell may deserve the fame that surrounds him, even though he has yet to be evaluated as a man apart from his reputation. At the same time, it seems undeniable that in the period *before* 1879 Hayden was much more significant than Powell. This fact has been obscured, and a general appreciation of Hayden delayed, by Powell's success *after* 1879, and the rapid decline of Hayden after that time. Needless to say, Hayden's story might have been dramatically different had he been chosen the first director of the USGS.

So it becomes crucial to understand why Hayden did *not* become the first director of the USGS. There are three parts to the explanation: Hayden made some critical mistakes; the tide of the times was turning against his kind of surveying; and Powell was involved with a small nucleus of men who wished to displace Hayden. In Chapter 20 I noted several of the ties from as early as 1875 and 1876 that bound Powell, Newberry, Marsh, and King, and it is beyond doubt that the cement of their continued alliance was mutual hostility toward Hayden and a desire to undermine his preponderant influence in exploratory science. Newberry's vituperative letters to Hewitt and Garfield, and Powell's hopeful sponsorship of Newton's study on the Black Hills, show this deliberate opposition to Hayden coming to fruition.

The tie between Powell and Clarence King was central to this alliance and quite surprising because the leaders of the four rival surveys had no reason to wish each other well, much less to cooperate. Yet cooperate was precisely what we find Powell and King doing in January 1877. Desperate to influence the appropriations committee to keep his survey funded, Powell wrote King: "I beg of you to come and help me pull through this year. You can do me great good in exactly the direction in which I am needing assistance." Such a candid and unadorned request does not suggest two men who were just becoming acquainted. They had cooperated before. Hayden certainly thought so, and he complained that half of Powell's map of the Uinta Mountains (published in 1876 with Powell's *Report on the Geology of the Eastern Portion of the Uinta Mountains*) was directly traced from King's earlier unpublished map of the same region. "To this is to [be] added the fact," said Hayden, "that the only good part of Maj. Powell's map is that stolen from Mr. King." This sounds like an overheated Hayden, but interestingly Powell did not deny the charge (indeed, he all but admitted it in a letter to Secretary Schurz). A private letter between two of Powell's friends summarized the matter.

> Since writing you I have seen Prof. Marsh, who has had an interview with Clarence King. From this, and another source, it seems that King allowed Powell to use his topography to complete his maps, and that no credit was to be given because King, being under the Engineer Dept., had no right to communicate the matter. Powell seems to be no more in fault than King.

During spring 1878 four events took place in a relatively short span of time that dramatically accelerated and congealed the alliance against Hayden. On 8 March Representative John Atkins of Tennessee introduced a resolution asking the secretary of the interior to summarize the operations of all the geological and geographical surveys under his department over the previous ten years, mentioning expenses and overlaps between the surveys. The resolution revived the whole question of consolidation. Atkins was chairman of the House Appropriations Committee, and he had been a spokesman of consolidation for some time and an open admirer of Powell's since at least 1874.

On 1 April Powell handed to Schurz his *Report on the Lands of the Arid Region of the United States,* his formal plan of reform for the western lands, including ideas about restructuring the surveys. Two days later Schurz sent it to the House, which had it printed and then sent it to Atkins for study by the appropriations committee.

Then on 13 May Joseph Henry died. In addition to being the chief executive officer of the Smithsonian, he was also president of the National Academy of Sciences. By one of those fortuitous coincidences of history that seem small but prove momentous, the vice president of the Academy and the man who thus became acting president was none other than Professor Othniel Charles Marsh.

The fourth event of that spring was no coincidence: it was orchestrated by those who saw the picture emerging from the first three events. On 20 June Representative Abram Hewitt attached a clause to the Sundry Civil Bill requiring the National Academy of Sciences to review all the scientific surveys; the bill, including Hewitt's clause, passed the same day. By the way, Hewitt was also a member of the appropriations committee and a man whose professional interests put him in the camp of those who wanted a unified survey that would emphasize economic geology. Hewitt was an executive in the iron and steel business; he was also a founding member of the American Association of Mining Engineering, and its president in 1876; he was a personal friend of Clarence King, whose survey had precisely the economic emphasis Hewitt wanted, and he was also a business associate of King's in a cattle venture. Since coming to the House in 1875, Hewitt had shown himself friendly to fiscal reforms, especially in reducing the role of the army and in promoting the idea of a consolidated geological survey.

Several aspects of Hewitt's clause in the Sundry Civil Bill betray a direct debt to Powell's reforming ideas. In requiring the Academy to review the surveys, he was precise in saying exactly the ones he intended: "all surveys of a scientific character under the War or Interior Department, and the surveys of the Land Office." Previously, Atkins had asked for a review of only the surveys managed by Interior, but that was before Powell suggested in his *Lands of the Arid Region* that the problems presented by the surveys ought to be tackled in conjunction with problems of parceling and selling the public lands. This linkage was new with Powell. No one before him had thought of reforming the surveys from this broad a perspective. Wallace Stegner, one of Powell's biographers, has made a case for the fact that it was Powell who first suggested the clause in the Sundry Civil Bill requiring the Academy's sweeping review. King's biographers think perhaps King suggested the idea to Hewitt. Whoever first thought of it, the important point is that Hewitt's clause grew directly out of Powell's ideas.

But Hewitt's clause makes two other interesting points, both stemming from Powell's influence. The essential charge to the Academy, after reviewing the existing surveys, was to furnish Congress with "a plan for surveying and mapping the Territories of the United States." This was odd because a plan already existed in the Department of the Interior; it had been in effect since 1 July 1874, when Secretary Columbus Delano established guidelines for Powell and Hayden to follow in mapping their respective territories.[1] Though the mechanics of the 1874 plan were sound, by implication they assumed a role for Hayden, indeed a major role, because in 1874 Hayden was the most ambitious mapper in the department.

But Powell wanted to eliminate Hayden, which was also clear from the last phrase of Hewitt's clause that asked for "a suitable plan for the publication and distribution of reports, maps, and documents, and other results of the said surveys." Again, such a request was not necessary under the existing order of things because publication and distribution of reports had been progressing perfectly well, in the same way Congress had always authorized work for the government printer. The implication was that "the said surveys" were about to end, and therefore some "suitable plan" would be needed to determine how much of their unfinished "results" should be published. It was plain to anyone familiar with the rival surveys that this clause was aimed specifically at Hayden who had a mass of unfinished material, some of which never came to print; even the work that was eventually published after 1878 took twelve years and resulted in ten more volumes. By contrast, after 1878, the three other surveys combined did not have half as much unfinished work in the pipeline as Hayden.

Even more telling evidence of a deliberate conspiracy to overthrow Hayden emerges from the work of the committee of the National Academy of Sciences, the one appointed in accordance with Hewitt's clause and known as the Academy's Committee on the Surveys. As acting president of the Academy, Marsh had the authority to appoint the committee, and he promptly made himself chairman. He also appointed Newberry. His other appointees are significant, too, but can be discussed in detail after observing how Marsh carefully steered the committee's work toward a predetermined goal of undermining Hayden. Marsh was in Europe at the time the Sundry Civil Bill passed, and he did not return home until August, which gave most people the impression that his committee's work did not begin until then. Indeed, the committee did not convene until October, when most of its members attended at least one of a series of meetings in New York; but well before those meetings Marsh had already worked out the purpose and agenda for the committee. The meetings in October only served to confirm what he had arranged privately over the previous two or three months.

Because these facts throw a different light on the origins of the U.S. Geological Survey, I will review them in detail. No sooner had Congress authorized the Academy in late June to make recommendations on the surveys than Powell sent Marsh advance copies of his *Lands of the Arid Region.* In an accompanying note he added, "I beg you to distribute [them] among those gentlemen who may be appointed members of the committee of the National Academy of Sciences to take into consideration the organization of a Bureau of Surveys." It is interesting that Powell's copy of this letter (in his

Letterpress volumes) is dated 24 September 1878; on Marsh's copy the letter is undated, but someone has penciled in a date of June 1877. Now "1877" cannot be correct because Powell had not finished his volume at that time, but "June" probably is correct and would more accurately fit the fact that Powell said, "I send you today eight copies of a report, just issued, on the Lands of the Arid Region." Because his report had been issued on 3 April, referring to it as "just issued" would have made sense in June 1878, but not in September.

So what was going on? It is not necessary to imagine Powell deliberately misdating letters. Probably he sent copies of his report in late June as soon as he realized Marsh would be involved with the Academy's Committee on the Surveys and before he discovered Marsh had already departed for Europe. Because he had no idea how many members would be on Marsh's committee, he sent several copies of *Lands of the Arid Region* for Marsh to peruse and circulate. He then sent more copies in September with the same covering letter. That he should send two sets of copies at different times is not at all strange: he wanted to broadcast his report as widely as possible, and he knew Marsh would place them in the right hands. In both his June and September letters to Marsh, Powell said: "When the committee is organized, I hope to have the privilege of making a statement before it, setting forth what I deem to be the proper organization for the United States Geographical and Geological Surveys." This is interesting. Supposedly Marsh was heading a disinterested committee charged to produce an objective recommendation about the surveys. Yet here is Powell assuming that it will be acceptable for one of the interested parties to give his partial views to that committee. I doubt he would have thought to do so had he not received some approving signal from Marsh; otherwise he was certainly taking improper initiatives.

But Marsh was more than willing to be influenced by Powell. Wallace Stegner has underlined how much the report of Marsh's Committee on the Surveys relied on Powell's *Lands of the Arid Region,* and Stegner has also discovered a telltale letter from Powell's secretary (James Pilling) to Powell: "I see the Academy has made its report and it sounds wonderfully like something I have read—and perhaps written—before."

What no one has noticed before is how swiftly and independently Marsh acted to focus the committee's efforts. By the time Powell sent his second letter on 24 September, Marsh had already produced a draft report for the committee. We know this because on 25 September Simon Newcomb, one of the committee members, sent Marsh a detailed critique of a plan Marsh had sent him some time earlier. Four days later another committee member, Alexander Agassiz, wrote indicating he, too, knew of Marsh's plan. It seems Marsh had circulated his draft report to all committee members by no later than mid-September. If Marsh granted Powell's wish to meet with members of the committee to convey his views on the future of the surveys, no record of it survives. But Marsh's report reflects Powell's views so strongly that it scarcely matters whether Marsh distilled those views from personal interviews or careful reading, or both. In any case, once Marsh had prepared his draft report, it seems likely he asked Powell for the additional copies of *Lands of the Arid Region* (which Powell sent on 24 September) to provide committee members with the full context and rationale that Marsh had so skillfully summarized in his draft report.

The timing is most instructive. On 28 September Marsh wrote Secretary Schurz saying a committee on the surveys had now been appointed, "and is now ready to consider the subject," giving the impression that nothing had yet been done when in fact a draft report had already been circulated. Marsh also asked Schurz to send "any information in regard to the plans and wishes of your department as to the above surveys you may think proper to lay before the academy," but this was strictly a pro forma request. The crucial work was being done in private without regard to any public documents Schurz would send. On 19 October Marsh met in New York with Newberry to go over the draft of his report; other members had seen it and communicated their reactions to Marsh, all favorable to judge by the surviving correspondence. About the same time Marsh and Newcomb met with King separately, probably in Washington. By the time Marsh received from Schurz on 2 November the formal statements of Hayden, Powell, and the commissioner of the General Land Office on their surveys, he and his committee had already finalized the report. On 5 November five members of the committee (all but Rogers and Dana) met in New York to review their strategy for presenting the report to the full Academy the next day. On 6 November the Academy heard Marsh's report and approved it.

It is important to realize how thoroughly Marsh controlled the events leading to the adoption of his report. He set the committee's agenda, drafted its report, and was the only member to attend all of the committee's meetings. His central and personal role in creating the report is obvious, even from the incomplete correspondence that survives with committee members. His personal dominance is also revealing. He moved much faster than others intended; he ignored suggestions about membership; he completely finessed the secretary of the Academy, J. E. Hilgard, who felt he should have some role in the committee's affairs; he visited Schurz in Washington to brief him on the evolving plans even before Schurz had collected the official responses he was obliged to submit to the committee. And he waved away a warning from W. B. Rogers of 17 October, who said: "I have heard that we are considered a secret comm[ittee.] This impression would be unfortunate, as nothing is more likely to arouse general opposition than any suspicion of secret management." Marsh could afford to laugh at such warnings: he had already covered all the bases and gathered support from the key players.

And he had already done something else that had a large impact on the way things turned out. For his fellow committee members, he had selected men who were disposed to favor Clarence King as director of whatever consolidated agency emerged, or at least men who were not inclined to Hayden and who might be turned to King. This fact is important because it shows how little the origin of the USGS derived from a dispassionate interest in scientific institutions and how much it owed to the quite passionate and personal disputes between scientific leaders of the period. Marsh had an enormous enmity for Hayden by 1878, partly due to Hayden's support for his archrival, E. D. Cope, but also because he had crossed swords with Hayden himself. Newberry, too, was a sworn enemy of Hayden's, partly due to jealousy over the rapid rise of a former protégé but also due to his own rivalry in the field of paleobotany with Leo Lesquereux, whom Hayden came to prefer over Newberry because Lesquereux produced while Newberry frittered. Also Hayden and Lesquereux had ideas about the Great Lignite that conflicted with Newberry's. With two such bitter opponents of Hayden's on the committee, it was already a stacked deck, particularly because both of them had congenial ties to King and Powell.

Two other committee members had strong preferences for King. Alexander Agassiz had met King in 1868, and King thought enough of Agassiz to name a mountain after him the following summer. Agassiz soon became an investing partner in King's cattle ranch, and before the end of 1878 they shared some mining interests too. It was not irrelevant that as president of several fabulously rich copper mines in Michigan, Agassiz had a strong interest in a survey that would emphasize economic geology. In a letter to Marsh of 20 September Agassiz tipped his hand rather candidly about the future he intended for Hayden: "I think that the matter of Hayden & Co. going on indefinitely will take care of itself. All their materials will naturally pass into the hands of <u>their successors!</u>" Agassiz wrote this letter even before Marsh's report was approved by the Academy and well before enabling legislation for a new survey was written.

Simon Newcomb was a superb mathematician and astronomer who directed the Nautical Almanac Office in Washington, where he was also a professor at the Naval Observatory. In 1877 he served as president of the American Association for the Advancement of Science. Unlike most intellectuals, Newcomb took pride in his political connections, and he was instrumental in arranging meetings for Marsh in official circles and in promoting the committee's plan with General Carlile P. Patterson, head of the Coast Survey, and with

Schurz, again even before Marsh presented his plan to the Academy. (It did not hurt, either, that Schurz was on close personal terms with King.) Even before Hewitt's rider to the appropriations bill that created the Academy's committee, Newcomb had thought King the best man to succeed Joseph Henry at the Smithsonian. And even before that committee had been formally organized, Newcomb was writing King desiring him to give his advice on the surveys to the future committee! This letter is interesting on several grounds: it shows the preference of another committee member for King even before the committee convened; it hints that Marsh had tapped Newcomb for membership even before he left for Europe; and it foreshadows in July the entire outcome of the committee's deliberations. At any rate, King did meet with Marsh and Newcomb during October to give his ideas on the surveys, which is another indication of Marsh's poorly disguised partiality.

At least none of the other three committee members had any reason to hate Hayden. James Dwight Dana had long encouraged Hayden's professional efforts, as well as those of King and Powell, and he remained scrupulously neutral when the choice came down to King versus Hayden. William Barton Rogers, a distinguished geologist, had also admired Hayden's early work in the Upper Missouri, though he was eventually persuaded to back King against Hayden. William Petit Trowbridge was a colleague of Newberry's at the Columbia School of Mines, formerly on the faculty at Yale with Marsh and a man with experience in the iron business and with the Coast Survey. He also eventually backed King.

Hayden was under no illusions about the situation. "These surveys have been referred to the National Academy," he wrote to a colleague, even before he knew the committee's membership, "and I presume some great plan will be proposed that will obliterate the present order of things, unless all our friends take hold and help." In a note to his English friend Joseph Hooker, he admitted his fears more candidly.

> I enclose in this letter a copy of a law passed last session for the purpose of killing off some of the surveys. As the man who proposed the law, Hon. Abram Hewitt, is an enemy of mine it is not intended to work to the interest of my survey. . . . We had a hard time this last session and came near being decapitated. It cost me about 4 months hard toil to save the survey. We had to cultivate the good will of over 300 members to counteract the vicious influence of the [Appropriations] Committee.

Hayden had difficulty deciding how to react to this challenge. He wrote Baird and Leidy, urging them to do what they could to keep Newberry off the committee. He worried out loud that Marsh would use this opportunity to settle old scores. Not being sure he would be back from the field in time to attend the Academy's meeting in November, he also urged friends to attend and support his interests. In mid-October, while in Cheyenne, he learned that Marsh had formed a committee, though he still did not know its membership, and now Schurz was asking for his statement to Marsh's committee. He showed a desperate state of mind in two notes he dashed off on 14 October, first to Leidy: "I am asked to make a reply. I do not know what to say. Think up something for me. Gather outside opinions. Will see you soon." And to Baird: "I do not know what to say or do. I do not wish to commit myself to anything and wish the whole matter were over."

Hayden had no choice but to submit a response to Schurz, and eventually he did so; but the contrast between the way he and Powell handled this similar opportunity betrays a shift in polarity. All the magnetic energy and leadership was draining away from Hayden and rushing to Powell. Hayden put together two and a half pages, but his whole argument was captured in one sentence: "In reply, I beg to say that any plans which I could offer for the survey of the Western Territories would naturally be based upon the organization now under my charge." He failed to advance any forceful arguments on his own behalf, relying instead on the lame point that he had been longer in the field and pointing with pride, but not very thoroughly, to his past accomplishments. It was a pathetic effort for a man once so fearless and aggressive, but now so obviously wounded and clearly failing.

By contrast, in a little more than thirteen pages Powell accomplished proportionally much more. While Hayden's meager summary of his splendid survey failed to do it justice, Powell's made his appear far greater than it was. He rehearsed his reasons for preferring a consolidated survey, buttressing them with persuasive cost comparisons. He borrowed arguments from his *Lands of the Arid Region* and blended them with specific recommendations that anticipated and elaborated upon points in Marsh's forthcoming report on surveys. In the process, he misrepresented the true worth of Hayden's survey and managed to leave the impression that Hayden's broadbrush approach to natural history was "unscientific." He also concocted a specious argument "that zoology and botany as branches of general science are not proper subjects of governmental patronage," which aimed to eliminate Hayden's publication of natural history research at public expense. In short, he gave Hayden a good drubbing, and he sustained not a scratch in the exchange.

The uncharacteristic weakness of Hayden's response to Schurz and the surprisingly desperate tone of his notes to Leidy and Baird were not typical and must give us a moment's pause. Certainly he was under great stress—worrying about Marsh's intrigues and concerned about Powell's growing strength—and his suspicious nature only pulled tighter the knots of tension that squeezed him, making him more nervous and excitable than usual. But there are signs that in this period of time Hayden was suffering from a physical ailment as well, one that exacerbated his nervousness and probably affected his judgment.

Consider his actions. After learning the Academy would be considering the future of the surveys, which he knew boded ill for his own enterprise, he still decided to head west and spend the summer in the field, where he had no particularly important work to do. Fieldwork was ably supervised by his assistants. Under the circumstances an alert combatant might have stayed in Washington for the summer to tend his political fences. That is precisely what Powell did; he spent most of the summer in Washington, then made a much briefer trip to the field before returning east just before Hayden. William Darrah, another of Powell's biographers, cited letters to Hayden from some of his friends in Washington showing Hayden was anxious to follow Powell's movements; but surely the larger point is that if Hayden had been aware of the genuine peril he faced he would have stayed in town to be directly in touch with developments. Unless—as I believe—he realized his physical and mental health were both in such jeopardy that he needed the restorative tonic of a summer in the field.

Even after recuperating in Wyoming his spirits were not sufficiently restored to face up to the forthcoming battle. This is evident in his pathetic notes to Leidy and Baird and in his intention of avoiding the Academy's meeting entirely by asking friends to protect his interests for him. Hayden had never hesitated to recruit friends to intervene on his behalf or do things for him while he was away; but here we see something quite different: not a request for help so much as a desperate plea for rescue. Thinking he could stay away from the most critical meeting of his career and rely on his friends to pull him through demonstrates a serious deterioration of judgment.

Later he realized he must attend the Academy's meeting, and he did; but he failed to put his best foot forward. At each of the Academy's meetings, time was given to members who wanted to read papers on their recent work. Hayden volunteered to give no less than three, but none of his topics conveyed the resounding impression he needed—of a dynamic scientist, an imaginative administrator, or even of a capable man at the height of his powers who was looking for wider responsibilities. He spoke on the peculiar topography surrounding Two Ocean Pass in Wyoming; he mentioned finding evidence of true glaciers in the Wind River Range; and he outlined his plan for a general geological map of the territories. Under the circumstances, only the latter made any impact. Newberry's reading of a paper summarizing the conflicting interpretations of Hayden's Great Lignite reemphasized his (and King's) opposition to Hayden. It was a conscientious scholarly review, but the critical interpretation of Hayden and the timeliness of the presentation in view of the larger political rivalry between the surveys were lost on nobody.

After the Academy meeting in November, Hayden continued to show signs of poor judgment and discursive attention. Even though Marsh's plan for the surveys had made it abundantly clear there would be no role for the military in future surveys of the West, Hayden could not shake off his fears of the army. He alternated between gloating about Wheeler's demise and worrying about a resurgent role for the army. He gave undue attention to an unfriendly but flimsy report of his work that appeared in a foreign journal at a time he should have been carefully orchestrating a counterattack on Powell. Faced with great danger, he seemed to lose his nerve, to pull in his horns and fritter away his efforts on inconsequential matters. He intervened to help Archibald Geikie get an invitation to give the Lowell lectures; he sent around to museums the models of Indian villages his survey had prepared; he arranged for a fourth edition of the *Catalogue of the Publications of the U.S. Geological and Geographical Survey of the Territories.* It appeared in early 1879. Meanwhile, he wrote fatalistically to Hooker, "What ever may be the destiny of the organization in the future, its career has been an honorable one so far & will form a part of the scientific history of the country."

The most certain sign that Hayden's judgment was deserting him appeared in a letter he wrote to Geikie on 13 December. Out of the blue, in the course of a long letter, he said, "Since I began this letter I have been assured that no one but myself would get the chief directorship of the new Bureau if it is formed." Supposedly, Hayes conveyed this promise to Hayden through mutual friends in Congress. We will never know what was said or done to put such an idea into Hayden's head, but for the time being he may have believed it. (I will look at this letter again from another point of view in the next chapter.) He abandoned his normally suspicious frame of mind; worse, he seems to have ignored the very real evidence that now he faced the political fight of his life. Over the next few months he did continue the battle, but without the fire and vigor that were characteristic of him. (By contrast, Powell moved forward with confidence, and he gained in public acclaim: in October he was elected one of the vice presidents of the AAAS and a month later he organized the influential Cosmos Club in Washington.) I think Hayden decided he was licked and began to look for explanations or excuses, and he had no trouble finding them in the concerted opposition of Marsh, Powell, and Newberry. That much seems inescapable from the facts at hand. But what could explain this surprising change in Hayden's demeanor? I believe part of the answer lies in his physical health and to understand that we must go back to spring 1878.

On 2 May Emma Hayden wrote a letter to Emily Peale, the wife of Hayden's colleague A. C. Peale. In the course of this very intimate letter she said: "But of course all disappointments seem trivial compared to the great one—I could not trust myself to allude to it when I wrote you, for it was one of the hardest trials I have ever known." Out of context, these painful remarks seem difficult to interpret, but in view of some other aspects of Hayden's life not yet mentioned the circumstances point to only one explanation. Hayden was to die in nine years—of syphilis. I will discuss his disease fully later on, but for now it is enough to say that syphilis is a progressive, degenerative disorder that affects the central nervous system, and it proceeds in distinct but irregular stages—that is, the stages are clinically distinct, though their timing and intensity can vary considerably in individual cases. Though it will always be uncertain when (and, for that matter, under what circumstances) Hayden contracted syphilis, his strange behavior in spring and summer 1878 and his wife's letter both suggest he had recently experienced one of the typically debilitating bouts of illness that accompany the disease.

Though less was understood about syphilis in the 1870s than is known now, the congenital risk to an unborn child from an infected mother was appreciated. I believe Emma's great disappointment in May 1878 was the realization that she might never be able to have a healthy child. This interpretation demands some evidence of Hayden's sickness in 1878 and assumes that he knew of his problem at that time. He knew for certain of his condition by at least 1882 because he confessed it in a letter to Leidy in 1884, in which he asserted his sexual continence over the previous two years because of the disease. The situation was personally mortifying. Hayden revealed only enough of his problem to gain the sympathy of a friend in the midst of an embarrassing public scandal. There was no need to acknowledge a longer awareness of his problem, which would only have raised more questions and added to his humiliation.

As to his morbid condition in spring 1878, plenty of signals indicate that he was not well at the time. In June Hayden said to one friend that the political infighting during the previous few months to secure another appropriation had caused a breakdown in his health—a believable cover for a more sinister cause. Emma Hayden's letters to Mrs. Peale over the summer are full of concern for his health, and they refer to his "recovery" during the summer, once back in the field. That correspondence between Emma Hayden and Emily Peale began in spring 1878; doubtless it—and their deeper friendship—grew out of Emma's personal crisis, when she needed a sympathetic friend to lean on, to confide in. She needed somebody other than her husband toward whom she must have had terribly mixed feelings. Although she could still show compassion for him, perhaps even affection and sympathy in order to hold their marriage together, she needed somebody else to help assuage her anger, to dissipate her mostly unspeakable hurt.

No wonder Hayden was not himself. In addition to the physical discomforts of his condition and anxieties about its uncertain progress, he carried a heavy burden of sadness himself, not to mention guilt; yet, unless he wanted to invoke a ruinous scandal, he could confide in no one—no one, that is, except his wife, whose heart he must have nearly broken already. Despite the political threats that surrounded him, no wonder he might have felt drawn to the wilderness in summer 1878, to the forgiving solitude he could find nowhere else. But even a summer's recreation with congenial colleagues in an attractive setting where he could revive reassuring rhythms of his past was not enough to heal his own deep wound. His actions and words during autumn and winter 1878 are those of a broken man, a man who knew he was finished but who played out his hand gamely, unable, after a lifetime of ambitious self-promotion, to acknowledge publicly what he knew privately.

Meanwhile his enemies were preparing the coup de grace. Fresh from a triumphant approval by the Academy, Marsh took his committee's report to Washington, where he began to sell it to leaders of Congress, the head of the Coast Survey, and the president himself. King was brought in and introduced to key players who did not yet know him. In early December the report itself was delivered to both houses of Congress and subsequently turned over to a gleeful appropriations committee in the House. It was decided to introduce into law the gist of the Academy's recommendations through a series of clauses in the Legislative, Executive, and Judicial Expenses Bill, as well as in the Sundry Civil Bill. Powell drafted the clauses, which Schurz reviewed and approved. This set the stage for the final action.

23
CONSOLIDATING THE SURVEYS, 1879

His energies were so absorbed in the Geological Survey from this time out that his whole life and soul were in it, & I have always thought he was heart-broken when on the consolidation of the surveys, he was "rotated out" of the direction. For energy in work, I doubt if he had a superior. His administrative ability was great, notwithstanding his nervousness. He had wonderful influence with Congress, & I feel sure the consolidation of the surveys would not have been made except on the expectation that he was to be at the head. His honesty was undoubted. To him more than to any other man the U.S. Geological Survey owes its existence and scope. Of his strictly scientific standing I do not feel competent to judge, though the consensus of the world ought to be good authority for ranking it high.

—Jacob D. Cox to Professor A. A. Wright of Oberlin, 24 February 1888

THE REPORT OF the National Academy of Sciences' Committee on the Surveys recommended specific changes in the way the federal government managed its vast western territories. The plan embodied a spirit of reform that had been building for several years among legislators and scientists, and Major Powell had been the single greatest spokesman as well as the most influential architect of that spirit. Powell's forceful presence led to the creation of the Academy's committee, and Marsh's initiative codified a reform package suitable for legislative enactment.

Three intricate and interrelated problems had become obvious to those who knew about the western lands during the 1870s. The major challenge was to revise public lands policy in order to reconcile the needs of settlers with the realities of western geography. At first the homestead acts had provided a satisfactory method of transferring title for unsettled public lands to private landowners. And the homestead concept made sense as long as American geography continued to offer an expandable series of agricultural lots similar to midwestern farms. But beyond the 100th Meridian (which includes the western half of the Dakotas and Nebraska and the western third of Kansas) the arid and rugged terrain demanded more flexibility in parceling the land. The westerners who opposed reforms in the public lands were not unaware of the problems, but they feared changes would jeopardize their control over development in the region.

The second challenge was to prepare an inventory of the West's economic resources in a way that would serve the needs of an expanding industrial nation; for example, by classifying the lands as arable, pasture, timber, mineral, and so on. The difficulty was that no acceptable definitions existed—at least not until Powell published his *Report on the Lands of the Arid Region.*

Related to both these problems was the greatest need of all: to provide accurate maps—maps that would comprehend the entire West, rely on uniform standards, and serve federal officials, landowners, prospectors, and scientists as well as the whole tide of persons, corporations, and interests that had been flooding westward since the end of the Civil War. When Congress tacked on Representative Hewitt's clause to the Sundry Civil Bill in June 1878, what it specifically asked the Academy for was "a plan for surveying and mapping the Territories of the United States."

It was a reasonable request (assuming Hewitt did not know that Interior already had a plan) and a necessary beginning because all plans for the West assumed the existence of good maps. Good maps in turn depended on a single mapmaker boasting competence in the latest technology and brandishing a plenary jurisdiction to include the entire region, perhaps the whole nation. Awkwardly, there were six mapping agencies of varying competence to choose from, none of which possessed a writ for national mapping. Of the six, three were permanent federal bureaus (the General Land Office, the Coast Survey, and the army's Corps of Engineers), and three were temporary organizations surviving on annual grants from Congress—namely, the Hayden, King, and Powell surveys. Wheeler carried the banner of the Corps of Engineers.

Marsh focused his committee's attention on an institutional solution that would pave the way for standardized maps. It is worth repeating that Marsh borrowed heavily from Powell when he drafted the committee's report and that he talked personally with King about the committee's emerging plans; but he scorned any similar input from Hayden. Essentially, Marsh's plan (adopted by the Academy) aimed to accomplish three things: (1) reorganize the Coast Survey into the Coast and Geodetic Survey under the Interior Department with an expanded and exclusive authority to perform a general geographic and topographic survey of the "public domain"—an undefined phrase that was generally understood to mean the western territories; (2) create a geological survey to study the structure and economic resources of that region; and (3) turn over to a commission questions of classifying and parceling the public lands.

The implications of this plan were revolutionary. Of the six mapping agencies only the Coast and Geodetic Survey would now triangulate across the West, applying the more accurate but also more costly methods it had been employing in the East. Henceforth, even mapping for the General Land Office would be done by a reformed Coast Survey; thus the posts for sixteen surveyors-general in that office would be abolished, along with the separate surveys of Hayden, King, Powell, and Wheeler. The Corps of Engineers would continue its work on harbors, rivers, lakes, flood control, and tidal lands, but it would no longer have a role in western exploration or mapping. To assure administrative efficiency and prompt sharing of information, the Coast Survey and the new USGS along with the General Land Office would all be placed under the authority of the secretary of the interior. Geology and topography, once pulling in tandem, would now haul for separate agencies. The broad and unifying matrix of natural history would now decompose, dispersed by the spray of specialization.

Hayden found no reason to support such reforms, but he dared not show his opposition to them. On the day the Academy reviewed Marsh's recommendations sixteen members took part in a general discussion. Though Hayden was present, he said nothing, and when the Academy voted he supported the committee's report. The vote was 31–1, only Edward Cope opposing, doubtless out of pique for the large role played in the proceedings by his rival, Professor Marsh. Hayden could afford to bide his time, for he realized the whole report would be reconsidered when translated into specific pieces of legislation, and Hayden had many friends in both houses of Congress.

The process of converting the Academy's report into legislation began when it was turned over to the House Appropriation Committee. Chairman Atkins supervised its incorporation into the Legislative, Executive, and Judicial Expenses Bill, which he delivered to the House on 28 January 1879. In his introductory speech on the bill Atkins characterized the section consolidating the scientific surveys under the Interior Department as "the most important feature in this bill." At the same time he reminded his western colleagues, who were deeply suspicious of reforms in parceling and selling the public lands, that the rectilinear surveys of the Land Office would continue until such time as the commission suggested by the Academy should propose remedies and until such time as Congress should enact a solution.

During the debate that followed in the House over the next two weeks a current of opinion favoring more efficiency in the scientific surveys gathered momentum. Not even Hayden's friends resisted it; significantly, they saw nothing in it that threatened him. Two speeches in particular reveal the prevailing mood in the House. On 11 February Hewitt asked his colleagues:

> What is there in this richly endowed land of ours which may be dug, or gathered, or harvested, and made a part of the wealth of America and of the world, and how and where does it lie? These are the questions which the enterprise, the capital, and the labor of the United States are engaged in working out with such signal energy, and it is to the solution of these questions, the greatest of all national problems, that the scientific surveys of the public domain should be directed.

Behind Hewitt's swelling rhetoric was the desire for a survey that would identify economic resources, especially coal and metals. In view of Hewitt's business interests, his question was remarkably self-serving. Yet many Americans at the time hoped to join self-interest with progress; that dream had motivated Hayden's entire career.

Shortly afterward, Garfield rose to make the point that most science could be done by privately funded individuals and societies. Only that which pertained to the national interest required federal funding. Because geologic surveys were in the national interest, they should be consolidated under one head to eliminate overlapping. As to whether the broader concerns of natural history belonged in such a survey, Garfield quipped, "Ornithology is a delightful and useful study; but would it be wise for Congress to make an appropriation for the advancement of that science? In my judgment manifestly not." How convenient that Garfield's speech relied on material provided through the courtesy of Major Powell.

But votes are mightier than speeches, and specific clauses of the Legislative, Executive, and Judicial Expenses Bill needed approval. By 12 February the House was debating clauses of the proposed bill under the five-minute rule. On 15 February the section regarding the transfer of the Coast Survey to the Interior Department came up, but it was linked to a proposal to abolish the posts for sixteen local surveyors-general in the General Land Office. This linkage was deliberate; it had been crafted by Atkins and other reformers on the appropriations committee to test the waters, to see how broad a reform the House would accept, for it joined one of the most desirable proposals (transferring and extending the powers of the Coast Survey) with one of the most controversial (tampering with the existing system of surveying the public lands). But Horace Page of California spoke for many members who wanted to separate the two issues. Page favored consolidating the scientific surveys, but he worried about the local effects of centralizing in Washington all the authority of the sixteen surveyors-general. On 18

February Page offered an amendment that preserved a consolidated survey but deliberately omitted any mention of the land office surveys.

This move unsettled both sides of the House. On the one hand it created consternation among the reformers who wanted both issues decided together, some of whom felt Page's amendment must be opposed because it did not go far enough; on the other hand it caused confusion among proponents of the traditional land surveys, some of whom feared that to vote with Page would eliminate the old system entirely because his amendment did not specifically mention the land surveys.

Before a vote could be taken, Dudley Haskell of Kansas managed to interject a bit of doubt about the Academy's intentions. He read from a letter claiming that a number of Academy members actually opposed the proposed reforms, despite the near unanimity of the Academy's recent vote on Marsh's report. Even after repeated requests, Haskell declined to identify the author of the letter. (It was probably Edward Cope.) The result was a very close vote on Page's amendment: 81 in favor, 80 opposed. The closeness invoked a vote by tellers, and after some scurrying by party leaders a final tally of 98 for and 79 against was recorded. Atkins then further amended the main bill to assure language in favor of the Academy's other recommendations, including the provision for a commission to study the public lands system. Thus was the gist of Marsh's report converted to a legislative bill.

Although apparently signaling a victory for the reformers, these actions actually demonstrated the limits of their power. An important choice between reforms had been made. The scientific surveys would be consolidated, but the public land surveys would remain separate. Once that distinction was made, the urgency for further reform dissipated. Some progress had been made, for which all could take credit. On 25 February the House voted decisively (121 to 62) to retain the local surveyors-general, free of the more stringent requirements of the Coast Survey. On the same day the House passed the entire Legislative, Executive, and Judicial Expenses Bill and sent it on to the Senate.

Also on the 25th the House sent to the Senate the other major appropriations bill, the Sundry Civil Expenses Bill. It had only been introduced into the House on the 24th and passed the same day, after the House approved a suspension of the rule about approving a bill without debate. Understandably, some members protested because so far only members of the appropriations committee had seen the bill, but the two-thirds vote to suspend the rule on debate was forthcoming. Time was running out on the third session of the Forty-Fifth Congress, and if the Legislative, Executive, and Judicial Expenses Bill ran into trouble in the Senate, as many expected, the Sundry Civil Bill became even more important. Interestingly, that bill did not

attempt to duplicate the language of the other appropriations bill regarding
the reformed scientific surveys or a reorganized General Land Office.
Ignoring all else in the package recommended by the National Academy of
Sciences, the Sundry Civil Bill contained only a clause providing $100,000
for "the expenses of the geological survey and classification of the public
lands and examination of the geological structure, mineral resources, and
products of the national domain." We will understand this curiously selective clause better after reviewing the progress of the two appropriations bills
in the Senate.

The Senate's various committees got to work amending the two bills
promptly, and on the 28th both bills were reported back to the full Senate.
Because the session was expiring rapidly, it was necessary to work fast. After
some difficulty in settling down, and after objections to proceeding due to
the late hour, at 10:00 P.M. the Senate commenced reading through the
Sundry Civil Bill, considering the proposed amendments of committees. The
senators did not recess until 3 A.M., but they began business again the next
morning, 1 March, at 10:30. The Senate Appropriations Committee modified
the language of the House bill just quoted by adding the words "of the territories" just after "the geological survey." In order that no mistake could be
made, Senator William Windom, the chairman of the appropriations committee, moved on the floor of the chamber to further modify the wording to
read "for the expenses of the Geological and Geographical Survey of the
Territories [the full title of Hayden's survey], and the classification of the
public lands, . . . [then repeating the previous language] to be expended
under the direction of the Secretary of the Interior, $100,000." To demon-
strate beyond any doubt the Senate's preference for Hayden's survey, Windom
then moved that a clause granting Powell's survey $20,000 for the com-
pletion of its publications be transferred to Hayden's survey. Similar clauses
to complete the publications of Wheeler's and Hayden's surveys were proposed, showing that with one hand the senators approved the House's initiative of abolishing the old surveys while with the other they restored Hayden's
survey under different auspices. All these amendments were approved without objection.

The Senate showed a similar disposition in dealing with the Legislative,
Executive, and Judicial Expenses Bill. Recall that the bill contained the
essence of the Academy's recommendations on a reformed and consolidated
system of surveys. Following the advice of its appropriations committee, the
Senate struck out section two of that bill, which contained the entire language about scientific surveys and a commission on the public lands. Thus
in two quick strokes the Senate abolished the Academy's proposals as drafted
by the House, eliminated all the old surveys, and revitalized Hayden's with a

new authority. All this was achieved by the evening of 1 March—without dissent.

Oddly, this clear preference of the Senate for continuing Hayden's survey with a fresh mandate was reversed two days later. This feat was accomplished on the last day of the session by the report of the conference committee acting for the House and Senate to reconcile their differences on the Sundry Civil Bill. In a previous study of this situation, Henry Nash Smith attributed to Representative Hewitt, one of the conference committee members, the initiative in pushing through the compromise language regarding a new geological survey that would have no tie to Hayden. The difficulty with this interpretation is that it fails to explain why the Senate should have felt constrained to follow the lead of Representative Hewitt. Smith says that Hewitt's last-minute tinkering with the Sundry Civil Bill passed because of "dubious parliamentary propriety," implying that perhaps the full Senate did not understand what it was approving in the final compromise language. A more satisfactory explanation is possible once we realize that Hewitt was not the giant killer he claimed to be.

Hewitt was no friend of Hayden's survey, but his parliamentary role in destroying it has been exaggerated. There were actually two conference committees—one for the Sundry Civil Bill, another for the Legislative, Executive, and Judicial Expenses Bill. Each committee had six members, three from the House, three from the Senate. Two men, and only two men, served on both committees: Representative Atkins and Senator Windom, each the chairman of his chamber's appropriations committee. These are the key players, not Hewitt, and they offered the compromises finally accepted by the two conference committees.

Let's look carefully at the final version of the Sundry Civil Bill, approved on 3 March, the last day of the session. Although four paragraphs discuss a new geological survey, most of the wording concerns peripheral matters: the old surveys are abolished; officers of the new organization are forbidden to have personal interests in the lands they survey; publications of the new survey are outlined; the National Museum is to receive all collections of any federal surveys; and a commission to study and make recommendations on the public lands is authorized. The essentials regarding the structure and duties of the new survey are brief, even cursory, and derive directly from the earliest version of the Sundry Civil Bill as drafted in the House by Atkins: "For the expenses of the Geological Survey and the classification of the public lands and examination of the geological structure, mineral resources, and products of the national domain, to be expended under the direction of the Secretary of the Interior, $100,000."

Notice that this clause omits any reference to Hayden or his survey of the territories. This would seem an enormous concession to Atkins, especially in view of the clear and obvious preference in the Senate for Hayden's survey to continue. But consider what Atkins gave up. Gone was any reference to a streamlined scientific enterprise, whereby the work of three separate agencies (the USGS, the Coast Survey, and the General Land Office) would be coordinated under the secretary of the interior. This was what the Academy recommended and what Atkins and the reformers wanted. Under the compromise wording, however, these separate agencies remained separate, and the Coast Survey did not move under the authority of the Department of the Interior. The only change was to abolish the old temporary surveys and create a new and permanent one in their place. Hayden might still direct this new geologic survey should the president appoint him. The new survey Atkins and Windom agreed upon was a much more independent body than the one Atkins originally envisioned, and because the issue of mapping the territories was still not resolved, the new geologic survey stood to become even more powerful should it eventually add that responsibility to its duties. Considered as a warrant for his future operations, Hayden could not have asked for more. An independent and permanent geologic survey was created, and the man the Senate (and probably most of the House) desired to direct that new bureau was waiting in the wings. It seems Windom gave up little in the compromise with Atkins. It was Atkins the reformer who had to surrender most of what he had wanted—and for a very good reason.

Remember there was the other appropriations bill to consider: the Legislative, Executive, and Judicial Expenses Bill. What became apparent as the conference committee began work on that bill was that it contained a number of politically divisive problems, and neither house seemed prepared to budge on its particular wishes. The chief difficulties were the test-oath amendment, the supervisors' amendment, and a question about using troops to keep the peace at polls—legacies from the era of Reconstruction following the Civil War. Those issues are not related to Hayden's story, but all the explosive problems wound up in this bill, and partisan feeling about them precluded any compromises. In fact, the Forty-Fifth Congress failed to pass a Legislative, Executive, and Judicial Expenses Bill, and it was the acknowledgment of this looming reality that put tremendous pressure on Atkins especially to pass a Sundry Civil Bill, or the government would go without funding for its next fiscal year.

Given the hastiness with which the USGS was created in the waning moments of the Forty-Fifth Congress, it is appropriate to ask if the Senate realized what it was approving. Beginning with Nash, most historians have supposed Hewitt conjured some sleight of hand that bamboozled Hayden's supporters into accepting a legislative compromise they did not understand

and that furnished a result they did not intend. But there is no indication in the Senate's proceedings that members were confused about the final vote they took on the Sundry Civil Bill. Some senators objected to the procedure of creating a new agency by means of a rider to an appropriations bill, but that was nothing new. Hayden's survey, for example, had always been approved by this means in the past. Some members wanted to debate further the merits of a new versus an old system of surveying, but that was a luxury the expiring session could not allow. And the entire four paragraphs regarding the survey were read aloud before being voted on. If, at the end of the session, there was any misunderstanding at all in either house about the new survey, it would have been the failure of reformers to appreciate how thoroughly Senator Windom had forged the compromise in a way that favored the likely continuance of Hayden's influence.

Lobbying on behalf of those who wished to become director of the newly created geologic survey had begun even before the two appropriation bills came to the floor of the House. Passing the Sundry Civil Bill on 3 March only cranked up the pressure a few notches. In Washington Newcomb and Powell did most of the arm-twisting for King, though King himself arrived on the scene to visit with potential backers. Elsewhere, Marsh and Newberry spread their private contempt for Hayden as widely as possible; Alexander Agassiz assisted, though with less personal animus.

Josiah Whitney was also a candidate, if only a wishful one, who let it be known that he would take the place if it were offered, but he would not seek it. When King visited Whitney in Cambridge during summer 1878, specifically to ask for Whitney's backing, King thought he heard words of support; however, either he misinterpreted Whitney or Whitney later changed his mind. Alexander Winchell, the former state geologist of Michigan, also took a fancy for the position, though no one took him seriously; in the end even Winchell was not serious. Some of Powell's admirers urged him to step forward, and he might have done so in a different climate; that is, had most westerners in Congress not cordially despised him because of his reforming ideas. Besides, through the courtesy of his friend, the Honorable J.D.C. Atkins, that same Sundry Civil Bill approved a new federal agency for ethnology, which everyone realized was created for Powell. Powell decided to give his reforms a rest until the climate cooled; meanwhile, having secured his own place, he could afford to throw all his weight behind King.[1]

As a political idealist, as a social reformer, or as a witness before congressional committees, no doubt Powell was a heavyweight who earned wide respect even from those who disagreed with him. In the campaign for King, however, he showed his other side: conniving, mean-spirited, and willing to twist the truth for his own purposes. The man who wrote the *Report on the*

Lands of the Arid Region is the same man who prepared a widely circulated memorandum of 7 March on Hayden's survey. Though sent to James Garfield, it was written for other eyes as well; its intention was to discredit Hayden's work and denigrate his character. It is so distorted and nasty that it would not be worth noticing did it not embody many of the negative opinions that have become part of Hayden's standard image.

In brief, Powell aimed to insinuate that Hayden was a fraud. Powell claimed Hayden took personal credit for publications he had nothing to do with. Next he blasted Hayden for "fritter[ing] away splendid appropriations upon work which was intended purely for noise and show—in photographs—in utterly irrelevant zoological works which were designed to be scattered broadcast over the United States and Europe with his name blazoned on them and to attract the attention of every accessible class of scientific people as well as the wonder-loving populace." One can feel Powell nearly choking on his rage and his inflated rhetoric.

Of course, Powell was trying to destroy Hayden, not provide a balanced appraisal of his work. Hayden never pretended he wrote the many publications produced by his survey; it was clear to anyone who read them that Hayden acted as general editor for a variety of articles, reports, and monographs on geology as well as many aspects of natural history. In condemning Hayden for venturing to publish material not strictly derived from his own geologic investigations, Powell deliberately failed to add that Hayden's whole understanding of geology depended upon a generous linkage with natural history. Powell failed to credit Hayden's pioneering role in providing basic descriptions of the territories he explored. Powell belittled Hayden's part in producing the survey's *Final Reports,* without mentioning how many of them pertained to the Great Lignite and without admitting that Hayden himself had instigated and encouraged this emphasis. Powell tried to tarnish the value of Hayden's maps by saying they conjectured regarding the boundaries between geologic formations. Yes, those maps sometimes surmised without verification, but so did every geologic map; Hayden's maps compiled an abundance of information on territory no one else had touched. Also Powell completely falsified Hayden's role with the Entomological Commission, and so on. It is not necessary to elaborate each issue, for Powell's deceptive purpose is plain enough.

Powell's report was a diatribe, filled with invective and personal attacks on Hayden. Here is his summation: "There is not a third rate scientist in America who knows Hayden who is not perfectly aware that he is a charlatan who has bought his way to fame with government money and unlimited access to the Government Printing Office." We will shortly mention some of the first-rate scientists in America who thought Hayden should be the director of the USGS, but Powell's tone is worth noting: it demonstrates the polemical purpose of his report (and reminds us it was aimed at politicians not scientists), and it typifies the tone used by Marsh and Newberrry and some others who opposed Hayden.

Notable in this regard is a letter written by President Charles Eliot of Harvard on King's behalf to President Hayes. Beneath the uncouth portrait of Hayden the letter carried a more subtle message: that the gentlemen who saw themselves as leaders of American science did not want to admit to their ranks an upstart roughneck.

> I have often heard Dr. Hayden discussed among scientific men, but I have never heard either his attainments or his character spoken of with respect. On the contrary, I have often heard his ignorance, his scientific incapacity, and his low habits when in camp, commented on with aversion and mortification. He has never shown that he is himself a geologist, a topographer, a botanist, or a zoologist.

Another man who could be counted on to say some ugly things was Hayden's old enemy, James Hall. "Besides this, could I do anything in your favor," Hall wrote King, reporting he had recommended him to Hayes, "I would think it some atonement for my sin against science which I have committed, through my sympathy and misjudged liberality to a man, who but for my acts, would have remained unknown to us all." To another ally in the cause, Hall wrote: "I did not think it possible that so notorious a charlatan in geology and so positively dishonest a man could have any chance when coming in competition with such a man as Clarence King." On such sentiments was the campaign against Hayden built.

Hayden and his sponsors had their ways of turning aside such slanders. Over the years Hayden had assembled quite a flattering portfolio of letters regarding his survey. Now he edited some of the best ones, combined them into a pamphlet, and printed the results with a title that revealed both purpose and contents: *Extracts from Letters and Notices of Eminent Scientific Men and Journals in Europe and America, Commendatory of the United States Geological and Geographical Survey of the Territories.* Here appeared endorsements from some of Europe's most prominent scientists, men like Joseph Hooker, Archibald Geikie, Laurent de Koninck, Edward Desor, John Evans, Gaston de Saporta, Ferdinand von Hochstetter, Oswald Heer, Henry Benedict Medlicott, Richard Owen, William Boyd Dawkins, T. C. Archer, among others.

Always the master of effective public relations, Hayden managed to publish this pamphlet just as the lobbying contest with King was heating up.

None of the selected letters bore dates (they had been received over several years), but the impact of printing them in early 1879 was to suggest that the authors supported Hayden's bid for the directorship of the new geologic survey. It was a brilliant if typically Haydenesque touch, enabling him to brandish favorable quotes from men like Judge Charles Daly, W. B. Rogers, and William H. Brewer—each of whom subsequently endorsed King for the new position.

Still, the names of those who did specifically endorse Hayden for that position formed an impressive list. Geikie and Hooker wrote on his behalf, as did Asa Gray; Joseph and John LeConte; Eugene Waldemar Hilgard, the geologist and brother of King-supporter J. E. Hilgard; John William Dawson of the Canadian Geological Survey; the geological brothers, Newton and Alexander Winchell; S. H. Scudder; Alpheus Hyatt; J. A. Allen; William Harmon Niles; Arnold Henry Guyot; and a number of others, including Leidy, Packard, Cope, and Lesquereux. I will quote one letter at length, that of J. P. Lesley, partly because it counters the tone of Powell's remarks but also because it offers a perceptive portrait of Hayden. Having objected to what seemed to him a political role for the National Academy of Sciences' Committee on the Surveys, and after opposing the idea of consolidating the surveys, Lesley asked, if one man were to head up such a bureau,

> that Dr. F. V. Hayden's claims to such a position be not entirely over-looked; but that his many years services, inexhaustible energy, fairness in the treatment of subordinates, and really broad views be offset against his often disagreeable & violent & dictatorial manners, which have won against him many powerful and bitter enemies; while on the other hand his extraordinary executive abilities and a certain evident sterling honesty & singleness of purpose <u>in the direction of science,</u> has kept many who dislike him personally his staunch friends & supporters as a <u>pioneer geologist</u> of the very highest rank.
>
> His career has been a most extraordinary one, and to this career I for one have no hesitation in ascribing much of the popularity & consequent progress of my science on this side of the Atlantic. To call him a great geologist would be absurd; but to speak of him as <u>the man</u> who by his unaided & undisciplined pluck & force of will commenced twenty years ago the <u>real</u> survey of the territories, and has been ever since unswervingly and most successfully enlarging & organizing & glorifying that immense survey, until other & better geologists have been inspired and helped to come in and appropriate parts of it to themselves, to the effect of lifting American geology far above European geology in renown—this is no more than just. <u>To set aside</u>

such a hero, now, because more exact workers have taken the field, and find their interest in exposing his mistakes (the best of us have made quite as many & as flagrant ones) and the personal peculiarities of the man (we all have some such) I think would not redound to the benefit or to the honor of geology.

Hayden later claimed that he was supported by no less than forty members of the National Academy of Sciences, most of the state geological surveys, and over thirty colleges, universities, and scientific societies. Even his opposition acknowledged that he had a numerical edge. Newcomb wrote to W. B. Rogers on 14 March, "The question of the director of the geological survey is so far from settled that the President inclines to Hayden, who brings a vast preponderance of numbers in his favor."

Regarding King's support and the eventual success of his campaign, less needs to be said, as King has received a fairer share of attention from historians. However, there are a few interesting points about King that have never been mentioned. Who realizes, for example, that as early as February 1878 King was telling friends he now sought another post; or that over the summer he told Carl Ochsenius he would enter the contest against Hayden; or that by November he was already gathering memorials on his behalf from Europe? Or that on 2 January 1879 King composed a bold outline of what he would do with a newly organized geologic survey, sent the memo to Marsh, and urged Marsh to line up each member of his Committee on the Surveys behind him? Or that one of King's influential supporters was the wealthy lawyer and financier Samuel L.M. Barlow, who had close ties to Abram Hewitt and was currently involved in mining investments with King? Such facts emphasize—contrary to the reluctant posture he adopted in public—how early and how eagerly King entered the lists against Hayden.

A strong sense of personal antagonism against Hayden motivated King and his supporters and gave them an urgency of purpose that was lacking among Hayden's more numerous friends. Another point in their favor was the prestige and influence of key King supporters. All of Marsh's committee except Dana urged President Hayes to appoint King, as did Representatives Hewitt and Atkins; Secretary Schurz; the faculties of Columbia, Yale (again with the significant exception of Dana, who remained neutral), and Harvard (with the equally significant exception of J. D. Whitney, who wound up supporting Hayden); geologists the caliber of Clarence Dutton, G. K. Gilbert, James Hall, Thomas Sterry Hunt, Raphael Pumpelly, J. J. Stevenson, among others, and not forgetting Major Powell.

Such potent sponsors helped King's cause, but they still faced a stiff challenge to divert the limelight away from Hayden and toward King. King's friends tried to emphasize subjects that seemed to favor their candidate even if the issues bore no direct relevance to the new USGS. Consider, for instance, the topic of mapmaking. People who understood such technical matters generally conceded that the methods of accurately surveying alpine environments had been worked out in California. In particular, Charles Hoffmann developed the refinements while working for the California survey, and King learned his topography from Hoffmann. Thus, on 15 March, Professor Marsh paid a visit to the White House and brought along his colleague William Henry Brewer, who held the chair of agriculture at Yale. During the 1860s Brewer had been the chief assistant to J. D. Whitney on the California Geological Survey, and Brewer had given King his first job as a scientist when he hired him in 1863 to assist on the California survey.

Bringing in Brewer to talk about geographic excellence might seem a strange tactic, however, because the new USGS had been given no mandate for general mapping. Besides, Hayden had hired two other topographers trained by Hoffmann who between them produced Hayden's *Atlas of Colorado,* which was generally conceded—by the same experts who understood such things—to be the finest geographic product of all the topographic surveys. Of course, Brewer would have omitted to mention that detail. Also, had the issue of mapmaking been important, Brewer's letter to Hayes, written more than two months earlier, on 11 January, would have sufficed to make the point. But the point was not mapmaking; rather, it was to create the appearance that the president was consulting prominent men. That was the real reason Brewer accompanied Marsh to the White House.

Newcomb employed a similar strategy shortly thereafter. I will let Newcomb relate his own anecdote because it shows how President Hayes helped procure the kind of advice he wanted to hear. Newcomb is describing a meeting he had with President Hayes and telling how he steered the conversation around to a strong supporter of King's.

So, when the occasion arose, he [Newcomb himself] gently introduced the name of the gentleman.

"What view does he take?" inquired the President.

"I think he will be favorable to Mr. King," was the reply; "but would you give great weight to his opinion?"

"I would give great weight to it, very great weight, indeed," was the reply.

The expression was too decided in its tone to leave any doubt, and the geologist in question was on his way to Washington as soon as electricity could tell him that he was wanted.

The mysterious geologist was J. S. Newberry, who had been state geologist of Ohio during Hayes's tenure as governor of that state. Shortly after Newberry's visit to the White House, the president felt adequately fortified in announcing the decision he had wanted to make all along. The result: King was appointed, Hayden retired to Philadelphia.

As it happens, there are two pieces of evidence suggesting Hayes made up his mind for King during December 1878—in other words, even before Congress began debating the clauses that would create the USGS. The first was a meeting between the president and Hayden that took place on 20 December. On that day Hayes's private assistant, C. M. Hendley, sent a telegram to Hayden's executive officer, Jim Stevenson, saying the president would visit Hayden that afternoon in the survey's offices. We don't know what the two talked about, but ten days later in a letter to Joseph Hooker Hayden reported, "I have been promised an appointment as one of the jury to Paris." He referred to a forthcoming international geological meeting, and Hayes would have been the man to promise him an honorary assignment there. Nothing was said on 20 December about the rival surveys or the future director of a consolidated bureau; otherwise Hayden would have mentioned this more crucial bit of news. In other words, Hayden undoubtedly saw Hayes's offer regarding the geological conference for what it was—a consolation prize. Had Hayes any inclinations for Hayden as director of the consolidated surveys, would he not have communicated them in person during their meeting of 20 December? Let us recall that letter Hayden wrote to Geikie on 13 December, in which he reported astonishing news: "Since I began this letter I have been assured that no one but myself would get the chief directorship of the new Bureau if it is formed." Hayden never claimed Hayes made this promise in person; on the two occasions he mentioned it he said it came to him indirectly through friends in Congress. But when, on 20 December, he was offered only a trip to Paris, Hayden realized the president had no intention of nominating him to direct any newly constituted survey.

On 4 January Postmaster General David Key wrote an interesting letter to the president. In it he said, "Having been apprised by you of your anxiety that Mr. Hayden should be provided for, I have instituted an examination to see whether anything could be done for him in this Department." He went on to report that there was nothing he could find for Hayden; this was the second part of a strategy to compensate the man who would have to be let down gently. Once Hayden grasped the president's preference, the fight went out of him.

By contrast, once word of Hayes's choice was leaked, the news had a rejuvenating effect on the other camp. Had King's supporters received anything less than a secret nod from the president, it is doubtful whether they could have sustained such a vigorous campaign—especially in view of the over-whelming sentiment in Congress for Hayden. For King's stalwarts the strat-egy now became obvious: to parade as many of his champions through the White House as possible until the popular preference for Hayden could be offset. Over the next ten weeks that is exactly what they did. The president's meetings with Brewer and Newberry provided the finishing touches.

The critical influence on Hayes was probably Schurz. Schurz had been in favor of reform a long time; he had learned to respect Powell; and he was a warm personal friend of King's. Marsh came to town in mid-November to begin selling the Academy's program to key officials in Washington, and he met with President Hayes at that time. Marsh would have said enthusiastic things about economic geology and King's fitness to direct a survey with that emphasis. Schurz would have reinforced everything Marsh said.

By 20 December I think Hayden realized he had lost his chance for the consolidated survey. This awareness would explain the lackluster attitude he took toward the greatest political crisis of his career. He continued writing letters urging his friends to back him, and naturally he stayed in Washing-ton to oversee his campaign. But by comparison with earlier struggles, espe-cially the one in 1874 with the army engineers, an irresistible energy had deserted him. On 3 February Hayden wrote fatalistically to a friend, "Unless I am appointed director, my career in western work is cut short off." The next day he said to another friend, "Unless my friends make some strong points for me I am afraid I shall go overboard." Meanwhile he bemoaned King's support in New England. Recall his distracted activity at this time, when he busied himself on minor survey business and seemed to take as much interest in securing the Lowell lectures for Geikie as the directorship of the survey for himself. Perhaps the continuing disability of his disease discouraged him too, but I think Hayden picked up a distinct signal from Hayes during late December that foretold his downfall.

The best indication of his mood appears in early April, just after the Senate confirmed Hayes's nomination of King. Rather than showing anger or humili-ation—which he might have had he been genuinely surprised at the out-come—he was relieved not to be out of work. "I think K[ing] will do as fair as he can in my case . . . I have seen Powell and had a very satisfactory talk with him. I think I shall be comfortable again." Even more revealing is Hayden's terse statement regarding King: "King was duly confirmed without much dif-ficulty. I aided as much as I could." Did Hayden really "aid" in King's confir-mation? Knowing he was licked and given his concern to keep some position in the government, it would have been good tactics. Also, it would explain the surprising fact, given Hayden's considerable following in the Senate, that King was "duly confirmed without much difficulty," which he was.

Perhaps there was an additional reason for Hayden's docile behavior and the surprising turnabout of the Senate in King's favor. Recall that Hayes wanted to find some compensation for Hayden, after deciding to give the position to King if sufficient support could be found for his nomination. The postmaster general had been unable to arrange anything for Hayden, and Hayden had been unable to travel to the international geological conference in Paris. What if leading supporters of Hayden in the Senate had agreed to support King, provided that Hayden be given a place in the new USGS? Wouldn't Hayes have welcomed this compromise? Couldn't King have lived with it?

Hayden dealt with his disappointment by distancing himself as much as possible from his former affairs. Having secured what amounted to a sinecure under the USGS, he gained a leave of absence from any duties over the summer, went to the White Mountains for a month with his wife, then resettled quietly in Philadelphia. By October he and Emma moved into their own house. Meanwhile, he asked Elliott Coues to look after the unfinished writings his survey had not yet published.

Marsh and Powell and their coterie had done a good job of blocking Hayden's appointment to the position nearly everyone expected him to win. The passing of years and the antiseptic requirements of institutional history have disguised the viciousness stirred up during the founding of the USGS. "I think all good men may congratulate themselves," Newberry gloated to Garfield, "that King is nominated for the directorship of the Govt. Survey, rather than Hayden." Similar remarks circulated among the other conspirators, who reveled in what they felt was a personal victory. Rogers wrote to Marsh, "As you may imagine, we have rejoiced over it [King's confirmation] not a little," and Rogers passed the good news on to Agassiz. Henry Adams crowed, "Our fight ended so satisfactorily that we shall never be happy till we've had another and got licked." Writing to Powell, Marsh summed up the victors' mood: "Now the battle is won, we can go back to pure science again." An editorial in the British periodical *Nature* caught the same flavor: "We fear that personal interests have had more weight in bringing about the new state of things than the interests of science."

Even after the passions of the moment had been spent, a sense of personal triumph lingered. Clarence King best articulated this feeling, when he boasted eight years after the affair: "The one important fact of my twenty years Washington career, and the most important contribution I ever made to science, is wisely omitted, for it might throw the biography all out of balance. That act was the crushing of the old system of personal surveys." Since Hayden's was the leading survey in the days of "personal surveys," King was taking credit for "crushing" Hayden. It was a private remark to be sure, not meant for circulation, but its timing was doubly ironic. Four months after King uttered those words, Hayden died.

It is also instructive of the contemporary mood, so completely forgotten now, that virtually no one viewed the USGS as anything very new. Letters from the sponsors of both King and Hayden emphasized the fitness of their candidate to continue the work of a geological survey, and everyone appreciated, some grudgingly, that it was Hayden who had originated and developed that geological survey. What the USGS became and has become must not prevent us from seeing what it was at its inception. Compared to the powerful agency envisioned by the National Academy of Sciences, the infant USGS seems a pretty pale and puny creature. Its jurisdiction was uncertain, its ability to survey mineral lands was severely limited, and the powers of its director were unclear. Lost for the time being was the opportunity to produce a reliable map of the territories (the desire for which had been the inspiration for reform in the first place), and postponed was the most pressing problem of all—reforming the way public lands were surveyed, classified, and parceled. Considering the meager results of the reform effort and the highly personal motivations of the conspirators, I conclude that a change in personal leadership for the geologic survey was the chief accomplishment of the reformers.

24
CONSUMMATION,
1879–1887

Hayden's sun has set forever, and "the dream of his life is ended." It was a glorious dynasty, and the H of history is to be honored forever, whatever may be the H in person. The hand was played for all it was worth—and more—and never in the history of our government was such a thing before, nor ever will there be anything like it again. To think that for twelve years our government has been coaxed and bullied into enormous scientific enterprises it did not want by the intensity of a strange genius, backed by the sagacity of a shrewd henchman!

—Elliott Coues to Joseph Leidy, 15 July 1879

HAVING WON THE prize, Clarence King had difficulty settling down to his new duties. Even before Hayes officially nominated him, King drove his sponsors to exasperation by dashing out of town to look after mining cases, and he could not be corralled and brought back to swear his oath of office until the month following his confirmation. He then proposed to travel abroad for six months, ostensibly to gather firsthand information about European geological surveys. Schurz had to be quite firm with his good friend in squashing that venture. During his first six months in office King managed to draft an organizational plan for the survey and appoint its first officers, all the while flitting between Washington, New York, Newport, and San Francisco. Hayden was hired as U.S. geologist at an annual salary of $4,000, though he received no instructions, no responsibilities, and no assignment for fieldwork as did the other appointees. King was puzzled about what to do with a man he did not want to employ but obviously could not dump. For the time being he asked an intermediary to obtain summaries from Hayden of his recent activities, which King could use in his own formal reports.

Meanwhile Hayden's retreat from Washington and its limelight was swift and unceremonious. He was out, and no one thought to give him a testimonial dinner or even a hail and farewell. Perhaps he left town before anyone had time to think of it. But from abroad came welcome recognition. Memberships in the Geologists' Association of London, the Society of Natural History of Toulouse, and the Geographical Society of Geneva arrived in the spring, to be followed by a dozen more from similar groups over the next year and a half.

Hayden viewed his departure from Washington almost as a banishment, and occasionally he spoke of it in those terms. Emma also missed her circle of friends, the picnics, the receptions, the buzzing activity of Washington. Nearly a decade later she still complained, "The Philadelphia streets look indeed narrow and dreary after the broad spaces and bright sunshine of Washington." Who can blame either of them? Retiring to Philadelphia must have been a bitter draft to swallow; it quenched no thirsts, especially after the potent elixirs Hayden had been imbibing at the capital. Yet the metaphor of drink may be apt in one sense: staid old Philadelphia offered a dram of solace, which helped assuage his pain.

He quickly settled into a comfortable routine. He began attending meetings at the Academy again and at the American Philosophical Society, even taking part in their discussions, which was unusual for him. In May 1880 he attended the gala celebration of the Society's one hundredth year as an incorporated body. (It had been founded in 1743 without a formal charter.) He visited museums. He took Emma to New Hampshire again for part of the summer of 1880, and during the fall they hosted English geologist William Boyd Dawkins in their home for a week. He resumed his habit of broad reading. Daily he digested the newspapers of Philadelphia and Washington. He subscribed to a variety of magazines and scientific periodicals, read the reports of the Smithsonian, of Baird's Fish Commission, even Powell's volumes on Indians. He complained of trouble with his eyes, which he blamed on too much reading, though the cause could have been his progressive disease. He wrote a couple of short articles, relics of his survey really, and a couple of book reviews that were more lively than the articles. Still thrilled to see a knowledge of science spreading far and wide, he was especially delighted to applaud the second edition of A. S. Packard, Jr.'s, *Zoology for High Schools and Colleges*.

One thing he did *not* do was attempt to reverse the order of things in Washington. He had no intention of undermining King in hopes of succeeding him at the head of the geological survey. There has been misunderstanding on this point because of a few remarks in his letters. For instance, during summer 1880 Hayden heard the rumor, which everyone else in scientific circles heard too, that King might soon resign as director. In passing the rumor along to Geikie, Hayden said that should King step aside, "justice may come to me then, as there is a great demand for the restoration . . . " (of my survey in its original form, he implies). And to Packard he said, "I understand that King intends to resign. I hope then my friends will take hold strong . . . Something may be done next winter . . . Let me hear from you when you can & when you are in W[ashington] find out what you can."

Out of context those statements sound like Hayden was keen to succeed King at the survey. But Packard was one of those who wanted very much for Hayden to succeed King in order to make the survey more attentive to the broader concerns of natural history. Packard wrote to Hayes to say as much. Geikie, too, had been sympathetic to Hayden for a long time, and his flattering articles in *Nature* regarding Hayden's former survey implied to some readers that Hayden's survey was superior to the existing one. In the face of such warm endorsements, Hayden's pride was stirred sufficiently that he mustered some fighting talk about getting back into harness. But fighting talk is all he mustered. His heart was not in the cause of restoring his survey. A far more typical expression of his feelings was sent to Baird, regarding a proposed visit to Washington: "I am so located here and so utterly removed from all my old troubles that I have put off the time [for the visit to Washington]. I do not wish to be in W. much during Congress, so I will start today . . . I wish to do up my business as quickly as possible and return. Please make no mention of my coming. I wish to attract as little attention as possible." Nearly a year later he wrote in a self-mocking but not unhappy tone, "I am working away here quietly about as much secluded from the world and its cases [sic] as if I were in Africa."

Naturally, it pleased Hayden to hear his friends say kind things about him or fantasize about restoring him to a position of influence in Washington. It also suited him to supply Geikie with information for articles, but his intention was not so much to make King look bad as to make his own lost survey look good. Similarly, pouring out his complaints to a few friends about losing the directorship proved therapeutic to Hayden, and he did so the more confidentially by confining such comments to men who were abroad, away from the center of action in Washington—men like Geikie and Joseph Hooker.

In fact, Hayden was content with his retired lifestyle in Philadelphia; he had no desire to reimmerse himself in the hurly-burly of Washington. Reminiscing about pleasant aspects of his former life was one thing; plunging back into the political crosscurrents quite another. He had been in poor health since at least spring 1878 as the result of his resurgent syphilis, but his general physical decline seems to have started somewhat earlier. He mentioned to James Hall during May 1879, "I have not been well for two years past. Am just able to get about now. <u>Worn out early.</u>" After retiring to Philadelphia, he told friends he was having trouble sleeping. He didn't admit it, but obviously his spirit was shattered too.

Under the circumstances he had not the remotest yearning to reinstate himself at the head of the survey. By early 1881 it was apparent that King would shortly resign, which he did formally on 11 March. Powell succeeded him on 19 March, "so noiselessly," as Clover Adams wrote to her father, "that Professor Hayden, who would have done his best to upset it, knew nothing of it till it was done." Some of Hayden's old enemies wrongly assumed he would want the place that had previously been denied him, and the fact that he visited Washington in late February seemed to reinforce their suspicions. But he wrote to Baird following that visit: "I intended to call on Maj. Powell. Will you present him my kind regards and say to him that I shall make him a special call soon. I hope all will work out to our success in the end. King was very kind." This remark is interesting, as it shows how widespread was the understanding that Powell would quietly succeed King as soon as King stepped down. Hayden offered no opposition. In fact, once it was certain King would resign, Hayden confided his real concern to Baird: "I beg of you to do me the kind office to ask Maj. Powell to continue me in my position, the same as Mr. King has. He will no doubt be confirmed and with our slender means we would be in sore trouble. I hope the unparalleled success of Maj. Powell will lead him to be generous toward me." Hayden was trying to retain his position, and his salary, without having to come live in Washington. To Baird again on the 16th he wrote, "I prefer to remain quietly here in Phila and do my work." To his old comrade W. H. Holmes, who was curious to know whether Hayden would want to succeed King, Hayden was more explicit: "I do not really desire the responsibility of such a place. I am satisfied as I am." And to another old friend, A. C. Peale, he was even more candid. "You know of course how I feel and I shall never feel any differently. My gratitude to Maj. P will always be sincere and great. He has been more than just. I am wholly passive in the matter. . . . I wish while I live to maintain a nominal connection with the Survey so that I can watch its progress. If you have another talk with the Major [say] that nothing will change my good feeling and gratitude to him." These are not the words of a man anxious to thrust himself back into power. His actions are even more revealing: he stayed in Philadelphia and wrote letters to assure his friends he was not interested in the directorship and that he would not oppose Powell—a point he had to make repeatedly to allay the suspicions of his old enemies.

How utterly defeated and desolate Hayden felt after being passed over is best seen in the way he wound up the business of his own survey. It would have been more convenient to complete these affairs in Washington in order to deal personally with the various details. But he chose to retreat to Philadelphia, to be "removed from all my old troubles." By delegating Elliott Coues to take charge of the survey's daily business in Washington, Hayden supervised from afar with occasional help from Stevenson, Peale, and Holmes, each of whom visited in Philadelphia during the first year of Hayden's retirement to confer on survey business. Until July 1880 Hayden kept the authority to sign all vouchers for approved expenses. Peevishly, he tried to sustain this impractical arrangement, but when Congress granted the survey a final $10,000 to publish all its unfinished works Secretary Schurz ended this practice, thus wiping out the last vestige of Hayden's direct involvement in federal science. Coues kept the reins in his hands until December 1880, when Holmes took over to take care of the final details. It was a pathetic denouement for a man who had once so aggressively and imaginatively promoted his own interests; yet Hayden preferred it that way.

It was more comforting, and more healing too, to sit quietly in his study in Philadelphia and reflect on the past glory of his work. He reinforced this mood by writing Baird regularly about minor matters, like circulating his survey's publications (often in exchange for works that became the property of the Smithsonian) or allowing scholars to copy some of the survey's illustrations or seeing to the distribution of Leidy's *Fresh Water Rhizopods of North America* (1879), and all the while insisting that the artifacts he had accumulated in Washington over many years (journals and topographic notes, furniture and equipment, fossils and plaster casts, miscellaneous specimens, pottery, photographs, and illustrations) be kept together until he found it convenient to attend to their dispersal. He never found time for that duty, which would have symbolized the final depletion of his survey; eventually others did it for him.

But there was more to Hayden's retirement than plaintive reverie. In 1883 he would retake the field for several seasons. Before that, though, in addition to his pleasant amusements in Philadelphia and his sentimental puttering on behalf of his survey, he was writing parts of two books. The first of them, *The Great West* (1880), tells us nothing new about Hayden or his ideas about the West, but his selection as author says much about his reputation at the time. The publisher, Charles R. Brodix, conceived the book as a "popular description of the marvelous scenery, physical geography, fossils, and glaciers of this wonderful region," and he recruited Hayden to lend the authority of science to what amounted to a promotional tract Brodix hoped to sell to every traveler and potential settler who ventured west of the Mississippi. The wide recognition of Hayden as a scientist who could write for the masses made him the ideal author of a general introductory essay on the West. What Hayden may not have realized, because he had nothing to do with it, was that the bulk of the book would be devoted to a superficial dusting of facts and fables regarding "climate, health, mining, husbandry, education, the Indians, Mormonism, the Chinese," and summaries of "the homestead, pre-emption, land, and mining laws." Mostly written by an anonymous "corps of able contributors," the book played up the happy mythology of the West as a ripe garden awaiting only the touch of the immigrant to burst into bloom.

The Great West was yet another vulgar blandishment for western settlement, but Hayden's introduction dressed it up a bit. His cooperation with Brodix was unfortunate in one sense: the book only added to Hayden's reputation as a superficial popularizer. Work like *The Great West* has obscured Hayden's more solid contributions, both to geology and to an appreciation of western landscape and aesthetics. However, Hayden believed sincerely in the potential of the West, and he yearned passionately to be recognized as a sponsor for that new land, perhaps even a prophet for it.

Hayden's admirers doubtless wished he had not let his desire for fame overpower his judgment about the use of his name. Hayden himself did not imagine he had done anything infelicitous. So what, he probably thought, if his name was associated with some exaggerations or simplifications. In a region where mystery still dominated, who could reliably distinguish fact from fiction? The fullness of time would reveal the West for the stupendous marvel it was, Hayden believed, and for his early appreciation of it, his name would be linked forever with its glory.

The second book Hayden contributed to at this time was *Stanford's Compendium of Geography and Travel,* which appeared in 1883. Conceived and published by Edward Stanford of London, the book was based on Friedrich von Hellwald's massive geographic handbook, *Die Erde und ihre Völker,* which surveyed all the world's continents except Antarctica. Thinking along the same lines as Brodix, Stanford wanted to expand the relatively small section Hellwald devoted to North America, have it translated, and sell it to the growing audience on both sides of the Atlantic that was fascinated by the American West. Accordingly, he hired as editor the one man whose name could sell such a book just by its being on the title page, and he gave him carte blanche on the revisions.

Hayden had a small ax to grind with Hellwald, which added a little animus to his work on the book. As editor of the journal *Ausland,* Hellwald had published an article critical of Hayden's survey, written, Hayden thought, by "a small idiotic looking man named Oscar Loew, who was chemist to

Wheeler's survey, [and] is now wandering over Germany traducing me." Having learned of Loew's article, Hayden pitched into Hellwald with a vengeance. "I am now editing Hellwald's America for Stanford," he told Geikie. "It is worthless, and ought not to have been taken from its oblivion. It is so incorrect that I must rewrite the whole work."

Well, he didn't quite rewrite it. In fact, he reproduced Hellwald's format of a geographic overview of the United States and its western territories plus Alaska in the first half of the book, and a broad political, social, economic, and religious survey in the second. He was content to follow the translator's wording for most of the second half, which held no interest for him at all. In the first half he covered the same ground as Hellwald, but he did make substantial changes, nearly doubling the text on the United States and its territories. He also wrote a first draft of the section on Canada, but it would not pass muster. In the preface to the book Stanford put a tactful face on the matter. "The complete volume was originally undertaken by Professor Hayden, then Chief of the United States Geological Survey; but on the receipt of his MS it was considered, both by him and myself, better that the British American portion should be edited by some gentleman resident in the Canadian Dominion, and whose knowledge and predilection for the Dominion were quite equal to Professor Hayden's for the United States."

Restricted to his own province, as it were, Hayden added original material on the regions he knew best in Colorado and Wyoming, especially in Yellowstone. Hellwald had scarcely spoken of geology, but Hayden had much to say about it, and where he could not rely on his own experience he summarized the most recent scholarship, including works of Dana, King, and Whitney. Even in sections he had nothing original to say, he used his more current knowledge of the literature to revise and improve the first half of Hellwald's book. I suspect he had stylistic help from Stanford or one of his assistants, for the language is more polished than one usually finds in Hayden's works and there are some phrases (references to "the Great Maker," for instance) not characteristic of him.

It was fortunate he had the two books to work on because for most of the four-year period beginning in summer 1879 Hayden was fighting a painful battle against declining health. He struggled often with insomnia, and an inflamed spinal cord was leading to increased paralysis. In December 1882 he gave Geikie a very personal insight into his sad condition: "In March last I was taken very sick with an acute condition of a chronic nervous disease which rapidly carried me down to an almost helpless condition. My case was pronounced hopeless, incurable and I prepared for the worst. I was unable to walk and was supposed to be helpless for life. I cannot describe the mental as well as physical suffering I endured. Within a month or two I have been convalescing so that I can write a few letters, though I do little or no work." After March 1882 he was being treated for the deteriorating condition of his back.

Meanwhile, in June 1881 he and Emma moved to 1803 Arch Street, one square away from their previous residence at 1910 Arch. They relaxed in Atlantic City briefly that month, then spent most of the summer back in the White Mountains to escape the heat of Philadelphia. By May 1882 the $10,000 appropriated to bring out his survey's last publications had been exhausted. Hayden appealed directly to Powell to have the USGS underwrite the cost of his final publications, and in July Powell agreed.

As was typical of the sporadic nature of his disease, the symptoms remitted in early 1883, allowing Hayden to move about and to think seriously about fieldwork for the first time in five years. In April he traveled to Washington for a meeting of the National Academy of Sciences, during which he met with Powell to confirm his plans for the summer. Like King before him, Powell was in a quandary about employing his former rival, whose traditional interests did not suit the current needs of the survey. King and Powell justified the anomaly of a highly paid but idle assistant by pointing to his disability. Powell would have been delighted to continue this arrangement as the price for keeping a popular renegade from having real influence. But what to do with the man in a healthier condition? Apparently, Peale and Holmes together prevailed upon Powell to let Hayden roam around some of his old haunts in Montana on the Upper Missouri, with the understanding that Peale would accompany him and assist Hayden in preparing some kind of report.

Hayden took the field for a little over a month in 1883, beginning in late July. He and Peale followed the line of the Northern Pacific Railroad from Bismarck (Dakota Territory) west up the Missouri and Yellowstone Rivers to the vicinity of Helena. They gathered fossils and examined the relations between formations, focusing on Hayden's old concern with the Cretaceous-Tertiary border. They made several side trips to examine coal outcrops and looked at Paleozoic beds near Helena. Hayden worked a little more around Bozeman on the way back east, then headed straight home. Peale remained in the field another month. Hayden was not moving well, and his joints and bones were pained by changes in the weather. To Holmes he wrote, "I cannot get about much but I am thankful to be able to be here and see these old mountain peaks again. I can say with Wm Tell, 'Ye crags and peaks, I'm with you once again.' The old spirit comes over me to work but I am chained down by disease."

A fruitful result of that summer was the completion and publication of a geologic map of the entire area previously examined by the Hayden survey.

On a scale of 41 miles to the inch, it covered the region between the 90th and 114th meridians, and the 35th to 48th parallels. Large parts of eastern Montana, the western Dakotas, eastern Colorado, and areas around the Wind River–Powder River Basin of Wyoming were colored "Post Cretaceous," showing Hayden finished as he had begun over two decades earlier, believing in the survival of his Great Lignite. Holmes colored the geologic formations on the map.[1]

In early August 1884 Hayden and Peale returned to Montana ready to re-examine the region between the Bridger Range (north of Bozeman) and Three Forks to the west. The area provided splendid exposures of the entire series between Precambrian metamorphics up to Quaternary gravels, and though early September snows prevented them working as long as they had intended they were able to compile a stratigraphic column of the early Paleozoic rocks. They also found the first confirmed Devonian rocks in the northern Rockies, though Meek had thought (correctly) some of the survey's finds from 1872 might prove to be Devonian.

During summer 1885 Mrs. Hayden and Mrs. Peale accompanied their husbands. The Peales and Haydens left Philadelphia in early July on a long railroad voyage to Denver, Colorado Springs, Manitou Springs, Pueblo, Ogden, Salt Lake, and Helena, before arriving on 22 July in Bozeman where the two veterans resumed their work of the previous season. Along the way Peale gathered samples for his studies of hot springs and mineral waters. They began on the southern and eastern sides of the Bridger Range, then returned to the western slopes to explore each of the major drainages on that side. Hayden concluded the season in early September after studying the ancient lake beds of the Gallatin Valley. An important secondary result of their work was the discovery of extensive coal beds. While he and Peale were busy at work, their wives enjoyed a trip through Yellowstone Park.

In 1886 Hayden made his last visit to the country he so loved along the Upper Missouri. He and Peale took the field from 18 August to 20 September; George Merrill of the U.S. National Museum accompanied them. Merrill was curious to see for himself the strata whose samples he had studied during the previous winter. They collected extensively from the ancient lake beds stretching between the Gallatin and Madison rivers, but because of high concentrations of igneous detritus in the samples they were unable to determine the age of the beds.

Once Hayden renewed fieldwork, he was obliged to account for his activities, and from August 1883 through December 1886, when he retired from the USGS, he dutifully filed monthly reports with Powell. (During the previous four years, when he had been an inactive member of the survey, he filed no reports.) The reports contain nothing remarkable from a geological point of view. They are valuable because they reflect Hayden's state of mind at the end of his career. Contrary to what some of his enemies said, Hayden did not make a lot of money in government service and he did not have sufficient means to thumb his nose at a good salary. He needed money and was anxious to create a reserve for medical expenses. As a result, this once proud and even arrogant man was now remarkably deferential and obviously grateful for a sinecure, even if it carried no influence. At the same time these monthly reports restate a powerful continuity of interest, a prideful disdain for the oblivion to which he had been assigned, and a heartfelt if rather feeble summary of the favorite themes that had dominated his work for more than three decades—the Great Lignite, the age of Tertiary lake beds, and the historical advance of geological exploration. Hayden was calmer, more relaxed now, certainly a humbled man, but a man who could accept professional disappointment and declining health with an equanimity that would have been impossible for him ten years earlier.

A similar mellowness pervades most of what is known of his last years. He was a founding member in December 1883 of the American Society of Naturalists. He served on the local committee that made arrangements for the AAAS meeting in Philadelphia during September 1884. He went out of his way to promote and broadcast Leidy's monograph on rhizopods. Despite ups and downs in their relationship, Leidy had become Hayden's most supportive colleague and closest male friend since Meek's death; they were now on more confidential and intimate terms than ever before. Now that the reasons for so much frantic stroking were gone, a good deal of the original warmth and mutual admiration of his relationship with Baird returned. He wrote sentimentally (though inaccurately) to the wife of Senator Logan that "the General was always the best friend I ever had," and he reminisced fondly with another old friend about "the old aboregains [aborigines]," whom he characterized as "a fertile set. Variety was the spice of life to them."

This warmth and spirit of reconciliation was most evident in his relationship with Emma. He became increasingly dependent upon her for companionship—especially as he lost the ability to move outside the house—and for countless small acts. During his last year, when he was virtually bedridden, she took most of her meals with him, read to him, and wrote whatever letters he was strong enough to dictate. He showed no signs of rebellion at this dependency, and she gave no hint of a resentment she might justifiably have felt. On the contrary her confidential letters to Emily Peale exude an abiding affection and respect for Hayden. More than a year after his death she wrote from Hoboken, "I go over to New York every day, and find some sort of satisfaction in wandering where Dr. Hayden and I have been together. There seems some companionship still." All this shows that their marriage more than survived the crisis thrust upon it in the late seventies when Hayden became aware of his morbid condition. That Emma and Ferdinand traveled together as much as they did during his last years speaks of personal friendship and affection. That Emma devoted herself so wholeheartedly to his care suggests she had successfully resolved her own conflicted feelings. She could easily have left him in the hands of others; instead she seems to have cherished their time together.

Not even public embarrassment could shake their revitalized relationship. In August 1884 Hayden and Dr. Betton Massey were implicated in a sex scandal. A young woman named Grace Gardner alleged that Hayden had got her pregnant, then taken her to Dr. Massey for an abortion. Hayden claimed, and the evidence sustains him, that out of friendship he and a lawyer had tried to protect a patent belonging to the woman's father. They succeeding in increasing his income for the patent, but not enough to satisfy the daughter, who trumped up the sexual charges in order to extort blackmail. Taken to court and required to testify, she dropped her charges against Hayden.

Alongside the new mellowness, Hayden remained the same provocative individualist he had always been. His mind was still capable of knocking off sparks. He had some sharp insights into the futile ruckus Cope stirred up against the USGS in 1885. Cope yearned to unseat his old rival O. C. Marsh as paleontologist of the survey, and simultaneously he was trying to generate sufficient noise to force Powell to publish a volume he had completed for Hayden's survey on Mesozoic vertebrates. Hayden called Cope a "bull head," said his tussle with Powell would not succeed, and predicted (correctly) that "it will be Cope's last fight." In the same letter and a subsequent one, Hayden mentioned "Taitt cure," a humorous reference to Mind Cure, an offshoot of Christian Science. His allusion is vague but suggests he may have been involved in the Mind Cure church. (At just about the same time and three thousand miles away in California, one of Hayden's former colleagues, Franklin Rhoda, was involved with the same group.) Such an inclination would have been wholly in keeping with Hayden's unorthodox beliefs, of which his friends had always complained, and which must have exasperated his pious and more conventional wife. When he and Emma sojourned in Jacksonville for the month of February, 1886, he complained that the South had not been worth fighting for. The remark was prompted by his dislike of Florida. Until he was no longer able to write or dictate letters, he was eagerly pumping friends for gossip, reminiscing about former colleagues, making sharp comments on their wives, and asking people to come visit him. He teased his old friend James Monroe, the congressman and former Oberlin professor: "I had heard that Oberlin was holding fast to some of the sixteenth century idols, that it was not receiving the great wealth of new truths which the last half century has revealed to mankind; but I think I am mistaken."

During his last year Hayden was mostly confined to his bed, but he occasionally sat up in the library, where a servant read to him. He was incontinent from time to time and often in pain. For two months during his last summer, Emma managed to find them rooms in Bryn Mawr, where he rallied briefly. In June the University of Pennsylvania awarded him an honorary Doctor of Laws.[2] Because he suffered a number of painful disorders near the end, the last one seemed to Emma just another attack; it swept him away before she realized its seriousness. He died on 22 December 1887 at age 59.

Hayden left the stage much as he had first appeared on it years earlier: self-absorbed and manifesting unconventional behavior. Less than a month before he died he sent an extraordinary note to another old friend at Oberlin, Professor James Harris Fairchild; it was his last letter.

> I do not wish you to misunderstand me. I do not think that you would regard my religious views as orthodox but they are the only ones that give me any security. I have spent two years or more in their study [probably meaning Mind Cure]. When I was told by my physician that my disease was fatal I felt that I ought to have some sure foundation for a hope beyond. It became necessary for me to evolve it from my inner consciousness, following the inner light. I laid the Old Testament aside and studied the real teachings of Christ, reading such books as I could secure that threw any collateral light on the matter. I soon began to receive such light as gave me confidence that I was on the right course and I have had no doubts since. I was obliged to strip my mind of all tradition and I do not think there is now a trace of Calvinism about me, and I do not see occasion for any fear of falling into the hands of the living God. All fear of the future has gone from me.

The rhetoric and structure here are rather smoother than in his other late letters, suggesting that Emma (who actually wrote the letter) cleaned up the sense of what Ferdinand was trying to say. But the meaning of the letter and its similarity to other late letters is unmistakable: Hayden had found his own undogmatic way to a relationship with Christ through study and personal experimentation.

Considering the probable cause of his death, there is reason for saluting the brave demeanor of his last months. Even worse than the physical agony he endured was the social stigma accompanying syphilis, which to most people in the 1880s signified sheer moral depravity. The venereal etiology of syphilis had been known since the sixteenth century, but in Hayden's day an understanding of the specific cause of disease was still mysteriously entwined with the ancient notion of bad humors. Since the Middle Ages in Christian Europe, health and disease had been linked to morality, which is why for centuries so many doctors had been priests. The nineteenth century saw the secularization of the medical profession, but medical knowledge still depended heavily on prejudices and ignorance handed down through the centuries, which made it possible, even logical, to assume God's direct involvement in dispensing health and sickness. Doctors had been treating syphilis since the era of Columbus (and still in the 1880s) by introducing strong metals into the body, especially mercury or potassium iodide, which were thought to expel the evil humor of the disease by inducing salivation or perspiration. Because doctors had only a general awareness of the toxicity of metals, many victims were hastened to their deaths by well-intentioned doses of poison.

The germ theory of disease began to be accepted by American physicians during the 1870s, and by the 1880s many illnesses could be linked to specific germs. In the case of syphilis a period of confusion ensued, for scientists implicated scores of microscopic agents that might cause the disease. The true one, the spirochete bacteria, was not discovered until 1905, and penicillin was not used against it until 1943.

Meanwhile both an understanding of the disease and the discovery of an effective treatment were delayed by social attitudes. The public had not been as quick as the medical profession in accepting the germ theory, largely because it suited conventions of Victorian morality to continue believing that venereal disease was the badge of the depraved. From the 1870s a growing campaign by various private organizations against pornography and prostitution reinforced this notion, making it more difficult to understand venereal problems as disease. As a result, syphilis was not discussed in polite society; it was mostly ignored in the popular press that was increasingly talking about other kinds of disease. Until well into the twentieth century, moral repugnance prevented many doctors and hospitals from treating syphilitics. Even thoughtful people argued that to provide protection against the disease might accelerate promiscuity. The only acceptable prophylactic was the absolute restriction of sexual activity to married couples, which worked as well as it did because this prohibition reflected two other cherished assumptions of Victorian society: motherhood was the supreme role for married women; and sin (and therefore disease) was more common among minorities, the poor, and especially immigrants.

So, in addition to the debilitating symptoms of the disease, Hayden carried an enormous psychological burden. But did he really die of syphilis? His death certificate testifies, confusingly, that his cause of death was locomotor ataxia. Locomotor ataxia is not a disease but a descriptive summary of various symptoms, including deteriorated motor control, partial paralysis, loss of bladder control, problems with vision, cardiovascular complications, and various neurological complaints, at least the first four of which Hayden had. It was known at the time that syphilis was one of the possible causes of locomotor ataxia, and given the stern moral climate of the times it was universally regarded as *the* cause. Today syphilis is seen as the major cause of locomotor ataxia, but modern medical opinion is only good circumstantial evidence in deciding Hayden's case. Technically, we cannot go further than this.

But a number of facts in Hayden's life support the circumstantial evidence. We know of his susceptibility to romantic love from his days at Oberlin and his unashamed fascination with sexual contact that dates from the same period. We know he had numerous short-term liaisons all through his bachelor days, and that he did not marry until his forties. Back East, his obviously robust libido may have been held in check by social convention or the scruples of his sweethearts, but in the West morals were looser, especially around army posts, which were hotbeds of venereal disease. Recall that William Henry Jackson mentioned meeting Hayden for the first time in a brothel in Cheyenne. But the best evidence for his syphilis comes from Hayden himself. In 1884, at the time Grace Gardner made allegations about his sexual behavior, Hayden defended himself in a confidential letter to his close friend Joseph Leidy, in the following words: "As to any intimacy, proper or improper, I have had none with any woman not even my wife for over two years. The incurable chronic nervous disease from which I suffer renders that a physical impossibility." So whether Hayden had syphilis or not, which cannot now be clinically proven, he thought he did, and that is what matters in assessing his psychological burden.

How early others began to understand his condition is difficult to pinpoint. I have found no evidence that people even suspected his condition until well after 1880, which means that his loss of the directorship of the USGS in 1879 had nothing to do with knowledge of his medical condition. In fact, given the irregular progression of the disease, and based on the periodic descriptions Hayden gave of his health, I doubt that he himself began to think seriously of syphilis until around 1878. Thereafter, even as he became more aware of his condition, he had practical reasons for keeping things quiet, not least his need for an income from the survey. I wonder to what extent his ventures into the field between 1883 and 1886 were, in part, a bold assertion of physical competence designed to hide his affliction.

His final decision about coping with the problem showed self-confidence and courage. He retired from the survey at the end of 1886 because he knew he was no longer physically strong enough to continue. Once out of the survey and revitalized by religious faith, he resolved to make a clean breast of the situation. He authorized Peale to pass the word. Accordingly, on 20 April 1887 Peale wrote privately to Marcus Benjamin stating that Hayden was suffering from "progressive locomotor ataxia." Hayden felt Benjamin was entitled to know the facts because he was then preparing an article about Hayden for *Appleton's Cyclopaedia of American Biography,* to be published later in the year. (Benjamin discreetly ignored the subject in his printed article.) Charles Aldrich, a journalist who had accompanied Hayden's survey to Colorado, was also informed. Subsequently, in the course of a sympathetic summary of Hayden's career (published in the *Critic* on 25 June 1887), Aldrich mentioned "progressive locomotor ataxia." Given the circumstances, this deliberate public announcement of Hayden's true condition cannot have occurred without Hayden's approval.

Or Emma's. After all, it was his wife who would bear the brunt of any opprobrium, for they both realized Ferdinand would soon die. Following his death, Emma wore the same mask of bravery, and she declared her affection and respect for her fallen husband in several public ways. She buried him beneath a splendid monument at Woodlands Cemetery. She gave the remainder of his books to Oberlin College, the University of Pennsylvania, and the Academy of Natural Sciences. (In her will Emma made no mention of Hayden's personal papers, which included their letters to each other, other personal correspondence of Hayden, and his field journals; I suspect Emma destroyed all this material after his death.) In May 1888 she gave $2,500 to the Academy to create the Hayden Memorial Geological Fund. Accrued interest from the fund was to be awarded annually, along with a bronze medal, "for the best publication, exploration, discovery or research in the sciences of geology and palaeontology, or in such particular branches thereof as may be designated."[3] She had a fountain erected in his memory at 40th and Woodland Avenue, which she maintained for almost thirty years. In her will of 4 November 1909 she paid tribute to him, leaving the "rest and residue" of her estate to Oberlin "as an endowment fund in memory of my late husband Ferdinand V. Hayden, M.D." Following her death on 16 September 1934, she was buried beside him at Woodlands Cemetery.

25
IN SEARCH
OF REPUTATION

One cannot fail to feel that Dr. Hayden was a man of strong will power, of remarkable fixity of purpose, of unusual self-abnegation, of broad training, a great explorer, and at the same time a man possessing a shyness and point of view that made him more misunderstood by his associates and contemporaries than any one of the group of men who were exploring and studying the great West. As a creator of public interest and sentiment in favor of surveys and explorations, he helped to clear the way for Government support, and finally for the combination of the four independent and rival organizations then existing into one great survey in 1879. He was also largely responsible for the inception of the great Biological and Botanical surveys of the Government. . . . Often laughed at by his fellows and treated as of unbalanced mind by the red man, he ignored the one and smiled at the childishness of the other, and went forward as though neither were in existence.

—Charles D. Walcott, 7 January 1907,
on the occasion of accepting the Hayden Medal

REPUTATION! TO SPEAK the word is to enrich the air with the sound and feel of solidity. To define its tangible qualities is as difficult as painting a cloud, yet we all know and value its essence even if we are often brought to think of it more by its absence than its presence. Thus Shakespeare, in *King Richard II,* has the Duke of Norfolk say,

The purest treasure mortal times afford
Is spotless reputation; that away,
Men are but gilded loam or painted clay.

Spotless Hayden was surely not, but how much more is he than "gilded loam or painted clay"? Everything has a history, and Hayden's reputation, too, has evolved against a background of changing circumstance and according to the varying interests of his interpreters. Not surprisingly, because of the controversies that swirled around his well-publicized deeds, we find divergent opinions about Hayden. By the time of his death or shortly thereafter, two distinct reputations vied with each other.

The earliest coincides with what I have previously called his popular image, which took form at the time of Hayden's explorations of the Yellowstone region in the early 1870s. Seizing upon stories of exploding geysers and boiling hot springs, American and European journalists hailed Hayden as the discoverer of natural wonders, though they overlooked most of his more important work in geology, geography, and natural history.

A particular slant was given to the popular image by Samuel R. Wells, who edited the *Phrenological Journal and Life Illustrated.* At first phrenology was a theoretical attempt to understand the structure and operation of the human brain, but popularizers promised it would unlock all secrets of the human mind and character. Promoters took over the movement in the 1840s and made it irresistible to practical-minded Americans who exuded enormous faith in self-improvement. Wells specialized in "character readings," or the determination of a subject's strengths and weaknesses by measuring parts of the skull in accordance with a chart purporting to map the "thirty-seven faculties" of the brain. Even though experiments had demonstrated the futility of phrenology's scientific claims by around mid-century, character readings retained a powerful hold on the popular imagination. To the dubious assumptions behind character readings were added the timeless abuses incident to creating good copy about the rich and famous. In July 1874 Wells published his character reading of Hayden. The reading was based entirely upon a photograph. Hayden probably never met Wells; he certainly never corresponded with him.

The character reading is an intriguing mixture of facts, hunches, and shrewd observations that produced an apparently convincing mental profile. Wells begins by recording a number of accurate comments that would have been easy to assume from Hayden's achievements. He speaks of Hayden's self-reliance, his ability to combine literary and scientific interests, his skill with words, his capacity to influence people, and his eagerness for reputation. Perceptively, Wells even catches a few personal traits, such as "watchful relative to dangers, but not afraid to meet them" and "fond of society, is gallant and loving toward women." The latter perception is not so impressive as might be thought because Hayden made no secret of his admiration for women, and this detail is the sort anyone who knew Hayden might have offered to an interviewer. During a sojourn in the West in summer 1873 Wells traveled with a number of journalists, some of whom certainly knew Hayden and any one of whom could have supplied the requisite anecdotes.

But then Wells departs from facts he might have learned and begins to invent. Hayden "is spirited and courageous without being quarrelsome or severe in his spirit." Not quarrelsome? What would Hayden's opponents in the Permian controversy have thought of this? Or after enduring Hayden's petulant demands for years, how would Baird or Leidy have reacted to this? What would Warren or Raynolds have said, or Engelmann, or Coues? And what about his rivals, for whom Hayden sustained an aggressive paranoia?

Next Wells makes Hayden appear more open than is good for him. "He needs more Secretiveness to give him policy. He is frank almost to a fault. People who have a right to his acquaintance will know him like a book. He has few concealments, and if he were to go into a political or a strictly business pursuit, he would find occasion for more personal service and policy." Hayden would have been delighted to hear this, for it coincided well with the self-image he wished to promote: that of the sincere advocate of science. But how does this reconcile with plagiarizing Denig's work on Indians? And arranging for Gardner's report on coal in Colorado, which secretly served the purposes of Hayden's friend William Blackmore?

Although Wells tries to paint a favorable picture, he vastly underestimates Hayden. More than once he remarks on Hayden's quick wits: he "lives more in a day than some men do in a week"; he "reads character at a glance"; he "picks up knowledge as if it were on the wing." Admittedly, Hayden was a mercurial sort in all the senses of that word, but the inference Wells draws from his correct premise completely misses the mark. He puts the reader in mind of a brilliant meteor that attracts attention readily, then burns itself out. "He has inherited a tendency to overexertion; his mind is so active and his feelings so intense that he is liable to work too hard for the strength and endurance of his body." Wells turns Hayden's brilliance into something effervescent and makes the man appear to be an enthusiast, adept at making only dazzling impressions. Thus was codified for all time the image of Hayden as the frenzied popularizer.

But does this image capture the indefatigable collector who gathered more specimens in more fields than anyone else in his day and did so for nearly thirty years? Is this the tenacious administrator and lobbyist who for twelve years campaigned to have his survey transformed into a national scientific bureau? Is this the naturalist whose insatiable appetite would engorge all the natural sciences in one gulp? Is this the editor who initiated hundreds of publications?

Inaccurate and misleading though the popular image was, it provided a persuasive verbal portrait of Hayden just at the time when he was becoming a celebrity. The popular image seemed to fit what little the public knew of the man, and Wells's version appealed because it offered personal details not available in the standard press clippings. This popular image appeared suitable and was easy to remember; thus it was almost impossible to obliterate. Years later,

Marsh and Powell and Newberry were able to draw on it in order to mythologize Hayden as a popular personage lacking in substantial credentials.

That image of Hayden persists to the present. It surfaces periodically (for example, in a 1978 master's thesis by Sarah Oliver entitled "Ferdinand V. Hayden, Scientist or Charlatan?" and in a 1987 Harvard honor's thesis by Claudia Polsky called "The Unmaking of a Scientific Reputation"). These authors have not accepted the superficial image of Hayden, even though they showed it lives on. My own experience in talking to historians of science confirms that the popular image is alive and well. Among academics Hayden is often perceived as a shallow character who did nothing worthy of extended attention. Field geologists have a much higher regard for him.

Hayden's second reputation derives from the testimony of colleagues. We find it best articulated in the obituaries they wrote about him. A first group characterized him as a brilliant field explorer. Charles Aldrich said, "If the history of Western scientific exploration is ever written, and it doubtless will be, its central and commanding figure will be Prof. Hayden." J. P. Lesley focused on Hayden's sweeping contributions in the field of geology. "Dr. Hayden will be remembered as one of the great discoverers of the world in the history of the science of geology." E. D. Cope took a similar stance. "He is the founder of our knowledge of the geographical geology of North America from the eastern border of the plains to the Wasatch Mountains." C. A. White went even further: "There is, in my opinion, no room for doubt that the labors of Dr. Hayden, directly or indirectly, accomplished more for the general advancement of geological science in America than those of any one else." White worked with both Hayden and Powell, including years under Powell as head of the USGS. Recall that White's earlier view of Hayden had not been so flattering; he changed his mind after years of working with Hayden.

Other colleagues saw Hayden's wider impact on his times. S. H. Scudder said: "To the general interest in science excited by the enthusiastic labors of Dr. Hayden . . . is due in a great degree the existence and continuance of the present United States Geological Survey." White, Cope, and Lesley said words to the same effect. Archibald Geikie recalled Hayden's role in stimulating the patronage of government for the benefit of science. "No one who has not been in some measure admitted behind the scenes of political wire-pulling in the States, can realize what had to be undertaken by the man of science who would obtain and retain an annual subsidy from Congress for scientific investigation in the days when Hayden carried on his explorations." Cope thought that "Dr. Hayden's influence was only second to that of Baird in securing for science the aid and recognition which it has received from the government." Others remembered how much Hayden contributed indirectly to science by encouraging a host of talented younger men coming up through the ranks and by sponsoring a virtual library of publications.

Although they paid tribute to his accomplishments, it is puzzling how little Hayden's eulogists said about him personally. Three of his more important obituary writers—J. D. Dana, Marcus Benjamin, and A. C. Peale—had nothing to say in this regard. Dana stressed Hayden's unique contributions to geological science. Benjamin compiled the most complete summary of Hayden's career. But Peale was content to summarize the opinions of others and to spend most of his space on the details of expeditions, almost as if he were afraid to raise the specter of the man he had known as teacher, mentor, colleague, and friend. During the late nineteenth century obituary writers prided themselves on a tactful reticence regarding personalities and a bland disguising of anything disagreeable. Those who knew Hayden best would have been the most aware of his controversial reputation and they seem to have been the most reluctant to speak of it.

What little they said is to be treasured as a rare articulation of his friends' judgment. We must remember to allow for their gentlemanly habit of accentuating the positive. Here is Cope's reminiscence.

> The most prominent features of his character were: restless activity, ambition to accomplish a useful career, love of scientific truth, sympathy for unpretentious merit, and a certain flexibility of character which enabled him to adapt himself to his environment more readily than is possible to many men.

Geikie had similar thoughts.

> The first impression which the late geologist made on those who came to know him was of gentleness, almost of timidity . . . It was some time before one could see the real underlying secret of his success. This was undoubtedly a quiet enthusiasm for science, supported by an undemonstrative but indomitable courage, and a determination to gain the proposed end, cost what it might in bodily and mental endurance.

Lesley was the most candid: "There was a vehemence and a sort of wildness in his nature as a man which won him success, cooperation, and enthusiastic reputation among all classes, high and low, wherever he went."

If we translate their language into a modern idiom, we can identify a Hayden that is already familiar to us: ambitious, determined, impetuous, forceful, deceptive, and difficult to get along with. But also generous, charming, unpretentious, and unpredictable.

To summarize the two competing reputations at the time of Hayden's death: His colleagues painted a broad and balanced picture of him as a pioneering geologist, the founder of an influential survey, and the man who taught the government how to invest in science. The image created by the popular press implied a range of abilities especially for organizing and persuading, but it spotlighted an explorer who discovered and explained novelties of the natural world. His only memorable personal trait was an enthusiasm to popularize these wonders. This popular image has been the most enduring and the most influential on later writers.

In trying to decide how important he was, his contemporaries faced several difficulties; the most severe was that Hayden left no definitive written work, no single masterpiece that resoundingly stated his conception of nature and its secrets. Though not at all systematic, his writings do contain some original points, and I have shown earlier that he espoused some consistent ideas and was guided by a discernible interpretation of nature. But that only became apparent after a thorough study of his scattered writings on diffuse topics. During Hayden's lifetime no one gave him the same patient attention, and who can blame them? They had their own work to keep them busy. The one idea everyone associated with Hayden was the Great Lignite, but when later research dismembered the empire of the Great Lignite, common opinion also denigrated the great proponent of that concept.

Another difficulty his contemporaries faced was their unconscious bias in favor of geological studies. Most of Hayden's eulogists were geologists, and by the year of his death nearly all of them agreed that a specialized approach to geology was the correct one. In so believing they reflected the spirit of the times. Yet, as a result, they unwittingly overlooked one of Hayden's most distinctive attitudes—that geology was not a separate specialty but an aspect of natural history, along with paleontology, zoology, and botany, and that to understand the Earth and its life forms, past and present, the scientist must approach them with a united vision, not with an array of specific prisms.

Some of the shortcomings of his contemporaries can be corrected by considering another viewpoint on Hayden—the one he created himself, which amounts to a third reputation. This third reputation is unique and revealing, especially as a contrast to the other two, but it went to the grave with Hayden. It has not influenced later thought because no one has known of it. No single document embodies Hayden's thoughts about his place in the greater scheme of things; instead, there are hundreds. His reports to the secretary of the interior, the articles he wrote about his survey, even his private correspondence are full of his own pretensions. Producing a string of quotations won't suffice to make my point for not one hits the nail on the head.

Also Hayden was an active man who rarely gave even his closest friends a window into his thoughts, much less into thoughts about himself; therefore, I have codified his sense of himself from a lot of verbiage and by extracting a deeper meaning from what otherwise would seem to be frenetic and point-less activity.

From the beginning Hayden saw himself as a tireless explorer trying to perpetuate the example of Lewis and Clark. He wanted to discover the mys-teries of the Great American West—all of them: the topography, the geol-ogy, the fossils, the living creatures, the Indians, their forebears, and their artifacts. These different aspects added up to a wholeness, an intangible to-tality, the uniqueness of which could only be appreciated by studying all the aspects together. Since the Civil War Hayden felt that he, almost single-handedly, was working to preserve this pioneering vision of the West. At the same time he was going well beyond discovery because he was assisting in the physical development of the West by making known its abundant re-sources and by preparing blueprints for its settlement. Linking his many and diverse activities was the thread of increasing knowledge, and his rampant curiosity served a variety of learners. For scholars he found old bones and new species, and he described both the ancient structures of the Earth and its modern movements. But knowledge was not just for scholars, particu-larly because much that Hayden learned was of practical use to the ordinary people who lived in the West. For Hayden there was always a unity between his esoteric researches and his popular descriptions. Even as he took pride in sharing his practical knowledge, he delighted in expounding on the higher purposes of the naturalist in order to draw the layman into an appreciation of paleontology, of natural wonders, and of aesthetics. Hayden saw himself as a heroic synthesizer of knowledge.

For Hayden the West was not merely a geographic region, and it was much more than an embodiment of certain values that over time have con-tributed to the enduring legacy of the West. To Hayden the West was a vast living laboratory that offered virtually endless instruction, and in his travels across it (which he hoped science would continue indefinitely) Hayden saw himself and those who would follow him as pious students, soaking up like sponges whatever knowledge they could by direct immersion, then squeez-ing it out through publications for the benefit of those less fortunate mortals who could not experience the West directly. It is through his sense of him-self that we catch Hayden's unity of purpose, his idealism, his desire to in-struct and improve, which otherwise have been overlooked.

Another problem for contemporaries in evaluating Hayden was the fact that he was too much in the public eye, so much so that it became difficult to separate applause from praise or to distinguish popularity from merit.

Every age has sneered at reputations too easily won, and in Hayden's day a cutting edge was honed to this natural skepticism by the elitist prejudice against scientific men who were popular. This was unfortunate because it blinded nearly everybody to one of Hayden's greatest contributions, certainly the one where he was ahead of his times, though he has never been sufficiently appreciated for it: his popularization of science. The growing financial support of government for science was a direct result of the huge enthusiasm Hayden stirred up for his broadbrush approach to natural history and of his popular approach to the West, which blended development and knowledge and tourism. For all this accomplishment his colleagues merely found him strange, without recognizing his powerful genius for shaping new events.

As his eulogists recognized, and as even the popular image of Hayden admitted, his enduring monument and his true claim to fame was his Survey of the Territories. But recognizing this fact has had, and continues to have, a distorting effect on understanding Hayden. The survey is easy to track through the archives: its achievement is clear, its importance manifest (and a great deal less controversial than its leader), but all this institutional emphasis makes it seem as though the survey made Hayden. On the contrary, it was very much the other way around. The uniqueness of the man behind the institutional accomplishment becomes blurred and eventually is lost.

How much of this strange genius has been understood by the historians, biographers, and scientists who came after Hayden? No final verdict regarding Hayden has been handed down. He has been the subject of numerous articles, and he has been mentioned prominently in several books—none of them, however, devoted entirely to Hayden or to an unabashed look at the whole man.

Naturally, biographers of Powell and King and James Hall have been under no obligation to search out the source materials unique to Hayden. The result has been that biographies of these men, however valuable in their own right, tend to adopt the attitudes about Hayden held by their protagonists. More favorable judgments of Hayden appear in books about Baird and Leidy and Cope, though their authors have relied more on shopworn anecdotes than original research, at least in what concerns Hayden. None of these books provide much insight into Hayden.

The two autobiographical books by William Henry Jackson (1929, 1940) are not much better. Jackson's views should be useful because he alone among Hayden's many colleagues published extensive comments about him. Of course Jackson had a bias as well as an impediment. Jackson spent the greater part of his very long life making images of the West and promoting a romantic interpretation of that region, enterprises that admirably suited

Hayden's own purposes of popularizing the West and his survey along with it. Jackson shows what a lively personality Hayden was, how much his men venerated him, and how loyally Hayden supported them. Jackson idealized Hayden because of what he accomplished, but these accomplishments just happened to draw attention back to Jackson. Jackson's impediment was that he did not know Hayden intimately. He only knew the public man, the dazzling impresario of a natural history circus. He missed the manipulative, secretive aspects of his hero.

In his massive history of geology George Merrill (1924) compiled a detailed summary of the survey's field activities, which emphasized the originality of much that Hayden did. Interestingly, he gave far more space to Hayden than to Powell and King and Wheeler. Charles Keyes (1924) concluded that Hayden was the foremost exploring geologist in American history. Both Keyes and Merrill thought Hayden laid the foundations for the USGS in his Survey of the Territories. Though fortified with more specific arguments, their conclusions add nothing to the general picture of Hayden painted by the eulogists at the time of his death and in two respects were less comprehensive. Both abstracted Peale and White regarding Hayden's character and personal life and both neglected to consider Hayden's contributions to science in general, beyond geology, not to mention his wider impact on social history.

Richard Bartlett (1953, 1955, and 1962) went farther than anyone else in presenting a lively description of the four rival surveys in action. What interested Bartlett was how the surveys glorified the West and became popular in the process. Unfortunately from Hayden's perspective, this approach touts the wonders of the West and his survey's role in discovering them, all of which reinforces aspects of the old stereotype of Hayden as the superficial popularizer. In trying to give equal attention to each of the postwar surveys Bartlett missed the formative nature of Hayden's solo work before the war, which influenced all the subsequent surveys. The most unfortunate effect of Bartlett's selective approach is that it played down or ignored Hayden as a creative individual: his preeminence as a collector, his original work in geology, his sponsorship of important publications, and his enormous influence in promoting government sponsorship of science.

Although his figure of Hayden is small on the huge canvas of the American West, William Goetzmann (1959, 1966) limned the first balanced composition by a historian and the fullest one since the eulogists. Goetzmann gave Hayden credit for his originality as a geologist, his versatility in creating a diverse scientific enterprise, and his genius as a popularizer, without exaggerating that last aspect into a stereotype. Goetzmann is aware of Hayden's flaws, at least some of them, and my major criticism of his sketch is that it fails to blend the defects and the talents into a convincing overall portrait. But Goetzmann had little concern for individuals like Hayden; he worked with a grander design in mind. He chose to see exploration as "a process with cultural significance." This focus on ideas makes for exciting reading, but to me it also subordinates men to abstractions and thereby diminishes their contribution. But such is the bias of a biographer.

To the debate about Hayden's reputation Claudia Polsky (1987) brought a refreshing reliance on high standards of scholarly research. She insisted that an evaluation of Hayden's achievement could only be valid if it appreciated science as it was in Hayden's day. At that time massive empirical work was needed, the kind of relentless fact-gathering that both precedes and later tests sophisticated theories. Hayden provided this in spades—and much more fully than his rivals, Polsky might have added. Moreover, in addition to forwarding a practical understanding of the West, his earnest pursuit of paleontology and natural history stimulated pure research. Polsky reminded us that Hayden's success in both endeavors was won by persuading the government to broaden its support for both pure and applied science. She was the first since Cope (in 1888) to notice that Hayden's bad reputation was consolidated by his opponents during the struggle for the directorship of the USGS. She pointed out that the materialistic climate of the times favored Clarence King's emphasis on economic geology over Hayden's broadbrush natural history. Although I agree with that observation, I draw a different conclusion regarding the origin of the USGS. I believe that personal hostilities were paramount, that Hayden's survey was abolished in order to get rid of Hayden. After all, with Hayden comfortably out of the way, Powell reinstated paleontology and natural history into the survey—under the direction of Othniel Charles Marsh.

The work of other scholars has added specific pieces to a knowledge of Hayden. Frances Binkley (1945) had some perceptive insights about the debilitating influence of Hayden's ambition on his career. Jesse Howell (1959) was the first to expose the myths surrounding Hayden's childhood. Bonnie Hardwick (1977) demonstrated Hayden's superlative publicity skills. Gerald Cassidy (1991) showed that in addition to being a skillful promoter Hayden was an innovative administrator. As valuable as these discoveries are, they leave a great many empty spaces in the jigsaw puzzle that is Hayden.

Why has Hayden not attracted a biographer? Or received fuller treatment from historians? A large part of the answer is in the sources. The materials for Hayden's life are extensive but scattered, not always readily located, and demand considerable time to ponder, sift, and evaluate.

Rather than benefiting from comprehensive biographical appraisal, Hayden has been subjected to a number of specialized topical studies. Like most earlier writing, this work emphasized Hayden's survey more than Hayden himself, but even the picture of the survey that emerged was fragmented and incomplete. Hayden himself disappeared even further into the institutional haze. Without a unifying vision of the whole man, based on a knowledge of all his various involvements, how can an author interpret the many pieces or put them into their proper places? It is useful to learn more about Hayden's collaborative work with Meek (Nelson and Fryxell, 1979), but to see this relationship as a harmonious partnership in science is to miss the bitter rivalry that partnership mobilized against other scientists, not to mention the sharp tension between Meek and Hayden. Rediscovering the sites of Hayden's collections can be fascinating, and reexamining the specimens he gathered perhaps necessary (Waage, 1968, 1975; Hartman, 1984). Such work demonstrated the continuing relevance of questions Hayden raised; but looking too closely at the details obscures the revolutionary implications for the history of life Hayden drew from that evidence. Joseph Gregory (1969) reviewed the rise and fall of the notion that ancient lakes once stretched across the West and the prominent role Hayden played in promoting this concept. It proved to be another wrong idea. Though Gregory did not say so, Hayden's authority as a field explorer probably prolonged its existence.

A similar problem of imbalance has resulted from too much concentration on a local dimension of the survey's work.[1] Some authors uncovered unique circumstances in Hayden's background and emphasized his breadth, whether in terms of versatile skills or the diverse regions in which he deployed them. But unless such divergent essays are related to general themes, they add up to antiquarianism, not history. In too many local studies Hayden becomes an attractive diorama in a museum, a frozen embodiment of some particular event, instead of a dynamic individual in the process of defining his life. The same criticism can be made of articles that have examined only a part of Hayden's whole career (Nelson, Rabbitt, and Fryxell, 1981; Schubert, 1984). Hayden has eluded them all.

As the literature on Hayden has grown more specialized, it has become increasingly diffuse. Authors from several disciplines have been attracted to Hayden, but few have read each other's work; none have consulted all the available sources. As the literature discloses more about different aspects of his career, it also reveals less about the whole man. A related difficulty is that specialized emphasis tends to reflect present-mindedness, but a preconceived focus isolates an author from those surprising but fruitful encounters with historical reality that lead to an understanding of the past.

In criticizing particular examinations of Hayden my purpose is to remind that Hayden's reputation suffers unjustly when he is seen only through a microscope, no matter how well-intentioned the observer. The challenge for a biographer is to reassemble from dusty records and disparate clues a complete picture, a living person, with all the virtues and warts well displayed. There is great privilege in this work but also much responsibility, for it brings the scholar into the most direct and intimate contact with someone's whole being—their humanity as well as their lack of it.

A few moments ago I asked why Hayden had not received more attention from historians and biographers. I mentioned that the sources present formidable hurdles. I have also said that his professional colleagues and their successors—the geologists and paleontologists—have staked the first claims on the Hayden territory, but that they have been too preoccupied applying their picks and hammers to particular veins to map out and appraise the whole mine. I would be remiss not to mention a more general situation that has impeded an understanding of Ferdinand Hayden. Considering this problem brings us back to reputation and reveals something basic about the character of Hayden, but even more about certain tendencies in human nature. For all his patronage of scientific colleagues, for all his sincere promotion of protégés, Hayden was a loner who wrought great deeds for his own benefit. True, in his survey he created an important institution whose influence long outlived him, but the survey was a highly personal reflection of himself. Hayden was not a joiner, not a team player, not the clubby sort. And those who are can never quite forgive such an individualist. If it is a truism that victors usually write the history of the past, it is equally unfortunate that conformists tend to pronounce the reputations of mavericks.

We have seen an early example of this tendency in the admiring but patronizing way geologists told and retold the story of Hayden's nickname, "the man who picks up stones running." Here a smug group of geologists looked back with unguarded amusement on an eccentric character they esteemed as one of their progenitors. They knew more geology than Hayden had known, and naturally they took pride in their collegial approach to science. They could afford to be amused by Hayden, for eccentricity in a precursor is more tolerable than in a colleague.

Another example comes from the annual farce staged by the Pick and Hammer Club of the USGS. In 1965 and again in 1971 the club "burlesqued Hayden as a pompous, shallow, and opportunistic 'Herr Doktor Geheimrat,'" according to a triumvirate of geologist-authors. In the skit the actor playing Hayden was made to sing three verses of boastful rhyme, which doubtless produced the desired laughter. Harmless good fun perhaps, but consider the underlying attitudes from which it springs.

It is also revealing to look into the scientific societies of Hayden's day and realize that though they honored him with memberships, they never re-

garded him as truly one of their own. This seems odd because through his
natural history collections Hayden dramatically forwarded the purposes of
the Academy of Natural Sciences, the American Philosophical Society, the
Academy of Science of St. Louis, and most of all the Smithsonian Institution. Though he was a rather indifferent member of the National Academy
of Sciences, the American Association for the Advancement of Science, and
the Philosophical Society of Washington, the publications Hayden engendered and the survey he instigated directly promoted the wider purposes of
each of those groups. But clubs and societies instinctively look inward and
are somewhat parochial by nature, no matter how broadly they claim to look
upon the world. My point is to emphasize the extent to which Hayden's reputation has been formed by clubby men, if not actual clubmen.

A final example is so perfect that I will quote it in full; it seems to be the
earliest articulation of the attitude I am illustrating. Looking back over the
history of the Cosmos Club of Washington in 1904, on the occasion of its
twenty-fifth anniversary, G. K. Gilbert related the following anecdote regarding Hayden and Powell. By that time both Powell and Hayden were
dead, but within the club Powell—the leading spirit behind its founding in
1878—had been virtually apotheosized. Hayden had never become a member, not because he was excluded but because he chose not to join when he
had the chance.[2]

About thirty years ago Donn Piatt, the journalist, a clever and pun-
gent writer, entertained the readers of the Sunday *Capital* by witty attacks on various persons and things. Among his victims was Dr.
Hayden, the geologist and explorer, whom he dubbed "the triangulat-
ing Hayden," and who was goaded to wrath and misery by the weekly
thornings. He turned attention also, once or twice, to Major Powell,
but the result was different. The astute Major may have fumed inter-
nally—I do not know—but his visible action was to seek the acquaintance of the troublesome editor, and meet him socially a few times.
There was no discussion of the Sunday *Capital,* there were no favors,
nothing was done but to establish social relations—and the attacks
ceased.

It is revealing that Gilbert did not presume to read the mind of Powell,
whom he knew quite well, but he did not hesitate to guess at Hayden's,
with whom he had no personal relationship. But the ghost of Hayden was
only raised for the purpose of contrasting him unfavorably to the sainted
Major Powell. No one in the Cosmos Club knew Hayden well, not even the
former members of his survey because Hayden kept himself isolated from

congenial societies; but in doing so he helped to reinforce the stereotypes those societies created of him. Based on my knowledge of Hayden, I doubt he was perturbed at all by a teasing journalist; he fenced skillfully with so many. But Hayden was known to be restless, impetuous, and irritable; by drawing on a common awareness, Gilbert was able to pass off a likely distortion as a believable incident. Of such stuff are reputations made.

If these examples belittle and demean Hayden, another shows that even when trying to be objective scholars have misunderstood him. Except for the biographers of John Wesley Powell, most scholars have not taken seriously the scabrous slanders about Hayden circulated by his enemies. (I think Powell's biographers have taken them *too* seriously.) But in attempting to be nonpartisan by rising above personal polemics, other writers on Hayden have missed something essential about the man and his circumstances. Hayden annoyed almost everyone he knew at one time or another; he thrived on spiteful controversy. He was born and raised amid such strife; he matured while stimulating it. Eventually it overwhelmed him. His life and his accomplishments were heavily seasoned with the spice of personal and angry disputation.

Hayden was an outrageous character. A notorious womanizer, an abject flatterer, an unashamed self-promoter who was not above embroidering the truth for his own purposes, Hayden was widely admired but also deeply disliked. Such men do not find historians knocking at their door. But Hayden was also the most versatile naturalist and the most formidable collector of natural history specimens of his day. In the field his ability to find the representative fossil was uncanny; in Washington his knack of manipulating Congress and the press was amazing. He popularized science, and he influenced for all time the way Americans and Europeans would understand the western United States. He demonstrated to a reluctant government the value of federal sponsorship of science. He sponsored a large shelf of books and articles about natural history, and he epitomized more than anyone else a particular attitude toward nature. In short, Hayden is an apt reminder that ability does not always come wrapped in an attractive package.

I end this book with no illusions as to its finality, but still with a sense of fulfillment. The lesson for the biographer seems to be that one cannot rely on the subject's reputation. Each biographer must look at the subject anew and look with a wary eye on all those who have written before, just as those who come after must surely do the same. Perhaps, to modify a suggestion of Shakespeare's, the biographer should begin by killing all the historians. Metaphorically, it is an excellent idea and a necessary one if the biographer wants to arrive at independent conclusions.

But let us not kill history in the process, for the study of history—like the study of geology—is a cumulative effort, and some of what has been written in the past is still valid today. We only learn the value of history, and only distill what is valid from what is not, through a process of discovering *all* the previous Haydens that have been imagined. Only in that historical process do we learn that there is no *one and only* Hayden, true and real for all time. An awareness of historical writing teaches that interpretation is more tangible than the person. What saves biography and history from relativism is that objective writers looking at the original sources for themselves have found certain elements of the subject over and over again. There are reliable facts about the past and about Hayden, and over time different authors have added more to the common stock of knowledge. Alternatively, what saves history from positivism is that the accepted past is only discovered one piece at a time—by individual minds working alone, limited by subjective biases, but blessed with unique intuitions. Historical understanding is an imperfect process of knowing, but given the nature of biographers—and biographees— it may be the best method we have of comprehending human beings.

ABBREVIATIONS

THE FOLLOWING ABBREVIATIONS occur in the Notes and the Select Bibliography.

Am Jour Sci   *American Journal of Science and Arts*
Am Nat   *American Naturalist*
Am Phil Soc   American Philosophical Society
ANSP   Academy of Natural Sciences of Philadelphia
Bulletin   *Bulletin of the U.S. Geological and Geographical Survey of the Territories*
Eng & Min Jour   *Engineering & Mining Journal*
GPO   Government Printing Office
Jour ANSP   *Journal of the Academy of Natural Sciences of Philadelphia*
Jour Wash Acad Sciences   *Journal of the Washington Academy of Sciences*
Nat Acad Sci   National Academy of Sciences
Nat Acad Sci Biog Memoirs   *National Academy of Sciences Biographical Memoirs*
Proc Am Phil Soc   *Proceedings of the American Philosophical Society*
Proc ANSP   *Proceedings of the Academy of Natural Sciences of Philadelphia*
RG   Record Group
RU   Record Unit

SIA   Smithsonian Institution Archives
Trans Am Phil Soc   *Transactions of the American Philosophical Society*
USGS   U.S. Geological Survey
WRHS   Western Reserve Historical Society, Cleveland

NOTES

ALL NOTES APPEAR here. In order to interrupt the narrative as infrequently as possible, I have inserted numbered references in the text only for peripheral material that may interest the general reader. The numbered notes appear in **bold** typeface. For convenience, the page number is also shown; thus: **Note 3**, at p. 15.

Most notes are not indicated by a cipher in the text. If curious about the source of a quotation, the reader will find it below identified by the page number where the quotation appears. In other unnumbered notes, I make comments on various sources as well as extended remarks on topics that may interest scholars or specialists. (In the Notes, "Washington" refers to Washington, DC, unless otherwise noted.)

Notes for Chapter 1

1: The description of the interior of the House is based on DeB. Randolph Keim, *Washington and Its Environs* (Washington: D. R. Keim, 1874). In a letter of 9 January 1991 George M. White, architect of the Capitol, sent me a photograph of the desks and chairs in the House at the time of Hewitt.

2: Hewitt's speech is printed in *Congressional Record,* 45th Cong, 3d sess, 1879, 214:1207.

Notes for Chapter 2

Epigraph: Manly Root's letter to Professor A. A. Wright of Oberlin is one of several letters written by Hayden's classmates shortly after his death. The letters are in Wright's papers in the Oberlin College Archives. Typescript copies of these letters wound up in the Marcus Benjamin Papers at the Smithsonian Archives (RU 7085), probably because A. C. Peale arranged to have them copied. The typescripts contain a number of errors; therefore, when quoting these letters, I have gone back to the originals at Oberlin.

11–12: The background on Westfield is based on Wallace Nutting, *Massachusetts Beautiful* (Norwood, MA: Plimpton Press, 1923) and Rev. John H. Lockwood and others, *Western Massachusetts: A History, 1636–1925,* Vol. 2 (New York: Lewis Historical Publishing Co., 1926).

12ff: For the abbreviated genealogy (going back no further than Hayden's grandfather Joel), I have relied on the vital records of Sutton, Sudbury, Hopkinton, and Lee and the unpublished records of Westfield and Blandford. Even for the veteran, a genealogical search can become a maze of dead ends and dubious connections, and I am grateful to Shirley M. Pizziferri for help in finding the raw materials on which my summary is based. In the vain attempt to find Hayden's birth records, Ms. Pizziferri also checked a number of other sources, including the International Genealogical Index, the Corbin Collection on western Massachusetts towns, and the Barbour Index for Connecticut. The Fryxell and Howell collections at the University of Wyoming contain a great deal of biographical material on Hayden's family, but much of it is inaccurate and all of it requires checking against original records.

13: Joel Hayden's will, dated 9 June 1834, was admitted to probate 5 April 1842 and is found at the office of the Register of Probate, Berkshire Division, in Pittsfield, Massachusetts. His Revolutionary War pension documents (claim number: W. 14864) provided useful confirmations and were found on Roll 1232, in drawer 27/7, at the Denver Branch of the National Archives.

14: Melinda Hayden's divorce petition is in Vol. 10, p. 316, of the papers of the Berkshire County Supreme Judicial Court.

15: Frances Hayden to Ferdinand, regarding their mother, undated letter of c. 1849. The letter is in MS 3154 at WRHS, which is an invaluable source on family, Oberlin, and Hayden's early years. All letters referred to in this and the next two chapters are in this collection, unless noted otherwise.

16: Lucretia Stevens to Hayden, 12 December 1850.

16: Hayden's recollections about his early years are quoted from an article by Joseph Savage, "Around the Camp Fire," *Kansas Magazine* 4 (July 1873), 46. Savage was a general assistant to Hayden's survey one summer; he erred in reporting Hayden's birthday, giving it as 27 September instead of 7 September. Marcus Benjamin recorded a similar version of Hayden's boyhood in "Ferdinand Vanderveer [sic] Hayden," *Scientific American,* 7 January 1888, 9.

A. C. Peale, "Ferdinand Vandiveer Hayden," *Bulletin of the Philosophical Society of Washington* 11 (1892), 476.

C. A. White, "Memoir of Ferdinand Vandiveer Hayden, 1839 [sic]–1887," *Nat Acad Sci Biog Memoirs* 3 (1895), 397.

18: Lucretia Stevens to Hayden, 1 November 1849.

Frank Hayden to Ferdinand, 4 July [year unspecified, probably 1849]; "Frank" was the nickname of Hayden's brother, Henry Franklin, who would have been twelve in 1849.

Notes for Chapter 3

The essential sources for this chapter are the records of Oberlin College (all found in the Oberlin College Archives), especially the Alumni Records, College Catalogues, Treasurer's Files, Theological Society Records, and Union Society Book of Minutes. Cox's letter to Professor Wright is in the Wright papers. All letters to Hayden mentioned in this chapter are in MS 3154 at WRHS.

19–20: Hayden was quoted by Joseph Savage in "Around the Camp Fire," *Kansas Magazine* 4 (July 1873), 46.

20: Hayden's residence at Oberlin has been constructed from facts in the R. W. Howard file in the Oberlin College Archives.

The anecdote about Professor Penfield's botany class is printed in *Oberliniana: A Jubilee Volume of Semi-Historical Anecdotes connected with the past and present of Oberlin College,* 1833–1883 (Cleveland: Home Publishing Co., 1883), pp. 99–100.

Letters of Thomas Robinson, Manley Root, and N. W. Hodge, all written to Professor A. A. Wright of Oberlin shortly after Hayden's death.

21: Keith J. Hardman, *Charles Grandison Finney, 1792–1875: Revivalist and Reformer* (Syracuse: Syracuse Univ. Press, 1987).

Edward H. Madden and James E. Hamilton, *Freedom and Grace: The Life of Asa Mahan* (Metuchen, NJ: Scarecrow Press, 1982).

Robert S. Fletcher, *A History of Oberlin College: From Its Foundation Through the Civil War* (Oberlin: Oberlin College, 1943); the quote is from p. 809.

22: Thomas Robinson, "Reminiscences of the Class of 1850" [c. 1870], Oberlin College Archives, p. 39.

On Hayden's religion, Robinson's letter to Professor Wright, A. A. Wright papers.

Robinson's "Reminiscences of the Class of 1850," p. 39.

24: The quote on Hayden's interest in natural science comes from Savage, "Around the Camp Fire," 47.

24–25: Allen's notes for his natural history and geology lectures.

27: Savage, "Around the Camp Fire," 47.

28: John Martin's letters to Hayden, 5 August 1846, 28 March 1849, and 6 December 1849.

Notes for Chapter 4

The letters to Hayden that are found at WRHS (MS 3154) go up to April 1853, when he left Cleveland for St. Louis to take his first journey up the Missouri. It is not known how this valuable collection came to be saved or how it wound up at WRHS. Obviously, Hayden did not want to carry these letters around the West, nor did he want to dispose of them. So he gave them to a trusted friend for safekeeping, and later, after he had a permanent office, either forgot to retrieve them or found it difficult to do for some reason.

Who was this trusted friend? Certainly not Newberry, who later soured on Hayden (besides he was residing most of the time after 1866 in New York). Kirtland is a much better possibility, especially because of his close ties to Cleveland and because some of his own papers also came to WRHS. But would Hayden have wanted a respected mentor and a rather severe moralist to glance through this material, some of which is risqué?

A more likely candidate is one of his personal friends, probably one of the ladies. Hattie Brooks? Yes, on two counts. She and Hayden were still in each other's minds and apparently tried to reconcile around 1857–1858. Hayden might have given her his letters in 1853 as a signal of his affection and a tangible reminder of himself while he went off to explore the West. Once their reconciliation failed, it would have been awkward to ask Hattie to return the papers and equally difficult for her to know what to do with them. Probably she held on to them for a number of years until Hayden became a well-known figure, prompting her to dispose of them, though whether she acted out of vengeance or public interest we will never know. The second reason for believing he gave Hattie these papers is that her letters are notably absent from the collection, which suggests she disposed of them before handing the rest over to WRHS.

Fortunately, just as this valuable series of letters comes to an end, another begins. This more substantial group now resides in the National Archives in RG 57: Letters of the Hayden Survey; they date from 1853 to May 1879, when Hayden retired from Washington to Philadelphia. (Therefore, all Hayden's letters cited in this chapter are from MS 3154 at WRHS. Reference to letters from RG 57 begins in Chapter 6.) Most, but not all, of the letters in RG 57 have been photographed on Microcopy 623. They were preserved because they were regarded as official records of a government agency, though they span a longer time than Hayden was employed by the government (1867–1879). Between 1853 and 1867 there are a number of hints in his correspondence that Baird and Leidy were each at different times saving his papers for him. Once he gained a permanent office, he merged his accumulated papers with those of his survey. When his survey was abolished in 1879, these papers became the property of the newly formed U.S. Geological Survey, which held them in its library until some time after 1934 (the year the National Archives was organized), when, during a departmental cleanup, the papers were transferred.

Four other repositories have major collections of Hayden's letters written to Hall, Baird, Meek, Leidy, and Engelmann. Hall's papers are divided between the New York State Archives and the New York State Library, both in Albany. Baird's letters are mostly at the Smithsonian Institution in several collections, most importantly RU 7002 and RU 52; copies of his outgoing correspondence are in RU 53. Consult the *Guide to the Smithsonian Archives* (Washington: Smithsonian Press, 1983). Another vast body of Baird's letters resides in the National Archives; most of it concerns his work with the Fish Commission, but because he touched more than one base in many of his letters, some of this material is of a broader interest. Meek's papers at the Smithsonian are brought together in RU 7062. Leidy's are at ANSP in several collections. See the Academy's published guide for the many other valuable papers there. Engelmann's papers are gathered at the Missouri Botanical Gardens in St. Louis.

30: Hayden to Perry Ransom, 20 November 1852.

31–32: Robert Kennicott's comments about Hayden are from a letter of 17 February 1863 to his father; the letter is at the Grove National Historic Landmark, Glenview, IL.

32: Letter of Hank to Jim, no date, written in Cleveland.

33: Esther wrote Hayden on 9 December 1850.

The warning was from Richmond Winsor to Hayden, 8 March 1851.

George Hall sent his comments on the broken engagement on 16 May 1851 and 17 January 1852.

33–34: Hayden's reading list is on an undated sheet in his correspondence at WRHS.

Note 1, p. 34: Hayden had contracted to teach another term in a district school, this time in Cuyahoga Falls, north of Akron and only a short distance from Cleveland. He seems to have commuted back and forth for three or four months, beginning his studies in Cleveland while finishing up his teaching duties, but not settling in Cleveland until around March 1852. Thereafter, except for brief excursions growing out of his natural history studies, Hayden remained in Cleveland until the following spring, when he transferred briefly to Albany in preparation for going west.

34: Kirtland's lectures are summarized in the 1850 notes of a student, W. H. Mattchett (MS 1169 at WRHS).

On Kirtland and the first geological survey of Ohio, see Herbert Thoms, *The Doctors Jared of Connecticut: Jared Eliot, Jared Potter, Jared Kirtland* (Hamden, CT: Shoe String Press, 1958), especially pp. 59–60.

35: Kirtland's quote on science is from *Timeline* 2:2 [the magazine of the Ohio Historical Society], April-May (1985), 49.

35–36: Alphonso Wood to Hayden, 29 October 1852.

36: Dr. Sterling's comments about Hayden have a kernel of truth in them, but the parts I chose not to quote are based on the same hostility Newberry later demonstrated. Sterling's letter of 25 June 1888 to A. C. Peale is among the Marcus Benjamin Papers at SIA.

On Newberry, Herman Le Roy Fairchild, "A Memoir of Professor John Strong Newberry," *Proceedings of the Second Joint Meeting of the Scientific Alliance of New York,* 27 March 1893 (New York: L. S. Foster, 1893), pp. 7–23; J. J. Stevenson, "John Strong Newberry," *American Geologist* 12:1 (July 1893), 1–25; and Michael C. Hansen and Horace R. Collins, "A Brief History of the Ohio Geological Survey," *Ohio Journal of Science* 79:1 (January 1979), 3–14.

Note 2, p. 36: It is especially annoying to have to resort to such mawkish nonsense in the case of Newberry, who was a major scientific figure of the period; but no critical biography of the man exists. The problem is typical of virtually all biographical essays of the period: when it involved one colleague writing about another, critical assessment yielded to gentlemanly tact every time.

37: George Washington Hall to Hayden, 20 April 1852.

Letter from Maria, 28 November 1852.

Letter from Aunt Lucretia, 7 June 1852.

Letter from Hayden's father, 20 June 1852.

38: Stevenson's letter about James Hall was written 1 August 1906 to G. P. Merrill, and Merrill quoted it in his *The First One Hundred Years of American Geology,* pp. 694–695.

Hall's recollections of meeting Hayden were written in 1890 in a letter to Persifor Frazer, and were quoted in the *Philadelphia Public Ledger,* 10 March 1890. Both Hall and his biographer, John Clarke, remembered (inaccurately) Hayden coming to Albany in early 1852. Hayden's letters, however, tie him closely to Cleveland from December 1851 until early April 1853.

38–39: Hall to Hayden, 16 January 1853; the letter is incorrectly dated 1852.

39: Kirtland to Baird, 10 January 1853. For the location of Baird's papers, see the fifth paragraph of notes for Chapter 4.

Hayden to Baird, 16 February 1853.

40: David Dale Owen, *Report of a Geological Survey of Wisconsin, Iowa and Minnesota and Incidentally of a Portion of Nebraska Territory* (Philadelphia: Lippincott, 1852), p. 197.

Hall's papers are in Albany, divided between the New York State Archives and the New York State Library; both collections contain valuable letters. Engelmann's papers are at the Missouri Botanical Gardens in St. Louis. Leidy's are at ANSP.

41: Hall to Engelmann, 27 March, and to Baird, 31 March 1853.

Newberry to Hall, 27 March 1853.

Letter of Melinda Hayden, 10 March 1853.

42: Meek's papers are in RU 7062 at SIA.

Notes for Chapter 5

44: Prout's letter to Hall declining to lead the Bad Lands trip was dated 27 April, three days after Hall's to Hayden announcing that Meek would be in charge of their forthcoming trip. This suggests that Prout had sent an earlier letter, which has not survived, warning Hall that he would probably not be able to accept his offer.

Hayden to Hall, 16 May 1853.

46ff: All quotes regarding the voyage upstream between St. Louis and Fort Pierre are from Meek's letters to Hall. Merrill printed these in his *The First One Hundred Years of American Geology.*

Note 1, p. 48: Today scientists note the ratio of lead to uranium in certain rocks, and because the rate at which uranium disintegrates into lead is known, the ratio tells the actual age of the uranium-bearing rocks. The same can be told from the ratios of other radioactive elements in rocks. In Hayden's day, however, only a relative or comparative method of dating existed; it was based on comprehensive observations in the field and a knowledge of which fossils commonly existed in particular formations. Thus, the most Hayden could ever do was provide a correct sequence of deposition without having a clue about the absolute age of each formation.

49: The description of the quadroon and the other quotes that follow regarding their experiences in the Bad Lands come from Meek's diary, covering the period 20 June through 18 July.

50: Hayden, *The Great West* (1880), p. 43.

52: Meek to Leidy, 12 November 1856.

"Descriptions of New Species of Fossils, from the Cretaceous Formations of Nebraska," *Memoirs of the American Academy of Arts and Sciences,* New Series 5:2 (1854), 411.

Notes for Chapter 6

54: Hall to Engelmann, 12 December 1854.

55: Hayden to Baird, 8 January 1854.

Hayden to Meek, 27 March 1854.

Hayden to Hall, 16 May 1853.

56–57: Hayden to Baird, seriatim: 5 March, 19 April, 27 January, 8 January, 19 April, 10 April, and 5 March—all 1854.

58: Hayden to Baird, 8 February 1854.

Hayden to Baird, 26 April; and to Meek, 14 May 1854.

Hayden to Baird, 5 May 1854.

Vaughan served in several political capacities in Virginia before moving to St. Joseph, Missouri, where he gained a seat in the state legislature. He joined the Indian Bureau in 1842 and, after working at several agencies, became responsible in 1853 for all the Upper Missouri tribes.

59: Hayden to Baird, 2 July 1854.

Baird to Hayden, 9 May 1854. From here on, letters to Hayden are in RG 57 at the National Archives, which I discussed in the fourth paragraph of the notes to Chapter 4. Most of the letters from Baird are also in RU 53 (copies of Baird's outgoing letters, at SIA).

Note 1, p. 60: Several excerpts from Hayden's field journals, or diaries, found their way into his later publications regarding the years 1854–1855: see pp. 23–26 of his *Sun Pictures* (1870) for Hayden's remarks on the Indian hieroglyphics and the anecdote about Chief Blackbird (in the next paragraph of the text). What he called his "meteorological notes" (mostly comments on birds and plants) of 7 March to 1 June 1855 appear in "A Catalogue of the Collections . . . " (1858), 727–28. His diary of the third trip to the Bad Lands, 7 May to 6 June 1855, is in "A Brief Sketch of the Geological and Physical Features of the Region of the Upper Missouri . . . " (1856), 71–76. After pondering the likely migration of the original journals, then fruitlessly searching for them for several years, I have concluded that they were probably destroyed, most likely by his wife after his death. Given his acquisitive habits, I doubt Hayden would have destroyed any of his papers.

60–61: The anecdote about Hayden's nickname comes from E. D. Cope's obituary of Hayden in the February 1888 issue of *American Geologist.* Scott's remark is from his *Some Memories of a Palaeontologist* (1939), p. 57. McPhee's rendition appears in his "Annals of the Former World," *New Yorker,* 10 March 1986, 73. The original quote about Hayden's reputation for insanity among the Indians is from the *Daily Missouri Republican* of late January or early February 1856, a copy of which is in Meek's papers at the Smithsonian, accompanied by an approving letter of 6 February from Hayden. Walcott's remarks were made 7 January 1907 on the occasion of his receiving the Hayden Medal and are recorded in the archives of ANSP in Collection 547.

61: Vaughan to Baird, 4 July 1854.

62: Hayden to Baird, 2 July 1854.

Hayden's quote on the Yellowstone country in 1854 comes from Vaughan's official report of which Hayden claimed to have written the parts concerning natural history, amounting to four paragraphs. "Report of Agent Alfred J. Vaughan [1854]," No. 28, 33d Cong, 2d sess, 1854, Senate Exec Doc 1, 287–97.

63: Hayden to Meek, 6 October 1854.

Newberry's letter about carrying the Bible is in the G. P. Merrill Papers at SIA, RU 7177/8.

Hayden to Baird, 11 November 1854.

65: Hayden to Baird, 21 April 1855.

Hayden to Meek, 5 April 1855.

65–66: Hayden to Baird, 10 June [incorrectly dated 10 May] 1855.

66: Hayden to Engelmann, 5 April 1855.

Baird to Leidy, 14 February 1856.

67: Meek to Hayden, 4 February 1856.

Meek to Hayden, 25 February 1856.

68: Stevens to Baird, 22 October 1855.

69: Hayden to Baird, 30 January 1856.

70: Hayden to Meek, 25 and 30 January 1856.

Notes for Chapter 7

73: Warren's diary, which mentions the terms of Hayden's employment, is part of a large manuscript collection of G. K. Warren Papers in the New York State Library at Albany.

Warren to Baird, 24 May 1856, and Hayden to Baird, 21 April 1856.

Hayden to Meek, 18 June 1856.

74: Captain La Barge's remarks were noted during an interview with Hiram Martin Chittenden, who later recorded them in his *History of Early*

Steamboat Navigation on the Missouri River (New York: Francis P. Harper, 1903), I, pp. 208–10.

74: Hayden to Baird, 11 July 1856.

Hayden published these recollections about Bridger in his *Fifth Annual Report* (1872), p. 7.

75: The interview with Hayden was published in the *Republican* [*Daily Missouri Republican*] 16 December 1857.

The collections of 1856 are itemized in Hayden's letter to Meek of 6 October and in the Smithsonian's *Annual Report for 1856* (Washington: Cornelius Wendell, 1857), p. 50, which was published by the 34th Cong, 3d sess, 1856, House Misc Doc 55.

The contract for the Philadelphia Academy's purchase of Hayden's material is in MS Collection 567, dated 30 March 1857. This pertained only to Hayden's half of what he collected with Vaughan's financial backing in 1854–1855. The St. Louis Academy of Science, with a large assist from Charles Chouteau, purchased Vaughan's half. Incidentally, all the mollusks from Hayden's half of this collection went to the Smithsonian. The Smithsonian in turn, and possibly the Philadelphia Academy too, later gave away to other institutions duplicate sets of fossils and particular specimens.

76: Hayden to Baird, 11 February 1857.

Note 1, p. 76: Meek's masterpiece on the Paleozoic and Mesozoic invertebrates, *Palaeontology of the Upper Missouri* (*Smithsonian Contributions to Knowledge* 14:172) was followed by a similar review of the Cretaceous and Tertiary invertebrates of the West, completed only weeks before his death in 1876; it was published as Vol. 9 of the *Final Reports* of Hayden's Survey.

77: Hayden to Leidy, 4 March 1857.

Hayden to Baird, 22 May 1857—the first of two letters Hayden wrote Baird that day.

Hayden's quote on the buffalo, originally in his field notes, was reprinted in his *Sun Pictures* (1870), p. 40.

79: Hayden to Baird, 21 August 1857.

80: Hayden to Baird: 1 and 22 November 1857.

Hayden to Meek, 18 December 1857.

Leidy summarized Hayden's remarkable vertebrate finds of 1857 in letters to Hayden of 17 and 26 January 1858 and in a letter to Warren published in *Am Jour Sci,* 2d series, 25 (May 1858), 441–42. His comments on the wolf *(Canis haydeni)* appear at p. 30 of his authoritative *Extinct Mammalian Fauna of Dakota and Nebraska* (Philadelphia: J. B. Lippincott, 1869).

81: Baird to Hayden, 21 November 1857.

On the insects, see the Academy's *Proceedings* 10 (8 June 1858), iii.

Stimpson's house was at 539 17th at G Street; he described it as being next to the Winder's Building. Stimpson said it contained eleven rooms, was near the Smithsonian, and he paid $250 a year for it.

Note 2, p. 81: These megatheres began cohabiting and enjoying their social traditions well before they thought of a name for themselves. The earliest reference I have found to the name is in a letter of Stimpson to Hayden of 13 June 1857. There is also an early tie of the group to the Rugby boardinghouse, where Stimpson seems to have preferred living when no other close friends were in town.

82: Hayden to G. N. Allen, 7 March 1859.

Hayden to George Engelmann, 26 March 1859.

Note 3, p. 82: They left the Missouri at Leavenworth, traveled overland to Indianola (Topeka), then went up the Kansas River to Junction City. From there they ascended the Smoky Hill River to above Salina and then explored part of the Smoky Hills before walking south and east through the present counties of McPherson and Harvey. In the latter they found and followed the Santa Fe Railroad (because railroad beds often expose the surrounding strata) to the Cottonwood River, whose banks they explored for many miles. From Cottonwood Falls they headed north to Council Grove, then west to Lost Springs, and northwest back to the Smoky Hill River in the vicinity of Sand Spring. From here they descended the south bank to Lawrence, where they crossed the river and returned to Leavenworth.

Hayden's comments on grasshoppers are in Meek's journal for 1858, in which Hayden also wrote occasional entries. The journal is part of Meek's papers at SIA.

Stimpson to Hayden, 14 September 1858.

83: His salary with Raynolds and the equipment are listed in MS 393 of the Raynolds Papers, Vol. 3 (the account books) at Yale University's Beinecke Library.

Diary of Elias J. Marsh, 31 May 1859, Missouri Hist. Society.

Note 4, p. 83: Heading northwest from Fort Pierre, they joined the Cheyenne River in the vicinity of Hermaphrodite and Plum creeks, at both of which Hayden hunted fossils. From here they aimed for the north end of the Black Hills, moving along the hilltops dividing the drainages of Cheyenne and Cherry creeks, which enabled Hayden to study the upper reaches of the country whose riverbanks he had walked along in 1855. Continuing west, Hayden took another look at Butte Creek and Bear Butte before swinging slightly north to find the Little Missouri, which he explored southwest nearly to its head (in modern Wyoming), then he turned west to the Little Powder, which he descended beyond its junction with the Powder (in Montana) to a point perhaps 10 miles south of Mizpah. From there he moved west across Mizpah and Pumpkin creeks, across the Tongue River and Rosebud Creek to a point on the West Fork of Armell's Creek.

83: The Raynolds Papers at Yale, Vol. 1 (his field journal, 1859–1860), and his official report contain valuable details on this expedition. The report was published as "Report of Brevet Brigadier General W. F. Raynolds on the Exploration of the Yellowstone and Missouri Rivers in 1859–60," by the 40th Cong, 1st sess, 1867–1868, Senate Exec Doc 77, 1–174.

84: Hayden to Leidy, 16 October 1859.

Note 5, p. 85: The party had proceeded southeast from the Bighorn River to explore the several creeks between the Bighorn and the Little Bighorn, continued south along the eastern flank of the Big Horn Mountains, swung to the east once more to examine the divide between the Tongue and Powder rivers, then followed the Powder Valley itself for a while until turning south once again to the Platte River, where they established winter quarters. They arrived at Deer Creek by 16 October. Along the way Hayden succeeded in instigating three side trips, none violating a Sunday however.

85: Hayden to Baird, 13 October and 24 November 1859.

Hayden to Meek, 22 February 1860.

Hayden to Baird, 21 March 1860.

Hayden to Meek, 1 December 1859.

Note 6, p. 86: Heading west from Deer Creek, they crossed Rattlesnake Hills, turned north to the base of the Big Horn Mountains, then came down Badwater Creek to the Wind River. As he had done before, Raynolds directed his lieutenants to explore adjacent territories and to rendezvous periodically, but Hayden stayed with Raynolds.

86–87: Raynolds to Humphreys, 4 October 1860; a copy of the letter is among the Raynolds Papers at Yale.

Notes for Chapter 8

94: Hayden to Hall, 11 October 1856.

Hayden to Meek, 16 April 1857.

Hayden to Meek, 27 April 1857.

95: Hayden to Meek, 21 April 1857.

Hayden to Meek, 1 June 1857.

On Swallow, see an article in *American Geologist* 24:1 (July 1899), 1–6; G. C. Broadhead and others, *Dedication of Swallow Memorial Monument, June 5, 1928, 4 p.m., Columbia Cemetery, and Facts Concerning the Life of George Clinton Swallow, M.D., L.L.D.* (Columbia, MO: Boone County Historical Society, 1928).

96–97: Hawn to Meek, 22 February 1858.

97: Swallow to Meek, 20 March 1858.

The secretary of the Albany Institute recorded his acknowledgment of Swallow's earlier article in *Transactions* (1858) 4:248.

98: Details on the Permian controversy will be found in my article, "The Permian Controversy of 1858: An Affair of the Heart," *Proc Am Phil Soc* 133:3 (1989), 370–90.

100: This first draft of the plant catalog survives at the Missouri Botanical Gardens among Engelmann's papers.

Hayden to Engelmann, 18 March 1862.

101: Stimpson to Hayden, 13 June 1857.

Notes for Chapter 9

105: The anecdotes on Leidy come from Chapter 4 of a manuscript biography ("Joseph Leidy") by David H. Wenrich at ANSP.

107: In identifying sixteen of their joint publications as the "major" ones, I am omitting several short announcements penned to gain publicity for their views in the Permian controversy. These shorter pieces are reviewed in my article, "The Permian Controversy of 1858."

Meek drew a number, probably most, of the illustrations of Hayden's fossils, but he farmed out some of this work to other illustrators. Hayden drew none of them, though he arranged the financing for the illustrators.

Note 1, p. 108: My remarks on who contributed what are based on a careful reading of the jointly authored articles as well as the articles Hayden wrote alone; a review of their private correspondence; an awareness (based on other letters in Hayden's correspondence) of where Hayden was and for how long; and a knowledge of which of them had the greatest interest in particular topics. For example, Meek obviously wrote most of the fossil descriptions, and Hayden just as certainly added the facts that he alone knew from his experience in the field.

Let me amplify a bit on the particular role of Hayden in his partnership with Meek. For instance, the four-page introduction to their article of June 1856 (see the Bibliography for the full titles of articles) was "based upon the observations and collections of Dr. Hayden" (p. 115). Hayden probably wrote that introduction, too, while working with Meek in Albany for three weeks during spring 1856. His essay traced the extent of the Great Lignite Formation, with notes on previous explorers who had encountered it.

Of the other four articles of 1856 (two in March, one each in April and November), the first three are Meek's fossil descriptions; the geological notes and vertical section in the fourth, though put into final form by Meek, were based on notes and specimens Hayden sent him from the field. Meek did the part on parallelism of the Cretaceous and the connecting narrative pulling the whole essay together as well as the catalog at the end.

In May 1857 Hayden continued the historical account of those who had previously studied the strata of the Upper Missouri. He discussed the question of parallelism between the Great Lignite and the beds of the White River, both Tertiary, but decided that they were not equivalent; the former was older. Meek compared the Cretaceous of the Upper Missouri with similar formations elsewhere in the states. Significantly, they were able to work together for seven weeks during winter 1857, which explains the large contribution each of them made to this, their most important article up to that time.

Of their two articles of March 1858, Meek wrote all of the one appearing in the *Transactions of the Albany Institute.* In the one for the *Proceedings* Meek did most of the fossil descriptions, of course, but their correspondence suggests Hayden may have helped with the descriptions during January 1858 when they worked together in Washington. The seven-page "remarks" on geology came directly from Hayden's field notes of 1857, though regarding his rough draft of the vertical section on the Black Hills, Hayden urged Meek to "alter it somewhat and make it a little nicer."

Aside from the fossil descriptions in December 1858, the narrative introduction to this article and the whole of the succeeding essay (January 1859 in the *Journal*) contain elements that either author could have written. In light of the typical interests of each man and considering the style of each article, I find reasons for saying they collaborated on both of these essays, each writing different parts. Both pieces grew out of their trip to Kansas in the late summer and autumn of 1858, and upon returning to Washington they continued to live and work together.

January 1859 (in the *Proceedings*) also resulted from the Kansas trip and is mostly the work of Hayden, though Meek probably wrote the part on synonymy of fossils and, of course, most of the fossil descriptions.

January 1860, May 1860 (fossil descriptions), and October 1860 (a catalog of fossils) are entirely the work of Meek, done, incidentally, while Hayden was in the field with Raynolds, but based on Hayden's earlier collections and notes while with Warren.

December 1861 seems to have been another cooperative venture, again because they had plenty of time to work together, this time in Washington. Hayden provided the geological commentary and the revised vertical section; Meek described the fossils and undoubtedly wrote the comparative sections regarding the Cretaceous, which he had started in November 1856 and continued in May 1857. Meek also suggested the names for the five divisions of the Cretaceous.

February 1862 is mostly the work of Meek (descriptions of Cretaceous fossils from Lieutenant John Mullan's expedition of 1858–1860). Hayden had nothing to do with gathering this collection, but he did arrange with Mullan to have the fossils delivered to Meek for description and he may have written the preliminary comments, though I suspect Meek did because of the brief remarks on the Judith River beds, which conflict with what Hayden had written on the same not long before.

Note 2, p. 109: Since 191 was the total number of all mollusks ever found on the Upper Missouri up to November 1856, it is another testament to Hayden's skill as a collector that he was the first to find nearly two-thirds of them. After his second year with Warren (1857), Hayden could boast of having found 80 percent of the new shells brought back from the West.

110: The *Proceedings* of the Philadelphia Academy did publish three other miscellaneous pieces by Hayden, but these were summaries of informal speeches made at the Academy, not a basis for articles.

111: The quote is from "Some Remarks in Regard to the Period of Elevation . . . ," May 1862, p. 306.

112: The quote locating the eruptive rocks is from March 1861, p. 233.

Note 3, p. 113: On Hayden's laccoliths: June 1858, pp. 140–41. The man usually credited with identifying laccoliths for the first time, William Henry Holmes, did so in Colorado during the 1870s, while working for Hayden. Is this a coincidence or was Holmes inspired to look carefully at these strange structures only after learning Hayden's insights about them?

113: May 1862, p. 312. Hayden returned to this concept with examples from the Gallatin River in Montana. See his *Sixth Annual Report* (1873), p. 85, and the Survey's *Bulletin* 2 (1876), No. 3, p. 200.

Notes for Chapter 10

116: The quotes are from pp. 68, 70 of "A Brief Sketch" (1856).

117: The table of lists is in "A Catalogue" (1858), p. 675.

Hayden wrote the introduction for Leidy's *The Extinct Mammalian Fauna of Dakota and Nebraska* (Philadelphia: J. B. Lippincott, 1869).

119: *Roadside Geology* is published for several states by the Mountain Press Publishing Company of Missoula, Montana.

Note 1, p. 120: He made the following changes as a result of his two years with Raynolds: he expanded his lists, contributed some new thoughts on the Quaternary, tacked on a few more vertical sections of the Great Lignite, summarized his recent expedition in a Resume (which borrows heavily from his article of March 1861), argued more forcefully for the Triassic, and attached a new edition of his geologic map.

120: *Geology and Natural History* (1862) made a few other points that had not appeared in his earlier publications or were revisions of earlier findings. For example, Hayden had previously supposed the existence of the New Red Sandstone, or Triassic beds, in the West, and at p. 123 he made a better argument for their existence than any he had made before. However, he had earlier thought he might have found the Old Red Sandstone, or Devonian beds, but he did not repeat that claim here. The disproportionate amount of space devoted to the Permian was to solidify his and Meek's recent claim to its discovery and to explain their latest thoughts on it.

Note 2, p. 121: On the natural history essay: Philip M. Hicks, *The Development of the Natural History Essay in American Literature* (Philadelphia: Univ. of Pennsylvania, 1924); Hans Huth, *Nature and the American: Three Centuries of Changing Attitudes* (Berkeley: Univ. of California, 1957); Paul Brooks, *Speaking for Nature* (Boston: Houghton Mifflin, 1980). Such books sometimes mention Powell or King in their surveys, but never Hayden.

122–23: On Hayden's grasp of theological literature: "I did not meet Hayden until 1866, when for a week or two I saw a good deal of him in Philadelphia. He had then become distinguished, of course. One thing I noted, that he knew a good deal more about current literature and a good deal more about current theology than I did, who had had nothing else to take off my attention from them. I dare say I knew more of German religious literature than he, but certainly much less of American." (Charles C. Starbuck, of Andover Theological Seminary, to A. A. Wright, 21 February 1888.)

Note 3, p. 123: Hayden caused confusion by talking about a "Judith River Basin," but also the "Judith River Bad Lands," and apparently used these terms interchangeably to refer to the various outcrops near the mouth of the Judith. Though he later lumped all these rocks together into his "Judith River Group," a close reading of his articles shows that despite his loose terminology, his real intent was always to focus on the problematic "fresh water and estuary beds at the mouth of the Judith," which occurred at the top of his "group."

124: "Descriptions of New Species of Acephala and Gasteropoda . . ." (1856), p. 114.

"Notes Explanatory of a Map and Section . . ." (1857), p. 116.

126: "Explanations of a Second Edition of a Geological Map . . ." (1858), p. 139.

Note 4, p. 127: Hayden could also sing the praises of paleontology as an exact measure of a fossil's age—as he did in his *Preliminary Report of the Field Work of the U.S. Geological and Geographical Survey of the Territories for the Season of 1877.* Unclassified Publication, No. 13 (Washington: GPO, 1877), pp. xxvi–xxvii. In that same report he was able to show that C. A. White had just found paleontological evidence supporting his own view that the Great Lignite was equivalent to the Fort Union and Laramie formations.

127: Meek to Hayden, 12 April 1860.

Note 5, p. 128: Cooper's letter to Baird is quoted in Eugene Coan, *James Graham Cooper,* p. 96. It may be more than coincidence that the man who did bring out a revised edition of Lewis and Clark's journals was Elliott Coues (it appeared in 1893, not long after Hayden's death). Coues was a versatile naturalist who became involved in the work of Hayden's survey during the 1870s, and he later had a special responsibility for publishing some of the survey's unfinished work after the USGS was formed in 1879. He knew Hayden well and had ample opportunity to hear him mention his unfulfilled dreams. He may have borrowed from Hayden the idea about a new edition of Lewis and Clark, just as W. H. Holmes borrowed Hayden's pioneering interest in what became known as laccoliths.

Notes for Chapter 11

130: His research on the Cheyenne proved of value to later scholars. See Karen Daniels Peterson, "On Hayden's List of Cheyenne Military Societies," *American Anthropologist* 67:2 (April 1965), 469–72.

132: The quotations come from p. 380 of Hewitt's introduction and p. xxxvi of Ewers's edition of *Five Indian Tribes of the Upper Missouri* (Norman: Univ. of Oklahoma Press, 1961). In a note on p. 63 Ewers said that the beginning of the Assiniboine chapter in Denig's manuscript was missing, and he supposed that the beginning of Hayden's chapter on the same might supply what was needed. Indeed Hayden's pp. 379, 381–82 come directly from Denig's other longer work on the Assiniboine, which Hewitt edited as *Indian Tribes of the Upper Missouri,* pp. 395–97. Denig prepared that manuscript in reply to queries sent by H. R. Schoolcraft, who was preparing a report on Indians for Congress (published 1851–1857). I assume Hayden had access to it through Schoolcraft, from whom he also borrowed some books on Indians. On the probable theft of the Hidatsa (Hayden called them Minitari) and Mandan sections, see Ewers, "Literate Fur Trader: E. T. Denig," *Montana* 4:2 (Spring 1954), 1–12.

133: Hayden, *Contributions* (1862), p. 234.

133–34: For biographical information on Culbertson and Denig, and for the background on Denig's two manuscripts, I have used Ewers's works, cited above. Denig's will is reproduced in Chris Vickers's article, "Denig of Fort Union," *North Dakota History* 15:2 (April 1948), 134–43.

136: The letter of Hayden to Leidy is dated only May 1862, though another hand has penciled in "about May 10–15" on it.

137: Hayden's letter to Longfellow is in the Houghton Library at Harvard University. Longfellow sent a polite thank you for the book, but no comments.

138: That Dr. Miner did the Winnebago work for Hayden is clear from a letter of H. H. Brown to Baird, of 5 September 1867, in Collection RU 26 of Baird's papers at the Smithsonian.

Hayden's quote is from p. 444 of the *Contributions* (1862).

Some lesser known Indian photographs Hayden acquired are at the National Anthropological Archives (a branch of the Smithsonian Institution), as a part of Photo Lot 37, especially Catalogue 261,080. For other un-cataloged Indian photographs in the same archive, also gathered through Hayden's efforts, look for the photographs of William Henry Jackson or for "Hayden Survey Photographs." Hayden's claim on the extent of his Indian photographs is in a draft letter he wrote on 25 June 1877 to Secretary of the Interior Schurz, and it is found in Microcopy 623, Roll 21.

Notes for Chapter 12

140: Letter of 28 December 1860 to William Barton Rogers (Rogers Papers, Massachusetts Institute of Technology Archives).

141: Letter of 4 January 1861 to George Engelmann.

Letter of 15 April 1861 to Meek.

Letter of 5 May 1861 to Frederic Ward Putnam (Putnam Papers, Harvard University Archives).

Letter from Newberry of 15 April 1861.

Meek to Hayden, 18 April 1861.

Hayden to Meek, 24 May 1861.

Sheldon M. Novick, *Honorable Justice: The Life of Oliver Wendell Holmes* (Boston: Little, Brown & Co., 1989).

142: Hayden to James Abram Garfield, 4 October 1880 (Garfield Papers, Library of Congress).

Hayden to Henry Augustus Ward, 7 November 1861 (Ward Papers, Rochester University).

Hayden to Mrs. Martin Brewer Anderson, 21 March 1862 (M. B. Anderson Papers, Rochester University).

Hayden to Lewis Henry Morgan, 28 August 1862 (Morgan Papers, Rochester University).

142–43: Ronald L. Numbers, ed., *The Education of American Physicians* (Berkeley: Univ. of California, 1980), and Richard T. Beebe, *Albany Medical College and Albany Hospital: A History, 1839–1982* (Albany: New Art Printing, 1983).

143: Hayden told Baird about his connection with *Hospital Record* in his letter of 9 February 1863.

143–44: Hayden to Baird, 17 March 1863.

144: Hayden to Baird, 23 August 1863.

145: Hayden to Baird, 13 June 1863.

146ff: On Hammond: Bonnie Ellen Blustein, *Preserve Your Love for Science: Life of William A. Hammond, American Neurologist* (New York: Cambridge: Univ. Press, 1991). On the medical disputes, see Alex Zeidenfelt, "The Embattled Surgeon, General William A. Hammond," *Civil War Times Illustrated* 17:6 (1978), 24–32; Gert H. Breiger, "Therapeutic Conflicts and the American Medical Profession in the 1860s," *Studies in Visual Communication* 8:1 (Winter 1982), 98–109; Edward M. Brown, "Neurology and Spiritualism in the 1870s," *Bulletin of the History of Medicine* 57:4 (1983), 563–77.

147: Hayden to Leidy, 11 November 1863.

Hayden to Baird, 20 November 1863.

148: Material on the Potomac Side Naturalists' Club is in RU 7210 at the Smithsonian Archives.

Notes for Chapter 13

150: Letter to Frederic Ward Putnam, 19 June 1865, in the Putnam Papers of the Harvard University Archives.

Letter to Leidy, 18 August 1865.

151: The background to the auxiliary professorships comes from David H. Wenrich's unpublished biography of Leidy, Chapter 19, which is held by the library of ANSP.

Lesley's letter (25 September 1865) to George B. Wood, one of Penn's trustees, is in the George P. Merrill Collection at the Library of Congress, Box 2.

152: Letters to Leidy of 30 September and 31 October 1865.

Hayden to Baird, 6 April 1866.

Hayden to Martin Brewer Anderson, 3 July 1866 (University of Rochester Archives).

Hayden to Leidy, 14 February 1868.

Note 1, p. 152: After Hayden's western surveys were rolling again, he contributed some of his own samples to the permanent cabinet of the university. Thoughtfully, he suggested combining all such objects into a "Wood Museum of Practical Geology, Mineralogy and Paleontology," to be named for George Bacon Wood, a distinguished physician, professor of medicine at Penn, and one of the university's trustees. Boldly, Hayden asked that Wood contribute $10,000 toward the proposed museum. Wood's reply is not recorded, though he was a generous benefactor of the university who eventually donated the money and specimens for a botanical garden.

Note 2, p. 153: Starting in a southwesterly direction they came to the Niobrara River, which they ascended to the Rapid River (today known as Minnechaduza Creek), then followed it north until it evaporated in the hills separating the Niobrara from the White River. They traveled west along the crest of this divide and explored several drainages new to Hayden that emptied into the White River south of the Bad Lands. Eventually reaching his old collecting sites at Bear and Sage creeks, he worked several days there before returning eastward along the hills north of the Bad River. The party gathered more specimens while descending the west side of the Missouri between Fort Pierre and Fort Randall.

153: Baird to Hayden, 12 January 1867.

On the Yale purchase see 3 January 1867 to Hayden from Dana, and 13 May from Marsh. On the Boston purchase, see S. H. Scudder to Hayden of 4 March.

154: Hayden to Baird, 10 March 1867.

155: Wilson to Hayden, 29 April 1867, for his instructions.

Hayden to Wilson, 24 September, on the photographer. Hayden's letters to Wilson are in the National Archives, RG 49, series E. The same series contains copies of Wilson's letters to Hayden, most of which are also found in Hayden's own papers in RG 57.

156: Wilson to Hayden, 10 May 1867, for the probable uses Hayden made of the photographer and for the quote.

On Hayden suggesting what his instructions should be, compare his letter to Wilson of 9 July 1868, with Wilson's to him of 28 July.

Wilson's letter to Hayden of 28 July 1868.

158: Once Hayden begins reporting directly to the secretary of the interior, his letters to the secretary are found in RG 48, Miscellaneous and Patents Division, Geological Survey, Miscellaneous Letters Received. A few letters from Hayden are also in RG 48, Lands and Railroad Division, Miscellaneous Letters Received. Both collections are in the National Archives.

158ff: The background on Blackmore comes from Herbert O. Brayer, *William Blackmore: A Case Study in the Economic Development of the West,* 2 vols. Vol. 1: *The Spanish-Mexican Land Grants of New Mexico and Colorado, 1863–1878* (Denver: Bradford-Robinson, 1949). For Hayden's involvement with him, see especially pp. 48–49, 54, 73–74, 80–81, 91–93, 99–100, 147, 185, 201–02, 271, and, in Vol. 2, p. 186, note 46; and letters from Blackmore to Hayden, 1869–1878, in Hayden's letters at the National Archives.

160: Gardner's report was published in Colorado Springs by the Out

West Printing & Publishing Company, 1875. A copy of the report is among Gardner's papers at the New York State Library in Albany.

160: The story of Blackmore's involvement with the D & RG is told in Brayer's Vol. 2: *Early Financing of the Denver & Rio Grande Railway and Ancillary Land Companies, 1871–1878.*

Endlich to Hayden, 31 August 1875.

161: Stimpson to Meek, 21 March 1867.

Meek to Dana, 16 March 1867. The letter is in the Marsh Papers at Yale University. Other letters of Dana's have been preserved in the Dana Family Papers, Yale University, Collection 164.

Note 3, p. 161: Nebraskans were bullish on coal largely because of George Swallow's comments on Kansas coal in his *Preliminary Report of the Geological Survey of Kansas* (Lawrence: John Speer, 1866), pp. 55–57.

Hayden to Meek, 15 May 1867.

Hayden's articles in the *Journal* appeared in January, March, and May 1868 (2d series, Vol. 45, pp. 101–02, 198–208, 326–30).

Hayden to Meek, 2 November 1867.

White to Meek, 6 April 1868.

162: Newberry to Hayden, 10 March 1868 on the lignites of New Mexico; on 19 January 1871 Newberry communicated similar conclusions regarding the Green River plants Hayden found in Wyoming, Colorado, and Utah.

163: Newberry to Hall, in G. P. Merrill's collection at the Library of Congress.

Newberry to Powell, 11 January 1876, on Microcopy 156, Roll 4 (Powell's papers at the National Archives).

Lesquereux to Hayden, 15 January 1875.

164: Dana to Hayden, 13 January 1870.

Dana to Cox, 7 February 1870 (in RG 48 at the National Archives, Miscellaneous and Patents Division, Geological Survey, Miscellaneous Letters Received).

See pp. 754–56 of C. H. Hitchcock and W. P. Blake, "Geological Map of the United States [and Territories], Prepared for the 9th Census [1870]," published as Vol. 3 of the Ninth Census: *The Statistics of the Wealth and Industry of the United States* (Washington: GPO, 1872).

Whitney to Hayden, 19 April 1868.

165: George Washington Hall to Hayden, 14 November 1870.

Notes for Chapter 14

Note 1, p. 168: Incidentally, Hayden did not pack his survey with congressional favorites, as his enemies liked to claim. All the western surveys accommodated the friends and relatives of influential politicos, and Hayden received more requests than others to do so, because his survey enjoyed greater popularity. He did take along a few such individuals, usually in the capacity of unpaid "general assistant," which meant honored guest without specific duties. It was an inevitable consequence of working in a political system that tied government jobs to patronage. But for every honored guest Hayden considered, he turned down scores. The picture of the survey as riddled with political appointments is false.

169: Jackson's diary for 28 June 1869, which is in the custody of the New York Public Library.

Note 2, p. 170: Beginning in 1871 Hayden was too busy with administrative aspects of his surveys to write much of interest about fieldwork in his letters, with a few exceptions. In compensation, his reports become fuller, though they lack the kind of shrewd, offhand comments he formerly confided to his letters.

171: *First Annual Report,* p. 32. My page references to the *First, Second, and Third Annual Reports* are from the combined edition Hayden had reprinted in 1873.

On local newspaper reactions to Hayden, see Robert N. Manley's article, "Wealth Beneath the Prairie: The Search for Coal in Nebraska," *Nebraska History* 47:2 (June 1966), 157–76.

Hayden to Henry Hartshorne, 10 October (Haverford College Library).

172: Henry's locked book is in RU 7001, Box 39 at the Smithsonian; the entry quoted is from 15 December 1868.

173: *Second Annual Report,* p. 94.

Note 3, p. 174: Hayden pushed hard to submit a summary of each summer's work as soon after returning from the field as possible, but he was not always successful at squeezing in everything. Sometimes part of what he accomplished in one season was only mentioned in the report for a succeeding summer. For example, after his first trip across Wyoming in 1868 he wrote Part One of "Notes on the Geology of Wyoming and Colorado Territories," which he published in the October issue of *Proc Am Phil Soc.* He reproduced the entire article in his *Second Annual Report,* with only minimal changes, which also appeared in autumn 1868. He discussed the balance of his 1868 season in Part Two of "Notes on the Geology of Wyoming and Colorado Territories," which came out in the *Proceedings* of February 1869. Subsequently, large chunks of Part Two reappeared in his *Fourth Annual Report,* where he reviewed the work of several seasons in Wyoming.

174: *Third Annual Report,* p. 106.

175: *Fourth Annual Report,* p. 4.

176: *Fourth Annual Report,* p. 6.

176–77: *Fourth Annual Report,* p. 135.

178: *Fourth Annual Report,* pp. 6, 7.

Note 4, p. 179: James Cassidy tells me, from looking at the Faculty Minutes at Penn, that Hayden attended few faculty meetings and that he exasperated his colleagues by rushing to finish his lectures in order to get out West. This is a source I had overlooked, but I am pleased to discover that it reveals just the kind of man I have sketched.

179: Hayden's letter to Leidy of 9 August 1868 on the professorship he wanted.

Note 5, p. 179: Hayden certainly wanted the marriage earlier, for he wrote to Representative John Logan on 21 September 1870 (letter in the Logan Papers at the Library of Congress) that he expected to be married in December and he wanted Logan at the wedding. I have no explanation for the unusually long engagement. Hayden's marriage certificate is in the Philadelphia City Hall Annex. It shows his age as forty and Emma's as twenty-one, but both bride and groom lied about their ages. For Hayden's correct age, review my discussion in Chapter 2. For Emma, records of the Woodlands Cemetery in Philadelphia show her age as ninety at her death in 1934, which means she was twenty-seven in 1871, not twenty-one.

Notes for Chapter 15

181–82: Thomas's remarks are in Hayden's combined edition of his *First, Second and Third Annual Reports* (1873), pp. 236–38.

182: See pp. 14–15 of *First, Second and Third Annual Reports* for Hayden's initial comments about rainfall in his first annual report.

On the desert idea, see Ralph G. Morris, "The Notion of a Great American Desert East of the Rockies," *Mississippi Valley Historical Review* 13:2 (September 1926), 190–200. The contemporary difficulty in categorizing the climate of the plains is nicely captured in the fact that Josiah Gregg's book was cited by both those who saw a desert there as well as those who thought settlement was increasing rainfall. A review of how the climate of the plains has been interpreted is John L. Allen's, "The Garden-Desert Continuum: Competing Views of the Great Plains in the Nineteenth Century," *Great Plains Quarterly* 5:4 (Fall 1985), 207–20; Allen points out that people's opinions varied with their economic interests in the West and their proximity to it.

For background to the theory about increasing rain, I have used Charles R. Kutzleb's doctoral dissertation (Univ. of Colorado, 1968), "Rain Follows the Plow: The History of an Idea." While interesting and valuable for other reasons, Henry Nash Smith's article, "Rain Follows the Plow: The

Notion of Increased Rainfall for the Great Plains, 1844–1880," *Huntington Library Quarterly* 10:2 (February 1947), 169–93, unjustly criticizes the theory as "false" on the basis of information only obtained long after 1880. Smith chose to overlook the fact that rainfall *was* increasing into the 1880s, according to the various techniques then available for measuring it. Not until well after the 1880s did more reliable meteorological records demonstrate that the apparently greater rainfall accompanying postwar settlement of the Great Plains was a coincidence resulting from cyclical weather patterns. Smith repeated these distortions in his widely read book, *Virgin Land* (Cambridge: Harvard Univ. Press, 1950), pp. 180–81, and Smith was not the only writer who judged the issue with the benefit of hindsight. David Lavender did the same in his very popular *The Great West* (New York: American Heritage Publishing Co., 1965), p. 350. Many lesser writers have borrowed the same theme without looking at the contemporary facts. The result has been the portrayal of Hayden as an uncritical booster of Western development, which, as the balance of this book shows, is simply not justified.

182: Thomas's second reference to the theory appears in Hayden's *Sixth Annual Report,* p. 310; after showing that western farmers still trusted in increased rainfall, Thomas himself calls the theory "very doubtful." H. N. Smith must have missed this quote (which is at the bottom of the page in a note by Thomas), enabling him to confuse what Thomas himself believed at that point with what Thomas found (through his questionnaires) farmers still believed. Hayden's other references to the theory appear in his *Sun Pictures* (1870), p. 35, and again in his *Fourth Annual Report* (1871), pp. 103–04.

183: Elliott's remarks are in *Fourth Annual Report,* pp. 455–56, and *Fifth Annual Report,* p. 279.

183–84: Aughey's quote is from pp. 264–65 of Hayden's report.

184–85: *Contributions to the Fossil Flora of the Western Territories. Part Two: The Tertiary Flora* (1878), p. v.

185ff: For summaries on the Laramie, see Willis T. Lee and F. H. Knowlton, "Geology and Paleontology of the Raton Mesa and Other Regions in Colorado and New Mexico," USGS Professional Paper 101 (Washington: GPO, 1917); F. H. Knowlton, "The Laramie Flora of the Denver Basin, With a Review of the Laramie Problem," USGS Professional Paper 130 (1922); and G. P. Merrill, *The First One Hundred Years of American Geology* (1924), Chapter 11.

186: Newberry to Meek, 20 July 1874.

On the Cretaceous lignites Hayden found in 1868, see his article of 19 February 1869 in Proc Am Phil Soc, p. 48.

Hayden's quotes are from his *Fourth Annual Report* (1871), pp. 94, 165.

187: Preface to Lesquereux's *Contributions to the Fossil Flora of the Western Territories, Part Two* (1878), p. v, which was Vol. 7 of Hayden's *Final Reports.*

Meek's views on the Judith appear in Vol. 9 of Hayden's *Final Reports,* which was *A Report on the Invertebrate Cretaceous and Tertiary Fossils of the Upper Missouri Country* (1876), p. xlvii.

For Peale's and White's numerous contributions to the whole issue, see Hayden's *Annual Reports,* mentioned before, and their articles in the *Bulletin.*

189: *Fourth Annual Report,* p. 165.

Bulletin, 1st series, no. 2 (9 April 1874), p. 1.

190: On the development of the lakes theory, I have summarized Joseph T. Gregory, "Tertiary Freshwater Lakes of Western America—An Ephemeral Theory," *Journal of the West* 8:2 (April 1969), 247–62.

190–91: March 1868, p. 205.

191–92: "Remarks in Regard to the Geology of the Missouri Valley," a paper given before the American Philosophical Society in December 1866; it was summarized at p. 295, of the *Proceedings.*

192: Summary of article printed in the *Proceedings* of February 1867; quote on pp. 319–20.

Monographs of North American Rodentia (1877) by Elliott Coues and Joel Asaph Allen, Vol. 11 of Hayden's *Final Reports,* p. iv.

192–93: The quote is from my article, "Ferdinand Vandeveer Hayden as Naturalist," *American Zoologist* 26 (1986), 347.

193: All Hayden's publications are listed in the Bibliography. I abbreviate the references to each by their date of publication. The five mentioned first in the text are: January 1867 ("Sketch"), February 1867, May 1870, May 1869, and October 1867. The three on coal are January, March, and May 1868. The professional arguments: March and July 1867. The "Brief Notes" appeared in April 1868; the quote is from pp. 389–90.

194: The *Final Report of Nebraska* was not published until 1872, though Hayden had mostly finished it by spring 1868. His private correspondence shows he continued to revise it even after submitting it for Commissioner Wilson's approval in March 1868. Wilson acknowledged receiving it in April 1869, which was probably the time of Hayden's last revisions. When Congress finally authorized publication, in March 1871, Hayden was preparing for his summer's fieldwork, so he asked Meek to go over the whole volume one last time for errors. The book appeared as the first volume in the Hayden Survey series known as *Unclassified Publications.*

194–95: Hayden's remarks are in Elliott Coues's *Birds of the Colorado Valley,* Vol. 11 of Hayden's *Miscellaneous Publications* (Washington: GPO, 1878), p. vi.

Bulletin III:1 (5 April 1877), p. iv.

195: *Eighth Annual Report* (1876), p. 17.

195–96: Hayden to Thomas Durant, 1 September 1868 (Union Pacific Railroad Correspondence, University of Iowa, Iowa City).

196: On Russell: Susan Danly Walther, "The Landscape Photographs of Alexander Gardner and Andrew Joseph Russell," Brown University, Doctoral Dissertation, 1983.

    Sun Pictures (1870), p. 18.

197: *Sun Pictures,* p. 39.

Harper's of September 1869 carried some woodcuts based on O'Sullivan's photographs, but the earliest published photographs I have found were prepared for the Vienna World's Fair of 1873.

Note 1, p. 198: In his "A History of the Popularization of Geology in America: A Bibliographical Survey," *Jour Wash Acad Sciences* 49:7 (July 1959), 224–227, Mark W. Pangborn, Jr., does not even mention Hayden. It is another measure of how little Hayden's impact on social history has been appreciated.

Notes for Chapter 16

202: Doane's report is reprinted in Orrin H. Bonney and Lorraine Bonney, *Battle Drums and Geysers* (Chicago: Swallow Press, 1970).

    In a letter to General William T. Sherman of 28 August 1871 Hayden refers to the meeting of the Washington Philosophical Society (without mentioning a date), where Baird read Doane's report; the letter is on Reel 17 of the Sherman Papers, Library of Congress. The Philosophical Society of Washington was founded 7 February 1871, and Hayden was a charter member.

202–03: Hayden to J. P. Lesley, 13 February (American Philosophical Society, Lesley Papers).

203: The four authorities are: (1) Aubrey L. Haines, *The Yellowstone Story: A History of Our First National Park* (Boulder: Colorado Associated Univ. Press, 1977), pp. 138, 140; (2) anonymous pamphlet written by researchers at the USGS, *Ferdinand Vandiveer Hayden and the Founding of Yellowstone National Park* (Washington: GPO, 1980), p. 8; (3) Hiram Martin Chittenden, *The Yellowstone National Park,* ed. Richard A. Bartlett (Norman: Univ. of Oklahoma Press, 1964), p. 75; (4) Wallace Stegner, *Beyond the Hundredth Meridian: John Wesley Powell and the Second Opening of the West* (1st ed 1954). Bison Book Edition, Univ. of Nebraska Press, 1982, p. 178.

    Nettleton wrote Hayden about Moran on 7 and 16 June 1871.

204: Jackson's article, "With Moran in the Yellowstone," appeared in *Appalachia* 21:82 (December 1936), 151; his autobiography is *Time Exposure* (New York: G. P. Putnam's Sons, 1940), p. 196.

207: "Around Montana," *Helena Daily Herald,* 10 July 1871.

208: Hayden's *Sixth Annual Report* (1873), p. 43.
Sixth Annual Report, p. 85.

209: *Fifth Annual Report* (1872), pp. 144, 146.
Fifth Annual Report, pp. 8–9.

210: Hayden to Allen, 13 April 1871 (Allen Papers, Oberlin College).
Hayden to Meek, 9 April 1871.

211: Hayden to Baird, 14 September 1872.

Notes for Chapter 17

Note 1, p. 214: The contrasting style of their reports suggests that Hayden and Clarence King viewed nature quite differently. From the start King adopted a specific and more limited block of territory, and he published nothing significant until he had finished studying the block. His final reports were systematic historical studies of rocks, from oldest to youngest. Perhaps King's topical emphasis and the fact that he chose a limited region to study grew out of his belief that nature is susceptible to rational understanding, whereas Hayden's descriptive studies relied on a more intuitive approach. I suspect that Hayden was less confident about understanding nature through systematic rational inquiry and that he felt his impressionistic glimpses might describe its reality more accurately.

Hayden was capable of writing systematic, historical studies of rocks: that is what he did before the Civil War, in reporting on the strata of the Upper Missouri. And he recognized the value of comprehensive analysis, for he several times alluded to a final report he would write eventually, summarizing the geology of all the regions he had seen. Furthermore, he encouraged his collaborators to codify their own final reports. But he never wrote his own overview of western geology. Certainly his detractors would argue that he lacked the intellectual power to forge such a synthesis. However, he never finished his intended plan of exploration—a survey of all the western territories—on which his synthesis would depend. From early in his explorations, he realized that no single overview could adequately comprehend the West's diversities and that the West could only be portrayed through a series of impressions.

214–15: The quotes on hot springs and geysers appear respectively at pp. 66, 69, and 70.

215–16: The quotes on basalt are from pp. 75, 76, and 79.

217: In addition to Jackson, two other photographers accompanied the party; we know of them from a letter written by Henry Elliott to Baird on 16 July: "Our photographers are in fine trim. There are only three of them:

Jackson, Hines, and a man from Virginia City." Thomas J. Hines (also Hine or Hyne) was not officially with Hayden because the army hired him as part of the corps of engineers' party led by Captain John W. Barlow, but it is clear he was welcome to tag along with both parties; his specific route in Yellowstone and how much time he spent with each party are not known. Most of his pictures were lost in the Chicago fire of 1871. The "man from Virginia City" seems to have been J. Crissman of Bozeman, according to Jackson's recollections. Apparently Crissman never circulated his pictures outside Montana, though Marlene Merrill tells me some are now in the National Archives.

Note 2, p. 217: It seems that officials of the Northern Pacific Railroad had in mind to hire Bierstadt as well as Moran to accompany Hayden in 1871, to judge from a letter sent by A. B. Nettleton to Hayden on 7 June and another from Hayden to Baird of 22 June.

217: In his catalog of pictures taken during 1871, Jackson only listed about 130 images, but there is no knowing how many duplicate prints Hayden may have had Jackson prepare, considering their use in lobbying the Yellowstone Bill and for the survey's own promotional uses. The number 300 is conservative, and I use it because when Hayden agreed to supply Barlow with a set of images to replace his lost in the Chicago fire of 1871 the number he agreed to send was 200, but Barlow made his selection from a total of 126 large views and 144 stereopticons (Barlow to Hayden, 13 and 17 January 1872). I am assuming Hayden did not send samples of all his available pictures, only enough to show a diverse selection.

218: Regarding the geological section, Hayden says at p. 72, "In figure 21 I have attempted to present an ideal section of the strata on Gardiner's [Gardner] River." This is not quite an assertion of authorship because he could have been trying to present the section through the hand of Henry Elliott, which I suspect was his meaning. To my knowledge, none of Hayden's field sketches survives except for a crude map now in Albany, done for Warren. In my opinion, none of the illustrations printed in Hayden's many reports can be attributed to him.

Note 3, p. 219: It is an open question whether Hayden himself or "his men" were mostly responsible for this kind of imaging. Jackson and Moran (along with others) were making the actual images, but my sense is that Hayden gave a lot of general guidelines for the pictures he wanted, though he left his artists free to find the specific examples. I have found no letters of instruction regarding images (probably instructions would have been verbal), but Jackson, for example, was well aware that his pictures would be used for scientific as well as aesthetic purposes as he acknowledged in his original contract with Hayden: ". . . I hereby agree to furnish the

Government or the said F. V. Hayden, all the prints, transparencies, etc. that may be required, or the use of the negatives in any way that shall promote the interests of the expedition or advance its scientific results . . ." (1 August 1870 letter to Hayden). No doubt Hayden suggested from time to time the views that would best illustrate particular principles of geology and geography, and probably also scenery, because that was of great interest to Hayden.

220: Merriam's diary, 14 August 1872 (Merriam Papers, Bancroft Library, Berkeley).

Note 4, p. 221: At least one scholar doubts Jackson's photographs had a direct impact on passing the Yellowstone Park Act: Howard Bossen, "A Tall Tale Retold: The Influence of the Photographs of William Henry Jackson on the Passage of the Yellowstone Park Act of 1872," *Studies in Visual Communication* 8:1 (Winter 1982), 98–109. One of the questions in this issue is whether in addition to the numerous separate prints he developed, Jackson ever prepared bound volumes of selected prints to give to various congressmen. In his book on Jackson *(William Henry Jackson and the Transformation of the American Landscape),* Peter Hales denies Jackson ever prepared such volumes (p. 109). There are contemporary references to such volumes, but until recently none had been found. I found one volume of this kind at the University of Wyoming (Hebard Folio/F722/Y47/1872). The volume is bound in red leather and has gold lettering on the spine: "Yellowstone Views." There is no title page, dating, or any internal information about its preparation. It was not considered a publication of the Hayden survey because it is not listed in any of Hayden's catalogs of his publications. The catalog information prepared by the University of Wyoming is incorrect on two counts: from the size of the pictures (8" by 10") and from a comparison of each picture to Jackson's published catalogs, it is clear that all the pictures were taken in 1871, not 1872 as implied by the reference number. Also the catalog states there are 52 pictures; in fact there are 75, in two irregularly numbered series. The volume came to the library from Jesse V. Howell, a geologist who collected Hayden material for years. To judge by a penciled note in the front endpapers, "P. Decker NY May 1957, $67.50," I infer that Howell bought the volume in 1957 from a dealer in New York named Decker. I believe that no similar volumes have been found because Hayden had only a few prepared: I would guess less than ten, and the rest no doubt remain in private hands or have been lost. Strictly speaking, they were not used for lobbying (Hayden used the 300 separate prints for that), but rather as presentation copies or thank-yous for such key players as Representatives Dawes and Dunnell, and Senators Pomeroy and Lyman Trumbull.

222: Richard A. Bartlett, *Nature's Yellowstone* (Albuquerque: Univ. New Mexico Press, 1974), chapter 9; Aubrey L. Haines, *Yellowstone National Park:*

Its Exploration and Establishment (Washington: Dept. Interior [National Park Service], 1974), Part 3.

222: Hayden's letter to Schurz is found at the National Archives, RG 48, Microcopy 62, Roll 6. Hayden repeated his claim in identical language in the introduction to his *Twelfth Annual Report, Part 2* (1883), p. xvii, which he wrote on 1 February 1883.

Haines, *Yellowstone National Park,* note 50 on p. 183, is the authority for saying the House Committee on the Public Lands adopted Hayden's synopsis of his draft report. The report itself appears in 42d Cong, 2d sess, 1872, as Report 26.

Note 5, p. 223: Langford's claim, written over thirty years after the events described, appears in *The Discovery of Yellowstone Park, 1870* (St. Paul, MN: J. E. Haynes, 2d ed., 1923 [1st ed., 1905]), pp. 36, 38. There is no evidence Langford thought of a national park as early as he claimed. For instance, his own notes for the lectures he delivered over winter 1870–1871 (at the Yellowstone Park Library) make no mention of a national park idea. Neither the *New York Times* nor the *New York Tribune,* both of which summarized his New York lecture, reported anything about setting aside the region as a park. Neither did the *Evening Star* in Washington, which covered his lecture in that city. H. M. Chittenden in *The Yellowstone National Park,* ed. Richard A. Bartlett (Norman: Univ. of Oklahoma Press, 1964), p. 81, goes so far as to quote Langford's lecture, as supposedly recorded in the *New York Tribune* of 23 January 1871, as saying ". . . this new field of wonders should be at once withdrawn from occupancy, and set apart as a public National Park. . . ." However, careful inspection of the original newspaper shows no such language ("The Wonders of Montana," p. 5, cols. 5–6.) It seems Chittenden relied on language his friend claimed to have uttered and no doubt wrote out for Chittenden *after* the fact. It is more difficult to understand how William Turrentine Jackson fell under Langford's spell, but in two scholarly articles he also claimed Langford's lectures ended with an appeal for a national park. I suspect Jackson relied on what he read in Chittenden, for in checking his citations I find no references to the park idea, even after allowing for mistakes Jackson made in naming the newspapers: it was the *Helena Daily Herald,* for example, that mentioned Langford's lecture in its edition of 19 November, not the *Helena Herald* for the 18th, and it was the *Evening Star,* not the *Washington Star.* Jackson, "Government Exploration of the Upper Yellowstone," *Pacific Historical Review* 11:2 (June 1942), 188; and "The Creation of Yellowstone National Park," *Mississippi Valley Historical Review* 29:2 (September 1942), p. 191.

Note 6, p. 223: I doubt that Hayden himself ever conceived of a national park; he had never shown any interest in this sort of idea. Activity was his forte, and his hands were full with his survey. Of course, he would have recognized immediately the publicity advantages of riding the coattails of such an idea. But it was irrelevant to Hayden whether or not the region became a national park; he knew he and his survey would prosper from association with it in either case. I believe it was Jay Cooke (or someone close to him) who imagined the park idea. In that case Cooke could have called on Hayden to take action when the moment seemed right. Thus on 27 October 1871 Nettleton suggested that Hayden introduce the idea into his formal report on Yellowstone. From Cooke's viewpoint Hayden was the logical frontman to lobby on behalf of the idea because he was so well known in Congress. He could also become the scapegoat should the scheme go awry. Hayden proved a willing accomplice to this plan. His correspondence with R. W. Gilder (editor of *Scribner's*) shows that he finished writing during November 1871 the article (not published until February 1872) in which he made a strong plea for the park idea. In January 1872 he plugged the park idea again in what he wrote out for the Senate and House committees on the public lands.

Notes for Chapter 18

226: Hayden to Garfield, 28 July 1872 (Garfield Papers, Library of Congress).

Garfield to Hayden, 4 April 1872; Hayden's appropriation passed with the Sundry Civil Bill of 10 June 1872.

Hayden to Leidy, 20 September 1872.

Hayden to Meek, 14 September 1872.

Hayden to James Monroe, 14 October 1871 and 21 May 1872 (Monroe Papers, Oberlin College).

Garfield's *Diary of a Trip to Montana in 1872,* ed. Oliver W. Holmes, *Sources of Northwest History,* no. 21, general editor, Paul C. Phillips (Missoula: Montana State Univ. Press, 1934); on Garfield Peak, see p. 6.

227: Several general assistants wrote books about the West. Sidford Hamp wrote the most, though his stories went well beyond his experiences with the survey. Capturing some of their adventures (which they obviously embellished) while working under Hayden are Alonzo Merritt Welles, *Reminiscent Ramblings* (Denver: W. F. Robinson Co., 1905) and Sid H. Nealy, *In the Trail of the Pack Mule* (New York: F. T. Nealy, 1902).

228: See Haines, *Yellowstone National Park,* pp. 203–06, for a list of some of the newspaper articles on Yellowstone. Elliott wrote: "The Hayden Geological Survey," *Omaha Daily Herald* (28 September 1871); "The New Wonderland," *Cincinnati Daily Gazette* (18 October 1871); "Great Soda Mountain and Jupiter's Baths, in the Yellowstone Region," and "The New Wonderland," both for *Frank Leslie's Illustrated Newspaper* (31 September 1871 and 6 January 1872). Adams's lecture was extensively covered in the *Daily Evening Telegraph (Philadelphia)* of 3 April 1874. His articles in the *Philadelphia Inquirer* appeared on 14 June, 25 July, 8, 15, and 26 September, 24 October 1871, then 1 and 26 July, 2 and 19 September, 15 and 28 October, and 25 November 1872. A draft of Taggart's article, "Wonders of the Yellowstone," dated 31 January 1873, appears among his papers in the Fryxell Collection, University of Wyoming; a copy of the MS version is in Box 20, and a typed version is in Box 38. I have not found that it was published anywhere. Peale's articles for *Philadelphia Press* appeared on 15 and 29 June, 14 and 29 July, 11 and 29 August, 19 and 25 October 1871; then 10 and 30 July, 13 September, 11 and 12 October 1872; and for the *Illustrated Christian Weekly* on 3 August and 30 November 1872, and 3 May 1873. Peale continued to publish in both places after the survey moved to Colorado.

229: Oliver B. Bunce, "Our Great National Park: The Valley of the Yellowstone," *Picturesque America,* vol. 1, ed. William C. Bryant (New York: Appleton, 1872), pp. 292–316. The article in the *World* appeared on 3 March 1873.

"A Gigantic 'Pleasuring Ground': The Yellowstone National Park of the United States," *Nature* (12 and 26 September 1872). *Weekly Montanian* [Virginia City], 12 December 1872. August H. Petermann, "Die neu entdeckten Geyser-Gebiete am oberen Yellowstone und Madison River," *Petermann's Geographische Mittheilungen* 18 (Gotha: Justus Perthes, 1872), pp. 241–53, 321–26. "Esplorazioni del dottore F. V. Hayden nella regione delle Montagne Rocciose," *Cosmos* 2 (Torino, Guido Cora, 1874), pp. 312–16. "Le Parc National des Etats-Unis," *Le Tour du Monde* 28, Nos. 722–725 (Paris: Librairie Hachette, 1874), pp. 289–352.

Blackmore quoted in Herbert O. Brayer, ed., "Exploring the Yellowstone with Hayden, 1872. The Diary of Sidford Hamp," *Annals of Wyoming* 14:4 (October 1942), 261.

230: *Am Jour Sci,* 3d series, 4 (October 1872), 313–16. *Eng & Min Jour* 14 (12 November 1872), 312.

Bonnie Skell Hardwick, "Science and Art: The Travel Writings of the Great Surveys of the American West After the Civil War," University of Pennsylvania Doctoral Dissertation, 1977, pp. xxii–li. By my count, Hayden's survey collected 182 notices, Powell's 65, Wheeler's 42, and King's 37.

"Wonders of the Rocky Mountains. The Yellowstone Park, How to Reach it," pp. 277–92 of *The Pacific Tourist,* ed. Henry T. Williams (New York: Henry Williams, 1876). Two other editions of this popular guide appeared within the next ten years.

231: Boston: L. Prang and Co., 1876.

I have found no letters from Hayden to Prang, but over eighty from Prang to Hayden during a period of two years tell the story of the book.

232–33: *The Grotto Geyser* appeared as Vol. 7 in the survey's *Unclassified Publications.*

233: *Report on the Proposed Yellowstone National Park* gives every indication of being published by the Government Printing Office as an official publication of Hayden's survey. However, it is not listed in L. F. Schmeckebier's authoritative *Catalogue and Index of the Publications of the Hayden, King, Powell, and Wheeler Surveys* (Washington: GPO, 1904). The only copy I have found is at the USGS Library in Reston, Virginia; it is possible Schmeckebier missed this work, which he undoubtedly would have listed among the Hayden survey's *Unclassified Publications.*

Johnson's New Universal Cyclopaedia, 3:717 and 4:1526–30 (New York: Alvin J. Johnson & Son, 1877, 1878).

233–34: Among the papers of A. C. Peale at the Smithsonian Archives (RU 7208) is a manuscript biography of Hayden (never published), which includes a partial list of his society memberships.

234: Josiah Curtis to Hayden, 26 February 1874. Curtis was writing to complain he had never received his set of pictures.

Note 1, p. 234: A long-standing dispute has focused on whether Langford and Stevenson actually reached the true summit of "the Grand" or only the stone enclosure somewhat beneath it. Doubts of their claim centered on the fact that in Hayden's mention of the climb in his *Sixth Annual Report,* p. 2, and in Langford's article on the subject (*Scribner's Monthly* 6:2 [June 1873], 129–57) the area of the stone enclosure is confused with the true summit. However, William M. Bueler, a historian and mountaineer, has made a convincing case for their ascent based on a study of Langford's field diary, which describes the real summit as accurately as any mountaineer could have under the circumstances (*The Teton Controversy: Who First Climbed the Grand?* [Terrace Heights, Winona, MN: St. Mary's Press, 1981]).

Note 2, p. 234: Hayden twice said he named the island for Stevenson: in a letter to Baird (8 August 1871), then at p. 5 of his *Fifth Annual Report* (1872). But Marlene Merrill mentioned to me that an entry in Peale's diary for 29 July claims Henry Elliott named the island. It is a small point, but it illustrates the great difficulty in knowing for certain who named what.

234: Hayden, in his *Fifth Annual Report,* p. 8.

235: Holmes made the claim in his "Random Records," Vol. 4.

237: Leidy to Hayden, 2 September 1872.

Hilgard to James Hall, 3 April 1873 (New York State Library, Hall Papers).

238: See Doane's quotation in Orrin H. Bonney and Lorraine Bonney, *Battle Drums and Geysers* (Chicago: Swallow Press, 1970), p. 245.

Notes for Chapter 19

240: Hayden's letter to Delano is at the National Archives, RG 48, Miscellaneous and Patents Division Geological Survey, Miscellaneous Letters Received; part of it was quoted in the *New York Times,* 5 February 1873.

241: On Hayden's relations with Blackmore, see Chapter 13; and Hayden's letter of 15 February 1873 to Congressman Nathaniel P. Banks (Banks Papers, Library of Congress). Blackmore no longer depended exclusively on Hayden for help. A letter he wrote his agent on 11 August 1877 shows he was trying to get maps from any of the surveys that might have information on the extent of his grant (letter quoted in Brayer, *William Blackmore* I:307).

Dana to Hayden, 8 February 1873.

242: *Seventh Annual Report* (1874), p. 2.

Gardner's numerous letters to members of his family have never been brought together in one place. Some reside at the New York State Library in Albany (Gardner Papers), some remain in the hands of his descendants. Extracts from several of his Colorado letters, including the one to his mother of 10 September 1873, have been printed by Roger W. Toll in the *Colorado Magazine* 6:4 (July 1929), 146–56.

243: Anna E. Dickinson wrote an important early impression of the West in *A Ragged Register* (New York: Harper & Brothers, 1879); pages 268–71 describe her climb of Longs Peak on 13 September 1873 with Hayden and Gardner.

King's letter of 15 February 1873 is in the Gardner Papers at the New York State Library.

244: Gardner to his mother, 10 September 1873 (quoted in the *Colorado Magazine* collection).

244: Gardner to Baird, 21 September 1873 (Smithsonian Archives, RU 52, volume 4: 259).

Jackson, *Time Exposure,* p. 190.

245: *Eighth Annual Report* (1876), p. 48.

Eighth Annual Report, p. 55.

246: Hayden to Archibald Geikie, 25 October 1875 (Geikie Papers, Edinburgh University Library).

246–47: Hayden's letter to Zachariah Chandler, 1 October 1875, is reprinted in the *Eighth Annual Report,* pp. 16–17.

247: On expenses of the survey, see Hayden's letter of April 1878 to

Secretary Schurz, printed in 45th Cong, 2d sess, 1878, House Exec Doc 81, 19–20.

Note 1, p. 248: After Gardner left Hayden's survey in 1875, it was the job of Allen Wilson to finish up the *Atlas.* I found Wilson to be one of the most interesting but neglected men who made their mark in western exploration. See my article, "Mapping Mountains: A. D. Wilson, Nineteenth-Century Colorado Cartographer," *Colorado Heritage* no. 4, (1988), 22–33.

248: Holmes to A. C. Peale, 11 May 1875 (letter in Box 34 of the Howell Collection at the University of Wyoming).

248–49: *Ninth Annual Report* (1877), p. 26.

249: Ramsay quoted in the *Am Nat* 12:11 (November 1878), 767.

Note 2, p. 249: On the number of Jackson's pictures, see Hayden's article, "The Progress of the U.S. Geological Survey," *Republic* (April 1877), 225. A year earlier in his *Ninth Annual Report,* pp. 21–22, he said the survey had accumulated over 2,000 photographs, and though he doesn't specifically say so, this undoubtedly meant only landscapes.

Jackson, *Time Exposure* (1940), p. 236. Though it was common by 1940 to epitomize all the cliff dwellings of the Four Corners area as "Mesa Verde," Jackson himself never saw the specific ruins at Mesa Verde.

250: Ingersoll's best material appeared in *Scribner's Monthly* (see especially April, May, and June 1880). He also published in *Cosmopolitan,* the *New York Herald,* and the *New York Tribune.* After his years with Hayden, he wrote two popular books about his years in the West.

Peale's quote is from the *Illustrated Christian Weekly,* 12 August 1876.

See Hardwick, "Science and Art," for the newspaper coverage.

Note 3, p. 250: Rhoda's report is one of the classics in the literature of western exploration and it had long been out of print; I prepared an edited version of it for modern readers: *Summits to Reach: Report on the Topography of the San Juan Country, by Franklin Rhoda* (Boulder, CO: Pruett Publishing Co., 1984).

250: Hayden's quotes appeared in the *Rocky Mountain News,* 21 and 13 September 1875, 10 August 1875.

251: J. D. Whitney's article was in the *North American Review* 121:248 (July 1875), 37–85; 121:249 (October 1875), 270–314.

Geikie's articles: 5 August and 4 November 1875. Geikie wrote a number of other reviews on particular aspects of the American surveys and was consistently a strong supporter of Hayden.

252: Two of the circulars he prepared appear on Microcopy 623, Roll 21 (Hayden's incoming letters at the National Archives), for 1872. The ad was in *Am Nat* 7:3 (March 1873), 127.

This letter to Hall of 4 February 1874 is one of several that did not wind up in Hall's Papers in Albany (perhaps it was later removed from that source). At any rate it is at the University of Wyoming, Box 47 of the Fry-xell Collection.

Baird's correspondence at the Smithsonian records the details of ship-ping publications abroad for exchanges; a sense of how much of this baggage came from Hayden's publications is in RU 28 and RU 33.

Baird to Hayden, 19 May and 4 June 1880 (SIA, RU 33).

Powell to Baird, 27 April 1881 (RU 28, No. 15334).

253: Baird to Hayden, 18 May 1882 (RU 33).

Hayden to Gardner, 6 February 1873 (Joseph Bradley Murray Papers, Yale University).

254: Hayden to Congressman James Monroe, 18 July 1873 (Monroe Papers, Oberlin College).

The Diary of James A. Garfield, 4 vols., ed. Harry James Brown and F. D. Williams (East Lansing: Michigan State Univ. Press, 1967–1981), 2:141; entry for 19 January 1873.

Merriam outlined his plan for a scientific board in a draft act, which he never submitted to the House; it is among the papers of his son, Clinton Hart Merriam, at the Bancroft Library. Hayden's letter to Gardner of 2 Feb-ruary 1873 suggests Hayden was instrumental in persuading Merriam to abandon this scheme.

254ff: The Townsend committee report, "Geographical and Geological Surveys West of the Mississippi," was printed in 43rd Cong, 1st sess, 1874 (Serial Set 1626), House Report 612.

255: Hayden's remarks are in the Townsend Report, pp. 8, 39, 9.

256: Hayden to W. D. Whitney, 30 May 1874 (Whitney Papers, Yale University).

257: J. D. Whitney to W. D. Whitney, 13 May 1874.

W. D. Whitney's articles about the Hayden survey appeared in the *Rocky Mountain News* (24 and 31 August and 7 September 1873), and the *New York Tribune* (Extra no. 14, Scientific Series, 30 December 1873).

Notes for Chapter 20

258: On the Academy, see A. Hunter Dupree, "The Founding of the Na-tional Academy of Sciences, A Reinterpretation," *Proc Am Phil Soc* 101: 5 (1957), 434–40.

258–59: Leidy to Hayden, 28 April and 7 June 1863; both letters are printed in *Science in Nineteenth Century America: A Documentary History,* ed. Nathan Reingold (New York: Hill and Wang, 1964), pp. 209, 212.

259: Hall to J. E. Hilgard, 19 February 1873 (Hall Papers, New York Library). The quotation is from a messy draft letter penned by Hall, who was in the habit of keeping handwritten copies of the letters he sent; it is not certain how much of what he said in the draft wound up in the final version mailed to Hilgard.

The five who nominated Hayden were Hall, Newberry, J. E. Hilgard, Dana, and Meek (Minutes of the Academy, 18 April 1873, p. 400).

W. D. Whitney to Hayden, 6 November 1873.

259–60: I found only one case of Hayden consulting at this time: he seems to have taken $500 for writing up a report on a private property in Colorado for a Scottish owner, but he did so only after being approached by the owner's banker.

260: Their house in Philadelphia, at 1708 Vine Street, actually belonged to Emma's family. The Haydens did not have their own house in that city until September 1879, when they moved from Washington and resettled at 1910 Arch Street.

Engelmann to Charles Christopher Parry, summer 1873; letter quoted in Andrew Denny Rodgers, *American Botany, 1873–1892, Decades of Transition* (Princeton: Princeton Univ. Press, 1944), p. 52.

Note 1, p. 260: Hayden's name has been given to forty-five topographic features in six states, including three towns, one mountain, five peaks, a number of creeks, gulches, lakes, passes, and even a cemetery. The most famous, of course, is Hayden Valley in Yellowstone National Park (USGS Topographic Division, *Colorado Geographic Names: Alphabetical Finding List* [Reston, VA, 1981]; and similar lists for Idaho, Montana, Nevada, Utah, and Wyoming). Four of the twenty features named Hayden in Colorado are not for F. V. Hayden (Louisa W. Arps and Elinor E. Kingery, *High Country Names: Rocky Mountain National Park* [Estes Park: Rocky Mountain Nature Association, 1977], p. 98). There are also at least three geological formations: the Hayden Group in Wyoming and South Dakota; the Hayden Gulch Sandstone Member, and the Hayden Peak Latite in Colorado. A. C. Peale compiled a list (completed by 1891) of forty-five species or genera, mostly fossils, that colleagues named for him. The list is in Peale's manuscript, "Biographical Sketch of F. V. Hayden, M.D., with Bibliography," pp. 41–48, which is in RU 7208 at the Smithsonian Archives.

261: Raymond's article: "The National Surveys," *Galaxy* 21 (January 1876), 40. Even before Whitney's two-part article of 1875, Edwin L. Godkin had been focusing on the rivalry over the national surveys in the *Nation,* of which he was editor. Articles appeared there on the subject irregularly between 1874 and 1879, written by such authors as W. D. Whitney, Charles Raymond, W. H. Brewer, Simon Newcomb, and Godkin himself.

Hayden to Geikie, 4 January 1876.

262: Gardner's article appeared in the *Am Jour Sci,* 3d series, 6 (October 1873), 297–300.

Gardner to his mother, 28 October 1875 (Gardner Papers, Albany).

263: Hayden to Baird, 19 May 1873.

Letter to Secretary of the Interior Delano, 1 July 1874, printed in the survey's *Seventh Annual Report,* p. 13.

265: Hayden to Leidy, 12 May 1874.

Note 2, p. 266: A colleague Hayden did not abandon was Archibald Geikie, to whom Hayden wrote some of his most candid letters and with whom he stayed in touch long after Geikie could do him any practical good. Geikie epitomized the unqualified praise Hayden received from Great Britain and Europe in general; thus their correspondence was a constant tonic to Hayden. Being a foreigner, whom Hayden met only once during their twelve-year acquaintance, Geikie was one of the few unthreatening men Hayden ever encountered to whom he felt safe in opening his heart, at least as much as he opened it to anyone.

267: Hayden to Meek, 9 June 1873, in which he also says, "We cannot afford to lose you. Let your health be of the first importance."

268: White to Meek, 17 July 1875. The other letter on the subject was 6 June 1875.

Note 3, p. 268: White left Powell's survey to join Hayden's during summer 1876, ostensibly because Powell could not afford to pay him. There may have been more to it than that because the "disappointed member" of Powell's survey Hayden mentions in the epigraph introducing this chapter was probably White.

269: *The Diary of James A. Garfield,* 4 vols., ed. Harry James Brown and F. D. Williams (East Lansing: Michigan State Univ. Press, 1967–1981), 4:158–59, 181–82. Vols. 2 and 3 give examples of the building friendship of Garfield and Powell from 1874.

269: Newberry to Powell, 4 and 15 March 1875, 11 January 1876 (Microcopy 156, Rolls 3 and 4: Letters of the Powell Survey at the National Archives).

On the growing alliance of King and Powell, see the letters of King and Marsh to Powell, March and April 1876.

On Marsh's election to the Century Club, Newberry to Marsh, 2 March 1876 (Marsh Papers, Yale University).

Hayden to Meek, 29 January and 10 July 1876.

Notes for Chapter 21

270: "Obituary Notice of Ferdinand Vandevere Hayden, M.D., Ph.D., LL.D.," *Proc Am Phil Soc* 25:127 (January-June 1888), 59–61.

273: Hayden's article of April 1877 in the *Republic,* pp. 225–26.

274: Hayden claimed 2,050 copies of the *Bulletin* were printed per issue, of which 500 went abroad and 200 were reserved for authors. Authors were not normally paid for their contributions, though this generous circulation gave them intangible rewards for their efforts. Hayden to J. L. LeConte, 22 January 1878 (Collection 913, ANSP).

Note 1, p. 274: To the monographs in the *Final Reports* should be added three other studies that Hayden found it convenient to publish in his annual reports: Joel Allen's "History of the American Bison" (in the *Ninth Annual Report*), Packard's study of phyllopod crustaceans *(Twelfth Annual Report, Part One),* and A. C. Peale's massive study of thermal springs *(Twelfth Annual Report, Part Two).*

275: "Professor Leidy's 'Fresh Water Rhizopods of North America,'" *Science* 1 (31 July 1880), 54–57.

Hayden to Logan, 6 March 1876 (Box 2 of the Merrill Collection at the Library of Congress).

276: Riley to Hayden, 13 October 1876; Thomas to Hayden, 12 October 1876.

See the Introduction to Jenks Cameron, *The Bureau of Biological Survey: Its History, Activities, and Organization* (Baltimore: Johns Hopkins Univ. Press, 1929), which was prepared by the Brookings Institute as *Service Monograph of the U.S. Government, No. 54.*

Note 2, p. 277: George Peabody endowed museums at both Yale and Harvard and other institutions in Salem and Baltimore, as well as an educational fund for Danvers, Massachusetts, and another one for the southern states—not to mention his philanthropy in England.

278–79: On Hayden's role in the "bone rivalry," see his letters to Baird, 13 November 1868, and to Leidy, 11 September and 13 October, 12 and 13 November 1870. Even after Leidy withdrew from the collecting competition with Marsh and Cope in summer 1872 he continued to have the first option to describe Hayden's vertebrates.

279: For insight into Cope, see Cope to Baird, 20 November 1873 (SIA, RU 52), Vol. 2, p. 411; and Hayden to Leidy, 26 April 1873.

279–80: Hayden to Marsh, 20 April 1874 (Marsh Papers, Yale University).

280: Marsh to Hayden, "April" 1874.

Hayden to Hall, 21 December 1858.

281: The Academy's *Proceedings* mention Hayden's paper: Vol. 1, p. 103.

Notes for Chapter 22

283: Hayden's obituary in the *Am Nat* appeared in Vol. 21, no. 12, pp. 1134–35, and was written by the journal's coeditor, E. D. Cope.

285: Newberry to Hewitt, and to Garfield, 20 January 1877 (Stegner Papers, American Philosophical Society). Powell thanked Newberry on 25 January for sending him copies of the two letters.

Newberry to Garfield, 11 February 1878 (Garfield Papers, Library of Congress).

285–86: The letters concerning Newton's survey were all written during March and are found on Microcopy 156, Roll 6 (records of Powell's survey at the National Archives). On the setting, see G. P. Merrill, *The First One Hundred Years of American Geology,* pp. 482–83, and Wallace Stegner, *Beyond the Hundredth Meridian,* pp. 206–07. Powell's political motives in this whole matter are also apparent from the people he enlisted to write Schurz, urging publication of Newton's report: among them were the editors of the *Engineering and Mining Journal* and the *Army and Navy Journal,* neither of whom had any particular knowledge of the Black Hills; they were recruited because of their previous criticisms of Hayden's survey.

286: Hayden to Scudder, 21 May 1877 (Scudder Papers, Boston Museum of Science).

Hayden to Monroe, 21 May 1877 (Monroe Papers, Oberlin College).

Monroe to Hayden, 23 May 1877, suggesting he also ask Cox to help.

286ff: Hayden's and Powell's letters to Secretary Schurz are found in the National Archives, RG 48, Miscellaneous and Patents Division Geological Survey, Miscellaneous Letters Received. Schurz's letters are in the same record group and are also found among Powell's papers (Microcopy 156) and Hayden's (Microcopy 623).

287: Henry to Powell, 10 October 1876 (Microcopy 156, Roll 4).

288: The drafts of Hayden's 15 November letter to Schurz appear in Microcopy 623, Roll 21; they are much stronger and more argumentative than the letter he finally sent.

289–90: Townsend hearings, 43rd Cong, 1st sess, 1874, House Report 612, p. 10.

290: Patterson's speech of 11 February 1879 is in *Congressional Record,* 45th Cong, 3d sess, 1879, Appendix, 215: 217–21.

Hayden to Geikie, 17 February 1876 (Geikie Papers, Edinburgh University).

290ff: This assessment of Powell's strategy is based on a reading of his letters in Microcopy 156, Roll 7. The letter he wrote to Elias Loomis in February 1878 is probably the single best example of what I am talking about.

293: Powell to King, 23 January 1877 (Stegner Papers, American Philosophical Society).

Hayden memo, April 1878 (Microcopy 623, Roll 21).

Powell's remarks on cooperating with King are in his letter to Schurz of 27 April 1878 (45th Cong, 2d sess, 1878, House Exec Doc 80, p. 13).

Simon Newcomb to Alexander Agassiz, 17 May 1878 (Agassiz Papers, Museum of Comparative Zoology, Harvard University).

Hayden's and Powell's responses to Atkins's resolution were given to Schurz and appear in, respectively, 45th Cong, 2d sess, House Exec Doc 81 (Hayden) and 80 (Powell). Hayden's reply was dated only "April, 1878" though Schurz submitted it to the House on 18 April; Powell's was dated 27 April and was submitted on the 29th.

294: Hewitt's clause was part of H.R. 5130, 45th Cong, 2d sess., 1878.

On Hewitt's debt to Powell, see Stegner, *Beyond the Hundredth Meridian,* chapter 3, especially p. 233.

Note 1, p. 294: The 1874 plan for mapping the territories is found in the National Archives, RG 48, Miscellaneous and Patents Division, Geological Survey, under date 1 July. A printed version appears as part of House Exec Doc 80, p. 2 (cited above).

295: Powell's copy of the letter to Marsh is in his Letterpress Vol. 2, pp. 769–70, in the National Archives. Marsh's copy, the one Powell sent in June, is among Marsh's papers at Yale.

296: Stegner, *Beyond the Hundredth Meridian,* p. 235. Pilling wrote Powell on 5 December, a month after the Academy accepted Marsh's committee report on the surveys.

296ff: The workings of Marsh's committee are revealed in his correspondence, especially in letters from Newcomb of 25 and 30 September, 5, 18, 23 October, and 1 November; also W. B. Rogers to Marsh of 17 October and 1 November; and Marsh to Rogers of 12 October (all 1878): a copy of this letter is in Marsh's papers at Yale, among his incoming letters.

297: Marsh's letter to Schurz and the other relevant letters and statements collected by Marsh's committee on the surveys appear in 45th Cong, 3d sess, 3 December 1878, House Misc Doc 5.

298: The best guide to King's activity and connections is Thurman Wilkins, *Clarence King;* pp. 233ff concern his investment partners, including Agassiz and Abram Hewitt.

298–99: Agassiz to Newcomb, 22 April 1878 (Newcomb Papers, Library of Congress) and Newcomb to King, 13 July 1878 (Newcomb's Letterpress books at the same place) on Newcomb's early preference for King; Newcomb to Marsh, 23 October 1878 on their recent meeting with King.

299: Hayden to Scudder, 7 July 1878 (Scudder Papers, Boston Museum of Science).

Hayden to J. D. Hooker, 24 July 1878 (Hooker Papers, Kew Gardens).

300: Hayden and Powell's letters to Schurz are in 45th Cong, 3d sess, 1878, House Misc Doc 5.

301: William Culp Darrah, *Powell of the Colorado,* pp. 246–47.

302: Hayden to Geikie, 24 November 1878, and to Hooker, 25 November 1878.

Hayden to Geikie, 13 December 1878; Hayden repeated the same claim about Hayes's promise in another letter to Geikie of 31 May 1879.

303: Emma Hayden to Emily Peale, 2 May 1878 (Howell Collection, Box 34, University of Wyoming). The letters of Mrs. Hayden to Mrs. Peale were among A. C. Peale's papers at his death, which were found by Edwin Kirk, who had worked with Peale at the U.S. National Museum. In 1955 Kirk turned them over to geologist Fritiof Fryxell, who, along with Jesse V. Howell, was by then gathering materials for a biography of Hayden. Their accumulated materials now reside at the University of Wyoming.

Hayden to Leidy, 27 August 1884.

Hayden to Scudder, 23 June 1878.

Emma Hayden to Emily Peale, 25 August 1878.

Notes for Chapter 23

305: A. A. Wright Papers, Oberlin College.

307: *Congressional Record,* 45th Cong, 3d sess, 1879, 214:1170 for Atkins's remark.

308: *Congressional Record,* 214:1203.

Congressional Record, 214:1209.

310: *Congressional Record,* 215:2084.

311: Henry Nash Smith, "Clarence King, John Wesley Powell, and the Establishment of the United States Geological Survey," *Mississippi Valley Historical Review* 34:1 (1947), 52. Smith accepts too readily Hewitt's claim to have pushed through the language that established the USGS, which ignores the roles of Atkins and Windom I discuss hereafter.

Congressional Record, 215:2298.

313ff: Marsh's private correspondence, cited in Chapter 22, is the best guide to the workings of King's supporters.

For King's understanding of Whitney's position, see his letters to W. H. Brewer of 15 January 1879 (MS 27832 at the Huntington Library), to Whitney of 16 January (W. D. Whitney Papers, Yale University), and to G. J. Brush of 16 January (Brush Papers, Yale University). In the latter, King acknowledges that Whitney has thrown his influence to Hayden. Whitney wound up supporting Hayden in a backhanded sort of way; see his private letter to Hayden of 15 March 1879, in Edwin T. Brewster, *Life and Letters of Josiah Dwight Whitney* (Boston: Houghton Mifflin, 1909), pp. 337–39.

Note 1, p 313: Concerning Powell's backing of King, it is an interesting coincidence that Powell organized the Cosmos Club in Washington in autumn 1878 after the meeting of the National Academy of Sciences in November and before Congress assembled to take up the Academy's recommendations on the surveys in early 1879. J. Kirkpatrick Flack has argued that Powell did not found the Cosmos Club to promote his aims for the consolidated surveys or to insert King as first director. In a strict sense that may be true because there were other interests leading to the club's founding and other men besides Powell who desired it. See Flack's *Desideratum in Washington: The Intellectual Community in the Capital City, 1870–1900* (Cambridge, MA: Schenkman Publishing Co., 1975), pp. 86–93. But the overlooked point is that once the club existed, Powell and King took advantage of their connections within the membership in whatever ways they thought would aid their political struggle against Hayden. To deny this possibility on the grounds of no specific documentation is to ignore the resourcefulness of Powell and his enmity for Hayden, both of which are abundantly documented elsewhere.

314–15: Powell's report to Garfield accompanied his letter of 7 March 1879 and is found among Garfield's papers in the Library of Congress; a typescript copy is among Wallace Stegner's papers at the American Philosophical Society.

315: Eliot to Hayes, 28 February 1879 (Hayes Papers, Fremont, Ohio). Just after Eliot sent the letter, he received requests from W. B. Rogers and Simon Newcomb to support King, showing King's sponsors thought Eliot would write the sort of letter they wanted. Rogers made his request of Eliot through Walcott Gibbs (a professor at Harvard and a mutual friend), to judge by his letter to Gibbs of 26 February 1879 (Marsh Papers, Yale University).

315: Hall to King, 23 February 1879.

Hall to J. T. Gardner, 5 March 1879 (both letters among Hall's Papers, New York State Archives).

Hayden's *Extracts* was printed in Washington by R. O. Polkinhorn.

316–17: Lesley to President Hayes, 10 February 1879 (Lesley Papers, Am Phil Soc).

317: Hayden's claims on support are in his letter to A. Geikie of 31 May 1879. The extant records on who supported whom for the directorship are in several places: the Hayes Papers in Fremont, Ohio; RG 48 at the National Archives, Appointments Division, Director of Geological Surveys, Misc. Box 1; several letters in the G. P. Merrill Papers at the Library of Congress; various letters in Hayden's correspondence as well as in collections of men like J. P. Lesley. Probably the single largest collection regarding Hayden's support has not survived because Hayden wrote Hayes's secretary on 20 September 1880 asking that the file of letters in his favor be sent to him; his request was honored, but the papers have never been seen since. Probably Hayden's wife destroyed them and a number of other personal and professional papers that have disappeared.

King to George Brush, 28 February 1878 (George Jarvis Brush Papers, Yale University).

Ochsenius to Hayden, 24 October 1878, suggesting they meet soon in New York; and Hayden to Geikie, 24 January 1879, saying that he learned of King's potential competition from Ochsenius.

Ferdinand Zirkel to King, 14 November 1878 (among the Hayes Papers, Fremont, Ohio).

Barlow's papers at the Huntington Library reveal his ties to Hewitt and King.

318: That Marsh was present the day Brewer came to give his testimonial to President Hayes is established by a letter of H. N. Smith to Francis Farquhar, 11 April 1947, in the Farquhar Papers at the Bancroft Library, Berkeley.

Newcomb's autobiography, *The Reminiscences of an Astronomer* (Boston: Houghton Mifflin, 1903), p. 259.

319: A copy of Hendley's telegram is among the Hayes Papers in Fremont, Ohio.

The other letter to Geikie regarding the supposed presidential promise is 31 May 1879.

Key's letter to Hayes is among the president's papers at Fremont.

320: Hayden to L. H. Morgan, 3 February 1879 (Morgan Papers, Rochester University).

Hayden to Leidy, 4 February 1879.

Hayden to Alexander Winchell, 5 April 1879 (Winchell Papers, University of Michigan).

321: During part of summer 1879 Hayden and his wife lived with her family at 1708 Vine Street before moving into their own home at 1910 Arch Street in October.

Newberry to Garfield, 21 March 1879 (Garfield Papers, Library of Congress).

Rogers to Marsh, 4 April 1879 and Adams to Marsh, 9 April 1879 (Marsh Papers, Yale University).

Marsh to Powell, 6 April 1879 (Microcopy 156, Roll 10).

Nature 20 (8 May 1879), 40.

King to Marcus Benjamin, 21 August 1887 (Benjamin Papers, RU 7085, SIA). Benjamin was preparing a biographical sketch of King.

Notes for Chapter 24

323: Leidy Papers, Collection 1, ANSP. The "shrewd henchman" is Jim Stevenson.

324: Emma Hayden to Emily Peale, 3 December 1888 (Howell Collection, Box 34, University of Wyoming).

324–25: In regard to Hayden's activities in his later years, the authors of an article have misread him in two respects. He did not try "to prevent King from securing congressional approval to extend the Survey's operations east of the Mississippi River." He was indifferent to that issue and only provided Geikie and Dana with information on the USGS in order to make his own, now defunct, survey look better in the eyes of history. Secondly, the authors say Hayden "clung to the hope of vindication," and they imply that Hayden wished to succeed King as head of the survey—a view that is incompatible with the facts I relate in the following paragraphs. See Clifford M. Nelson, Mary C. Rabbitt, and Fritiof M. Fryxell, "Ferdinand Vandeveer Hayden: The U.S. Geological Survey Years, 1879–1886," *Proc Am Phil Soc* 125:3 (June 1981), especially 239–40.

325: Hayden to Geikie, 21 September 1880 (Geikie Papers, Edinburgh University).

Hayden to Packard, 17 October 1880 (Packard Papers, Museum of Comparative Zoology, Harvard University).

Hayden to Baird, 19 November 1879 and 14 September 1880.

326: Hayden to Hall, 11 May 1879.

Clover Adams's letter of 27 March 1881 is reprinted in *The Letters of Mrs. Henry Adams, 1865–83,* ed. Ward Thoron (Boston: Little, Brown & Co., 1937), p. 278.

Hayden to Baird, 1 March 1881.

Hayden to Baird, 15 and 16 March 1881.

Hayden to Holmes, 16 March 1881 (RU 7084 at SIA).

Hayden to Peale, undated [probably 18 March 1881] (original in Howell Collection, Box 24, University of Wyoming).

327: After 1879, the remaining work of the survey was to bring to press several unfinished publications: J. A. Allen's book on pinnipeds (1880); Vols. 5 (1880) and 6 (1882) of the *Bulletin,* containing a variety of natural history articles; the *Twelfth Annual Report* (1883); a general geological map of the entire area covered by Hayden's survey (1883); and three volumes in the *Final Reports.* See notes for p. 330 below.

327–28: The quotations about *The Great West* (1880) are taken from its title page. It was published simultaneously in Bloomington, Illinois, and Philadelphia.

328: Friedrich Anton Heller von Hellwald, *Die Erde und ihre Völker,* 2 vols. (Stuttgart: W. Spemann, 1877–78). The work was translated into English by someone named Keane.

328–29: Hayden to Geikie, 15 November 1878.

329–30: Hayden to Geikie, 9 December 1882.

330: Hayden to Powell, 28 June and 27 July [incorrectly written as June] 1882, Microcopy 590 (Letters Received by the USGS), Roll 12, item 734, and Roll 13, item 1294. These last publications were three volumes of the *Final Reports* series: Vol. 3 by Cope on Tertiary vertebrates (1883); Vol. 8 by Lesquereux on Cretaceous and Tertiary floras (1883); and Vol. 13 by Scudder on Tertiary insects (1890).

330ff: Hayden's fieldwork is summarized in his reports to Powell, published in the Fifth, Sixth, and Seventh annual reports of the USGS, at pp. 28–30, 48–53, and 85–87, respectively. Peale's report for summer 1886 (pp. 146–48 of the *Eighth Annual Report*) summarizes Hayden's last field season.

330: Hayden to Holmes, 21 August 1883 (W. H. Holmes, "Random Records of a Lifetime, 1846–1931," 3:153; at the Library of the National Collection of Fine Arts and the National Portrait Gallery, Washington).

Note 1, p. 331: Hayden's geologic map of 1883 is available in the Map Room of the Library of Congress; it was enclosed with some of the copies of his *Twelfth Annual Report.*

332: Hayden to Mrs. J. A. Logan, 23 December 1883 (Logan Papers, Library of Congress).

Hayden to F. W. Putnam, 3 June 1885 (Putnam Papers, Harvard University Archives).

Emma Hayden to Emily Peale, 30 December 1888 (Howell Collection, Box 34, University of Wyoming).

333: On the scandal, see press reports of 9 August 1884 in the *Philadelphia Record,* p. 6, c. 4; the *Times-Philadelphia,* p. 1, c. 6; and the *Philadelphia Press,* p. 3, c. 1. Hayden wrote his side of the matter in a confidential letter to Leidy of 27 August 1884.

Cope had been studying Tertiary and Mesozoic vertebrates for years; his report on the Tertiary species came out in Vol. 3 of Hayden's *Final Reports* in 1883; Vol. 4 of the same series, which would have been on the earlier species, was never published.

Hayden to A. C. Peale, 28 October 1885 (Merrill Papers, Library of Congress).

333–34: Hayden to Monroe, 7 July 1887 (J. H. Fairchild Papers, Box 10, Oberlin College).

Note 2, p. 334: Hayden had previously been awarded an honorary Doctor of Laws by Rochester University in 1878, which had also awarded him an honorary Master of Arts in 1863. Penn also renamed one of its buildings for him—a structure originally built in 1896 for the School of Dentistry. By 1968 the Geology Department had taken up residence there and during a renovation of the building during the 1970s members of the Geology Department suggested calling it Hayden Hall. (My sources on Hayden Hall are a fact sheet from the university and a personal telephone conversation with Carol Faul of 27 October 1987.)

334: Hayden to J. H. Fairchild, 30 November 1887 (Fairchild Papers, Box 11, Oberlin College).

334ff: The most valuable studies on the historical context of syphilis I have found are Terra Ziporyn, *Disease in the Popular American Press: The Case of Diphtheria, Typhoid Fever, and Syphilis, 1870–1920* (New York: Greenwood Press, 1988); and Allan M. Brandt, *No Magic Bullet: A Social History of Venereal Disease in the United States Since 1880* (New York: Oxford University Press, 1985). I verified the conclusions of these authors by browsing through the *Medical Record* for the 1870s and 1880s. An excellent medical overview, "Syphilis" by John Thorne Crissey and David A. Denenholz, appears in *Clinics in Dermatology* 2:1 (January-March 1984); I am grateful to Don Friday King for pointing it out to me.

336: Calvin B. Delaplain, "Venereal Diseases Among Frontier Troops," *True West* 31:1 (January 1984), 17–19.

27 August 1884 to Leidy. Strictly speaking, intercourse is not "impossible" for a syphilitic, though Hayden's statements may be taken as evidence of the painful symptomatic chancre that appears in the first stage of syphilis, which can reappear irregularly thereafter. That Hayden abstained from intercourse during the later stages of his disease shows he was mindful of the consequences for Emma.

337: Peale's letter to Benjamin is in RU 7085 at the SIA.

Note 3, p. 337: The award of the Hayden Medal was annual until after 1899, when it became triennial. It would have amused Hayden that Cope was an early recipient, and it would have pleased him that Geikie was another. However, in what must be the supreme irony of Hayden's career, which was full of them, the Academy awarded the first Hayden Medal in 1890 to none other than James Hall. The irony was not lost on Hall, who wrote to Leidy on 5 April 1890: "Nothing in the way of honors which I have ever received can equal my appreciation of this one." He went on, without once mentioning Hayden, to praise Leidy so fulsomely that one begins to wonder if he understood the award commemorated Hayden, not Leidy; one wonders, that is, until his last sentence, where Hall wreaks a final vengeance on his dead rival: "I have known you and have revered your name and your work since my very beginnings in scientific pursuits, and no other name could have carried with it the gratification and satisfaction which I have in this award, coming from a committee of which you are the head" (Hall Papers, New York Library, Albany.)

The "fountain" was probably the watering trough Emma gave to the Women's Pennsylvania Society for the Prevention of Cruelty to Animals (a predecessor of the SPCA). The fountain no longer exists, but apparently it endured into the 1950s. (See a letter of 24 May 1955 of H. J. Weeks to Robert H. Dott in the Howell Collection, Box 23, University of Wyoming.)

Emma's will: W3102-1934, Register of Wills, Philadelphia.

Notes for Chapter 25

338: Walcott's speech is preserved in Collection 547 at the ANSP.

King Richard II, Act I, Scene 1, line 177, the first half of which is quoted in John Bartlett, *Familiar Quotations,* 13th edition (Boston: Little, Brown and Co., 1955), p. 138.

339: *Phrenological Journal and Life Illustrated* 59 (Old series), 10: no. 1 (New series), whole number 427 (July 1874), pp. 5–7. The *Journal* was published in New York and edited by Samuel R. Wells. My summary of phrenology is based on John D. Davies, *Phrenology, Fad and Science: A 19th Century American Crusade* (New Haven: Yale Univ. Press, 1955), and Madeleine B. Stern, *Heads and Headlines: The Phrenological Fowlers* (Norman: Univ. of Oklahoma Press, 1971).

341: Sarah Ireland Oliver, "Ferdinand V. Hayden, Scientist or Charlatan? The Wyoming Years," University of Wyoming, Master's Thesis, 1978. Claudia Polsky, "The Unmaking of a Scientific Reputation: Ferdinand Vandiveer Hayden and the Geological and Geographical Survey of the Territories," Harvard University, Bachelor's Honors Thesis, 1987.

Aldrich's view was not in an obituary, but in an article written six months before Hayden's death and published in the *Critic,* 182 (25 June 1887), 320.

Lesley, in the *Proc Am Phil Soc,* 20 January 1888, 61.

Cope, in *American Geologist* 1:2 (February 1888), 111.

White, in *Nat Acad Sci Biog Memoirs* 3, p. 408.

Scudder, in *Science* 11 (6 January 1888), 2.

Geikie, in *Nature* 37 (2 February 1888), 325.

Cope wrote two obituaries on Hayden; this quote comes from *Am Nat* 21:12 (December 1887), 1135.

342: Dana, in *Am Jour Sci,* 3d series, 35 (February 1888), 179–80.

Benjamin, in *Appleton's Cyclopaedia of American Biography,* Vol. 3 (New York: D. Appleton & Co., 1887), p. 131; and in *Scientific American,* 7 January 1888, 9.

Peale wrote two obituaries: *Ninth Annual Report* of the USGS (Washington: GPO, 1889), pp. 31–38; and *Bulletin of the Philosophical Society of Washington* 11 (1892), 476–78. (In my article on Hayden that appeared in *American Zoologist* 26 [1986], 349, I attributed the anonymous obituary in the *Ninth Annual Report* to Charles D. Walcott, but I have since found reasons for changing my mind, mostly the similarity of the two essays, the second of which is signed by Peale.)

Cope, *American Geologist,* 112.

Geikie, *Nature,* 326.

Lesley, *Proc Am Phil Soc,* 61.

346: Goetzmann, *Exploration and Empire,* p. xi. Besides the fact that he underestimated Hayden (everyone else has too), my specific criticisms of Goetzmann are that he misunderstood Hayden's role in collaborating with Meek, and that he misrepresented Hayden and Cyrus Thomas regarding the "rain follows the plow" issue.

Note 1, p. 348: Examples of these local studies are: Willard C. Hayden, "The Hayden Survey," *Idaho Yesterdays* 16:1 (Spring 1972), 20–25; Bill Mahan, "The Hayden Survey in the San Luis Valley, 1873–1876," *San Luis Valley Historian* 14:4 (Fall 1982), 26–36; Marshall Sprague, *The Great Gates: The Story of the Rocky Mountain Passes* (Boston: Little, Brown, 1964); Gilbert F. Stucker, "Hayden in the Badlands," *American West* 4:1 (February 1967), 41–45, 79–85; Larry S. Thompson, "Ferdinand Vandiveer Hayden," chap. 10 in *Montana's Explorers: The Pioneer Naturalists* (Helena: Montana Magazine, 1985).

349: Nelson, Rabbitt, and Fryxell (1981) reproduce the lyrics of the three verses at page 242 of their article.

Note 2, p. 350: During December 1878 the new Cosmos Club invited all members of the older Philosophical Society of Washington to become members. Hayden was a member of the latter, but he declined to join the former. Gilbert's quote is in *The Twenty-Fifth Anniversary of the Founding of the Cosmos Club* (Washington: Cosmos Club, 1904), p. 4.

SELECT
BIBLIOGRAPHY

Hayden's Publications and Writings

This is a chronological list of all known articles, books, and unpublished papers that Hayden authored, including several he published through his Survey of the Territories. It does not include numerous other studies issued by Hayden's survey, most of which Hayden edited for publication; these are listed by L. F. Schmeckebier in his *Catalogue and Index of the Publications of the Hayden, King, Powell, and Wheeler Surveys.* USGS Bulletin No. 222. Washington: GPO, 1904.

Schmeckebier noticed several of the introductions Hayden wrote for his *Annual Reports* series, but he overlooked introductions Hayden wrote for nearly every volume in the *Final Reports,* the *Miscellaneous Publications,* the *Unclassified Publications,* and for several of the volumes of the *Bulletin.* I have not listed these introductions because they are more administrative than scholarly in nature.

Though he lists them all, Schmeckebier gives no attribution for several volumes in the *Unclassified Publications* series. In view of their contents and the timing of their publication, I believe Hayden compiled them, doubtless with assistance from members of his survey. These include volumes 5, 7, 8, 13, 15, 16, and 17 of that series.

"The Digestive Process." Thesis for the M.D. degree, Albany Medical College, 1853. Albany, New York.

With Fielding Bradford Meek. "Descriptions of New Species of Gasteropoda from the Cretaceous Formations of Nebraska Territory." *Proc ANSP* 8 (March 1856), 63–69.

With Meek. "Descriptions of New Species of Gasteropoda and Cephalopoda from the Cretaceous Formations of Nebraska Territory." *Proc ANSP* 8 (March 1856), 70–72.

With Meek. "Descriptions of Twenty-Eight New Species of Acephala and One Gasteropod, from the Cretaceous Formations of Nebraska Territory." *Proc ANSP* 8 (April 1856), 81–87.

With Meek. "Descriptions of New Species of Acephala and Gasteropoda, from the Tertiary Formations of Nebraska Territory, with Some General Remarks on the Geology of the Country about the Sources of the Missouri River." *Proc ANSP* 8 (June 1856), 111–26.

With Meek. "Descriptions of New Fossil Species of Mollusca, Collected by Dr. F. V. Hayden in Nebraska Territory, Together with a Complete Catalogue of All the Remains of Invertebrata Hitherto Described and Identified from the Cretaceous and Tertiary Formations of That Region." *Proc ANSP* 8 (November 1856), 265–86.

"A Brief Sketch of the Geological and Physical Features of the Region of the upper Missouri, with Some Notes on its Soil, Vegetation, Animal Life, etc." In *Explorations in the Dacota Country in the Year 1855,* pp. 63–79. Ed. Lieut. G. K. Warren. 34th Cong, 1st sess, 1855–56, Sen Exec Doc 76. Washington: A.O.P. Nicholson, 1856.

"Notes Explanatory of a Map and Section Illustrating the Geological Structure of the Country Bordering on the Missouri River, from the Mouth of the Platte River to Fort Benton, in Lat. 47° 30′ North, Long. 110° 30′ West." *Proc ANSP* 9 (May 1857), 109–16.

With Meek. "Descriptions of New Species and Genera of Fossils Collected by Dr. F. V. Hayden in Nebraska Territory under Direction of Lieut. G. K. Warren, U.S. Topographical Engineer, with Some Remarks on the Tertiary and Cretaceous Formations of the North-West and the Parallelism of the Latter with Those of Other Portions of the United States and Territories." *Proc ANSP* 9 (May 1857), 117–48.

"Notes on the Geology of the Mauvaises Terres of White River, Nebraska." *Proc ANSP* 9 (June 1857), 151–58.

With **Meek.** "Descriptions of New Organic Remains from North-Eastern Kansas, Indicating the Existence of Permian Rocks in That Territory" [read 2 March 1858]. *Transactions of the Albany Institute* 4 (1858–64), 73–88.

With **Meek.** "Fossils of Nebraska." *National Intelligencer,* 16 March 1858.

With **Meek.** "The Probable Existence of Permian Rocks in Kansas Territory." *Proc ANSP* 10 (March 1858), 9–10.

With **Meek.** "Descriptions of New Organic Remains, Collected in Nebraska Territory in the Year 1857 by Dr. F. V. Hayden, Geologist to the Exploring Expedition under the Command of Lieut. G. K. Warren, Top. Engr. U.S. Army, Together with Some Remarks on the Geology of the Black Hills and Portions of the Surrounding Country." *Proc ANSP* 10 (March 1858), 41–59.

With **Meek.** "Geology of Nebraska: Important Discoveries." *Mining and Statistic Magazine* 10:4 (April 1858), 292–95.

With **Meek.** "Fossils of Nebraska." *Am Jour Sci,* 2d series, 25 (May 1858), 439–41.

"Explanations of a Second Edition of a Geological Map of Nebraska and Kansas, Based upon Information Obtained in an Expedition to the Black Hills, under the Command of Lieut. G. K. Warren, Top. Engr. U.S.A." *Proc ANSP* 10 (June 1858), 139–58.

"Tertiary Basin of White and Niobrara Rivers." *Am Jour Sci,* 2d series, 26 (November 1858), 404–08.

With **Meek.** "Remarks on the Lower Cretaceous Beds of Kansas and Nebraska, Together with Descriptions of Some New Species of Carboniferous Fossils from the Valley of Kansas River." *Proc ANSP* 10 (December 1858), 256–66. A modified version of this article appeared in *Am Jour Sci,* 2d series, 27 (March 1859), 219–27.

"A Catalogue of the Collections in Geology and Natural History, Obtained in Nebraska and Portions of Kansas." In *Report of the Secretary of War,* pp. 673–747. 35th Cong, 2d sess, 1858–59, House Exec Doc 2, vol. 2, part 2. Washington: J. B. Steedman, 1858. The same report was printed simultaneously in 35th Cong, 2d sess, Sen Exec Doc 1.

With **Meek.** "On the So-Called Triassic Rocks of Kansas and Nebraska." *Am Jour Sci,* 2d series, 27 (January 1859), 31–35.

With **Meek.** "Geological Explorations in Kansas Territory." *Proc ANSP* 11 (January 1859), 8–30.

"Geological Sketch of the Estuary and Fresh Water Deposit of the Bad Lands of the Judith, with Some Remarks upon the Surrounding Formations" [read 4 March 1859]. *Trans Am Phil Soc,* New series, 11:123–38. Philadelphia: The Society, 1859.

"Comparative Crow and Hidatsa Vocabulary" [a six-page manuscript, c. 1859]. RDM/68 at the National Anthropological Archives, Washington.

"Lakota Vocabulary" [a six-page manuscript, c. 1859]. RDM/67 at the National Anthropological Archives, Washington.

With Meek. "On a New Genus of Patelliform Shells from the Cretaceous Rocks of Nebraska." *Am Jour Sci,* 2d series, 29 (January 1860), 33–35.

"Explorations in Nebraska: A Letter to Prof. Dana." *Am Jour Sci,* 2d series, 29 (March 1860), 286.

"Notes on the Geology of Nebraska and Utah Territory [sic]." *Am Jour Sci,* 2d series, 29 (May 1860), 433–34.

With Meek. "Descriptions of New Organic Remains from the Tertiary, Cretaceous and Jurassic Rocks of Nebraska." *Proc ANSP* 12 (May 1860), 175–85.

With Meek. "Systematic Catalogue with Synonyma, etc., of Jurassic, Cretaceous and Tertiary Fossils Collected in Nebraska by the Exploring Expeditions under the Command of Lieut. G. K. Warren of U.S. Topographical Engineers." *Proc ANSP* 12 (October 1860), 417–32.

"Sketch of the Geology of the Country about the Headwaters of the Missouri and Yellowstone Rivers." *Am Jour Sci,* 2d series, 31 (March 1861), 229–45.

With Meek. "Descriptions of New Lower Silurian, (Primordial), Jurassic, Cretaceous, and Tertiary Fossils Collected in Nebraska, by the Exploring Expedition under the Command of Capt. Wm. F. Raynolds, U.S. Top. Engrs., with Some Remarks on the Rocks from Which They Were Obtained." *Proc ANSP* 13 (December 1861), 415–47.

"The Primordial Sandstone of the Rocky Mountains in the Northwestern Territories of the United States." *Am Jour Sci,* 2d series, 33 (January 1862), 68–79.

With Meek. "Descriptions of New Cretaceous Fossils from Nebraska Territory, Collected by the Expedition Sent out by the Government under the Command of Lieut. John Mullan, U.S. Topographical Engineers, for the Location and Construction of a Wagon Road from the Sources of the Missouri to the Pacific Ocean." *Proc ANSP* 14 (February 1862), 21–28.

"Physics and Hydraulics of the Mississippi River." *Am Jour Sci,* 2d series, 33 (March 1862), 181–89. Peale (1891, p. 58) attributed this unsigned review article to Hayden.

"Some Remarks in Regard to the Period of Elevation of those Ranges of the Rocky Mountains near the Sources of the Missouri River and its Tributaries." *Am Jour Sci,* 2d series, 33 (May 1862), 305–13.

"Colorado River of the West." *Am Jour Sci,* 2d series, 33 (May 1862), 387–403. Peale (1891, p. 59) attributed this unsigned review article to Hayden; mostly it quotes Lt. Joseph Ives's original report.

"A Sketch of the Mandan Indians, with Some Observations Illustrating the

Grammatical Structure of Their Language." *Am Jour Sci,* 2d series, 34 (July 1862), 57–66.

"United States Government Surveys." *Am Jour Sci,* 2d series, 34 (July 1862), 98–101.

On the Geology and Natural History of the Upper Missouri. Philadelphia: C. Sherman, 1862. First published in *Trans Am Phil Soc,* New series, 12:1–218.

Contributions to the Ethnography and Philology of the Indian Tribes of the Missouri Valley. Philadelphia: C. Sherman, 1862. First published in *Trans Am Phil Soc,* New series, 12, part 2, article 3, pp. 231–461.

With Meek. *Palaeontology of the Upper Missouri: A Report upon Collections Made Principally by the Expeditions under Command of Lieut. G. K. Warren, U.S. Top. Engrs., in 1855 and 1856. Invertebrates. Part I.* Washington: Smithsonian Institution (*Smithsonian Contributions to Knowledge,* vol. 14, no. 172), 1865.

"Brief Journey to the Black Hills." *The Union and Dakotaian* 2:28 (20 October 1866), 2. Reprinted in *South Dakota History* 4:2 (Spring 1974), 190–94. A talk to the Dakota Historical Society, 4 October 1866.

"Remarks in Regard to a Side Trip to the Celebrated Pipestone Quarry of North-Eastern Dakota." *Proc ANSP* 18 (October 1866), 291–92. Summary of a talk to the academy.

"Remarks on a Short Visit to the Celebrated Pipestone Quarry." *Proc Am Phil Soc* 10 (November 1866), 274–75. Summary of a talk to the society.

"Remarks in Regard to an Extensive Chalk Deposit on the Missouri River." *Proc ANSP* 18 (November 1866), 314. Summary of a talk to the academy.

"Remarks in Regard to an Extensive Chalk Deposit on the Missouri River." *Proc Am Phil Soc* 10 (November 1866), 277. Summary of a talk to the society.

"Discovery of Two Mastodon Teeth." *Proc ANSP* 18 (November 1866), 316. Summary of a talk to the academy.

"Remarks in Regard to the Geology of the Missouri Valley." *Proc Am Phil Soc* 10 (December 1866), 292–96. Summary of a talk to the society.

"Sketch of the Geology of Northeastern Dakota, with a Notice of a Short Visit to the Celebrated Pipestone Quarry." *Am Jour Sci,* 2d series, 43 (January 1867), 15–22.

"Remarks and Observations in Regard to the Lignite Beds of the Country on the Upper Tributaries of the Missouri." *Proc Am Phil Soc* 10 (January 1867), 300–07.

"Geographical Distribution of Plants." *Proc Am Phil Soc* 10 (February 1867), 315–20. Summary of a talk to the society.

"The Great Scarcity of Timber in Certain Parts of the Country about the Upper Waters of the Missouri." *Proc Am Phil Soc* 10 (February 1867), 322–26. Summary of a talk to the society.

"Remarks on the Cretaceous Rocks of the West Known as No. 1, or the Dakota Group." *Am Jour Sci,* 2d series, 43 (March 1867), 171–79.

"Notes on the Geology of Kansas." *Am Jour Sci,* 2d series, 44 (July 1867), 32–40.

"Observations in Regard to Indian History." *Proc Am Phil Soc* 10 (10 October 1867 letter to the secretary of the society), 352–53.

"Rocky Mountain Coal Beds." *Am Jour Sci,* 2d series, 45 (January 1868), 101–02.

"Notes on the Lignite Deposits of the West." *Am Jour Sci,* 2d series, 45 (March 1868), 198–208.

"Brief Notes on the Pawnee, Winnebago and Omaha Languages." *Proc Am Phil Soc* 10 (April 1868), 389–421.

"Remarks on the Geological Formations along the Eastern Margins of the Rocky Mountains." *Am Jour Sci,* 2d series, 45 (May 1868), 322–26.

"Remarks on the Possibility of a Workable Bed of Coal in Nebraska." *Am Jour Sci,* 2d series, 45 (May 1868), 326–30.

"Notes on the Geology of Wyoming and Colorado Territories, No. 1." *Proc Am Phil Soc* 10 (2 October 1868), 463–78.

"Observations in Regard to Indian History." In *Annual Report of the Board of Regents of the Smithsonian Institution for 1867,* pp. 411–12. 40th Cong, 2d sess, 1867–68, Senate Misc Doc 86. Washington: GPO, 1868. Revised version of letter of 10 October 1867 in *Proc ANSP.*

"Notes on the Geology of Colorado and Wyoming Territories, No. 2." *Proc Am Phil Soc* 11 (19 February 1869), 25–56.

"A New Species of Hare from the Summit of Wind River Mountains." *Am Nat* 3 (May 1869), 113–16.

Geological Report of the Exploration of the Yellowstone and Missouri Rivers in 1859–60. Washington: GPO, 1869. This "Report on Geology" was a part of William F. Raynolds's *Report on the Exploration of the Yellowstone River* (40th Cong, 2d sess, 1867–68, Senate Exec Doc 77), but it was not approved for printing until the next year.

"On the Geology of the Tertiary Formations of Dakota and Nebraska." Introduction to *On the Extinct Mammalian Fauna of Dakota and Nebraska* by Joseph Leidy. *Jour ANSP,* 2d series, 7:9–21. Philadelphia: J. B. Lippincott, 1869.

"Report on San Luis Park." In *Colorado: Its Resources, Parks, and Prospects,* pp. 196–200. Ed. William Blackmore. London: Sampson Low, Son & Marston, 1869.

"Sections of Strata Belonging to the 'Bear River Group' near Bear River City, Wyoming Territory." *Proc Am Phil Soc* 11 (6 May 1870), 420–25.

Sun Pictures of Rocky Mountain Scenery. New York: J. Bien, 1870.

"The Wonders of the West—II: More About the Yellowstone." *Scribner's Monthly* 3 (February 1872), 388–96.

[Report on the Yellowstone Park]. In *The Yellowstone Park,* pp. 1–2. 42d Cong, 2d sess, 27 Feb. 1872, House Report 26. This is Hayden's synopsis of his draft report on Yellowstone, which the Committee on the Public Lands approved and passed along over Chairman Mark Dunnell's signature.

"The Hot Springs and Geysers of the Yellowstone and Firehole Rivers." *Am Jour Sci,* 3d series, 3 (February 1872), 105–15, and (March 1872), 161–76.

"The Yellowstone National Park." *Am Jour Sci,* 3d series, 3 (April 1872), 294–97.

"A Gigantic 'Pleasuring Ground': The Yellowstone National Park of the United States." *Nature* 6 (12 September 1872), 397–401, and (26 September 1872), 437–39.

"Hayden Rocky Mountain Geological Expedition." *Am Jour Sci,* 3d series, 4 (October 1872), 313–16.

"The Rocky Mountain Expedition." *Eng & Min Jour* 14 (12 November 1872), 312.

Final Report of the United States Geological Survey of Nebraska and Portions of the Adjacent Territories. 42d Cong, 1st sess, 1871, House Exec Doc 19. Washington: GPO, 1872. This report was published through Hayden's Survey in the *Unclassified Publications.*

"The Yellowstone: Story of Last Year's Explorations." *The World* (New York) 3 (March 1873), 2.

"The Hayden Expedition: Origin, Organization, History, Work and Publications." *Rocky Mountain News* (Denver), 20 July 1873, p. 2.

"The Hayden Expedition." *Rocky Mountain News,* 13 September 1873, p. 2.

"The Hayden Expedition." *Rocky Mountain News,* 17 September 1873, p. 2.

"Letter in Regard to a Plan for the Improvement and Protection of the Yellowstone National Park." In *Yellowstone Park,* p. 6. 43d Cong, 1st sess, 14 November 1873, House Exec Doc 147.

"The Survey of the Territories." *New York Tribune,* Extra no. 14, scientific series, 30 December 1873.

"Prefatory Note." *Bulletin,* 1st series, 1 (9 April 1874), 1–2. On the Lignitic Group.

"Our Great West, and the Scenery of Our National Parks." *Journal of the American Geographical Society of New York* 6 (1874), 196–211. Based on Hayden's talk to the society on 15 April 1874.

"Explorations in Colorado: Wonderful Peaks." *New York Times,* 16 November 1874, p. 6.

"Notes on Some Peculiar Forms of Erosion in Eastern Colorado, with Heliotype Illustrations." *Bulletin,* 2d series, 1 (15 May 1875), 210–11.

"Notes on the Surface Features of the Colorado or Front Range of the Rocky Mountains." *Bulletin,* 2d series, 1 (10 June 1875), 215–20.

"The Hayden Survey: Mapping the Centennial State." *Philadelphia Press,* 14 July 1875, p. 8.

"Out in the Wilderness." *Rocky Mountain News,* 10 August 1875, p. 4.

"The Hayden Survey: Colorado Deserts and Cañons." *New York Times,* 31 August 1875, p. 1.

"Exploits of the Explorers." *Rocky Mountain News,* 7 September 1875, p. 4.

"Rocky Mountains," In *American Cyclopaedia,* 14: 374–82. Eds. George Ripley and Charles A. Dana. New York: D. Appleton and Co., 1875.

"Notes on the Lignitic Group of Eastern Colorado and Portions of Wyoming." *Bulletin,* 2d series, 1 (8 January 1876), 401–11.

"Explorations in Colorado Under Professor Hayden in 1875." *Am Nat* 10 (March 1876), 161–65.

"Summary of the Field Work of the Hayden Geological Survey During the Season of 1875." *Republic* 6 (March 1876), 149–60.

"Notes Descriptive of Some Geological Sections of the Country about the Headwaters of the Missouri and Yellowstone Rivers." *Bulletin* 2 (5 June 1876), 197–209.

"On the Ore-Bearing Rocks of Colorado." *Am Jour Sci,* 3d series, 12 (July 1876), 71.

"Hayden Geological and Geographical Survey." *Rocky Mountain News,* 12 December 1876, p. 2.

The Grotto Geyser of the Yellowstone National Park. Unclassified Publication, No. 7. Washington: GPO, [1876].

With Albert Charles Peale. "Wonders of the Rocky Mountains. The Yellowstone Park. How to Reach it." In *The Pacific Tourist: Williams Illustrated Trans-Continental Guide of Travel,* pp. 277–92. Ed. Henry T. Williams. New York: Henry Williams, 1876.

With Louis Prang. *The Yellowstone National Park and the Mountain Regions of Portions of Idaho, Nevada, Colorado and Utah.* Boston: L. Prang & Co., 1876.

Report on the Proposed Yellowstone National Park. Washington: GPO, 1872 [1876]. A copy of Hayden's report on Yellowstone from 1872, along with later extracts from the books done with Peale and Prang.

"Explorations Made under the Direction of F. V. Hayden, in 1876." *Am Jour Sci,* 3d series, 13 (January 1877), 68–74.

"Explorations Made Under the Direction of Prof. F. V. Hayden in 1876." *Republic* 8 (January 1877), 17–24.

"Notes on Some Artesian Borings along the Line of the Union Pacific Railroad in Wyoming Territory." *Bulletin* 3 (5 April 1877), 181–85.

"The United States Geological and Geographical Survey of the Territories—Explorations in 1876." *Quarterly Journal of Science* [London], New series, 7 (April 1877), 238–51.

"Progress of the U.S. Geological Survey." *Republic* 8 (April 1877), 217–26.

"The Hayden Survey: Work for the Season." *New York Times,* 2 July 1877, p. 5.

"The Hayden Survey: In the Bear River District." *New York Times,* 21 August 1877, p. 2.

"Geographical Progress and Discovery in 1876: United States." In *Appleton's Annual Cyclopaedia,* New series, I: 333–35. New York: D. Appleton and Co., 1877.

Sketch of the Origin and Progress of the United States Geological and Geographical Survey of the Territories. Washington: Darby & Duvall, 1877.

"National Parks." In *Johnson's New Universal Cyclopaedia,* 3:717. New York: Alvin J. Johnson & Son, 1877.

"Summary of Field Work of the United States Geological and Geographical Survey of the Territories." *Am Jour Sci,* 3d series, 15 (January 1878), 56–60.

"The Field-Work of the United States Geological and Geographical Survey of the Territories, under the Direction of Prof. F. V. Hayden, for the Season of 1877." *Am Nat* 12 (February 1878), 96–114.

[Report to the Secretary of the Interior]. In *Geological and Geographical Surveys,* pp. 1–22. 45th Cong, 2d sess, April 1878, House Exec Doc 81. Hayden's response to House resolution of 8 March 1878.

[Letter to Secretary Schurz]. In *Surveys of the Territories,* pp. 11–13. 45th Cong, 3d sess, 29 October 1878, House Misc Doc 5. Hayden's comments for the National Academy of Sciences' Committee on the Surveys.

"Letter to the Editor." *New York Daily Tribune,* 5 November 1878.

"Glaciers in the Wind River Mountains. *Science News* 1 (15 November 1878), 20–21.

"The Two Ocean Pass." *Science News* 1 (1 December 1878), 34–35.

"Discovery of Recent Glaciers in Wyoming." *Am Nat* 12 (December 1878), 830–31.

"Wasatch Group." *Am Nat* 12 (December 1878), 831.

"Yellowstone National Park," In *Johnson's New Universal Cyclopaedia,* 4: 1526–30. New York: Alvin J. Johnson & Son, 1878.

"Summary of the Field Work of the U.S. Geological and Geographical Survey of the Territories . . . During the Season of 1878." *Am Nat* 13 (January 1879), 55–56.

Extracts from Letters and Notices of Eminent Scientific Men and Journals in Europe and America. Ed. F. V. Hayden. Washington: R. D. Polkinhorn [January or early February], 1879.

"The So-Called Two-Ocean Pass." *Bulletin* 5 (6 September 1879), 223–25.

"List of the Geological Formations in Colorado and Nebraska." In *An American Geological Railway Guide*, pp. 162–64. Ed. James MacFarlane. New York: D. Appleton & Co., 1879.

"Professor Leidy's 'Fresh Water Rhizopods of North America.'" *Science* 1 (31 July 1880), 54–57.

"Prof. Wm. Boyd Dawkins." *Am Nat* 14 (August 1880), 615.

[Book review of] *Zoology for High Schools and Colleges* by A. S. Packard, Jr. *Science* 1 (18 December 1880), 308.

"Twin Lakes and Teocalli Mountain, Central Colorado, with Remarks on the Glacial Phenomena of that Region." *Am Nat* 14 (December 1880), 858–62.

With others. *The Great West: Its Attractions and Resources.* Bloomington, IL: Charles R. Brodix, 1880.

"Lesquereux on the Tertiary Flora as Related to the Tertiary Animals of the West." *Am Nat* 16 (July 1882), 602.

"Administrative Report." In *Second Annual Report, USGS (1880–81)*, pp. 42–44. Washington: GPO, 1882.

With Alfred Richard Cecil Selwyn. *Stanford's Compendium of Geography and Travel: North America.* London: Edward Stanford, 1883.

"A Scientific Swindler." *Science* 3 (20 February 1884), 245.

"A Scientific Swindler." *Am Nat* 18 (April 1884), 448.

"Administrative Report." In *Fifth Annual Report, USGS (1883–84)*, pp. 28–30. Washington: GPO, 1885.

"Administrative Report." In *Sixth Annual Report, USGS (1884–85)*, pp. 48–53. Washington: GPO, 1885.

"Administrative Report." In *Seventh Annual Report, USGS (1885–86)*, pp. 85–87. Washington: GPO, 1888.

Books and Articles

The essential sources for this book are the manuscript collections mentioned in the notes. Books and articles cited for specific reasons in the notes are not repeated here, except for the few that show a general interest in Hayden or his times. Included here are all the printed materials I could find about Hayden himself, but only a few of the many publications discussing his Survey of the Territories. Also listed are the studies I found most valuable, either because of factual content or because of a suggestive point of view on the period.

Academy of Natural Sciences, Philadelphia. *The Joseph Leidy Commemorative Meeting. Held in Philadelphia, December 6, 1923.* Philadelphia: privately printed, 1923.

Agassiz, G. R., ed. *Letters and Recollections of Alexander Agassiz.* Boston: Houghton Mifflin, 1913.

Aldrich, Charles. "Dr. Hayden and His Work." *Critic* 182 (25 June 1887), 320.

Aldrich, Michele L. "Ferdinand Vandiveer Hayden." *Dictionary of Scientific Biography* 6, pp. 186–88. New York: C. Scribner's Sons, 1970.

Allard, Dean Conrad, Jr. "Spencer Fullerton Baird and the U.S. Fish Commission: A Study in the History of American Science." Doctoral Dissertation, George Washington Univ., 1967.

Anonymous. "F. V. Hayden." [Two newspaper clippings dated 22 December 1887.] Marcus Benjamin Papers, RU 7085, Smithsonian Archives.

_____ . "F. V. Hayden." *Philadelphia Inquirer,* 22 December 1887.

_____ . "F. V. Hayden." *Philadelphia Press,* 23 December 1887.

_____ . "F. V. Hayden." *Philadelphia Telegram,* 23 December 1887.

_____ . "Ferdinand Vandeveer Hayden." *Am Jour Sci,* 3d series, 35 (February 1888), 179–90.

_____ . "Ferdinand V. Hayden, Born September 1829, Died 23 December 1887." *Geological Magazine* 5:3 (March 1888), 143–44.

_____ . "Dr. Ferdinand Vandeveer Hayden." *Albany Medical Annals* 9 (1888), 26–27.

_____ . "Ferdinand Vandeveer Hayden." *Chambers' Encyclopaedia* 5:597. Philadelphia: J. B. Lippincott, 1890.

_____ . "Ferdinand Vandeveer Hayden." *Lamb's Biographical Dictionary of the United States* 3, pp. 604–05. Boston: J. H. Lamb, 1900.

_____ . "Ferdinand Vandiveer Hayden." *National Cyclopaedia of American Biography* 11, pp. 97–98. New York: James T. White & Co., 1909.

Barrell, Joseph. "A Century of Geology: The Growth of Knowledge of Earth Structure." In *A Century of Science in America With Special Reference to the American Journal of Science, 1818–1918,* pp. 161–91. Ed. Edward Salisbury Dana. New Haven: Yale Univ. Press, 1918.

Bartlett, Richard A. "The Great Surveys in Colorado, 1867–1879." Doctoral Dissertation, Univ. of Colorado, 1953.

_____ . "The Hayden Survey in Colorado." *Colorado Quarterly* 4:1 (Summer 1955), 73–88.

_____ . *Great Surveys of the American West.* Norman: Univ. of Oklahoma Press, 1962.

_____ . *Nature's Yellowstone.* Albuquerque: Univ. of New Mexico Press, 1974.

Beach, Mark. "Was There a Scientific Lazzaroni?" In George H. Daniels, ed., *Nineteenth-Century American Science: A Reappraisal,* pp. 115–32.

Benjamin, Marcus. "Ferdinand Vandeveer Hayden." *American Cyclopaedia* 3, p. 538. New York: D. Appleton & Co., 1881.

————. "Ferdinand Vandeveer Hayden." *Appleton's Cyclopaedia of American Biography* 3, p. 131. New York: D. Appleton & Co., 1887.

————. "Ferdinand Vanderveer Hayden." *Scientific American* 7 January 1888, 9.

Bigglestone, William E. "George Nelson Allen: Teacher In Spite of Himself." *Northwest Ohio Quarterly* 48:1 (Winter 1975–76), 3–23.

Binkley, Frances Harriet (Williams). "The Hayden Survey." Master's thesis, Univ. of Colorado, 1945.

Boller, Paul F., Jr. *American Thought in Transition: The Impact of Evolutionary Naturalism, 1865–1900.* Chicago: Rand McNalley & Co., 1969.

Bowler, Peter J. *Evolution: The History of an Idea.* Berkeley: Univ. of California Press, 1984.

Brayer, Herbert O. *William Blackmore: A Case Study in the Development of the West,* 2 vols. Denver: Bradford-Robinson, 1949.

Bredeson, Robert C. "Landscape Description in Nineteenth Century American Travel Literature." *American Quarterly* 20 (1968), 86–94.

Brown, F. Martin. "Hayden's 1854–55 Missouri River Expedition." *Denver Westerners Roundup* 27 (May-June 1971), 3–66.

Browne, Janet. *The Secular Ark: Studies in the History of Biogeography.* New Haven: Yale Univ. Press, 1983.

Bruce, Robert V. "A Statistical Profile of American Scientists, 1846–1876." In George H. Daniels, ed., *Nineteenth-Century American Science,* pp. 63–94.

Burnham, John C. *How Superstition Won and Science Lost: Popularization of Science and Health in the United States.* New Brunswick, NJ: Rutgers Univ. Press, 1987.

Cassidy, Gerald J. "Ferdinand V. Hayden: Federal Entrepreneur of Science." Doctoral Dissertation, Univ. of Pennsylvania, 1991.

Cassino, S. E., ed. *The Naturalists Directory.* Boston: S. E. Cassino & Co., 1884.

Chambers, Frank. *Hayden and His Men: Being a Selection of 108 Photographs by William Henry Jackson of the U.S. Geological and Geographical Survey of the Territories for the Years 1870–78.* Hoosick, NY: Francis Paul, 1988.

Chickering, J. W., Jr. "The Potomac-Side Naturalists' Club," *Science,* New series, 23 (16 February 1906), 264–65.

Chittenden, Hiram Martin. *History of Early Steamboat Navigation on the Missouri River,* 2 vols. New York: F. P. Harper, 1903.

Chorley, Richard J.; Dunn, Antony J.; and Beckinsale, Robert P. *The History of the Study of Landforms.* New York: John Wiley & Sons, 1964.

Clark, Barzilla Worth. *Bonneville County in the Making.* Idaho Falls: privately printed, 1941.

Clarke, John M. *James Hall of Albany, Geologist and Paleontologist, 1811–1898.* New York: Arno Press, 1978; reprint of 1923 first edition.

Coan, Eugene. *James Graham Cooper: Pioneer Western Naturalist.* Moscow, ID: Univ. Press of Idaho, 1982.

Cochrane, Rexmond C. *The National Academy of Sciences: The First Hundred Years, 1863–1963.* Washington: The Academy, 1978.

Colbert, Edwin H. *Men and Dinosaurs.* New York: E. P. Dutton, 1968.

Cope, Edward Drinker. "Ferdinand V. Hayden, M.D., Ph.D." *Am Nat* 21:12 (December 1887), 1134–35.

———. "F. V. Hayden, M.D., LL.D." *American Geologist* 1:2 (February 1888), 110–13.

Cowie, Anne Elizabeth. "Two Views of the Yellowstone Region: Nathaniel P. Langford and Ferdinand V. Hayden." Master's Thesis, Univ. of Washington, 1974.

Cramton, Louis C. *Early History of Yellowstone National Park and its Relation to National Park Policies.* Washington: GPO, 1932.

Crosby, Harry H. "So Deep a Trail: A Biography of Clarence King." Doctoral Dissertation, Stanford Univ., 1953.

Curti, Merle. *The Growth of American Thought,* 3d ed. New York: Harper & Row, 1964.

Cutright, Paul R., and Brodhead, Michael J. *Elliott Coues: Naturalist and Frontier Historian.* Urbana: Univ. of Illinois Press, 1981.

Dall, William Healey. *Spencer Fullerton Baird.* Philadelphia: Lippincott, 1915.

Dana, Edward Salisbury, ed. *A Century of Science in America With Special Reference to the* American Journal of Science, *1818–1918.* New Haven: Yale Univ. Press, 1918.

Dana, James Dwight. "On American Geological History." *Am Jour Sci,* 2d series, 22 (November 1856), 305–34.

———. "Review of Hall and Whitney's Report on the Geology of Iowa." *Am Jour Sci,* 2d series, 27 (January 1859), 103–117.

———. "Ferdinand V. Hayden." *Am Jour Sci,* 3d series, 35 (February 1888), 179–80.

Daniels, George H. *American Science in the Age of Jackson.* New York: Columbia Univ. Press, 1968.

———. *Science in American Society: A Social History.* New York: Knopf, 1971.

———. "The Process of Professionalization in American Science: The Emergent Period, 1820–1860." In Nathan Reingold, ed., *Science in America Since 1820,* pp. 63–78.

Daniels, George H., ed. *Nineteenth-Century American Science: A Reappraisal.* Evanston: Northwestern Univ. Press, 1972.

Darrah, William Culp. *Powell of the Colorado.* Princeton: Princeton Univ. Press, 1951.

Deiss, William A. "Spencer F. Baird and His Collectors." *Journal of the Society for the Bibliography of Natural History* 9:4 (1980), 635–45.

————. "The Making of a Naturalist: Spencer F. Baird, the Early Years." In *From Linnaeus to Darwin: Commentaries on the History of Biology and Geology,* pp. 141–48. London: Society for the History of Natural History, 1985.

Dickason, David H. "Henry Adams and Clarence King, the Record of a Friendship." *New England Quarterly* 17:2 (June 1944), 229–54.

Dippie, Brian W. *Catlin and His Contemporaries: The Politics of Patronage.* Lincoln: Univ. of Nebraska Press, 1990.

Dott, Robert H., Jr. "James Hall's Discovery of the Craton." In Ellen T. Drake and William M. Jordan, eds., *Geologists and Ideas: A History of North American Geology,* pp. 157–67.

Drake, Ellen T., and Jordan, William M., eds. *Geologists and Ideas: A History of North American Geology.* Boulder: Geological Society of America, 1985.

Dupree, Anderson Hunter. "The Founding of the National Academy of Sciences, A Reinterpretation." *Proc Am Phil Soc* 101 (1957), 434–40.

————. *Asa Gray.* Cambridge: Harvard Univ. Press, 1959.

Elliott, Clark A. "Hayden, Ferdinand Vandiveer." In *Biographical Dictionary of American Science: The Seventeenth Through the Nineteenth Centuries,* p. 121. Westport, CT: Greenwood Press, 1979.

English, Donald E. "William H. Jackson: Western Commercial Photographer." *Colorado Heritage* 1 & 2 (1983), 60–68.

Ewan, Joseph. *Rocky Mountain Naturalists.* Denver: Univ. of Denver Press, 1950.

Fairchild, Herman Le Roy. "A Memoir of Professor John Strong Newberry." In *Proceedings of the Second Joint Meeting of the Scientific Alliance of New York,* pp. 7–23. New York: L. S. Foster, 1893.

Fenton, Carroll L., and Fenton, Mildred A. *Giants of Geology.* Garden City, NY: Doubleday, 1952.

Fisher, Donald W. "James Hall, Patriarch of American Paleontology, Geological Organizations, and State Geological Surveys." *Journal of Geological Education* 26:4 (September 1978), 146–52.

————. "Emmons, Hall, Mather and Vanuxem—The Four 'Horsemen' of the New York Geological Survey (1836–1841)." *Northeastern Geology* 3 (1981), 29–46.

Flanagan, Vincent J. "The Life of General Gouverneur Kemble Warren." Doctoral Dissertation, City Univ. of New York, 1969.

_____ . "Gouverneur Kemble Warren, Explorer of Nebraska Territory." *Nebraska History* 51:2 (Summer 1970), 171–98.

Foster, Mike. "Ferdinand Vandeveer Hayden as Naturalist." *American Zoologist* 26 (1986), 343–49.

_____ . "Hayden in Wonderland: Exploring Yellowstone." *Timeline* 6:4 (August-September, 1989), 36–47.

_____ . "The Permian Controversy of 1858: An Affair of the Heart." *Proc Am Phil Soc* 133:3 (September 1989), 370–90.

Frazer, Persifor. "The Life and Letters of Edward Drinker Cope." *American Geologist* 26:2 (August 1900), 67–128.

Freeman, Larry. *Louis Prang, Color Lithographer, Giant of a Man.* Watkins Glen, NY: Century House, 1971.

Fryxell, Fritiof M. "Albert Charles Peale: Pioneer Geologist of the Hayden Survey." *Annals of Wyoming* 34:2 (October 1962), 175–92.

_____ . [An unfinished, untitled manuscript biography of F. V. Hayden.] Deposited at the Univ. of Wyoming, Laramie, c. 1965.

Fuess, Claude M. *Carl Schurz, Reformer.* New York: Dodd, Mead & Co., 1932.

Gannett, Henry. "The Geodetic Work of the Hayden and Wheeler Surveys." *Science* 3 (11 April 1884), 447–48.

Gardner, James Terry. "Hayden and Gardner's Survey of the Territories, Under the Direction of the Department of the Interior." *Am Jour Sci,* 3d series, 6 (October 1873), 297–300.

Geikie, Archibald. "American Geological Surveys," etc. *Nature* 12 (5 August 1875), 265–67; 13 (4 November 1875), 1–3; 18 (12 September 1878), 516–17, 694–95; 19 (9 January 1879), 213–14; 21 (1 January 1880), 197–98.

_____ . "Ferdinand Vandeveer Hayden." *Nature* 37 (2 February 1888), 325–27.

Gilman, Daniel C. *The Life of James Dwight Dana.* New York: Harper & Brothers, 1899.

Glick, Thomas F., ed. *The Comparative Reception of Darwinism.* Austin: Univ. of Texas Press, 1974.

Goetzmann, William H. *Exploration and Empire: The Explorer and the Scientist in the Winning of the American West.* New York: W. W. Norton & Co., 1978; reprint of 1966 first edition.

_____ . "The Heroic Age of Geological Exploration: The U.S. Geological Survey and the Men and Events That Created it." *American West* 16:5 (September-October 1979), 4–13, 59–61.

_____ . *Army Exploration in the American West, 1803–63.* Lincoln: Univ. of Nebraska Press, 1979; reprint of 1959 first edition.

Gray, John S. "The Story of Mrs. Picotte-Galpin, a Sioux Heroine." *Montana* 36:2 (Spring 1986), 2–21.

Green, Constance McLaughlin. *Washington: Village and Capital, 1800–1878.* Princeton: Princeton Univ. Press, 1962.

Greene, Mott T. *Geology in the Nineteenth Century: Changing Views of a Changing World.* Ithaca: Cornell Univ. Press, 1982.

Gregory, Joseph T. "Tertiary Freshwater Lakes of Western America—An Ephemeral Theory." *Journal of the West* 8:2 (April 1969), 247–62.

Guralnick, Stanley M. "Science and the Ante-Bellum American College." *Memoirs of the Am Phil Soc* 109 (1975).

———— . "Sources of Misconception on the Role of Science in the Nineteenth-Century American College." In Nathan Reingold, ed., *Science in America Since 1820,* pp. 48–62.

———— . "The American Scientist in Higher Education, 1820–1910," In Nathan Reingold, ed., *The Sciences in the American Context: New Perspectives,* pp. 99–141.

Haines, Aubrey L. *Yellowstone National Park: Its Exploration and Establishment.* Washington: GPO (Department of the Interior, National Park Service), 1974.

Hales, Peter B. *William Henry Jackson and the Transformation of the American Landscape.* Philadelphia: Temple Univ. Press, 1988.

Hansen, Michael C., and Collins, Horace R. "A Brief History of the Ohio Geological Survey." *Ohio Journal of Science* 79:1 (January 1979), 3–14.

Hardwick, Bonnie Skell. "Science and Art: The Travel Writings of the Great Surveys of the American West After the Civil War." Doctoral Dissertation, Univ. of Pennsylvania, 1977.

Hartman, Joseph Herbert. "Systematics, Biostratigraphy, and Biogeography of Latest Cretaceous and Early Tertiary Viviparidae (Mollusca, Gastropoda) of Southern Saskatchewan, Western North Dakota, Eastern Montana, and Northern Wyoming." Doctoral Dissertation, Univ. of Minnesota, 1984.

Hicks, Philip M. *The Development of the Natural History Essay in American Literature.* Philadelphia: Univ. of Pennsylvania Press, 1924.

Hoogenboom, Ari. *The Presidency of Rutherford B. Hayes.* Lawrence: Univ. of Kansas Press, 1988.

Howell, Jesse V. "Geology Plus Adventure: The Story of the Hayden Survey." *Journal of the Washington Academy of Sciences* 49:7 (July 1959), 220–24.

———— . "Ferdinand V. Hayden, Surveyor of the Yellowstone." *American Scene Magazine* 5:3 (1963), 11–20.

Huth, Hans. *Nature and the American: Three Centuries of Changing Attitudes.* Berkeley: Univ. of California Press, 1957.

Jackson, William Henry. *The Diaries of William Henry Jackson.* Volume 10 of

The Far West and the Rockies Historical Series. Eds. L. R. Hafen and A. W. Hafen. Glendale, CA: Arthur H. Clark, 1959.

Jackson, William Henry, with Driggs, Howard R. *The Pioneer Photographer: Rocky Mountain Adventures with a Camera.* New York: World, 1929.

Jackson, William Henry, with Brown, Karl. *Time Exposure.* New York: G. P. Putnam's Sons, 1940.

Karnes, Thomas L. *William Gilpin: Western Nationalist.* Austin: Univ. of Texas Press, 1970.

Karrow, Robert W., Jr. "George M. Wheeler and the Geographical Surveys West of the 100th Meridian, 1869–1879." In *Exploration and Mapping of the American West: Selected Essays,* pp. 121–57. Ed. Donna P. Koepp. Occasional Paper No. 1. Map and Geography Round Table of the American Library Association. Chicago: Speculum Orbis Press, 1986.

Keyes, Charles Rollin. "Last of the Geological Pioneers: Ferdinand Vandiveer Hayden." *Pan American Geologist* 41 (March 1924), 80–96.

Kinsey, Joni Louise. *Thomas Moran and the Surveying of the American West.* Washington: Smithsonian Press, 1992.

Klett, Mark; Manchester, Ellen; and Verburg, Jo Ann. *Second View: The Rephotographic Survey Project.* Albuquerque: Univ. of New Mexico Press, 1985.

Kohlstedt, Sally Gregory. *The Formation of the American Scientific Community: The American Association for the Advancement of Science, 1848–60.* Urbana: Univ. of Illinois Press, 1976.

————— . "Curiosities and Cabinets: Natural History Museums and Education on the Antebellum Campus." *Isis* 79 (1988), 405–26.

Kramer, Howard D. "The Scientist in the West, 1870–80." *Pacific Historical Review* 12:3 (September 1943), 239–51.

Kuritz, Hyman. "The Popularization of Science in Nineteenth-Century America." *History of Education Quarterly* 21 (Fall 1981), 259–74.

Lanham, Urless Norton. *The Bone Hunters.* New York: Columbia Univ. Press, 1973.

Laudan, Rachel. "Tension in the Concept of Geology: Natural History or Natural Science?" *Earth Sciences History* 1:1 (1982), 7–13.

Lavender, David. *Fort Laramie and the Changing Frontier.* Washington: Department of the Interior (National Park Handbook 118), 1983.

Lesley, John P. "Obituary Notice of Ferdinand Vandevere Hayden, M.D., Ph.D., LL. D.," *Pro Am Phil Soc* 25:127 (January-June 1888), 59–61.

Leutze, Willard P. "Ferdinand V. Hayden, 1829–87." In *Biographies of Geologists,* p. 54. Columbus: Ohio State Univ. Press, 1961.

Lurie, Edward. *Louis Agassiz: A Life in Science.* Chicago: Univ. of Chicago Press, 1960.

Manarin, Louis H. "Major General Gouverneur Kemble Warren: A Reappraisal." Master's Thesis, Duke Univ., 1957.

Manning, Thomas G. *Government in Science: The United States Geological Survey, 1867–1894.* Lexington: Univ. of Kentucky Press, 1967.

Marzio, Peter C. "Mr. Audubon and Mr. Bien: An Early Phase in the History of American Chromolithography." *Prospects* 1 (1975), 139–54.

_____ . *The Democratic Art: Pictures for a Nineteenth Century America, 1840–1900.* Boston: D. R. Godine, 1979.

Mayer, Alfred G. "Biographical Memoir of William Stimson, 1832–72." *Biographical Memoirs* 8:419–33. Washington: Nat Acad Sci, 1918.

McLaird, James D., and Turchen, Lesta V. "Exploring the Black Hills, 1855–1875: Reports of the Government Expeditions." *South Dakota History* 3:4 (Fall 1973), 359–89, and 4:1 (Winter 1973), 18–62.

_____ . "The Scientist in Western Exploration: Ferdinand Vandiveer Hayden." *South Dakota History* 4:2 (Spring 1974), 161–97.

Merrill, George P. "Ferdinand Vandiveer Hayden." *Dictionary of American Biography* 8:438–40. New York: C. Scribner's Sons, 1932.

_____ . *The First One Hundred Years of American Geology.* New York: Hafner Pub. Co., 1969; reprint of 1924 first edition.

Miller, Howard S. *Dollars for Research: Science and its Patrons in Nineteenth Century America.* Seattle: Univ. of Washington Press, 1970.

Moore, Frank, ed. *The Rebellion Record: A Diary of American Events.* Vols. 3 (1864) and 5 (1871). New York: G. P. Putnam.

Naef, Weston J., and Wood, James N. *Era of Exploration: The Rise of Landscape Photography in the American West, 1860–1885.* Boston: New York Graphic Society, 1975.

Nash, Roderick. *Wilderness and the American Mind.* New Haven: Yale Univ. Press, 1967.

Nelson, Clifford M. "William Henry Holmes: Beginning a Career in Art and Science." *Records of the Columbia Historical Society of Washington, D.C.* 50 (1980), 252–78.

_____ . "Paleontology in the United States Federal Service, 1804–1904." *Earth Sciences History* 1:1 (1982), 48–57.

Nelson, Clifford M., and Fryxell, Fritiof M. "The Ante-Bellum Collaboration of Meek and Hayden in Stratigraphy." In Cecil J. Schneer, ed., *Two Hundred Years of Geology in America,* pp. 187–200. Hanover: Univ. Press of New England, 1979.

Nelson, Clifford M., and Yochelson, Ellis L. "Organizing Federal Paleontology in the United States." *Journal of the Society for the Bibliography of Natural History* 9:4 (1980), 607–18.

Nelson, Clifford M.; Rabbitt, Mary C.; and Fryxell, Fritiof M. "Ferdinand

Vandeveer Hayden: The U.S. Geological Survey Years, 1879–1886." *Proc Am Phil Soc* 125:3 (June 1981), 238–43.

Nevins, Alan. *Abram S. Hewitt, With Some Account of Peter Cooper.* New York: Octagon Books, 1967; reprint of 1935 first edition.

Newberry, John Strong. "Modern Scientific Investigation: Its Methods and Tendencies." *Am Nat* 1:9 (November 1867), 449–69.

Nolan, Edward J. *A Short History of the Academy of Natural Sciences of Philadelphia.* Philadelphia: The Academy, 1909.

Novak, Barbara. *Nature and Culture: American Landscape and Painting, 1825–75.* New York: Oxford Univ. Press, 1980.

Oliver, Sarah Ireland. "Ferdinand V. Hayden, Scientist or Charlatan? The Wyoming Years." Master's Thesis, Univ. of Wyoming, 1978.

Osborn, Henry Fairfield. "Biographical Memoir of Joseph Leidy." *Biographical Memoirs* 7:335–96. Washington: Nat Acad Sci, 1913.

————. *Impressions of Great Naturalists.* New York: C. Scribner's Sons, 1924.

————. *Cope, Master Naturalist.* Princeton: Princeton Univ. Press, 1931.

O'Toole, Patricia. *The Five of Hearts.* New York: Clarkson Potter Publishers, 1990.

[Peale, Albert Charles.] "Ferdinand Vandiveer Hayden." *Ninth Annual Report of the United States Geological Survey* (1889), 31–38.

Peale, Albert Charles. "Biographical Sketch of F. V. Hayden, M.D., with Bibliography" [c. 1891]. Peale Papers, RU 7208, Smithsonian Archives.

————. "Ferdinand Vandiveer Hayden." *Bulletin of the Philosophical Society of Washington* 11 (1892), 476–78.

Penick, James. "Professor Cope and Professor Marsh: A Bitter Feud Among the Bones." *American Heritage* 22:5 (August 1971), 4–13, 91–95.

Pike, Donald G. "Four Surveyors Challenge the Rocky Mountain West: Fighting Bureaucracy and Indians in a Wild Land." *American West* 9:3 (1972), 4–13.

Plate, Robert. *The Dinosaur Hunters: Othniel C. Marsh and Edward D. Cope.* New York: David McKay Co., 1964.

Polsky, Claudia. "The Unmaking of a Scientific Reputation: Ferdinand Vandiveer Hayden and the Geological and Geographical Survey of the Territories." Bachelor's Honors Thesis, Harvard Univ., 1987.

Porter, Charlotte M. *The Eagle's Nest: Natural History and American Ideas, 1812–42.* Tuscaloosa, AL: Univ. of Alabama Press, 1986.

Pyne, Stephen J. *Grove Karl Gilbert: A Great Engine of Research.* Austin: Univ. of Texas Press, 1980.

Rabbitt, Mary C. *Minerals, Lands, and Geology for the Common Defence and General Welfare.* Vol. 1: *Before 1879.* Washington: GPO, 1979.

Raynolds, William Franklin. *Report on the Exploration of the Yellowstone River in 1859–60.* 40th Cong, 2d sess, 1868, Senate Exec Doc 77. Washington: GPO, 1868.

Reingold, Nathan, ed. *Science in Nineteenth Century America: A Documentary History.* New York: Hill and Wang, 1964.

_____ . *Science in America Since 1820.* New York: Science History Publications, 1976.

_____ . *The Sciences in the American Context: New Perspectives.* Washington: Smithsonian Press, 1979.

Rivinus, E. F., and Youssef, E. M. *Spencer Baird of the Smithsonian.* Washington: Smithsonian Press, 1992.

Rodgers, Andrew D., III. *American Botany, 1873–1892, Decades of Transition.* Princeton: Princeton Univ. Press, 1944.

Rogers, Emma Savage, ed. *Life and Letters of William Barton Rogers,* 2 vols. Boston: Houghton Mifflin, 1896.

Romer, Alfred S. "Cope Versus Marsh." *Systematic Zoology* 13:4 (December 1964), 201–07.

Rose, Phyllis. *Parallel Lives: Five Victorian Marriages.* New York: Knopf, 1983.

Ross, Dorothy. "Historical Consciousness in Nineteenth-Century America." *American Historical Review* 89:4 (October 1984), 909–28.

Rothman, David. *Politics and Power: The United States Senate, 1869–1901.* Cambridge: Harvard Univ. Press, 1966.

Salisbury, Stephen. "Prof. Ferdinand Vandeveer Hayden, M.D., Ph.D., LL.D." *Proceedings of the American Antiquarian Society* (April 1888), 180–82.

Schmeckebier, Laurence Frederick. *Catalogue and Index of the Publications of the Hayden, King, Powell and Wheeler Surveys.* USGS Bulletin No. 222. Washington: GPO, 1904.

Schubert, Frank N.S. *Vanguard of Expansion: Army Engineers in the Trans-Mississippi West, 1819–1879.* Washington: Historical Division, U.S. Army Corps of Engineers, 1980.

_____ . "Troublesome Partnership: Gouverneur K. Warren and Ferdinand V. Hayden on the Northern Plains in 1856 and 1857." *Earth Sciences History* 3:2 (1984), 143–48.

Schubert, Frank N.S., ed. "Explorer on the Northern Plains: Lieutenant Gouverneur K. Warren's Preliminary Report of Explorations in Nebraska and Dakota in the Years 1855–56–57." *Engineer Historical Studies* 2 (October 1981). Washington: Historical Division, U.S. Army Corps of Engineers.

Schuchert, Charles, and LeVene, Clara Mae. *O. C. Marsh, Pioneer in Paleontology.* New Haven: Yale Univ. Press, 1940.

Scott, William Berryman. "Memoir of Edward Drinker Cope." *Bulletin of the Geological Society of America* 9 (1898), 401–08.

_____ . "Leidy's Paleontological and Geological Work." *Scientific Monthly* 18:4 (April 1924), 433–39.

Scudder, Samuel Hubbard. "Ferdinand Vandeveer Hayden." *Science* 11 (6 January 1888), 1–2.

Sears, John F. *Sacred Places: American Tourist Attractions in the Nineteenth Century.* New York: Oxford Univ. Press, 1989.

Secord, James A. *Controversy in Victorian Geology: The Cambrian-Silurian Dispute.* Princeton: Princeton, Univ. Press, 1986.

Shor, Elizabeth N. *The Fossil Feud Between E. D. Cope and O. C. Marsh.* Hicksville, NY: Exposition Press, 1974.

Simpson, George Gaylord. "Hayden, Cope, and the Eocene of New Mexico." *Proc ANSP* 103 (25 April 1951), 1–21.

Skelton, Lawrence H. "Kansas Skirmishes in the Cope/Marsh War." *Earth Sciences History* 3:2 (1984), 117–22.

Smith, Henry Nash. "Clarence King, John Wesley Powell and the Establishment of the United States Geological Survey." *Mississippi Valley Historical Review* 34:1 (1947), 37–58.

Sonnichsen, C. L. *The Ambidextrous Historian: Historical Writers and Writing in the American West.* Norman: Univ. of Oklahoma Press, 1981.

Stegner, Wallace. *Beyond the Hundredth Meridian: John Wesley Powell and the Second Opening of the West.* Lincoln: Univ. of Nebraska Press, 1982; reprint of 1954 first edition.

Sterling, Keir Brooks. *Last of the Naturalists: The Career of C. Hart Merriam.* New York: Arno Press, 1974.

Sternberg, Charles H. *The Life of a Fossil Hunter.* New York: H. Holt, 1909.

Stevenson, John J. "John Strong Newberry." *American Geologist* 12:1 (July 1893), 1–25.

_____ . "Memoir of James Hall." *Bulletin of the Geological Society of America* 10 (1898), 425–51.

Sunder, John E. *The Fur Trade on the Upper Missouri 1840–65.* Norman: Univ. of Oklahoma Press, 1965.

Taylor, Emerson Gifford. *Gouverneur Kemble Warren: The Life and Letters of an American Soldier, 1830–82.* Boston: Houghton Mifflin, 1932.

Thom, William B. "Dr. F. V. Hayden—Pioneer Geologist." *Eagle Valley Enterprise* (Colo.), 30 December 1921 and 6 January 1922.

Toll, Roger W. "The Hayden Survey in Colorado in 1873 and 1874." *Colorado Magazine* 6:4 (July 1929), 146–56.

Trefousse, Hans L. *Carl Schurz, A Biography.* Knoxville: Univ. of Tennessee Press, 1982.

True, Frederick W. *The National Academy of Sciences, 1863–1913: A History of the First Half Century.* Washington: The Academy, 1913.

Turner, James. *Without God, Without Creed: The Origins of Unbelief in America.* Baltimore: Johns Hopkins Univ. Press, 1985.

Waage, Karl M. "The Type Fox Hills Formation, Cretaceous (Maestrichtian), South Dakota." Part 1: Stratigraphy and Paleoenvironments, *Bulletin of the Peabody Museum of Natural History* [Yale] 27 (1968), 18–37, 168–71.

———— . "Deciphering the Basic Sedimentary Structure of the Cretaceous System in the Western Interior." In W.G.E. Caldwell, ed., *The Cretaceous System in the Western Interior of North America,* pp. 55–81. Special Paper no. 13. Waterloo, Ontario: Geological Association of Canada, June 1975.

Warren, Gouverneur Kemble. *Explorations in the Dacota Country, in the Year 1855.* 34th Cong, 1st sess, 1855–56, Senate Exec Doc 76. Washington: A.O.P. Nicholson, 1856.

———— . *Preliminary Report of Explorations in Nebraska and Dakota in the Years 1855–'56–'57.* 35th Cong, 2d sess, 1858, Senate Exec Doc 1. Washington: GPO, 1875; reprint of 1858 first edition.

Wells, Samuel R. "Ferdinand V. Hayden, of the United States Geological Survey." *Phrenological Journal and Life Illustrated,* Old series 59; New Series 10:1 (July 1874), 5–7.

Wenrich, David H. "Joseph Leidy." Manuscript biography, deposited at ANSP, 1967.

Wheat, Carl I. *Mapping the Transmississippi West.* Vol. 5, pt. 2. San Francisco: Institute of Historical Cartography, 1963.

White, Charles A. "Memoir of Ferdinand Vandiveer Hayden, 1839 [sic]– 1887." *Biographical Memoirs* 3:394–413. Washington: Nat Acad Sci, 1895.

White, Leonard D. *The Republican Era: A Study in Administrative History, 1869–1901.* New York: Macmillan, 1958.

Wilkins, Thurman, with Hinkley, Caroline. *Clarence King,* 2d ed. Albuquerque: Univ. of New Mexico Press, 1988.

Wright, A. A. "Death of Dr. F. V. Hayden." *Oberlin Review* 15 (10 January 1888), 92.

Yochelson, Ellis L. "Monuments and Markers to the Territorial Surveys." *Annals of Wyoming* 43:1 (1971), 113–24.

Zochert, Donald. "Notes on a Young Naturalist." *Audubon* 82:2 (1980), 34–47.

INDEX